THE
FORMATION
OF Q

STUDIES IN ANTIQUITY AND CHRISTIANITY

The Institute for Antiquity and Christianity
Claremont Graduate School
Claremont, California

STUDIES IN ANTIQUITY & CHRISTIANITY

THE FORMATION OF Q

Trajectories in Ancient Wisdom Collections

John S. Kloppenborg

FORTRESS PRESS   **PHILADELPHIA**

Library of Congress Cataloging-in-Publication Data

Kloppenborg, John S., 1951–
  The formation of Q.

  (Studies in antiquity and Christianity)
  Bibliography: p.
  Includes indexes.
    1. Q hypothesis (Synoptics criticism) 2. Wisdom literature. I. Title. II. Series.
  BS2555.2.K568   1986   226'.066   86–45225
  ISBN 0–8006–3101–3

2543F86   Printed in the United States of America   1–3101

For Leanne

Contents

Foreword

John Kloppenborg's impressively wide-ranging survey of the various genres of sayings collections in antiquity and his placing of Q within that context have elevated this dimension of the study of Q to a new niveau of sophistication. With its publication, all previous studies of the genre of Q are rendered inadequate, irrespective of how near or far they may have been from the truth. For they have sought to place Q on a very partial grid of alternatives, in contrast to the vast panorama, the carefully textured background, on the basis of which Q receives its profile in *The Formation of Q: Trajectories in Ancient Wisdom Collections.*

The comparison of Kloppenborg's achievement with that of his predecessors seems so one-sided as to be hardly kind. Such a brief earlier study as that of Ernst Bammel,[1] to the effect that Q is to be considered a testament comparable to the *Testaments of the Twelve Patriarchs*, seems by comparison hardly worthy of discussion, based as it was on little more than a single and, at that, uncertain, Q saying, which is compared with but one segment of the Jewish background of Christianity. Such a study betrays the narrowness of vision that ignores the whole Hellenistic world, from Egypt to Greece to Babylonia to Persia, in which early Judaism and primitive Christianity were bathed, and in which Kloppenborg's study is thoroughly at home. Again, such a recent study as that of Robert Hodgson,[2] to the effect that Q belongs to the *testimonia* literature that has been sporadically assumed to lie behind primitive Christian literary production, a view that has been given added impetus by Qumranian *testimonia*-like texts, seems likewise to suffer from the limited scope surveyed in Hodgson's Heidelberg dissertation on *testimonia*. In the case of Q, such a study projects a cozy biblicism back upon the Q

---

1. Ernst Bammel, "Das Ende von Q," *Verborum Veritas: Festschrift für G. Stählin zum 70. Geburtstag* (Wuppertal: Rolf Brockhaus, 1970) 39–50.
2. Robert Hodgson, "On the Gattung of Q: A Dialogue with James M. Robinson," *Biblica* 66 (1985) 73–95.

community's much more uninhibited proclamation. In effect it makes the last stage of Q, characterized by the three Deuteronomic responses to the temptations, itself a worthy anticipation of the Gospel of Matthew's biblical erudition, the anachronistic model for reconstructing the sayings of Jesus and his original disciples. What Kloppenborg's presentation brings home again and again is that such limited approaches, even if the conclusions were nearer the truth than they happen to be in these cases, are simply methodologically unacceptable. Such whimsical, almost anecdotal approaches, even if by accident they were to fall on the right conclusion, would not deserve to be right!

A somewhat more awkward comparison would have to do with my own article of a generation ago, "LOGOI SOPHON: On the *Gattung* of Q."[3] There I broke with the prevalent critical view of the *Gospel of Thomas*, commonly held to be a gnosticizing reduction of the canonical Gospels into a haphazard scattering of sayings worthy of the Gnostic redeemer, who saves not by his saving work but only through the gnosis latent in his word. Yet it had been the anti-Bultmannian forces, represented by such prestigious names as Oscar Cullmann and Gilles Quispel, who had argued that the *Gospel of Thomas* was primarily to be understood not as a reduction of the canonical Gospels but as based on noncanonical gospels. I surely had no interest to aid and abet such an approach, with its disinterest in the genre question and its conservative bias.

What had actually triggered my essay was the view bluntly expressed by Werner Georg Kümmel, to the effect that the genre of the *Gospel of Thomas*, whatever it might be, had absolutely nothing to do with Q. Thus my motivation was not to strengthen a correlation of the *Gospel of Thomas* with lost apocryphal gospels, about which hardly more was known than their titles and a very few sayings shared with the *Gospel of Thomas*. For it seemed a moot question whether one text was dependent on the other, and if so which on which, or whether the texts were independent of each other but shared a dependence on oral tradition. Hence to designate such lost apocryphal gospels or even Q as "sources" of the *Gospel of Thomas* seemed uncritical. Rather I had in view a form-critical trajectory which Q and the *Gospel of Thomas* might share. This working hypothesis was based on their strikingly similar divergence

---

3. James M. Robinson, "*LOGOI SOPHON:* On the *Gattung* of Q," *The Future of Our Religious Past: Essays in Honor of Rudolf Bultmann* (ed. James M. Robinson; New York/Evanston/San Francisco: Harper & Row, 1971) 84–130; repr. *Trajectories Through Early Christianity* (Philadelphia: Fortress Press, 1971) 71–113.

from what one normally expects of a gospel: a narrative text in which some sayings are embedded, culminating in the passion narrative and Easter, oriented to the kerygma of cross and resurrection as *the* Christian message. There must be *some* historical explanation for this deficiency shared by Q and the *Gospel of Thomas*, a deficiency that seems related to the problem of defining the gospel as a literary genre. But I never actually worked through this working hypothesis.

To put the matter a bit baldly, my article was at the time conceived of as one chapter of a book on Q that was never written—one of several casualties resulting from my being trapped into a sudden career shift, motivated by fear that the Nag Hammadi texts, with whatever relevance they might have beyond the *Gospel of Thomas* for such matters, would not become accessible during my lifetime. By the time I completed in 1984 *The Facsimile Edition of the Nag Hammadi Codices,* I had settled upon Q as the area where I proposed to work myself back into New Testament scholarship in the traditional sense of the term. I was not only motivated by the central position of Q in any assessment of primitive Christianity, in spite of its almost complete neglect in the Bultmannian synthesis. I was also impressed by the many creative monographs on Q that had appeared in the post-Bultmannian period, which had catapulted this area of research onto a completely new level after a half century of neglect. The whole topic of Q seemed ready for plucking. I decided to devote a major part of my career from now on to reconstructing a critical text of Q and producing a commentary on that text, both for the Hermeneia series.

I first read *The Formation of Q* in typescript at this critical juncture in my own career, and experienced it as a fine confirmation of this sense of the times. Indeed it seemed to me to compensate in large part for the two decades I had lost in my own New Testament scholarship relevant to Q, between the article "LOGOI SOPHON" of 1964, and the plan of 1984 to return to Q studies. In fact my relation to *The Formation of Q* was much like the compliment one occasionally finds in book reviews: it is the kind of book I would like to have written. For Kloppenborg's much more detailed analysis of the kinds of sayings collections in antiquity did not just rubber-stamp my conclusions, much less validate my limited methodological scope. Rather it improved upon what I had to say in my premature article, as well as providing the equivalent of the rest of the chapters of the nonexistent book. Thus I can to a very large degree identify with the book and even claim its conclusions as mine, in the sense that I think my position would have modulated into much the same as that of the book, had I taken the time to carry out such careful and extensive research. Thus I can only welcome it at this quite personal level as the kind of follow-through by a junior colleague that I have learned to accept with satisfaction, when I have launched a working hypothesis that I have not found time to work through to definitive conclusions.

It is with such a mixture of objective academic assessments and personal feelings of identification that I read this book in typescript, recommended its inclusion in the Institute's recently launched Studies in Antiquity and Christianity, and here commend it to the reading public as a landmark in the study of Q. My own future work on Q will be advanced considerably by the materials and conclusions that Kloppenborg presents here. And I look forward to comparable assistance from the continuing research on Q in which Kloppenborg, as a member of the Institute's Q Project, the Society of Biblical Literature's Q Seminar, and Robert W. Funk's Jesus Seminar, is currently quite actively engaged.

Institute for Antiquity and Christianity   JAMES M. ROBINSON, *Director*
Claremont, California

Preface

The impetus for this study came in part from the germinal essay of James M. Robinson, "ΛΟΓΟΙ ΣΟΦΩΝ: Zur Gattung der Spruchquelle Q," which appeared in the Bultmann Festschrift over twenty years ago, and in part from a remark of Hans-Dieter Betz, who noted that both the structure of Q and its *Gattungsgeschichte* deserved to be clarified.

As a contribution to this needed clarification, I have considered Q from two perspectives, one diachronic and redaction-critical, and the other, synchronic and comparative. The goal of this approach is to trace the literary evolution of Q as a document of primitive Christianity and then to view that development within the context of antique literary genres, their immanent tendencies and their theological or ideological proclivities.

To do full justice to the topic of Q in the context of antique sayings collections would take more than a lifetime, since it would entail, presumably, a detailed analysis of a vast body of wisdom collections in Egyptian, Semitic languages, Greek, Latin, Arabic and a variety of more exotic tongues, and a synthesis of the results of the analysis. Obviously such a mammoth task has never been attempted nor, in all likelihood, will it be. I have chosen to compare Q with the "instruction," a well-defined genre in ancient Near Eastern and late antique wisdom literature, and a representative number of Hellenistic gnomologia and chriae collections. My discussion of the "instruction" is indebted at many points to the analysis of this genre by several Egyptologists. I owe another debt to Max Küchler, who has begun the task of situating the wisdom writings of second-temple Judaism within the broader context of Hellenistic gnomologia.

Reconstruction of the wording of the Q text is a difficult yet important matter, and one which is the concern of the SBL Consultation (and now Seminar) on Q, founded in 1983 by James Robinson. Since the thesis argued herein does not depend upon establishing the most probable wording of each Q text, I have discussed reconstruction only in those cases where the redaction of Q by Matthew or Luke may have effected changes in the overall hermeneutical framework of Q or of a significant portion of Q. For our purposes, the problems of the original order and the extent of Q are more immediate and will be dealt with in detail.

For citing Q texts, I have adopted the convention of the SBL Q Seminar (see below, p. xvii). Unless otherwise stated, biblical quotations are from the RSV and translations of German secondary literature are my own (designated by "trans. by auth."). Both English and German page references are given when citing Harnack's *Sprüche und Reden Jesu* and Bultmann's *Geschichte der synoptischen Tradition*.

I owe a deep debt of gratitude to many, especially to Heinz O. Guenther, who read through earlier forms of the manuscript with a critical and careful eye, and who gave generously of his learning and time. Hans-Dieter Betz provided both encouragement to pursue this topic and sage advice along the way. Like so many others, I am indebted to James M. Robinson for his continuing encouragement and stimulating comments and, in particular, for recommending this study for inclusion in "Studies in Antiquity and Christianity." I am also grateful to Schuyler Brown, John Coolidge Hurd, Jr., and Michael G. Steinhauser for many criticisms and comments, and to Harold W. Rast and John A. Hollar at Fortress Press. My gratitude goes especially to Wendy J. Cotter, C.S.J., who has read through most of the text and discussed with me many aspects of the argumentation, and to Raymond C. Van Leeuwen, who shared with me his expertise in Hebrew wisdom and paroemiography. James Robinson and Ron Cameron have kindly provided me with materials in advance of their publication. Mary Catherine McKenna provided invaluable assistance in compiling the indices.

Abbreviations and Short Titles

1. QUOTATIONS OF Q TEXTS

In order to avoid confusion, Q texts are cited by their Lucan position, prefaced by "Q" (e.g., Q 6:20b = Luke 6:20b // Matt 5:3). This in no way is meant to suggest that the Lucan wording or location is necessarily that of Q. "Luke 6:20b" refers to the text *as it functions in the Third Gospel* and "Matt 5:3" refers to the text *as it functions in Matthew*.

2. ABBREVIATIONS

Abbreviations used in this volume for journals, series and standard reference works are found in the *Catholic Biblical Quarterly* 46 (1984) and the *Journal of Biblical Literature* 95 (1976). Ancient authors and works are abbreviated in accordance with the conventions listed in the *Theological Dictionary of the New Testament I* (ed. Gerhard Kittel, trans. Geoffrey W. Bromiley; Grand Rapids: Wm. B. Eerdmans, 1964) xvi-xl. In addition to these, the following abbreviations are used:

CH	Corpus Hermeticum
ClassQ	*Classical Quarterly*
CP	*Classical Philology*
CR	*Classical Review*
diff	differs (from)
FzB	Forschung zur Bibel
HSCP	*Harvard Studies in Classical Philology*
JHS	*Journal of Hellenic Studies*
NA[26]	E. Nestle and K. Aland, ed. *Novum Testamentum Graecum.* Stuttgart: Deutsche Bibelstiftung, 1979[26].
NHC	Nag Hammadi Codex
OBO	Orbis biblicus et orientalis
RdÉ	*Revue d'égyptologie*
red	redactional

Sond   *Sondergut*
trad   traditional
TuscB   Tusculum Bücherei
ZÄS   *Zeitschrift für Ägyptische Sprache und Altertumskunde*
ZPE   *Zeitschrift für Papyrologie und Epigraphik*

3. SHORT TITLES

Short titles are used in the notes for anything listed in the Secondary Works section of the Bibliography. In addition, the following short titles are employed:

Diels and Kranz, *Vorsokratiker*

H. Diels and W. Kranz. *Die Fragmente der Vorsokratiker.* 3 vols. Berlin: Weidmann, 1951–52[6].

Mayser, *Grammatik*

E. Mayser. *Grammatik der griechischen Papyri aus der Ptolemäerzeit.* 2 vols. in 7. Berlin and Leipzig: Walter de Gruyter, 1926–38.

Moulton-Howard-Turner, *Grammar*

J. Moulton, W. F. Howard, N. Turner. *A Grammar of New Testament Greek.* 4 vols. Edinburgh: T. & T. Clark, 1906–76.

NHLE

James M. Robinson, ed. *The Nag Hammadi Library in English.* San Francisco: Harper & Row, 1977.

OTP

James H. Charlesworth, ed. *The Old Testament Pseudepigrapha.* Vol. 1, *Apocalyptic Literature and Testaments.* Garden City, N.Y.: Doubleday & Co., 1983.

Pack[2]

Roger Pack. *The Greek and Latin Literary Texts from Greco-Roman Egypt.* Ann Arbor: Univ. of Mich. Press, 1965[2].

SAIW

James L. Crenshaw, ed. *Studies in Ancient Israelite Wisdom.* New York: Ktav, 1976.

Smyth, *Grammar*

H. Smyth. *Greek Grammar.* Cambridge: Harvard Univ. Press, 1920; repr. 1956.

Spengel, *Rhetores Graeci*

L. Spengel. *Rhetores Graeci.* 3 vols. Leipzig: Teubner, 1853–56.

1

Introduction

FORMS AND GENRES

No study of the writings of the New Testament is possible without paying attention to the formal and generic conventions which govern those writings. This was one of the basic insights which guided the form-critical enterprise of Bultmann, Dibelius and Taylor, whose attention was directed to the small units which the Synoptic tradition comprises. Form criticism was not, and is not a dispensable exercise in taxonomy. On the contrary, analysis of the structural features of these small units, cataloguing the motifs and themes which appear within them, and drawing inferences regarding the typical social situations in which they functioned, are essential components for understanding the *type of communication* which these units intend.

It might be expected that a logical extension of form criticism would have been the investigation of the structure, typical content and function of the larger compositional units such as "gospel," "acts," and "sayings collection." But for reasons which will be discussed below, this was not the case. In fact, form criticism refused to award any independent importance to these larger structural units, preferring to regard them simply as extensions and functions of the smaller oral units. The result is that the study of the literary genres employed in early Christian writing was for a long period largely ignored.

Among the literary genres which have not as yet received much attention is the collection of maxims or wise sayings.[1] *A fortiori* this is also true of the Synoptic Sayings Source, or Q. With the notable exceptions of articles by James M. Robinson and Helmut Koester,[2] most Q

---

1. A preliminary examination of some sayings collections from second-temple Judaism has been made by Küchler, *Weisheitstraditionen*.
2. Robinson, "ΛΟΓΟΙ ΣΟΦΩΝ," repr. with alterations as "LOGOI SOPHON"; Koester, "Apocryphal and Canonical Gospels."

1

studies have focused on other problems: reconstruction, order, redac-
tion-history, tradition-history, theology, relation to Mark, etc. Yet the
determination of the genre of the Synoptic Sayings Source is necessary if
we are to assess properly the type of communication it represented.
Each literary genre carries within itself a hermeneutical framework
which points the reader in one or another direction. Several suggestions,
many of them casual, have been made concerning the intention of Q as a
whole; so far, the subject has not been explored in detail. This study will,
I hope, contribute to filling this lacuna.

The Importance of Genre in Interpretation

The recent attention to the question of the genres of religious discourse is not simply a matter of scholarly whim. On the contrary, it
reflects, whether self-consciously or not, new understandings of the
importance of "genre conception" which have emerged from linguistic
philosophy and from modern literary criticism.

Fundamental to the present study of Q is the proposition that meaning in texts is "genre-bound." This notion cannot be explored and
defended fully in this context, but some explanation is warranted. The
idea of genre is not simply a heuristic device or a classificatory schema
which can be discarded once it has served its purpose. It is not an
artificial taxonomic concept. On the contrary, the understanding of the
genre of a text is always constitutive to the act of understanding. This
insight has been expressed variously. A genre conception, according to
E. D. Hirsch, "is constitutive of speaking as well as of interpreting, and it
is in virtue of this that the genre concept sheds its arbitrary and variable
character."[3] Or again, "It [a genre conception] is that sense of the whole
by means of which an interpreter can correctly understand any part in
its determinacy."[4] The importance of grasping correctly a speaker's
genre intention is most dramatically illustrated by those cases in which
misapprehensions occur. When a serious anecdote is misconstrued as a
joke, interpretive difficulties and even embarrassment result.

Even Paul Ricoeur, who otherwise de-emphasizes the author and
his/her intention (as belonging to the "background" of the text) in favor
of the "world" which is disclosed "before the text,"[5] agrees that the idea
of genre mediates between the production of a text and its under-

---

3. E. D. Hirsch, *Validity*, 78.
4. Ibid., 86.
5. Paul Ricoeur, "Philosophical Hermeneutics and Theological Hermeneutics," *SR* 5
(1975–76) 15–33, esp. 24–26.

standing. The function of genre is "to mediate between the speaker and hearer by establishing a common dynamics capable of ruling both the production of discourse as a work of a certain kind and its interpretation according to the rules provided by that genre."[6] Other formulations of the notion of "intrinsic genre" could be given.[7] The main point is that an idea of the genre of a particular work is integral to any act of interpretation.

The assumption that meaning in texts is "genre-bound" is of immediate significance to a study of Q. One sometimes encounters the assertion that Q is a Christian composition *sui generis*. That is, it falls into no known taxonomic slot. But such a view only postpones the problem; it does not solve it. No one would seriously deny that almost every literary product is unique in some respect. And few would argue that there is no diachronic change in the field of genres. New genres emerge through the transformation of older genres. The use of a genre in a new situation may affect the way that genre is interpreted. And within the tradition-history of a work, new motifs and structures may be added which alter the way in which that work is read. But such "new" genres must be understood in their diachronic and synchronic relations to existing literary codes and conventions.[8] Otherwise, so our assumption would dictate, the reader would be unable to judge *what kind* of work was before him or her.[9] If genres are shared cultural conventions for linguistic organization, then writer and reader must share some understanding of genre intention if the text and its constituent parts are to be grasped adequately. An utterance which is entirely idiosyncratic or "idiolectal" with respect to genre would be unintelligible to all but its author.

Kleinliteratur and the Question of Genre

The past neglect of the question of literary genres in biblical works may be traced to an understanding of the nature of early Christian literature which was dominant throughout the era of early form criticism. It was widely affirmed, and not without some justification, that the Gospels were not "literature in the strong sense" comparable with the

6. Paul Ricoeur, "The Hermeneutical Function of Distanciation," *Philosophy Today* 17 (1973) 136.

7. See Edgar V. McKnight, *Meaning in Texts* (Philadelphia: Fortress Press, 1978) 205–15; Mary Gerhart, "Generic Studies," *JAAR* 45 (1977) 309–25.

8. See Norman Peterson, *Literary Criticism for New Testament Critics* (Philadelphia: Fortress Press, 1978) 44.

9. Peterson, "Notion of Genre," esp. 136–39.

"high literary products" of classical culture. The alternative was that early Christian literature was the sedimentation or crystallization of oral tradition. This accounted for the general lack of literary conceits. The written aspect of Christian literature was virtually incidental. Bultmann's statement on the subject typifies this understanding:

> [The literary composition of the Gospels] involves nothing new in principle, but only completes what was begun in the oral tradition . . . it can only be considered in organic connection with the history of the material as it lay before the evangelists.[10]

This form-critical assumption was rooted in the work of Franz Overbeck (1837–1905). Overbeck was impressed with the fact that in form-critical terms, there seemed to be no continuity between the New Testament and patristic literature. Within the former, one finds either *non-literary* forms (e.g., personal letters—the Pauline epistles) or *literary* forms which were atypical of both later patristic literature and contemporary Hellenistic literature.[11] This observation provided the empirical basis for positing a distinct class of *Urliteratur*, distinguishable from literature proper, which "Christianity so to speak created from its own resources, insofar as it grew up on the basis of, and for the unique inner interests of, the Christian community, before its intermixture with the surrounding world."[12] Such literature, elsewhere called "pre-literature" and *Kleinliteratur*, was the immediate expression of the practical interests of the primitive church, and not the product of a mediation of the literary traditions of antiquity. *Kleinliteratur* was, for that reason, *sui generis*. Overbeck conceded that early Christians did borrow the form of "apocalypse" from Judaism and that they relied upon Hellenistic forms for the production of the Sibyllines. However, "what it [early Christian literature] in fact wholly avoids are the existing forms of profane literature; therefore to that extent it can be called, if not a purely Christian literature, then purely religious."[13]

A corollary to the characterization of *Kleinliteratur* as a surrogate for oral tradition was the minimizing of authorial activity. Dibelius typifies this approach to the Gospels:

---

10. Bultmann, *Tradition*, 321 [347]. Dibelius also posited a continuum between oral tradition and the written Gospels and at the same time refused to ascribe full literary status to the written Gospels: "The literary understanding of the synoptics begins with the recognition that they are collections of material" (*Tradition*, 3).
11. Overbeck, "Über die Anfänge."
12. Ibid., 443 [trans. by auth.].
13. Ibid.

The position taken by the evangelists in forming the literary character of synoptic tradition is limited. It is concerned with the choice, the limitation, and the final shaping of the material, but not with the original moulding. The form in which we hear of the words and deeds of Jesus is due only in a certain degree to the personal work of the evangelist.[14]

In his classic study of the gospel form Karl Ludwig Schmidt stated, "The gospel is fundamentally not *Hochliteratur* but *Kleinliteratur*, not the production of an individual but a folk book, not a biography but a cult legend."[15] Again the legacy of Overbeck is evident.[16] The written gospels are not literary creations of authors but surrogates for the oral tradition of a community. They represent the spontaneous emanations of early Christian cultic activity. Final texts are regarded as little more than "collections of material" (Dibelius). Given this view of the production of early Christian literature, it is not at all surprising that investigation of literary genres played hardly any role.

Many of the observations of Dibelius in respect to the character of the Synoptic tradition are still of considerable value. The marks of oral production and transmission are still visible in the "small units." And indeed one cannot really speak of "authorship" of those units; the dynamics of oral performance and transmission obscures almost entirely the individuals who stand behind the oral units. But to admit this does not demand that we concede to Overbeck the essentially non-literary character of the compositions which employ these "small units." Overbeck and those form critics who were so influenced by him consistently undervalued the factors involved in the transition from the oral to written medium. Several factors have provoked a reassessment of the idea of *Kleinliteratur* and the literary-critical agenda which that idea dictated.

The first is the rise and success of redaction criticism with its attention to the theological and literary intentionality of a redactor. Redaction

14. Dibelius, *Tradition*, 3; see also *Die Geschichte der urchristlichen Literatur* (ed. F. Hahn; TBü 58; Munich: Chr. Kaiser, 1975) 42.

15. Karl Ludwig Schmidt, "Die Stellung der Evangelien," 76 [trans. by auth.]. The congeniality of this conclusion with the program of dialectical theology did not escape Schmidt's notice: "Thus the form-critical approach is a theological matter. The general philosophical question about content and form carries over into the theological question of God and the world, Christianity and culture. Radical and positive consideration of the Gospels is an exponent of the main theological question" (p. 134; [trans. by auth.]). Similarly Bultmann, "Gospels (Form)," 89: "Thus [the Gospels] are a unique phenomenon in the history of literature and at the same time are symbolic of the distinctive nature of the Christian religion as a whole."

16. See Güttgemanns, *Candid Questions*, 125–39; Philipp Vielhauer, "Franz Overbeck und die neutestamentliche Wissenschaft," *Aufsätze zum Neuen Testament* (TBü 31; Munich: Chr. Kaiser, 1965) 248–49.

criticism has successfully demonstrated that the evangelists were more
than simple tradents of oral units; on the contrary, they shaped, rewrote and arranged their materials in such a way that it is legitimate to
call them authors. The rise of redaction criticism did not, however,
automatically open up the question of the genre of the Gospels (or Q); in
fact many critics still maintain the form-critical view that the gospel
form arose essentially as an expansion of the (oral) kerygma, and hence
is a function of the oral tradition, uninfluenced by the genres of *Hochliteratur*. Nevertheless, redaction criticism had the effect of driving a
wedge between the tradition and the redactor, and this, in turn, made
the questions of authorial and genre intention allowable, at least in
principle.

In the second place, one of the essential presuppositions of the idea of
Kleinliteratur was subject to a serious objection. Ehrhart Güttgemanns
has shown that the idea of *Kleinliteratur* emerged as a corollary to the
thesis that the church was an eschatological community which was not
oriented towards the world.[17] To quote Dibelius:

> The company of unlettered people which expected the end of the world
> any day had neither the capacity nor the inclination for the production of
> books, and we must not predicate a true literary activity in the Christian
> Church of the first two or three decades.[18]

But as Güttgemanns rightly points out, "this represents a very general
psychological conclusion from analogy"[19] and one which is scarcely consonant with the historical analogy provided by Jewish apocalyptic.
Naherwartung did not prevent apocalypticists or the Qumran covenanters from writing. Indeed the form of apocalypse, with its narrative
format and pseudonymous mode of presentation, necessarily entails a
written document. To argue that the apocalypse is itself *Kleinliteratur*[20]
only obfuscates the matter; the production of apocalypses can in no way
be conceived of as simply a process of sedimentation of oral apocalyptic
tradition. Moreover, it can be shown that apocalyptic *did* employ literary
patterns represented also in Graeco-Roman, Gnostic and Persian writings.[21] Even though we can agree with Overbeck that patristic writers

17. Güttgemanns, *Candid Questions*, 130–31.
18. Dibelius, *Tradition*, 9.
19. Güttgemanns, *Candid Questions*, 131 [emphasis original].
20. Thus H. Thyen, "Positivismus in der Theologie und ein Weg zu seiner
Überwindung," *EvT* 31 (1971) 472–95, esp. 491–92.
21. See John J. Collins, "Towards the Morphology of a Genre," *Semeia* 14 (1979) 18
and passim.

did not continue many of the forms which are encountered in the primitive Christianity, we should not adopt too quickly the dogmatic assumption that early Christianity did not, in view of its eschatology, use the literary conventions of antiquity.

Third, observations made by modern folklorists have given cause to doubt Overbeck's thesis. Folklorists have noted that the distinction between oral tradition and written texts becomes critical in regard to the way in which the two function. Folklore exists only as the objectification of a community. It is continuously variable in form, and exists in a "homoeostatic balance." If the "oral text" no longer functions in the act of social communication it is modified so that it will fulfil that function. If it cannot be modified it disappears. This is the "censorship" of oral performance. Literary texts, by contrast, are completely determinate in form, and they achieve independence from the process of modification and censorship precisely by their written character.[22] A text is meant to be read, not performed. In his classic study of the Homeric epic, A. B. Lord showed from empirical investigation of contemporary Yugoslav epic poets that the transition from oral to written composition consti- tutes a fundamental and significant shift in form and function.[23] The formulaic pattern of oral performance may be altered or abandoned, thematic variations may be introduced and stylistic changes may occur.[24] In some cases, the transition from oral to written is precipitated or facilitated by borrowed and foreign *literary* genres.[25] In other words, the production of a literary work from oral tradition can involve *non- traditional* factors. The production of a literary work cannot be reduced to sedimentation of its oral past. The genre of a written work cannot be assumed to be a pure continuation or function of the prior oral tradi- tion.[26]

Finally, careful literary examination of various NT writings in fact indicates that Overbeck's characterization of early Christian texts as *sui generis* and "non-literary" in nature is inadequate. To illustrate the point:

22. See Hermann Bausinger, *Formen der Volkspoesie* (Berlin: Schmidt, 1968) 40–50; P. Bogatyrev and Roman Jacobson, "Die Folklore als eine besondere Form des Schaffens," *Donum Natalicum Schrijnen* (Nijmegen: N. v. Dekker; Utrecht: van de Vegt, 1929) 900– 913; Güttgemanns, *Candid Questions*, 193–96.

23. Lord, *Singer*.

24. Ibid., 129–32.

25. Ibid., 138.

26. Güttgemanns (*Candid Questions*, 204–11) tends to exaggerate the discontinuous aspects of oral and written phases whereas Lord (*Singer*, 130) notes that "non-formulaic expressions will be found in an oral text" as "seeds of the 'literary' style" and that formulaic speech perdures in written texts as vestigial oral style.

Recent studies on both Galatians and Romans have shown that the constructions of these letters have been heavily influenced by the literary and rhetorical traditions from Hellenistic literature.[27] These texts simply cannot be regarded as the sedimentation of oral tradition; they are works produced through the mediation of established literary genres.

There is indeed validity in Overbeck's refusal to classify early Christian literature as *Hochliteratur*; for example, compared with Hellenistic biography, the Gospels may be found wanting. But it should be realized that if for this reason the Gospels are considered as *Kleinliteratur*, then there are a substantial number of non-Christian compositions which belong to the same category: the *Sentences of Secundus* and Lucian's *Demonax* also display an episodic and rather disjointed presentation of materials. As a matter of fact, the Synoptics are in many regards better organized than, for example, *Demonax*. The rigid distinction between *Hochliteratur* and *Kleinliteratur* and the attendant characterizations "literary" and "non-literary" must give way to a more adequate heuristic. The literature of early Christianity, just like Hellenistic literature, admits of more and less sophisticated literary forms. To regard the less sophisticated forms as merely surrogate oral tradition is to miss the real literary character of those simple forms.

Conclusion

An investigation of the genre of Q is both necessary and timely. Necessary, because of the theoretical considerations discussed above: a genre conception is constitutive to every act of interpretation. And the investigation is timely: the emerging awareness of the inadequacy of the idea of *Kleinliteratur* and criticism of any attempt to segregate Christianity from its Hellenistic environment invites a re-evaluation of the significance of the literary forms with which Christians chose to articulate their message.

STATUS QUAESTIONIS

In the 150 years since Schleiermacher's essay on the sayings source used by Matthew, there has been remarkably little attention paid to the genre or *Gattung* of this source. For many critics, the designation *Spruch-*

---

27. E.g., Hans-Dieter Betz, *Galatians* (Hermeneia; Philadelphia: Fortress Press, 1979); Stanley K. Stowers, *The Diatribe and Paul's Letter to the Romans* (SBLDS 57; Chico, Calif.: Scholars Press, 1981).

quelle, Redensammlung or "the Logia" adequately described the nature of
Q. Only a few made more specific suggestions. Schleiermacher himself
referred to the Sermon on the Mount (i.e., the first speech in his *Redenquelle*) as a gnomologium but said nothing of the genre of the collection
as a whole.[28] Holtzmann compared Q with the *Aphorisms* of Hippocrates,[29] presumably on the basis that both Q and these aphorisms were
thematically organized, and both were thought to represent the authentic teachings of Jesus and Hippocrates which were compiled and elaborated by disciples.[30] In a somewhat casual aside the classicist F. H.
Colson spoke of Q as a collection of chriae similar to those collected by
Hecaton and Zeno of Citium and used in philosophical propaganda.[31]
For the most part, however, comparisons between Q and other Graeco-
Roman literature were not made. Nevertheless, most critics have ven-
tured some opinion on the general character of Q. These opinions are
usually based upon a variety of factors: the assessment of the content
and extent of Q, its probable use and its age relative to other documents
of primitive Christianity. Opinion falls into two general classes: those
which characterize Q as biographical and as having narrative aspects,
and those which term it a sentence or speech collection.

Q as a "Gospel"

In his introduction to the New Testament, Bernhard Weiss contended
that "the oldest source" (as he termed Q) contained not only material
from the double tradition but also speech material found in Mark (2:24–
28; 3:31–35; 10:28–34; 13:5–31) and "such pieces of Mark's narrative as
have a simpler and more original form in the first Gospel."[32] These
included the healing of the Syro-Phoenician woman's daughter, the
feedings of the multitudes, the transfiguration and the anointing.[33] He
conceded that the source did not contain a passion narrative. Nor did it

---

28. Schleiermacher, "Zeugnisse," esp. 373.

29. Holtzmann, *Lehrbuch*, 364.

30. The approximately 400 sentences constituting the *Aphorisms* are divided into
seven groups of related pronouncements on diet, diagnostics, purgatives, etc. In fact,
the authenticity of nearly every item in the Corpus Hippocraticum has been questioned,
including the *Aphorisms*. See H. Gossen, "Hippokrates 16," *PW* 8 (1913) 1844–46; F.
Kudlien, "Hippokrates," *Der kleine Pauly* 2 (1979) 1169–72.

31. Colson, "Quintilian," 150.

32. Bernhard Weiss, *Introduction*, 2:224–25.

33. Ibid., 224–26. Weiss argued that Mark used Q, abbreviating it and adding
narrative. But since both Matthew and Luke also had access to Q, they often preserved
a simpler and more original form of sayings and narratives (even those in the triple
tradition).

aim at biographical completeness.[34] Nevertheless, most of the sayings had "historical introductions"[35] and could legitimately be regarded as "fragments of preliminary history."[36] The source began with the words of the Baptist, the baptism and the temptations and concluded with Jesus' anointing. Short narratives were used to divide the smaller collections of sayings and discourses.[37]

The source conjectured by Weiss was intended more for edification than it was for historical knowledge, and it did not contain a continuous narrative or intend to provide a complete account of Jesus' ministry.[38] Nevertheless the historicizing introductions to the sayings, and the presence of narratives in Q distinguished it from a pure sentence collection. It was for Weiss the beginning of a biography.

Another approach was taken by B. W. Bacon. In his search for a text which would provide the hermeneutical key for the whole document, Bacon seized upon Matt 12:18–21, the quotation from Isa 42:1–4, which he ascribed to Q.[39] The kind of ministry described in Q 7:18–35—characterized especially by rejection and unbelief—is consonant with the description of the Suffering Servant of Isa 35:3–10; 42:1–7; 52:7; and 61:1–2. According to Bacon the Isaiah quotation offers "the key to a precanonical outline of the gospel story."[40] Q is not simply a sayings collection but

> a presentation of the *kind of ministry* represented by Jesus' career, a true *Gospel* (*pace* Harnack), in which Jesus was set forth as the redeeming "Wisdom" of God, the Suffering Servant of Isian prophecy, humbled in obedience unto rejection and death and, therefore, also "highly exalted." It will have been a gospel more akin to Paul and John than many of our extant Synoptics.[41]

Weiss and Bacon diverge vastly in their understandings of the extent and importance of Q. For both, however, Q was a "gospel": it aimed at a presentation of an account and interpretation of the career of Jesus. The

---

34. Ibid., 227.
35. Ibid., 222.
36. Ibid.
37. Ibid., 226–27.
38. Ibid., 227, 235, 238.
39. Bacon, "Nature and Design." Bacon argued that Matt 12:18–21 was not due to Matthaean redaction since (1) it was not entirely consonant with Matthew's context (as summary of Mark 3:7–12); (2) the quotation was non-Septuagintal (unlike other Matthaean instances) and (3) it cohered with other non-Marcan (i.e., Q) material such as Matt 11—12 (pp. 680–86).
40. Ibid., 688.
41. Ibid. [emphasis original].

difficulty with both such evaluations consists in the fact that they rest on imputing to Q a good deal of the triple tradition, in the case of Weiss, and in the case of Bacon, a text attested only in Matthew. Many arguments could be raised against the inclusion of each of the texts mentioned by Bacon and Weiss. But there is a methodological problem with their procedure which is of more importance: both rely upon what is *least* certain as components in Q for what is *most* determinative of its character.

While Weiss and Bacon stopped short of attributing passion and resurrection texts to Q, several others did precisely that. F. C. Burkitt, W. E. Bundy and Emanuel Hirsch attempted to conceive of Q in biographical terms by ascribing Lucan *Sondergut* to Q or by tracing "minor agreements" between Matthew and Luke in the passion accounts to a Q passion story.[42] These will be examined in greater detail in the next chapter. Here it is sufficient to make two observations. First, even if all of the texts considered by Burkitt, Bundy and Hirsch were admitted to Q, we would still be very far from a continuous passion narrative, to say nothing of a narrative-biographical format such as the Synoptics represent. Second, the conclusion that Q contained a passion narrative seems to have been based as much on *a priori* assumptions as upon actual literary evidence. Burkitt states, "I find it difficult to believe that a document Q, which on any hypothesis goes into some detail about the Ministry of Jesus, could have been silent about the end of his earthly career."[43] Hirsch adopted the view that there was only one literary form in which the Jesus materials could be related: the gospel form created by Mark.[44] Collections of sayings and parables and catanae of miracle stories are phantoms created by source critics; it is only within the gospel form that interest in speeches, parables and miracles could find adequate expression.[45] Since in Hirsch's view, a sayings collection was a "non-concept," Q must be regarded as a complete gospel with passion and resurrection narratives. In fact Hirsch asserts that Q borrowed this form from the earliest form of Mark, upon which Q was dependent.[46]

The attempt to solve the problem of the genre of Q by considering it a "gospel" was not very satisfactory. It rested upon arguments which are ultimately unconvincing: that Q originally contained narrative materials

---

42. Burkitt, *Gospel History*, 134–45; idem, *Earliest Sources*, 109–10; Bundy, *Jesus*, 481, 499, 502; Emanuel Hirsch, *Frühgeschichte*; idem, "Fragestellung," 106–24.
43. Burkitt, *Earliest Sources*, 111.
44. Emanuel Hirsch, *Frühgeschichte*, 2:33.
45. Ibid., 33; idem, "Fragestellung," 109.
46. Emanuel Hirsch, "Fragestellung," 115.

from the triple tradition or from *Sondergut*, and that any recounting of the words of Jesus would necessarily also include an account of his death and resurrection. The attempt to conceive Q along biographical lines was, nevertheless, symptomatic of the dis-ease felt with respect to the theological "place" of sayings of Jesus within early Christianity. This problem found other expression in the work of Harnack, Wernle and Jülicher, and still another in the form-critical assessments of Q.

Q as the "Gospel of Jesus"

Relatively few have believed that Q had a narrative-biographical framework, still less a passion and resurrection narrative. But if there was agreement on what Q was not, there was no consensus on an alternate generic designation or on the setting in which Q functioned.

At the turn of the century several scholars promoted Q as a document of extremely great historical and theological value. As a result of the way in which this conclusion was defended, the literary and editorial features of Q were minimized or completely overlooked. Adolf Jülicher, who in the early editions of his *Introduction to the New Testament* placed Q earlier than Mark,[47] declared that it was "a collection of the Sayings of Jesus composed without any exercise of conscious art, though doubtless not without some regard to the connection between them . . . "[48] The purpose of the collection was to hand on the sayings of Jesus "*in an authentic form.*"[49] Nevertheless, Jülicher noted that sayings were grouped thematically, and concluded from this that Q was intended to function catechetically.

Paul Wernle agreed with the basic characterization of Q by Jülicher. Although he posited a late Jewish Christian redaction of the collection prior to its reception by Matthew,[50] he declared that in its earlier stages it revealed "the free, almost revolutionary Gospel of Jesus himself," and at the same time afforded "the best portrait of the early Church."[51] Like Jülicher, Wernle held that the collection was for catechetical purposes and that it contained no additions on the part of a compiler.[52]

The position adopted by Harnack was very similar. Q expressed most

---

47. Jülicher, *Einleitung*; ET: *Introduction*, 364.
48. Jülicher, *Introduction*, 356.
49. Ibid., 358 [emphasis original].
50. Wernle, *Synoptische Frage*, 229–30. Wernle regarded this as a corrupting Judaizing redaction consisting of the addition of Matt 5:17–20; 10:5–6 and 23:3.
51. Ibid., 230, 228. Also idem, *The Beginnings of Christianity* (trans. G. A. Bienemann; 2 vols.; New York: G. P. Putnam's Sons; London: Williams & Norgate, 1914) 1:149.
52. Wernle, *Beginnings* 1:148, 149.

clearly the message of Jesus and indeed the essence of Christianity: the acknowledgment of God as father and the morals of repentance, faith and renunciation of the world.[53] As a historical source Q eclipsed Mark, whom Harnack accused of exaggerating apocalypticism and subordinating the "purely religious and moral element" of Jesus' message.[54] Q was compiled for catechetical purposes and aimed to give "with a certain degree of completeness a representation of the major features of our Lord's relationship with His environment."[55] He continued,

> Q is a compilation of discourses and sayings of our Lord, the arrangement of which has no reference to the Passion, with an horizon which is as good as absolutely bounded by Galilee, without any clearly discernible bias, whether apologetic, didactic, ecclesiastical, national or anti-national.[56]

So important was Q theologically that Harnack declared one Q saying, Q 10:22 (Matt 11:27), to be the "basis of faith and of theology."[57] As a document compiled without significant editorial intrusion, Q provided a historical source of unparalleled value, and as a relatively complete account of the "gospel of Jesus" it served as the foundation for theology.

Several aspects of the treatments of Jülicher, Wernle and Harnack invite their being grouped together. Each tended to isolate Christianity from its environment, declaring, on the one hand, that it transcended Jewish forms of expression and, on the other, that it was not yet contaminated by Hellenism or re-Judaizing influences. Even more important is the view that Q was a record of the preaching of Jesus. The obverse of this characterization of Q as the "pure gospel of Jesus" was the assertion that the collector of Q did not significantly reshape or otherwise influence it. Whereas Harnack was ready to ascribe to Mark real literary and theological activity, he conceded no such role to the tradents of the Q material. Owing to the desire to see in Q the teachings of the historical Jesus, Q could not come into focus as a document with its own distinctive theological and literary intentionality. So long as the editorial contribution to Q was minimized or overlooked, and the document was treated in isolation from its literary environment, the question of the literary genre of Q could not even arise.

---

53. Harnack, *Sayings of Jesus*, 250 [173].
54. Ibid., 250–51 [173].
55. Ibid., 171 [121].
56. Ibid.
57. Adolf von Harnack, *History of Dogma* (7 vols.; New York: Dover Pubs., 1961) 7:273.

The Subordination of Q to the Kerygma

The consensus developed by Jülicher, Harnack and Wernle was not to last long. Jülicher, who had once affirmed the priority of Q to Mark, was later to be persuaded of the contrary position. In the 1906 revision of his *Introduction*, he argued that Q was post-Marcan.[58] This did not mean that a literary dependence upon Mark could be established; some of the Q tradition could be traced back to the apostle Matthew. But, Jülicher held, it was only under the influence of Mark that Q reached its final form.[59] Beginning as a "loose list of sayings" it gradually grew into a "half-gospel" (*Halbevangelium*)[60] which functioned as a catechetical supplement to the Second Gospel.[61]

Instrumental in this reassessment was Julius Wellhausen's *Einleitung in die drei ersten Evangelien*.[62] Wellhausen sought to prove not only that Mark was anterior to Q, but also that Q depended upon Mark in a literary way.[63] The conclusion which Wellhausen reached had far-reaching effects. Like others he supposed that Q was intended as a catechetical collection;[64] but more important, he contended that Q *intentionally* omitted narrative accounts, of which the most prominent were the passion and resurrection stories, *because* it presupposed the Marcan passion:

> On the surface the difference is that while Mark combines narrative and didactic material, the other documentary source restricts itself mainly to the didactic. It omits the narrative *intentionally*. That it knew the passion, which it passes over in silence, goes without saying. . . Thus it is not out of the question that it presupposes and attempts to elaborate on Mark.[65]

Hence Q was not only historically secondary to Mark, but theologically and hermeneutically dependent upon the Second Gospel.

The appropriateness of the notion of Q as a "half-gospel" (to use Jülicher's term) depends entirely upon the prior assumption that Q was formulated with a "full gospel" in sight. For Jülicher this assumption

---

58. Jülicher, *Einleitung*[5.6] §28; continued in Jülicher and Fascher, *Einleitung*[7].
59. Jülicher, *Einleitung*[5.6] 322.
60. Ibid., 322; Jülicher and Fascher, *Einleitung*[7] 347–48.
61. Jülicher, *Einleitung*[5.6] 348, 364.
62. Jülicher (*Einleitung*[5.6] 320) accepted Wellhausen's thesis that Q was composed after Mark, but did not follow Wellhausen's assertion that Q depended upon Mark in a literary way.
63. Wellhausen, *Einleitung*[1] §8, [2] §6. He argued that Q was consistently secondary and inferior to Mark, and since he rejected the possibility of mutual independence, he concluded that Q depended upon Mark.
64. Wellhausen, *Einleitung*[1] 84, [2] 75.
65. Wellhausen, *Einleitung*[2] 159–60 [trans. and emphasis by auth.].

becomes especially problematic since he was unwilling to concur with Wellhausen that Q depended upon Mark literarily.[66] This meant that he left himself with no independent support for his hermeneutical conclusions. Wellhausen indeed tried to demonstrate literary dependence by showing that in the instances of Mark-Q overlap, the Q version was always the more recent.[67] He was not, however, successful in disposing of the objection that even if Mark's traditions were more primitive than those of Q—a thesis which has not met with critical acceptance—that did not necessitate the conclusion that Q depended upon Mark in a literary way. In view of the relative paucity of Mark-Q overlaps, it is difficult to show that the *plan* of Mark influenced the construction of Q in any way at all. The fact that the Baptist's preaching and the temptations of Jesus occur first in both documents is hardly unexpected given the nature of these pericopae. The attempt to supply the hermeneutic for Q by appeal to Mark was notably unsuccessful because it could not be demonstrated that Q knew Mark or was dependent upon it.

Although Wellhausen did not succeed in attracting many to his position of the literary dependence of Q on Mark, his influence was far-reaching in two other respects. First, he had cast doubt upon the idea that Q was the "pure gospel of Jesus" by pointing to the significant degree of Christianizing of the Q material through retrojection of later ecclesial and christological concerns.[68] Second, he introduced the notion that theologically and hermeneutically, Q was not to be interpreted solely on its own terms. Later critics in both England and Germany, while rejecting Wellhausen's late dating of Q, agreed that theological priority was to be given not to Q but to the kerygma of the Crucified and Risen One and Q was to be interpreted in this light.

That Q should be understood as a supplement to the passion kerygma found one of its earliest exponents in B. H. Streeter.[69] According to Streeter, Q lacked references to the passion because the events of the passion were already well known in Palestine, the putative provenance of Q. What was not so well known were the details of Jesus' teaching.[70]

---

66. Jülicher, *Einleitung*[5,6] 321. He also rejected Wellhausen's skepticism regarding the historical value of the Q tradition (p. 335).

67. Wellhausen, *Einleitung*[1] §8, [2] §6.

68. Wellhausen, *Einleitung*[1] 84, [2] 75. Bultmann ("Synoptic Gospels," 22) quotes with approval Wellhausen's conclusions that "the sayings-document, like Mark, has been influenced by the theology of the primitive community; it grew out of the primitive community and is steeped in its views and interests and therefore gives us no infallible reflection of the preaching of Jesus."

69. Streeter, "Literary Evolution," esp. 215, 219.

70. Ibid., 215–19. Streeter contended that Q supplemented the (Palestinian) oral passion tradition, and that Mark was written in Rome to supplement Q (where the

Q provided a convenient handbook for missionaries, dealing with the problems which arose in the early years of the Christian mission. Q 3:7–9, 16–17 and 7:18–35 responded to the problem of the relation of John and his disciples to Jesus; Jesus' relation to Pharisaic teaching was clarified by the controversies and woes; and the temptation account explained the relatively unassuming and unspectacular appearance of Jesus.[71] Q did not intend to offer a complete summary of doctrine; it lacked the central affirmation of the death and resurrection of Jesus. Hence, the oral passion kerygma figured importantly in the hermeneutical situation which Streeter proposed for Q. For its theological intelligibility it depended upon that kerygma, and as literary effort it ranked as a rather incomplete *vade mecum*.

Dibelius took a similar position. Whereas Harnack and Wernle treated Q as preaching, Dibelius considered it under the rubric of parenesis.[72] The sayings in Q had not been transmitted as the heart of the Christian tradition; that position was reserved for the kerygma. Sayings of Jesus were employed as parenetic supplement to the kerygma. Q was Christian halakha.[73]

The key to Dibelius' interpretation was provided by the parenetic sections of Pauline epistles. With the exception of 1 Thess 4:15–17 (which Dibelius believed to come from an apocalypse), words of Jesus appear in hortatory contexts. They are not found in conjunction with christological proofs or in the exposition of the kerygma. By using such sayings for parenetic purposes, Dibelius urged, Paul was only conforming to a much broader practice in early Christianity. Missionaries not only preached the kerygma, they also gave ethical instructions to their congregations. It was to meet this need for moral instruction that sayings of Jesus were transmitted and collected.[74]

---

details of the passion were not so well known). Streeter accounted for the paucity of sayings in Mark by the assumption that Q had reached Rome some 20 years prior to the composition of Mark. Later (1924) he rejected Marcan dependence upon Q and confessed that geographical considerations were of less importance than he had previously held.

71. Ibid., 212–14.

72. Dibelius, *Tradition*, chap. 9.

73. Ibid., 28, 238.

74. Ibid., 239–40. Brown ("Parallels") has pressed this even further: the parenetic sections of various NT epistles depend upon Q, whose primary function was parenetic/catechetical. "The manner in which the Epistles use Q is nothing other than the *Sitz im Leben* where the early Church modified the sayings of Jesus into something more useful: that is, into the ecclesiastical revision of Q which has been preserved in Matthew" (p. 29).

As a group which expected the imminent end of the world, the early Christians were "in no way prepared for the necessity of bringing forward hortatory sentences for everyday life."[75] Therefore they relied upon models of Jewish and Hellenistic parenesis, examples of which are found in *Did.* 1–6, Ps-Phocylides, Tobit 4, 12, Ahikar, Isocrates (*Ad Nicoclem*) and Ps-Isocrates (*Ad Demonicum*). Sayings of Jesus were pressed into service and were transmitted alongside Jewish and Greek parenetic sentences.[76] While emphasizing the parenetic motive for the collection of sayings of Jesus, Dibelius also conceded that secondary interests were served, notably the desire to assemble authentic and authoritative pronouncements of Jesus.[77] And in spite of the original parenetic thrust, the sayings were eventually made to serve biographical and theological interests. As Dibelius puts it, "[W]hat had first been seen as containing Halacha were now seen also to contain Haggada."[78]

Dibelius' comparison of early Christian parenesis with Hellenistic models might have resulted in the treatment of Q in the context of parenetic documents such as Ps-Phocylides or Ahikar. But Dibelius completely avoided the question of the genre of Q. Under the influence of Overbeck's idea of *Kleinliteratur* he minimized the literary aspects of early Christian compositions. Q, in fact, was to be treated not as a document (*Schrift*), but as a stratum (*Schicht*).[79]

In *The Four Gospels*, the classic British formulation of the two-document hypothesis, B. H. Streeter took a similar position.[80] In the years since the publication of *Oxford Studies in the Synoptic Problem* he had become convinced that Mark did *not* know Q and instead argued that Q and Mark were essentially independent of each other. However, he maintained the view that Q presupposed the oral tradition of the passion and "its redemptive significance."[81] Thus for Streeter as for Dibelius, Q was ethical supplement to the kerygma, not the heart of Christian preaching. Unlike Dibelius, however, he made some explicit literary comparisons: Q was "a collection of the 'Wise Sayings' of Christ comparable to a book like Proverbs or the *Pirke Aboth*, with very little attempt at arrangement."[82] He also drew attention to the fact that like the

75. Dibelius, *Tradition*, 240.
76. Ibid., 238, 240.
77. Ibid., 242.
78. Ibid., 246.
79. Martin Dibelius, *Die Formgeschichte des Evangeliums* (Tübingen: J. C. B. Mohr [Paul Siebeck], 1959³) 236.
80. Streeter, *Four Gospels*, 187–91.
81. Ibid., 292.
82. Ibid., 286.

Didache, "a first century manual of Christian instruction," Q ended with an apocalyptic section.[83] Another analogy for Q was provided by Jeremiah: like prophetic books, Q consisted mostly of discourse with only an occasional narrative to explain the teaching:

> The baptism and temptation are described because the author regarded these as virtually the "call" to the Messianic office. The author would regard them, like the "call" of the Prophet so often given in the Old Testament, as of great apologetic value as evidence of the Divine authorisation of our Lord's mission.[84]

Unfortunately Streeter did not work out these suggestions in any detail, nor did he decide which of these rather diverse literary analogies best approximated Q in form and function.

T. W. Manson showed himself to be under the influence of the kerygma/didache schema too:

> For the primitive Church the central thing is the Cross on the Hill rather than the Sermon on the Mount . . . Christian doctrine and Christian ethics may be the inevitable corollaries of the Christian gospel; but they are corollaries.[85]

Again, Q was treated as catechetical supplement to the kerygma.[86] While Manson did not propose any literary analogies for Q, he did outline the probable motives for its collection. Primary was the need for catechesis following missionary preaching. But three secondary interests could be detected: a personal interest in Jesus himself; an apologetic interest in the words of Jesus as a means by which to attract Gentiles already exposed to Stoic moralizing propaganda; and an interest in guarding and defending against distortions and misrepresentations of Jesus' words by opponents.[87]

The weaknesses inherent in this view are evident. As with Dibelius and Streeter, the priority of the kerygma is presupposed rather than demonstrated. No attention was given to the fact that Q reflects none of the language of the kerygma—something of an embarrassment if Q is indeed circulated in churches in which the preaching of the cross was central. In addition, the assumption that the kerygma occupied the

---

83. Ibid., 287–88.
84. Ibid., 291. Gilbert ("Jesus") compared the *contents* of Q with those of Isaiah and Jeremiah, emphasizing Jesus' role as a prophet. He observed that Q attached no more importance to Jesus' death than did the prophetic books to the death of the prophets.
85. Manson, *Sayings,* 9.
86. Ibid., 13, 14, 17.
87. Ibid., 9–11.

dominant *theological* position had important *hermeneutical* ramifications for Q. Manson marginalized the non-parenetic portions of Q—in particular the polemical passages against "this generation" and in fact asserted,

> A . . . striking feature in Q is the exceedingly small [*sic*] quantity of polemical matter it contains . . . This fact again is explicable on the assumption that the work was intended for use within the Christian community as a manual of instruction.[88]

The characterization of Q as parenesis is a mark of Bultmann's treatment of Q. Deeply influenced by the historical skepticism of Wellhausen, Schmidt and Wrede,[89] Bultmann was ready to acknowledge that the early church progressively elaborated its ethical teaching and created or co-opted sayings which were then transmitted as dominical sayings. Q was therefore not primarily a source for the teachings of the historical Jesus, as Harnack had believed, but for those of the primitive church.

From the outset Bultmann posited a fundamental continuum between the oral and written phases of tradition. Consequently, Q was treated as an extension of the sayings tradition. The "laws" governing the development of the tradition continued through both oral and written phases. Therefore "it is of no consequence whether the tradition is oral or written since due to the unliterary character of the material there is in principle no difference between the two."[90]

Bultmann's treatment of the contents and collection of Q appears in the section of *History of the Synoptic Tradition* devoted to the "Logia" and "Jesus as the Teacher of Wisdom."[91] His model for the growth of Q was taken from the realm of Old Testament wisdom books. The collection and editing of Q could be compared with that of Sirach: the editor of Sirach took over ancient sayings collections, enlarging and combining them with other proverbial materials.[92] According to Bultmann, Q may have begun as a collection of exclusively dominical sayings.[93] During the course of transmission, however, popular wisdom, proverbs, prophecies and laws which had parenetic value were treated as dominical and for

88. Ibid., 16.
89. Bultmann, "New Approach."
90. Bultmann, *Tradition*, 6 [7] [trans. modified by auth.]. See the penetrating critique of this by Kelber ("Mark").
91. Bultmann, *Tradition*, 69–108 [73–113].
92. Ibid., 88–89, 99–100 [92–93, 104].
93. Ibid., 102 [106].

that reason added to Q. The written Q was simply a precipitation of oral "wisdom utterances" analogous to other examples of *Kleinliteratur* such as the Wisdom of Solomon, Proverbs, and *m. 'Abot*.[94]

Speech material was grouped thematically, by formal similarity or by catchword.[95] Bultmann envisaged a rather long period of "editing" and collecting, beginning with an Aramaic version of Q, continuing with its translation into Greek, and coming to completion on Hellenistic soil with the addition of Q 4:1–13; 7:1–10 and 10:21–22.[96] This process of editing found a partial analogy in rabbinic writings, although Bultmann thought that a closer parallel was presented by writings such as *1 Enoch* and the *Didache* which like Q embrace both parenesis and apocalyptic prophecy.[97]

The motives for transmitting and collecting the Q materials were, first, the need for edification in the case of the apocalyptic and prophetic words, and second, parenesis and church discipline in the case of the dominical sayings.[98] Q was not the centre of Christian preaching, but a supplement. Indeed Bultmann was insistent on the theological centrality of the kerygma:

> ... the Christian faith did not exist until there was a Christian kerygma; i.e., a kerygma proclaiming Jesus Christ—specifically Jesus Christ the Crucified and Risen One—to be God's eschatological act of salvation.[99]

Again, the decision in regard to the theological centre of the Christian faith had important implications for the assessment of the place and hermeneutic of Q.

While Bultmann's position in *History of the Synoptic Tradition* is clear and relatively unambiguous, a new perspective is introduced in *Theology of the New Testament*. In this work Bultmann began with the message of the historical Jesus which he characterized programmatically as "among the presuppositions for the theology of the New Testament rather than

94. Bultmann, "New Approach," 50. Interestingly, Bultmann (*Tradition*, 48 n. 2 [50 n. 2]) notes that in the case of apophthegms, the transition from oral to written was facilitated by the influence of the *literary Gattung* of "rabbinic stories," but he does not pursue the implications of this insight for the Q materials.

95. Bultmann, *Tradition*, 322–26 [349–52].

96. Ibid., 328 [354].

97. Ibid., 368–69, 373 [393–94, 399]. More recently Luz ("Logienquelle," 533) draws attention to the parallels between Q and *1 Enoch*, although he focuses on material rather than formal similarities: "An earthly figure was also expected as the Son of Man in the circle which produced the Enoch literature, but in this case it was a figure of the mythic primeval time" [trans. by auth.].

98. Bultmann, *Tradition*, 368 [393].

99. Bultmann, *Theology* 1:3.

part of that theology itself."[100] The primitive church, however, did not simply pass on this message without change. For them, the proclaimer had already become the proclaimed. Jesus was not simply a teacher or prophet or critic of the Law or even coming Son of Man:

> If Jesus' significance to the earliest Church were exhausted in its expecting him as the coming Son of Man, it would still be only a Jewish sect and would not properly be called Christian Church. Nor would the additional fact that it proclaimed the Crucified and Risen One, change matters. For so long, at least, as the resurrection means no more than proof of the exaltation of the Crucified to Son of Man, it is not yet understood as an event that breaks the frame of Jewish eschatology.[101]

The early church did, however, grasp Jesus' person and fate as the decisive eschatological event, if only implicitly. For Q this consciousness is manifest in the fact that the collection begins with the eschatological preaching of John, continues with the beatitudes, "full of eschatological consciousness,"[102] and closes with sayings dealing with the parousia. In an important way, Bultmann's theological assessment of Q is the opposite of Harnack's. For Harnack, Q expressed the "gospel" in its pristine purity, prior to its contamination by polemical, ecclesiastical, apocalyptic and Hellenistic features. For Bultmann, by contrast, the proximity of Q to the message of the historical Jesus was precisely its weakness; Q had taken the decisive theological step to constitute itself as properly Christian, but that step was grasped in only an imperfect and implicit manner.

It will be seen immediately that this is not the understanding of Q given in *History of the Synoptic Tradition*. In *Theology* Q is not simply a hortatory supplement to the kerygma; on the contrary, it had a theological integrity despite its failure to grasp fully the eschatological significance of Jesus' person and fate. Here the kerygma/didache distinction invoked by Dibelius, Manson and Streeter is no longer dominant; it has given way to the understanding of Q as a transitional stage between the unmessianic preaching of Jesus and the fully self-conscious kerygma of the Hellenistic churches.

This raises an important question: If Q is not merely parenesis but preaching of the eschatological event itself—however imperfectly or inadequately that event is grasped—how may we account for its transmission and preservation? We must either posit two somewhat asymmetrical "kerygmas" existing side by side in the same churches, or

100. Ibid., 3 [trans. modified by auth.].
101. Ibid., 37.
102. Ibid., 42.

alternatively presume that Q's "kerygma" derives from circles different
from those which created the "Crucified and Risen Lord" kerygma.
Streeter, in fact, identified the ambiguity which Q presented. While
asserting that Q presupposed the oral teaching of "the Passion and its
redemptive significance"[103] and served as an ethical supplement to this
kerygma, he also noted that for Q the parousia, not the passion, was the
centre of the gospel. The passion "was still one of those calamities which
darken men's understanding of His Purpose, rather than the one act that
has unveiled the mystery."[104] In other words, Q had an understanding of
soteriology which was at variance with the passion kerygma, the alleged
centre of Christian theology. In what sense, then, can it be regarded as a
supplement to the kerygma?

Bultmann and Streeter raised problems which their own treatments of
Q could not solve. As long as it was supposed that the passion kerygma
was theologically and hermeneutically determinative, the distinctive-
ness of Q could not come to the fore. Moreover, important elements
within Q such as the polemical speeches and the properly kerygmatic
statements could not be given their full weight. Although Bultmann did
not pursue this matter—probably because his interest lay not in Q as
such but in the development of the kerygma of the Hellenistic churches
—he planted the seeds for a new assessment of Q as an independent
kerygma reflecting a "second sphere" of Christian theology.

Q as Kerygma

The ambiguities raised by Bultmann's treatment of Q were directly
addressed in 1956 by H. E. Tödt.[105] He began by observing that if one
assumed that the life of Jesus was first regarded as non-messianic, it
would be necessary to account for the fact that it was transmitted at all:

> A community which expected the coming of the one exalted to be the Son
> of Man, as Bultmann sees it, might have been content with the voice of this
> exalted one. Why did they accept the authority of the words of the one on
> earth?[106]

He continued that many pericopae in Q betray no parenetic interest at
all, e.g., the Beelzebul accusation (Q 11:14–26), the request for a sign (Q

---

103. Streeter, *Four Gospels*, 292.
104. Ibid.
105. Heinz E. Tödt, *Der Menschensohn in der synoptischen Überlieferung* (diss.,
Heidelberg, 1956; Gütersloh: Mohn, 1959, 1963²); ET: *Son of Man*.
106. Tödt, *Son of Man*, 241.

11:29–32) and the thanksgiving for revelation (Q 10:21–22).[107] Taking his clue from Bultmann's statement that the earliest church resumed the preaching of Jesus,[108] and from Q's own references to the preaching of the kingdom (Q 9:60 [?]; 10:9), Tödt characterized Q not as parenetic supplement but as the renewed preaching of the kingdom. The resurrection of Jesus was not understood as the subject of the preaching, but as the enablement to preach and as the validation of that preaching:[109]

> The community which preserved the Q material for us, concentrating its attention almost exclusively on Jesus' preaching, was convinced that Jesus' pointing to the coming of God's reign had not lost its meaning in the post-Easter situation, but must be proclaimed anew . . . The meaning of the hortatory sections, too, was not understood separately but in connection with "the most essential subject of our Lord's preaching, namely the kingdom of God is at hand."[110]

Tödt's position is in some ways comparable with Harnack's: Q has independent theological significance as the re-presentation of the preaching of Jesus. The crucial disagreements with Harnack are twofold: Q *has* a Christology and it reflects the views of its redactor and the community in which it circulated. According to Tödt, "christological cognition" had occurred: the resurrection was comprehended as God's confirmation of Jesus' authority. Jesus was the Son of Man:

> Since Jesus was recognized as having the future task of acting as the Son of Man, he had to be recognized correspondingly as having *exousia* while acting on earth. After this recognition, the material from Jesus' teaching could not be rendered otherwise than in a manner imbued with Christological concern.[111]

This provided the *raison d'être* for the collection of Jesus' sayings: since the earthly Jesus had spoken with the *exousia* of the Son of Man his promises were not void but deserved to be proclaimed anew.

Tödt's thesis marked a decisive shift in this historical, theological and hermeneutical valuation of Q. His arguments were soon echoed by his teacher, Günther Bornkamm,[112] and by others. W. D. Davies rejected the

107. Ibid., 246.
108. Bultmann, *Theology* 1:33.
109. Tödt, *Son of Man*, 250.
110. Ibid., 249. The quotation is from M. Dibelius, "Die Bergpredigt," *Botschaft und Geschichte I* (Tübingen: J. C. B. Mohr [Paul Siebeck], 1953) 98.
111. Tödt, *Son of Man*, 253.
112. Bornkamm, "Evangelien, synoptische," 759: "Its [Q's] principal motif is Jesus' proclamation of the coming of the kingdom of God and entry into the kingdom. . . The additional motif of Jesus' authority in word and deed stands in close relationship to the message of the coming kingdom (and the Son of Man)" [trans. by auth.].

designation of Q as catechetical on the grounds that the many important *topoi* of Christian catechesis were lacking in Q.[113] On the contrary,

> Q sets forth the crisis constituted in the coming of Jesus, and it is as a part of this crisis that it understands the ethical teaching of Jesus: it is itself an expression of this crisis.[114]

Yet Davies seems to presume that the passion kerygma existed alongside the tradition of Jesus' sayings:

> . . . the ethical teaching of Jesus in Q was preserved not merely as catechetically useful, and not only as radical demand, but as *revelatory*: it illumines the nature and meaning of the coming of the Kingdom as demand, which is the concomitant of the coming of the Kingdom as grace. It is, therefore, not the case that the words of Jesus were handed down, at first, in isolation from the kerygma and later were found to be necessary in catechetical work and so introduced alongside the kerygma. To judge from Q, concentration on them antedates any catechetical concerns because, from the first, they were included within the kerygma. In Q, crisis and commandment are one.[115]

Ulrich Wilckens attempted to clarify further the relation between Q and the passion kerygma by positing two spheres of Christian tradition.[116] In the Hellenistic churches of the Stephen-group and of Paul, the passion kerygma was central and the few sayings of Jesus which had infiltrated this circle were employed only as hortatory sentences. It was the Jewish Christian church of Palestine which preserved sayings of Jesus, and these were used in the context of the didactic activity of the "Christian synagogue."[117] The same group also transmitted the account of the passion and resurrection which it used in cultic recitation and which functioned as an authorization and legitimation of their continued existence as a group of disciples of Jesus.[118] In this context, words of Jesus were not simply ethical supplement to the central proclamation. The resurrection had confirmed the eschatological authority of Jesus and

---

113. W. D. Davies, *Setting*, 370–80. He relies upon Selwyn's discussion of primitive Christian catechesis in *Epistle*, 363–466.

114. W. D. Davies, *Setting*, 385.

115. Ibid., 386 [emphasis original].

116. Wilckens, "Tradition de Jésus." See also idem "Jesusüberlieferung und Christuskerygma: zwei Wege urchristlicher Überlieferungsgeschichte," *Theologia Viatorum* 10 (1965–66) 310–39.

117. Wilckens, "Tradition de Jésus," 12.

118. Ibid., 13–14. See also idem, "The Tradition-History of the Resurrection of Jesus," *The Significance of the Resurrection for Faith in Jesus Christ* (ed. C. F. D. Moule; SBT 2/8; London: SCM Press, 1968) 51–76, esp. 72.

his words; his words had become the basis for the transformed relation of Jesus with his disciples.[119]

The supposition that the passion narrative co-existed with the Q materials in different *Sitze im Leben* in the same churches was adopted by Käsemann, Steck and Balz.[120] But Q was not understood simply as instruction for the Christian synagogue. Käsemann contended that so long as Q was conceived solely in terms of edification for the community, "it remains absolutely inexplicable why what is undoubtedly the most important element for all time—the narrative of Passiontide and Easter—was omitted."[121] Accordingly, Q must be seen as mission instruction compiled from words of Jesus and from primitive prophetic pronouncements.[122] Steck took a similar position. Q was "a sayings collection for the instruction of these preachers to Israel . . . from which they could take their message for Israel, for supporters and for themselves, but also woes and judgment sayings for the obstinate."[123]

Three observations may be made here. First, knowledge of the passion narratives is assumed rather than proved. As will be argued below, there is substantial evidence to indicate that Q was not influenced by either the passion kerygma or the passion stories. Second, the mission to Israel is too narrow a *Sitz* for Q given the presence of several texts which indicate that Q was already well disposed to Gentiles and relatively less inclined to believe that Jews would respond in any significant numbers.[124] Third, a rather significant proportion of Q is not obviously "mission instruction" at all. The inaugural sermon (Q 6:20b–49) and Q 12:22b–31, 33–34 are directed at a much broader group than simply missionaries. The chriae which recount the antagonism of "this generation" do not function as actual threats aimed at outsiders but instead serve to interpret for the community their relative lack of success in preaching to their countrymen. Steck's description in fact recognizes the diversity of types of material within Q. In the face of this recognition, his description of Q as "instruction for preachers to Israel" is less than adequate.

119. Wilckens, "Tradition de Jésus," 13.
120. Käsemann, "Primitive Christian Apocalyptic"; Steck, *Israel*, 288; Horst R. Balz, *Methodologische Probleme der neutestamentliche Christologie* (WMANT 25; Neukirchen-Vluyn: Neukirchener Verlag, 1967) 170–71.
121. Käsemann, "Primitive Christian Apocalyptic," 119.
122. Ibid., 119–20.
123. Steck, *Israel*, 288 [trans. by auth.]; similarly Balz, *Methodologische Probleme*, 170–71.
124. E.g., Q 7:1–10; 10:13–15; 11:29–32; 13:28–29; 14:16–24.

While Wilckens, Käsemann and Steck conceived Q in relation to the passion story which eventually found its way into Mark, Siegfried Schulz attempted to understand Q solely on its own terms.[125] In contrast to the chronological, geographical and biographical schema of Mark, the Pauline gospel which lacked both Palestinian and Hellenistic Jesus tradition, and the revelatory speeches characteristic of John, Q reflects "the pharisaic-nomistic and apocalyptic structure of thought." Q, however, is not written in the form of an apocalypse, but instead presents the "messianic Torah and halakah of Jesus in the style of *m. 'Abot*."[126] What is innovative about Q is that "for the first time in the Pharisaic-Jewish-Christian tradition, the coming of the Messiah was conceived and controlled in a literary and catechetical way."[127] Q located the saving event not like Mark in the history of Jesus nor like Paul in the death and resurrection, but in Jesus' "messianic Torah, his prophetic-apocalyptic proclamation and his priestly instruction."[128]

By the use of Dibelius' term "halakah," Schulz did not mean to suggest that Q was parenetic. Quite the contrary:

> Behind Q there is a special sphere of tradition with an independent kerygmatic tradition, i.e., a distinct community which preserved and continued to proclaim Jesus' message in the post-Easter situation.[129]

The importance of Schulz's formulation lies in the fact that he tried to understand Q without appealing to a passion kerygma upon which it was theologically and hermeneutically dependent, or to the pre-Marcan passion story alongside which Q functioned as "teaching of the Christian synagogue." That is, Q was treated as a discrete entity from tradition-historical, theological and hermeneutical standpoints. The strength of this view is not difficult to see. It provides a ready explanation for the fact that the contents of Q are not merely parenetic but are sometimes also properly kerygmatic. And it explains the ambiguity which Streeter observed: the reason why Q has a different view of the passion than that of the kerygma (or even the Marcan passion story) is that it derives from a different orbit of tradition.

This point, indeed, can be made more forcefully. Although Q does not contain a passion narrative, or direct reference to Jesus' death, it does contain several references to the murder of Sophia's envoys, among

125. Schulz, "Bedeutung."
126. Ibid., 138 [trans. by auth.].
127. Ibid., 139 [trans. by auth.].
128. Ibid. [trans. by auth.].
129. Schulz, "Gottesherrschaft," 58 [trans. by auth.]; similarly idem, *Spruchquelle*, 30–32.

whom Jesus is undoubtedly the most prominent (Q 6:23; 11:47–51; 13:34–35; cf. 7:31–35). As Arland Jacobson has recently shown, this motif derives from the deuteronomistic understanding of Israel's history.[130] Q apparently conceived of the death of Jesus in accordance with the deuteronomistic pattern: it was the expected fate for a messenger of Sophia. Hence, at precisely the point at which one would expect influence of either the passion kerygma of the Crucified and Risen Messiah, or the narratives of the passion with their apologetic use of the OT, and the motif of the suffering Just One, Q moves in an entirely different direction. This is best explained by supposing, as Schulz does, that Q represents a theologically autonomous sphere of Christian theology.

While Schulz's treatment of Q in its theological integrity is decidedly an advance, his proposed hermeneutic is not very helpful. To assert that Q is "messianic Torah and halakah" presupposes that Q as a document aims at the reinterpretation of the Law. It will be argued in chapter five that Q 6:27–35 (which Schulz apparently has in mind) is not framed as a reinterpretation of the Torah. Moreover, there is a significant portion of Q which is descriptive of Jesus' relations with his contemporaries rather than prescriptive for his followers. For these reasons, "messianic Torah" is not a very appropriate description for Q.

LOGOI SOPHON

A major step toward the solution of the question of the hermeneutic of Q was taken by James M. Robinson in his contribution to the 1964 Bultmann Festschrift.[131] Taking his clue from Bultmann's treatment of the "logia" of Jesus in a chapter entitled "Jesus as the Teacher of Wisdom," Robinson tried to work out the implications of the association of Jesus' sayings with sapiential sentences and their eventual compilation in Q.

Robinson posited a "trajectory" of sayings genres which he termed "sayings of the sages" or "words of the wise," extending from Proverbs on one extreme, to Gnostic collections and *m. 'Abot* on the other. The *Gos. Thom.* is an important representative of the genre. Its incipit reads,[132]

---

130. Jacobson, "Wisdom Christology"; a summary is conveniently available in idem, "Literary Unity."

131. Robinson, "ΛΟΓΟΙ ΣΟΦΩΝ," repr. with alterations as "LOGOI SOPHON"; all references are to the English translation, "LOGOI SOPHON."

132. Robinson ("LOGOI SOPHON," 76–80) has argued convincingly that the title contained in the colophon of Thomas, ⲡⲉⲩⲁⲅⲅⲉⲗⲓⲟⲛ ⲡⲕⲁⲧⲁ ⲑⲱⲙⲁⲥ (NHC II, 99:27–28) is secondary, and that the incipit contains the more original designation.

These are the secret sayings which the living Jesus spoke and which
Didymos Judas Thomas wrote down.
And he said, "Whoever finds the interpretation of these sayings will not
experience death." (NHC II, 32:10–14)[133]

Other early Christian examples of sayings collections designated as *logoi*
may be found in *Did.* 1:3—2:1[134] and in small clusters of sayings
imbedded in early patristic writings, most notably 1 *Clem.* 13:1–2; 46:7–8;
Ptolemaus *Ad Floram* 3.8 and throughout Justin.[135] Within the NT itself
Robinson found the term *logoi* associated with small collections of
sayings of Jesus: the Matthaean sermons are designated as *logoi* (7:28;
19:1; 26:1). Although it uses the term *parabolai* rather than *logoi*, the
Marcan collection of parables and sayings (4:1–34) resembles in both
construction and hermeneutic the *Gos. Thom.* Sayings are gathered by
means of the repeated formula "he said/says"—which is also typical of
other collections such as *Demonax*, and *m.* *'Abot*—and like Thomas,
Mark presents his sayings as riddles or "secret sayings" in need of
interpretation.[136] More recently Robinson has gathered evidence for the
existence of several other first-century Christian sayings collections
which found their way into the NT.[137]

The origin of this trajectory of sayings collection is to be found,
according to Robinson, in Jewish wisdom collections such as Prov 30; 31
and 22:17—24:22, all of which bear the term *logoi* in their openings, and
ultimately in Near Eastern collections such as Ahikar and Amenemope.[138] Other examples are *m.* *'Abot*, whose earliest title seems to have
been "the sayings of 'Nezekin'" and "the sayings of the fathers" (*b. B.*

---

133. *P. Oxy* 654, 1–5 represents the incipit of the Greek Thomas: οὗτοι οἱ λόγοι οἱ
[ἀπόκρυφοι οὓς ἐλά]λησεν Ἰη(σοῦ)ς ὁ ζῶν κ[αὶ ἔγραψεν Ἰούδας ὁ] καὶ Θωμᾶ(ς). καὶ εἶπεν
[ὃς ἂν τὴν ἑρμηνεί]αν τῶν λόγων τούτ[ων εὑρήσῃ θανάτου] οὐ μὴ γεύσηται.

134. *Did.* 1:3: τούτων δὲ τῶν λόγων ἡ διδαχή ἐστιν αὕτη. Robinson draws attention to
the sapiential formula "my son" in 3:1, 3, 4, 5, 6; 4:1; 5:2 and to the exhortation to revere
τοὺς λόγους διὰ παντός, οὓς ἤκουσας (3:8).

135. Robinson, "LOGOI SOPHON," 95–103. Helmut Koester (*Synoptische Überlieferung*, 4–6) first drew attention to the formula "remember the words (sayings,
commandments) of the Lord" (1 *Clem.* 13:1; 46:7; Polycarp *Phil.* 2.3; Acts 20:35; 2 *Clem.*
17:3) which, he argued, derived from a time in which sayings were not yet quoted from
authoritative gospels, but from oral or written collections such as Q. Cameron (*Sayings
Traditions*, 91–131) has explored the use of the term "remembering" in *Ap. Jas.* and notes
the coincidence of "remembering" Jesus' words and the appearance of the Savior (187). I
am indebted to the author for providing me with a pre-publication copy of the final
chapter.

136. Robinson, "LOGOI SOPHON," 89–95.

137. Robinson, "Early Collections." A copy of this paper, which was read at the 32d
session of the Colloquium Biblicum Lovaniense (1981), was kindly provided me by the
author before it became available in *Logia*.

138. Robinson, "LOGOI SOPHON," 103–11.

Qam. 30a); the *T. 12 Patr.*, seven of which contain the term *logoi* in their incipits, and which employ the typically sapiential exhortation to hearken to the sages' words (*T. Dan.* 1:2; *T. Naph.* 1:5, etc.);[139] and portions of *1 Enoch* whose earliest designation seems to have been "the words of Enoch the righteous" (*T. Benj.* 9:1).

Robinson noted the tendency inherent in the *Gattung* to associate the sayings with a sage. The presence of wisdom sayings among Jesus' sayings no doubt accounted for their organization in the *Gattung logoi sophon*. This had important theological ramifications: the tendency at work in the *Gattung* was coordinated with Q's association of Jesus with the heavenly Sophia (Q 7:35; 11:49). When this in turn was coordinated with "the trajectory from the hypostasized Sophia to the gnostic redeemer,"[140] the outcome was the "hidden sayings" of Gnosticism. The ease with which this *Gattung* could undergo gnosticizing distortion explains in part the fact that "orthodox" circles preferred the "gospel" form to that of sayings collections. Elsewhere Robinson speaks of the gnosticizing proclivity of the *Gattung* itself.[141]

In Christian usage the *Gattung* was transitory. On one hand, the "orthodox" eventually adopted the gospel form. Robinson implies that the genre had its main function within an oral context of remembering Jesus' sayings, and depended for its existence upon that context:

> With the final discontinuation of the oral transmission of Jesus' sayings, the *Sitz im Leben* of the gattung was gone; hence orthodoxy contented itself with the canonical gospels . . .[142]

On the other hand, Gnostics came to prefer the dialogue over the simple sayings collection. *Thom. Cont.* (NHC II,7) is indicative of this shift: it begins very much like *Gos. Thom.* ("The secret words that the Savior spoke to Judas Thomas") but is framed as a dialogue between the risen

---

139. Bammel ("Das Ende") adopts the view that Q reflects the form of a testament. He argues that Q 22:28–30 recalls the final instruction and conferral of goods by the patriarch in the testament form; both Q and the testaments are composed largely of parenetic sentences; and Q's Christology can be understood as a development of the view of the patriarch as "a semi-divine being" (pp. 49–50). While Bammel's attempt to understand Q without appeal to a passion narrative is insightful, his comparison with testaments is unconvincing: Q lacks most of the standard features of a testament including the address "my children," the formulaic introduction and closing and the fairly consistent first-person speech characteristic of the *T. 12 Patr.*

140. Robinson, "LOGOI SOPHON," 113.

141. Robinson, "The Problem of History in Mark Revisited," *USQR* 20 (1965) 135; idem, "Kerygma and History in the New Testament," *Trajectories*, 43.

142. Robinson, "LOGOI SOPHON," 102–3.

Jesus and Thomas.[143] Koester in fact has observed the beginning of the transition to dialogue within Gos. Thom. itself.[144]

The term *logoi sophon* has been accepted by many as a suitable generic designation for Q, Thomas and other similar literature.[145] But Robinson's achievement is much more than the coining of a term. First, he recognized that the transition from oral to written stages of the Jesus tradition was enabled by the mediation of literary genres. Additionally, he addressed the related questions of why Jesus' sayings came to be transmitted in such a genre and what theological influence the genre itself exerted upon the interpretation of those sayings. Finally, his use of *Gattungsgeschichte* to analyze Q and the Gos. Thom. represented a methodological advance since, by its presupposition of diachronic change within the field of genres, it allowed Q to be situated not on a static grid of generic traits, but within a matrix of inner dynamisms and polarities expressed within the entire range of documents of a certain class.

Robinson's thesis that Proverbs, *m. 'Abot*, Q and the Gos. Thom. are comparable in form and belong on the same line of generic development is predicated on the fact that all of these collections comprise wisdom sayings and that they are represented as the pronouncements of various sages.[146] It must be recognized that almost all of the examples which Robinson adduces are, from a form-critical and history-of-traditions standpoint, much more homogeneous than Q. In fact Q is a composite of

143. Following Robinson ("LOGOI SOPHON," 83), J. D. Turner (*The Book of Thomas the Contender* [SBLDS 23; Missoula, Mont.: Scholars Press, 1975] 106–8) argues that the incipit originally belonged with the collection of woes and blessings found at the end of the document (142:26—145:16). The final form of *Thom. Cont.* suggests that the sayings format had exhausted its usefulness in the Gnostic or ascetic circles and the dialogue form proved more serviceable.

144. Koester, "Dialog," 544–48.

145. See, e.g., C. E. Carlston, "On Q and the Cross," *Scripture, Tradition and Interpretation* (Grand Rapids: Wm. B. Eerdmans, 1978) 27–33; idem, "Wisdom and Eschatology in Q," in *Logia*, 111–12 (where he tries to distinguish between a "tradition" and a *Gattung* of "wise men's sayings"); Polag, *Christologie*, 21 n. 58; Küchler, *Weisheitstraditionen*, 562–63; Lührmann, *Redaktion*, 89–92; Schenke, "Tendenz," 360–61; Vielhauer, *Urchristlichen Literatur*, 316; Stevan L. Davies, *Gospel of Thomas*, 13–17.

146. There has been resistance to Robinson's comparison of Q with Gos. Thom. though little criticism of consequence. D. Guthrie (*New Testament Introduction: The Gospels and Acts* [London: Tyndale Press, 1965] 145) and Neirynck ("Q") assert that Thomas depends upon the Synoptics and that its gnosticizing tendency distinguishes it from Q. However, the question of Thomas' *sources* is very different from its *genre*, and the fact that Thomas differs theologically from Q is not itself a reason to reject generic similarity. Devisch ("Le Document Q") unconvincingly tries to distinguish Q as a "composition théologique" from Thomas, "un simple recueil," and Dehandschutter ("L'Evangile de Thomas") emphasizes the dialogical elements (which he concedes are secondary developments) and the incipit as distinguishing features of Thomas.

not only wisdom sayings, but chriae, prophetic and apocalyptic words and the temptation story. Is such variety compatible with its inclusion in the genre of *logoi sophon*? The answer to this question is, I think, yes. However, it is necessary to establish more clearly the range of forms which the genre permitted. In addition, Robinson's focus on Jewish sapiential collections is, in view of the international nature of wisdom, too narrow. As a document penned and read in Greek (see below, chapter two), Q must be seen in the context of the literary forms available in Greek.

The assertion that the genre *logoi sophon* was gnosticizing in tendency also requires some qualification. It has been pointed out repeatedly that apart from *Gos. Thom.* none of the other examples of the genre shows any gnosticizing tendency.[147] This suggests that the presentation of "wise sayings" as "secret words" requiring special interpretation was only *one* possibility of the genre. This particular hermeneutical outcome must be understood in terms of a complex matrix of the sociological and historical settings in which the genre was employed, and in terms of the particular forms (e.g., parables, paradoxes) and motifs (e.g., seeking and finding, rest, knowing oneself, heavenly Sophia)[148] which were selected by its editor. In other words, without denying that genres exert theological pressure on their contents (and vice versa!), it would be wise to acknowledge that the specific hermeneutic of Thomas, or Q, or *m. 'Abot* is the product of formal, material and sociological factors.

Robinson's conjecture regarding the disappearance of *logoi sophon* asks for further investigation (though this is beyond the scope of this work). That the genre functioned in a situation of oral transmission of sayings is not at all clear. Although both Q and the *Gos. Thom.* may derive from oral tradition, both are unquestionably written, and as such not subject to the "censorship" of oral transmission. Long after the triumph of textuality, sayings collections such as the *Sentences of Sextus* were still employed. Sextus, at least, does not depend upon an oral hermeneutic. Moreover, it is not obvious that concern about the tendencies of the genre accounts for its disappearance as a vehicle for the transmission of sayings of Jesus. The abandonment of the apocalyptic genre in Judaism after the Bar Cochba revolt is as much a result of historical and social factors as it is a matter of genre-related consider-

---

147. Lührmann, *Redaktion*, 91; Schenke, "Tendenz," 361; Küchler, *Weisheitstraditionen*, 562–63.

148. Stevan L. Davies (*Gospel of Thomas*, 36–61) has recently catalogued the numerous contacts between the *Gos. Thom.* and sapiential tradition.

ations. In the case of sayings of Jesus, it may well be that just as the form
of a post-resurrection dialogue better served the needs of Gnosticism, so
too a narrative presentation of sayings of Jesus came to be regarded as a
more adequate vehicle for transmission of the Jesus tradition.

Robinson's seminal contribution was developed further by Helmut
Koester in a series of articles. Although he accepts Robinson's term *logoi*
sophon, Koester proposes a more specific term for Q and Thomas:
"wisdom gospel."[149] This term signifies not only the fundamentally
sapiential character of the two documents, but also the fact that they
constitute kerygmatic statements, intelligible in themselves without
appeal either to the passion kerygma or to the Synoptic passion narratives.[150] Koester describes the internal principle of the genre itself. The
controlling interest is

> the authority of the word of wisdom as such, which rests in the assumption
> that the teacher is present in the word which he has spoken. If there is any
> "Easter experience" to provide a Christology congenial to this concept of
> the *logoi*, it is here the belief in "Jesus, the Living One" (incipit of the *Gospel*
> *of Thomas*).[151]

Or again:

> Faith is understood as belief in Jesus' words, a belief which makes what
> Jesus proclaimed present and real for the believer. The catalyst which has
> caused the crystallization of these sayings into a "gospel" is the view that
> the kingdom is uniquely present in Jesus' eschatological preaching and that
> eternal wisdom about man's true self is disclosed in his words. The gnostic
> proclivity of this concept needs no further elaboration.[152]

Effects of this gnosticizing "wisdom theology" may be seen directly in
the *Gos. Thom.* But it also bore fruit among Paul's Corinthian opponents,
whom Koester conjectures had access to a collection of Jesus' sayings.[153]

A guiding assumption for Koester is that the so-called apocryphal
gospels are not necessarily subsequent and inferior to the canonical
products in genre and theological tendency. Concretely, this means that
an analysis of the *Gos. Thom.* may reveal the *primary tendencies and*
character of the genre "wisdom gospel." Koester observes that the forms

---

149. Koester, "Apocryphal and Canonical Gospels," 113.
150. Koester, "GNOMAI DIAPHOROI," esp. 135–36; idem, "One Jesus," esp. 166–87;
idem, "Early Christian Beliefs"; idem, *New Testament* 2:147–55.
151. Koester, "GNOMAI DIAPHOROI," 138–39.
152. Koester, "One Jesus," 186.
153. Koester, "Gnostic Writings," 249. Koester posits a "lost sapiential writing" as the
source for Q 10:21–22 and the Synoptic-like sayings in 1 Cor 1—4.

most typical of the wisdom gospel or *logoi sophon* are wisdom sayings, legal pronouncements, prophetic sayings ("I"-words, blessings and woes) and parables. Least typical of this genre are apocalyptic sayings, especially apocalyptic Son of Man sayings.[154] Therefore, as far as *Gattungsgeschichte* is concerned, the *Gos. Thom.* reflects a stage antecedent to the final form of Q. By including Son of Man sayings, Q produced a secondary version of a "wisdom-gospel."[155] Koester conjectures that the introduction of apocalyptic eschatology was a means to attenuate the radicalized eschatology and gnosticizing tendencies at work in earlier forms of Q.[156]

Koester's main purpose was not to analyze the genre of Q in detail, but to establish a methodological principle: that apocryphal gospels may not simply be dismissed as worthless for the understanding of early Christian genres and theological developments.[157] However, his comments on Q suggest an approach which may be able to disentangle the form-critical heterogeneity which has plagued attempts to discuss the genre of Q. Koester proposes,

> If the genre of the wisdom book was the catalyst for the composition of sayings of Jesus into a "gospel" and if the christological concept of Jesus as the teacher of wisdom and as the presence of heavenly Wisdom dominated its creation, the apocalyptic orientation of the *Synoptic Sayings Source* with its christology of the coming Son of Man is due to a secondary redaction of an older wisdom book.[158]

That is, Koester looks not to the final form of Q but to its *formative* elements, which he thinks are sapiential. From this he attempts to describe the later forms of Q by understanding the tendencies and pressures immanent in the basic genre. Like Robinson, he recognizes that "genre" is not a static grid, but a set of dynamisms which influence the hermeneutic of the contents of the collection, and which account in some measure for diachronic change within the history of a given genre.

Before evaluating the strengths and weaknesses of Koester's method-

154. Koester, "GNOMAI DIAPHOROI," 138; idem, "One Jesus," 166–75.
155. Koester, "One Jesus," 186–87; idem, "GNOMAI DIAPHOROI," 138; idem, "Apocryphal and Canonical Gospels," 113.
156. For this reason Koester does not hold that Thomas was dependent upon Q. Instead, Thomas reflects smaller collections, some of which were also incorporated into Q, and others which were directly available also to Mark and Luke. Koester ("GNOMAI DIAPHOROI," 136) characterizes the relation between the *Gos. Thom.* and Q: "Thomas does not use Q, but he does represent the eastern branch of the gattung *logoi*, the western branch being represented by the Synoptic *logoi* of Q . . ."
157. Koester, "Apocryphal and Canonical Gospels," 112.
158. Ibid., 113.

ological insight, and his actual procedure and results, let us turn briefly to a proposal which developed and transformed the Robinson-Koester view of Q.

Q as Prophetic Utterance

Two recent authors have attempted to come to terms with the form-critical heterogeneity which Koester noticed, but with rather different results. In what is perhaps the most systematic attempt to defend the thesis that oracles of Christian prophets made their way into the Synoptic tradition as sayings of Jesus,[159] M. Eugene Boring has argued that a substantial number of Q sayings (22 by his count) are the products of Christian prophets and almost as many (20) have been reformulated or re-presented by such prophets.[160] But Q not only contained oracles; it should be understood as *the address of the Risen Lord to his community*. It is an oracle collection. Boring does not deny that there are some histor-icizing forms in Q: he acknowledges the presence of some chriae which he regards as historicizing in form. But the dominant *Tendenz* of Q is contemporizing:

> While the dissolution of the word of the historical Jesus into the word of the heavenly Jesus had not yet occurred in Q, the center of gravity had shifted, so that Q was moving in the direction of a collection of "sayings of the living Jesus" such as the Gospel of Thomas.[161]

Werner Kelber makes a similar point.[162] From Robinson he adopted the view that Q functioned in the *Sitz* of the oral transmission of Jesus' sayings. In fact, "Q represents an oral genre."[163] The hermeneutical situation which Kelber envisages for Q is its "oral performance" within the community, a performance which makes present the Exalted Lord. Hence it is not the historical figure of the past who authorizes the preachers to continue the proclamation of the kingdom (Q 10:9) but the Risen Lord who speaks through their words.

According to Kelber, this prophetic and contemporizing tendency of Q becomes visible in several ways. The Christology of Q is centered on

---

159. Boring, *Sayings of the Risen Jesus*. See my review in *CBQ* 46 (1984) 144–45.

160. Boring, *Sayings of the Risen Jesus*, 137–79, 180. The following are designated by Boring as oracular: Q 6:22–23; 10:3, 4, 5–12, 13–15, 16, 21–22; 11:29b–30, 39–52; 12:8–9, 10, 11–12; 13:34–35; 16:17; 22:28–30. Prophetic reformulations include Q 6:20b–21; 10:2–16, 23–24; 11:14–23, 29a, 31–32; 12:2–3, 4–7, 22–34, 51–56, 57–59; 13:23–30; 17:22–37. This accounts for 53 percent of Q or 49 percent of the actual word count (p. 198).

161. Ibid., 182.

162. Kelber, *Oral and Written Gospel*.

163. Ibid., 201.

the present and the future, not as in Mark on the past and crucified, Messiah. Moreover, Q has a strong interest in the OT prophets, and portrays both Jesus and his disciples in fundamental continuity with them. Q's prophetic character provides the rationale for its silence about Jesus' death: "A tradition that focuses on the continuation of Jesus' words cannot simultaneously bring to consciousness what put an end to his speaking."[164]

Both Boring and Kelber try to distinguish between the "historicizing" and "contemporizing" tendencies within the Q material. Numerically and hermeneutically the contemporizing forms, typified by the *legō hymin* mode of address, take precedence over the historicizing or *kai eipen autois* form.[165] Boring rejects the appropriateness of Robinson's term *logoi sophon* on the grounds that Q is neither timeless gnomic wisdom nor words of some historic authority, but the prophetic address of the exalted Jesus. It is closer to Jeremiah in genre than it is to Proverbs.[166] More sympathetic to Robinson's term, Kelber argues that "Jesus' identity as prophetic speaker of words of wisdom could easily modulate into that of a gnostic redeemer, bringer of secret sayings."[167] With Koester he affirms the gnosticizing proclivity of the genre. Numerous factors point in this direction:

> the canonical rejection of the sayings genre *in its own right*, Paul's defensive attitude in 1 Corinthians, the paucity of sayings in Mark, Matthew's and Luke's absorption of the oral genre into gospel textuality, and its privileged status in gnosticism.[168]

Even before the explicitly gnosticizing transformation of the sayings, Q's "oral ontology" proved unacceptable to the wider church. Kelber formulates the bold thesis that Mark was composed as a counter-form to the suspicious hermeneutic of Q, and that Q itself was neutralized by its inclusion in Matthew and Luke: sayings of the exalted Jesus were tied to a pre-resurrection Jesus and thus attached to an authority of the past rather than to the exalted Lord.[169]

Several comments are in order here. First, the "oral" nature of Q is asserted rather than proved. Both Kelber and Boring presumably accept the *opinio communis* that Q was a document. The "oral" nature of the

---

164. Ibid.
165. Kelber, *Oral and Written Gospel*, 202; Boring, *Sayings of the Risen Jesus*, 181.
166. Boring, *Sayings of the Risen Jesus*, 180–81.
167. Kelber, *Oral and Written Gospel*, 200.
168. Ibid., 199.
169. Ibid., 203.

genre resides, apparently, in the fact that it was intended for "oral performance." But what then is the precise relationship of the document to the oral performance? Was it a memory aid? Or a casual transcription of what had been performed orally? It is the latter which Kelber has in mind.[170] But this brings us back to all of the problems raised by the idea of *Kleinliteratur:* it does not take sufficient account of the significance of the transition to the written medium.[171] Nor is this model capable of explaining the careful *literary* stylization which is present in Q. Moreover, the example of the *Gos. Thom.* sabotages the hypothesis that the genre as such presupposed oral performance. As the incipit of Thomas clearly shows, its hermeneutic is explicitly *scribal:* interpretation and appropriation of the "truth" of the sayings is accomplished not by oral performance but by penetration of the opacity of the written word.

Secondly, the importance which Boring and Kelber have attached to the *legō hymin* formula as an index of prophetic and contemporizing speech is problematic. As will be indicated below (chapter five), the formula *legō hymin* followed by an imperative corresponds more closely to sapiential usage found, for example, in the *T. 12 Patr.* than it does to prophetic usages.

Finally, it is precarious to infer from the presence of oracular forms among the Q material that Q itself presupposes a prophetic hermeneutic. To take one example: Q 3:7b–9 is indeed a prophetic announcement of judgment. But it has received a *historicizing* setting by its ascription to the Baptist and by the details provided concerning the occasion on which the oracle was delivered (3:7a). That Q contains a number of prophetic forms does not prove that they were *framed* as sayings of the Exalted Lord. What is decisive is the way in which prophetic (and sapiential) materials have been compiled and the compositional patterns which have been imposed. Q does not, for example, employ the most obvious device for signaling the presence of prophetic speech: the unambiguously prophetic *tade legei ho kyrios* or some variant of this. It does not follow the pattern of Hellenistic oracle collections, which preface the oracles with the formula *he Pythia echrēsen* or *ho theos*

---

170. Kelber, "Mark," 22: "Oral traditions can fixate into texts, while texts in turn may stimulate oral impulses. A case of the former would be the possible transfer of the sayings source Q into literary form . . ."

171. Kelber is already thoroughly familiar with these questions and indeed the insight into the inadequacy of the idea of *Kleinliteratur* is fundamental to his work on Mark.

echrēsen.[172] These observations point to the need for compositional analysis when posing the question of the genre and hermeneutic of Q.

The Formative Principle of Q

That there can be such sharp disagreement between those who characterize Q as sapiential and those who see it as prophetic is in part due to the lack of clarity in the definition of such terms and in part, to the ambiguity of the Q material itself. We are still far from agreement as to what constitutes "wisdom"[173] and "prophecy."[174] It is clear, however, that an attempt to distinguish the two on the material grounds that "wisdom" is eudaemonistic, anthropocentric and fundamentally debatable while "prophecy" is theological, theocentric and categorical is too schematic. Recent discussion has also recognized that the sage's counsel presupposes an appeal to divine authority no less than the prophet's oracle.[175] A difference exists in the extent to which human intellect plays a mediating role in the disclosure. But this is not a very helpful criterion when it comes to designating a given saying as prophetic or sapiential.

No one would confuse Proverbs with prophecy, or Isaiah with wisdom—this despite the facts that Prov 8 contains prophetic motifs, and 1 Isaiah has absorbed sapiential elements. But what of the Delphic saying "Know thyself"? Is it an oracle of the Pythian Apollo, or a wisdom saying of Chilon? Ancient writers saw no difficulty in assigning it to both. Certain sayings in Q, e.g., the woes in Q 10:13–15 and 11:49–51, are obvious imitations of prophetic forms. But what of Q's "persecution beatitude" (6:22–23)? Does it rest on "prophetic insight"? Or is it an expression of that "wisdom" which makes its declarations not on the basis of, but in spite of, ordinary experience. The statement by Sirach that the prayer of the poor man is heard immediately (21:5) is similar: it is not arrived at nor is it supported by empirical observation.

---

172. These formulae are used to introduce (respectively) the pronouncements of the Pythia (Herodotus 1.67; 3.57; 4.157, 159) and those of Apollo in the "Tübingen Theosophy" (H. Erbse, ed., *Fragmente griechischer Theosophien* [Hamburg, 1941]).

173. See Crenshaw, "Prolegomenon," esp. 3–13; Murphy, "Hebrew Wisdom," esp. 25–26.

174. David E. Aune, *Prophecy in Early Christianity and the Ancient Mediterranean World* (Grand Rapids: Wm. B. Eerdmans, 1983), passim.

175. James L. Crenshaw, "*'esā* and *dabar*: The Problem of Authority/Certitude in Wisdom and Prophetic Literature," *Prophetic Conflict* (BZAW 124; Berlin: Walter de Gruyter, 1971) 116–23. Crenshaw concludes, "In short, between 'Thus saith the Lord' and 'Listen, my son, to your father's advice' there is no fundamental difference" (p. 123).

Sirach's statement is identified as sapiential because it occurs in the context of a wisdom instruction. Were it to occur in the middle of a prophetic indictment of the rapacity of the rich and powerful, it would doubtless be read differently. This illustrates the importance of the framing devices and formulae for determining the overall genre. Content is not enough because it is too often ambiguous.

We return to the suggestions of Koester. His conclusions regarding the formative elements of Q are based on two assumptions: that Q belongs to the genre of "wisdom gospel" and that only certain kinds of sayings and theological tendencies are typical of the genre. According to Koester, apocalyptic Son of Man sayings and sayings which evince a strongly future-oriented eschatology run counter to the tendencies of the genre, and for that reason are to be judged secondary. In practice, Koester's method is comparative and the *Gos. Thom.* serves as a criterion for deciding what was formative in Q. *Gos. Thom.* lacks an apocalyptic thrust and has only one (non-apocalyptic) Son of Man saying (saying 86).

This requires some nuancing. On the surface, apocalyptic Son of Man sayings do indeed seem inappropriate to a sapiential collection. But the more important question is, Are such sayings presented in a way which is compatible with the sayings genre? Miracle stories, which are likewise atypical of sapiential collections, are also found in Q (7:1–10; 11:14). But both stories are presented for the sake of the saying which they occasion. This seems compatible with the intent of a wisdom gospel. Similar analysis is needed for the "apocalyptic" elements in Q.

Moreover, Koester's method requires the presupposition that *Gos. Thom.* is the best representative of the genre of which Q also is a member. But such an assumption is question-begging. In an investigation of the genre of Q, Koester's procedure must be revised and turned on its head: one must first determine the principles of composition of Q and the portions of it which were formative from a literary-critical perspective.[176] Only then is it possible to compare Q with antique genres and determine the extent to which Q shares or fails to share the characteristics and tendencies of those genres. It must be shown on redactional grounds that certain elements (e.g., apocalyptic Son of Man sayings)

---

176. Herein lies the difference between our investigation and that of Schulz. Schulz clearly recognizes the form-critical and tradition-historical heterogeneity within Q. But he treats this problem not by asking how Q was formed as a literary work, but by investigating the tradition-history of each component and by assigning the materials to one of two tradition strata. See further my comments in "Tradition and Redaction."

belong to a secondary compositional level and that compositionally and literarily the wisdom sayings, and the wisdom-gospel format, are foundational and formative for the document. Such a conclusion can be obtained in the first place only from an analysis of Q itself, not by comparative analysis.

Summary

A review of the history of Q studies reveals several issues which have affected the assessment of the nature, genre and function of Q. The characterization of Q as *Kleinliteratur* impeded rather than furthered the investigation of its literary intentionality. On this view, the appropriate instrument of investigation was form criticism and the conclusions regarding the function and *Sitz* of the individual components of Q could simply be extended to Q as a whole. As we have seen, however, the construct of *Kleinliteratur*, however useful it may be as a heuristic, obscures significant features of Q as a literary composition which deserve attention in their own right.

A second issue which appears throughout the history of the Q question is that of the "place" of Q within the theological history of early Christianity. Assessments of the function and hermeneutic of Q vary greatly depending on whether one posits (*a*) an essential equivalence between the preaching of Jesus in Q and the theology of Paul (Harnack), (*b*) a theological and hermeneutical dependence of Q upon the passion kerygma (Bultmann, Dibelius, Streeter, Manson), (*c*) a "second sphere" of Christian tradition uninfluenced by the passion kerygma but familiar with the passion stories (Wilckens, Steck, Käsemann) or (*d*) a discrete group in which Q functioned as the central theological expression (Tödt, Schulz, Koester). As indicated above, the fourth position has the most to recommend it. Consequently, Q must be understood without recourse to theological harmonization with either the passion kerygma or the passion stories.

Finally, an understanding of the subtle relationship between the literary genre of Q, its constituent forms and the setting in which it was used has become a desideratum because of the work of Robinson and Koester on the one hand, and that of Boring and Kelber on the other. Important questions have been raised. Why were sayings of Jesus compiled into a collection such as Q? And what were the theological and hermeneutical ramifications of this compilation?

The following chapters are designed to investigate these questions. Before turning attention to the examination of Q's formative principle, several preliminary issues must be clarified: whether Q was in fact a written document, its language of composition and the methods appropriate to the reconstruction of its order and extent (chapter two). The next chapters will consider the overall compositional patterns in Q and the methods appropriate to the analysis of a sayings collection (chapter three), followed by an analysis of the blocks of material controlled by the theme of the announcement of judgment (chapter four) and by sapiential forms and motifs (chapter five). Chapter six treats the somewhat anomalous temptation story. Once the literary formation and composition have been described, we shall be in a position to consider possible parallels to Q in genre, construction, intention and setting. The various modalities of antique sayings collections will be sketched with a view to situating Q within the range of compositional techniques, applications and hermeneutics at work in such collections (chapter seven).

2

The Document Q

If the discussion of the literary genre of Q is to have much sense, Q must be shown to have been a document with an identifiable order and arrangement. This is now widely assumed by critics. However, since there are a few distinguished authors who have held other views, it is advisable to examine in some detail the evidence for and against this hypothesis.

A related question, and one which arises repeatedly in the literature on the Synoptic Sayings Source, is that of the original language. Opinion is sharply divided between two hypotheses: that Q was originally composed in Aramaic and only subsequently translated into one or more Greek versions; and that Q was compiled in a Greek-speaking community even though some of its sayings may have circulated earlier in Aramaic formulations. Although a solution to this problem is not absolutely necessary to a discussion of the genre of Q, it will aid in the determination of the provenance of the document.

A third area of dispute is whether the "original" order of the sayings in Q was fixed, and if so, whether this order may be recovered. While the majority of authors have either argued or assumed that the Lucan order best represents that of Q, there are important dissenters. And among the proponents of Lucan order there is no consensus on how best to demonstrate the priority of Luke. The question of order is an important one for obvious reasons. Any examination of the genre of Q must take into account the principles of composition and arrangement operative in the document, and this in turn requires some idea of the order of pericopae. It must be said, however, that it is beyond the reasonable expectations of modern scholarship to determine the exact wording and the exact position of every Q pericope. It is impossible, for example, to rule out the possibility that both Matthew and Luke occasionally altered the wording and location of some sayings. It is, nevertheless, both necessary and feasible to address the question of order and, as will be seen, it is possible to reconstruct a considerable measure of this order, and with a relatively high degree of probability.

This raises a fourth question. As the history of Q research shows, it is sometimes held that the double tradition represents either more than the original extent of Q, or considerably less. That is, some of the double tradition may not in fact derive from Q at all,[1] or Q may have contained more than is present in the double tradition (e.g., the baptism story, or sayings such as Matt 11:28–30; Luke 9:61–62). The question of reconstruction is crucial if, for example, there is any possibility that Q contained elements (such as extended narratives) which would require a radical reassessment of the character of Q. It is necessary, then, to reflect briefly upon the methodological principles which should govern a discussion of the genre of a reconstructed document such as Q.

Q: WRITTEN OR ORAL?

Although disputed in the past, the written nature of Q[2] has been conceded by the majority of critics even if this conclusion was not always defended in a very systematic fashion. The available evidence indeed is such as to sustain only this conclusion; the principal alternative, namely an oral Q, collapses in the face of four considerations: the presence of strong verbal agreements of Matthew and Luke, the use of peculiar or unusual phrases by both evangelists, agreements in the order of Q pericopae and the phenomenon of doublets.

Verbal Agreements

As is well known, the degree of agreement between Matthew and Luke in the reproduction of the double tradition materials varies widely from extremely high in such passages as Q 3:7–9; 4:1–13; 7:24–28, 31–35; 9:57–60; 10:21–22, 23–24; 11:31–32; 13:34–35, etc., to minimal in the

---

1. E.g., double-tradition passages which display a low degree of Matthew-Luke agreement (Matt 5:13 // Luke 14:34–35; Matt 22:1–10 // Luke 14:15–24, etc.); or those passages which are of a proverbial nature and may have been used independently by the evangelists (e.g., Matt 20:16 // Luke 13:30); or passages which differ in form or content from the rest of Q (Matt 4:1–11 // Luke 4:1–13).

2. Early advocates of a written Q include Weizsäcker, *Evangelische Geschichte*, 130; Holtzmann, *Synoptische Evangelien*, 128; idem, *Lehrbuch*, 362–67; Bernhard Weiss, *Introduction* 1:203–23, 226; Wernle, *Synoptische Frage*, 224–27, 228–29; Jülicher, *Introduction*, 356–57 (a later revision of Jülicher's *Einleitung* [1931[7] 348] reveals some hesitation on this point); Johannes Weiss, *Schriften*, 35–37; Harnack, *Sayings of Jesus*, passim; Wellhausen, *Einleitung*[1] 66, [2] 57–60; Moffatt, *Introduction*, 197–202; Bacon, "Nature and Design," 674; Manson, *Sayings*, 15. More recently the documentary status of Q is assumed by virtually all except Jeremias and Wrege.

parable of the talents and the parable of the great supper. In the past, authors who emphasized the almost verbatim agreements generally opted for a written Q and explained the divergences as a result of redactional modifications or the influence of other sources.[3] On the other hand, those who stressed the disparities concluded that Q was oral. The agreements were due to a relatively fixed oral tradition, and the disparities were readily explicable by appeal to the vicissitudes of oral tradition or to the activity of redactors.[4] A mediating position posited written sources for the high-agreement passages, and oral sources for those with lesser similarities.[5] It should be noted, however, that most exponents of the documentary hypothesis concede that pericopae displaying extremely low agreement may derive from oral sources and that only those with moderate to high agreement derive from Q. Hence the mediating position is tacitly allowed by the documentary hypothesis.

What is the significance of the Matthew-Luke agreements? In an important challenge to the documentary hypothesis, Theodore Rosché examined the Matthew-Mark and Mark-Luke agreements (in both wording and order) and compared these with Matthew-Luke agreements in the Q sections. Finding the Matthew-Luke agreements to be significantly less than the agreements with Mark, Rosché concluded that the double tradition must have been oral.[6] In 1971, however, Rosché's essay was subjected to a probing examination and critique by C. E. Carlston and D. Norlin.[7] They rightly pointed out the fallacy of Rosché's inference. Rosché had compared Mark *individually* with Matthew and Luke in the triple tradition but Matthew and Luke *directly* in the double tradition instead of comparing Matthew and Luke directly in both sets of material. Carlston and Norlin performed this direct comparison and assessed the faithfulness with which Matthew and Luke transmitted double- and triple-tradition material in three categories: narrative mate-

3. E.g., Streeter (*Four Gospels*, 281–84) argues that Matthew sometimes conflated Q and M versions of the same saying.

4. W. C. Allen ("Did St. Matthew and St. Luke use the Logia?" *ExpT* 11 [1899–1900] 424–26) and Wright ("Oral Teaching," *ExpT* 11 [1899–1900] 473–74) conclude that the disagreements between Matthew and Luke in wording and order are fatal to any documentary hypothesis. Wrege (*Bergpredigt*) attempts to show that, on the one hand, the strong verbal agreements are found only in particularly memorable sayings and that, on the other, the differences are not due to redaction but to variations within the oral tradition.

5. Thus Barrett, "Q—A Re-examination," 320–23; W. Sanday, "A Plea for the Logia," *ExpT* 11 (1899–1900) 473. Knox (*Sources*, 3–6) proposes multiple written sources. This view has been recently revived by C. J. A. Hickling, "The Plurality of Q," *Logia*, 425–29.

6. Rosché, "Words," 210–20.

7. Carlston and Norlin, "Statistics and Q," 59–78.

rials, words of Jesus and miscellaneous sayings. As might be expected, in both the double and triple traditions, speech material was transmitted more faithfully than narrative. But the double tradition was consistently *better* preserved than the triple in all three categories![8] They concluded,

> [Our samplings] are surely large enough to establish beyond reasonable doubt that Matthew and Luke used Q, as far as the wording of their material is concerned, at least as conservatively as they used Mark. There seems to us to be no reasonable explanation of this phenomenon except a second *written* source for Matthew and Luke.[9]

There can be no serious doubt that a written source can account for the strong agreements of Matthew and Luke and that allowance for the redactional activity—of the same nature that is visible in the Matthaean and Lucan treatment of Mark—can account for the disagreements. The essential issue is whether purely oral transmission is sufficient to explain the strong agreements. It can surely account for the disagreements.

The oral hypothesis must in fact be rejected. This is not because certain oral techniques could not in principle be faithful, but because there is no evidence that such techniques were in use in primitive Christianity (or in contemporary Judaism for that matter!). The thesis of Gerhardsson and Riesenfeld of a rabbinic-type transmission of tradition in early Christianity has been rejected decisively on the grounds that primitive Christianity was not Torah-centered but Christ- or Spirit-centered.[10] There is no evidence that Jesus himself taught by memorization

---

8. Ibid., 71. The definition of agreement used was "the use of approximately the same word in both Matthew and Luke . . . expressed . . . as a percentage of the total words used by either author" (pp. 62–63). The most extreme case of synonyms being considered as agreements is ἰάθη/ὑγιαίνοντα in Matt 8:13/Luke 7:10 (pp. 61–62). Since this principle is applied to both the triple and the double tradition, it is self-correcting. To insure objectivity, Carlston and Norlin defined the double tradition as those non-Marcan passages "in which Matthew and Luke are clearly treating the same material, even though verbal correspondence is not very close" (p. 61). They excluded from both sets of materials: (a) introductory phrases, (b) *Sondergut*, (c) summary statements and (d) material which occurs only in Matthew and Mark, or Mark and Luke (pp. 61–62). The results of their study (expressed as a percentage of the total words):

Triple Tradition	Matt	Luke	Avg.	Double Tradition	Matt	Luke	Avg.
Narrative	50.2	46.9	48.5		55.7	51.8	53.7
Words of Jesus	63.5	68.3	65.8		69.5	73.6	71.5
Misc. words	56.7	60.6	58.5		87.5	80.9	84.1
Average	56.0	56.0	56.0		69.8	72.2	71.0

9. Ibid., 72 [their emphasis].

10. B. Gerhardsson, *Memory and Manuscript* (Uppsala: Gleerup, 1961); H. Riesenfeld, *The Gospel Tradition* (London: A. R. Mowbray & Co., 1957). See the critical reviews by W. D. Davies, "Reflections on a Scandinavian approach to 'the Gospel Tradition,'" *Neotestamentica et Patristica* (NovTSup 6; Leiden: E. J. Brill, 1962) 14–34; Howard Teeple, "The Oral Tradition That Never Existed," *JBL* 89 (1970) 56–68; C. K. Barrett, *Jesus and the*

or that early Christians modeled themselves after rabbinic schools. Such a thesis would in fact be seriously anachronistic, representing the rabbinic techniques of the mid to late second century CE as those of pre-70 Judaism.[11] Moreover, early Christian literature betrays no trace of the institutions and professional classes of memorizers which an accurate transmission of oral tradition would require and which later rabbinic Judaism presupposed.[12]

If one turns to the Q materials in search of evidence of oral composition and transmission, the results are far from encouraging. According to the American Homeric critic Milman Parry, what betrays the oral character of Homeric verse is the abundance of formulaic diction.[13] The oral composition of heroic hexameter was made possible by a large stock of noun-epithet formulae each with a fixed metrical value.[14] In Christian and rabbinic traditions, of course, metrical considerations play a much less significant role than they do in Homer. Nevertheless, oral composition and transmission still depend upon fixed formulae and mnemonic devices.

In his masterful treatment of the evidence of oral transmission of traditions about the Pharisees before 70 CE, Neusner provides a useful classification of the mnemonics which appear in the small and presumably easily memorized units of tradition. These include (a) the use of

---

Gospel Tradition (London: SPCK, 1967) 9–10; Geo. Widengren, "Tradition and Literature in Early Judaism and in the Early Church," *Numen* 10 (1963) 42–83.

11. Jacob Neusner has forcefully called into question the uncritical assumption that rabbinic mnemonic techniques were in widespread use prior to 70 CE. No one seriously disputes the fact that there were extra-biblical traditions transmitted by pre-70 teachers (some of whom were *scribes*!). But the texts which are routinely cited in support of the antiquity of oral techniques (*b. 'Erub.* 54b; *b. Git.* 60b = *b. Tem.* 14b) are no earlier than mid-Yavnean times (ca. 100 CE). See Neusner, "Pharisees," 73–89; idem, "Oral Torah and Oral Tradition: Defining the Problematic," *Method and Meaning in Ancient Judaism* (Brown Judaic Studies 10; Missoula, Mont.: Scholars Press, 1979) 59–75; idem, "Written Traditions in Pharisaism Before 70," *Early Rabbinic Judaism* (SJLA 13; Leiden: E. J. Brill, 1975) 90–99; idem, *Rabbinic Traditions*, 3 and passim.

12. Thus Morton Smith, "A Comparison of Early Christian and Early Rabbinic Tradition," *JBL* 82 (1963) 169–76.

13. Parry, "Homer and Homeric Style." Parry observes that the first 25 lines of the *Iliad* and the *Odyssey* contain respectively 29 and 34 fixed formulae which appear in the same form elsewhere in Homer. One-quarter of these are found more than eight times, whereas in all of Euripides there is only one phrase which occurs more than seven times.

14. Parry, *Homeric Verse*, 272. Thus θεὰ γλαυκῶπις Ἀθήνη (50x), δῖος Ὀδυσσεύς (60x), πατὴρ ἀνδρῶν τε θεῶν τε (15x), etc., are repeatedly used in Homer for metrical reasons to express much simpler ideas. Parry comments: "Without writing, the poet can make his verses only if he has a formulaic diction which will give him his phrases all made, and made in such a way that, at the slightest bidding of the poet, they will link themselves in an unbroken pattern that will fill his verses and make his sentences" (p. 317).

fixed opposites, (b) balanced two-part lemmas with equal syllable counts and a balanced metre, (c) metrically balanced lemmas with a single change of letter between the two lemmas, (d) two-part lemmas with an alteration in word order or in a syntactical detail, (e) unbalanced lemmas differing principally in the choice of a key word and (f) lemmas containing numerical sequences which facilitate memorization.[15] According to Neusner, many of the sayings attributed to Hillel and Shammai, and most of the House sayings display mnemonic patterns; sayings pertaining to other pre-70 masters tend not to exhibit such patterns.

Within the material usually assigned to Q such devices are almost entirely lacking. The closest to balanced lines with fixed opposites is the proverbial saying Q 16:13:

Οὐδεὶς (οἰκέτης) δύναται δυσὶ κυρίοις δουλεύειν
ἢ γὰρ τὸν ἕνα μισήσει καὶ τὸν ἕτερον ἀγαπήσει,
ἢ ἑνὸς ἀνθέξεται καὶ τοῦ ἑτέρου καταφρονήσει.
οὐ δύνασθε θεῷ δουλεύειν καὶ μαμωνᾷ.

In this saying, the agreement between Matthew and Luke is remarkable: Luke differs only by adding οἰκέτης but in all other respects agrees with Matthew. To be sure, oral techniques might account for the preservation of the substance of this saying. But how, for example, are we to explain the agreement in the use of the pair μισέω/ἀγαπάω when other synonyms could easily have been used without destroying the parallelism? The *Gos. Thom.* 47 in fact uses τιμάω/ὑβρίζω in the same saying. Even in so stylized a saying as this, oral techniques cannot fully account for the almost verbatim agreements. It is fair to say that other Q sayings are much less stylized than Q 16:13. And while parallelism is used in Q, it is not of the sophisticated sort which Neusner describes as necessary for mnemonic transmission.

There is, in sum, insufficient evidence either from primitive Christianity in general or from Q in particular for the institutions or techniques which would have been required to preserve the words of Jesus as faithfully as they in fact have been preserved. There is no doubt, however, that a written document can explain such strong agreements.

Peculiar Phrases

John C. Hawkins pointed out the presence of several "peculiar or very unusual words" and grammatical constructions such as ἐν γεννῆτοις γυναικῶν (Q 7:28), ἵκανος ἵνα (Q 7:6), εἰπὲ λόγῳ (Q 7:7), φοβεῖσθε ἀπό (Q

15. Neusner, *Rabbinic Traditions* 3:120–38.

12:4) and ὁμολογεῖν ἐν (Q 12:8).[16] Such phrases are very rare in the LXX and in other early Christian literature. If it were a matter of oral transmission, Hawkins reasoned, these peculiar phrases would undoubtedly have been replaced by more common expressions in at least one of the Synoptic versions. Hawkins' list could be expanded by adducing various verbs which are rare or unattested in the LXX and the rest of the NT: ἀμφιέννυμι (Q 7:25; elsewhere only in Matt 6:30), διχοτομέω (Q 12:46),[17] σαρόω (Q 11:25; elsewhere only in Luke 15:11). It is difficult to suppose that such unusual verbs would appear in both Matthew and Luke were it not for a written source.

Order

A third argument for the written status of Q relies on the phenomenon of order. This question will occupy us in the third major part of this chapter, but a few preliminary observations can be made here. It is fair to say that if little or no common order existed in the Matthaean and Lucan reproduction of the sayings, or if the order which existed fell within the range of probabilities of random or accidental agreement, or again if all of the agreements could be explained on the basis of casual oral associations, then the case for a written Q would be greatly weakened.

A. M. Honoré, in his 1968 statistical study,[18] argued that there were only two agreements in sequence in the double tradition: Luke 3:7–9, 16–17 (Matt 3:7–12) followed by Luke 4:1–13 (Matt 4:1–11), and Luke 7:18–23 (Matt 11:2–6) followed by Luke 7:24–28 (Matt 11:7–11). But, Honoré observed, the probability of two sequential agreements within a set of materials as large as Q is well within the range of *accidental* agreements which might obtain in any two random orderings of elements. Carlston and Norlin, however, pointed out that Honoré's argument from order rested on the sequence of Huck-Lietzmann sections, not *individual sayings*. There is no reason to suppose that Matthew and Luke understood the present Huck-Lietzmann divisions as inviolable. In fact, if one con-

16. Hawkins, "Probabilities," 99.
17. This verb appears only in Exod 29:17 with the (usual) meaning "to cut in two" (BAGD 200). In Q 12:46 it presumably means "to punish severely," a meaning unattested elsewhere. The use of the verb, in view of its meaning, has caused embarrassment. Some exegetes propose a mistranslation hypothesis to explain διχοτομέω. See Weiser, *Knechtsgleichnisse*, 198–200. But this only serves to emphasize the unusual nature of the Matt-Luke agreement. Surely if it were a matter of oral tradition, such an unusual word would have been dropped in one or the other version.
18. Honoré, "Statistical Study," esp. 133–34.

siders the order of basic sense units or *form-critical units*, a considerable measure of sequential agreement is found (see below).[19]

In 1916 Thaddeus Soiron challenged the documentary view of Q on the basis that *ad vocem* associations of sayings could be found throughout the collection. Since Soiron regarded this technique as typical of oral composition, he reasoned that it was superfluous to posit a written Q.[20] His argument was further refined by Jeremias, who pointed out that not only are there numerous sayings which stand in *ad vocem* associations, but there are at least 17 cases in which a saying stands in different *ad vocem* associations in Matthew and Luke.[21] Thus, for example, Matt 5:15 is connected to the preceding and following Matthaean verses by the catchwords φῶς (5:14, 16) and λάμπω (5:15, 16) while its parallel, Luke 11:33, is attached to 11:34 (whose Matthaean parallel is placed in an entirely different context) by the word λύχνος.[22] This indicated to Jeremias that (at least) two different oral arrangements of the sayings existed, each composed by means of oral catchwords, though not necessarily the same set of catchwords. Although Jeremias allowed that some of the catchword associations might be due to the initiative of one of the evangelists, he insisted that on the whole his observation of differing catchword associations rendered the thesis of a written Q unnecessary.

Catchword composition, however, belongs as much to the literary sphere as it does to the oral, and is employed widely in *literary* compositions, especially of a sapiential variety (e.g., Ps-Isocrates *Ad Demonicum*, Sirach, Tobit, Proverbs, *Sent. Sext.*). The mere presence of catchword connectives neither proves nor excludes oral composition and transmission. However, Petros Vassiliadis has pointed out that Soiron and Jeremias' explanation of the phenomenon of order can be regarded as satisfactory only if it can cover all of the agreements in the entire double tradition.[23] Vassiliadis' point may be illustrated by looking at three Q pericopae:

1. The Beelzebul accusation in Q is met by three responses: "A kingdom divided against itself . . ." (11:17–18), "If I cast out demons by

---

19. Carlston-Norlin, "Statistics and Q," 74.
20. Soiron, *Logia Jesu*, 133–34 and passim.
21. Jeremias, "Zur Hypothese," 147–49.
22. See also the respective settings of Matt 5:18 // Luke 16:17; Matt 5:25–26 // Luke 12:57–59; Matt 6:25–33 // Luke 12:22–32; Matt 7:21 // Luke 6:46; Matt 7:22 // Luke 13:26–27; Matt 10:19–20 // Luke 12:11–12; Matt 10:34–36 // Luke 12:51–53; Matt 11:12–13 // Luke 16:16; Matt 12:32 // Luke 12:10; Matt 12:34–36 // Luke 6:45; Matt 18:6–7 // Luke 17:1–2; Matt 18:12–14 // Luke 15:3–7; Matt 23:37–39 // Luke 13:34–35; Matt 24:26–28 // Luke 17:23–24; Matt 24:37–39 // Luke 17:26–27; Matt 24:42–44 // Luke 12:39–40.
23. Vassiliadis, "Nature and Extent," 52.

Beelzebul, how do your sons cast out demons?" (11:19) and "If I cast out demons by the finger of God . . ." (11:20). Then follows the saying about binding the stronger one (11:21–22, if this was in Q), and finally the saying "He who is not with me is against me" (11:23). The association of these five units with the accusation is undoubtedly due to the common themes of exorcism and of opposition to Jesus. But this alone does not explain the fact that Matthew and Luke reproduce the three answers and the two sayings in precisely the same order, especially since the answers need not logically appear in the present order. In oral tradition, one would expect more variation.

2. The same argument can be made with respect to Q 7:24–35, which contains Jesus' eulogy of John to the crowds (vv. 24–26), a quotation from Malachi (v. 27), another saying about John (v. 28), the parable of the children in the market place (vv. 31–32), its interpretation (vv. 33–34) and finally a Sophia saying (v. 35). While 7:33–34 necessarily follows 7:31–32, the order of vv. 27 and 28 is not the only possible one (as the manuscript evidence itself shows)[24] nor are the association and placement of the parable with the Sophia saying inevitable. In such an instance, it would seem simpler to posit literary dependence than two independent oral renderings.

3. Several Q pericopae display not only strong verbal agreement but extremely high agreement in word order. In Q 3:7–9, for example, the words of John's oracle (63 in Matt; 64 in Luke) follow in precisely the same order, notwithstanding the addition of καί by Luke and a minor disagreement in word choice. There is agreement not only in the most important vocabulary, but also in the selection and placement of particles, prepositions and other highly variable sentence elements. In a language as highly inflected as Greek, it is highly unlikely that such minute agreements would occur in two independent oral versions except in the event that metrical constraints were operative. Evidence such as this—and Q 3:7–9 is certainly not the only such case—point irresistibly in the direction of a written document.

Doublets

Recently Fitzmyer, Vielhauer and Kümmel[25] have used the presence of doublets to argue not only for the existence of Q but also for its documentary status. The following examples serve to illustrate the

24. Codex Beza (D) inserts v. 28a after v. 26.
25. Fitzmyer, "Priority of Mark," 152–53; Vielhauer, *Urchristliche Literatur*, 312; Kümmel, *New Testament*, 66–67; Devisch, "Le Document Q," 72 n. 6.

point.[26] A request for a sign occurs in Mark 8:11–12 which is taken over by Matthew in 16:1–4. But it also appears in a Q context and in a slightly different form in Matt 12:38–40 (Luke 11:29–30). Similarly, the saying "for to the one who has will more be given" appears in Mark 4:25 (= Matt 13:12 // Luke 8:18) but also in Matt 25:29 // Luke 19:26 (from Q). The same phenomenon may be observed with the sayings concerning self-denial and following Jesus (Mark 8:34–35 // Matt 16:24–25 // Luke 9:23–24 and Matt 10:38–39 // Luke 14:27) and those concerning confessing Jesus (Mark 8:38 // Matt 16:27 // Luke 9:26 and Matt 10:32–33 // Luke 12:8–9). In all these instances the most probable explanation for the doublet is a second *written* source. If the Q traditions were oral we might more reasonably expect that Matthew and Luke would have conflated the oral version with Mark. It is also significant to note that in a few of the doublets (e.g., the sign of Jonah/request for a sign), one version is placed by Matthew in Marcan sequence while the other occurs in what appears to be its relative position in Q.[27] This phenomenon virtually demands a written source.

To summarize. Four types of evidence support the thesis of a written Q: the presence of strong verbal agreements in the Matthaean reproduction of the double tradition, the survival of peculiar formulations in both versions, significant agreements in order of pericopae and the phenomenon of doublets. On the other hand, none of the criticisms of the documentary hypothesis has carried the day,[28] and the chief alternative, namely, oral tradition, raises many more problems than it solves. Q does not exhibit the kind of mnemonics which would be required for verbatim or near-verbatim agreements, and the external evidence for mnemonic practice in contemporary Christianity is wanting. Moreover, catchword composition, which curiously is regarded by some as *evidence*

26. For a more complete list of doublets, see Hawkins, *Horae Synopticae*, 80–107.

27. Matt 16:1–4 appears in the Marcan sequence, i.e., parallel to Mark 8:11–12, following the feeding of the four thousand (Matt 15:32–39 // Mark 8:1–10), and just before the "leaven of the Pharisees" (Matt 16:5–12 // Mark 8:14–21). The Q version (Matt 12:38–40) follows the Beelzebul complex (12:22–30 // Luke 11:14–23) and is immediately followed by the double saying about Jonah and the Queen of the South (Matt 12:41–42 // Luke 11:31–32).

28. G. Schille (*Das vorsynoptischen Judenchristentum* [Arbeiten zur Theologie 1/43; Stuttgart: Calwer, 1970] 69) observed that the Q materials display conflicting Christologies which, in his view, are incompatible with the assumption of a single document. In the Sermon on the Mount, Jesus appears as a judge offering "judgment-parenesis in the style of Jewish-Christian prophecy" (p. 69; [trans. by auth.]) while other Q passages seem to be informed by a divine man Christology (pp. 67–68). Such an argument is hardly convincing. It naively assumes that all materials in a given document are from the same tradition-historical stratum. Any familiarity with the literature of early Christianity tells us otherwise. The Gospel of John, e.g., contains multiple Christologies as well as a variety of eschatologies. Yet it is a single (if composite) document.

of oral composition, does not in fact belong exclusively to that domain. And in any case, appeal to oral catchword composition cannot explain enough of the sequential agreements to constitute a serious alternative to a written Q.

THE ORIGINAL LANGUAGE OF Q

One of the most persistent claims made with respect to the Synoptic Sayings Source is that it was originally composed in Aramaic and only then translated into Greek. Although this claim was by no means new with Harnack,[29] it proved highly congenial for those who, with Harnack, sought an ancient and reliable source for reconstructing an image of Jesus uncontaminated by the influences of Hellenism.[30] It is perhaps not too much to say that this desire for a source close to the *fons et origo* was responsible for at least some of the momentum for the thesis of an Aramaic Q. Notwithstanding such concerns, there are two main evidences for the contention: the testimony of the "elder" mentioned by Papias and quoted in Eusebius' *Hist. eccl.* (3.39.16) and the alleged presence in Q of "translation variants" and "translation mistakes" which can be explained by positing an Aramaic *Vorlage*. On the other hand, the marks of good Greek style and the fact that Matthew and Luke knew Q in a Greek version are factors which may be invoked to support the contention that Q originated in a Greek-speaking sphere.

The Testimony of the Elder (apud Papiam)[31]

Friedrich Schleiermacher was the first to infer from the testimony of Papias that an Aramaic sayings collection existed and served as the

29. More than a century before Harnack, J. G. Eichhorn (*Einleitung in das Neue Testament* [Leipzig, 1820²] 1:365) opined that the source common to Matthew and Luke was originally composed in "Hebrew or Chaldaic-Syriac."

30. Harnack (*Sayings of Jesus*, 249–50 [173]) contrasts Mark, "wherein page by page the student is reduced to despair by the inconsistencies, the discrepancies, and the incredibilities of the narrative," with Q, "which alone affords us a really exact and profound conception of the teaching of Jesus, and is free from bias, apologetic or otherwise . . ."

31. Eusebius *Hist. eccl.* 3.39.15–16: Καὶ τοῦτο ὁ πρεσβύτερος ἔλεγε· Μάρκος μὲν ἑρμηνευτὴς Πέτρου γενόμενος, ὅσα ἐμνημόνευσεν, ἀκριβῶς ἔγραψεν, οὐ μέντοι τάξει, τὰ ὑπὸ τοῦ Χριστοῦ ἢ λεχθέντα ἢ πραχθέντα· οὔτε γὰρ ἤκουσε τοῦ Κυρίου οὔτε παρηκολούθησεν αὐτῷ, ὕστερον δέ, ὡς ἔφην, Πέτρῳ, ὃς πρὸς τὰς χρείας ἐποιεῖτο τὰς διδασκαλίας, ἀλλ᾽ οὐχ ὥσπερ σύνταξιν τῶν κυριακῶν ποιούμενος λογίων, ὥστε οὐδὲν ἥμαρτε Μάρκος, οὕτως ἔνια γράψας ὡς ἀπομνημόνευσεν ἑνὸς γὰρ ἐποιήσατο πρόνοιαν, τοῦ μηδὲν ὧν ἤκουσε παραλιπεῖν ἢ ψεύσασθαί τι ἐν αὐτούς.

Ταῦτα μὲν οὖν ἱστόρηται τῷ Παπίᾳ περὶ τοῦ Μάρκου. Περὶ δὲ τοῦ τοῦτ᾽ εἴρηται· Ματθαῖος μὲν οὖν ἑβραΐδι διαλέκτῳ τὰ λόγια συνετάξατο, ἡρμήνευσε δ᾽ αὐτὰ ὡς ἦν δυνατὸς ἕκαστος.

source of Matthew.[32] Arguing that Papias' description of Matthew as
λόγια does not accord with the actual contents of the canonical Gospel,
he reasoned that Papias was alluding to an Aramaic sayings collection
which, in his view, must have contained sayings from Matt 5—7; 10; 13;
18; 23—25, and which the editor of the First Gospel combined with a
narrative source. Although Schleiermacher wrote long before the articu-
lation of the two-document hypothesis in its classical form, his line of
argument has been borrowed and rehearsed many times in reference to
Q.[33] Manson put the case most succinctly: two of Papias' assertions—
viz., that Matthew was composed in Aramaic and that it was variously
interpreted (i.e., translated)—are demonstrably false if applied to canonical Matthew. That Matthew is the work of an apostle is improbable, and
the term λόγια is "singularly inept" as a description of the canonical
Gospel. All of Papias' statements, however, are quite intelligible if they
refer to an Aramaic collection such as Q.[34]

Several points can be made in response to this interpretation. First, it is
necessary to interpret the elder's comments on Matthew in the context
of his remarks on the Second Gospel.[35] In the latter case, a strong
apologetic tone is evident. The elder wishes to exonerate Mark of any
charge of inaccuracy and to apologize for the account's lack of order
(τάξις).[36] He states that although Mark's knowledge of the details of
Jesus' activities was not complete, his information nonetheless derived
from a reliable informant, and his account was a careful and accurate
rendition of those things which he had heard.[37]

32. Schleiermacher, "Zeugnisse."
33. Harnack, *Sayings of Jesus*, 247–49 [171–72] (who refers also to linguistic evidence
of a Semitic *Vorlage*); V. H. Stanton, *The Gospels as Historical Documents* (3 vols.;
Cambridge: At the Univ. Press, 1903–20) 2:44–45, 47–48; Hawkins, "Probabilities," 104–
5; Moffatt, *Introduction*, 194. Most recently, Koester, "Apocryphal and Canonical
Gospels," 108 n. 12; idem, *New Testament* 2:172.
34. Manson, *Sayings*, 17–18.
35. Thus Josef Kürzinger, "Das Papiaszeugnis und die Erstgestalt des Matthäus-
evangeliums," *BZ* NF 4 (1960) 19–38, esp. 21; more recently, idem, "Die Aussage des
Papias von Hierapolis zur literarischen Form des Markusevangeliums," *BZ* NF 21 (1977)
245–64. Cameron, *Sayings Traditions*, 108–10.
36. The meaning of τάξις is disputed: (*a*) F. H. Colson ("Τάξει in Papias," *JTS* 14
[1912–13] 62–69) suggests that it is a rhetorical term, referring to the lack of appropriate
and pleasing arrangement of the contents. When compared with Matthew, Mark
displayed poor τάξις in his abrupt beginning and his incomplete ending. Thus also
Kürzinger, "Papiaszeugnis," 23–25. (*b*) A. Wright ("Τάξει in Papias," *JTS* 14 [1912–13]
298–300) advocates a chronological interpretation, contending that Papias' standard of
comparison was John, whose chronology was markedly different from Mark's. A
decision in this matter is not absolutely necessary since in either case, Mark is regarded
as deficient when compared with another Gospel.
37. The phrase οὕτως ἔνια γράψας I take to mean that Mark recorded only a selection

It is in this context that the elder's statements about Matthew must be seen. Ματθαῖος ... τὰ λόγια συνετάξατο is in explicit contrast to οὐ μέντοι τάξει and οὐχ ὥσπερ σύνταξιν τῶν κυριακῶν ποιούμενος λογίων. The most probable explanation for the elder's apologia on Mark's behalf is not that in itself Mark gave the impression of an incomplete and disorganized account, but that when compared *with another gospel* which had both a different arrangement and more material, Mark appeared deficient. Although Papias' standard for comparison is disputed,[38] canonical Matthew seems to be the most probable candidate in view of its prominence in the primitive church and in view of the fact that Papias mentions Matthew virtually in the same breath.[39]

It is important to note that the elder refers to the contents of Mark as τὰ ὑπὸ τοῦ Κυρίου ἢ λεχθέντα ἢ πραχθέντα but later simply states that Mark did not make an orderly arrangement of τὰ κυριακὰ λόγια. This implies that the elder considered Mark to be λόγια. Although the basic meaning of this term is "oracle," it is used of individual OT verses, sayings of Jesus and, in the plural, of the Old Testament as a whole.[40]

---

of the stories about Jesus. T. Zahn (*Introduction to the New Testament* [2 vols., Edinburgh: T. & T. Clark, 1909] 2:440–41) rejects this, arguing instead that Papias expressly limits the dependence of Mark's Gospel upon the speeches of Peter to *some* portions of the Gospel. But this gratuitously assumes that Mark had some other source, an assumption which has no foundation in the comments of the elder. T. Y. Mullins ("Papias on Mark's Gospel," *VC* 14 [1960] 216–24) argues that ἔνια . . . ὡς ἀπομνημόνευσεν implies that Mark had been attacked for writing *some* things from memory, i.e., for adding extraneous details from memory. But this interpretation is forced, since Papias intimates at the outset that the *whole* of the account was from memory. What ἔνια, "a few things," implies is that Mark did not record *all* that was in theory available, but only such things as he heard from Peter's unsystematic preaching. That explains the incompleteness and lack of order of his Gospel.

38. Johannes Munck ("Das Matthäusevangelium bei Papias," *Neotestamentica et Patristica* [NovTSup 6; Leiden: E. J. Brill, 1962] 25) thinks that Luke was the standard; Robert M. Grant (*A Historical Introduction to the New Testament* [London: William Collins Sons, 1963] 106) and Wright ("Τάξει in Papias," 299–300) argue that it was John. Haenchen (*Der Weg Jesu*, 7) does not think Papias had a norm.

39. See Kürzinger, "Papiaszeugnis," and W. A. Meeks, "Hypomnemata from an Untamed Sceptic," *The Relationship Among the Gospels* (San Antonio: Trinity University Press, 1978) 165–66. The numerical dominance of Matthew among the manuscripts of the NT is well known, and a perusal of the recently published *Biblica Patristica: Index des citations et allusions bibliques dans la littérature patristique* (3 vols.; Paris: CNRS, 1975, 1977) shows that Matthew was quoted almost twice as frequently as any other Gospel in the first three centuries CE.

40. Individual verses: Justin *Apol.*, 32.14; Eusebius *Hist. eccl.* 9.9.7; 10.1.4; 10.4.7, 28. Sayings of Jesus: Polycarp *Phil.* 7.1; *Acts of Thomas* A. 39; Justin *Dial.* 18.1; Eusebius *Hist. eccl.* 9.7.15; Irenaeus *Haer.* 1.8.1. OT as a whole: 1 *Clem.* 19:1; 53:1; 62:3; Clement of Alexandria *Strom.* 1.31.124; *Protrept.* 10.107.1; *Quis Dives* 3.1; Eusebius *Hist. eccl.* 5.17.5; 6.23.2; 10.4.43.

Papias' use of the term in connection with Mark suggests that for him it included τὰ πραχθέντα, i.e., narratives.[41] This conclusion is confirmed by the description of the contents of Papias' Λογίων κυριακῶν ἐξηγήσις, which reportedly included lists of disciples and accounts from Acts as well as sayings of Jesus.[42] One can only conclude from this that Papias' use of the term λόγια is imprecise and that by λόγια he meant canonical Matthew.

Papias' testimony, consequently, is of no probative worth in the quest for an Aramaic Q. His claims are apologetically motivated, and they refer to the canonical Gospels, not to their sources.

Internal Evidence of an Aramaic *Vorlage*

The second pillar of the hypothesis of an Aramaic Q is the more important one, involving linguistic evidence. If it can be shown, so the argument runs, that Q contains a number of peculiarities and obscurities which can be explained only by recourse to an Aramaic word or syntactical feature, then the probability is high that Q was first composed in Aramaic. There are several types of evidence which have been adduced: (1) Bussby pointed to the "poetic features" of Q which, he argued, indicated a Semitic original.[43] (2) He also adduced a number of Semitic names and transcriptions of Semitic words, and along with others (3) he listed passages displaying Semitic idioms.[44] Another type of evidence has to do with discrepancies between Matthew and Luke which can be explained by positing an Aramaic original which was either (4) translated in different ways by Matthew and Luke (or their respective sources) or (5) mistranslated by one of the evangelists. In the latter case it would be especially significant if the mistranslation occurred because of an optical confusion (e.g., the confusion of a waw for a yod or a resh for a daleth).

Not all of these evidences lead to the same conclusion. The presence of Semitic stylistic features and Semitic personal names is only to be expected given the fact that the Q materials were formed in some proximity to Semitic-speaking areas and deal with biblical themes and

41. Thus G. Kittel, "Λόγιον," *TDNT* 4 (1967) 140–41; William Schoedel, *The Apostolic Fathers V: Polycarp, Martyrdom of Polycarp, Fragments of Papias* (London: Thomas Nelson & Sons, 1967) 109 and others.

42. See the texts in J. B. Lightfoot, *The Apostolic Fathers* (London: Macmillan & Co., 1898) 515–35.

43. Bussby, "Aramaic Document?" 272–75. Bussby has in mind various kinds of parallelism, *qal wehomer* conclusions, *kinah*- and three-beat rhythms and assonance.

44. Ibid., 272–75. See also C. C. Torrey *Our Translated Gospels* (New York: Harper & Bros., 1936) passim.

persons. While they are consistent with an Aramaic Q, they are consistent with a variety of other options too. As Nigel Turner remarked, the presence of Aramaisms or Semitic idioms "does no more than indicate that the author was thinking in Semitic forms or writing in a dialect of Greek which was influenced by Semitic idiom."[45]

The two other types of evidences are of a different order. Translation variants would provide strong circumstantial evidence of an Aramaic *Vorlage* (either oral or written), while *optical* translation mistakes would require a written source. But even supposing that such phenomena could be found, several possible explanations could be offered. Since a substantial portion of Q texts exhibit strong verbal agreements in Greek, one must rule out the possibility of two independent translations of the *whole* of Q. Two possibilities remain: either (a) Q was available to both evangelists in Greek and one (or both) occasionally revised that version by recourse to an Aramaic original, or (b) Q must be sub-divided into two documents, a Greek source and an Aramaic source, which the evangelists translated independently of one another. The first solution was proposed by Manson, the second by Bussmann.[46] On the other hand, if no optical mistranslations can be demonstrated and only the occasional "translation variant" is in evidence, then it would be arguable that (c) while Q was composed in Greek, variant Greek and Aramaic versions of individual sayings continued to exert influence upon later recensions of Q or upon the Synoptic evangelists themselves.[47] If, finally, the evidence of mistranslations and translation variants is wanting, it would be legitimate only to conclude that Q was compiled in Greek.

Bussmann compiled a list of no fewer than 122 "translation variants" which, he contended, showed that Q was in part the translation of an Aramaic document (designated "R").[48] Evaluation of his proposal is complicated by the fact that he did not indicate *which* Aramaic words might have produced such variants. Moreover, closer inspection of his list shows that the majority of the "translation variants" are simply synonyms, e.g., ἀγαπάω/φιλέω, αἴρω/λαμβάνω, ἐνώπιον/ἔμπροσθεν,

---

45. Turner, *Grammatical Insights*, 175.
46. Manson, "Problem of Aramaic Sources," 7–11; Bussmann, *Redenquelle*, 110–56. Bussmann's sigla are "T" (composed in Greek by a former Baptist disciple) and "R" (composed in Aramaic).
47. Koester (*Synoptische Überlieferung*) has convincingly demonstrated that a free tradition of sayings of Jesus continued to exert influence on writers well into the second century.
48. Bussmann, *Redenquelle*, 151–55.

μέχρι/ἕως, προσεύχομαι περί/ὑπέρ τινος. One hardly need posit an
Aramaic original here; simple re-wording of Q by one of the evangelists
is the more economical solution. In other cases, Bussmann's "variants"
are more plausibly explained as redactional.[49]

Matthew Black produced a much more modest list of Synoptic variants which might bespeak an Aramaic original.[50] These may be divided
for our purposes into two groups: cases of alternate translations of an
Aramaic idiom or word, and cases of mistranslation which allegedly
arose from optical confusion. The translation variants include the following:

1. Luke 6:22, ἐκβάλωσιν τὸν ὄνομα ὑμῶν ὡς πονηρόν // Matt 5:11, εἴπωσιν πᾶν
   πονηρὸν καθ᾽ ὑμῶν. Since Wellhausen[51] it has been argued that Luke
   provided a literal translation of the Hebraism hws᾽ šm r᾽ (cf. Deut 22:14, 19)
   or the Aramaism ᾽pq šm bys ᾽l . The Semitic character of Luke's phrase must
   be conceded. It in no way follows, however, that Matthew was offering an
   alternative translation of that idiom since he frequently eliminates Marcan
   Semitisms and might reasonably be expected to do the same with a Greek
   version of Q.[52]
2. Luke 6:23, σκιρτήσατε // Matt 5:12, ἀγαλλιᾶσθε. Black suggests that the
   Vorlage read dwṣ, which can mean either "leap" or more generally
   "rejoice."[53] Presumably the pre-Lucan translator rendered the verb rather
   literally and Matthew (or a predecessor) provided a freer translation. But
   again, the assumption of an Aramaic Vorlage is not the only possible
   explanation: redactional modification of the Greek text by either Luke or
   Matthew is the more parsimonious solution.[54]

Several other "translation variants" are listed by Black. Each could be
the result of varying translations from Aramaic, but since all have to do
with substitutions of synonymous or nearly synonymous terms, it could
likewise be a matter of redactional modification by Matthew or Luke.

---

49. E.g., Bussmann adduces πατήρ μου ὁ ἐν οὐρανοῖς (Matt 10:32; cf. 5:45), which,
however, must be regarded as redactional. See Matt 5:16, 45, 48; 6:1, 9, 32; 7:1; 10:32, 33;
12:50; 15:13; 16:17, etc. Similarly, the Lucan use of compound verbs such as ἀπαρνεῖσθαι
and ἐκδιώκειν is redactional, as Cadbury (Style, 166–67) has shown.

50. Black, Aramaic Approach, 187–96, 203–8.

51. Julius Wellhausen, Das Evangelium Lucae (Berlin: Reimer, 1904) 24.

52. See E. P. Sanders, The Tendencies of the Synoptic Tradition (SNTSMS 9;
Cambridge: At the Univ. Press, 1969) 190–255.

53. Black, Aramaic Approach, 193; Jeremias, Sprache, 139.

54. Schulz (Spruchquelle, 453–54) observes that Luke does not attach a strongly
eschatological significance to ἀγαλλιᾶσθαι (1:47; 10:21; Acts 2:26 [= Ps 16:9]; 16:34) and
suggests that he substituted σκιρτᾶν because of its eschatological significance in Ps
113:4, 6; Mal 3:20. Schürmann (Lukasevangelium 1:334 n. 64, 336 n. 84), however, thinks
that σκιρτᾶν is original and that Matthew added ἀγαλλιᾶσθαι under the influence of Isa
61:10–11 LXX.

They include

Luke 6:46, τί δέ με καλεῖτε // Matt 7:21, οὐ πᾶς ὁ λέγων μοι[55]
Luke 10:5, λέγετε· εἰρήνη τῷ οἴκῳ τούτῳ // Matt 10:12, ἀσπάσασθε αὐτήν[56]
Luke 11:3, καθ᾽ ἡμέραν // Matt 6:11, σήμερον[57]
Luke 11:4, τὰς ἁμαρτίας ἡμῶν // Matt 6:12, τὰ ὀφειλήματα ἡμῶν[58]
Luke 12:10, ἐρεῖ λόγον εἰς τινά // Matt 12:32, εἴπῃ λόγον κατὰ τινός[59]
Luke 14:27, ἔρχεται ὀπίσω μου // Matt 10:38, ἀκολουθεῖ ὀπίσω μου.[60]

Of more importance for sustaining the hypothesis of an Aramaic Q are translation mistakes, especially those arising from optical confusions. Black lists the following:[61]

1. Luke 6:23c, οἱ πατέρες αὐτῶν // Matt 5:12, τοὺς πρὸ ὑμῶν. Wellhausen had already suggested that this variant arose from a confusion of קדמיכון ("who

---

55. Black (*Aramaic Approach*, 193) suggests that '*mr* was translated in two different ways: καλεῖν and λέγειν. However, καλεῖν is also a favorite Lucanism, occurring frequently in *Sondergut* (30x) and redactional passages (at least 8x) and in Acts (18x). Moreover, Cadbury (*Style*, 171) has shown that Luke often substitutes verbs of more distinctive significance for Mark's εἴπειν or λέγειν.

56. Luke's version here clearly preserves the Semitic greeting, but it is also evident that Matthew has seen this in Q, since his subsequent verse (10:13) presupposes this greeting of peace.

57. This variant is probably due to the difficult term ἐπιούσιος (Matt = Luke) which the evangelists have construed variously. See below n. 61.

58. Matthew's ὀφείλημα, used to mean "sin," is, as Black (*Aramaic Approach*, 140) notes, a Semitism representing Aram. *hobā*, "sin," "debt" (see Jastrow, *Dictionary*, 429). Since this appears in liturgical material which has a life of its own apart from its function within the document, it is unwise to attach too much significance to it. It could be said, however, that Luke's ἁμαρτία would be more intelligible to a Greek-speaking audience.

59. Black (*Aramaic Approach*, 195) argues that "to say a word εἰς" is an Aramaism, from *millin lᵉsad . . . yᵉmallil*, "to speak words against" (Dan 7:25). But Matthew's formulation is good Greek (Plato *Apol.* 37B; BAGD 226A) and should be regarded as a stylistic improvement on Matthew's part.

60. The MT *b' 'hry, hlk 'hry* is translated by (εἰσ)έρχομαι ὀπίσω τινός (Exod 14:9), ἀκολουθεῖν ὀπίσω τινός (3 Kgdms 19:20; Hos 2:5 [7]; Isa 45:14; Amos 2:4) and πορεύεσθαι ὀπίσω τινός (3 Kgdms 18:21; Gen 45:15; Deut 4:3; 6:14; 13:14, etc.). The prepositional use of ὀπίσω is septuagintal and extremely rare elsewhere. Matthew's use of ὀπίσω with ἀκολουθεῖν (which normally takes the dative or μετά) is unclassical and redundant. Whether Matthew introduced the redundancy or whether Luke eliminated it is not certain. A translation hypothesis, however, does not alleviate the problem since the "Semitism" is present in both Matthew and Luke, and it is, moreover, a *septuagintalism*, appearing more than 300 times.

61. In addition to the variants attributed to translation mistakes, Black (*Aramaic Approach*, 203–8) attempts to trace ἐπιούσιος in the Lord's Prayer to an Aramaic idiom. But since the meaning of the Greek word is not itself clear, any Aramaic equivalent remains quite hypothetical. Black also suggests that νεκροί in Matt 8:22 = Luke 9:60 obtains from a confusion of מתנין, "waverers," from "to delay" with מיתיהון, "their dead." But this posits a mistranslation in order to avoid the most obvious way of reading the text: Let the (spiritually) dead bury the dead. Thus Bultmann, "νεκρός," *TDNT* 4 (1967)

were before you," which Matthew took as appositional to "the prophets") and קדמיהון ("their predecessors," which Luke used as the subject).[62] Black took this one step further, reconstructing the "original" saying from Matt 5:10a, 12b + Matt 5:11a // Luke 6:22a + Luke 6:23b.[63] For Black it is not really a matter of two alternate translations; on the contrary, he thinks that the saying originally contained *both* words and that deliberate paranomasia was intended. This is highly ingenious but quite unconvincing. It overlooks the fact that Luke tends to specify subjects (as in 6:22a, οἱ ἄνθρωποι)[64] and that οἱ πατέρες ὑμῶν/ἡμῶν is a favorite Lucan expression, appearing frequently in contexts having to do with the rejection of God's messengers and message.[65] This obviates the need for a mistranslation hypothesis which, in any event, is unable to account for the several other disagreements between Matthew and Luke.

2. Luke 11:41, τὰ ἐνόντα δότε ἐλεημοσύνη // Matt 23:26, καθάριον πρῶτον τὸ ἐντός. Again it was Wellhausen who proposed an Aramaic explanation:[66] the verb דכי, "to cleanse, purify," was misread by Luke as זכי, "to give alms." It should be noted, however, that זכי can mean *both* "to purify" and "to give alms"[67] and hence דכי is not needed to explain Matthew's reading. On the other hand, appeal to mistranslation does not explain the other (substantial) differences between Matthew and Luke. Moreover, giving alms appears to be a Lucan interest;[68] Luke 11:41 is best regarded as a Lucan reformulation and explication of a Q saying which is perhaps best represented by Matthew.[69]

3. Luke 11:42, πήγανον // Matt 23:23, ἄνηθον. E. Nestle was first to propose that this variant could be attributed to Luke's misreading of שבתא (= ἄνηθον, "dill") as שברא (= πήγανον, "rue").[70] This is problematic on two counts. In the first place, it is doubtful whether πήγανον stands for שברא

893; Schulz, *Spruchquelle*, 439–40; M. Hengel, *The Charismatic Leader and His Followers* (New York: Crossroad, 1981) 8.

62. Wellhausen, *Das Evangelium Lucae*, 24.

63. Black, *Aramaic Approach*, 192–93. His reconstruction: "Blessed are you when men persecute you, for thus did they persecute the prophets before you. Blessed are you when men reproach and revile you, for thus did their fathers do to the prophets."

64. Cadbury, *Style*, 150.

65. Luke 1:17, 55, 72; 6:26; 11:47, 48; Acts 3:25; 7:11, 12, 15, 38, 39, 44, 45, 51, 52; 15:10; 26:26; 28:25.

66. Wellhausen, *Einleitung*[2] 26–27; thus Black, *Aramaic Approach*, 2.

67. Jastrow, *Dictionary*, 398–99. *Lev. Rab.* 34 (בהר) 7: "The poor man says to his neighbor: Give me alms (זכי בי) or give me charity (דכי בי) by which he means, become pure through me (זכי גרמך בי)." C. F. D. Moule (*An Idiom Book of New Testament Greek* [Cambridge: At the Univ. Press, 1971²] 186) cautions, however, that "the evidence for the currency of the word [זכי] in Palestinian Aramaic seem[s] precarious."

68. Luke 12:3; Acts 3:2, 3, 10; 9:36; 10:2, 4, 31; 24:17.

69. Turner (*Grammatical Insights*, 57) points out that Luke's version is quite intelligible without appeal to Aramaic if τὰ ἐνόντα is taken as an adverbial accusative ("give alms inwardly," i.e., sincerely).

70. E. Nestle, "Anise and Rue" *ExpT* 15 (1904) 528; Black, *Aramaic Approach*, 194. Nestle relied upon Immanuel Löw's identification of שברא with πήγανον (*Aramäische Pflanzennamen* [1881] §§317–18).

since πήγανον has an exact Aramaic equivalent, פיגם.[71] Moreover, translation mistakes cannot explain the discrepancy between Matthew's κύμινον ([א]כמונ, "cummin") and Luke's λάχανον (ירק, "herb").

4. Luke 11:48, ὑμεῖς δὲ οἰκοδομεῖτε // Matt 23:31, υἱοί ἐστε. Black traces this to an "intentional word play" on אתון בנין אתון which could be rendered as "you are building" or "you are children of."[72] But this is unnecessarily speculative. Luke 11:48b is a carefully constructed climax to the woe, employing a μὲν . . . δέ construction impossible in Aramaic. And again, Matthew and Luke differ so radically in other respects that it is very doubtful that a translation hypothesis could ever be convincing.[73]

While Black has convincingly demonstrated the presence of Semitisms in Q, the case for a mistranslation hypothesis is insecure at best. Moreover, this type of explanation hinges on so many imponderables—such as both Matthew and Luke knowing Aramaic, and only occasionally using that knowledge—that in comparison with the redactional solution it is clearly the more cumbersome one. To be convincing a translation hypothesis would have to explain not only the occasional variation but extensive portions of the Matthew-Luke disagreements. Moreover, it would have to show that the variations cannot be accounted for by the more proximate explanation, namely, redactional modification. In the absence of such demonstrations, we are obliged to conclude that while parts of Q betray a Semitizing Greek style, and possibly an origin in an Aramaic-speaking milieu, there is no convincing proof of a literary formulation in Aramaic.

Q as a Greek Compilation

Black himself willingly concedes that "it is doubtful if we are justified in describing Q, without qualification, as a translation of Aramaic . . . [I]t *is the Greek literary factor which has had the final word with the shaping of the Q tradition.*"[74] This conclusion finds support in the detailed observations of Nigel Turner.[75] Turner began by observing that the typically Greek μὲν . . . δέ construction appears in Q relatively more frequently

---

71. Jastrow, *Dictionary*, 1159. I. Löw (*Flora der Juden* [Vienna and Leipzig, 1924] 3:468) later rejected the identification of שברא with πήγανον. Thus also Dietrich Correns, "Die Verzehntung der Raube," *NTS* 6 (1963) 110–12.

72. Black, *Aramaic Approach*, 12–13; Torrey, *Translated Gospels*, 103–4.

73. Black (*Aramaic Approach*, 211 n. 2) notes that the discrepancy between 11:12 (βιάζεται) and Luke 16:16 (εὐαγγελίζεται) might be explained by a confusion of פרץ, which "is used idiomatically of Jahweh's 'breaking in violently (in judgment) upon' (2 Sam v. 20) . . . ," with בשר, "to bring good news." But he concedes that "in such a notoriously *unheilbare Stelle* as Mt. xi.12 we are thrown back on conjecture of this kind."

74. Ibid., 191 [emphasis original].

75. Turner, "Recent Thought," 324–28.

than it does in the LXX of the Pentateuch, which represents fairly good Koine.[76] He also argued that the use of the genitive absolute is much higher than would be expected in translation Greek.[77]

Turner then proposed four tests of non-translation Greek:

1. First, coordinating particles (δέ, γάρ, οὖν, etc.) in second position tend to occur relatively more frequently in non-translation Greek than in translation works. Turner's statistics give the ratio of particles in the first position to those in second:[78]

Matthew's Q	104:117	(1:1.125)
Luke's Q	108:119	(1:1.102)
Acts 16—19	54:131	(1:2.425)
2 Macc 1—4	63:143	(1:2.270)
Wisdom 1—4	83:55	(1:0.663)
Tobit B 1—4	96:17	(1:0.177)

A cursory glance at Gen 1 and 1 Kgdms 1 (1 Sam 1) shows significantly lower ratios:

| Gen 1 | 59:1 | (1:0.017) |
| 1 Kgdms 1 | 60:0 | (1:0.000) |

From his statistics, Turner concludes that "the language of Q is somewhere between the idiomatic Greek of St. Luke's travel diary and the Second Book of Maccabees on the one hand and the translation Greek of such books as Tobit on the other, which in any case is not slavish."[79]

Further examination of individual particles confirms this conclusion. The use of γάρ compares favorably with that of Acts 16—28 and 4 Macc,[80] while the frequency of οὖν is close to that of non-translation books of the LXX.[81]

---

76. Turner ("Recent Thought," 326) counts μέν . . . δέ nine times in Q. Many of these instances, however, appear only in Matthew (10:13; 13:32; 16:3; 22:5, 8; 23:27, 28; 15:15) and may be due to redaction. This leaves Matt 9:37 // Luke 10:2 and Matt 3:11 // Luke 3:16 (unnoticed by Turner) as secure instances, although some of the Matthaean examples might also derive from Q. Μέν . . . δέ occurs only 10x in the LXX Pentateuch, i.e., 10x in approximately 5700 verses; never in historical books but frequently in Wisdom, 2—4 Macc.

77. Turner (Grammatical Insights, 177). Caution must be exercised here, however, since there are only two probable instances of a genitive absolute (Matt 11:7 // Luke 7:24; Matt 9:33 // Luke 11:14) but in both cases there are vocabularic differences. Turner (ibid., 177–78) counts Matt 11:7; 8:5; 16:2; 17:5 (!); Luke 3:21 (!) but fails to notice Luke 11:14.

78. Turner, "Recent Thought," 326.

79. Ibid., 326.

80. Ibid., 326. Q, 1x in 8 verses; Heb, 1x in 3 verses; Mark, 1x in 10 verses; Acts 16—28, 1x in 9 verses; Gen, 1x in 15 verses; Exod, 1x in 13 verses; Minor Prophets, 1x in 350 verses; 4 Macc, 1x in 6 verses.

81. Ibid., 326–27. Matt's Q, 1x in 10 verses; Luke's Q, 1x in 25 verses; 2 Macc, 1x in 19 verses; 3 Macc, 1x in 25 verses; 4 Macc, 1x in 27 verses; Gen, 1x in 37 verses; 1 Macc, 1x in 39 verses; Wisdom, 1x in 44 verses; Job, 1x in 63 verses; Isa, 1x in 430 verses; Minor Prophets, 1x in 1049 verses.

To Turner's observations can be added the following: ἄρα occurs at least twice in Q (Q 11:20; 12:42).[82] This classical, literary particle is very infrequent in the translated books of the LXX, except Job, which represents a very free rendering of the original.[83] Likewise, ὅθεν (Q 11:24) is uncommon in the LXX except in Job and 2–4 Macc. The appearance of such particles in Q provides some evidence of a freer Greek style than would be expected in a literary translation of an Aramaic document.

2. A second index mentioned by Turner is the frequency of καί and δέ in introductory clauses. When statistics from non-translation works are compared, it is obvious that Q is by no means as idiomatic as authors such as Plutarch, Polybius or Epictetus.[84] But Q performs on par with Luke 1—2, the Epistle of Barnabas, 4 Macc and the LXX Pentateuch.[85] Inconclusive in itself, this finding is compatible both with a translation hypothesis (in which case, Q would be a free rendering) and with that of composition in Greek (but presumably in proximity to Semitic-speaking areas).

3. Word order can also serve as a test of translation Greek.[86] In his study of Semitic style in Mark, E. C. Maloney points out that in Hellenistic Greek the strong preference is for a subject-verb order in main clauses.[87] Word order is more variable in dependent clauses. The verb may precede the subject when the verb is an imperative, in the case of an apodosis following a subordinate clause, with verbs of saying, when the verb "to be" means "to exist" and when a single verb has a double subject.[88] By contrast, the normal

---

82. On the usage of the particle, see BDF §452 (2); Smyth, *Grammar*, §§2782–99; Moulton-Howard-Turner, *Grammar* 3.330; Mayser, *Grammatik* II/3:119. The unclassical (prepositive) use found in Luke 11:20 is also found in Paul and in the Hermetic Corpus (11.13).

83. Pentateuch, 2x; historical books, 2x; Job, 12x; Pss, 10x; rest of LXX, 12x. On the character of Job in the LXX, see E. C. Colwell, "Greek Language," *IDB* 2 (1962) 485; R. A. Kraft, "Septuagint," *IDBSup* (1976) 814.

84. Plutarch, 0.24:1; Polybius Bks. 1—11, 0.06:1; Epictetus, 0.44:1. These statistics are from Martin, *Syntactical Evidence*, 19.

85. Turner, "Recent Thought," 327: the LXX ranges from 188:1 (Jeremiah β) to 2.4:1 (Gen) and 2.1:1 (Exod 1—24). Matthew's Q is comparable to Exod (2.1:1), while Luke's Q performs even better (1.6:1). Turner (in Moulton-Howard-Turner, *Grammar* 3:332; "Recent Thought," 327) gives Luke 1—2 as 5:1; *Barn.* as 1.3:1 and 4 Macc as 1:1. Martin (*Syntactical Evidence*, 19) gives other statistics including Gen 1—4: 6; 39 (6.0:1); 1 Sam 3—4; 22 (178:1); 1 Kgs 17 (58:1); 2 Kgs 13 (61:1); Dan LXX [Hebrew sections] (58:1), [Aram. sections] (7.2:1); Dan Theod [Hebrew sections] (343:1), [Aram. sections] (82:1); Ezra [Heb.] (134:1), [Aram.] (82:1).

86. Turner ("Recent Thought," 327) examines only declarative sentences having nominal subjects and objects. This provides seven examples, six having S-O-V order and one having the (Semitic) V-S-O order.

87. Maloney, *Semitic Interference*, 51–52; E. Schwyzer, *Griechische Grammatik* (Handbuch der Altertumswissenschaft 2/1; Munich: Beck, 1953) 2:693. According to E. Kiekers (*Die Stellung des Verbs im Griechischen und den verwandten Sprachen* [Strassburg: Trübner, 1911] 5), the S-V order occurs in 86 percent of main clauses in Polybius and 82 percent in Xenophon. H. Frisk (*Studien zur griechischen Wortstellung* [Göteborgs Högskolas Arsskrift 39/1; Göteborg: Elanders, 1932] 16): from 71 to 87 percent in Herodotus, Thucydides, Xenophon, Lysias, Demosthenes and Polybius; 72 percent in papyri surveyed.

88. Schwyzer, *Grammatik* 2:694–95; Maloney, *Semitic Interference*, 52.

word order in Biblical Hebrew, in the LXX and in Middle Aramaic is verb-subject. Only Biblical Aramaic reverses this.[89]

An examination of the independent declaratory sentences with nominal or pronominal subjects (and excluding those above-mentioned clauses in which verb-subject order is normal) reveals that the preference in Q is for subject-verb (Matt's Q, 66.6 percent; Luke's Q, 65.3 percent).[90] This finding is admittedly somewhat less that what one would expect in good literary Koine (namely, 72–87 percent) but very much higher than that of the LXX, where even Genesis, an otherwise idiomatic translation, maintains the Semitic order.[91]

4. The final test of style mentioned by Turner is the separation of the article from its substantive. Since in Hebrew and Aramaic the noun and article (or its equivalent in Aramaic, the determined state) form one unit, it is *a priori* likely that in translation Greek, articles would only infrequently occur apart from their substantives. Studies of J. M. Rife and R. A. Martin[92] confirm this: LXX books translated from Hebrew or Aramaic display article-substantive separation in only 0 to 4 percent of arthrous substantives. This compares with up to 11 percent in non-translation LXX books, and 18 percent in NT epistles, and between 18 percent and 43 percent in Epictetus, Plutarch, Polybius, Josephus and a selection of papyri.[93] When the Q sections of Matthew and Luke are examined, it can be seen that Q performs somewhat better than the translation parts of the LXX: Matt's Q, 9.19 percent; Luke's Q, 8.37 percent.[94] This is significantly higher than Mark, which, according to Maloney's figures, exhibits this phenomenon in only 6.5 percent of arthrous substantives.[95] Again, the syntactical evidence does not support a translation hypothesis although, to be sure, Q is far from idiomatic Greek.

Several other indices of non-translation Greek may be applied to Q.

5. A few cases of hyperbata or artificial displacement of sentence parts occur in Q. These are very rare indeed in translation Greek but are commonly used in Greek prose and poetry to achieve emphasis. In Q the clearest cases of hyperbata are εἰ υἱὸς εἶ τοῦ θεοῦ (Q 4:3, 9) and perhaps καθήσεσθε ἐπὶ θρόνων τὰς δώδεκα φυλὰς κρίνοντες τοῦ Ἰσραήλ (22:30 diff Matt).[96] In addition, phrases such as τὴν (δὲ) ἐν τῷ σῷ ὀφθαλμῷ δόκον (Matt 7:3 diff

---

89. F. Rosenthal, *A Grammar of Biblical Aramaic* (Wiesbaden: Otto Harrassowitz, 1974[4]) §143. In Aramaic, with sentences containing no direct object, the preference is S-V; with an object it is O-V-S.

90. V-S: Matt's Q, 30x // Luke's Q, 25x. S-V.: Matt's Q, 60x // Luke's Q, 47x. These and the following statistics are based on the Q texts listed in table 3 (below, pp. 74–76).

91. In Gen 1—2, only 11.1 percent (5/45) of independent clauses are S-V.

92. J. M. Rife, "The Mechanics of Translation Greek," *JBL* 52 (1933) 244–52, esp. 248; Martin, *Syntactical Evidence*, 21–23.

93. Rife, "Translation Greek," 248; Martin, *Syntactical Evidence*, 21; Moulton-Howard-Turner, *Grammar* 3:348.

94. According to my count, Matt's Q has 609 arthrous substantives (including 56 separated substantives); Luke's Q has 585 (49 separated).

95. Maloney, *Semitic Interference*, 63.

96. This may be due to Lucan redaction. Luke introduces hyperbaton at 18:18 (cf. Mark 10:17).

Luke), ὁ δὲ ὀπίσω μου ἐρχόμενος (Matt 3:11),[97] τὸν δυνάμενον καὶ ψυχὴν καὶ σῶμα ἀπολέσαι ἐν γεένῃ (Matt 10:28 diff Luke) and οἱ δὲ ἱματισμῷ ἐνδόξῳ καὶ τρυφῇ ὑπάρχοντες (Q 7:25) are quite unexpected in translation documents.

6. The frequency of adjectives in first attributive position also serves as an index of Semitizing or translation Greek. While the normal position for the adjective in Hebrew as well as in both biblical and Middle Aramaic is following the substantive, Greek adjectives can appear in first or second attributive position, with the first being the more common.[98] Translated books of the LXX tend to follow the Semitic order: Martin's study shows that the ratio of first- to second-position adjectives in translated books ranges from 0:1 to 0.33:1,[99] whereas in books which were originally penned in Greek, the ratio always exceeds 1:1.[100] When the style of Q is examined, it can be seen that Q does not exhibit translation frequencies. The preference is for first attributive position in both Matthew's Q (2:1 [i.e., 16:8]) and Luke's Q (4:1 [i.e., 12:3]). Although the sample is rather small, even these ratios are probably conservative since several second-position adjectives are almost certainly due to Matthaean redaction (e.g., ὁ πατὴρ ἡμῶν ὁ οὐράνιος, Matt 5:48; 6:26, 32).

7. In Greek, dependent personal pronouns may precede or follow their substantives,[101] while in Hebrew and Aramaic the equivalent of a genitive regularly follows the *nomen regens*. This means that cases of dependent personal pronouns preceding their substantives *cannot* represent literal

---

97. Since Luke 3:16 follows the Marcan form of the saying, it is most probable that the Matthaean formulation reflects that of Q. Thus Schulz, *Spruchquelle*, 368; Hoffmann, *Studien*, 23.

98. Smyth, *Grammar*, §§1157–59; Mayser, *Grammatik* II/2:52–54.

99. Martin (*Syntactical Evidence*, 30) gives the following statistics (1st position::2d position):

Gen 1—4; 6; 39	0.14:1
1 Sam 3–4; 22	0.00:1
1 Kgs 17	0.33:1
2 Kgs 13	—
Dan LXX (Heb)	0.27:1
Dan Theod (Heb)	0.05:1
Dan LXX (Aram)	0.15:1
Dan Theod (Heb)	0.04:1

Turner (in Moulton-Howard-Turner, *Grammar* 3:349) states that in Gen 1—19 the ratio is 0.30:1 (i.e., 17::56) and in 1 Kgs 1—6 it is 0.062::1 (or 1::16).

100. Martin, *Syntactical Evidence*, 30 (1st position::2d position):

Plutarch's Lives	1.3:1
Polybius Bks. 1, 12	6.1:1
Epictetus *Diss.* 3—4	3.4:1
Josephus *Contra Apionem, Ant.*	5.6:1
Papyri	1.4:1

The papyri examples collected by Mayser (*Grammatik* II/2:52–54) show an even stronger preference for the first position (35:1)!

101. The forms τὸ βιβλίον μου and μου τὸ βιβλίον are both quite proper in classical and Hellenistic Greek. See Smyth, *Grammar*, §1185; Mayser, *Grammatik* II/2:64–65. Maloney (*Semitic Interference*, 199) points out that papyri from G. Milligan's *Selections from the Papyri* (Cambridge: At the Univ. Press, 1927) [III BCE—I CE] display a strong preference for post-positive pronouns with *anarthrous* substantives. Only seven of 60 are prepositive.

translations of Aramaic. Pronouns following their substantives do not, however, give evidence of a Semitic *Vorlage* since that order is quite acceptable in Greek. Q in fact contains several instances of preceding dependent personal pronouns, and this suggests that even if there were a Semitic *Vorlage*, it was not translated literally.[102]

The balance of the linguistic evidence does not favor a translation hypothesis. Two of the indices, the frequency of post-positive particles and the καί:δέ frequency, are consistent with either a translation or a non-translation hypothesis since Q's linguistic profile falls on the boundary between translation and non-translation frequencies. Other statistics, however, tip the balance in favor of a non-translation hypothesis. The presence of μέν . . . δέ constructions, the use of ἄρα and οὖν, the preference for the subject-verb order, the separation of articles from their substantives, cases of hyperbaton and the relatively high frequency of adjectives in first attributive position—all unexpected in translation Greek—point to the same conclusion: Q was composed originally in Greek. Of course, it must be conceded immediately that the style of Q is not literary Koine. And no one would seriously dispute that Q was formulated in proximity to a Semitic-speaking area, under the influence of the Semitizing Greek of the LXX, and in part, from orally transmitted sayings which had their origin in Aramaic-speaking circles.

To conclude: The many instances of strong Matt-Luke agreements compel us to assume that the two evangelists at least had before them a Greek copy of Q. Were there earlier recensions in Aramaic? The evidence for this is not strong. The search for "translation variants" has not turned up many candidates, and even those it has adduced are subject to other explanations. On the other hand, syntactical analysis provides good evidence of non-translation Greek. In this light the most economical solution is this: Q was compiled and composed in Greek. Litterae non sunt multiplicandae praeter necessitatem!

THE ORIGINAL ORDER OF Q

If Q was a document, is it possible to ascertain the order of pericopae? To this question many critics have responded in the affirmative, and the majority have concluded that Luke's order best reflects that of Q.[103]

---

102. Luke 6:29, 47 (= Matt); 9:60 (= Matt); 11:19; 12:30; 13:34; 14:26 (= Matt); 14:27 (= Matt); Matt 7:26; 8:8; 13:16. Some of these may be due to redaction although it is to be noted that Luke's preference is for a post-positive position (thus Cadbury, *Style*, 153), and thus more of the Lucan instances may be from Q.

103. Thus Holtzmann, *Synoptische Evangelien*, 141; B. Weiss, *Introduction* 2:200;

On the other hand, a few, most notably Harnack, Ewald and Moffatt, urged that Matthew better preserves the Q order.[104] Harnack, for example, concluded that it was Luke who broke up the speech in Matt 10 and distributed its sayings—following Matthaean order!—throughout his chapters 9, 10, 12, 14 and 17.[105] Apart from a few sayings which defied placement (and for that reason may not have belonged to Q at all!),[106] Matthew's order could be taken as the Q order. Luke "separated and distributed [the sayings] throughout his work *for reasons which can no longer be discovered.*"[107]

Moffatt took another tack. Arguing that the closing formula, καὶ ἐγένετο ὅτε ἐτέλεσεν ὁ Ἰησοῦς κτλ, derived from Q, he suggested that Q had been divided into five discourses connected by fragments of narratives. Such fivefold divisions, Moffatt held, could be observed in other Jewish and Christian documents of the time.[108] Moffatt explained the Lucan order with the conjecture that Luke restructured Q on the basis of "some other source" or "possibly now and then . . . the oral tradition."[109]

Neither of these defenses of Matthaean originality is particularly convincing. Harnack has to assume that Luke's editorial technique was "highly capricious"[110] and Moffatt's solution, apart from its speculative explanation of Lucan order, naively assumes that the closing formulae of the Matthaean sermons are pre-Matthaean, an assumption which is highly questionable.

There have been three systematic and detailed treatments of the problem of order in Q. Two somewhat different methods are used: one

---

Wernle, *Synoptische Frage*, 228; J. Weiss, *Schriften*, 36; Wellhausen, *Einleitung*[1] 67 [2] 58–59; Bussmann, *Redenquelle*, 109; Manson, *Sayings*, 15, 30. More recently, L. Cerfaux, "L'Utilisation de la source Q dans Luc," *L'évangile selon Luc: Mémorial Cerfaux* (BETL 32; Gembloux: Duculot, 1973) 63; Edwards, *Sign of Jonah*, 70; Fitzmyer, "Priority of Mark," 146–47; Josef Ernst, *Das Evangelium nach Lukas* (RNT 3; Regensburg: Pustet, 1977) 26; Vielhauer, *Urchristliche Literatur*, 314; Jacobson, "Wisdom Christology," 6–8; Worden, "Redaction Criticism," 533–34.

104. Harnack, *Sayings of Jesus*, 172–82 [121–28]. P. Ewald (*Das Hauptproblem der Evangelienfrage und der Weg seiner Lösung* [Leipzig: J. C. B. Mohr [Paul Siebeck], 1890] 27–33) argues that the Lucan form—a mere collection of aphorisms—is not likely to have been the work of the apostle Matthew. The connection of Matthew's name with the "Logia source" (by Papias) supports the originality of Matthew's presentation. See also Moffatt, *Introduction*, 195. C. F. Burney (*The Poetry of Our Lord* [Cambridge: At the Univ. Press, 1925] 7) prefers Matthew to Luke on the basis that Matthew preserves the poetic format of the sayings better than Luke.

105. Harnack, *Sayings of Jesus*, 175 [123].

106. E.g., Matt 5:13, 15, 18, 25, 26, 32; 6:9–13, 19–21, 22–23; 7:7–11, 13–14.

107. Harnack, *Sayings of Jesus*, 180 [127] [emphasis added].

108. Moffatt, *Introduction*, 197.

109. Ibid., 195.

110. Harnack, *Sayings of Jesus*, 181 [127].

advocated by Streeter and De Solages, and another by Taylor. The conclusions, however, are identical: Luke best preserves the Q order. Moreover, there has been no real attempt to refute their conclusions.[111]

Streeter (and De Solages)[112]

Streeter begins by isolating five major blocks of Q sayings and shows that within these blocks, considerable agreement in the order of sayings either already exists, or can be achieved by a single transposition (see table 1). This leaves only (a) the materials collected in Matt 5—7 and 10 but scattered in Luke, (b) the transpositions just mentioned and (c) seven "detached sayings." Streeter works from the principle that Matthew and Luke would undoubtedly have treated Q as they did Mark. For example, Matthew regularly transposed Marcan passages while Luke in general preserved Marcan order. As well, it can be shown that in Matt 10; 13; 18 and 23–25 Matthew has combined not only different documents (i.e., Mark and Q) but passages from *different parts of the same document*.[113] In other words, we know that Matthew combined several distinct documents and made rearrangements within some of these sources. This establishes the general probability that Matthew's reproduction of Q is suspect, and that Luke's is more to be believed.

Streeter resolved the disagreements between Matthew and Luke in favor of Luke. Some differences were attributed to Matthew's practice of

---

111. S. Petrie's article ("Q Is Only What You Make It," *NovT* 3 [1959] 28–33) is nothing more than a list of disagreements among writers on Q designed, presumably, to "prove" that the reconstructions of Q are sheer guesswork. He fails to treat either the logical and theoretical issues, or any of the primary evidence. Rosché and Honoré (above, nn. 6, 18) were apparently unaware of the articles of Streeter and Taylor and consequently do not speak directly to their arguments. D. Dungan ("Mark—The Abridgement of Matthew and Luke," *Jesus and Man's Hope* [2 vols.; Pittsburgh: Pittsburgh Theological Seminary, 1970] 1:51–97) simply dismisses Taylor's work as "special pleading" but treats none of the issues.

112. Streeter, "Original Order," 141–64; De Solages, *Composition*, 153–82. De Solages uses a procedure very similar to that of Streeter (although he refers to neither Streeter nor Taylor). Dividing Q (his siglum is "X") into 64 pericopae (including nine in which Mark and Q overlap), he points out that 27 pericopae, accounting for 52 percent of the word total, are already in order in Matt and Luke. Next, he observes that the majority of the remaining texts appear in Luke's long interpolation and in the five Matthaean sermons. Since there is no conceivable reason for Luke to have collected the sayings into the long interpolation (which does not appear to be thematically coherent), De Solages assigns the priority to Luke. This leaves only 11 texts. Except for four which defy placement, these disagreements are due to Matthew's transporting a Q text to a Marcan context or to a more suitable Q context. In only one instance was Luke responsible for the transposition (Luke 6:43–44; *Composition*, 159). Hence the majority of Q texts either already manifest common order or can be brought into order by taking into account Matthaean editorial techniques.

113. Streeter, "Original Order," 145–50.

TABLE 1

Matthew	Luke
1. John's preaching	John's preaching
Temptation	Temptation
Great sermon	Great sermon
Centurion's servant	Centurion's servant
2. Jesus' followers	John's question
Harvest is great	Jesus' followers
Mission speech	Harvest is great
John's question	Mission speech
3. Woes against the cities	Woes against the cities
Jesus' thanksgiving	Jesus' thanksgiving
Beelzebul	Beelzebul
Sign of Jonah	Return of the evil spirit
Return of the evil spirit	Sign of Jonah
4. Mustard seed and leaven	Mustard seed and leaven
Concerning offenses	Lost sheep
Lost sheep	Concerning offenses
On forgiveness	On forgiveness
5. Woes against Pharisees	Woes against Pharisees
Lament over Jerusalem	On the day of the Lord
On false Christs	Lament over Jerusalem
On the day of the Lord	On false Christs
Parable of the pounds	Parable of the pounds

This leaves only (1) passages gathered in Matthew's two great sermons (5—7, 10) but scattered in Luke, and (2) 7 detached sayings:

Matthew	Luke
8:11–12	13:28–29
11:12–13	16:16
13:16–17	10:23–24
15:14b	6:39b
17:20	17:6 (cf. Mark 11:23)
19:28b	22:30b
23:12	14:11; 18:14

B. H. Streeter, "On the Original Order of Q," *Oxford Studies in the Synoptic Gospels*, ed. W. Sanday (Oxford: At the Clarendon Press, 1911) 141–64.

attaching Q sayings to Marcan contexts.[114] For others, he appealed to the dictates of the Matthaean editorial schema, while in other instances the priority of Luke was defended by an argument from general probability (based on Lucan treatment of Mark)[115] or from the improbability that Luke would have scattered sayings which were already collected and thematically organized in Matthew.[116]

Streeter's argument is impressive but not without problems. In the first place, his division of Q into units disguises some disagreements of order *within* these units, e.g., in the woes against the Pharisees and in the mission speech. His grouping also hides the fact that, for example, Luke's woes precede the parables of the mustard seed and the leaven, while Matthew's woes follow them (see table 1). A second problem is his use of an argument from general probability. It is indeed true that Matthew conflates and rearranges his sources. This may establish the general probability that Luke is original, but such an argument should be used as a last, not a first, resort. Especially in the case of the disagreements in the two large sermons (Matt 5—7, 10) Streeter too quickly resolves the issue by appealing to this argument.

Taylor

The problem presented by the Matthaean and Lucan sermons was addressed by Taylor in two articles.[117] Rather than comparing Matthew and Luke in two parallel columns, Taylor offered the brilliant solution of dividing Matthew into six components: the five large sermons and the remainder of the Gospel (see table 2). When this was done, Taylor was able to show that there is a large measure of agreement in order when one compares *each* of the six Matthaean columns with Luke. In effect, Taylor suggested that Matthew scanned Q several times, removing material appropriate to each of the five sermons, and reproducing these smaller sets of sayings in Lucan order.[118] He conceded, however, that the agreement in order is "not continuous throughout [each sermon] but visible in groups and series of passages in the same order in both Gospels."[119] Finally, he tried to provide explanations for each transposi-

---

114. E.g., Matt 13:16–17, 31–32; 15:14b; 17:20; 19:28b; 23:37–39; 24:26–28, 31–41, 43–51.

115. Streeter ("Original Order," 154) explains the transpositions within the Sermon on the Mount and the mission charge in this way.

116. E.g., Matt 8:11–12; 11:12–13; 12:38–42.

117. Vincent Taylor, "Order of Q"; idem, "Original Order of Q."

118. Because the degree of Matt-Luke agreement is slight, Taylor disregards several possible Q texts: Luke 10:25–28; 12:54–56; 13:23–24, 25–27; 15:3–7, 10; 19:12–27.

119. Vincent Taylor, "Original Order," 97. In fact, some of these "groups" consist of only two (six groups) or three (five groups) sayings in the same order.

tion or dislocation of Q material, almost invariably attributing the change to Matthew. Conflation with Mark and influence of M tradition were his most usual ways of accounting for Matthaean alterations.

Despite the ingenuity of this solution, one caution must be observed. Given a sufficient number of scannings, *any two lists* of common elements can be reconciled in order. Put differently, the more scannings that are required, the more cumbersome and the less convincing is this kind of solution. Taylor, in effect, permits 15 scans (see table 2). Given the initial common order, it is hardly surprising that 15 scannings can reconcile the other disagreements.

Methodological Considerations

Reconstructing the original order of Q is in effect the obverse of understanding the redactional rearrangement of Q by one or both of the evangelists. If the reconstruction is to be convincing, the solution must entail explanations which are both editorially plausible and in keeping with redactional procedures evidenced elsewhere in the author's work. Resort to explanations which must posit arbitrariness or caprice on the part of the editor, or which rely on uncontrollable factors such as the influence of *Sondergut*, or which require us to imagine complicated or inexplicable editorial maneuvers only serves to diminish the overall persuasiveness of the solution.

In the treatments of Streeter, De Solages and Taylor there is no real attempt to stratify the arguments with respect to the degree of probability which obtains from each. Their explanations of dislocations are adduced *ad hoc* and arguments from general probability are applied too frequently. Five types of arguments are regularly adduced:

1. Common order already exists between Matthew and Luke in some of the sayings.
2. Matthew tends to conflate Mark with Q; Luke keeps the two separate. This favors Lucan priority.
3. Matthew rearranges his Marcan material and for this reason it is *a priori* likely that he did the same with Q. On the other hand, Luke is more faithful to the Marcan order and hence would be expected to be more faithful to Q.[120]
4. It is more likely that Matthew would collect sayings into thematically organized groups than that Luke would scatter them.

120. G. B. Caird (*St. Luke* [London: Penguin, 1965] 24–25) lists 17 Lucan divergences from Marcan order. But in 11 (or 12) cases, the Lucan text is almost certainly from Q, not Mark, and it follows Q order. In four cases (4:16–30; 5:1–11; 10:25–37; 7:36–50) the Lucan version differs so radically from Mark that the presence of non-Marcan tradition must be suspected. This leaves only 12:1 (Mark 8:15) and 22:25–27 (Mark 10:42–45) as genuine transpositions.

TABLE 2

Luke	Matt 5—7	Matt 10	Matt 13	Matt 18	Matt 23—25	Other
3:7–9, 16–17						3:7–12
3:21–22						3:16–17
4:1–13						4:1–11
6:20–23	5:3–6, 11–12					
6:27–30	5:39–44					
6:31	(7:12)					
6:32–36	5:45–48					
6:37–38	7:1–2					
6:39						(15:14)*
6:40		(10:24)*				
6:41–42	7:3–5					
6:43–45	7:16–20					12:33–35
6:46	7:21					
6:47–49	7:24–27					
7:1–10						8:5–13
7:18–23						11:2–6
7:24–28						11:7–11
7:31–35						11:16–19
9:57–60						8:19–22
10:2						9:37–38
10:3–12		10:9–16*				
10:13–15						11:21–24
10:16		(10:40)*				
10:21–22						11:25–27
10:23–24			13:16–17			
11:1–4	6:9–13					
11:9–13	7:7–11					
11:14–23						12:22–30
11:24–26						12:43–45
11:29–32						12:38–42
11:33	(5:15)*					
11:34–35	6:22–23					
11:49–51					23:34–36	
12:2–3		10:26–27				
12:4–7		10:28–31				
12:8–9		10:32–33				
12:10						(12:32)*
12:11–12		(10:19–20)*				
12:22–31	6:25–33					
12:33–34	(6:20–21)*					
12:39–46					24:43–51	
12:51–53		10:34–36				

Luke	Matt 5—7	Matt 10	Matt 13	Matt 18	Matt 23—25	Other
12:57–59	5:25–26	↑	↑			
13:18–21			13:31–33			
13:28–29						8:11–12
13:34–35					23:37–39	
14:11				(18:4)*		
14:26–27		10:37–38				
16:13	(6:24)					
16:16						(11:12–13)
16:17	(5:18)					
16:18	(5:32)					
17:1–2				18:6–7		
17:3–4				18:15, 21–22		
17:5–6						17:20
17:23–24					24:26–27	
17:26–27					24:37–39	
17:33		10:39				
17:34–35					24:40	
17:37					(24:28)	
22:30b						19:28b

( ) denotes passages which break continuous sequence.
* denotes passages in which conflation is possible.

Vincent Taylor, "The Original Order of Q," *New Testament Essays* (Grand Rapids: Wm. B. Eerdmans, 1972; London: Epworth Press, 1970) 92–93.

5. Matthew may have conflated Q with M material, or may have transported Q sayings to M contexts.

The last explanation is particularly weak since we have no independent access to M. Indeed, it is far from clear that M was written; hence it may be meaningless to speak of an M context.

By far the most secure argument is that of *already existing order*. Such agreement is of two sorts: agreements in absolute order, i.e., with respect to the whole of Q; and agreements in relative order, i.e., with respect to sayings in subsets of Q. That there is agreement, for example, in the initial and closing sections of Q as reproduced by Matthew and Luke is good evidence in itself that Q began and closed with these sections.[121] Groups of sayings which agree internally in order but disagree in overall placement present another problem. The original position of such groups can be determined only by reference to the respective editorial techniques of the evangelists and by observation of the relation of the Q material to the framework which is external to Q, i.e., the Marcan framework.

It is here that the second consideration has value. That Matthew both conflates Q with Mark and displaces Marcan stories is a matter of empirical fact. When we encounter a Q pericope which is conflated with a Marcan story, we may assume that the setting is secondary. Similarly, when a cluster of Q sayings is placed in such a way as to fulfil a specific function in respect to the *Marcan framework or Marcan materials* (i.e., a function it could not originally have had in Q), then its position is certainly secondary.

It is also a matter of empirical observation that Matthew transposed Marcan passages. From this derives the probability that in the case of disagreements, Matthew *may* be secondary in his setting of Q. It should be remembered, however, that such generalizations are precarious and should not be employed too liberally. Similarly, the fourth argument— that it is more likely that Matthew would have collected sayings than it is that Luke would have scattered them—provides only a general consideration which may or may not apply in specific instances.

Order in Q (see table 3)

A considerable degree of agreement between Matthew and Luke already obtains in the presentation of Q sayings. Of 106 units (by my

---

121. There is agreement in the fact that Q 3:7–9, 16–17; 4:1–13; 6:20b–21, 22–23 pars. are the first Q texts cited by Matthew and Luke and in the fact that 19:12–27 occurs as the last or second-last Q text cited.

division) of the double tradition, 35 already exhibit a common order, providing the following framework:

John's preaching	##1, 2
Temptation account	3
Sermon on the Mount/Plain	4–5, 7–8, 10–12, 15–16, 18–19
Centurion's son	20
Sayings concerning John	21–26
Woes against Galilee	38
Jesus' thanksgiving	40
Beelzebul accusation	45–50
Request for a sign	52–54
Lost sheep	90
On forgiveness	96
Parable of the talents	105

It should be kept in mind that this agreement exists in spite of the fact that Matthew and Luke did not insert their respective Q texts into the same Marcan contexts. To this list we may reasonably add two sayings (##6, 51) which do not occur in quite the same sequence but which are found in the same groups of sayings.[122] A single transposition in each group produces considerable sequential agreement (viz., 1–8; 45–54).

Of the remaining pericopae, 24 have been conflated with Mark, attached to Marcan stories or transposed to a new position in the Marcan framework: ##13, 41, 57–64, 70, 71, 79–80, 84, 95, 97, 98–99, 100–101, 103 and 105. In these cases, we know the Matthaean setting to be secondary. But there is no corresponding reason to suspect the Lucan setting as specially contrived, and for this reason it is preferable to assume that Luke reproduced the original order of Q.

There are several groups of sayings which are differently placed by Matthew and Luke but in which there is some measure of internal agreement in the order of individual sayings. Q 9:57–60 (##27, 28) is one such group. This cluster occurs just before the mission charge in Luke, but in the midst of a cycle of miracle stories in Matthew. As several authors have recently noted,[123] Matt 8—9 does not simply present Jesus

---

122. It is most likely that Matthew inverted the order of 12:38–42, 43–45. His addition of the phrase οὕτως ἔσται καὶ τῇ γενεᾷ ταύτῃ τῇ πονηρᾷ (v. 45) suggests that he intended this pericope as a summary of the preceding section which treats the rejection of Jesus and his resurrection (v. 40) by Israel. See Strecker, Weg, 103, 105–6.

123. H. J. Held, "Matthew as an Interpreter of Miracle Stories," in G. Bornkamm, G. Barth, H. J. Held, Tradition and Interpretation in Matthew (Philadelphia: Westminster Press, 1963) 200–202; W. G. Thompson, "Reflections on the Composition of Mt 8:1—

TABLE 3

The Order of the Double Tradition (in Lucan Order)

No.	Name	Luke	Matthew	Mark
1.	John's preaching (1)	3:7–9 ‖	3:7–10	
2.	John's preaching (2)	3:16–17 ‖	3:11–12	
3.	Temptation story	4:1–13 ‖	4:1–11	
4.	Beatitudes (1)	6:20b–21 ‖	5:3–6	
5.	Beatitudes (2)	6:22–23 ‖	5:11–12	
6.	Love your enemies	6:27–28	5:43–44	
7.	On retaliation	6:29 ‖	5:39–41	
8.	Giving freely	6:30 ‖	5:42	
9.	Golden Rule	6:31	7:12	
10.	Be sons of God	6:32–35 ‖	5:45–47	
11.	Be merciful	6:36	5:48	
12.	On judging	6:37–38 ‖	7:1–2	
13.	Blind guides	6:39	15:14 ———— 7:1–23	
14.	Disciples and teachers	6:40	*10:24–25	
15.	On hypocrisy	6:41–42 ‖	7:3–5	
16.	Good and bad fruit	6:43–44	7:16–20/12:33–34	
17.	Treasures of the heart	6:45	12:35	
18.	Lord, Lord	6:46 ‖	7:21	
19.	Parable of the builders	6:47–49	7:24–27	
20.	Centurion's son	7:1–10	8:5–10,13	
21.	John's question	7:18–23	11:2–6	
22.	Jesus' eulogy	7:24–26	11:7–9	
23.	Quotation of Mal 3:1	7:27	11:10	
24.	None born of woman ...	7:28	11:11	
25.	Children in the marketplace	7:31–34	11:16–19a	
26.	Sophia saying	7:35 ‖	11:19b	
27.	Discipleship chria (1)	9:57–58	8:19–20	
28.	Discipleship chria (2)	9:59–60	8:21–22	
29.	"The harvest is great ... "	10:2	9:37–38	
30.	Sheep among wolves	10:3	10:16	
31.	Carry no purse	10:4	10:9–10a ——— 6:8–9	
32.	Greeting of peace	10:5–6	10:12–13	
33.	Remain in one house	10:7a,c	10:11b ——— 6:10	
34.	On support of missionaries	10:7b	10:10b	
35.	Activity of missionaries	10:8–9	10:7–8	
36.	Concerning rejection	10:10–11	10:14 ——— 6:11	
37.	Threat	10:12	10:15	
38.	Woes against Galilee	10:13–15 ‖	11:21–24	
39.	"Whoever hears you ... "	10:16	10:40	
40.	Jesus' thanksgiving	10:21–22 ‖	10:25–27	

No.	Name	Luke	Matthew	Mark
41.	"Blessed are the eyes . . ."	10:23–24	13:16–17——4:12	
42.	Lord's Prayer	11:2–4	6:9–13	
43.	On prayer (1)	11:9–10	7:7–8	
44.	On prayer (2)	11:11–13	7:9–11	
45.	Beelzebul accusation	11:14–15	12:22–24	
46.	A kingdom divided	11:17–18	12:25–26	
47.	Jewish exorcists	11:19	12:27	
48.	Exorcism by the finger of God	11:20	12:28	
49.	Binding the stronger one	11:21–22	12:29	
50.	"He who is not for me . . ."	11:23	12:30	
51.	Return of the evil spirit	11:24–26	12:43–45	
52.	Demand for a sign	11:29	12:39	
53.	Sign of Jonah	11:30	12:40	
54.	Jonah and Solomon	11:31–32	12:41–42	
55.	Light saying	11:33	5:15	
56.	Sound eye	11:34–36	6:22–23	
57.	Woe: cleansing the outside	11:39–41	23:25–26——}	
58.	Woe: neglect of justice	11:42	23:23————}	
59.	Woe: the best seats	11:43	23:6–7————}	
60.	Woe: unseen graves	11:44	23:27–28——}12:37b–40	
61.	Woe: you burden men	11:46	23:4—————}	
62.	Woe: murderers of the prophets	11:47–48	23:29–31——}	
63.	Sophia's oracle	11:49–51	23:34–36——}	
64.	Woe: you lock the kingdom	11:52	23:13————}	
65.	Revelation of the hidden	12:2	*10:26	
66.	What is said in the dark	12:3	*10:27	
67.	Do not fear	12:4–5	*10:28	
68.	You are worth more . . .	12:6–7	*10:29–31	
69.	Confessing Jesus	12:8–9	*10:32–33	
70.	Blasphemy of the Spirit	12:10	12:32————3:28–30	
71.	Assistance of the Spirit	12:11–12	10:19–20——13:11	
72.	Anxiety about daily needs	12:22–32	6:25–33	
73.	Treasures in heaven	12:33–34	6:19–21	
74.	Parable of the householder	12:39–40	24:43–44	
75.	Parable of the faithful servant	12:42–46	24:45–51	
76.	I cast fire on the earth	12:49,51	*10:34	
77.	On divisions	12:52–53	*10:35–36	
78.	Agreeing with one's accuser	12:57–59	5:25–26	
79.	Parable of mustard seed	13:18–19	13:31–32——}4:30–32	
80.	Parable of leaven	13:20–21	13:32–33——}	
81.	Two ways	13:24	7:13–14	
82.	I do not know you . . .	13:25–27	7:22–23	
83.	They will come from east and west	13:28–29	8:11–12	
84.	First will be last	13:30	19:30————10:31	
85.	Lament over Jerusalem	13:34–35	23:37–39	

No. Name	Luke	Matthew	Mark
86. Great supper	14:16–24	22:1–10	
87. Loving one's parents	14:25–26 |	*10:37	
88. Take up your cross	14:27 |	*10:38	
89. Salt	14:34–35	5:13	
90. Lost sheep	15:3–7 ||	18:12–14	
91. Serving two masters	16:13	6:24	
92. Law and prophets	16:16	11:12–13	
93. Endurance of the Law	16:17	5:18	
94. On divorce	16:18	5:32	
95. On scandal	17:1–2	18:7———————9:42	
96. Forgiveness	17:3–4 ||	18:21–22	
97. Faith as a mustard seed	17:5–6	17:20———————9:28	
98. "Lo, here, lo, there"	17:23 |	24:26———————13:21	
99. The day of the Son of Man (1)	17:24 |	24:27———————13:21–23	
100. The day of the Son of Man (2)	17:26–27 |	24:37–39c———13:33–37	
101. The day of the Son of Man (3)	17:28–30 |	24:39b———————13:33–37	
102. He who saves his life	17:33	*10:39	
103. Two in the bed	17:34–35 |	24:40–41———13:33–37	
104. Where the corpse is . . .	17:37	24:28———————13:21–23	
105. Parable of the talents	19:12–27 ||	25:14–30	
106. Twelve thrones	22:28–30	19:28———————10:29–31	

Sigla

Double vertical lines: agreements in absolute sequence.

Single vertical lines: agreements in relative sequence.

Solid horizontal line: Matthaean sayings joined to Marcan context.

* denotes sayings collected into second part of the Matthaean mission speech.

as "der Messias der Tat," to use Schniewind's term;[124] these chapters are permeated with the themes of Christology, discipleship and faith. The verb ἀκολουθέω appears seven times in the two chapters (8:1, 10, 19, 22, 23; 9:9, 27), twice in 8:18–22, and Matthew has edited his materials from Mark and Q in order to show what it means to be a disciple. Seen in this light, it is clear why Matthew would have moved 8:18–22 into this collection of Marcan stories:[125] it suited the theme of discipleship which he wished to develop there.

Another important disagreement of Matthew and Luke is in the relative placement of the mission speech. In Luke it follows the sayings about John, while in Matthew it precedes this material and follows the "miracle and discipleship" chapters (8—9). Again it is most likely that the change is due to Matthew. Jesus' answer to the Baptist has special significance in the structure of the First Gospel. It has long been recognized that Matthew transposed several miracle stories which occur later in Mark into chapters 8—9 so that Jesus' claim in 11:5 (τυφλοὶ ἀναβλέπουσιν καὶ χωλοὶ περιπατοῦσιν . . .) would have an obvious referent.[126] The commissioning and sending of the Twelve (10:1–5a; 11:1), which brackets the mission speech (10:5b–42), was used by Matthew to provide the point of reference for πτωχοὶ εὐαγγελίζονται. By contrast, Luke solved the problem of referents for 7:22 by stating that Jesus was performing miracles at the time at which the question was asked (7:21). In other words, Luke had no reason to tamper with the order of Q sayings. But Matthew's use of John's question obliged him to rearrange both Mark and Q.

A similar situation obtains in the parables of the householder and the faithful servant (## 74–75). Matthew places the two in his apocalyptic discourse whose structure is primarily determined by a Marcan schema (Mark 13:1–32 // Matt 24:1–36). Luke, on the other hand, places these parables in a predominantly Q context. His setting should be regarded as the original one.

Attention to Matthaean editorial habits can also resolve some of the

---

9:34," CBQ 33 (1971) 365–88; C. Burger, "Jesu Taten nach Matthäus 8 und 9," ZTK 70 (1973) 272–87; J. D. Kingsbury, "Observations on the 'Miracle Chapters' of Matthew 8—9," CBQ 40 (1978) 559–73.

124. J. Schniewind, Das Evangelium nach Matthäus (NTD 1/1; Göttingen: Vandenhoeck & Ruprecht, 1937) 103.

125. Matthew drastically rearranges Marcan pericopae, reproducing them in the order Mark 1:40–45, 29–31, 32–34; 4:35–41; 5:1–20; 2:1–12, 13–14, 18–22; 5:21–43; 10:46–52; 3:22.

126. Wellhausen, Evangelium Matthaei, 42, 53.

disagreements within the mission charge (##29–37). While the second part of the charge is constructed from a transferred Marcan section (Mark 13:9–13), he constructed the first part of the speech from (presumably) the first saying of the Q speech (Q 10:2, #29), parts of Mark 6:7; 3:13–19 (= Matt 10:1–4), an M saying (10:5–6) and then a conflation of the remainder of the Q speech with Mark 6:8–11. Q 10:3 (= Matt 10:16) was transferred to the end of the first section of Matthew's speech undoubtedly because it served as an appropriate transition to the theme of persecution which is developed in Matt 10:17–25. In other words, Matthew has placed Q material in a context partially determined by non-Q materials, and has conflated Q sayings with parallel Marcan sayings (thus explaining the disagreements in order with Luke 10:3–7). By contrast, Luke keeps the Q speech (Luke 10) distinct from its Marcan counterpart (Luke 9:1–6). Again, Luke's literary procedures suggest that he better represents the Q order of sayings in the mission speech.

As argued above, the observation that Matthew collected related materials is of only limited value in defending Lucan priority in order. In many instances it does not yield particularly convincing conclusions. In one case, however, its force is considerable. The mission speeches in Matthew and Luke begin with a cluster of Q sayings (see above). At 10:16 Luke finished his speech and turns to other subjects. But Matthew continues, employing diverse materials, some drawn from Mark (13:9–13) and some from Q passages which are scattered throughout Luke. What is striking is that Matt 10:24–39, comprising ten Q sayings, reproduces these sayings *in Lucan order* (##14, 65–69, 76–77, 87–88) even though they do not appear together in Luke. Here it appears that Taylor's type of explanation has special merit (even though Taylor did not treat these particular sayings). After reproducing and rearranging the Q mission speech, and after interpolating part of Mark 13, Matthew scanned Q and removed, *in the original Q (= Lucan) order*, 11 sayings appropriate to the theme of mission and used these as the balance of his mission speech. Only in the case of Q 17:33 (Matt 10:39), which occurs with a cluster of discipleship sayings (Q 14:26, 27 // Matt 10:37, 38), is it likely that the Matthaean order is primary.[127] Otherwise, it is the most economical and intelligible solution to suppose that Matthew scanned Q and collected these sayings than to argue that Luke distributed them in a capricious fashion.

Thus far, considering only those Q sayings which are either already in

127. See below, chapter four, pp. 158–59.

order, and those in which the Matthaean (but not the Lucan) setting is demonstrably secondary, we have treated 85 of the 106 units:

Existing order: 1–8, 10–12, 15–16, 18–26, 38, 40, 45–54, 90, 96, 105
Texts conflated with Mark by Matthew: 13, 41, 57–64, 70, 71, 79–80, 84, 95, 97, 98–101, 103, 106
Texts transferred to function in Marcan settings: 27–28, 29–37, 74–75
Texts collected in Matt 10:24–39: 14, 65–69, 76–77, 87–88, [+ 102]

There are a few individual sayings whose position in Matthew is suspect as redactional: (a) Q 13:28–29 // Matt 8:11–12 (#83), connected by Matthew with 8:5–10, 13 but reproduced separately by Luke;[128] (b) Q 6:43–45 // Matt 7:16–20 // 12:33–35 (#17), which Matthew uses twice, once in its Q position (= Luke 6:43–44) and once in connection with the "sin against the Holy Spirit" (Matt 12:31–37), where it is expanded by the addition of other materials;[129] (c) Q 10:16 // Matt 10:40 (#39) (despite the fact that Matthew transposed the mission speech [see above] and greatly expanded it with other Marcan and Q sayings, he, like Luke, used this saying as the conclusion of the speech; this undoubtedly indicates that he saw it functioning that way in Q);[130] (d) Q 16:18 // Matt 5:32 (#94), presumably transferred to the Sermon on the Mount by Matthew and used in his antitheses on adultery and divorce (there is scarcely any reason for Luke to move this saying from its Matthaean position to its present Lucan location); (e) finally, Q 16:17 (#93), which is probably secondary in its Matthaean setting. Matt 5:17–20 is composite and betrays strong Matthaean redactional interests.[131] It is placed programmatically at the beginning of the antitheses, where Matthew's redactional activity is clearly visible. The Lucan setting, by contrast, does not appear to be a redactional construction.[132]

This leaves only 16 sayings, of which 13 (##9, 42–43, 55–56, 72–73, 81–82, 91) belong to the Matthaean Sermon on the Mount. That Matthew collected various scattered Q sayings is a strong possibility, given the editorial procedures of the first evangelist as observed elsewhere. Yet such a conclusion must remain tentative because factors beyond our

128. See Josef Schmid, *Matthäus und Lukas*, 254; Lührmann, *Redaktion*, 57; Schulz, *Spruchquelle*, 324 n. 12.
129. See Josef Schmid, *Matthäus und Lukas*, 247–48; Schürmann, *Lukasevangelium* 1:375–76; Steinhauser, *Doppelbildworte*, 317.
130. Thus Josef Schmid, *Matthäus und Lukas*, 278–79; Lührmann, *Redaktion*, 60, 110; Grundmann, *Matthäus*, 302. Schulz (*Spruchquelle*, 458) is undecided.
131. See G. Barth, "Matthew's Understanding of the Law," in G. Bornkamm, G. Barth, H. J. Held, *Tradition and Interpretation in Matthew* (Philadelphia: Westminster Press, 1963) 65–73.
132. Thus Josef Schmid, *Matthäus und Lukas*, 221.

grasp may have been at work, e.g., the structure of *Sondergut* or the presence of fixed catechetical or liturgical schemata.[133] The original position of certain passages such as 13:34–35 and 16:16 is quite problematic and will be treated later.[134] Similarly, the original order of the individual woes against the Pharisees is a matter which requires detailed examination.[135]

Notwithstanding these few uncertainties, it is striking that for a very high proportion of the Q texts, it is possible either to ascertain the common order, or to determine which evangelist disturbed the common order by appealing to only the most secure observations. In fact, this determination can be made in 90 of the 106 cases—or about 85 percent of the sayings, and an even higher percentage if word count is considered. Even if some sayings ultimately defy placement, it can safely be said that Q was a document with a largely discernible order, and that in general Luke best represents that order.

THE ORIGINAL EXTENT OF Q

One of the perennial problems of Synoptic studies is that of the original extent of Q. This arises in redaction-critical studies, for example, when attempting to determine whether a given passage which occurs in a Q context is to be ascribed to that source, to *Sondergut*, or to redaction. For investigations of Q itself, the question of the original extent of Q has considerable bearing on the assessment of the character, theology and genre of the document. If it could be shown, for example, that Q contained a passion account, the genre and theology of Q would require substantial re-evaluation. Or if it contained narratives and a continuous

---

133. The placement of the Lord's Prayer (#42) in Matthew may be due to the presence of the theme of prayer in special Matthaean material. Betz ("A Jewish-Christian Cultic *Didache* in Matt 6:1–18," *Essays,* 55–69) argues that Matt 6:1–18 is a pre-Matthaean composition, consisting of a Jewish Christian cult didache on almsgiving (6:2–4), prayer (6:5–6) and fasting (6:16–18), which was later supplemented by vv. 7–15. This would imply not only a complex tradition-history for the Q material which eventually found its way into the Matthaean Sermon, but presumably also an overlap between the putative pre-Matthaean Sermon and Q. For Betz's advocacy of pre-Matthaean portions of the Sermon see *Sermon on the Mount,* passim. The arrangement of 7:12 (#9), 7:13–14 (#81), 7:15–20 (warning against false prophets; good and bad fruits), 7:21–23 (## 18 + 82) and 7:24–27 (#19) may reflect a catechetical "two ways" schema. On this see M. J. Suggs, "The Christian Two Ways Tradition: Its Antiquity, Form and Function," *Studies in New Testament and Early Christian Literature* (NovTSup 33; Leiden: E. J. Brill, 1972) 60–74.

134. See below, chapter four, pp. 113–114 and chapter five, pp. 227–28.

135. See below, chapter four, pp. 139–40.

narrative framework, the usual designations "Logienquelle" and "Spruchquelle" would obviously be inappropriate.

The question, then, is whether the double tradition and Q are roughly identical in extent and in character. Some have argued that Q is almost completely preserved by Matthew and Luke. Reasoning that Matthew and Luke would have treated Q as they did Mark, Streeter concluded that although one evangelist occasionally may have omitted material which the other preserved, such omissions were relatively few.[136] G. D. Kilpatrick came to the same conclusion, contending that the eventual disappearance of Q was explicable only on the assumption that it was almost completely absorbed in Matthew and Luke.[137]

On the other hand, several authors believe that Q was much larger than the present double tradition. Honoré calculated that the double tradition represents only 10.5 to 14 percent of the original Q, while Carlston and Norlin estimate 22 percent.[138] Such calculations are precarious for several reasons. Honoré's estimate is predicated on two highly dubious assumptions: that Matthew and Luke did not regard Q as highly as Mark, and that sayings material was treated no differently than narrative. Both assumptions are questionable in light of the Carlston-Norlin study which showed that both Marcan and Q sayings are treated more conservatively than narrative, and that the reproduction of Q is slightly better than that of Mark in both sayings and narrative.[139] Moreover, all of Honoré's calculations are based on verbatim agreements. Thus despite the fact that Matthew takes over all but ten of Mark's 128 pericopae,[140] Honoré sets the agreement of Matt-Mark

---

136. Streeter, *Four Gospels*, 185, 289–90.

137. Kilpatrick, "Disappearance of Q," 182–84. Kilpatrick reasons that if Q was contained in Matthew and Luke, it could disappear relatively quickly, especially if it was anonymous, and considering its primitive structure. If a considerable part of Q was preserved by only one or other evangelist, Q could disappear only when both Gospels came into circulation, and the process would be even slower if a considerable part was absorbed by neither.

138. Honoré, "Statistical Study," 134–35. Honoré arrives at this figure by assuming that the portion of Mark (and hence of Q) preserved verbatim by Matthew (x) multiplied by the portion preserved by Luke (y) will yield the material common to Matt-Luke (t). Thus if $x = 35$–40% and $y = 30$–34%, then the extent of Matt-Luke agreement = 10.5–14% of the original Q. Since Matthew and Luke presumably did not preserve the *same* parts of Q, Honoré reckons that between them 65 to 75 percent (less the 10 to 14 percent overlap) of Q is preserved, and hence about 40 percent of Q is irretrievably lost. Carlston and Norlin ("Statistics and Q," 76–77) accept Honoré's formula ($xy = t$) and his 10.5–14% statistic but note that Q contains proportionally about twice as much sayings material as Mark and adjust the estimate accordingly.

139. Carlston and Norlin, "Statistics and Q," 71.

140. I use the divisions of R. Morgenthaler's *Statistische Synopse* (Zurich and Stuttgart: Gotthelf, 1971) 66–68.

at only 38 to 43 percent. The more probable assumption upon which to base an estimate of the size of Q is that the Synoptists could be expected to treat Q as they did the corresponding type of Marcan materials. If one examines the Marcan sayings which are most like what we know of Q, i.e., individual sayings and chriae (excluding the dialogue portions of miracle stories except where the story is used to introduce a pronouncement),[141] it may be seen that Matthew retains a very high proportion of such Marcan sayings although he does not necessarily reproduce Mark verbatim. Luke retains a lesser proportion, but it should be noted that he often uses a similar Q or L passage in place of Mark when confronted by an apparent overlap or redundancy.[142] This suggests that Luke regarded Q *even more highly* than he did Mark. Statistics are very imprecise and potentially misleading indicators of the extent of Q. We may surmise, however, that if Matthew and Luke treated Q at least as conservatively as they did Mark, a substantial portion of Q is preserved in them. Since both evangelists occasionally omitted Marcan sayings (e.g., 2:27; 4:26–27; 12:32–34), we must reckon with the possibility that parts of Q are now irretrievably lost,[143] and further, that some Matthaean and Lucan *Sondergut* may in fact derive from Q.

It is, of course, not possible to recover sayings which have been omitted by both evangelists. *Sondergut* is another matter. A method employing "verbal reminiscences" devised by Heinz Schürmann provides one means of determining whether *Sondergut* derives from Q.[144] Schürmann observes that even when Marcan passages are omitted or completely reformulated by one or another of the evangelists, verbal reminiscences of such passages persist. Reasoning that the same would apply *mutatis mutandis* to Q, he sought reminiscences of Matthaean

---

141. E.g., in Mark 1—10: 1:7–8, 11, 15, 17; 2:5–11, 14, 16–17, 18–20, 21–22, 24–26, 27, 28; 3:4, 22–27, 28–29, 32–35; 4:3–9, 11–12, 13–20, 21–25, 26–29, 30–32; 6:4, 8–11, 14–16; 7:5–13, 14–16, 18–23; 8:12, 15–21, 27–29, 31, 33; 8:34—9:1; 9:7, 9, 11–13, 28–29, 31, 35–37, 39, 41, 42–48, 49–50; 10:2–9, 10–12, 15, 17–21, 23–27, 28–31, 33–34, 35–40, 42–45 (= 53 units of sayings).

142. Of the 53 units in Mark 1–10 (see previous note) Matthew retains 46 and offers at least two Q or M substitutes for Marcan sayings; Luke retains 33 but replaces Mark with Q or L in at least nine instances.

143. Vassiliadis ("Nature and Extent," 72–73) suggests that some of Q may have been omitted "because of the Q-document's heretical [*sic*] orientation," which consisted in an over-estimation of the Baptist. Although he argues that the baptismal story in Luke 3:21–22 was not from Q (p. 69) he gratuitously assumes that Q had a baptismal account which "differed widely from that of the canonical synoptics" (p. 73). One does not have to posit such conjectural explanations for the occasional omission of Q pericopae from the Gospels.

144. Schürmann, "Reminiszenzen." Schürmann uses this method not only to treat *Sondergut* but to aid in determining the wording and order of Q.

Sondergut in Luke and *vice versa*. For example, Matt 8:21 (ἕτερος δὲ ...
εἶπεν) agrees not with its parallel in Luke 9:58 (εἶπεν δὲ πρὸς ἕτερον) but
with 9:61 (εἶπεν δὲ καὶ ἕτερος). Moreover, Matt 8:21 inserts κύριε (diff
Luke) in agreement with Luke 9:61. These, according to Schürmann, are
evidences that Matthew saw the saying which is now preserved only in
Luke.[145]

The use of "reminiscences" is undoubtedly useful although it entails
subtle—perhaps over-subtle—arguments. And, as Schürmann con-
cedes, it is not by itself proof of the existence of a given passage in Q.[146] It
is worthwhile noting, however, that even if all of Schürmann's candidates were to be accepted as belonging to Q,[147] our estimation of the
genre of Q would not change appreciably since all are similar in character to what is already generally conceded as part of that document.[148]

More recently Vassiliadis proposed a set of criteria for dealing with
Sondergut. He argued that *Sondergut* passages could be admitted to Q if
(*a*) they were components of texts which on other grounds could be
ascribed to Q,[149] (*b*) they accorded theologically and stylistically with the
rest of Q, (*c*) they exhibited the language of "country life,"[150] (*d*) they

145. Ibid., 121.
146. Ibid., 125.
147. Neirynck ("Study of Q," 38 n. 38) provides a convenient tabulation of
Schürmann's candidates for membership in Q: Matt 4:4b; 5:19; 10:5b–6; 10:23; [21:14–
16]; Luke 3:2b–4, 5–6, 21–22; 4:14–15, 16–30, 31a, 37; 4:42–43, 44; 6:12–16, 17–20a, 24–26,
35a, 37b–38a; 7:1b–6a, 29–30; 8:1; 9:60b, 61–62; 10:1, [4b], 17–20, 23a, 25–28; 11:2a, 5–8,
21–22, 27–28, 37–39a, 45; 12:1b, 13–21, 32, 35–38, 49–50, 54–56; 13:25; 14:1–6;
14:11/18:14; 14:25, 35b; 15:8–10; 16:1–8, 9–12, 14–15; 17:5, 20–21, 22, 28–29, 31; 19:37, 39–
40; 22:24–27. Passages in square brackets should be added to Neirynck's list.
148. The most obvious exception is Matt 21:14–16, which Schürmann ascribes to Q
because of the presence of the catchword αἰνεῖν in Luke 19:37, which he takes to be a
reminiscence of Matt 21:16 (αἶνος). This is, however, rather slender evidence upon
which to base such a conclusion.
149. Vassiliadis, "Nature and Extent," 60–71. Q can reasonably be said to include (1)
"all extensive or consecutive sayings" which display "an almost verbatim agreement in
wording" (proverbs and short apophthegms, especially those placed differently by
Matthew and Luke, are excluded); (2) "all large units of the double tradition with no
close agreement in their narrative parts, but which agree verbatim or almost verbatim in
their sayings matter"; (3) "all extensive discourses in Luke with components found in
Matthew in a slightly or even quite modified form but in the same overall context"; (4)
doublets of a Marcan story or saying, especially if components are found in the other
Gospel (usually Matthew) in a conflated form; (5) Matthew-Luke agreements against
Mark (e.g., Luke 3:16–17; 4:1–13; 11:14–26; 13:18–21); (6) "semi-extensive sections of the
double tradition which although they do not disagree completely nevertheless show
considerable variation," which at the same time do not break the original Q (= Lucan)
order, and fit into the context of the document as reconstructed by principles 1–5,
provided that reasons may be adduced for the variations (e.g., Luke 12:49, 51–53; 11:2–
4).
150. The allusion to "country-life language" is evidently influenced by J. M. C.
Crum's *The Original Jerusalem Gospel* (New York: Macmillan Co., 1927), chap. 4, "Q and
Country Life."

betrayed no signs of redaction by Matthew or Luke, (e) good reasons
could be adduced for their omission by the other evangelist or (f) they
occurred in Luke 9:51—18:15, i.e., where about two-thirds of Luke's Q is
placed.[151]

These are sound and responsible criteria. Application of these criteria
does not, in fact, lead to a significant expansion of Q.[152] Moreover, the
principle of coherence implied in (b) insures that Q remains relatively
homogeneous both theologically and stylistically.

Neither the candidates promoted by Schürmann nor those of Vassiliadis would seriously affect the genre of Q. Several critics, however,
have contended that Q had a baptismal and a passion account. Such
hypotheses deserve some attention.

The Baptism of Jesus

Harnack and Streeter championed the view that Q contained a baptismal account.[153] The claim was based upon several grounds: (1) There
are a few agreements of Matt 3:16–17 // Luke 3:21–22 against Mark 1:9–
11: the use of a participial form of $\beta\alpha\pi\tau\iota\zeta\omega$ instead of a finite verb,
$\dot{\alpha}\nu o\iota\gamma\omega$ in place of $\sigma\chi\iota\zeta\omega$, $\dot{\epsilon}\pi$ $\alpha\dot{\upsilon}\tau\acute{o}\nu$ in place of $\epsilon\dot{\iota}s$ $\alpha\dot{\upsilon}\tau\acute{o}\nu$ and the placement of $\kappa\alpha\tau\alpha\beta\alpha\acute{\iota}\nu\omega$ before $\dot{\omega}\sigma(\epsilon\grave{\iota})$ $\pi\epsilon\rho\iota\sigma\tau\epsilon\rho\acute{\alpha}\nu$.[154] (2) Both Harnack and
Streeter regarded the western reading of Luke 3:22, $\upsilon\acute{\iota}\acute{o}s$ $\mu o\upsilon$ $\epsilon\hat{\iota}$ $\sigma\acute{\upsilon}$, $\dot{\epsilon}\gamma\grave{\omega}$
$\sigma\acute{\eta}\mu\epsilon\rho o\nu$ $\gamma\epsilon\gamma\acute{\epsilon}\nu\nu\eta\kappa\acute{\alpha}$ $\sigma\epsilon$, as Q's version of the voice from heaven.[155] (3)
Others add that the Son of God Christology presupposed by the temp-
tations demands the existence of a baptismal account containing this
motif.[156]

It must be said in response that the linguistic data are not very
compelling. The agreements against Mark are readily explained as

151. Vassiliadis, "Nature and Extent," 67.
152. Vassiliadis (ibid., 70) proposes only Luke 9:61–62; 11:27–28; 12:32–38, 54–56;
13:23–30; 21:34–36; Matt 10:16b; 11:12–13 (cf. Luke 16:16).
153. Harnack, Sayings of Jesus, 310–14 [216–18]; Streeter, Four Gospels, 188. Recent
proponents include Grundmann, Lukas, 106–7; Schürmann, Lukasevangelium 1:197, 218;
Hoffmann, Studien, 4, 39; Jacobson, "Wisdom Christology," 35–36, 152; Polag, Fragmenta,
30–31.
154. Thus Jacobson, "Wisdom Christology," 35; Schürmann, Lukasevangelium 1:197 n.
70; Marshall, Luke, 152.
155. The western reading is attested by D it Ju Cl Or Meth Hil Aug; "συ ει ο υιος μου
ο αγαπητος, εν σοι ευδοκησα" $\mathfrak{p}^4$ ℵ A B W Θ λ φ vg sa bo[pt]. See Harnack, Sayings of
Jesus, 311–12 [216–17]; Streeter, Four Gospels, 188; Polag, Fragmenta, 30–31.
156. Schürmann, Lukasevangelium 1:197, 218; followed by Marshall, Luke, 150. Both,
however, concede that the linguistic evidence is weak, and both reject the western
reading of Luke 3:22 as that of Q. They are obliged, therefore, to suppose that Q's
baptismal account was virtually identical with that of Mark.

redactional.[157] The western reading of Luke 3:22, even if it could be shown to be the original reading of Luke, scarcely proves anything about Q. Finally, that a Son of God Christology is presupposed by 4:1–13 is obvious; but that in itself is no reason to posit a special narrative justifying that Christology any more than there is reason to posit a narrative which grounds the Son Christology of 10:21–22 or the Son of Man Christology observed elsewhere in Q.

One may surmise that a baptismal account was thought appropriate to Q because of the relatively large amount of Baptist material present. The evidence, however, is not supportive of such a claim, and it should be noted that Q is much more interested in John's *preaching* and his *prophetic status* than in his baptizing practice as such.

A Passion Narrative in Q?

Several authors have posited a passion account for Q. Observing that Luke elsewhere preferred Q to Mark, W. E. Bundy suggested that portions of the passion story peculiar to Luke in fact derived from Q.[158] Specifically, he advanced the candidacy of Luke 22:25–27, 28–30, 35–36. Burkitt's reasoning was similar: Luke 22:24–30 was a conflation of Mark 10:41–45 and Q (cf. Matt 19:28).[159] Such proposals do not, however, succeed in proving the existence of a passion *narrative* since in all cases they concern *sayings* which do not even deal directly with the passion.

---

157. (a) Both Matthew and Luke show a marked tendency to use participial constructions to avoid Marcan parataxis. Moreover, Matthew ($\beta\alpha\pi\tau\iota\sigma\theta\epsilon\grave{\iota}s$ $\delta\grave{\epsilon}$ $\acute{o}$ $'I\eta\sigma\sigma\hat{v}s$) differs considerably from Luke's absolute genitive construction, which, as Cadbury (*Style*, 133–34) has shown, is a mark of Lucan style. Thus the "agreement" is not due to Q but is due to the redaction of the evangelists. (b) The verb $\sigma\chi\acute{\iota}\zeta\omega$ with $o\grave{v}\rho\alpha\nu\acute{o}s$ is quite unusual (see only *Joseph and Asenath* 14.3), whereas $\grave{a}\nuo\acute{\iota}\gamma\omega$ is well attested (Ezek 1:1; Isa 63:19; Ps 77:23; 3 Macc 6:18; John 1:51; cf. Rev 4:1; Philo *Quod Deus Immut.* 156; *Heres* 76; *Fuga* 192). Luke and Matthew are apparently simply substituting the more usual verb for Mark's unusual one. (c) The change of $\epsilon\grave{\iota}s$ $a\grave{v}\tau\acute{o}\nu$ to $\grave{\epsilon}\pi'$ $a\grave{v}\tau\acute{o}\nu$ is best explained as an accommodation to more usual biblical style, which commonly uses $\grave{\epsilon}\pi\acute{\iota}$ with $\pi\nu\epsilon\hat{v}\mu\alpha$ and a verb of motion (Judg 11:29; 14:6, 19; 15:4; 1 Sam 10:6, 10; 11:6; Isa 11:2; 32:15; 44:3; Joel 3:1, 2). More particularly, it represents an assimilation of the account to Isa 42:1 (cf. Matt 12:18) in the case of Matthew and Isa 61:1–2 (= Luke 4:18) and general Lucan usage (Acts 1:8, 17, 18; 10:44, 45; 11:16; 19:16) in the case of Luke. See on this Schürmann, *Lukasevangelium* 1:195; H. Greeven, $\pi\epsilon\rho\iota\sigma\tau\epsilon\rho\acute{a}$, *TDNT* 6 (1968) 68 n. 56. (d) The alleged agreement in word order is more apparent than real when the entire phrases are compared. (e) Jacobson ("Wisdom Christology," 35) adds that the explicit mention of Jesus constitutes an agreement against Mark, apparently overlooking Mark 1:9. In any event, Matthew tends to introduce the name Jesus at the beginning of pericopae even when Mark lacks it (at least 27x) and Luke tends to specify subjects (see Cadbury, *Style*, 150).

158. Bundy, *Jesus*, 481, 499, 500, 502.

159. Burkitt, *Gospel History*, 134–35; idem, *Earliest Sources*, 109–110.

One of the sayings, Luke 22:28–30, is regularly claimed as a part of Q, but it is an eschatological promise, not a passion prediction.[160]

More serious Lucan candidates for a Q passion were nominated by Hirsch:[161]

22:48: φιλήματι τὸν υἱὸν τοῦ ἀνθρώπου παραδίδως;
22:62: καὶ ἐξελθὼν ἔξω ἔκλαυσεν πικρῶς. (= Matt 27:75)
22:64: προφήτευσον, τίς ἐστιν ὁ παίσας σε; (= Matt 26:68)
22:69: ἀπὸ τοῦ νῦν δὲ ἔσται ὁ υἱὸς τοῦ ἀνθρώπου καθήμενος ἐκ δεξιῶν τῆς δυνάμεως τοῦ θεοῦ. [70]εἶπαν δὲ πάνες· σὺ οὖν εἶ ὁ υἱὸς τοῦ θεοῦ; ὁ δὲ πρὸς αὐτοὺς ἔφη· ὑμεῖς λέγετε ὅτι ἐγώ εἰμι.
24:47: καὶ κηρυχθῆναι ἐπὶ τῷ ὀνόματι αὐτοῦ μετάνοιαν εἰς ἄφεσιν ἁμαρτιῶν εἰς πάντα τὰ ἔθνη, ἀρξάμενοι ἀπὸ Ἰερουσαλήμ.

Since this is rather meager evidence upon which to build a continuous narrative, Hirsch was obliged to suppose that in other respects the Q passion account resembled that of Mark.[162] But examination of the proposed passages casts doubt upon the thesis. Luke 24:47 is strongly Lucan, as a recent treatment by Dillon shows.[163] And while in the view of Taylor and Rehkopf, Luke 22:48 may be pre-Lucan, there is nothing here to suggest that the pre-Lucan source was Q.[164] The words of Jesus to the high priest (22:69–70) are heavily influenced by Mark 14:62 and even if, as Taylor and Schneider contend,[165] Luke turned to another tradition here, there is no evidence that this tradition was Q. The "minor agreements" of Matt-Luke against Mark might offer stronger evidence of Q. However, Luke 22:62 is beset with textual difficulties[166] and even if it

160. See Bammel, "Das Ende." Luke 22:28, referring to those who remain "through my temptations," whether pre-Lucan or not, does not refer specifically to the passion but to the "temptations" incurred throughout Jesus' ministry. See further, S. Brown, *Apostasy and Perseverance in the Theology of Luke* (AnBib 36; Rome: Pontifical Biblical Institute, 1969) 8–9 and passim.

161. Emanuel Hirsch, *Frühgeschichte* 2:245–48.

162. Ibid., 248.

163. R. J. Dillon, *From Eye-Witnesses to Ministers of the Word* (AnBib 82; Rome: Pontifical Biblical Institute, 1978) 207–15. Τὸ ὄνομα (᾽Ιησοῦ) connected with preaching, baptizing, belief and forgiveness is typically Lucan. See Luke 21:21; Acts passim (32x), esp. 2:38; 10:43; 22:16, etc. Luke 24:27b, ἀρξάμενοι ἀπὸ Ἰερουσαλήμ is, of course, Lucan (cf. Acts 1:8).

164. Vincent Taylor, *The Passion Narrative in St. Luke* (ed. O. E. Evans; SNTSMS 19; Cambridge: At the Univ. Press, 1972) 74; F. Rehkopf, *Die lukanische Sonderquelle* (WUNT 5; Tübingen: J. C. B. Mohr [Paul Siebeck], 1959) 55–56.

165. Taylor, *Passion*, 82–83; G. Schneider, *Verleugnung, Verspottung und Verhör Jesu* (SANT 22; Munich: Kösel, 1969) 118–27.

166. Luke 22:62 is missing in 0171, a fourth-century Western ms and in some Old Latin mss (a b e ff² i l* m r¹). S. McLoughlin ("Le problème synoptique: Vers la théorie des deux sources—Les accords mineurs," *De Jésus aux évangiles* [BETL 24; Gembloux: Duculot; Paris: Lethielleux, 1967] 17–40, esp. 29) points out that without v. 62 Luke

does constitute a genuine "minor agreement" against Mark (which does not seem to be the case), the statement that Peter "went out and wept bitterly" is not a solid basis for a Q passion account. The same is true of 22:64: textual uncertainties abound.[167]

The search for Matt-Luke agreements and Lucan *Sondergut* from which to construct a passion account produces very few real candidates and falls far short of a continuous narrative, or even the beginnings of one. It would be unjustified to account for the paucity of Matt-Luke agreements against Mark in the passion sections by arguing that the Marcan and putative Q passion accounts were largely identical, differing only in a few minor aspects. Given the nature of early Christian literature, such a case of strong and extended agreement in two independent accounts is unlikely in the extreme. And the other instances of Mark-Q doublets do not display anything near verbatim agreement. The thesis of a Q passion account must accordingly be rejected.

SUMMARY

In summary the following points deserve to be repeated:

1. Q must be regarded as a written document, not simply a stratum of oral tradition.

2. Although the presence of Semitisms (both Aramaisms and Septuagintalisms) points to the pre-literary formulation of some of the Q tradition in, or in proximity to, Semitic-speaking areas, the linguistic evi-

---

flows better. ʽΩς in v. 61 introduces a final clause which does not require continuation in v. 62, while the αὐτόν in v. 63 refers not to the subject of v. 62 (Peter) but to that of v. 61 (Jesus). This suggests that v. 62 is an interpolation.

167. Here Matt 26:28 = Luke 22:64. This is a notorious crux, representing one of the most important apparent Matt-Luke agreements against Mark (14:65). It is complicated by several textual difficulties and has been treated variously:

1. Streeter (*Four Gospels*, 325–28), C. H. Taylor ("Western Readings in the Second Half of St. Mark's Gospel," *JTS* 29 [1927–28] 10–11) and McLoughlin ("Le problème synoptique," 31–35) argue that the lack of καὶ περικαλύπτειν αὐτοῦ τὸ πρόσωπον in Matt 26:67–68 (which is the necessary presupposition of the question "Who struck you?") and its absence in Mark 14:65 (D a f sy^s bo^mss) suggests that the original Marcan text (and hence the Matthaean exemplar) lacked the veiling of Jesus' face. Hence Matthew's question must also be a secondary assimilation to the text of Luke. This would mean that Luke's reading is due to redaction, not the influence of Q.

2. It is possible that the longer Marcan reading of 14:65 is original, but in that case the absence of the veiling in Matthew is inexplicable. Moreover, even the shorter reading has good attestation.

3. Bammel ("Das Ende," 43–44) considers the possibility of "the influence of oral tradition" (p. 44) while Schneider (*Verleugnung*, 102–3) is undecided whether it is a matter of textual assimilation of Matt to Luke or the presence of a non-Marcan *Vorlage* in Matthew and Luke. In any case, he does not think that this was Q.

dence is not such as to support a translation hypothesis. In fact, the contrary is true: Q appears to have been formulated in Greek.

3. That Q was a document implies that the sayings were ordered. In spite of the fact that in its present reproductions there are disagreements in order, a substantial degree of the original order can be restored by positing only a minimum of easily recognized editorial dislocations. As it turns out, and as the majority of critics have already affirmed, the Lucan presentation of Q is superior to that of Matthew, at least in regard to order.

4. To judge from the treatment of Marcan sayings by Matthew and Luke, and from the relatively more conservative handling of the double tradition when compared with the triple, it is safe to assume that a substantial portion of Q is already preserved in the double tradition, with a few sayings being present in Matthaean and Lucan *Sondergut*. There is no convincing evidence to suggest that Q contained either a baptismal story or a passion account. On the contrary, rigorous examination of the Matt-Luke agreements and application of the criteria suggested by Vassiliadis lead to the conclusion that essentially Q was composed of sayings and chriae. Even the Q "narratives" such as 7:1–10 can still be described as dominated by concerns endemic to sayings materials.

3

The Composition of Q

THE STRUCTURE AND UNITY OF Q

The Synoptic Sayings Source is not, as is sometimes thought, a "random collection of sayings" but manifests a variety of types of literary organization.[1] Not only are the sayings grouped into several topically coherent clusters, there is also a measure of unity and coherence among the several clusters as well as logical and thematic development throughout the course of the entire collection.

That Q has been viewed as a primitive or inferior literary product is not, of course, surprising. When placed alongside the Gospels of Matthew and Luke, both of which employ narrative as a framing device, Q seems deficient. But this is to compare apples and oranges. In fact, I will argue in chapter seven that when placed with its real literary family, namely, that of sapiential instructions, gnomologia and chriae collection, the Synoptic Sayings Source ranks with the most sophisticated literary products of its class.

The fact that the caricature of Q as a random collection of sayings could commend itself betrays significant historical and sociological assumptions about the nature of early Christianity. To those like Harnack who sought in Q an unimpeachable source for the consciousness of the Jesus of history, the denial of significant editorial intervention by the compilers of Q was essential. Q could not reflect strongly the literary and theological interests of its tradents and compilers if it was to reflect the historical Jesus. But even for those who, following Wellhausen's critique of Harnack's historical over-assessment of Q, found in it an expression of the earliest post-Easter Palestinian church, the assumption came easy

---

1. Schürmann, ("Reminiszenzen," 111) has criticized the use of the term *Logienquelle* and advocated *Redequelle* on the grounds that Q consists not in a collection of individual sayings, but in several "complexes of speeches." Koester ("Apocryphal and Canonical Gospels," 112) also rejects the designation "random collection of sayings."

that Q's lack of literary finesse was consistent with *anthropoi agrammatoi kai idiotai* who transmitted and used it. But have we been misled by a romantic notion of the constitution of earliest Christianity? Were the first purveyors of the Jesus tradition really so "primitive"? Recent investigation of other early Christian documents has challenged such a view, and social analysis of early Christian groups suggests that the Jesus movement had significant numbers of adherents from the "middle classes." The very fact that Q was *written* and not simply a set of oral folk sayings of a pre-literate group is evidence of use by Christians with access to literary technology.

Topical Groupings

What types of literary organization does Q exhibit? Perhaps the most obvious form is *topical*. Sayings are not simply strung together but gathered into coherent groupings. Some sayings are juxtaposed on the basis of formal similarities, e.g., four beatitudes in 6:20b–23 or seven woes in 11:39–52. Other clusters cohere thematically (e.g., 11:2–4, 9–13: on prayer). And these smaller compositions in turn combine to produce larger structural groupings.

Various attempts have been made to articulate the overall structure of Q. T. W. Manson proposed a fourfold division of Q:[2]

a. Q 3:7—7:35	John the Baptist and Jesus
b. Q 9:57—11:13	Jesus and his disciples
c. Q 11:14—12:34	Jesus and his opponents
d. Q 12:35—17:37	The future

Drawing on Jacobson's treatment of Q, Crossan proposes a similar division:[3]

a. Q 3:1—7:35	Jesus and John
b. Q 9:57—11:13	Jesus and disciples
c. Q 11:14–51	Jesus and opponents
d. Q 12:2—22:30	Jesus and apocalypse

The appropriateness of these headings may be questioned. There is much in 3:7—7:35 that has nothing at all to do with John the Baptist and his relation with Jesus (namely, 6:20b–49; 7:1–10). Manson's third section (11:14—12:34) is not solely concerned with opponents, but contains

---

2. Manson, *Sayings*, 39–148.
3. Crossan, *In Fragments*, 156, 342–45; Arland D. Jacobson, "Wisdom Christology in Q."

hortatory words directed at the community (12:2–7, 11–12, 22–31). And Crossan's fourth section (12:2—22:30) contains not only apocalyptic words, but sapiential admonitions, parables and discipleship sayings.

The division of Q into smaller thematically organized units avoids some of the inexactitudes of the above classifications. Both Polag and Schenk use more headings although neither their respective divisions nor their headings correspond exactly:[4]

Q Text	Polag	Schenk
Q 3:7–9, 16–17	A. Exordium	1. Prologue: John the Precursor
Q 4:1–13		2. Introductory portrait of Jesus
Q 6:20b–49	B. Sermo in monte	3. Statement of principles
Q 7:1–10		4. Paradigm: Jesus' first Gentile follower
Q 7:18–35	C. Johannes Baptista	5. On the Baptist
Q 9:57–62	D. Missio discipulorum	6. Prologue of the commissioning speech
Q 10:2–24		7. The commissioning speech
Q 11:2–4, 9–13	E. De oratione	8. On prayer
Q 11:14–35	F. Contentiones	9. Controversy: the Beelzebul accusation and request for a sign
Q 11:39–52		10. Controversy: contemporary Jewish piety
Q 12:2–12	G. De confessione	11. On the church
Q 12:22–34	H. De sollicitudinibus et vigilantia	
Q 12:39–53		12. The first eschatological speech
Q 12:54—13:21	I. Parabolae ac diversae sententiae	
Q 13:23—16:18		13. The two ways
Q 17:1–6	K. De responsabilitate discipolorum	
Q 17:23–22:30	L. De iudicio	14. The second and concluding eschatological speech

Most of the disagreements between Polag and Schenk are minor. Schenk proposes finer divisions, for example, separating Polag's section "Missio discipulorum" (D) into two sections (##6, 7), and "Contentiones" (F) into two controversies (##9, 10). In my view it is preferable to treat 7:1–10, which puts Israel in an unflattering light, along with 7:18–35 rather than including it with the Sermon on the Mount (thus Polag).

4. Polag, *Fragmenta*, 23–26; Schenk, *Synopse*, 5–9.

This produces a unit which is bracketed by criticism of the lack of response of Israel to Jesus (7:9, 31–35). Contrary to Schenk, 13:18–19 and 13:20–21 (two parables of growth) do not fit well with 12:39–59, but neither do they cohere with the following materials. They are best left on their own. While 13:23—14:34 may be appropriately termed a "two ways" speech, the material in 15:3—16:18 is not so readily classifiable.

Disagreement about this or that outline of the contents of Q is hardly avoidable.[5] But at the same time it is clear that the Q sayings have been organized thoughtfully into topical groupings. For the purpose of my analysis, I propose the following heuristic division of Q. Detailed rationale for these divisions and an exposition of the structural principles governing the composition of each unit will be provided in chapters four and five.

1. John's preaching of the Coming One	Q 3:7–9, 16–17
2. The temptation of Jesus	Q 4:1–13
3. Jesus' inaugural sermon	Q 6:20b–49
4. John, Jesus and "this generation"	Q 7:1–10, 18–28; (16:16); 7:31–35
5. Discipleship and mission	Q 9:57–62; 10:2–24
6. On prayer	Q 11:2–4, 9–13
7. Controversies with Israel	Q 11:14–52
8. On fearless preaching	Q 12:2–12
9. On anxiety over material needs	Q 12:(13–14, 16–21), 22–31, 33–34
10. Preparedness for the end	Q 12:39–59
11. Two parables of growth	Q 13:18–19, 20–21
12. The two ways	Q 13:24–30, 34–35; 14:16–24, 26–27; 17:33; 14:33–34
13. Various parables and sayings	Q 15:3–7; 16:13, 17–18; 17:1–6
14. The eschatological discourse	Q 17:23–37; 19:12–27; 22:28–30

Thematic Unity of Q

That there is topical organization of various subsets of Q sayings is evident. But what can be said of the collection as a whole? Examination of the contents of Q reveals that there are several basic unifying motifs which elevate Q beyond a mere agglomeration of sayings and smaller sayings collections.

Arland Jacobson has recently demonstrated a large measure of thematic unity within the Q materials.[6] Q, he argues, stands within a

5. The definition of Q adopted here includes all of those pericopae listed in table 3 (above, pp. 74–76) supplemented by Luke 9:61–62 and 12:13–14, 16b–21.
6. Jacobson, "Literary Unity," 365–89.

prophetic tradition pervaded by deuteronomistic theology. According to this theology,

> Israel's history is pictured as a history of disobedience. God in his forbear-
> ance sent warning to the people through the prophets, yet they rejected
> and even killed the prophets. Therefore God's wrath was—or will be—
> experienced. References to the prophets are a recurring but not a constant
> element in the deuteronomistic tradition; the rejection of the prophets is
> cited as simply one indication of the stiff-neckedness of the people. Certain
> distortions of history are conventional: the prophets appear almost exclu-
> sively in the role of preachers of repentance; far more prophets are killed
> than actually were; there is a tendency to expand the list of prophets . . . It is
> noteworthy that the guilt of the fathers is said to remain even up to the
> present (Ezra 9:7; Neh 1:6; Ps 78:8; cf. Luke 11:49–51 par.). The primary
> concern of the tradition is to call for Israel to return to Yahweh.[7]

Jacobson detects the motif of persistent disobedience in Q 6:23c, 11:47–51; 13:34–35; and 14:16–24. Likewise, Q refers to God's continual send-ing of the prophets (11:47–51; 13:34–35; 14:16–24) and Israel's continual rejection of them (6:23c; 11:47–51; 13:34–35; 14:16–24). Examples of Gentile faith further expose Israel's impenitence (7:1–10; 10:13–15; 11:31–32), an impenitence which will be punished by the coming wrath (3:16–17; 11:47–51; 13:34–35). Q contains the new call to repentance (3:7–9, 16–17; 6:20–49; 7:31–35; 10:2–12; 11:29–32; 11:39–52) and the threat of rejection for those who reject this final call (10:10–12, 13–15, 16; 12:10).[8]

It will be noticed that deuteronomistic influence is in fact restricted to a relatively few passages; large portions of Q (including 6:20b–49 and 10:2–12, 16, notwithstanding Jacobson's attempt to label either a "call to repentance") lack this motif. Nevertheless, Jacobson's observations are of utmost significance since they are coupled with a redaction-critical judgment that this theology dominated one stage of Q redaction.[9] Hence, although he has not attempted to prove that deuteronomistic theology pervades the whole of Q, Jacobson successfully demonstrates that at one point in its literary evolution, Q was organized and redacted from a coherent theological perspective. This redaction lends to the collection an important unity.[10]

7. Jacobson, "Literary Unity," 384. Jacobson depends here upon Steck, *Israel*, passim.
8. Jacobson, "Literary Unity," 384–85.
9. Ibid., 388–89; idem, "Wisdom Christology," passim.
10. Additionally, Jacobson asserts the unity of Q on form-critical grounds, observing that in comparison with Mark, Q contains a relatively large number of beatitudes, woes, "eschatological correlatives" and prophetic threats (Mark has only three, all duplicated in Q). Conversely, Q contains very few controversies and miracle stories. The controversies present in Q do not touch on legal matters as they do in Mark, and the

Logical and Qualitative Progression in Q

In his socio-rhetorical analysis of Mark, Vernon Robbins describes Mark's art of persuasion.[11] Drawing on the work of Kenneth Burke, Robbins distinguishes two ways in which Mark's narrative is advanced: by "logical form," that is, "the form of a perfectly conducted argument, advancing step by step," and by "qualitative form," in which "the presence of one quality prepares us for the introduction of another."[12] In Mark, logical progressions occur as "Jesus, the narrator, or others make promises that begin to be fulfilled, or when they make assertions or give explanations that anticipate or suggest later events."[13] On the other hand, the appropriateness of some developments is seen only in retrospect: that Jesus heals, exorcises and calls disciples follows, though not in a syllogistic way, from his designation as "the stronger one" (Mark 1:7).[14] This is qualitative progression. Although Q lacks Mark's overarching narrative framework, it too manifests logical and qualitative progressions.

The collection opens with John's prediction of the imminent appearance of the Coming One (3:16–17), thereby raising in the audience the expectation of fulfillment. This in fact occurs in 7:18–23 where Jesus is expressly identified with the Coming One. Yet ambiguities persist, since John's Coming One is not obviously consistent with Jesus as he is described in 7:22–23. How is the miracle-worker of 7:22 who points to the presence of the kingdom equivalent to John's coming apocalyptic judge? But this is not the end of it. The title emerges a third time, now in a context (13:25–30, 34–35) which is replete with the motifs of apocalyptic judgment: the Coming One of Q 13:34–35 acquires again the ominous connotations and strongly futuristic orientation of John's figure. Hence this particular logical progression begins and ends in the idiom of apocalypticism, but makes a theological detour in which the motif of the presence of the eschaton in Jesus' activity comes to the fore.

---

miracle stories are strongly oriented to the sayings component, not to the miraculous as such. Such form-critical observations are much less telling than his comments on thematic unity. While in comparison with Mark, Q displays a distinctive profile of sayings types, it must not be forgotten that Mark is unified above all by a *narrative* framework which Q lacks. When compared with other speech and saying collections from antiquity, it is immediately apparent that Q contains a relatively wider range of sayings types than these other collections. That is, Q is relatively less unified *formally* than comparable collections.

11. Robbins, *Jesus the Teacher*.

12. Robbins, *Jesus the Teacher*, 9; Kenneth Burke, *Counter-Statement* (2d ed.; Berkeley and Los Angeles: Univ. of California Press, 1968) esp. 123–83.

13. Robbins, *Jesus the Teacher*, 77.

14. Ibid., 85.

Qualitative progression occurs in Q's use of the theme of judgment. Q opens with the spectre of a baptizing ascetic proclaiming the imminent judgment of God and the demand for repentance (3:7–9, 16–17). At first blush, there seems to be little affinity between this figure and Jesus. In the description of the appearance of Jesus in Q 4:1–13 and in his first pronouncements (6:20b–49) the motifs of judgment and repentance are largely absent. Jesus' comportment, even as an itinerant preacher (Q 9:58), is in sharp contrast with the austerity of John's appearance. Despite Jesus' brief visit to the desert (4:1–13), his life is lived in constant interaction with populated areas and his followers preach in the towns and villages (Q 10:4–11), not on the fringes of civilization. Itinerancy is the spatial concept which belongs to Jesus' relationship with others; pilgrimage is John's. However, the motifs which characterized John's preaching soon emerge in Q, figuring prominently in Jesus' own preaching (10:12, 13–15; 11:31–32, 49–51; 12:8–9; 13:28–29, 34–35). Moreover, Q includes a sequence (7:24–28, 31–35) which asserts programmatically the fundamental agreement of John and Jesus and thereby serves to effect a transition between their two ministries. The effect of such a qualitative progression is to affirm rhetorically the commonality which exists between two figures who, as Q 7:33–34 expresses well, were quite different.

A related qualitative progression pertains to Jesus' disciples. The verses which most probably concluded Q (22:28–30) promise that the followers of Jesus will themselves dispense the judgment which Jesus and John threatened over Israel. This pericope and Q 10:16 ("the one who listens to you listens to me, and the one who rejects you rejects me . . .") establish a continuity between the activity of Jesus and that of his followers. With these qualitative progressions the compiler of Q seeks to assert the basic coherence between the activities of John, Jesus and his followers, and to underline the importance of the announcement of judgment and the call to repentance. While Q lacks a unifying narrative format, these instances of logical and qualitative progression lend the collection a significant measure of logical and structural coherence.

THE REDACTIONAL ANALYSIS OF Q

To affirm that the final form of Q reveals some degree of structural and thematic coherence does not answer all of the questions that we may have. I have already noted that the deuteronomistic motif, which Jacobson has properly identified as fundamental to one stage of Q redaction, does not appear in significant portions of Q. This raises the question, Is it the deuteronomistic motif of the preaching of repentance to Israel which was formative for Q as a literary work? Or is this motif characteristic of a second level of redaction and expansion? The varying assessments of the nature of Q by Robinson and Koester on the one hand, and Kelber and Boring on the other, also demand some resolution. There can be no doubt that Q contains both sapiential and prophetic forms. But what is the relationship between these two types of sayings forms? It is possible at least that the sapiential statements have been fully co-opted into a prophetic genre to the extent that Q presents itself not as a wisdom book, but as an oracle collection. Alternatively, Wisdom's speech in Prov 8 affords an example of the incorporation of the motif of the prophet's call to repentance into a sapiential context. Do the various elements within Q interact in one of these ways? It is also possible that, as Koester has intimated, Q has experienced a shift in its generic trajectory, beginning in one genre and experiencing a transformation through redactional intervention.

What is called for is a method of analysis which permits us to see the literary and theological principles which informed the composition of individual clusters of Q sayings, and the association of those clusters into a literary whole. Such a method of analysis should allow us to distinguish the redaction of smaller collections which eventually found their way into Q, or earlier, formative recensions of Q, from the theological and literary perspective of the final edition.

Methodological Considerations

In the past a variety of analytic methods have been employed in the discussion of the composition of Q, not all of them entirely successful. Since I have discussed the history of such attempts in another place,[15] I shall not rehearse this here. One point, however, is important. For the analysis of Q *as a document*, neither a form-critical nor a purely tradition-historical method is adequate. The compositional history of Q cannot be reduced to the various histories of its component forms. On the other hand, the redaction-critical methods which have proved effective in the analysis of Mark and which depend on the isolation of "seams" and "summary statements" and on the analysis of narrative movements are not readily transferable to the study of Q.

---

15. Kloppenborg, "Tradition and Redaction, " 34–62.

The most satisfactory models for redactional analysis of Q have been offered by Dieter Lührmann and Arland Jacobson.[16] Redactional intention, Lührmann writes, becomes visible in three ways: (*a*) in the principles of association of form-critically independent units; (*b*) in the comparison of Q and Mark in those instances of Mark-Q overlap and (*c*) in the *Gemeindebildungen* which may be ascribed to the Q redactor or to that stratum of tradition from which the redaction was born.[17] When a particular theme occurs in several complexes of sayings, or is evident in several Mark-Q overlaps, or is dominant in the Q *Gemeindebildungen*, then it may justifiably be considered redactional.

One caution is appropriate here. In the Q materials, it is notoriously difficult to distinguish sayings which are the creation of the Q redactor from "community constructions." In fact the term "community construction" belongs more properly to the vocabulary of form criticism than to redaction criticism and it implies, rather tendentiously, a creativity on the part of the community *per se*. For redactional purposes, it would be wiser to distinguish a redactor's addition of a free-floating saying (whatever its origin) from his creation of material which frames, joins or comments upon the sayings he has inherited. In most cases it is virtually impossible to determine whether a particular saying is a creation of a redactor or whether it is simply a piece of tradition which was deemed appropriate for inclusion because it resonated with the interests of the redactor and his community. For these reasons, Lührmann's *Gemeindebildungen* cannot be controlled sufficiently to act as a secure basis for determining redaction history and should not be employed as he attempts to employ them.

Jacobson's criteria for determining redaction are quite similar to Lührmann's. He finds evidence of insertions and additions in "grammatical shifts, breaks in the train of thought, shifts in audience, shifts in tradition or theology"[18] —generally speaking, in aporiae created by redactional activity. In the second place, Jacobson, like Lührmann, considers the principles which govern the juxtaposition of form-critically independent units. Compositional analysis, as Jacobson calls his method, consists of identifying redactional insertions and the principles which control the construction of larger units within Q. It yields a profile of what from a literary perspective is primary and what is secondary in particular pericopae or series of pericopae. Working synthetically, Jacob-

16. Lührmann, *Redaktion*; Jacobson, "Wisdom Christology."
17. Lührmann, *Redaktion*, 20–22.
18. Jacobson, "Wisdom Christology," 9.

son constructs several redactional phases, each having a coherent set of characteristics. Unlike Lührmann, who detects only a single redaction, Jacobson posits three successive redactions: the initial compilation ("the compositional stage"), followed by an intermediate and a final redaction.[19]

In broad agreement with Lührmann and Jacobson, Dieter Zeller has recently outlined criteria for the detection of Q redaction.[20] To begin with, redaction may be seen in the interpretive expansions of individual sayings. But one caveat is necessary here: to the extent that it is possible, one must distinguish between expansions made while the sayings circulated orally and those which were made during the written stage. Only the latter are important for determining Q redaction. Second, as for Lührmann and Jacobson, the juxtaposition of originally independent units provides a key to editorial intention. And finally, Mark-Q comparison provides an additional criterion by which Q redaction can be set into relief.

The method which this study will adopt is similar to those employed by Lührmann, Jacobson and Zeller. The first analytic tool is the determination of the compositional principles which guide the juxtaposition of originally independent sayings and groups of sayings. Naturally this presupposes and builds upon the results from form-critical analysis. Once the component units within a Q section have been ascertained, the order in which sayings were added to one another and the method by which the association was accomplished (e.g., catchword, thematic or formal association or syntactical connective) can be determined.

Of course, one cannot assume that the compositional themes governing one Q section were those of the final redactor. It is entirely possible that several smaller compilations—each governed by a particular redactional interest—were assembled by a final redactor who had entirely different interests. Hence it is necessary to coordinate the results of the analyses of several Q sections and endeavor to reconstruct one or more redactional stages, each having a coherent set of thematic, tradition-

---

19. To the final stage Jacobson assigns only the temptation account ("Wisdom Christology," 36–46). Since this constitutes an anti-enthusiastic polemic (sic) directed at other elements within Q, Jacobson allocates another set of redactional pericopae (3:16; 7:18–23, 28; 10:21–22; 11:2–4, 9–13; 17:5–6)—some of which manifest "enthusiastic tendencies"—to the penultimate (intermediate) redaction (pp. 218–22). To the compositional phase belong 3:8b; 6:23c, 39, 42; 7:1–10, 31–35; 16:16; 9:57–62; 10:2–12, 13–15, 16; 11:14–20, 23, 24–26, 29–32, 33–36, 49–51 and 13:34–35 (apparently).

20. Zeller, "Redaktionsprozesse," 396–99.

historical and perhaps form-critical characteristics, and further, to stratify the redactional phases with respect to each other.

Second, redactional or compositional activity may be seen in insertions and glosses. These may be of several types. Some may be new creations of a redactor, either formations by analogy (*Analogiebildungen*) or some other secondary expansion. Others are more properly termed "commentary words" (*Kommentarworte*), i.e., originally independent sayings used to explain or modify another saying or group of sayings.[21] What is especially significant here is that we are dealing with materials which are secondary from a compositional perspective, irrespective of their age or ultimate provenance. Such insertions afford us a tool by which to stratify successive redactions of Q. For example, if the group of sayings "A," displaying a coherent set of formal and material characteristics and resembling other Q compositions, has been modified by the insertion of a secondary expansion or commentary word displaying a theology or style characteristic of a set of glosses or compositions elsewhere in Q ("B"), then we may assume that the "A" compilation or redaction is antecedent to the "B" redaction.

Naturally it is also possible that particular commentary words or secondary glosses were added at the oral stage or very early in the prehistory of Q. Schürmann, for example, has argued that the Son of Man saying in Q 11:30 was added to 11:29 prior to the addition of 11:31–32, and prior to the composition of the larger complex consisting of 11:14–26 + 11:29–32 + 11:33–36.[22] In such a case the theological content of the commentary word or secondary expansion does not contribute to the understanding of Q redaction.[23]

---

21. Bultmann's discussion of the various kinds of expansions is seminal here (see *Tradition*, 81–108 [84–113]). See further Wanke, "Kommentarworte"; idem, *"Bezugs- und Kommentarworte" in den synoptischen Evangelien* (Erfuhter Theologische Studien 44; Leipzig: Benno, 1981).

22. Schürmann, "Menschensohn-Titel," 134.

23. Schürmann ("Menschensohn-Titel," 124–47) observes that all of the Q Son of Man sayings function as interpretations of other sayings, or small clusters of sayings. But they do not modify the more extensive Q compositions. "That means two things: on the one hand, that the Son of Man title probably does not belong to the earliest stratum of the sayings-tradition, . . . and on the other, that Son of Man Christology is probably no longer the fundamental and leading Christology of the final redaction of Q . . ." (pp. 146–47; [trans. by auth.]). In a more recent article, "Basileia-Verkündigung," Schürmann analyzes the kingdom sayings using a similar method. He assumes a progressive development of Q, (*a*) from individual sayings (*Grundworte*) which were augmented by commentary words or other expansions (*Zusatzworte*), (*b*) to *Spruchreihen* (i.e., series of *Grundworte* with their expansions—connected by catchword or thematic association), (*c*) to *frühe Kompositionen* (sayings and series of sayings arranged under thematic perspectives and presented as speeches of Jesus), (*d*) to the final collection of finished speeches. Schürmann also allows that the final redaction did not simply collect and

Finally, as Lührmann has noted, comparison of Q with other streams of tradition—principally Mark—is a means by which to corroborate the conclusions obtained from the analysis of the compositional principles governing Q speeches and from the analysis of insertions and glosses. Strictly speaking, the Mark-Q comparison yields information only about the general tendency of the Q stream of *tradition*, not Q redaction as such. If, however, the manifest *Tendenz* of the Q version of a doublet coheres with the theology of one of the redactional levels identified from the analyses of compositional principles and insertions, then such a pericope could legitimately be included in that redactional phase.[24]

The Analysis of Sayings Groups in Q

The method which we have proposed for the redactional analysis of Q focuses primarily upon the redactional principles governing clusters of sayings, and the motive informing the interpolation of glosses into pre-existing speeches. There is one limitation to this method: it is not particularly helpful for examining those sayings whose position in Q cannot be determined with certainty, or those sayings which are not obviously part of a larger complex of sayings. Examples of the latter are 17:1–4, 5–6 (the sayings on scandal), 15:4–7 (the parable of the lost sheep) and 16:13 (serving two masters). In these cases it is virtually impossible to decide on *literary* grounds whether a saying or parable is a *Grundwort*—to use Schürmann's term[25]—or a commentary word, or whether it is formative or secondary. On material and thematic grounds, some of these sayings may be able to be placed, but this is only possible once a profile of the redactional strata of Q has been assembled from an analysis of the larger complexes of sayings.

Of the clusters of Q texts enumerated above, the most suitable for compositional analysis are:

1. John's preaching of the Coming One	Q 3:7–9, 16–17
3. Jesus' inaugural sermon	Q 6:20b–49
4. John, Jesus and "this generation"	Q 7:1–10, 18–28; (16:16); 7:31–35
5. Discipleship and mission	Q 9:57–62; 10:2–24
6. On prayer	Q 11:2–4, 9–13

---

arrange the *frühe Kompositionen* but may also have inserted additional *Grundworte* and *Spruchreihen*.

24. Schenk (*Synopse*) proposes a lengthy list of redactional passages in Q, but since he provides no rationale, it is difficult to consider his suggestions in this survey of redaction-critical methods. On this see Neirynck, "Study of Q."

25. Schürmann, "Basileia-Verkündigung," 128.

7. Controversies with Israel	Q 11:14–52
8. On fearless preaching	Q 12:2–12
9. On anxiety over material needs	Q 12:(13–14, 16–21), 22–31, 33–34
10. Preparedness for the end	Q 12:39–59
12. The two ways	Q 13:24–30, 34–35; 14:16–24, 26–27; 17:33; 14:33–34
14. The eschatological discourse	Q 17:23–37; 19:12–27; 22:28–30

As both Lührmann and Jacobson have seen, several of these complexes appear to be organized about the motifs of the coming judgment, the urgency of repentance, the impenitence of "this generation" and the ramifications of Gentile faith: #1 (3:7–9, 16–17); #4 (7:1–10, 18–35); #7 (11:14–52); #10 (12:39–59) and #14 (17:23–37). Since it is the motif of judgment which emerges prominently in the logical and qualitative forms which unify the collection as a whole, it is with these speeches that we shall begin (chapter four). In chapter five we shall turn to several other clusters of sayings which appear to be organized along entirely different lines, and which in general lack the motif of judgment and the call to repentance: #3 (6:20b–49); #5 (9:57–62 + 10:2–16, 21–24); #6 (11:2–4, 9–13); #8 (12:2–12) and #9 (12:22–34). In treating these speeches together we do not, of course, preclude the possibility that they may contain interpolations made from another perspective. Q 13:24–30, (34–35?) + 14:16–24, 26–27, 34–35 is a rather mixed speech, but will be considered here too. The temptation account (#2), which differs markedly from the rest of the Q materials in form and function, will be treated last (chapter six).

4

The Announcement of Judgment in Q

The call to repentance, the threat of apocalyptic judgment and the censure of "this generation" for its recalcitrance are prominent in several clusters of Q sayings. In fact, they are the formative and unifying themes for John's preaching (3:7–9, 16–17), the healing of the centurion's servant and the sayings about John (7:1–10, 18–35), the large block of material beginning with the Beelzebul accusation and ending with the woes against the Pharisees (11:14–52) and the two sections of Q dealing with the parousia (12:39–59 and 17:23–37). This can be seen not only from a compositional analysis of the sections in question, but also from a Mark-Q comparison in those pericopae where overlaps occur.

Q 3:7–9, 16–17[1]

Despite its brevity, this small section in Q is not an original unity but the result of the juxtaposition and editing of smaller units of tradition. The entire oracle of John has been supplied with a historicizing setting by the addition of two details: the identification of John as the speaker and the designation of his audience as those coming for baptism (3:7a). The oracle itself is composed of at least two parts: Q 3:7–9 is a threat of imminent judgment and a call to repentance,[2] while Q 3:16–17 is an

---

1. Reconstructions: Schulz, *Spruchquelle*, 366–69; Harnack, *Sayings of Jesus*, 2–3 [6–8]; Schürmann, *Lukasevangelium* 1:163–66, 169–78; Hoffmann, *Studien*, 15–25; Laufen, *Doppelüberlieferung*, 93–97; Polag, *Fragmenta*, 28. For our purposes, the only details which require comment are the following: (a) Luke's ἔρχεται . . . ὁ ἰσχυρότερός μου seems to follow the Marcan version while Matthew's participial form agrees with the independent Johannine version (1:15, 27) and may represent the Q wording. Thus Hoffmann, *Studien*, 23; Harnack, *Sayings of Jesus*, 2 [7]; Schulz, *Spruchquelle*, 368; Laufen, *Doppelüberlieferung*, 99. (b) It is disputed whether Q read πῦρ (thus Schulz, *Spruchquelle*, 368; Hoffmann, *Studien*, 30; Manson, *Sayings*, 40–41; Fuller, *Mission and Achievement*, 62 n.1) or πνεῦμα καὶ πῦρ (E. Schweizer, πνεῦμα, *TDNT* 6 [1968] 398–99; F. Lang, πῦρ, *TDNT* 6 [1968] 943; Schürmann, *Lukasevangelium* 1:175–76; Marshall, *Luke*, 147). A decision between the two is hardly possible.

2. Although Bultmann (*Tradition*, 117 [123]) and Lührmann (*Redaktion*, 31) note the

apocalyptic prediction concerning a figure who will effect both fiery judgment and salvation of the elect.

It is possible that 3:7b–9 is also composite. Schürmann notes that *two* different criticisms of false confidences are juxtaposed: that baptism by itself will save (7b, 8a), and that national privilege will exempt one from judgment (8b, c). Of the two, Schürmann regards the latter as the earlier one; the former betrays the interests of Christian parenesis.[3] Linnemann and Jacobson, however, contend that two distinct audiences are addressed here: Q 3:7b, 8a, 9 is directed at those *coming for baptism*, presumably the *'am ha-'ares*. But 3:8c inveighs against those who *reject baptism*, invoking national privilege, i.e., the Pharisees.[4] According to Jacobson, 3:8b, c was an insertion made in the first edition of Q when the blindness of Jewish leaders was singled out for special criticism.[5]

Such a change in audience is not required. That God elected "the children of Abraham" and that, consequently, he would maintain and save them was an extremely widespread view, scarcely restricted to the Pharisees or to Israel's religious leadership![6] But in tension with this was an equally widespread view: that God required repentance and faithfulness of Israel and would destroy those who resisted the preaching of the prophets. Implicit in this is a rejection of national privilege as the *sole* basis for salvation. Steck has successfully shown that this deuteronomistic pattern (of Yahweh's sending of the prophets with a message of repentance and the threat of judgment) had penetrated many streams of tradition current between 150 BCE and 100 CE, including Pharisaic teaching.[7] In other words, the appeal to descent from Abraham was not the exclusive property of the Pharisees, and the criticism of that appeal was likely part of Pharisaic preaching itself (as well as other kinds of preach-

---

congeniality of Q 3:7b–9 with Christian interests, there is nothing specifically Christian here and the oracle is congruent with what is known of John's preaching. See Philipp Vielhauer, "Johannes der Täufer," *RGG*[3] 3 (1958) 804–8; J. Becker, *Johannes der Täufer und Jesus* (BibS[N] 63; Neukirchen-Vluyn: Neukirchener Verlag, 1972) 27–37; Merklein, "Umkehrpredigt," 32.

3. Schürmann, *Lukasevangelium* 1:182.

4. Linnemann, "Jesus und der Täufer," 228–29 and n. 23; Jacobson, "Wisdom Christology," 31; similarly Hoffmann, *Studien*, 27.

5. Jacobson, "Wisdom Christology," 32.

6. See E. P. Sanders, *Paul and Palestinian Judaism* (Philadelphia: Fortress Press, 1977) passim. The designation "sons of Abraham" is found in the Pharisaic (?) *Pss Sol* (9:8–9; 18:34), in rabbinic literature (Str-B 1.116–21) but also in 3 Macc 6:1–15 and *T. Levi* 15:4. Paul's redefinition of the term "seed of Abraham" presupposes a rather widely held notion of salvation based upon election and physical descent from Abraham. See further, B. Byrne, *Sons of God—Seed of Abraham* (AnBib 83; Rome: Pontifical Biblical Institute, 1979).

7. Steck, *Israel*, 196–215.

ing). Nor is it possible to say that 3:8 is an acknowledgment of the possibility of Gentile salvation and to ascribe it for that reason to a later stratum. The statement "God is able to raise up sons of Abraham from these stones" is prophetic hyperbole and not comparable to the explicit commendations of the Gentiles such as one encounters in Q 7:1–10; 11:31–32 and 13:29, 28. Thus while it is possible that 3:8b, c was an insertion into an existing Baptist saying (3:7b, 8a, 9), the exact provenance of this addition cannot be specified more precisely. It cannot with confidence be ascribed to Q redaction.

The second component of John's preaching (Q 3:16–17) may also be composite. The prediction of the coming apocalyptic figure—either God himself or some supra-human (angelic?) figure—is arguably of Baptist provenance since the title[8] ὁ ἐρχόμενος is not obviously Christian and since the description of that figure accords so poorly with the activity of Jesus.[9] Nevertheless, in Christian circles, and certainly in Q, ὁ ἐρχόμενος was identified with Jesus (as Q 7:18–23 shows). Hoffmann contends that the phrase which compares the Coming One (Jesus) with John, ὁ δὲ (ὀπίσω μου) ἐρχόμενος ἰσχυρότερός μού ἐστιν, οὗ οὐκ εἰμὶ ἱκανὸς τὰ ὑποδήματα βαστάσαι, is a Q Interpretament which was added as a response to the problem posed by the relation of John to Jesus.[10] That this phrase, which emphasizes John's inferiority, is intrusive has long been recognized.[11] It is, however, present not only in both Q and Mark, but also in the Johannine versions of the saying (1:26) and in Acts (13:25). This is surely an indication that this qualification of John's significance is a very early addition to the saying. To credit it to Q redaction would raise more problems than it would solve. The rivalry between the

---

8. On the titular character of ὁ ἐρχόμενος, see Laufen, Doppelüberlieferung, 407–9.

9. Many have suggested a Baptist provenance for all or part of 3:16–17: Bultmann, Tradition, 111, 246–47 [116–17, 261–63]; E. Lohmeyer, Das Evangelium des Matthäus (MeyerK Sonderband; Göttingen: Vandenhoeck & Ruprecht, 1967⁴) 38; Hoffmann, Studien, 28–31; Merklein, "Umkehrpredigt," 32; Schürmann, Lukasevangelium 1:183.

10. Hoffmann, Studien, 32–33; similarly Merklein, "Umkehrpredigt," 32; Schenk, Synopse, 19. Jacobson ("Wisdom Christology," 33–35) ascribes 3:16b to a penultimate redaction of Q, subsequent to the polemic against "this generation."

11. It is frequently pointed out that a Jewish slave as well as a student was not obliged to loose a master's shoes (Str-B 1.121; b. Qid. 22b; Mek to Exod 21:1; b. Keth. 96a). On the secondary status of 3:16b, see M. Dibelius, Die urchristliche Überlieferung von Johannes dem Täufer (FRLANT 15; Göttingen: Vandenhoeck & Ruprecht, 1911) 54; Bultmann, Tradition, 246–47 [262]. Laufen (Doppelüberlieferung, 116–17) rather unconvincingly argues for the existence of two independent pre-Christian sayings: (1) ἔρχεται (ὁ) ἰσχυρότερός (μού ὀπίσω μου) οὗ οὐκ εἰμὶ ἱκανὸς λῦσαι τὸν ἱμάντα τῶν ὑποδημάτων αὐτοῦ (ὑποδήματα βαστάσαι) and (2) ἐγὼ βαπτίζω ἐν ὕδατι, ὁ δὲ ἐρχόμενος βαπτίσει ἐν πνεύματι (ἁγίῳ). Curiously he ascribes "and fire" to Q redaction (pp. 107, 117).

disciples of John and Jesus which elicited this qualification appears to belong to the early pre-history, not to the Q redaction, of this saying.

Analysis of the Baptist sayings reveals several layers: a composite threat of judgment (3:7b, 8a, 9 + 8b, c) and a Baptist oracle about the coming judge (3:16a, c, 17) which has been expanded by a very early Christian gloss (3:16b). The two sayings were joined and introduced by 3:7a. The effect of the juxtaposition of 3:7b–9 with 3:16–17 is to emphasize the fact of the coming judgment and the impending destruction of the impenitent. Whatever rivalry there may have existed between the disciples of John and Jesus is now submerged. John in effect stands together with Jesus (and the Q preachers) in proclaiming the coming judgment upon Israel.

The joining of the two sayings is due of course to the fact that both concern John. Although John's baptizing activity is presupposed by 3:7a and 3:16a, Q's interest in John resides elsewhere. John is primarily a prophet of the coming end. Formally as well as materially the composition is dominated by prophetic features. Q 3:7b–9 is a prophetic reproach of impenitence and the announcement of judgment, and 3:16–17 describes that judgment in detail.

Materially, the two pericopae reflect the deuteronomistic pattern in which the prophets are interpreted as preachers of repentance and as heralds of judgment.

O. H. Steck describes the salient features of this deuteronomistic schema as follows: (a) Israel exists in a permanent state of impenitence and disobedience (Neh 9:26–30; 2 Chr 30:7–8; 2 Kgs 17:11–12); (b) through the agency of the prophets God warns Israel to repent and return (Neh 9:26, 30; 2 Kgs 17:13); but (c) Israel refuses (Neh 9:26, 29–30; 2 Kgs 17:14–17, 19) for which cause (d) God brings chastisements (Neh 9:30b; 2 Kgs 17:18, 20). This schema was later expanded by the addition of appeals to (or reports of) repentance and obedience to the Law (e), and the expectation or prediction of the final restoration of Israel (f^1) and the destruction of Israel's enemies and the impious (f^2).[12]

The phrase γεννήματα ἐχιδνῶν (3:7b) should be regarded as a reproach for Israel's enduring disobedience (a). The admonition to "bring forth fruit worthy of repentance" corresponds to (e), which is in fact parallel to the earlier admonitions of the prophets (b).[13] Evidently Q does not

---

12. Steck, *Israel*, 62–64, 122–24.

13. Steck (*Israel*, 194) observes that apart from Zech 1:3–6, which assumes a continuity between Zechariah's renewed preaching of repentance (e) and that of the former prophets (b), the renewed preaching is usually ascribed to sages and scribes (4 Ezra 7:129–30; *As. Mos.* 9; 2 *Apoc. Bar.* 31–32, 44–45, 85). In Q, however, John is not portrayed as a scribe or sage, but as (more than) a prophet (Q 7:24–26).

expect any significant response to the preaching. In contrast to sermons such as 2 Chr 30:6b–9, the Q sermon is bitter and reproachful. The first saying speaks only of the coming judgment (f^2),[14] and in the second it is this motif which receives the emphasis (3:16c, 17b). The attitude betrayed here resembles that of the Qumran covenanters who regarded themselves as part of the reconstituted "remnant of Israel."[15] Other Jews were vilified as "men of the lot of Belial" (1QS 2:4–5), "men of lies, seers of error" (1QH 4:20) and "the wicked of Israel" (1QpPs 37 3:12). Although it is unlikely that either Q or Qumran absolutely precluded the possibility of the repentance of fellow Jews, neither can be said to have been particularly optimistic over the fate of its countrymen.

Comparison of Q with Mark corroborates these observations. The emphasis in Mark, as 1:8 shows, falls upon the two baptisms. John's baptism is relegated to the past ($\dot{\epsilon}\beta\dot{\alpha}\pi\tau\iota\sigma\alpha$)[16] while the baptism of the "stronger one" refers unmistakably to the Spirit baptism of Jesus himself and the gift of the Spirit to Christians. Q, on the other hand, places the stress on judgment. This is evident not only from the first of John's oracles (Q 3:7–9), which is absent in Mark, but also from the extension of the oracle of the Coming One—an extension which emphasizes his forensic function. The mention of fire in 3:16c must also be seen in this light. It is an open question whether the Q version read $\dot{\epsilon}\nu$ $\pi\nu\epsilon\dot{\upsilon}\mu\alpha\tau\iota$ $\kappa\alpha\dot{\iota}$ $\pi\upsilon\rho\dot{\iota}$ or simply $\dot{\epsilon}\nu$ $\pi\upsilon\rho\dot{\iota}$ and in the former case whether the baptisms of spirit (wind?) and fire represent one baptism of judgment,[17] one baptism with a dual character (i.e., both refining and destroying),[18] or two alternate baptisms: Spirit baptism for the just and fire baptism for the impious.[19] The presence of "fire" excludes the purely positive Marcan interpretation. In view of the single object $\dot{\upsilon}\mu\hat{\alpha}s$ and the coordinating conjunction between "spirit" and "fire" it does not seen very likely that

14. For similar threats of judgment, see *Jub.* 7:27–39; 20:6; 21:22 (using the image of uprooting of the impious); 22:22–23; 36:9–11 (burning and uprooting).

15. CD 1:3—2:1 provides an excellent example of the deuteronomistic schema: recalling Israel's former disobedience and her punishments (*a–d*: 1:3–5; cf. 1QS 1:21–24), the remnant of Israel confesses its sins (*e*: 1:8–9; cf. 1QS 1:24–26), for which reason God reconstitutes the community (f^1: 1:10–12).

16. Mark's aorist is often taken as a Marcan or pre-Marcan historicizing of John's saying. Thus Hoffmann, *Studien*, 20; Gnilka, *Markus* 1:48; Rudolf Pesch, *Markusevangelium* 1:84–85.

17. Thus Schweizer, $\pi\nu\epsilon\hat{\upsilon}\mu\alpha$, 398–99; Hoffmann, *Studien*, 30 (if $\pi\nu\epsilon\hat{\upsilon}\mu\alpha$ belongs to Q); Rudolf Pesch, *Markusevangelium* 1:85; Ernest Best, "Spirit Baptism," *NovT* 4 (1960) 236–43.

18. Marshall, *Luke*, 147; Fitzmyer, *Luke I–IX*, 474.

19. F. Lang, $\pi\hat{\upsilon}\rho$, TDNT 6 (1968) 943; Schürmann, *Lukasevangelium* 1:174; Laufen, *Doppelüberlieferung*, 106.

alternate baptisms are envisaged. Fitzmyer remarks that "if John's own water baptism were intended to produce 'repentance,' it might at least be thought that a baptism involving God's Spirit and fire would be expected to accomplish something positive too."[20] The reference to the gathering of the grain in 3:17 supports this interpretation. However, the prominence of terms such as $\mu\epsilon\lambda\lambda o\acute{v}\sigma\eta$ $\dot{o}\rho\gamma\acute{\eta}$ (3:7), $\pi\hat{v}\rho$ (3:9, 16) and $\pi\hat{v}\rho$ $\check{\alpha}\sigma\beta\epsilon\sigma\tau ov$ (3:17), coupled with the fact that both sayings (3:7–9, 16–17) end on a threatening note, indicates that Q's interest lay in the destructive side of the Coming One's role.

Summary. The first section of Q is clearly composite, consisting of two main units, each of which is also composite. The redactional intention at work in the juxtaposition of the two is to emphasize John's status as a prophet who, like Jesus and the Q preachers who will follow, announces judgment upon an impenitent generation. Polemic against Baptist circles belongs to a pre-redactional phase, and the apologetic interest in Christian baptism is not yet on the horizon of this saying (as it is in Mark).

Q 7:1–10, 18–23, 24–26, (16:16), 31–35

Immediately following the inaugural sermon of Jesus (6:20b–49) is a lengthy block of Q sayings (7:1–10, 18–35). While all but one of its constituent parts have to do with John and his relationship to Jesus, the overall composition is controlled by the motif of the opposition of both John and Jesus to "this generation."[21] Four subsections directly concern John:

Q 7:18–23[22]

Bultmann regarded this pericope as an apophthegm encapsulating an authentic saying of Jesus (7:22–23).[23] It is more likely, however, that the entire pronouncement story is a post-Easter creation, arising in the effort to attract Baptist disciples into the Christian fold. The story deliberately invokes Baptist expectations in its use of the title "the Coming One," but infuses the title with specifically Christian content. There is no indication that John expected a miracle-worker. Nor does 7:22 trade in traditional Jewish expectations about the messiah. The events listed in 7:22 are a pastiche of Isaiah's description of the coming time of peace (Isa

20. Fitzmyer, *Luke I–IX*, 474.
21. Thus Lührmann, *Redaktion*, 30–31.
22. Reconstructions: Schulz, *Spruchquelle*, 190–92; Vögtle, "Wunder und Wort," 219–22; Hoffmann, *Studien*, 191–93; Polag, *Fragmenta*, 40.
23. Bultmann, *Tradition*, 110, 126 [115, 133].

61:1-2 LXX;[24] 42:6-7; 35:5; 29:18-19). But these Isaian miracles seem to be selected with Jesus' miracles in view, and the mention of the cleansing of lepers, which does not occur in Isaiah, suggests that 7:22 is a post-Easter interpretation of Jesus' deeds as evidence of the presence of the kingdom.[25]

John's question "Are you the Coming One or should we expect another?" sufficiently establishes that John makes no exalted claims for himself. There is no polemic here, but John's inferiority to Jesus is obvious. It is as if John is "on the outside looking in," seeking the fulfillment of his own prophecy rather than actively engaged in the events of the kingdom. The answer to his question, though it represents a Christian reinterpretation of Baptist expectations, is affirmative. Even though he is not the fiery judge, Jesus is the Coming One. The concluding beatitude (7:23) appears to be added specifically for the benefit of Baptist disciples: it tacitly admits the incongruity between John's expectations and Jesus' activity but warns against rejecting Jesus. Since the eschatological events are occurring, Jesus must be the expected one.[26]

Q 7:24-28[27]

The next pericope is clearly composite. Q 7:24-26 reports in chriic form Jesus' own assessment of John as "more than a prophet."[28] This is followed by two commentary words, the first (7:27) a combination quotation of Exod 23:30 and Mal 3:1, which appears independently in a different literary context in Mark 1:2.[29] The second commentary word is an originally independent kingdom saying, introduced by λέγω ὑμῖν and

24. The phrase τυφλοὶ ἀναβλέπουσιν reveals dependence on the LXX of Isa 61:1-2.
25. Peter Stuhlmacher (Das paulinische Evangelium I [FRLANT 95; Göttingen: Vandenhoeck & Ruprecht, 1968] 218-25) regards the pericope as the word of a Christian prophet, portraying Jesus as the eschatological prophet. Rudolf Pesch (Jesu ureigene Taten, 36-44) draws attention to the prophetic character of not only restoration of sight and evangelization of the poor (Isa 61:1-2) but also the raising of the dead and the healing of lepers (1 Kgs 17:17-24; 2 Kgs 4:18-37; 5:1-27).
26. See Schulz, Spruchquelle, 196; Vögtle, "Wunder und Wort," 241.
27. Reconstructions: Schulz, Spruchquelle, 229-30; Polag, Fragmenta, 40.
28. On the question of authenticity, see Bultmann, Tradition, 165 [178]; Schürmann, Lukasevangelium 1:417-18. In Gos. Thom. 78 Jesus' word is transmitted as a saying, not a chria: "Jesus said: Why have you come out into the desert? To see a reed shaken by the wind? And to see a man clothed in fine garments like your kings and your great men? Upon them are the fine [garments] and they are unable to discern the truth" (trans. Lambdin, NHLE, 127).
29. The intrusive character of Q 7:27 is widely recognized. While 7:24-26 declares that John is greater than a prophet, 7:27 places him in the role of Elijah (as does Matt 11:14-15). See Bultmann, Tradition, 165 [178]; Klostermann, Das Matthäusevangelium, 96-97; Hahn, Titles, 367-68; Schulz, Spruchquelle, 230.

known in another form in *Gos. Thom.* 46.[30] The reason for the appending of these two commentary words is understandable: Q 7:26b invites further explication. However, the two explanations differ in their respective focuses. Q 7:28a, b, perhaps a dominical saying, emphasizes the greatness of the kingdom by asserting that even the greatest representative of the old order, John, paled in comparison with it.[31] Although the original saying did not intend to denigrate John's position, once joined with 7:24–26 it had the effect of mitigating the high estimate of John given in 7:26b. It relativizes John by relegating his function to an era prior to the kingdom and indeed, if ἐν τῇ βασιλείᾳ is understood ecclesiologically, to a realm outside the kingdom.[32]

By contrast, Q 7:27 explicitly identifies John as the precursor of Jesus and implicitly identifies him with Elijah *redivivus*.[33] Thus John's role is interpreted eschatologically: as the messenger of Yahweh, and as one with a positive, if subordinate, function in the inauguration of the kingdom.[34]

30. A few regard 7:28a as the original conclusion of Q 7:24–26: Bultmann, *Tradition,* 164–65 [177–78]; Dibelius, *Urchristliche Überlieferung,* 13–14. Manson (*Sayings,* 69) considers 7:28a, b as the original ending. However, *Gos. Thom.* 46 evidences the independent version of the antithetical saying. Moreover, it is unlikely that λέγω ὑμῖν (vv. 26, 28) would occur twice in an original unity; more likely, the formula in v. 28 is a redactional clasp. Bultmann and Dibelius suppose that v. 28b is a secondary expansion of v. 28a. But Schnackenburg (*God's Rule and Kingdom,* 133) argues that the parallelism between the two halves of the saying indicates an original unity. That Thomas also presents both halves of the saying is perhaps a further indication of this.

31. Jüngel, *Paulus und Jesus,* 176 n. 5: The substance of the saying is authentic, expressing Jesus' high opinion of John (as the greatest preacher of repentance), but at the same time, the view that "everyone who follows Jesus' recent proclamation of the kingdom which summons people into the new age, is greater than the Baptist." See, however, Schürmann ("Basileia-Verkündigung," 140): 7:28a,b attests "a salvation-historical and (implicit) ecclesiological understanding which can hardly be heard in the original *vox Jesu*" [trans. by auth.].

32. Wanke, "Kommentarworte," 215–16. Several attempt to rehabilitate the patristic notion (e.g., Tertullian *Adv. Marcionem* 4.18.8) that ὁ μικρότερος refers to Jesus himself. Thus, "he who is lesser [Jesus, as John's follower] is greater than [John] in the Kingdom." Thus F. Dibelius, "Zwei Worte Jesu," ZNW 11 (1910) 190–91; M. J. Suggs, *Wisdom,* 47; O. Cullmann, *The Christology of the New Testament* (London: SCM Press, 1963²) 24, 32; Hoffmann, *Studien,* 220–24; Schenk, *Synopse,* 43. However, ἐν τῇ βασιλείᾳ is parallel to ἐν γεννητὸς γυναικῶν and thus belongs with ὁ μικρότερος, not μείζων. In this case, "the least in the kingdom" can scarcely refer to Jesus.

33. As Fitzmyer (*Luke I–IX,* 672) points out, there is no pre-Christian attestation of the view that Elijah was to be the forerunner of the Messiah; this appears to be a Christian innovation, based upon Mal 3:1. J. L. Martyn ("We Have Found Elijah," *Jews, Greeks and Christians* [Festschrift W. D. Davies; SJLA 21; Leiden: E. J. Brill, 1976] 181–219) has made a good case for assuming that some early Christians identified *Jesus* with Elijah.

34. Thus Hoffmann, *Studien,* 219; Polag, *Christologie,* 159; Jacobson, "Wisdom Christology," 78; Wink, *John the Baptist,* 19; Schenk, *Synopse,* 43. Hahn (*Titles,* 368) and Schulz (*Spruchquelle,* 232 and n. 371), however, argue that 7:27 characterizes John as

Without doubt, Q 7:24–26 is the kernel to which these two conflicting commentary words were attracted. Of the two interpretations, 7:27 seems to be the later. Explicit identifications of John with the Elijanic precursor are found only in later levels of tradition (Matt 11:14–15; 17:10–13 [both redactional]; see also Mark 9:11–13; Luke 1:17). Moreover, the construction of 7:24–28 is telling. Q 7:27 tries to qualify in prophetic terms what is said in 7:26b, namely, that John does not fit into the usual categories, even that of prophet. Q 7:28a, b does not comment on 7:27 as its position might suggest, but relates back to 7:26b. It is connected to the cluster of sayings not because of any attraction to 7:27, but because of the affinities of μικρότερος/μείζων in 7:28 with περισ-σότερον in 7:26b. It could be noted that Codex Bezae reacted to this affinity by placing v. 28a *before* 7:27. Given these facts, the best solution is that Q 7:28 was attached to 7:26b first and only later was 7:27 interpolated. Hence, the most recent perspective on John in this pericope is that he belongs alongside Jesus as a precursor, not outside the kingdom as the representative of a bygone epoch.

Q 7:31–35[35]

This perspective is reflected also in the next (certain) Q text, Q 7:31–35. This, like 7:24–28, is composite and consists of an original parable (7:31–32), an interpretive saying introduced by γάρ (vv. 33–34) and a summarizing conclusion, "Sophia is justified in her children."[36] Its composite character is indicated by several features: (*a*) Q 7:33–34 is an attempt at allegorization of the parable. But (*b*) the interpretation, which refers to John first and then the Son of Man, does not accord with the order of the verbs in vv. 31–32 (αὐλέω . . . θρηνέω). (*c*) The Sophia saying is not intrinsically related to either vv. 31–32 or vv. 33–34 and may in fact be an originally independent saying.[37]

Although it seems apparent that the parable and its interpretation

---

"only the last and most important link in the chain of messengers from God who lead on to the time of salvation" (Hahn, 368) but sharply separated from the time of the kingdom. This seems unduly influenced by Lucan theology.

35. Reconstructions: Schulz, *Spruchquelle*, 379–80; Steinhauser, *Doppelbildworte*, 158–64; Polag, *Fragmenta*, 42.

36. Matthew's ἔργα is undoubtedly secondary to Luke's τέκνα. Matthew refers (redactionally) to the ἔργα τοῦ Χριστοῦ in 11:2. Luke's πάντων is secondary, probably resuming 7:29; there is no reason for Matthew to have omitted it.

37. See further Bultmann, *Tradition*, 172 [186]; Lührmann, *Redaktion*, 29; Schulz, *Spruchquelle*, 381; Arens, ΗΛΘΟΝ, 222–23; Steinhauser, *Doppelbildworte*, 173. Jeremias (*Parables*, 160–62), Perrin (*Rediscovering*, 119–21) and Franz Mussner ("Der Nicht Erkannte Kairos: Mt 11,16–19 = Lk 7,31–35," *Bib* 40 [1959] 605–6) argue that vv. 31–34 are a unity and dominical.

criticize "this generation," the *tertium comparationis* is far from clear. Are the uncooperative children those who were summoned by John to repentance and by Jesus to participation in the kingdom? Or is it "this generation" which calls the uncooperative John and Jesus? Or again, is "this generation" *both* groups of children, calling to one another and perversely refusing the other's summons?[38] The interpretive saying (vv. 33–34), which has to do with the response of opponents to John and Jesus, seems to exclude the final alternative for the parable as it existed in Q. The identification of John and Jesus with the children who do the calling, and "this generation" with those who refuse to respond, seems the most natural interpretation,[39] especially since v. 35 characterizes John and Jesus as children (τέκνα) of Sophia.

As Suggs has argued, this phrase should be seen against the background of Wis 7:27 which represents prophets and "friends of God" as created by Sophia.[40] Related, too, are Q 11:49–51 and 13:34–35 in which appears the deuteronomistic motif of Sophia's sending of the prophets to call Israel to repentance. It should be noted that only with the addition of 7:35 with its connections with deuteronomistic theology does it become clear that John and Jesus are *preachers*; the rejection of the two in vv. 33–34 is apparently not based upon their preaching, but upon their respective life styles.

The composition of Q 7:31–35 is relatively simple to outline. Q 7:33–34 is intelligible on its own and fits so artificially with the parable (7:31–32) that it is likely that it was an originally independent saying, now functioning as a commentary word.[41] Fiedler suggests that this saying (7:33–34) is indeed primary and that the parable was added to it.[42] But the reverse is more likely: the enigmatic nature of 7:31–32 invited further explication, and this was provided by vv. 33–34, (35).[43] The commentary word must have been added relatively early in the history of the cluster since it is by virtue of its mention of John (7:33) that 7:31–35 could be associated with the other Baptist-related sayings in 7:18–23, 24–28. It is

38. For a documentation of opinion see Zeller, "Bildlogik"; Hoffmann, *Studien*, 225 n. 124; Fitzmyer, *Luke I—IX*, 678–79.

39. Thus Schürmann, *Lukasevangelium* 1:426–27; Hoffmann, *Studien*, 226; Fitzmyer, *Luke I–IX*, 678; Steinhauser, *Doppelbildworte*, 175. Jeremias (*Parables*, 161–62) and Arens (ΗΛΘΟΝ, 238) argue that John and Jesus are the children who refuse to dance and weep.

40. Suggs, *Wisdom*, 38–58.

41. Thus Schürmann, *Lukasevangelium* 1:131; Wanke, "Kommentarworte," 216.

42. P. Fiedler, *Jesus und die Sünder* (BBET 3; Bonn and Frankfurt: Peter Lang, 1976) 138.

43. Thus Wanke, "Kommentarworte," 216.

possible, too, that 7:35 was an originally independent saying.[44] In the present context it serves to round off the composition (7:31–35) and to state expressly that John acts alongside Jesus, not in opposition to him. Since 7:35 most directly relates to 7:31–34,[45] it is best to assume that it was added prior to the joining of 7:31–35 to the other Baptist sayings.

Q 7:31–35 looks in retrospect at the careers of John and Jesus and at their lack of success with "this generation." Schulz takes the view that the superiority of Jesus to John is still at issue: John represents the old aeon and Jesus the new.[46] Wanke argues similarly: "The *Sitz im Leben* of the commentary points again to the conflict of the envoys of Jesus, the Son of Man, with the Baptist movement."[47] But this is surely not the case. Q 7:31–35 does not oppose John to Jesus, but both to "this generation." Whatever rivalry may have existed between John and Jesus (or their respective disciples) is no longer in view. In 7:33–34 the differences between John and Jesus are not ignored, but they are not the main point either. This is yet clearer in 7:35, about which Robinson remarks,

> It is precisely in relation to Sophia that John and Jesus stand in parallel . . . Of course that is not to ignore a superiority over John accorded to Jesus as Son of man through the apocalyptic tradition. This differentiation in status derived from apocalypticism is so familiar to us that we are more likely to ignore the parallel into which the use of the wisdom conceptualization tends to bring them.[48]

Q 7:31–35 exists in the same orbit of tradition as Q 11:49–51 and 13:34–35 in which Sophia is represented as sending a series of envoys to Israel with a message of repentance and judgment. As Steck has shown, this arises with the fusion of the well-known sapiential motif of Sophia as a preacher of repentance (Prov 1:20–33; 8:1–21) and as indwelling the prophets (Wis 7:27) with the theological schema of the deuteronomistic conception of the history of Israel.[49]

Q 16:16

Several scholars argue that Luke 16:16 // Matt 11:12–13 followed 7:28

---

44. That 7:35 was not created deliberately as an interpretation for 7:31–34 is suggested by the lack of correspondence in both image and vocabulary (7:31, παιδία; 7:35, τέκνα). Q 7:35 recalls Sir 4:11: ἡ σοφία υἱοὺς αὐτῆς ἀνύψωσεν.

45. Suggs (*Wisdom*, 33, 36) and Schürmann ("Menschensohn-Titel," 131–32) suggest that 7:35 has a summarizing function with respect to the entire complex Q 7:18–34.

46. Schulz, *Spruchquelle*, 382, 386.

47. Wanke, "Kommentarworte," 216 [trans. by auth.].

48. Robinson, "Jesus as Sophos and Sophia," 5–6.

49. Steck, *Israel*, 222–39, 164 n. 5.

in Q.[50] This pericope is a notorious *crux interpretum* and virtually every detail is disputed: its position in the order of Q, the original order of its two component statements (Matt 11:12–13 // Luke 16:16a, b), the reconstruction of the original saying and its meaning.[51]

Long ago Johannes Weiss observed that it is unlikely that if Luke had seen 16:16 in its present Matthaean context, he would have moved it to its current Lucan location.[52] This being so, Matthew's setting of 11:12–13 may be due to the catchwords Ἰωάννης and βασιλεία (in 11:11 and 11:12–13). In defense of the Matthaean setting, Lührmann has observed that Matthew's redactional concern emerges not in 11:12–13 but in the following verses.[53] Whereas 11:12–13 characterize the *time* since John as eschatological, Matthew's expansion, 11:14–15, drawing upon 11:10 and anticipating 17:10–13, interprets the significance of his *person*. Lührmann's point is well taken, but it does not overcome Weiss's observation. Moreover, the fact that Matthew's point is to be found in vv. 14–15 does not mean that he did not relocate vv. 12–13. Matt 22:1–10, 11–14 provides a pertinent analogy: the Q parable was relocated to a Marcan context, and then expanded (22:11–14) in such a way as to bring it into accord with Matthew's theology of "better righteousness."

Luke's setting of the saying is not above suspicion. Luke 16:16 occurs alongside another saying regarding the Law (16:17) and the saying on adultery (16:18). The wider context reveals other Lucan concerns: that the Law remains in effect despite the proclamation of the kingdom (16:17, 31), and that entering the kingdom is a matter of struggle (16:16b; 13:23–24), faithfulness in little things (16:10–12) and avoidance of avarice (16:13, 14–15, 19–31). Since in 16:16 (in the Lucan version) both the Law and the struggle to enter the kingdom are focal issues, it may have been artificially relocated by Luke.

Luke 16:16 is strongly marked by Lucan redactional features in both its wording and its position, e.g., in the relegation of John to a past epoch,[54] the use of εὐαγγελίζομαι and the positive interpretation of βιάζεται.[55] By contrast, it is almost universally acknowledged that Matthew reproduces Q in 11:12b: ἡ

---

50. Harnack, *Sayings of Jesus*, 16 [16]; Bultmann, *Tradition*, 164 [177]; Lührmann, *Redaktion*, 27–28; Jacobson, "Wisdom Christology," 82–83; Fitzmyer, *Luke I–IX*, 662; Schenk, *Synopse*, 44. Others hold that Lucan order represents that of Q: Josef Schmid, *Matthäus und Lukas*, 284–85; Schürmann, "Wer daher eines," 126–36; Trilling, "Täufertradition," 275–76. Undecided: Marshall, *Luke*, 627; Hoffmann, *Studien*, 51; Wink, *John the Baptist*, 20.

51. For an account of exegetical opinion, see Richard H. Hiers, *The Kingdom of God in the Synoptic Tradition* (Univ. of Fla. Humanities Monographs 33; Gainesville: Univ. of Fla. Press, 1970) 36–42.

52. Johannes Weiss, *Die Predigt Jesu vom Reiche Gottes* (Göttingen: Vandenhoeck & Ruprecht, 1964³) 192.

53. Lührmann, *Redaktion*, 28.

54. See Hans Conzelmann, *The Theology of Saint Luke* (London: Faber & Faber, 1960) 16–17, 21; Helmut Flender, *St. Luke: Theologian of Redemptive History* (Philadelphia: Fortress Press, 1967) 123–28.

55. Εὐαγγελίζομαι: Matt 1x/Mark-/Luke 10x; at least 5x red/Acts 15x. On βιάζεται, see W. Schrenk, *TDNT* 1 (1964) 612.

βασιλεία [τοῦ θεοῦ] βιάζεται, καὶ βιασταὶ ἁρπάζουσιν αὐτήν.[56] Moreover, while Luke's ἀπὸ τότε seems to be controlled by his *heilsgeschichtliche* schematizing, there is no good reason to suspect Matthew's ἀπὸ (δὲ) τῶν ἡμερῶν . . . ἕως ἄρτι as Matthaean.[57] It is frequently asserted that Matthew inverted the order of vv. 12 and 13 and that Luke's order (vv. 16a, b) is the more logical and original one.[58] But precisely for that reason Matthew is more difficult and to be preferred. In fact, it is difficult to imagine why, if Matthew found v. 12 following v. 13 in his *Vorlage*, he would have placed v. 12 first. Barth himself concedes that πάντες γὰρ οἱ προφῆται καὶ ὁ νόμος . . . intrudes between v. 12 and vv. 14–15, both of which deal with the violence done to John.[59]

Under the circumstances, it seems unwise to consider Q 16:16 as a part of the complex of Baptist sayings in Q 7:18–28, 31–35. Nevertheless, since this saying bears on Q's understanding of the relation of John to the kingdom and to Jesus, it is important here. Because of the lack of a clear literary context, it will be impossible to determine the redactional status of 16:16 on *literary or redactional* grounds; but theological and tradition-critical considerations may be brought to bear in order to locate the saying within the composition-history of Q.

If the Q saying began ἀπὸ δὲ τῶν ἡμερῶν Ἰωάννου ἕως ἄρτι ἡ βασιλεία τοῦ θεοῦ βιάζεται καὶ βιασταὶ ἁρπάζουσιν αὐτήν, then the saying implies, like 7:27, that John's activity inaugurated the end time.[60] The meaning of βιάζεται is disputed, but its juxtaposition with ἁρπάζουσιν suggests that it means: "The Kingdom of God is contested, attacked and hampered by contentious opponents."[61] This meaning accords well with other parts of Q which describe the opposition between Jesus (and John) on one side, and "this generation" on the other (Q 7:31–35; 11:14–23, 49–51). Q 16:16 thus places John alongside Jesus as an envoy of the kingdom, and as a

56. Thus Schulz, *Spruchquelle*, 262; Hoffmann, *Studien*, 51–52; Jacobson, "Wisdom Christology," 79; Merklein, *Gottesherrschaft*, 80–87, and authors cited in n. 301.
57. Trilling ("Täufertradition," 277–78) asserts that "days of . . ." is used redactionally by Matthew but can only adduce two examples (2:1; 23:30), both of which are in fact *Sondergut*. Matt 24:37 is taken from Q!
58. Favoring Matthaean order (vv. 12, 13): Johannes Weiss, *Predigt*, 194; Harnack, *Sayings of Jesus*, 16 [16]; Perrin, *Rediscovering*, 75–76; Schenk, *Synopse*, 44. Favoring Lucan order (vv. 16a, b): Jüngel, *Paulus und Jesus*, 190–91; Trilling, "Täufertradition," 277; Schulz, *Spruchquelle*, 261; Jacobson, "Wisdom Christology," 81; Merklein, *Gottesherrschaft*, 87.
59. Gerhard Barth, "Matthew's Understanding of the Law," *Tradition and Interpretation in Matthew* (trans. P. Scott; Philadelphia: Westminster Press, 1963) 64.
60. Thus Perrin, *Rediscovering*, 76; E. Käsemann, "The Problem of the Historical Jesus," *Essays on New Testament Themes* (trans. W. J. Montague; SBT 1/41; London: SCM Press, 1960) 42–43; Jeremias, *New Testament Theology*, 47. Schulz (*Spruchquelle*, 265) and Jüngel (*Paulus und Jesus*, 191) both reconstruct the saying in Lucan order, using ἀπὸ τότε, and interpret it in such a way as to exclude John from the kingdom.
61. Thus G. Schrenk, βιάζομαι, TDNT 1 (1964) 610–11; likewise Hoffmann, *Studien*, 68–71; Jacobson, "Wisdom Christology," 79–80.

target for the violence which the envoys of the kingdom are bound to suffer at the hands of the "violent" who oppose God's actions.

The Composition of 7:18–23, 24–28, (16:16), 31–35

Q 7:18–35 presents a variety of traditions and layers of traditions, each with a distinctive theological perspective. Some seem to separate John from the kingdom either implicitly (7:18–23) or explicitly (7:28) while others include him in the eschatological events either as prophetic precursor (7:27) or as a divinely sent co-worker for Jesus (7:31–35). Which of these is the dominant perspective in the composition of the speech?

Polag assigns Q 7:18–23, 24–26 to the *Kernstücke* of Q and (apparently) regards 7:31–35 and 16:16[62] as additions to this core made at the time of the main redaction of the collection.[63] Q 7:27 and 7:28 both belong to the "late redaction." This conclusion, however, is predicated upon rather doubtful premises. Since he regards the introductory pericopae (Q 3:7–9, 16–17, 21–22[!]; 4:1–13) as late, any motif appearing in these is also deemed to be late. Specifically, the subordination of John to Jesus and use of explicit quotations of the Scripture place 7:27, 28 into this stage according to Polag.[64] But this seemingly arbitrary relegation of the introductory pericopae and biblical quotations to the late redaction places into doubt any conclusions founded upon that assumption.

For Jacobson, anti-Baptist "polemic" is later than the tendency to view John and Jesus as colleagues. Thus Q 7:18–23 and 7:28 belong to the penultimate stage of redaction (only the temptation story belongs to the ultimate stage). Q 16:16 and 7:31–35 represent the compositional stage while 7:24–26 (originally attached to 6:47–49 by the catchwords ἄνεμος, σαλεύω) is relegated to a pre-redactional stratum.[65] The relative lateness of Q 7:18–23, according to Jacobson, is indicated by (*a*) its use of the LXX, (*b*) an uncharacteristic interest in the miraculous, (*c*) the subordination of John to Jesus (which occurs also in 3:16b) and (*d*) the use of ὁ ἐρχόμενος, which depends upon Q 3:16, also relegated to the penultimate stage of redaction.[66] Against this it must be said that (*a*) the use of the LXX is not of probative value for redaction-critical conclusions if, as I have argued in chapter two, Q was composed in Greek. And even though most of Q's allusions to the OT are not verbatim quotations, they usually accord

---

62. Although Polag follows the Lucan order for 16:16, he treats this verse along with the redaction of 7:18–35 (*Christologie*, 47–48).

63. Ibid., 47–48, 129–30.

64. Ibid., 16–17, 159–60.

65. Jacobson, "Wisdom Christology," 94–98.

66. Ibid., 72–73.

with the LXX.[67] (b) Secondly, while it is clear that 7:18–23 presupposes the tradition of Jesus' miracles, this does not in itself distinguish the text from other parts of Q. Q 7:1–10 and 11:14 relate two miracles of Jesus, even if the miraculous element is not itself the focus. More importantly, Q 10:9; 10:13–15 and 11:20—precisely as 7:22—associate the display of the miraculous with the manifestation of the kingdom. (c) The subordination of John to Jesus and (d) use of the title ὁ ἐρχόμενος in 7:18–23 would prove Jacobson's case only if Q 3:16 were redactional *and* if 7:18–23 were dependent *literarily* on 3:16. However, as I have argued above, the saying which subordinated John to Jesus is, from a tradition-historical as well as literary-critical perspective, relatively old. In any event, there is every reason to suppose that 7:18–23 had an existence independent of 3:16–17, functioning in the early church's attempt to win Baptist disciples. That is, it existed prior to any *literary* relationship with the Q pericope of John's preaching.

From a compositional point of view, 7:18–23 must be primary, not secondary. Q 7:24b–26, which contains no mention of John at all, depends upon 7:18–23 and upon the clearly redactional and transitional phrase Q 7:24a for its connection with John. Zeller, incidentally, points out that the use of a genitive absolute in 7:24a indicates redaction in a Greek-speaking area, thus confirming what we have said about the provenance of Q.[68]

Jacobson rightly notes the mitigating effect which 7:28 exerts on the preceding pericope (7:24–26).[69] However, his ascription of 7:28 to the penultimate redaction follows from his understanding of the redactional status of 3:16 and 7:18–23. If these are seen differently, the assessment of 7:28 will change too.

Lührmann contends that in the redactional perspective which controls the composition of 7:18–35, anti-Baptist sentiments are submerged. Q 16:16 in his view forms the conclusion for 7:24–28, mitigating the negative implications of 7:28b by making the inbreaking of the kingdom coincident with John's activity.[70] Moreover, the rivalry between John and Jesus plays no further role in 7:31–35; the opponent is now "this generation."[71]

Lührmann's solution requires only slight adjustment if Q 16:16 cannot

67. See Q 13:35 // Ps 117:27; 13:27 // Ps 6:9; 13:29 // Ps 106:3; 17:27 // Gen 7:7, 11.
68. Zeller, "Redaktionsprozesse," 402.
69. Jacobson, "Wisdom Christology," 78–79.
70. Lührmann, *Redaktion*, 28–29.
71. Ibid., 30–31. Similarly Zeller, "Redaktionsprozesse," 403.

safely be placed in Q 7:18–35. The negative effect of 7:28 is attenuated on both sides by 7:27 which makes John into an eschatological precursor, and by 7:31–35 which treats him as a colleague of Jesus over against this generation.

Thus the earliest components of the cluster are 7:18–23 and 7:24–26, the first a rather neutral, the second a positive assessment of John's role. Q 7:28 restricted the surprisingly high estimate of John given in 7:26b, but both 7:27 and 7:31–35—the latest additions from a literary point of view—treat John as a friend of the kingdom. John now stands at the dawning of the kingdom (7:27; also 16:16); as in 3:16–17 he is the herald of the one to come and like Jesus comes with a message of repentance and judgment. Despite the acknowledged differences between the Baptist and Jesus, both are messengers of Sophia. Both stand together against an unresponsive Israel. Both suffer rejection and violence at the hands of "this generation."

Q 7:1–10[72]

Closely associated with the second complex of Baptist-related sayings is one of the two miracle stories in Q. Its position in Q is quite certain since both Matthew and Luke place it after the Sermon on the Mount/ Plain and before John's question (Luke 7:18–23 // Matt 11:2–6). The connection of 7:1–10 with the immediately preceding Q pericope (Q 6:46–49) may be based on the catchwords κύριε (6:46; 7:6)[73] and λόγος (6:47, 49; 7:7). Otherwise the intrinsic affiliation is quite tenuous: the miracle story has little to do with any of the specific themes of the Sermon. True, the centurion manifests extraordinary faith in Jesus' word. But this is less related to Jesus' function as a teacher than it is to his ἐξουσία as a miracle worker.[74] On the other hand, 7:1–10 is connected with 7:18–23 undoubtedly because of the common subject of the mirac-

---

72. Reconstruction: Schulz, *Spruchquelle*, 236–40; Polag, *Fragmenta*, 39.

73. There is no need to assume that κύριε in either 6:46 or 7:6 originally had strong christological connotations. The parallel but independent version of the healing story in John 4:46b–54 also employs the respectful address κύριε, which probably indicates that this feature was part of the earliest versions of the story. There is no need, further, to construe it as meaning anything stronger than "sir." On the original connotation of κύριε in 6:46, see Betz, "An Episode in the Last Judgment," *Essays*, 132; Bultmann, *Tradition*, 116 n. 2 [122 n. 1].

74. Lührmann (*Redaktion*, 58) argues that the connection of 7:1–10 with the inaugural sermon is deliberate: the narrative serves as a paradigm of the relation of hearing to doing required in 6:46–49. Similarly Jacobson, "Wisdom Christology," 70. But Q 7:1–10 goes significantly beyond the didactic thrust of the Sermon. Like Q texts such as 11:14–23 and 11:29–32, (33–36), it focuses on the recognition of Jesus' ἐξουσία by *outsiders*, not members of the community (as in 6:46–49).

ulous even though the former does not expressly interpret the healing as evidence of the presence of the kingdom. Perhaps an even more important feature guiding the connection of 7:1–10 and 7:18–35 is the implicit criticism of Israel's lack of response to Jesus' ἐξουσία (7:9; cf. 7:35).

The peculiar nature of this story has long been recognized. Bultmann, along with many others,[75] classified it as an apophthegm. Taylor dissented from this view and called it a "story about Jesus" although he allowed that it may have begun as a pronouncement story.[76] Taylor's view raises the question of the relative priority of the narrative and speech components. Dibelius regarded the speech elements as primary and even suggested that the Q story concluded with 7:9.[77] In a yet more radical vein, Manson proposed that Q contained *only* the dialogue portions and that the evangelists independently supplied the narrative settings.[78] But although the hands of the evangelists are in evidence throughout both versions of the story,[79] the miracle narrative is too intrinsic to be considered redactional, and it seems hardly likely that such a story would have ended without confirming the healing. Lührmann argues that the account began as a miracle story and was only later apophthegmatized.[80] There is some warrant for this position since in both the Johannine and the Q story, the pronouncement is addressed not to the suppliant but to a wider audience as indicated by the use of the second-person plural (John 4:48b; Q 7:9b) and John 4:48 is widely regarded as redactional.[81]

As an independently circulating apophthegmatized miracle story, 7:1–10 may have had its *Sitz im Leben* in the controversy over the admission of Gentiles to the church.[82] Whether or not the petitioner was identified as a Gentile from the outset (contrast John), this identification is crucial to the Q story as it stands. Presupposing a world view in which faith among Gentiles is unexpected, the story stresses not only the *fact* of his

75. Bultmann, *Tradition*, 38–39 [39]; Schulz, *Spruchquelle*, 241; Lührmann, *Redaktion*, 57; Fitzmyer, *Luke I–IX*, 649.

76. Vincent Taylor, *Formation*, 76.

77. Dibelius, *Tradition*, 244–45.

78. Manson, *Sayings*, 63, 65.

79. See E. Haenchen, "Johanneische Probleme," *ZTK* 56 (1959) 23–31.

80. Lührmann, *Redaktion*, 57. Against this, Schulz (*Spruchquelle*, 241 n. 434) asserts that the account was an apophthegm from the beginning.

81. Robert T. Fortna, *The Gospel of Signs* (SNTSMS 11; Cambridge: At the Univ. Press, 1970) 41; W. Nicol, *The Semeia in the Fourth Gospel* (NovTSup 32; Leiden: E. J. Brill, 1972) 28–29.

82. Thus Schürmann, *Lukasevangelium* 1:396–97.

faith, but its *exceptional quality*. Such a narrative undermines the notion that Gentile participation in the kingdom is restricted to an eschatological pilgrimage and would undoubtedly serve as useful ammunition in support of the Gentile mission.[83]

When juxtaposed with 7:18–35 the account takes on an additional note of censure. The declaration "I have not found such faith in Israel" anticipates 7:31–35, where Q reflects upon Israel's lack of response to John and Jesus. Q 10:13–15 and 11:31–32 employ similar examples of real or predicted Gentile response to set into sharp relief the impenitence of "this generation." It may be that 7:1–10 by itself does not evidence the involvement of the Q community in the Gentile mission, but the frequency with which the theme of Gentile response and faith occurs in Q suggests that such faith was no longer regarded as quite so unusual as the story by itself suggests (cf. 7:9; 10:13–15; 11:31–32; 13:29, 28; 14:16–24). Matthew's insertion into the story (Matt 8:11–12) only strengthens what is already implicit in the pericope as it exists in Q: the opposition between Israel or "this generation" and the messengers of the kingdom is put into dramatic relief by the positive response of "unworthies" such as Gentiles, or tax collectors and sinners. The polemical implications of 7:1–10 cohere with, and are in fact enhanced by, its association with 7:18–35.[84]

These emphases are corroborated by a comparison of Q with John. The similarities between the two accounts suggest an ultimate tradition-historical relationship.[85] There is broad agreement among Johannine critics that John 4:48 represents an insertion into an earlier pre-Johan-

83. Haenchen ("Johanneische Probleme," 24) points out that whereas the pre-Matthaean version treats the centurion's faith as exceptional, in Matthew he is only "the first of the many who will come from east and west and sit down at table with Abraham, Isaac and Jacob in the kingdom of God" [trans. by auth.]. Both Schulz (*Spruchquelle*, 243–44) and Jacobson ("Wisdom Christology," 69) argue against Lührmann (*Redaktion*, 58) that 7:1–10 is not evidence of a Gentile mission. This conclusion may hold for the story in isolation, but other factors are to be considered for the story in the context of Q redaction.

84. Polag (*Christologie*, 16–17, 158) ascribes 7:1–10 to "late redaction" because of the presence of the motif of the "power of Jesus," also seen in 4:1–13 (which Polag also ascribes to late redaction). However, he concedes that for the tradents of the story what was important was the saying of Jesus since his power was self-evident to them (p. 158). But if this is so, the reason for his ascription to "late redaction" evaporates (even if Polag's analysis of the late redaction were otherwise convincing).

85. See C. H. Dodd, *Historical Tradition in the Fourth Gospel* (Cambridge: At the Univ. Press, 1963) 188–95; F. Schnider and W. Stenger, *Johannes und die Synoptiker* (Munich: Kösel, 1971) 54–88; Rudolf Schnackenburg, *The Gospel According to John* (trans. K. Smyth et al.; 3 vols.; New York: Crossroad; Freiburg: Herder & Herder; Montreal: Palm, 1968–82) 1:471–75; R. E. Brown, *The Gospel According to John* (AB 29–29A; 2 vols.; Garden City, N. Y.: Doubleday & Co., 1966–70) 1:192–94.

nine account, and that in the pre-Johannine version the actions of the miracle-worker, not the dialogue, occupied centre stage.[86] The official's faith (or lack of real faith) is only an issue in Johannine redaction;[87] for the earlier story his faith was only a consequence of the miracle itself (4:53), or possibly of Jesus' authoritative command (4:50b). It is also noteworthy that the nationality of the suppliant is of no importance in the Johannine story.[88]

The common denominator between John and Q is not the dialogue component but the miracle itself—a *Fernheilung*. On the usual view that John and the Synoptics are not directly related, this suggests that Lührmann is correct in supposing that the Q story ultimately began as a miracle story which was only later apophthegmatized. Bultmann supposed that it was John who changed ἑκατόνταρχος into βασιλικός, and thus made him a Jew.[89] But the reverse is the more likely. The "official" of the pre-Johannine story is not clearly Jewish or Gentile and there is little reason for a deliberate change since, for John, his rank and nationality are apparently irrelevant. Neither detail, however, is irrelevant to the Q version. Q has solidified the identity and rank of the suppliant and has substantially developed the exchange between the petitioner and the miracle-worker into the main point of the story. These aspects are clearly interrelated and in comparison with the Johannine version appear secondary.[90]

It would be unjustified to ascribe all of these modifications to Q redaction. More likely, this tendentious development of the healing story into an apology for Gentile inclusion occurred already in the oral stage. Its reception into Q is to be seen in the context of Q's polemic against Israel's lack of recognition of the authority of Jesus and his message, and Q's interpretation of Gentile faith as an *Unheilszeichen* for Israel.

86. Haenchen, "Johanneische Probleme," 28; Schnider and Stenger, *Johannes und die Synoptiker*, 79–80.

87. Rudolf Bultmann (*The Gospel of John* [trans. G. R. Beasley-Murray; Philadelphia: Westminster Press; Oxford: Basil Blackwell, 1971] 206) suggests that 4:48 replaced another saying "which must have corresponded to Matt 8:7–10." But in view of the intrusive nature of 4:48, this solution is quite unnecessary. Verse 48 is more likely a Johannine insertion, not a replacement.

88. Schnackenburg (*John* 1:465–66) plausibly suggests that the man was attached to the court of Antipas, either as an official or as a soldier. In either case he could be Jewish or Gentile. John does not seem to be interested in his nationality although in v. 48 it is conceivable that John treats him as representative of the "Jews" who do not have adequate faith.

89. Bultmann, *John*, 206.

90. Thus Fortna, *Gospel of Signs*, 45–46.

Summary

Although composed of multi-layered traditions, Q 7:1–10, 18–23, 24–28, 31–35 is organized so as to emphasize the theme of the unresponsiveness of "this generation" to what in Q's opinion are the obvious signs of the kingdom. This motif is seen especially at the beginning and at the end of the complex. Earlier uncertainties regarding the Baptist have disappeared; he is now an ally against Israel. Q 16:16, which can no longer be located with certainty, reflects the same view of John, placing him at the beginning of the manifestation of the kingdom, and as one of those who shared in its suffering.

CONTROVERSIES: Q 11:14–26, 29–32, 33–36, 39–52

The theme of the opposition between Jesus and "this generation" recurs in a lengthy block of Q material, 11:14–26, 29–32, 33–36, 39–52. Since this block comprises many originally independent traditions, and since several of them have Marcan parallels, the theological tendency of the Q composition may be discerned both in the principles of association of the smaller units, and in the comparison with Mark. Four subsections constitute this block:

The Beelzebul Accusation[91]

The agreements between the Matthaean and Lucan versions against the parallel Marcan version allow the profile of the Q story to be determined. In contrast to Mark 3:22–27, the Q story begins with an exorcism of a dumb demoniac (Luke 11:14 // Matt 12:22; 9:32). It is this which occasions the accusation that Jesus performs exorcisms by demonic power. Unlike Mark, who attributes the remark to "the scribes from Jerusalem," and unlike Matthew, who typically identifies the opponents as Pharisees,[92] Q (reflected in Luke) simply refers to the opponents as $\tau\iota\nu\acute{\epsilon}\varsigma$.[93] Mark treats Jesus' response as parabolic speech ($\dot{\epsilon}\nu\ \pi\alpha\rho\alpha\beta o\lambda\alpha\hat{\iota}\varsigma$ $\ddot{\epsilon}\lambda\epsilon\gamma\epsilon\nu\ \alpha\dot{\upsilon}\tau o\hat{\iota}\varsigma$); Q takes an entirely different tack, stating that the

---

91. Reconstruction: Schulz, *Spruchquelle*, 204–6; Laufen, *Doppelüberlieferung*, 126–32; Polag, *Fragmenta*, 50–52; John S. Kloppenborg, "Q 11:14–26: Work Sheets for Reconstruction," *SBLASP* (1985) 133–51.

92. R. Hummel, *Die Auseinandersetzung zwischen Kirche und Judentum im Matthäusevangelium* (BEvT 33; Munich: Chr. Kaiser, 1966) 12–17. "Pharisee" is used redactionally in Matt 3:7; 5:20; 15:12; 16:11, 21; 21:45; 22:34, 41; 23:2, 13, 15, 27; 26:62 (9:34? 12:24?).

93. Thus Schulz, *Spruchquelle*, 204 n. 206, and the authors cited there; Laufen, *Doppelüberlieferung*, 127.

response was provoked by supernatural knowledge of the thoughts of the opponents (Luke 11:17a // Matt 12:25a). Finally, Luke and Matthew agree against Mark in the wording of the response.[94]

Although it contains all of the typical features of a miracle story— description of the illness, healing, confirmation and reaction of the crowd—Q 11:14 is so spare and terse that it can hardly have circulated independently of the speech material. Whether it served as the occasion for the pronouncement from the beginning, or whether it was supplied in a pre-Q stratum of tradition can no longer be determined. Schulz sees in 11:15, 17 the original apophthegm which was subsequently expanded by vv. 18, 19 and 20.[95] But if 11:18a was not original, it must have been an early addition since it appears also in the Marcan version (3:26).[96] In Q, two additional sayings follow: 11:19, which compares Jesus' exorcisms with those of contemporary Jewish exorcists, and 11:20, which asserts that the kingdom of God is manifest in Jesus' exorcisms. The relation of these to the accusation is controverted. Following Bultmann, some regard vv. 19 and 20 as originally independent sayings, added to the original complex of 11:(14), 15, 17, (18a).[97] But while Q 11:20 might have been an originally independent and perhaps authentic kingdom saying,[98] Q 11:19 quite clearly presupposes (in a literary way) the accusation which was made in 11:15.

Three solutions have been advanced to meet this difficulty. (1) Schweizer holds that 11:14, 15, 19 constitutes the original apophthegm.[99]

94. Matt = Luke: πᾶσα βασιλεία (δια)μερισθεῖσα . . . ἐρημοῦται. Mark: καὶ ἐὰν βασιλεία μερισθῇ οὐ δύναται σταθῆναι.

95. Schulz, *Spruchquelle*, 206. Steinhauser (*Doppelbildworte*, 141) describes 11:18a as a "secondary interpolation of a Q redactor." The usual reason for considering v. 18a as secondary is the fact that the accusation uses the name Beelzebul whereas v. 18a uses Satan.

96. Bultmann (*Tradition*, 13 [11]), Ernst Käsemann ("Lukas 11,24–26," *Exegetische Versuche und Besinnungen* [2 vols.; Göttingen: Vandenhoeck & Ruprecht, 1964] 1:243) and Laufen (*Doppelüberlieferung*, 133) regard v. 18a as an integral part of the story. Luke 11:18b is usually considered a Lucan addition: see Bultmann, *Tradition*, 90 [94]; Josef Schmid, *Matthäus und Lukas*, 292; Meyer, "Community," 71; Lührmann, *Redaktion*, 33 n. 4; Schulz, *Spruchquelle*, 205; Laufen, *Doppelüberlieferung*, 129. Marshall (*Luke*, 472) asserts that it belonged to Q.

97. Bultmann, *Tradition*, 162 [174]; Kümmel, *Promise and Fulfilment*, 105; Hahn, *Titles*, 292, 332 n. 80; T. Lorenzmeier, "Zum Mt. 12,28; Lk 11,20," *Neues Testament und christliche Existenz* (Festschrift Herbert Braun; Tübingen: J. C. B. Mohr [Paul Siebeck], 1973) 289, 293 and elsewhere.

98. Hahn (*Titles*, 292) regards 11:20 as authentic, and originally transmitted independently of the controversy setting. Thus apparently Wanke, "Kommentarworte," 219. Schulz (*Spruchquelle*, 206) and Schürmann ("Basileia-Verkündigung," 155) deny that 11:20 could have circulated freely.

99. E. Schweizer, *Das Evangelium nach Matthäus* (NTD 2; Göttingen: Vandenhoeck & Ruprecht, 1981[15]) 184–85; thus also Wanke, "Kommentarworte," 219; Marshall, *Luke*, 471–72; Zeller, "Redaktionsprozesse," 406 (who revised his earlier views; see below, note 102).

This represents a variant development parallel to the Marcan story (3:22b–26). In this case, 11:20 must be a commentary word which obviates the potential misunderstanding that Jewish exorcisms have something to do with the kingdom. On this view 11:17, 18a must also be regarded as a secondary expansion.

(2) Another alternative is that the core of the Q tradition is 11:14, 15, 17, (18a[?]), secondarily expanded by vv. 19 and 20. While Polag holds that vv. 19–20 were already a unit when added to the core,[100] Schulz rightly observes against this that the two sayings (19, 20) do not fit together well.[101] Lührmann suggests that 11:19 is a transitional verse created in order to join 11:20 to 11:17–18.[102] A serious objection can be raised against this: Q 11:19 can hardly be a redactional clasp since it actually undermines 11:20 by inviting the inference that the kingdom is also manifest in the work of Jewish exorcists. Jacobson indeed takes precisely this view, suggesting that the redaction of Q intended to relativize the eschatological position of Jesus by concentrating not on the person of Jesus, but upon what comes to light through his activity and the activity of the other envoys of Sophia.[103] He adduces 12:10, which in effect exalts the Spirit above any individual messenger. Q 11:31–32 also provides a parallel to the statement of 11:19 that the "sons" will judge the "fathers": "this generation" is condemned for not responding to the power of God which was revealed in the response of the Ninevites and the Queen of the South just as "your fathers" (11:19) are judged for not perceiving God's working in contemporary exorcisms. It is manifestation of the power of God which, for Jacobson, is paramount in Q redaction.

(3) A final alternative is offered by Schürmann, who holds that 11:14, 17a, 20 is the original apophthegm and that v. 19 was created as a transitional phrase when, at some later stage, 11:17b–18b was interpolated.[104]

In my view it is very difficult to regard v. 19 as a redactionally created

---

100. Polag (*Christologie*, 40) suggests that the saying (vv. 19–20) poses an alternative: Jesus exorcises either by Beelzebul or by God. Verse 19 rejects the first option and v. 20 establishes the second. But if vv. 19–20 were formed together, the connection between the two is poor indeed.

101. Schulz, *Spruchquelle*, 206.

102. Lührmann (*Redaktion*, 33) takes 11:20 as dominical; thus Laufen, *Doppelüberlieferung*, 148; Steinhauser, *Doppelbildworte*, 141–42. Zeller ("Prophetisches Wissen," 263) proposes that v. 20 is a secondary addition to 11:14, 15, 17–18, serving as a positive antithesis to v. 18 and attached by the catchword "kingdom." He hesitates to pronounce on its authenticity.

103. Jacobson, "Wisdom Christology," 164–65.

104. Schürmann, "Basileia-Verkündigung," 155–56.

clasp between vv. 17–18 and 20 (thus both Lührmann and Schürmann) because v. 19 fits so poorly with the kingdom saying in v. 20. Q 11:19 does not build upon the logic or the imagery of either the preceding or the following verses as might be expected of a redactional transition. On the contrary, it appears to be a supplementary comment, added without particular regard to vv. 17–18 or 20. This leaves open two possibilities: (a) that 11:14, 15, 17–18a was the original core which was successively elaborated by v. 19 (a secondary expansion) and v. 20 (a commentary word), or (b) that 11:14–15, 19 was the kernel which, on the one hand, was fused with a variant form of the apophthegm (11:15, 17–18a; cf. Mark 3:22–26) and, on the other, was expanded by the commentary word 11:20. The weakness of the latter hypothesis is that it is obliged to posit a special pre-Q variant of the accusation when in fact *both* Mark and Q agree in making the double metaphor of the divided kingdom and household the first response to the accusation. The putative variant form of the apophthegm is nowhere independently attested. This objection applied *mutatis mutandis* to Schürmann's hypothesis that 11:14, 17a, 20 was the original core. By far the most economical solution is to assume that the basic tradition was 11:(14), 15, 17–18a, and that this was elaborated successively by vv. 19 and 20.

If vv. 19 and 20 are successive additions to the core, what is the significance of the juxtaposition of the two? It is unlikely that any interpretation can solve all the logical tensions which these verses create. Nevertheless, something must be said of the redactor's intention in connecting the two. In view of the exclusivity of the statement made in 11:23, it is hardly likely that Q intended to include Jewish exorcisms as evidence of the manifestation of the kingdom (*pace* Jacobson). Q 11:19 in fact does not draw this conclusion: the force of the rhetorical question is to reveal the absurdity of the Beelzebul accusation. However, the question is followed by the assertion "Therefore they will be your judges." The logic of the argument is strikingly similar to that of Q 11:31–32: like 11:31–32, which imputes a forensic function to the Queen of the South and the Ninevites, Q 11:19 confers this function on Jewish exorcists. Neither the double saying nor 11:19b states that the kingdom is manifest in the activity of these persons, but both imply that divine activity should be recognized as such, and that failure to do so brings the threat of judgment. Q 11:20 then functions in the same way as the phrase "and behold, something greater than Solomon (Jonah) is here." It takes the argument one final step: if it is a serious matter—provoking divine judgment—to mistake the workings of God in lesser phenomena (Jewish exorcisms), how much more is it to misapprehend the manifestation of the presence of the kingdom in Jesus' activity! Therefore the Q composition begins by exposing the absurdity of the Beelzebul accusation by appeal to the double metaphor of the divided kingdom and household, and by use of the *reductio ad absurdum* of 11:19a. But then it changes its rhetorical posture and shifts to the offensive, declaring that Israel's heedlessness of divine activity will lead to her eschatological condemnation.

It is possible that the parable of the stronger man (11:21–22) followed in Q[105]—in which case it served to elaborate further the point that Jesus does not cast out demons by demonic power. If the Lucan version represents that of Q, the image is not one of the *robbery* of the "strong man" (as in Mark and *Gos. Thom.* 35), but of a battle between armed soldiers and the seizure and distribution of the spoils of war. And the focus is not on the act of binding the "strong man" (so Mark), but on the supplanting of his kingdom and the seizure of his goods. This accords better with Q 11:17–18a, which evokes the spectre of a civil war, and with 11:17–18, 20, which implies two warring *kingdoms*, than does the Marcan and Matthaean version of the parable.

Q 11:23 offers an exclusivist variant of Mark 9:40. Bultmann is undoubtedly correct in considering this an originally independent saying.[106] The use of συνάγω/σκορπίζω suggests that the saying may originally have had its *Sitz im Leben* in missionary instructions, perhaps deriving from the same orbit as Q 10:2, which likewise describes missionary work as eschatological gathering.[107] In the present context, however, 11:23 functions in a polemical way. It continues the motif of the parable of the warring soldiers, declaring that one is either on the side of the conquering Stronger One or on the side of the vanquished and

---

105. While some regard 11:21–22 as a Lucan elaboration of Mark 3:27 (Schulz, *Spruchquelle*, 205; Lührmann, *Redaktion*, 33; Jacobson, "Wisdom Christology," 163; Meyer, "Community," 71), others point out that the Matt-Luke agreement in the placement of the parable after Matt 12:28 // Luke 11:20 suggests that the parable also occurred in Q. Thus Bultmann, *Tradition*, 14 [11]; Josef Schmid, *Matthäus und Lukas*, 292–93; Manson, *Sayings*, 85; Marshall, *Luke*, 476–77; Laufen, *Doppelüberlieferung*, 129–30; Polag, *Fragmenta*, 52; Steinhauser, *Doppelbildworte*, 143.

106. Bultmann (*Tradition*, 98 [103]) suggests that it was a profane proverb placed on Jesus' lips. Similarly E. Nestle, "Wer nicht mit mir ist, der ist wider mich," *ZNW* 13 (1912) 84–87.

107. Gathering and dispersing are actions normally reserved to God or to the angels in the context of judgment (or holy war). See 2 Sam 22:17; Pss 17:15; 143:6; Wis 17:3; Zech 13:7–9; Sir 48:15; Tob 13:5 (καὶ πάλιν ἐλεήσει καὶ συνάξει ἡμᾶς ἐκ πάντων τῶν ἐθνῶν, οὗ ἐὰν σκορπισθῆτε ἐν αὐτοῖς); Q 3:17; *Did.* 9:4. See further O. Michel, σκορπίζω, *TDNT* 6 (1968) 418–22.

despoiled. Neutrality is impossible. Those who fail to recognize God's activity in Jesus (by accusing him of partisanship with Beelzebul) are God's opponents and will lie among the defeated.

The following parable is, in view of its terminology, to be regarded as an originally independent saying.[108] While the preceding sayings speak of the casting out of δαιμόνια (11:14, 19, 20) and Σατανᾶς (11:18), this story concerns a πνεῦμα ἀκάθαρτον. Q 11:24–26 has been interpreted, perhaps rightly, as a demonological instruction.[109] In the context of Q, however, this is not its function. If taken as a teaching about the inevitable consequences of exorcism, the story makes nonsense of the preceding materials by implying that no exorcism can ultimately be effective. Schulz proposes that 11:24–26 is a polemic against the Jewish exorcists of 11:19 who ineffectually and only temporarily rid their patients of their demonic inhabitants. By contrast,

> since Jesus' exorcisms by the "finger of God" are at the same time the advent of the kingdom, the person who has been healed is placed decisively under the protection of the eschatological spirit and the in-breaking kingdom.[110]

But Laufen rightly observes that 11:19 does not hint at polemic against Jewish exorcists.[111] Even if Q did not naively identify the exorcisms of Jesus with those of contemporary Jewish exorcists, neither did it exaggerate the differences. In the context, the more likely interpretation derives from 11:23.[112] If, as Jeremias has suggested, the sweeping and decoration of a house constituted a preparation for the reception of a guest,[113] then the parable threatens those who, having been delivered of

---

108. Reconstruction: Schulz, *Spruchquelle*, 476–77; Polag, *Fragmenta*, 52; Kloppenborg, "Q 11:14–26." There is a general consensus that Matthew has transferred the parable (12:43–45) to a position following the Sign of Jonah so that it might serve as a summary to chap. 12. Matthew's addition of 12:45c clearly aids this summarizing function. See Schulz, *Spruchquelle*, 476 n. 562, and the authors cited there.

109. J. M. Hull, *Hellenistic Magic and the Synoptic Tradition* (SBT 2/28; London: SCM Press, 1974) 102: "In Luke it remains what it originally was in Q and no doubt in the teaching of Jesus—an actual description of behaviour and reaction under certain conditions of varieties of evil spirits. Such knowledge is an essential part of the battle. The church must know its enemy." O. Böcher (*Christus Exorcista: Dämonismus und Taufe im Neuen Testament* [BWANT 96; Stuttgart: Kohlhammer, 1972] 17) calls it a "summary of ancient demonology."

110. Schulz, *Spruchquelle*, 479 [trans. by auth.].

111. Laufen, *Doppelüberlieferung*, 142–43.

112. See Laufen, *Doppelüberlieferung*, 141–47, for a chronicle of the various interpretations of the parable. Jacobson ("Wisdom Christology," 171–79), somewhat fancifully, connects the parable with the "wisdom myth" in *1 Enoch* 42 on the basis of the common motif of "seeking rest."

113. Jeremias, *Parables*, 197–98.

a demon, invite it back by failing to respond positively to divine power. This interpretation is suggested by a remarkably similar rabbinic text:

> As if a king went into the steppe and found dining halls and large chambers, and went and dwelt in them. So with the evil inclination; if it does not find the words of the Law ruling (in the heart), you cannot expel it from your heart.[114]

Q 11:23 implies that failure to recognize and accept the kingdom in Jesus' preaching is tantamount to opposing the kingdom and allying oneself with Beelzebul. Q 11:24-26 serves as an illustration. It is impossible to be free of demonic occupation if one has not positively responded to the kingdom. Neutrality is not an option in the face of a confrontation with divine power.

The starting point for this complex of Q sayings is the traditional Beelzebul accusation and its refutation, 11:(14), 15, 17-18a, found in a parallel version in Mark 3:22-26. In Q this had grown by the addition of vv. 19 and 20, which turn from demonstration of the absurdity of the accusation to the denunciation of the accusers: those who fail to perceive divine working in exorcism and who are blind to the even greater phenomenon of the manifestation of God's kingdom are deserving of judgment. The urgency of recognition and response is expressed in the appended sayings Q 11:21-22, 23, 24-26. Neutrality and agnosticism are impossible; to reject the kingdom as proclaimed by its envoy and manifest in his works is tantamount to demonic opposition to God, and will indeed meet with a severe judgment.

Comparison with Mark 3:22-29 is instructive. In Mark the accusation is made by "scribes from Jerusalem," and Jesus is portrayed as responding to this by instructing the crowds in parables. This recalls 1:22, where Jesus' "new teaching with authority" is contrasted with that of the scribes. In Q the accusers are not specified. But Jesus' response, especially the phrase "your sons" (11:19), indicates that Q does not restrict the opponents to one group within Judaism, but enlarges the attack to Israel herself. Thus while the threat given by Mark in 3:28-29 applies only to those who accuse Jesus of complicity with Beelzebul, Q's threats (11:19, 24-26) apply to all who in any way oppose or reject the presence of the kingdom manifest in Jesus' miracles or preaching (11:23).

---

114. *Midr. Prov.* 24:31, attributed to R. Johanan (b. Nappaha), a second generation Palestinian Amora (d. ca. 279). Text cited in C. G. Montefiore and H. Loewe, *A Rabbinic Anthology* (New York: Schocken Books, 1974) 124.

Request for a Sign[115]

Synoptic comparison of Matt 12:38–42 // 16:1–4 // Mark 8:11–12 //
Luke 11:16, 29–32 indicates that a request for a sign existed in Q as well
as in Mark. The Q version of the request is considerably longer and more
complicated than the Marcan one, and form-critical analysis confirms
the composite nature of Q 16, 29–32. Q 11:31–32 is almost certainly an
originally independent threat of judgment. This double saying can easily
stand on its own, and unlike Q 11:29–30, which compares the activity of
Jonah and Jesus, 11:31–32 contrasts Gentile and Jewish *responses* to
preaching. Moreover, 11:31–32 attributes to the Ninevites and the
Queen of the South a forensic eschatological role; no such role is implied
in 11:29–30.[116] It should be noted too that once separated from the term
"Son of Man" in 11:30, there is no reason to construe 11:31–32 in a
christological way. The neuter πλεῖον does not invite such an interpretation; more likely, the original referents of the "something greater than
Jonah/Solomon" were the eschatological occurrences which signaled
the presence of the kingdom.[117]

Whether Q 11:29–30 was an original unity is a matter of dispute.
Vielhauer and Schulz affirm this,[118] while many others regard Q 11:30 as
a secondary expansion or commentary word added to 11:29.[119] Three
points should be considered. First, the Marcan parallel (8:12) lacks both
the phrase "except the Sign of Jonah" and the explanatory correlative
(11:30).[120] It is sometimes argued that if 11:29c and 11:30 already

115. Reconstruction: Schulz, *Spruchquelle*, 250–52; Polag, *Fragmenta*, 52–54.
116. Thus Jacobson, "Wisdom Christology," 169–70.
117. This double saying is widely held to be authentic. Bultmann (*Tradition*, 113, 126
[118, 135]) takes this view although he concedes that it also resembles church
formulations such as 10:13–15. Perrin (*Rediscovering*, 195) points to the unlikely use of
examples such as Jonah and Solomon, the "element of warning" (common to authentic
parables) and the presence of the Aramaism ἀνίστασθαι μετά (= *qam 'im*). See also
Joachim Jeremias, Ἰωνᾶς, TDNT 3 (1965) 408 n. 15. Schulz (*Spruchquelle*, 253), observes,
however, that κήρυγμα has no equivalent in Aramaic and suggests that the saying is a
secondary composition.
118. Vielhauer, "Jesus und der Menschensohn," 110–13; Schulz, *Spruchquelle*, 252 n.
527; 255–56. Neither regards the saying as dominical.
119. Kümmel, *Promise and Fulfilment*, 68; Perrin, *Rediscovering*, 192; Hoffmann,
Studien, 157, 181; Vögtle, "Spruch vom Jonaszeichen," 132–33; Edwards, *Sign of Jonah*,
esp. 49–58; Schürmann, "Menschensohn-Titel," 134.
120. There is virtual unanimity that Matt 12:40 is a Matthaean elucidation of the
somewhat enigmatic Q 11:30 (= Luke). To explain 11:30 as an interpretation of Matt
12:40 is highly implausible. However, because of the absence of 12:40 in Justin's
quotation of the Sign of Jonah text (*Dial.* 107.2) Krister Stendahl (*School of St. Matthew*,
132–33) argues that 12:40 is a post-Matthaean interpolation. However, Justin does
advert to the resurrection on the third day in the same context and thus seems to betray
knowledge of 12:40.

belonged to the earliest form of the tradition, it would be unlikely that Mark would have omitted them. On the other side, however, it is well known that Mark denies public legitimations of Jesus' identity to outsiders and hence he may have abbreviated an originally longer tradition concerning the Sign of Jonah, leaving only the flat refusal of a sign. It is also conceivable that Mark knew only the exceptive phrase (Q 11:29c) and omitted it either because of his aversion to public disclosures, or because he found the phrase unintelligible. Thus the absence of the phrase in Mark is not ultimately decisive.

Second, Edwards has defended the composite nature of Q 11:29–30 by attempting to show that both the exceptive phrase and the correlative were *creations* of the Q community, and that the original form of the tradition corresponded to the Marcan refusal. He bases this on the claim that the "eschatological correlative" ($\kappa a\theta\grave{\omega}s/\H{\omega}\sigma\pi\epsilon\rho\ \grave{\epsilon}\gamma\acute{\epsilon}\nu\epsilon\tau o\ (\mathring{\eta}\nu) \ldots o\H{\upsilon}\tau\omega s\ \acute{\epsilon}\sigma\tau a\iota$) occurs only in Q (and in documents dependent on Q).[121] According to Edwards, the juxtaposition of the absolute refusal (11:29a, b // Mark 8:12) with the double saying (11:31–32) led to the creation of the exceptive phrase and the correlative. This reflects the tendency of Q "to correlate Old Testament figures with the Son of Man in the context of judgment" (cf. 17:26, 28–30).[122]

This scenario is susceptible to criticism, however.[123] As Vögtle has noted, the connection of 11:29 to 11:31–32 depends on three catchwords which occur in 11:30: $\mathring{}I\omega\nu\hat{a}s$, $N\iota\nu\epsilon\hat{\iota}\tau a\iota$, $\gamma\epsilon\nu\epsilon\grave{a}\ a\H{\upsilon}\tau\eta$.[124] In other words, the joining of 11:29 with the double saying presupposes 11:30. Moreover, without 11:29c, there would be little reason to associate 11:29a, b with 11:31–32 in the first place. We must conclude that 11:31–32 was added only because of the presence of v. 30.[125] In addition, Edwards'

121. Edwards, *Sign of Jonah*, 47–58, 86.
122. Ibid., 86.
123. Lührmann (*Redaktion*, 41–42) also calls 11:30 a redactional clasp which connects 11:29a, b with 11:31–32. Hoffmann (*Studien*, 157, 181 n. 92) proposes that 11:30 was added by the redactor to connect 29a–c with 11:31–32, both authentic words of Jesus, and to show that the rejection of Jesus had as its consequence judgment by the Son of Man. Meyer ("Gentile Mission," 407–9), like Lührmann and Edwards, holds the flat refusal to be primary and regards 11:30 as the creation of "an anonymous prophet" of the Q community who perceived the threat to Israel in the Gentile mission. He gratuitously emends 11:30 to read "as Jonah became (was) a sign *to his generation* . . .*" Hence as Jonah's sign (the conversion of Nineveh) was a condemnatory sign for Israel, Q's success with the Gentiles served as an *Unheilszeichen* to "this generation." Schenk (*Synopse*, 71–72) treats not only 11:29c-30 as redactional but 11:31–32 as well and assumes a christological interpretation for the latter.
124. Vögtle, "Spruch vom Jonaszeichen," 116–17.
125. Similarly Jacobson, "Wisdom Christology," 169; Schürmann, "Menschensohn-Titel," 134; Zeller, "Redaktionsprozesse," 397 n. 19.

claims that the correlative form is unique to Q must be discounted. D. Schmidt has conclusively demonstrated the existence of a "prophetic correlative" form in the LXX,[126] and further examples of this form are to be found in the literature of Qumran.[127] This removes the justification for attributing 11:30 specifically to Q redaction. Whether it was an early addition to Q is another matter.

The most decisive point which bears on the nature of 11:29–30 is Schürmann's observation that *all* of the Son of Man sayings in Q are attached either to the preceding or following sayings and function to explain or interpret them.[128] That is, all have the appearance of being secondary additions. From this he concludes that the Son of Man title "probably does not belong to the oldest stratum of the sayings tradition, but should be assigned to an interpretive secondary stratum."[129] On the other hand—and this is certainly the case with Q 11:30—these interpretive sayings are not as late as the final redaction. Schürmann is not willing to suppose that all of the Son of Man sayings arose simply as *Interpretamente* of other sayings; some may have had an independent existence apart from their present contexts. But in the case of 11:30 this option is not open.[130] The correlative is constructed specifically as the explanation of 11:29, repeating the key words σημεῖον, Ἰωνᾶς and γενεὰ αὕτη.

If we assume with Schürmann that 11:30 is, like the other Q Son of Man sayings, secondary, the most likely solution to the tradition-historical problem is as follows: the original pronouncement contained the exception clause "except the Sign of Jonah" (11:29c). This represents a *lectio difficilior* which, on the one hand, was omitted by Mark because it entailed a concession to Jesus' opponents, and on the other, was elaborated in pre-Q tradition by the addition of an explicative phrase. Only then was 11:31–32 appended to the pronouncement story.

What was the significance of the joining of 11:29–30 and 11:31–32, and

126. Daryl Schmidt, "LXX *Gattung*." He mentions Jer 38 (31):28; 39 (32):42; 49 (42):18; 2:26; 5:19; 19:11; Isa 10:10–11; 20:3–4; 41:25; 55:10–11; 66:13; 24:13; Ezek 12:11; 20:36; 34:12; Amos 3:12; Obad 1:15; Lev 24:20; Deut 8:5.

127. 1Q27 i.6: "As smoke disappears and is no more, so will evil disappear forever and righteousness will appear like the sun" [trans. by auth.]. 4QpsDanA^a [= 4Q 246] ii.1–2: "As comets (flash) to sight, so shall be their kingdom" (trans. Fitzmyer, *Wandering Aramean*, 90–93).

128. Attached to the preceding saying: Q 6:22–23; 7:33–34; 11:30; 12:8–9, 10, 40; 17:24, 26–27, 28–30. To the following: 9:57–58.

129. Schürmann, "Menschensohn-Titel," 124–47, quote 146 [trans. by auth.].

130. Polag (*Christologie*, 90, 95) and Tödt (*Son of Man*, 54, 65, 270–71) posit an independent existence for 11:30 but fail to account for the remarkable similarities with 11:29.

what was Q's understanding of the "Sign of Jonah"? There are three possible interpretations.[131] First, Jeremias and Vögtle have urged that the sign must be manifestation of Jesus as the "One who was delivered from death."[132]

Vögtle (whose treatment is the most detailed) (1) argues that since the opponents of Jesus demand a legitimation sign, there is no exegetical warrant for assuming that the "Sign of Jonah" is other than a legitimation sign. Further, he (2) insists that the future tenses in vv. 29–30 exclude the view that the sign was Jesus' preaching. Finally he (3) holds that Jonah's miraculous deliverance from death was the only outstanding "sign" which could have formed the *tertium comparationis*. Vögtle holds that 11:30 is an explication of an authentic word of Jesus (11:29). In fact, he argues that the first interpretation was "as Jonah became a sign, so the Son of Man will be a sign to this generation" and only subsequently did a (second) redactor add "to the Ninevites" (pp. 132–33). For all this, the basic meaning did not change.

   Vögtle's assumption of a two-stage development of 11:30 is not only gratuitous, but serves to highlight the embarrassment that the Ninevites did *not* see Jonah's deliverance from death.

The Q context, however, does not support this conclusion. Indeed the opponents request a legitimation sign rather than some other type of miracle. For Q as for Mark, healings are called δυνάμεις, not σημεῖα (Mark 6:5; Q 10:13).[133] But as 11:29 makes clear, the request for a sign comes from an "evil" and unbelieving group. Under the circumstances, it

---

131. For a survey of opinion on the meaning of "Sign of Jonah," see Vögtle, "Jonaszeichen," passim; Edwards, *Sign of Jonah*, 6–24. More recently G. Schmitt ("Das Zeichen des Jona," ZNW 69 [1978] 123–29) proposed that "Sign of Jonah" was borrowed from the *Vitae Prophetarum* (on Jonah), which speaks of a "sign which Jonah gave to Jerusalem . . . that the city would be destroyed." According to Schmitt the original tradition comprised only 11:29a, b = Mark 8:12, and sometime after the composition of the *Vitae* the phrase "Sign of Jonah" was borrowed and reinterpreted as the preaching of Jonah. While this is an intriguing solution, it is excluded by chronological considerations. The *Vitae Prophetarum* were composed about the time of the war, i.e., at roughly the same time as the composition of Q. This does not leave enough time for the tradition to enter circulation, influence 11:29c and then be reinterpreted by 11:30.

132. Jeremias, Ἰωνᾶς, 409–10; Vögtle, "Jonaszeichen," 130; similarly Marshall, *Luke*, 485.

133. Berger (*Amen-Worte*, 59–60) assumes that an apocalyptic sign is requested, but it is much more likely that the opponents are asking for a sign which legitimates Jesus' teaching. Compare 2 Kgs 20:1–11; Isa 7:10–16; Deut 13:1–5; *b. B. Mes.* 59b; *b. Sanh.* 98a: "The disciples of R. Jose b. Kisma asked him [R. Joshua b. Levi] 'When will the Messiah come?' He answered, 'I fear lest you demand a sign of me.' They assured him, 'We will demand no sign of you.' So he answered them, 'When this gate falls down, is rebuilt, falls again, and is rebuilt again, and then falls a third time. Before it can be rebuilt the Son of David will come.' They said to him, 'Master, give us a sign.' [He protests, but accedes to the request.] 'If so, let the waters of the grotto of Paneas turn to blood.' And they turned into blood" (trans. I. Epstein, *The Babylonian Talmud. Seder Nezikin* [4 vols.; London: Soncino, 1935]).

is hardly likely that Q would comply by granting a legitimation sign; Q elsewhere refuses to provide special apocalyptic signs on demand (17:23–24), insisting instead that preaching (11:31–32), miracles (7:22; 10:13–15; 11:20) and the "signs of the times" (12:54–56) should be quite sufficient to convince of the necessity of repentance. It is doubly unlikely that the resurrection (or the manifestation of the Resurrected One) is intended by the phrase "Sign of Jonah" since Q never explicitly refers to the resurrection. Nor does the logic of Q 11:30 permit this interpretation since there is no evidence from either the biblical Jonah story or its subsequent elaboration that the *Ninevites* witnessed Jonah's deliverance from the sea or believed on account of that deliverance.

Two other interpretive possibilities exist. The "Sign of Jonah" is either the Son of Man coming in judgment, or the preaching of judgment by the earthly Jesus (and its continuation by his followers). The former view, suggested by Bultmann,[134] is supported by the analogy of the three correlatives in 17:24, 26–30, all of which concern the coming Son of Man. However, 11:30 does not employ the phrase "in the days of . . ." or "in his day" characteristic of the other correlatives, and hence the emphasis is not obviously upon a temporal aspect, i.e., upon the unexpected time or nature of the parousia. Moreover, an examination of the "prophetic correlatives" isolated by Schmidt shows that the future verb in the apodosis may refer to action in the immediate as well as distant future, and in some cases the future is virtually gnomic.[135] In other words, the sign in 11:30 need not be understood as still in the distant eschatological future; it may be present. The immediate context indeed suggests this: the future in 11:30 is parallel to $o\dot{v}\ \delta o\theta\acute{\eta}\sigma\epsilon\tau\alpha\iota$ in 11:29, which means "God will give you no sign, now or later." This suggests that 11:30 means "The only sign *is* the Sign of Jonah."

The sense in which Jonah became a sign to the Ninevites was not that he brought about the destruction of Nineveh; the predicted destruction, in fact, did not occur, at least in the near term.[136] The Jonah story thus does not provide an analogy for the eschatological coming of the Son of Man and the attendant destruction of sinners. It does, however, provide

134. Bultmann, *Tradition*, 118 [124]. See also Tödt, *Son of Man*, 270–71; Lührmann, *Redaktion*, 40, 41–42; Schürmann, "Menschensohn-Titel," 134. Similarly Perrin, *Rediscovering*, 194; Hoffmann, *Studien*, 157, 181; Polag, *Christologie*, 133.

135. See Ezek 34:12; Isa 55:10–11; Obad 1:15. In Lev 24:20 and Deut 8:5 the context is legal or sapiential, and the apodosis refers to the legal or inevitable consequence of a certain action.

136. Interestingly, the accounts which focus on Nineveh's eventual destruction (Tobit 14:4, 8; Josephus *Ant.* 9.206–14) say nothing of Nineveh's repentance, but treat Jonah's prophecy as in fact fulfilled.

an analogy for Jesus' announcement of judgment. That was the only "sign" which the Ninevites received, and it sufficed to effect repentance. And this is the only sign which "this generation" will receive.

Early Jewish exegesis of the Jonah story confirms this point. It focused upon Jonah's extraordinary success as a preacher of judgment and repentance, and further, interpreted Nineveh's repentance as an *Unheilszeichen* for Israel:

In a Proem to *Lamentations Rabbah* attributed to R. Simeon b. Yohai [mid II CE], Jerusalem is called the "oppressing city" (*ha'ir hayyonah*; cf. Zech 3:1). The commentary continues, "Ought she not have learnt from the city of Jonah, i.e., Nineveh? One prophet I sent to Nineveh and she turned in penitence; but to Israel in Jerusalem [*sic*] I sent many prophets . . . Yet she hearkened not."[137]

In *Mekilta de R. Ishmael*, Jonah's flight is explained by R. Eleazar b. Zadok [2d or 4th generation Tanna] as an attempt to avoid God's command to go to Nineveh. Jonah realized that the Ninevites were "more inclined to repent" than Israel, and that in preaching to them he "might be causing Israel to be condemned."[138] Another opinion, proffered by the fourth-generation R. Nathan [ca. 140–65] was to the effect that Jonah cast himself into the sea as atonement for Israel's sins because he knew that Gentile faith would compound Israel's guilt.[139]

The immediate Q context suggests the same interpretation. Q 11:31–32 comprises two judgment threats which focus precisely upon the success of two OT preachers among Gentiles and the onus which Gentile repentance places upon Israel. Moreover, the double saying pronounces judgment upon those who refuse to respond to some *present reality* which is greater than Jonah or Solomon. Given the context, this can only be the preaching of judgment. Vögtle objects to this, arguing that the probable Q order of the double saying (i.e., 11:31, 32) places Solomon, the exponent of "wisdom," before Jonah, the repentance preacher.[140] This, however, neglects the fact that in second-temple Judaism "wisdom" was not simply a matter of abstract cosmological knowledge, but included repentance (Sir 17:24; 44:16, 48; Wis 11:23; 12:10, 19). Solomon

137. *Lam. Rab.* Proem 31 (H. Freedman and M. Simon, *Midrash Rabbah* [London: Soncino, 1939] vol. 7/2).

138. *Mek.* Pisha 1.80–82. (J. Z. Lauterbach, *Mekilta de-Rabbi Ishmael* [3 vols.; Philadelphia: JPSA, 1933; repr. 1961]). A similar explanation is given by R. Jonah [fourth-century Amora]: Jonah knew that "these gentiles are nigh unto repentance, and lo, I shall go and prophesy against them, and they shall repent, the Holy One, blessed be he, consequently will come and inflict punishment on Israel. So what should I do? [I have no choice but to] flee" (*y. Sanh.* 11.5 II.A, *The Talmud of the Land of Israel*, vol. 31, *Sanhedrin and Makkot* (trans. Jacob Neusner; Chicago: Univ. of Chicago Press, 1984).

139. *Mek.* Pisha 1.103–5, 112–13.

140. Vögtle, "Jonaszeichen," 127. Matthew probably reversed the order of the double saying so as to bring the Jonah saying into closer relation with the Jonah sayings in 12:39, 40.

is represented as a repentance preacher, chastising kings for their sins (Wis 6:1–11) and threatening a swift judgment on evildoers (Wis 6:5; cf. 11–19). Hence *both* σοφία and κήρυγμα, especially when associated with Jonah and Solomon, contain connotations of the preaching of repentance and judgment. Far from excluding the interpretation of the Sign of Jonah as preaching, 11:31, 32 supports it.[141]

The history of Q 11:16, 29–32 is relatively complex, involving at least three stages: the original request for a sign and Jesus' somewhat enigmatic response (11:16, 29a–c), the addition of the explanatory correlative (11:30) and, finally, the appending of the double saying (11:31,32). Evident in the juxtaposition of 11:16, 29–30 and 11:31, 32 is the tendency to emphasize the unbelief of those who request the sign, and the fact that an adequate ground for repentance already exists in the preaching of Jesus. Mark's account also interprets the request for a sign in a negative light. But his absolute refusal of a sign is connected to the idea that the mystery of the kingdom and of God's Son is by divine design not publicly revealed. Q's understanding of Jesus' public preaching as an adequate ground for repentance and faith is implicitly rejected by Mark 4:11–12, 33–34 and 8:11–12.

The Sayings Concerning Light

The Matthaean setting of both sayings on light (Matt 5:15 // Luke 11:33; Matt 6:22–23 // Luke 11:34–36) is secondary: Matt 5:15 occurs in a series of Matthaean discipleship sayings, heavily redacted, which compare the disciples with salt (5:13) and light (5:14).[142] Likewise 6:22–23 is found in a series of Q texts which appear to have been collected by Matthew: 6:19–21 (Q 12:33–34); 6:22–23 (Q 11:34–36); 6:26 (Q 16:13); 6:25–34 (Q 12:22–31). Matthew's positioning of 6:22–23 between the saying on treasures (which ends with "for where your treasure is, there will your heart be also") and the saying on serving God or Mammon (6:24) accords with the focus of 6:22–23 upon inner dispositions, and it orients the saying toward the idea of the capacity to perceive and decide rightly. On the other hand, there are no signs of Lucan redaction, either in the transition between 11:29–32 and 11:33 or between v. 33 and vv.

---

141. Many scholars have adopted the view that the preaching of judgment is meant in 11:30: Harnack, *Sayings of Jesus*, 23 [21]; Vielhauer, "Jesus und der Menschensohn," 110–13; Schulz, *Spruchquelle*, 255–56, and those cited in n. 545; Jacobson, "Wisdom Christology," 168.

142. See Schnackenburg, "Ihr seid"; Wanke, "Kommentarworte," 221; Hahn, "Worte vom Lichte," 133; Marshall, *Luke*, 487–88; Schneider, "Bildwort," 183–209; Steinhauser, *Doppelbildworte*, 380.

34–36.[143] Luke, it should be noted, reproduces the light saying twice: once in its Marcan setting (8:16 // Mark 4:21), and here, in a strictly Q context. Given these facts, it is difficult to escape the supposition that Luke took over a pre-existing complex of Q sayings, 11:29–32, 33, 34–36.

That 11:33–36 is not an original unity is evident. The first saying, "No one after lighting a lamp puts it in the cellar . . . ," appears independently in Mark (4:21) and in the Gos. Thom. (33).[144] On the assumption that "light" served as a metaphor for the kerygma, 11:33 may have been employed as encouragement to preach of the kingdom openly.[145] But this is not the original Sitz for Q 11:34–36 which focuses not on the light itself, but on its subjective appropriation. If it had an independent existence, this Q saying may have functioned as a post-baptismal parenetic word stressing the importance of unclouded moral vision.[146]

The basis for the connection of v. 33 and vv. 34–36 is twofold: the catchword λύχνος (33, 34, 36) and the logical parallel between v. 33 (the lamp which gives light to the house) and v. 34 (the eye which gives light to the body).

Q 11:34 presents serious interpretive difficulties. What sort of theory

---

143. Hahn ("Worte vom Lichte," 132–33) suggests the possibility of Lucan editing in v. 36b. However, neither φωτίζω nor ἀστραπή is obviously Lucan.

144. The agreements of Gos. Thom. 33b with Luke 11:33 might suggest that Thomas depends upon canonical Luke: οὐδείς/negative (ⲙⲁⲣⲉ-) + ⲗⲁⲁⲩ, οὐδέ/ⲟⲩⲁⲉ, εἰς κρύπτην/ⲙⲁ ⲉϥϩⲏⲡ, ἵνα/ⲭⲉⲕⲁⲥ and οἱ εἰσπορευόμενοι τὸ φέγγος/ⲟⲩⲟⲛ ⲛⲓⲙ ⲉⲧⲃⲏⲕ ⲉϩⲟⲩⲛ ⲁⲩⲱ ⲉⲧⲛⲛⲏⲩ ⲉⲃⲟⲗ ⲉⲩⲛⲁⲛⲁⲩ ⲁⲡⲉϥⲟⲩⲟⲉⲓⲛ. Not all of these elements are clearly Lucan, however. Οὐδείς is typical of such Bildworte (e.g., Mark 2:21–22; 3:27; Luke 5:39). Moreover, Luke usually avoids asyndeton when composing freely. While καλύπτει αὐτὸν σκεύει in 8:16 is redactional, εἰς κρύπτην is not obviously Lucan. Similarly, οἱ εἰσπορευόμενοι is redactional in 8:16 but it cannot be excluded that 8:16 was influenced by the presence of the phrase in Q. It occurs at least once more in Q, in Q 11:52. Since C. H. Dodd ("Changes of Scenery in Luke," ExpT 33 [1921–22] 40–41) and Joachim Jeremias ("Die Lampe unter dem Scheffel," Abba [Göttingen: Vandenhoeck & Ruprecht, 1966] 99–102) it has become customary to argue that Matthew's version presupposes one-roomed Palestinian houses, while Luke envisages a "Hellenistic" (i.e., non-Palestinian) house with a vestibule; hence, Luke's version is a later adaptation of the saying for Greek listeners. However, S. Safrai ("Home and Family," The Jewish People in the First Century [CRINT 1/1–2; Philadelphia: Fortress Press, 1976] 730–35) points out that one-roomed houses were not the rule, and vestibules were common, as were windows. It should be noted too that architecture in Galilee was influenced by that of Hellenistic cities, as Josephus (B. J. 2.503–4) attests. The Luke/Thomas version, then, is not less compatible with a Palestinian or Galilean milieu than Matthew's. In an unpublished paper, Wendy J. Cotter ("Matthew's Concept of οἰκία") points out that Matthew regularly envisages one-roomed houses (2:11; 5:15; 8:14; 9:25) and introduces this image redactionally. Hence an alteration of Q 11:33 by Matt cannot be excluded.

145. See the thorough tradition-historical analysis by Steinhauser, Doppelbildworte, 352–83, esp. 381–82.

146. Thus Wanke, "Kommentarworte," 222. Schenk (Synopse, 73–74), however, asserts that vv. 34–35 were added only at the stage of Q redaction and thus had no independent existence.

of vision does the saying presuppose? In what way is "the eye the lamp of your body"? And how does the metaphor of illumination function?

According to some Greek theories of vision, the eye was composed of light.[147] Plato (*Timaeus* 45BC) referred to the eyes as φωσφόρα ὄμματα through which the "pure fire within us flows" (τὸ γὰρ ἐντὸς ἡμῶν . . . πῦρ). Cf. also Empedocles in Diels and Kranz, *Vorsokratiker* 31 A 86; B 85, 86; Plutarch *Quaestiones conviv.* 1.8.4 (626D). Plato articulated an active theory of vision according to which light streamed from the eyes to the object of vision, functioning as a kind of extended tactile organ. It distributes "the motions of every object it touches or whereby it is touched throughout the body, even unto the soul and brings about sensation which we now term 'seeing'" (45C). Passive theories of sight are expressed by Democritus and Alcmaeon (both quoted in Theophrastus *De Sensu* 25–26, 49–50) and by Aristotle (*De Sensu* 437b.11–12) although these theories make some allowance for the active side of vision.[148]

Since 11:34b, c makes the interior condition of the body contingent upon the condition of the eye, it appears that the eye is regarded as a transmitter of light to the body. Nevertheless, like the Greek theories of vision cited above, it does not seem that here the eye is entirely passive. As it stands, the contrast ἁπλοῦς/πονηρός could be taken either physiologically (healthy/impaired) or ethically (simple, generous/evil),[149] although ἁπλοῦς and ἁπλότης are somewhat unusual as medical terms.[150] As Betz points out, contemporary Jewish usage of ἁπλοῦς suggests that v. 34 is to be construed in a moral sense.[151] In *T. Issachar* the phrase ἁπλότης ὀφθαλμῶν (3:4) is used interchangeably with ἁπλότης καρδίας (3:8; 4:1) and εὐθότης ζωῆς (4:6) and denotes rectitude in both inner disposition and consequent action. *T. Benj.* 4:2 uses the contrasting term σκοτεινὸς ὀφθαλμός as a metaphor for the inability or unwillingness to show mercy. In Q 11:34 a further nuance is introduced: a "simple eye" is said to be the *cause or pre-condition* of an enlightened self. That is, a proper moral disposition permits the transmission of light to the body, and forms the basis for all consequent action.[152]

147. See P. Wilpert and S. Zenker, "Auge," *RAC* 1 (1950) 957–63; H.-D. Betz, "Matthew vi.22f and Ancient Greek Theories of Vision," *Essays*, 71–87.

148. Theophrastus provides an important summary of ancient opinion in *De Sensu* (G. M. Stratton, ed., *Theophrastus and the Greek Physiological Psychology* [London: George Allen & Unwin, 1917; repr. Amsterdam: Bonset, 1964]).

149. See Betz, *Essays*, 85.

150. LSJ 190–91; G. Harder, πονηρός, *TDNT* 6 (1968) 555–56.

151. Betz, *Essays*, 73, 85.

152. Ibid., 86: "This statement [11:34] is flatly directed against the Greek philosophical tradition, according to which the *lumen internum* is divine in nature and can never be turned into its opposite, 'darkness.' In other words, this suggestion must be another correction of the Platonic-Stoic anthropology, and it follows from the first correction. If the eye is affected by human sinfulness, the same must be true of the 'inner light,' because nothing human is exempt from sin."

The next verses (Luke 11:35–36 // Matt 6:23b) present several difficulties of reconstruction.

First, while there is agreement between Matt 6:23b and Luke 11:35 in the words τὸ φῶς τὸ ἐν σοὶ σκότος ἐστιν (ἔσται), Luke uses an imperative (σκόπει οὖν μή. . .) while Matthew has an exclamation (εἰ οὖν τὸ φῶς . . . σκότος ἐστιν, τὸ σκότος πόσον). The preference is to be given to Matthew since Luke displays a tendency to insert parenetic imperatives and summaries into his sources.[153]

The case of 11:36 is much more difficult. The occurrence of εἰ οὖν in Matt 6:23b might be taken as an indication that Matthew saw Luke 11:36 in his *Vorlage* but omitted it because it added nothing to his saying.[154] Indeed, the saying is extremely obscure, if not completely tautologous.[155] It is difficult to imagine why Luke would have added it, but equally difficult to determine what it might have meant in Q if it occurred there. Hahn suggests that ἔσται in v. 36 refers to the eschatological (not the logical) future and that Q 11:34–36 is an antithetically balanced saying: proposition (34a) + contrasting conditionals (34b, 34c) + contrasting results (Matt 6:23b // Luke 11:36a).[156]

It is frequently asserted that the juxtaposition of ὁ λύχνος in v. 33 with Q 11:31–32 imports a christological significance to "the lamp."[157] This presupposes in turn that πλεῖον Ἰωνᾶς has acquired a specifically christological significance from the Son of Man saying in 11:30. While the christological ramifications of the connection of 11:29–30 with vv. 31–32 must not be minimized, it is unwise to draw too sharp a distinction between Q's understanding of Jesus himself and his function as the envoy of the kingdom. Q 11:30, it must be remembered, has to do with the *preaching* of the Son of Man; hence πλεῖον in vv. 31 and 32 and the

153. Although σκόπει appears only here in the NT, Luke uses similar parenetic imperatives redactionally. In 12:1 he concludes the woes against the Pharisees with a warning taken from Mark 8:15, adds προσέχετε in 17:3; 20:46 and 21:34 and concludes the parable in 12:15 with summarizing parenetic imperatives (contrast the version in *Gos. Thom.* 72).

154. Thus Josef Schmid, *Matthäus und Lukas*, 239; Marshall, *Luke*, 488; Manson, *Sayings*, 93; Steinhauser, *Doppelbildworte*, 374; Hahn, "Worte vom Lichte," 115–16; Wanke, "Kommentarworte," 221–22. Schulz (*Spruchquelle*, 469) and Schenk (*Synopse*, 73) regard v. 36 as Lucan.

155. Manson (*Sayings*, 94), relying on a mistranslation hypothesis advanced by C. C. Torrey (*The Four Gospels* [New York: Harper & Bros., 1933] 309), holds that the saying suggests that "the man who is full of light lights the world around him." This is quite speculative and does not obviate the problem in Greek. It is to be noted, however, that the *Gos. Thom.* 24 follows this interpretation, no doubt understanding "light" as "gnosis": "Within a man of light there is light and he lights the whole world."

156. Hahn, "Worte vom Lichte," 128–31; thus Wanke, "Kommentarworte," 221–22. Hahn ("Worte vom Lichte," 130–31) suggests further that ὡς ὅταν ὁ λύχνος τῇ ἀστραπῇ φωτίζῃ σε (v. 36b), which recalls 11:33, serves as a redactional clasp holding v. 33 and vv. 34–36a together. But whether this clasp is Lucan or pre-Lucan is impossible to determine.

157. Thus Hahn, "Worte vom Lichte," 132; Steinhauser, *Doppelbildworte*, 270; Wanke, "Kommentarworte," 222.

λύχνος of v. 33 (and 36?) refer, at least in the first place, to the *preaching of the kingdom* (by its pre-eminent envoy).

Q 11:31–32 concerns the ultimate consequences of responding to or ignoring the preaching of the kingdom and its pre-eminent envoy. Q 11:33–36 should be seen as a continuation of the rhetoric. This saying implies that the preaching of the kingdom is not something obscure or hidden, but universally and openly manifest, so that all might respond. The "sound eye" saying which follows functions as a commentary word, directing attention away from the objective fact of the "light" to the pre-conditions for subjective appropriation of that light, and to the fearful prospects which await those who do not respond adequately. When the moral disposition of the audience prevents it from apprehending divine activity when it is so openly manifest in Jesus' preaching, his exorcisms and his person, then that audience is benighted indeed!

Schulz opines that 11:34–36 "concerns the eschatological 'either-or' of radical obedience with respect to Jesus' intensified Mosaic Torah and uncompromising discipleship."[158] But nothing indicates that a radical-ized Torah is at issue here. Instead, Q 11:33–36 must be interpreted in the context of the issues raised in 11:14–26, 29–32. Throughout, the conflict between Jesus and his opponents is based on faulty perception: the opponents mistake the workings of "the finger of God" (11:20), which should have been taken as evidence of the kingdom, as deeds of Beel-zebul. Then they request a sign from heaven, not perceiving that Jesus' preaching is itself the sign they request. Such a failure to grasp the presence of the πλεῖον Ἰωνᾶς can only be interpreted as abject moral blindness, worthy of judgment and condemnation.

The sequence in Q is rhetorically ordered to make this point. The Beelzebul accusation and response concludes with 11:23, which ex-presses in quasi-proverbial form the objective "facts of the matter" of allegiance to Jesus. You are either with him or against him. Then follows a parable (11:24–26) which in effect threatens those who do not ally themselves with the kingdom with a hopeless and disastrous end. Q 11:29–36 forms a parallel to the first sequence. The request for a sign, which bespeaks a perverse and unbelieving attitude, is answered by Jesus' defense of his preaching as the adequate sign. The gnomic state-ment in 11:33 implies that this preaching/sign is plain for everyone to see. Then follows the metaphorical saying about the eye, which, like 11:24–26, amounts to a threat pronounced upon all those who, because

---

158. Schulz, *Spruchquelle*, 470 [trans. by auth.].

of their impaired moral vision, do not respond to the preaching of the kingdom.

The Woes Against the Pharisees

The next section in Q[159] further articulates the element of threat developed in Q 11:24–26 and 33–36 and the contrast between adequate and faulty moral vision. Matthew's version of the woes (23:1–36) is fused with Marcan warnings against the Pharisees (Mark 12:37b–40) and occurs in Marcan sequence. Luke's woes, by contrast, appear in a predominantly Q context. Moreover, Matthew's version contains much more than Q, and it is generally assumed that the first evangelist combined Mark and Q with his special material.[160] In addition he has interpolated sayings from originally different contexts in Mark (23:11 // Mark 10:43–44 // Matt 20:26–27) and Q (23:12 // Luke 14:12 // 18:14b; 23:33 // Luke 3:7b). By contrast Luke has apparently provided only an introduction (based upon the motifs present in Mark 7:1–5),[161] a few transitional phrases such as 11:45 and a conclusion (11:53–54) for the Q complex.

There is considerable disagreement between Matthew and Luke in the order of the woes. Nevertheless, the two Synoptists agree in the relative order of Luke 11:42, 44, 47–48, 49–51 (Matt 23:23, 27–28, 29–32, 34–36). If the meal scene is regarded as a Lucan creation, Luke may have inverted the order of 11:42, 39–41 (cf. Matt 23:23, 25–26) in order to achieve a connection between the question of washing (11:38) and the corresponding woe concerning the washing of cups and plates. There is little reason for Matthew to have reversed the order of his woes at this point.[162] On the other hand, Matthew fused the condemnation of self-approbation (23:6–7 // Luke 11:43) with Mark 12:38 and placed the

---

159. Zeller ("Redaktionsprozesse," 398) holds that 11:33–36 was followed by 12:2–12 and connected by the catchwords "light," "darkness" (11:35; 12:3) and "body" (11:34; 12:4). Hence he is obliged to hold that Luke inserted the woes after the request for a sign because of the common anti-Pharisaic theme, and thus broke up an original connection in Q. However, in neither Luke nor Q 11:16, 29–32 are the Pharisees mentioned, and hence Zeller's justification disappears.

160. See Haenchen, "Matthäus 23," esp. 39; Garland, *Intention*, 8–23.

161. Marshall (*Luke*, 491) and Jeremias (*Sprache*, 205–6) hold that Luke reproduces a Q introduction. However, Luke 11:37–39 contains many Lucanisms: ἐν with an articular infinitive (see Jeremias, *Sprache*, 27–29), ὅπως with a verb of asking (red in 7:3; Acts 8:15, 24; 23:30; 25:2–3; trad only in Luke 10:2); ὁ κύριος (Fitzmyer, *Luke I–IX*, 202–3); πρός with verbs of speaking (see Cadbury, *Style*, 203). A few peculiarities are present: the historic present (although it occurs 18x in Acts with verbs of speaking); ἄριστον (2x in Luke) and βαπτίζω, meaning "wash." But these oddities are not sufficient to posit a Q introduction.

162. Thus Garland, *Intention*, 17; Schürmann, "Basileia-Verkündigung," 174.

criticism of Pharisaic halakah (23:4 // Luke 11:46) in the midst of either
M or redactional material where it serves as part of his programmatic
opening for the woes. Since Matthew's settings are obviously redactional, and since there is little reason for Luke to have altered the order,
11:43 and 11:46 are best retained in Lucan order.[163] This leaves only one
woe, 11:52 (Matt 23:13). In Matthew it appears between M (23:8–11, 15,
16–22) and rearranged Q + Marcan materials (23:11; 23:12), while in
Luke it occurs as the conclusion to the woes. Matthew's setting is the
more contrived, and in all probability, secondary. Hence, we arrive at a
probable order for the Q woes:[164]

Luke	Matt	
11:42	23:23	On tithing
11:39–41	23:25–26	Ritual washings
11:43	23:6–7	You love the chief seats!
11:44	23:27–28	You are like graves
11:46	23:4	You bind heavy burdens on men
11:47–48	23:29–32	You build the tombs of the prophets
11:49–51	23:34–36	The oracle of Sophia
11:52	23:13	You take away the keys

The compositional history of the woes and the Sophia oracle appears
to be quite complex. Even apart from the Sophia oracle in 11:49–51,
which is almost unanimously regarded as a secondary insertion, the
individual woes do not all operate from the same presupposition, and
are not of the same tradition-historical provenance. The first two (Q
11:42, 39–41) concern the tithing and purification of vessels and allege
that Pharisaic practice does not meet the fundamental demands of
God's covenant: justice and mercy.[165] But in neither woe is the ceremonial law rejected; the phrase ταῦτα δὲ ἔδει ποιῆσαι κἀκεῖνα μὴ παρεῖναι
(11:42b) makes this clear. The dispute with the Pharisees is still *intra
muros*.[166] According to Schürmann 11:42, 39–41 represents the "kernel"

163. Thus Garland, *Intention*, 17; Josef Schmid, *Matthäus und Lukas*, 322–23, 326;
Marshall, *Luke*, 492–93. Jacobson ("Wisdom Christology," 184) holds that Luke divided
v. 44 from v. 47 (which were originally joined by the catchword "tomb"). But this
association is more likely due to Matthaean redaction which brought Q 11:46 forward,
thus allowing 11:44 to come into closer relation with Q 11:47.

164. The woe cry has been omitted by Luke in 11:39 (it is present in the parallel Matt
23:25) and by Matthew in 23:4, 6 (present in Luke 11:46, 43). In each case the omission
is due to redactional reformulation.

165. For a discussion of these two woes, see Garland, *Intention*, 136–41, 141–50; Jacob
Neusner, "First Cleanse the Inside: Halakhic Background of a Controversy Saying," *NTS*
22 (1976) 486–95; Schulz, *Spruchquelle*, 95–103.

166. Thus Schulz (*Spruchquelle*, 97, 100), who compares similar accusations leveled by
the author of *As. Mos.* 7:1–10 at his co-religionists.

of the woes, transmitted by a group of "law-observant Jewish Christians who in contrast to Pharisaic legalism accentuated the ethical aspect of Torah, especially the law of love . . ."[167] Pharisaic interpretation is disputed, but Q's rejection of such interpretation is temperate. By contrast, 11:46 calls into question the very practice of scribal interpretation of the Law which multiplies rules and creates "grievous burdens."[168] In 11:43 the connection with legal matters disappears entirely; the issue is the undeserved prominence of the Pharisees in the synagogues. Q 11:43 and 11:46 signal a rejection of Pharisaic legal interpretation and leadership, but they do not yet provide evidence of a fundamental break with Judaism.

Legal matters play no more role in the remaining woes (Q 11:44, 47–48, 52). The tone is much more vituperative, a fact which leads one to suspect that the gulf between the community and the Pharisees (or perhaps even Judaism) has widened significantly. The accusation that the Pharisees are "unmarked graves"[169] is no longer a complaint about Pharisaic exegesis; it constitutes an attack on the very existence of that group since it portrays them as a source of ritual defilement. The next woe is just as strong, either indicting the Pharisees with complicity in the murder of the prophets, or declaring that in spite of their superficial piety, their guilt remains.

The wording of the woe (11:47–48) in Q is not certain and several interpretations are possible. (1) Hoffmann and Polag hold (with minor variations) that Luke 11:47 + Matt 23:31 represents the substance of Q:[170] ". . . you build the tombs of the prophets whom your fathers killed. Thus you witness against yourselves that you are sons of those who murdered the prophets." Hoffmann argues that the woe expresses the continuity in mentality and deed between the vaticidal

---

167. Schürmann, "Basileia-Verkündigung," 174 [trans. by auth.].

168. The import of this saying is not clear. (1) Some argue that the scribes evade the rules which they impose upon others. Thus Schulz, *Spruchquelle*, 107–8; Haenchen, "Matthäus 23," 41; Marshall, *Luke*, 500; Str-B 1.913-14. This interpretation is perhaps unduly influenced by Matthew's application of the saying and his placement of it beside 23:3b, "But do not act according to their works." (2) Alternatively, the woe may complain that scribes multiply ways of offending God without correspondingly assisting those who fail under such impossible burdens. Thus Manson, *Sayings*, 101; Garland, *Intention*, 51.

169. It is generally conceded that the Lucan version is more primitive. It is logical and presupposes Jewish law (Num 19:16; *m. Ohol* 17:5). See Schulz, *Spruchquelle*, 105–6, and the literature cited there. Matthew apparently borrowed the inside/outside dichotomy from 23:25–26 and extended it to 23:27–28, where he speaks of the hypocrisy of external righteousness and internal lawlessness (cf. a similar saying in *Ahikar* 2:2). His formulation creates an illogicality, since whitewashing tombs was precisely a means of marking them in order to prevent inadvertent defilement (Str-B 1.936-37).

170. Hoffmann, *Studien*, 162–63; Polag, *Fragmenta*, 56.

fathers and their sons. This is reflective of the deuteronomistic view of history: the history of sin of pre-exilic Israel continues not only as an abiding guilt but as a continuing state of disobedience. In the same vein Manson says, the "real object is to make permanent the work of your fathers. They killed the prophets: you make sure that they stay dead."[171]

(2) Steck and Schulz hold that Matt 23:30, "[You say,] 'If we had lived in the days of our fathers, we would not have taken part with them . . . ,'" also derives from Q.[172] Steck has shown that in the deuteronomistic view of piety, confession of the faults of one's ancestors is essential; thus the statement in 23:30 constitutes an attempt to avoid repentance. The very act of distanciation tacitly admits that guilt exists, and that act makes them like their fathers, who likewise attempted to avoid repentance. Hoffmann, however, points out that Steck's interpretation depends upon importing into the text the notion of repentance as acceptance of ancestral *guilt*. But 11:47–48 speaks only of the murder of the prophets and thus concerns the continuity of *action* (i.e., murder followed by burial).[173] Q 6:23c, which reflects the same understanding of history, also emphasizes continuity of *action*, not simply guilt.[174]

Q 11:47–48 thus accuses the scribes of complicity in the murder of the prophets and hence of opposition to God's actions in history. The final woe, 11:52, makes a similar accusation.[175] Although the first half of the saying seems to concede to them the custody of the keys of the kingdom (Matt) or "knowledge" (Luke),[176] the second part implies that the scribes have deliberately and maliciously conspired to prevent entry into the kingdom.[177] This woe, as several critics have observed, probably reflects

171. Manson, *Sayings*, 101.

172. Steck, *Israel*, 28–29; Schulz, *Spruchquelle*, 108–9.

173. Hoffmann, *Studien*, 163–64.

174. See further Garland, *Intention*, 163–67; Marshall, *Luke*, 500–501; Minear, "False Prophecy"; Derrett, "You Build."

175. The wording of the Q text is controverted. Bussmann (*Redenquelle*, 74), Marshall (*Luke*, 507) and Manson (*Sayings*, 103) prefer Luke; Matt is favored by Josef Schmid (*Matthäus und Lukas*, 332), Harnack (*Sayings of Jesus*, 100 [70]), Schulz (*Spruchquelle*, 110) and Meyer ("Community," 35). The phrase "scribes and Pharisees" is almost certainly Matthaean, but Luke's νομικοί may be his rendering of an original γραμματεῖς. The agreement between Matt and Luke in the use of οὐκ εἰσέρχεσθε (εἰσήλθατε) . . . τοὺς εἰσερχομένους suggests that the original saying concerned entry into the kingdom. Luke may have altered "kingdom" to "knowledge" because of reluctance to attribute the kingdom to lawyers. It is frequently argued that αἴρειν is Lucan (Schulz, *Spruchquelle*, 110 n. 125) despite the fact that there are no clear examples of its redactional use by Luke (8x from Mark; 3x from Q; 3x in *Sond*; 6x in Q contexts, Matt diff; Acts 9x). Κλεῖς occurs only in 11:52 (and Matt 16:19), γνῶσις only here and in 1:77; κωλύω might be red although there are no other clear examples of its redactional use in Luke.

176. Compare 1QH 4:11: "And they [preachers of lies and seers of deceit] have withheld the draught of knowledge from the thirsty ones . . ." (the context suggests that knowledge is Torah learning; trans. M. Mansoor, *The Thanksgiving Hymns* [STDJ 3; Leiden: E. J. Brill, 1961]).

177. Manson (*Sayings*, 103) and Garland (*Intention*, 127) argue that the complaint is against "an ever-increasing mass of traditions and precedents and pettifogging rules."

scribal or Pharisaic opposition to the mission of the community.[178] Schürmann notes that both the terms "keys of gnosis" (or "keys of the kingdom") and "enter" are employed without need of further explanation. This suggests a relatively late stratum of tradition in which the kingdom is viewed as a present reality and as a realm into which one can enter even now.[179] Q 11:52 reflects a similar situation as that indicated in 11:47–48: Pharisees are viewed as opposing God's attempt to invite persons into his kingdom. The Q community and the Pharisees stand in bitter confrontation, quite unlike earlier woes such as 11:42, 39–41.

As noted above, Schürmann believes that 11:42, 39–41 is the "kernel" of the woes, deriving from an early Jewish Christian and Torah-observant circle. He holds that 11:44, 46 represents the first expansion, with 11:43, 47–48, 49–51, 52 stemming from an "anti-synagogue 'ecclesiastical' redaction."[180] This is suggestive, but requires some modification. As will be argued below, 11:49–51 should be distinguished from the rest of the woes. Moreover, 11:44 should be grouped with 11:47–48 and 11:52 since like the latter it challenges the very existence of the Pharisees. Q 11:43 is much milder, dealing only with their leadership or aspirations to leadership. It coheres better with Q 11:46, which criticizes excessive halakah and duplicity in its application. Thus we suggest a three-stage growth for the woes: 11:42, 39–41, expanded by the mildly critical 11:43, 46 and finally supplemented with the highly polemical 11:44, 47–48, 52.

The Sophia oracle presents special difficulties.[181] Q 11:49–51 is connected with the preceding woe (11:47–48) on the basis of the catchwords "prophets" and "kill" and the deuteronomistic theme of the killing of Yahweh's prophets. But the connections of vv. 49–51 with 47–48 are even closer. As several critics have noted,[182] the entire unit of Q 11:47–51

According to Schulz (*Spruchquelle*, 111–12), Q concedes to the Pharisees that God rules wherever his Torah is observed. "The Pharisees, however, bar the kingdom to people by the fact that they give the ceremonial law precedence over the ethical Torah and even hinder those who are at the point of entering!" [trans. by auth.]. But the statement "You do not enter and you prevent those who are entering" indicates that it is not simply a matter of dispute over correct Torah interpretation or about the radicalization of Torah observance but concerns deliberate opposition to the kingdom.

178. Haenchen, "Matthäus 23," 47; W. Pesch, "Theologische Aussagen," 291; Schürmann, "Basileia-Verkündigung," 175; Meyer, "Community," 36.

179. Schürmann, "Basileia-Verkündigung," 175–76, quote 176 [trans. by auth.].

180. Ibid., 174–75.

181. Reconstructions: Hoffmann, *Studien*, 164–66; Steck, *Israel*, 29–34; Schulz, *Spruchquelle*, 336–38; Jacobson, "Wisdom Christology," 189; Polag, *Fragmenta*, 56; F. Christ, *Jesus Sophia* (ATANT 57; Zurich: Zwingli, 1970) 120–24. With minor variations all agree that Luke has reproduced the substance of Q.

182. Steck, *Israel*, 32 n. 1, and the literature cited there; Suggs, *Wisdom*, 16–18; Jacobson, "Wisdom Christology," 188–89.

corresponds in form to a woe oracle, well known from the OT and apocalyptic literature. The form can be described as follows: an accusation or reproach introduced by οὐαί or ὦ (Heb. hôy),[183] followed by the announcement of judgment, introduced by διὰ τοῦτο (lākēn) or τάδε λέγει κύριος (Heb. koh 'āmar YHWH), or both.[184] In Q the reproach is found in 11:47–48, and the announcement of judgment in vv. 50–51, introduced by διὰ τοῦτο καὶ ἡ σοφία τοῦ θεοῦ εἶπεν (v. 49a).

Despite the unitary appearance of 11:47–51, there is reason to believe that the woe-oracle form is a secondary construction of Q redaction, and that 11:49–51 is an interpolation into a series of woes—an interpolation which separated 11:52 from the rest of the woes. Whereas 11:47–48 (like the rest of the woes) is directed against the Pharisees or scribes, 11:49–51 broadens this criticism to "this generation," i.e., to those who reject Wisdom's messengers (cf. 7:31–35; 11:29–32). Moreover, in the midst of woes attributed to Jesus it is unexpected to find a saying of Sophia speaking, apparently from her standpoint at the beginning of history (ἀποστελῶ). Finally, the character of the Sophia saying differs from that of the woes: whereas the woes offer reproaches, the Sophia oracle is a threat of retribution on this generation. Thus it appears that a saying of Sophia has been joined to a series of woes through catchwords and thematic associations to form a judgment oracle against "this generation."[185]

The degree to which Q is quoting and adapting an earlier saying, and the degree of redaction, is somewhat unclear. At least v. 51b may be seen as an editor's contribution, functioning to effect the transition from the Sophia saying back to Jesus as speaker.

There are repeated suggestions that part of 11:49–51 is pre-Christian. Bultmann regarded the saying as a quotation from a lost sapiential book, but this has not met with wide acceptance.[186] Without subscribing to the thesis of a documentary

183. See, e.g., Jer 22:13; 23:1–4; Ezek 34:1–6; Isa 5:8–24; 10:1, 5; 28:1; 29:1, 15; 30:1; Hab 2:6–19; Mic 2:1–3 (not a woe in the LXX). See Claus Westermann, *Basic Forms of Prophetic Speech* (trans. H. C. White; Philadelphia: Westminster Press, 1967) 190–98.

184. The woes in *1 Enoch* regularly use ὅτι (99:6, 7; 95:5, 6; 96:6, 8; 97:8; 98:8, etc.) to introduce the announcement of judgment, and the woes have a sapiential flavor: the judgment or consequence of the condemned action seems to obtain by an immanent sapiential logic typical of sapiential reasoning. E.g., "Woe to you who requite your neighbor with evil, for you shall be requited according to your works" (95:5). This is similar to the Lucan woes (6:24–26) which are less prophetic in structure than they are sapiential.

185. Similarly Lührmann, *Redaktion*, 45–47; Schulz, *Spruchquelle*, 339; Steck, *Israel*, 50–52; Suggs, *Wisdom*, 16–21.

186. Bultmann, *Tradition*, 114 [119]; thus Grundmann, *Lukas*, 249; J. Ernst, *Das Evangelium nach Lukas* (RNT 3; Regensburg: Pustet, 1977) 388; Suggs, *Wisdom*, 19–20.

source, Steck has argued that it derived from circles of Jewish repentance preachers who were influenced by both deuteronomistic and sapiential traditions. He confines the Jewish component to vv. 49–50, attributing 51a, b to a Christian expansion which restricted the προφῆται καὶ ἀπόστολοι of v. 49a and τὸ αἷμα πάντων τῶν προφητῶν τὸ ἐκκεχυμένον ἀπὸ καταβολῆς κόσμου of v. 50 to the period of the Old Testament.[187] Lührmann and Schenk go further by ascribing to Q redaction the whole of v. 51, "inasmuch as it now clearly concerns the blood shed in Israel."[188]

Hoffmann also relegates v. 51 to Q redaction, but for slightly different reasons. The use of ἀπό in vv. 50 and 51a is confusing, suggesting somewhat clumsy editing:[189]

50 ἵνα ἐκζητηθῇ	τὸ αἷμα πάντων τῶν προφητῶν τὸ ἐκκεχύμενον ἀπὸ καταβολῆς κόσμου
ἀπὸ τῆς γενεᾶς ταύτης,	
51a	ἀπὸ αἵματος ῞Αβελ ἕως αἵματος Ζαχαρίου ...
51b ναὶ λέγω ὑμῖν· ἐκζητηθήσεται	
ἀπὸ τῆς γενεᾶς ταύτης.	

᾽Απὸ τῆς γενεᾶς ταύτης in vv. 50 and 51b belongs with ἐκζητηθῇ (vv. 50, 51b).[190] But ἀπὸ αἵματος ῞Αβελ ... specifies, somewhat awkwardly, the phrase τὸ αἷμα πάντων τῶν προφητῶν ... ἀπὸ καταβολῆς κόσμου. Hoffmann takes the awkwardness as a sign of Q editing, suggesting that v. 51a was added to illustrate the statements about shedding blood in v. 50 (and vv. 47–48).[191]

Material considerations also suggest that v. 51a is an insertion. Vv. 49–50 provide only a *terminus a quo* for the sending and persecution of the prophets, but v. 51a supplies the *terminus ad quem*. However, while Zechariah was arguably a prophet,[192] Abel was not. What is common to the two figures is the fact that innocent blood was shed.[193] Thus, while vv. 49–50 concern the sending

---

187. Steck, *Israel*, 51–53, 222–27, 282–83. He rejects the idea that "prophets" and "apostles" in v. 49 refer to the same group; "apostles" must refer to "figures of a later period." But for this reason, v. 51 (which restricts both prophets and apostles to the OT period) cannot have belonged to the Jewish tradition (p. 223). This reasoning is forced. 2 Chr 36:15–16 uses προφῆται καὶ ἄγγελοι, apparently in synonymous parallelism, to describe God's envoys to Israel, and Q 13:34 uses τοὺς προφήτας in parallel with τοὺς ἀπεσταλμένους πρὸς αὐτήν.

188. Lührmann, *Redaktion*, 47 [emphasis original; trans. by auth.]; Schenk, *Synopse*, 80.

189. Hoffmann, *Studien*, 168.

190. Steck (*Israel*, 32 n. 1) gratuitously regards "from this generation" in v. 50 as a post-Lucan gloss.

191. Hoffmann, *Studien*, 168.

192. Manson (*Sayings*, 103) and Haenchen ("Matthäus 23," 54) argue that Zechariah was not a prophet either because 2 Chr 24 calls him a priest rather than a prophet. However, 2 Chr 24:20 states that the spirit of God came upon him and employs the typical prophetic formula τάδε λέγει κύριος. Josephus (*Ant.* 9.168–69) also suggests that he was a prophet, as does the *Vitae Prophetarum*, which includes him in its list of prophets. For rabbinic portrayal of Zechariah as a prophet, and for the confusion of various Zechariahs, see Blank, "Death of Zechariah."

193. Thus Blank, "Death of Zechariah," 337–38. T. *Issachar* 5:4 implies that Abel was the first of the "holy": εὐλογήσει ὑμᾶς κύριος καθὼς πάντας τοὺς ἁγίους ἀπὸ Αβελ ἕως τοῦ νῦν.

and rejection of the prophets, v. 51a shifts the emphasis to the shedding of innocent blood. It is far from clear why the death of Zechariah should constitute the *terminus ad quem*;[194] it is possible that his death had achieved some special theological status in Judaism of the time.[195]

Although v. 51a appears to be an insertion, there is little reason to suppose that it derived from Q redaction. To select Zechariah's death as a *terminus ad quem* would seem strange for the redactor of Q who sees the persecution and killing of the prophets as extending into his own day (Q 6:23; 13:34–35). If v. 51a were due to Q redaction, as Lührmann and Schenk hold, one might expect the *terminus ad quem* to be John the Baptist (cf. Q 16:16). The death of Zechariah attracted no significant attention in Christian circles but, as (somewhat later) rabbinic evidence shows, it was a matter of reflection among Jewish writers.[196] Q 11:51a may be an addition to the original Sophia saying but it is likely to have been a very early (pre-Christian) addition.

If 51a was an early embellishment of the Sophia saying (vv. 49–50), what of v. 51b? Materially, v. 51b only repeats the threat made in v. 50. Haenchen has suggested that the repetition was called for because "the comment about Abel, etc., took things too far from the present."[197] More importantly, the λέγω ὑμῖν formula signals the end of the Sophia saying and a return to direct address by Jesus.[198] Q 11:51b appears to function like the redactional verse Q 10:12 (also introduced by λέγω ὑμῖν). Drawing upon the motifs present in 10:13–15, Q 10:12 provides a conclusion to 10:2–11 and a transition to 10:13–15. In the same way, 11:51b draws

194. The fact that Zechariah's death is narrated in the last book of the Hebrew canon may have something to do with this (although Jeremiah is mentioned subsequently in 2 Chr 36). If this is the rationale, it would presuppose that Chronicles was already accepted as the final book of the *Kethubim*.

195. Zechariah's dying cry, ἰδοὺ κύριος καὶ κρινάτω (2 Chr 24:22), seems to be the origin of various legends according to which (rather disproportionate) retribution for his murder was exacted from Israel. See *b. Git.* 57b (R. Hiyya b. Abin, III CE, and R. Joshua b. Karha, 130–60 CE) = *y. Ta'an* 4:9.69a; *Eccl. Rab.* on 3:16; *Lam. Rab.* introduction 23. See further, Blank, "Death of Zechariah," 327–46. According to the *Vitae Prophetarum*, Zechariah's murder was attended by τέρατα φαντασίας in the temple and the oracular functions of the temple ceased thereafter.

196. The location of the murder (i.e., between the altar and the temple, cf. 11:51) is indebted to development of the Zechariah legend. 2 Chr 24 reports only that he was stoned in the court of the temple (24:21). The *Vitae Prophetarum* locate the death beside the altar; rabbinic versions place it inside the court of priests (see Blank, "Death of Zechariah," 343–47).

197. Haenchen, "Matthäus 23," 55 [trans. by auth.].

198. Q 11:51b is regularly regarded as a Christian addition: Bultmann, *Tradition*, 114 [119–20]; Suggs, *Wisdom*, 16; Haenchen, "Matthäus 23," 55; Neirynck, "Study of Q," 66–67; Steck, *Israel*, 51. Schulz (*Spruchquelle*, 341) asserts that Sophia is still speaking in v. 51b.

upon the motifs present in 11:49–50 and provides a summary and transition to 11:52. Q 13:35b, incidentally, plays a similar role and is also introduced by λέγω ὑμῖν. Building on the traditional Sophia saying (13:34–35a), v. 35b strengthens the element of threat and introduces an allusion to the Son of Man coming in judgment. Q 11:51b, like both 10:12 and 13:35b, intensifies the threat of judgment articulated earlier and thus coheres with the major perspective of Q redaction.[199]

Summary. The woes in Q 11:39–52 have a complex tradition-history. From a tradition-historical standpoint the oldest are 11:42, 39–41. Q 11:43, 46 are somewhat younger, while 11:44, 47–48 and 52 reflect increasingly acrimonious relations between the synagogue and the community. The latest insertion was 11:49–51, which broke up the original connection of 11:47–48 with 11:52, and which broadened the polemic from groups within Judaism to "this generation" itself. From the perspective of the latest editing of the Q woes, Israel is guilty of rejecting God's envoys, and her leaders actively attempt to thwart the unfolding of the kingdom. The editing of the Q woes has transformed them from intramural disputes into full-blown oracles and threats of judgment.

Comparison with Marcan parallels highlights this. In Mark 12:38b–39 Jesus warns his followers not to emulate the scribes whom he accuses of ostentation, love of the best seats in the synagogue and at feasts and even theft. An element of threat appears: οὗτοι λήμψονται περισσότερον κρίμα (12:40b). But Mark goes no further; he does not widen the polemic to all of Israel, and his remarks on scribes must be tempered in light of an earlier statement that at least one scribe was "not far from the kingdom of God" (Mark 12:34).

The Composition of the Q Controversies

As has been shown, the smaller blocks which constitute Q 11:14–52 are themselves the products of rather complicated literary histories, including the secondary expansion of "core" sayings and the juxtaposition of originally independent units. Not only does the development of each unit reveal a marked theological tendency, but the assembling of the four blocks in Q reinforces this tendency: to censure and threaten "this generation" for its failure to comprehend the presence of the kingdom, and for opposing the preaching activity of God's messengers.

As noted above, the editor of Q has set the Beelzebul accusation and the request for a sign/sayings on light in parallel. In both cases, the

---

199. Thus Neirynck, "Study of Q," 66 n. 197, and the literature cited there.

interlocutors make statements which reveal their lack of perception of what, in Q's view, should be obvious: the presence of the kingdom in Jesus' activity. And in both cases, Jesus ends by turning to the offensive, threatening his opponents with "a worse state" and "darkness." Jewish exorcists (11:19) and responsive Gentiles (11:31–32) are summoned as examples of those who evidence the divine presence and thus serve as *Unheilszeichen* to Israel, intensifying and rendering even more public their unresponsiveness.

In the woes, Jesus maintains the offensive. As Lührmann points out,[200] the addition of 11:49–51 to the original set of woes broadens the attack from the Pharisees and scribes to all of Israel. The association of 11:39–52 with 11:14–26 and 11:29–36 is undoubtedly due to the fact that the woes have to do with failures of perception, in particular, the failure to perceive God's action through his envoys (11:47–48, 49–51, 52). And like 11:24–26 and 11:33–36, the woes end on a threatening note and prediction of a decisive judgment upon impenitent Israel.

It is worthwhile noting that very little if anything in this section of Q holds out to "this generation" an opportunity for repentance and rehabilitation. Quite the contrary. Everything suggests that in the community's view, Israel's rejection of the kingdom, Jesus and Sophia's envoys is final and that nothing remains but the inevitability of judgment and eschatological punishment. Lührmann rightly says, "A repentance by Israel is no longer anticipated in this preaching of judgment; there remains only the judgment."[201]

Q 12:39–40, 42–46, 49, 51–53, (54–56), 57–59

The threat of apocalyptic judgment recurs as the formative literary and theological motif in the cluster of Q sayings found in Q 12:39–40, 42–46, 49, 51–53, (54–56), 57–59.[202] This unit follows directly on another

200. Lührmann, *Redaktion*, 47–48.
201. Ibid., 47 [trans. by auth.].
202. Several critics hold that 12:(35) 36–38 also derives from Q: Bussmann, *Redenquelle*, 82 (with hesitation); Lührmann, *Redaktion*, 69 (uncertain); Manson, *Sayings*, 115–16; Polag, *Fragmenta*, 62; Schneider, *Parusiegleichnisse*, 30–37; Schürmann, "Reminiszenzen," 124; Streeter, *Four Gospels*, 279; Vassiliadis, "Nature and Extent," 70; Weiser, *Knechtsgleichnisse*, 166–77. There are no verbatim agreements between Matt 25:1–13 and Luke 12:35–38, and despite the common image of a wedding feast, the narrative logic is quite different. An argument for inclusion might be made on the grounds of coherence with other Q sayings: admonitions to watchfulness are found elsewhere in Q. But the description of the eschatological banquet as a wedding feast and that of the Son of Man *serving* at a banquet are unattested in Q.

large block of Q sayings (Q 12:22–34) but the differences in tone and basic motif are immediately apparent. Whereas 12:22–34 is hortatory in character and sapiential in its idiom and mode of argumentation, 12:39–59 is aggressive and threatening in tone, and marked by warnings of judgment. The former is presumably addressed to the community itself; the latter looks beyond the bounds of the community, threatening all with judgment.

This is not to say that there is no connection between 12:22b–34 and what follows. Q 12:39–40 is attached to 12:33–34 on the basis of two catchwords, κλέπτης (Matt 6:19, 20 // Luke 12:33, 39) and διορύσσω (Matt 6:19, 20 // Luke 12:39). The artificial nature of this association is evident not only in the radical difference in tone between the two sections, but also in the fact that 12:33–34 concerns acquiring treasure which a thief *cannot steal*, while 12:39 deals with measures to *prevent an actual theft*.

As many have noted, 12:39–40[203] is itself a secondary composition. The parable (12:39) has to do with the prevention of a theft through foresight and watchfulness. But 12:40 implies that the coming of the Son of Man cannot be foreseen nor its catastrophic results prevented. The *Gos. Thom.* contains the parable of the thief, without a parallel to the Son of Man saying in Q 12:40:

> Therefore I say to you, if the owner of a house knows that the thief is coming, he will begin his vigil before he comes and will not let him dig through into his house of his domain to carry away his goods. You, then, be on your guard against the world.[204]

Despite its slight anti-cosmic dualism Thomas interprets the parable in its more natural sense: knowledge and watchfulness "against the world" will prevent the loss of one's "goods" (presumably γνῶσις).

Elsewhere the parable of the thief's coming occurs in connection with the sudden coming of the Day of the Lord (1 Thess 5:2, 4; 2 Pet 3:10); only in Rev 3:3 and 16:15 is Christ himself the "thief." In view of the inconsistency in logic between v. 39 and v. 40 and the fact that the parable occurs elsewhere without the Son of Man saying, we must conclude that the Son of Man saying was a secondary interpretation of the parable.[205] It must be assumed, however, that 12:40 was already

---

203. Reconstructions: Schulz, *Spruchquelle*, 268; Schneider, *Parusiegleichnisse*, 20–23; Polag, *Fragmenta*, 62.

204. Saying 21b (trans. Lambdin, *NHLE*, 120).

205. Thus Jeremias, *Parables*, 48–49; C. Colpe, υἱὸς τοῦ ἀνθρώπου, TDNT 8 (1972) 451–52; Schürmann, "Menschensohn-Titel," 138; Schneider, *Parusiegleichnisse*, 22; Schenk,

attached to 12:39 prior to its association with the following materials since the basis of that association is undoubtedly the statement "You do not know in what hour (or day) the Son of Man (or Lord) is coming" (12:40, 46). It is worth noting too that the parousia is not regarded with the unmixed enthusiasm which seems to have been the case with the "Maranatha" exclamation of 1 Cor 16:22, Rev 22:20 and *Did.* 10:6. On the contrary, it is something to be described with ominous metaphors such as housebreaking, flood and cataclysm (17:26–30) and eagles gathering over carion (17:37). It is something fearful for Christians as well as for unbelievers and the impenitent.

The parable of the faithful and unfaithful servants (12:42–46)[206] gains its explicit connection with the coming Son of Man through its attachment to 12:39–40. The allusion to the delay of the parousia in 12:45 coupled with the use of the term δοῦλος suggests that it originally served as a warning for community leaders to be faithful stewards.[207] Nevertheless, what becomes important in the context of Q through its attachment to 12:40 is the *unexpected and sudden* coming of the parousia—in spite of its apparent delay—and the disastrous consequences which attend it. The evil servant's statement "My master is delayed" and his revelry (12:45) bespeak the reckless disregard of Q's proclamation of the unforeseen coming of the Son of Man[208]—an attitude which characterized the generation of Noah and Lot (Q 17:26–30) and continues to be the mark of "this generation." The Q composition 12:39–40, 42–46 takes on the character of a warning to be prepared in the face of the unforeseen and catastrophic coming of the Son of Man. The punishment of the unfaithful is nothing short of astonishing: καὶ διχοτομήσει[209] αὐτὸν, καὶ τὸ μέρος αὐτοῦ μετὰ τῶν ἀπίστων θήσει (12:46b). The final phrase, "and he will assign his portion with the unfaithful (ἀπίστων)"[210] signals not only a

---

Synopse, 94; Wolfgang Harnisch, *Eschatologische Existenz* (FRLANT 110; Göttingen: Vandenhoeck & Ruprecht, 1973) 84–85. Several regard 12:39–40 as a unity and as a secondary construction conceived "christologically from the beginning": Vielhauer, "Gottesreich," 73–74 n. 79; Strecker, *Weg,* 241; Hahn, *Titles,* 49 n. 107; Schulz, *Spruchquelle,* 268; Lührmann, *Redaktion,* 70.

206. Reconstruction: Schulz, *Spruchquelle,* 271–72; Weiser, *Knechtsgleichnisse,* 178–79, 203; Schneider, *Parusiegleichnisse,* 24–27; Polag, *Fragmenta,* 64.

207. For a full discussion of possible interpretations of the independent parable, see Weiser, *Knechtsgleichnisse,* 204–14.

208. Hoffmann (*Studien,* 48) comments, "The [remark about the] delay relates to the attitude of the one who did not assimilate the message of Q; it does not necessarily refer to internal doubts of the Q group" [trans. by auth.].

209. See above, p. 47 n. 17 for a discussion of this peculiar verb.

210. Matthew's ὑποκριτῶν is almost surely secondary. The word (Matt 13x // Mark 1x // Luke 3x) is a favorite Matthaean term—at least 7x redactional: 22:18; 23:15, 23, 25, 27, 29. Ἄπιστος on the other hand is not obviously Lucan and there is no reason for Luke to have altered "hypocrite" had it occurred in Q.

harsh judgment but utter exclusion from the possibility of salvation.[211] The similarity of this motif to that encountered elsewhere in Q is unmistakable (see, e.g., 3:8–9; 11:24–26, 34–36; 13:26–27, 28–29).

On the assumption that the Lucan sequence preserves that of Q,[212] the next Q pericope is to be found in 12:51–53. Several critics would include 12:49 as well.[213] There can be no doubt that this cluster was attached to the preceding two parables on the basis of the shared theme of the approaching eschaton. In the context, the "fire" of 12:49 can only refer to the coming judgment (as it does in 3:16–17).[214] The following saying, Q 12:51–53,[215] is connected to 12:49 on the basis of the common phrase ἦλθον βαλεῖν (ἐπὶ τὴν γῆν?).[216] Both the motif of war and that of division of families are traditional apocalyptic *topoi* used to signify the utter chaos and social disorder which will portend the eschatological inter-

211. Otto Betz ("The Dichotomized Servant and the End of Judas Iscariot," *RQ* 5 [1964] 43–58) draws attention to 1QS 2:16–17 as a parallel to Luke 12:46b: "May God set him apart for disaster! May he be cut off from the midst of the sons of light because he swerved from following God because of his idols and because of that which casts him into iniquity. May He place his lot in the midst of the eternally cursed."
212. Luke 12:47–48 relates directly to the redactional insertion in 12:41. Although a few entertain the possibility that 12:47–48 is from Q (Josef Schmid, *Matthäus und Lukas*, 340–41; Streeter, *Four Gospels*, 291; Manson, *Sayings*, 119; Polag, *Fragmenta*, 86 [uncertain]), there is little or nothing to recommend this except perhaps 12:48b, which resembles the proverbial assertions found elsewhere in Q. Weiser (*Knechtsgleichnisse*, 222–24) has shown that in vocabulary, 12:47–48 is closer to Lucan *Sondergut* than to Q.
213. Manson, *Sayings*, 120; H. Schürmann, "Protolukanische Spracheigentümlichkeiten?" *Traditionsgeschichtliche Untersuchungen* (Düsseldorf: Patmos, 1968) 213; Josef Schmid, *Matthäus und Lukas*, 276–77; and Polag, *Fragmenta*, 64 include vv. 49–50. Most of the evidence, however, supports only the inclusion of 12:49. Arens (ΗΛΘΟΝ, 64–65) notes that 12:49 contains nothing specifically Lucan. Luke 12:50, however, is probably redactional, influenced by Mark 10:38, which Luke does not take over in his chap. 18. Arens (ΗΛΘΟΝ, 65–66) notes the use of βάπτισμα + βαπτισθῆναι (cf. Luke 7:29 [*Sond*]; Acts 19:4); the use of ἔχω + infinitive (Luke 7:40, 42; 12:4, 50; 14:14; Acts 4:14; 23:17, 18, 19; 25:26; 29:19; see Jeremias, *Sprache*, 223, 169); συνέχω (Matt 1 /Mark - /Luke, at least 3x red; 3x *Sond* or red, Acts 3x). Luke 12:50 functions analogously to Luke 17:25, also redactional, to alert the reader to the necessity of Jesus' suffering. Moreover, τελέω is used in Luke-Acts only to refer to the completion of the divine plan (2:39; 12:50; 18:31; 22:37; Acts 13:29), which is, of course, a distinctively Lucan theme.
214. Thus Arens, ΗΛΘΟΝ, 79; E. Grässer, *Das Problem der Parusieverzögerung* (BZNW 22; Berlin: Walter de Gruyter, 1977³) 190–91; Jeremias, *Parables*, 164; F. Lang, πῦρ, TDNT 6 (1968) 944; G. Delling, "Βάπτισμα βαπτισθῆναι, Studien zum Neuen Testament und zum hellenistischen Judentum (Göttingen: Vandenhoeck & Ruprecht, 1970) 247–50. There is no warrant to interpret "fire" as the Spirit (thus Grundmann, *Lukas*, 270; E. E. Ellis, *The Gospel of Luke* [London: Oliphants, 1974²] 182; Polag, *Christologie*, 164).
215. Reconstruction: Schulz, *Spruchquelle*, 258–60; Polag, *Fragmenta*, 64. There is general agreement among those cited by Polag and Schulz that Luke's παρεγενόμην δοῦναι is secondary (see Jeremias, *Sprache*, 152–53, for statistics) and that Luke replaced μάχαιραν with διαμερισμόν (Schulz, *Spruchquelle*, 258 n. 562).
216. See Schürmann, "Spracheigentümlichkeiten," 213: ἦλθον βαλεῖν is original in Matt 10:34 diff Luke 12:51, and Q 12:49, which contains the same locution, was associated with 12:51–53 by catchword composition prior to Lucan redaction (which replaced the phrase in 12:51).

vention of God.[217] In the context of Q, 12:51–53 may be intended in the general sense that is encountered in apocalyptic literature. Or, it might have been understood concretely with reference to the rejection and violence experienced by members of the community itself.[218] In this case, it would be most closely related to sayings such as Matt 11:12–13.

The association of 12:49, 51–53 with the preceding parables serves to emphasize the motif of impending judgment introduced in 12:46b. Since the divisions described in vv. 51–53 are presumably part of the contemporary experience of the Q group, these sayings serve to qualify the present time as eschatological and thus to intensify the call to preparedness and faithfulness. Despite the tacit admission of the delay of the parousia, the effect of the Q composition is to insinuate that the time of the parousia is near. There is no time to lose!

This impression is further reinforced by 12:54–56, provided that it can be ascribed to Q.[219] Even though it does not spell out a specific apocalyptic timetable, this warning—which combines a Greek weather proverb[220] with an admonition which occurs independently in the *Gos. Thom.* 91—implies that the signs of the end are apparent to all, and that only blindness stands in the way of an appropriate response to the impending catastrophe. In this respect 12:54–56 resembles 3:7–9, which likewise presupposes the nearness of the end and chastises the impenitent for their lack of response to what, in the mind of the speaker, are the obvious signs of the end.

A final warning is recorded in 12:57–59.[221] Zeller observes that 12:58 //

217. Wars: see Isa 34:5; 66:16; 1 *Enoch* 63:11; 91:12; 100:1–2; 2 *Apoc. Bar.* 70:6. Division of families: 1 *Enoch* 99:5; 100:1–2; *Jub.* 23:16, 19; 2 *Apoc. Bar.* 70:6; Mark 13:12. Otto Betz ("Jesu Heiliger Krieg," *NovT* 2 [1958] 129–30) implausibly suggests that the saying borrows the motif associated with "holy war" and envisages a band of disciples who value God's word and covenant more highly than family.

218. Thus Hoffmann, *Studien*, 72–73.

219. The Matthaean parallel, 16:2–3, is attended by textual difficulties. A parallel to Luke 12:54–56 is attested in C D W Θ λ lat; omit: B ℵ V X Y Γ φ sy^{c.s} sa bo^{Pt}. Several regard 12:54–56 // Matt 16:2–3 as a Q text: Manson, *Sayings*, 121; Polag, *Fragmenta*, 66; Schürmann, "Reminiszenzen," 116; Vassiliadis, "Nature and Extent," 70; Steinhauser, *Doppelbildworte*, 252 (apparently); Edwards, *Theology of Q*, 128. Schürmann ("Reminiszenzen," 116) argues that κρίνετε in 12:57 is a reminiscence of διακρίνειν in Matt 16:3 (diff Luke 12:56: δοκιμάζειν) and on this basis ascribes 12:54–56 to Q. For a reconstruction and tradition-history, see Klein, "Die Prüfung"; Steinhauser, *Doppelbildworte*, 251–58; Polag, *Fragmenta*, 66.

220. See C. E. Carlston, "Proverbs, Maxims and the Historical Jesus," *JBL* 99 (1980) 100.

221. Reconstruction: Schulz, *Spruchquelle*, 421–22; Zeller, *Weisheitliche Mahnsprüche*, 64; Polag, *Fragmenta*, 66. The only disagreement is whether Matthew's ἴσθι εὐνοῶν τῷ ἀντιδίκῳ σου ταχύ (Schulz, Polag) or Luke's δὸς ἐργασίαν ἀπηλλάχθαι (ἀπὸ τοῦ ἀντιδίκου σου) (Zeller) is original. Otherwise, all three reconstruct the next lines following

Matt 6:25 is a sapiential admonition consisting of an imperative followed by a final clause.[222] Similar admonitions to settle speedily with one's creditors and to avoid judicial proceedings are found in Prov 6:1–5 and 25:7b–8, 9–10 and in other sapiential works.[223] But the concluding phrase (12:59) is more typical of a prophetic judgment statement. The formula λέγω ὑμῖν (σοί)· οὐ μὴ ... ἕως/μέχρις appears in predominantly prophetic and apocalyptic declarations (Mark 9:1; 13:30; 14:25; Matt 5:18; Luke 13:35) while λέγω ὑμῖν/σοί very frequently serves as an asseverative introducing solemn statement concerning punishment, reward and judgment.[224] Since 12:59 cannot be considered to have been an originally independent prophetic word (in view of ἐκεῖθεν), it must be supposed that an original sapiential admonition to settle quickly with creditors was transformed into a prophetic threat. Further, it must be assumed that this transformation was already complete when 12:57–58, 59 was attached to this section of Q, since the connection was evidently made on the basis of the theme of judgment and punishment which runs through 12:39–56.

Although it consists of a variety of originally independent sayings, some of which have already undergone secondary growth, Q 12:39–59 is unified by the motifs of the nearness and unexpectedness of the parousia and of judgment. Secondarily attached to Q 12:33–34 on the basis of catchwords, this cluster of Q parables and judgment sayings stresses the catastrophic nature of the parousia and the dire consequences which await the unfaithful, the intransigent and the blind. In spite of the apparent acknowledgment of the delay of the parousia, Q repeatedly implies that there is little time left, since the signs of the end are already in evidence.

This cluster of sayings reveals some skillful composition. The theme of the unforeseen nature of the judgment occurs programmatically in 12:39–40. Q 12:42–46 continues this motif and paints the judgment in

---

Matthew. Luke 12:57 is usually regarded as a redactional transition; see Schulz, *Spruchquelle,* 421, and literature cited in n. 122; Zeller, *Mahnsprüche,* 64; Jeremias, *Sprache,* 224 (who notes that δὲ καί and κρίνετε, meaning "discern, decide," are Lucan).

222. Zeller, *Mahnsprüche,* 65.

223. See also the Counsels of Wisdom, lines 30–32: "But if it is really your own quarrel, extinguish the flame; for a quarrel is a neglect of what is right" (trans. Pfeiffer, *ANET*[3] 426) and Ankhsheshonq 9.10: "Do not quarrel over a matter in which you are wrong" (trans. Lichtheim, *Literature III,* 166). Sirach transposes the idea to the plane of divine judgment: "Before judgment, examine yourself and in the hour of visitation you will find forgiveness" (Sir 18:20).

224. Mark 3:28; 9:41; 10:29; 14:9; Matt 5:22; 6:2, 5, 16, 21, 31; 8:11; 11:22, 24; 12:36; 21:43; 23:36 (= Luke 11:51); 24:47; 26:64; Luke 10:12; 12:8; 12:37; 19:26; 23:43. See Berger, *Amen-Worte,* 31.

strikingly ominous tones (12:46). Then the compiler incorporates two sayings expressing Q's characteristic notion that the signs of the end are already evident to all who wish to see (12:51–52, 54–56; cf. 3:7–9; 11:20; 11:30, 31–32). This adds a note of urgency to the concluding apocalyptic warning and exhortation to make amends quickly before the judgment comes (12:57–59).

THE LOGIA APOCALYPSE,
Q 17:23, 24, 26–30, 34–35, 37

Content, Extent and Order of the Logia Apocalypse

The coming of the Son of Man is the focus of the final cluster of Q sayings, a collection which Conzelmann aptly terms "the logia apocalypse."[225] Although Matthew and Luke agree in general in the order of the sayings (see the synopsis below), reconstruction is complicated by the fact that Matthew inserts Q into the Marcan apocalypse, conflating some texts. Luke, for his part, introduces special material and adds several editorial touches.

Mark		Matt		Luke	Mark
13:14–20	=	24:15–22			
13:21–23	=	24:23–25			
				17:20a (red)[226]	
				17:20b–21 (Sond?)	
		24:26	Q	17:23	
		24:27	Q	17:24	
13:24–27	=	24:29–31			
13:28–32	=	24:32–36			
				17:25 (red)	
		24:37–39	Q	17:26–27	
		—	(Q)	17:28–30	
				17:31 =	13:15–16
				17:32 (red)	
		10:39	(Q)	17:33	
		24:40–41	Q	17:34–35	
				17:37a (red)	
		24:28	Q	17:37b	

225. H. Conzelmann, *An Outline of the Theology of the New Testament* (trans. John Bowden; London: SCM Press, 1969) 135.

226. It is widely agreed that Luke 17:20a is Lucan. Luke frequently introduces statements with a question: 1:34; 3:10, 12, 15; 10:26; 12:41, 51, 57; 13:23; 20:13; 24:5; Acts 1:6; 2:6, 37; 8:30, 34; 9:5; 10:4; 16:30; 19:3. The use of "Pharisees" as dialogue partners of Jesus is also often redactional: 5:17, 21; 6:7; 7:36; 13:31; 14:1; 15:2. See further Schnackenburg, "Abschnitt," 227; Geiger, *Endzeitreden*, 29–30; Zmijewski, *Eschatologiereden*, 360–61.

Whether 17:20b–21 should be ascribed to Q is doubtful. Schnackenburg argues for its inclusion,[227] but the lack of a Matthaean parallel, the
change of interlocutors in v. 22 and the obviously Lucan interest in
mitigating the *Naherwartung* of 17:23–37[228] cast this into doubt. Most
critics prefer to consider 17:20b–21 as *Sondergut* which Luke introduced
here.[229] Linguistic features, as well as the presence of the Lucan agenda
of explaining that the contemporaries of Jesus will not witness the
parousia identify Luke 17:22 as a Lucan addition.[230]

According to Lührmann the Q apocalypse began with 17:24,[231] but it
seems likely that 17:23 // Matt 24:26 also derives from Q. This conclusion is suggested by the presence of a doublet in Matthew: Matt 24:23
derives from Mark 13:21, but Matthew also offers a second version of the
saying in 24:26. This probably indicates a Q *Vorlage*.[232] Disagreements
between Luke 17:23 and Matt 24:26 make reconstruction difficult; all
that can be said with assurance is that the saying contained ἐὰν εἴπωσιν
or καὶ ἐροῦσιν + ὑμῖν, ἰδού (twice) introducing the false opinion, and a
double prohibition of response.

Strong Matthew-Luke agreements show that Luke 17:24 // Matt 24:27
followed in Q.[233] There is disagreement about what came next. That
Luke 17:25 is redactional is widely acknowledged.[234] But does this mean

227. Schnackenburg ("Abschnitt," 215, 219) defends the original connection of
17:20b–21 with 17:23–37 on the following grounds: (1) vv. 21a, 23a appear to be
connected by an "early catchword composition" (viz., ἰδοὺ ὧδε ἤ ἐκεῖ/ἰδοὺ ἐκεῖ ἤ ἰδοὺ
ὧδε); (2) the affinity of 17:20b–21 with the following verses allows the possibility that
the connection goes back to Q and that Matthew omitted 17:20b–21; (3) nothing
militates against the juxtaposing of a kingdom saying with a Son of Man saying in Q,
even though this connection may not have belonged to earlier strata of tradition and (4)
the separation of the two units (17:20b–21, 23–37) is due to redaction and does not rule
out an earlier association.
228. Cf. similar Lucan redactional interventions at Luke 13:23; 19:11; 21:7; Acts 1:7.
229. Some regard 17:20b–21 as a Lucan creation: A. Strobel, "In dieser Nacht (Luk
17,34)," ZTK 58 (1961) 16–29, esp. 26; Geiger, *Endzeitreden*, 45–50; Schürmann, "Basileia-
Verkündigung," 124. Several non-Lucan features (on which see Jeremias, *Sprache*, 266)
and the presence of parallels in *Gos. Thom.* (3, 51, 113) suggest that the saying may be
pre-Lucan. Thus Perrin, *Rediscovering*, 68–69; Bultmann, *Tradition*, 25 [24]; Manson,
Sayings, 303–4; Zmijewski, *Eschatologiereden*, 389–90; Marshall, *Luke*, 653.
230. On the linguistic features see Jeremias, *Sprache*, 266–67; Schulz, *Spruchquelle*, 278
n. 90; Zmijewski, *Eschatologiereden*, 398–403, 417–19.
231. Lührmann, *Redaktion*, 71–72.
232. Thus Schnackenburg, "Abschnitt," 220; Lambrecht, *Redaktion*, 100–101; Laufen,
Doppelüberlieferung, 361; Schulz, *Spruchquelle*, 278; Zmijewski, *Eschatologiereden*, 403;
Schürmann, "Menschensohn-Titel," 139.
233. Reconstruction: Schulz, *Spruchquelle*, 279; Laufen, *Doppelüberlieferung*, 370;
Polag, *Fragmenta*, 76; Zmijewski, *Eschatologiereden*, 412–14.
234. Luke 17:25 resembles the redactional phrase δεῖ γὰρ ταῦτα γενέσθαι πρῶτον in
21:7 (diff Mark 13:7). Δεῖ is very frequent in Luke-Acts: 2:49; 4:43; 9:22; 12:12; 13:14, 16,
33; 15:32; 18:1; 19:5; 22:7; 26:37, 44; Acts 1:16, 21; 3:21; 4:12; 5:29; 9:6, 16; 14:22; 15:15,

that in Q, as in Luke, the second correlative (17:26–27) followed the first (17:24), or was the "eagle saying" (17:37b) attached to the "lightning saying" (17:24) as it is now in Matthew? Luke's introduction of the eagle saying (17:37a) is probably redactional.[235] But this in itself does not prove that Luke's location of the saying is also secondary. Tödt argues that Luke moved the saying to avoid the offensive connotations which it might have had when juxtaposed with the Son of Man saying in 17:24, and replaced it with 17:25.[236] Indeed, it may be argued that the redactional verse 17:25, with its reference to the suffering Son of Man, is a "reminiscence" of 17:37b and its reference to the "corpse." Lucan redaction has schematized the questions presented in this chapter: 17:20b–21 answers the question πότε; (17:20a), 17:23–25 answers the implicit question πῶς and 17:37b answers the question ποῦ.[237] We shall proceed on the assumption that Matthew better represents the order of Q at this point.[238]

At this point Matthew interpolates Marcan and special material.[239] Then he returns to Q, which he reproduces in the same order as Luke: Matt 24:37–39, 40–41 // Luke 17:26–30, 34–35. The two evangelists concur in having two correlatives but disagree in the wording: both of Matthew's correlatives deal with Noah while Luke presents parallel

---

etc. In 17:25 Luke adapted and interpolated the passion prediction, thus adapting chap. 17 to the context of his travel narrative, which emphasizes the approaching passion of Jesus.

235. For the use of introductory questions redactionally, see above, n. 226. "Lord" is frequently redactional in Luke: 5:8, 12; 9:54, 61; 10:17, 40; 11:1; 12:41; 13:23; 18:41; 19:8; 22:33, 38, 49. The use of the historic present, however, is somewhat unusual in view of Luke's tendency to eliminate it (Cadbury, *Style*, 158–59 [but Acts has 18 instances of the historic present with verbs of speaking]). The use of the dative rather than πρὸς after a verb of speaking is uncommon in Luke (Cadbury, *Style*, 203).

236. Tödt, *Son of Man*, 48; Schulz, *Spruchquelle*, 280.

237. Zmijewski (*Eschatologiereden*, 515–16) interprets the Lucan answer as a statement of the universality of separation and judgment: wherever there are people, there will be judgment. Similarly Marshall, *Luke*, 669. For other interpretations, see Zmijewski, *Eschatologiereden*, 513–15.

238. Thus, in addition to Tödt, Harnack, *Sayings of Jesus*, 105 [74]; Lührmann, *Redaktion*, 72; Meyer, "Community," 51; Marshall, *Luke*, 668–69; Laufen, *Doppelüberlieferung*, 370; Schulz, *Spruchquelle*, 278, 280; Zmijewski, *Eschatologiereden*, 506–10; Polag, *Fragmenta*, 67; Schenk, *Synopse*, 120. In favor of Lucan order: Josef Schmid (*Matthäus und Lukas*, 336) argues that Matthew's order is more difficult (but does not this suggest a *Lucan* transposition?); Vincent Taylor ("Original Order," 113) inclines towards Lucan order on the grounds of the "roughness of Luke's enigmatic form." See also Steinhauser, *Doppelbildworte*, 302; Schnackenburg, "Abschnitt," 225–26; Schürmann, "Menschensohn-Titel," 139; Bussmann, *Redenquelle*, 94; Manson, *Sayings*, 147.

239. On Matthew's sources in 24:29–31, see my article "Didache 16,6–8 and Special Matthaean Tradition," *ZNW* 70 (1979) 54–67.

correlatives, the first concerning Noah and the second, Lot. It is a matter of debate whether Matthew abbreviated Q or whether Luke expanded it. As Cadbury notes,[240] Luke tends to avoid, not create, the kind of parallelism evident in Luke 17:26–30. This would militate against 17:28–30 being Lucan. Luke's two correlatives make the point that the parousia will take many by surprise. But Luke's redactional interest lies in a parenetic application: attachment to possessions is pointless and indeed dangerous since the judgment will be sudden and unheralded. Geiger points out that it is difficult to maintain that 17:28–30 is Lucan since his interest in the following (redactional) verses focuses not upon Lot, but upon his wife.[241] Finally, Luke's interpolation of Mark 13:15–16 (Luke 17:31) and his interpretation of it with respect to Lot's wife was certainly not prompted by the Noah correlative. It could, however, have been occasioned by a reference to Gen 19 in his source.[242]

If all or part of 17:28–30 is pre-Lucan, how can the Matthaean omission be explained? Bultmann thinks it very unlikely that Matthew would have omitted the Lot correlative and accordingly posits a pre-Lucan recension of Q which Matthew did not know.[243] Others aver that 17:28–30 belonged to Q but was dropped by Matthew.[244] But is such a thesis likely? Schnackenburg's explanation that Matthew omitted the verses when he separated the lightning saying from the Noah correlative is not very compelling.[245] Matthew's editorial intention may provide some clues, however. Matthew alters the focus of the correlatives: in Q the list of mundane activities is at the center of the saying, and the point, accordingly, is that the parousia will occur in the midst of the ordinary, unheralded by spectacular signs. For Matthew the essential point is that the time of the end is unknown. He positions the correlatives immediately after 24:36 (περὶ δὲ τῆς ἡμέρας . . . οὐδεὶς οἶδεν), inserts καὶ οὐκ

---

240. Cadbury, *Style*, 85–88.
241. Geiger, *Endzeitreden*, 93.
242. Zmijewski (*Eschatologiereden*, 455) considers the opposite solution: that Luke created vv. 28–30 as an introduction for vv. 31–33. But this does not account for the differing foci of the two pericopae.
243. Bultmann, *Tradition*, 117 [123]; also Tödt, *Son of Man*, 49, 51; Vielhauer, "Gottesreich," 74; Lührmann, *Redaktion*, 74, 82–83; Steinhauser, *Doppelbildworte*, 210; Geiger, *Endzeitreden*, 140.
244. Manson, *Sayings*, 143; Josef Schmid, *Matthäus und Lukas*, 338–39; Schnackenburg, "Abschnitt," 223; Rigaux, "La petite apocalypse," 407–38, esp. 422; Schürmann, "Menschensohn-Titel," 139; Marshall, *Luke*, 662; Polag, *Fragmenta*, 78; Schenk, *Synopse*, 122.
245. Schnackenburg, "Abschnitt," 223; similarly Rigaux, "La petite apocalypse," 422.

ἔγνωσαν ἕως into v. 39 and then continues with admonitions to watchfulness (24:42, 43–44). He has also used the simple correlative in 24:37 as a preface for the grammatically unwieldy correlative in 24:38–39. Matthew's point is made sufficiently well with the example of the flood generation; to repeat an equally unwieldy Lot correlative (with another preface) would only detract from his main point. Thus he omitted the Lot story as superfluous. There is, then, a possibility that a Lot correlative existed in Q alongside the Noah correlative and that Matthew omitted it.[246]

As noted above, Luke inserted a saying from Mark (13:15–16 // Luke 17:31) and interpreted it in relation to Lot's wife (17:32).[247] The following saying (17:33 // Matt 10:39), which is probably derived from Q,[248] is reproduced by Matthew in a completely different context along with two discipleship sayings (10:37–38). This is one of the few instances in which the Matthaean location of a Q saying is to be given priority.

The Lucan Redaction of Q 17:33

It has long been argued that Luke himself is responsible for the placement of 17:33, and that Matt 10:39 provides the original Q setting. This thesis is supported by several considerations. The immediate context (17:31–32) is clearly a redactional insertion into Q. Schnackenburg, admitting this, nevertheless holds that 17:33 was originally attached to 17:29 by the catchwords ἀπολέσει/

---

246. Lührmann (*Redaktion*, 75–83) has shown that there existed an established tradition which associated the flood generation with the contemporaries of Lot, and used both as examples of divine punishment of the wicked. Lührmann himself argues that this tradition influenced a pre-Lucan expansion of Q, but this tradition could just as easily have influenced Q itself.

247. See Zmijewski, *Eschatologiereden*, 469–71, 478. Lambrecht ("Logia-Quellen, " 342–46) offers the implausible hypothesis that Luke 17:31–32 belonged to Q. This can scarcely be justified. The Matt-Luke agreements against Mark in Matt 24:17–18 // Luke 17:31 are insignificant: the use of a plural object for ἆραι, the omission of μηδὲ εἰσελθάτω, and ὁ ἐν τῷ ἀγρῷ instead of ὁ εἰς τὸν ἀγρόν. These do not justify positing a Q *Vorlage*.

248. Zmijewski (*Eschatologiereden*, 479–82) and Neirynck ("Study of Q," 49–51) argue that Luke 17:33 is a Lucan rewriting of Mark 8:35. Luke 17:33 agrees with Mark and against Matt 10:39 in the use of ὃς ἐάν (Matt: ὁ + participle) and ζητήσῃ/θέλῃ τὴν ψυχὴν αὐτοῦ + infinitive (Matt: ὁ εὑρὼν τὴν ψυχὴν αὐτοῦ). On the other hand, Luke 17:33 agrees with Matt 10:39 by introducing the apodosis with καί [A D R W Θ 063 f¹ sy sa; NA²⁵; "δέ" 𝔭²⁵ ℵ B L Ψ f¹³ 892; NA²⁶]. Even though some assimilation to Mark 8:35 has occurred (as it also has in Matt 10:39), it is to be noted that Luke usually avoids doublets. Of the 15 doublets examined by Schürmann ("Dubletten," esp. 276) only one (21:18) is a real repetition of a Q saying (12:7); two appear to involve overlaps in *Sondergut*, or between *Sondergut* and Mark (Luke 18:14 // 14:11; Luke 19:10 // 5:32 // Mark 2:17). The remaining 12 cases (11:43 // 20:46 // Mark 12:38–39; Luke 12:11–12 // 21:14–15 // Mark 13:11 and those noted by Schürmann, "Dubletten," 275–76, under §4) involve Mark // Q overlap. This, in all likelihood, is the case with 17:33 // Matt 10:39 // Luke 9:24 // Mark 8:35 // Matt 16:25.

ἀπώλεσεν.[249] However, if 17:33 were juxtaposed directly with the Lot correlative, it would suggest that those who tried to save themselves—Lot and his family—would lose their lives! This makes nonsense of the message of the Q apocalypse. Only the Lucan redaction of Luke 17:31, which adds καὶ τὰ σκεύη αὐτοῦ ἐν τῇ οἰκίᾳ to Mark 13:15–16,[250] makes sense of 17:33 in this context: whoever is intent on acquiring and keeping worldly goods will perish at the parousia. Luke evidently interprets the backward glance of Lot's wife as a desire for her possessions. The only conclusion which may be drawn from these observations is that 17:33 depends for its intelligibility upon the Lucan redaction of Mark 13:15–16 and his addition of 17:32. This implies that 17:33 was also imported into the Q apocalypse by Luke. Schürmann concurs, pointing out that τὴν ψυχὴν ἑαυτοῦ (added by Luke to 14:26 diff Matt 10:37) may have been influenced by the occurrence of τὴν ψυχὴν αὐτοῦ (17:33 = Matt 10:39) in its original Q position, i.e., after Luke 14:27 // Matt 10:38.[251] The obviously redactional setting of Luke 17:33 and the "reminiscence" of the Q saying in Luke 14:26 suggests that Matthew's presentation of the three discipleship sayings (10:37, 38, 39) corresponds to that of Q.[252]

As the Synoptic comparison shows, the "logia apocalypse" closed with the double metaphor of the two on a bed (Luke) or in a field (Matt) and the two women milling.[253]

The Construction of the Q Apocalypse

The Q apocalypse comprised several originally independent sayings: Q 17:23, 24, 37b, 26–27, (28–30), 34–35.

1. Q 17:23. Although its exact formulation is unclear, the initial saying (Matt 24:26 // Luke 17:23) apparently contained no mention of false messiahs (cf. Mark 13:21). Nevertheless, it must have originated as a warning against messianic pretenders. The fact that the following saying concerns the Son of Man does not alter this.[254] As Vielhauer observes, "Son of Man pretenders" are nowhere attested and are, indeed, incon-

---

249. Schnackenburg, "Abschnitt," 224; thus Geiger, *Endzeitreden*, 124.

250. This is clearly a Lucan addition to Mark 13:15 and expresses the Lucan disdain of wealth and possessions as a hindrance to entry into the kingdom. See 3:10–14; 6:20 (Q), 24; 12:13–15 (Q?), 16–21 (Q?), 33(Q); 16:13 (Q), 14–15, 19–31.

251. Schürmann, *Lukasevangelium* 1:544.

252. Thus Lührmann, *Redaktion*, 74–75; Schulz, *Spruchquelle*, 278; Meyer, "Community," 52 n. 1; Laufen, *Doppelüberlieferung*, 319–20; Lambrecht, "Q-Influence," 294–95; Schenk, *Synopse*, 110–11; Marshall, *Luke*, 664. Against this: Schnackenburg, "Abschnitt," 224–25; Josef Schmid, *Matthäus und Lukas*, 335 n. 2; Bussmann, *Redenquelle*, 93; Polag, *Fragmenta*, 78; Geiger, *Endzeitreden*, 123–25.

253. Reconstructions: Schulz, *Spruchquelle*, 280–81; Steinhauser, *Doppelbildworte*, 198–205; Zmijewski, *Eschatologiereden*, 500–501; Polag, *Fragmenta*, 78.

254. Bultmann (*Tradition*, 122 [128]) regards 17:23–24 as a unity, as authentic and as a saying about the Son of Man.

ceivable.[255] The pretenders are earthly figures who appear "here or there" (Luke), or "in the wilderness, or in the inner rooms" (Matt). The fact that 17:23 originates in the polemic against false messiahs, while 17:24 reflects the realm of Son of Man speculations, indicates that 17:23 was not always found alongside 17:24. The absence of a counterpart for 17:24 in the Marcan version of the saying points to the same conclusion.

2. Q 17:24, 26–27, 28–30. Included in the logia apocalypse are three of Q's four "prophetic correlatives." As noted above, the *form* is not unique to Q.[256] Some have regarded these Son of Man sayings as dominical; others treat them as secondary creations.[257] In the case of Q 11:30, there is good reason to suppose that it was deliberately created as an *Interpretament* for 11:29.[258] With Q 17:24 the case is not so clear cut, since 17:24 does not obviously build on the vocabulary of 17:23. There is, moreover, an intriguing parallel to 17:24 found at Qumran. A fragmentary Daniel apocryphon (4QpsDan A^a [= 4Q 246]) describes the acclamation of a figure as "Son of God" and "Son of the Most High":

> (col. i) [But your son] shall be great upon the earth. [O King! All (men) shall] make [peace] and all shall serve [him. He shall be called the son of] the [G]reat [God], and by his name shall he be named.
> (col. ii) He shall be hailed (as) the son of God, and they shall call him Son of the Most High. As comets (flash) to the sight, so shall be their kingdom. (For some) year[s] they shall rule upon the earth and shall trample everything (under foot); people shall trample upon people, city upon ci[t]y, (*vacat*) until there arises the people of God, and everyone rests from the sword.[259]

Because of the damaged state of the text it is unclear whether the "son of God" is a Gentile pretender to that title and that, consequently, the kingdom is to be short-lived as a comet, or whether the figure is an heir to the Davidic throne and his kingdom appears suddenly and unexpectedly.[260] The fact that the correlative appears in an eschatological context raises the possibility that Q 17:24 was not a Christian creation *ex nihilo*, but was an adaptation of a current apocalyptic slogan. In Q it

255. Vielhauer, "Gottesreich," 75.
256. See above nn. 126, 127.
257. Those who regard the (coming) Son of Man sayings as authentic attribute the correlative to Jesus: e.g., Bultmann, *Tradition*, 122 [128]; Tödt, *Son of Man*, 48–54; Hahn, *Titles*, 31–32; Marshall, *Luke*, 660–63; Zmijewski, *Eschatologiereden*, 451–52. Against this: Vielhauer, "Gottesreich," 74–75; Edwards, *Sign of Jonah*, 55; Lührmann, *Redaktion*, 72–75; Schulz, *Spruchquelle*, 282–83; Perrin, *Rediscovering*, 191–97 and others.
258. See above, pp. 129–130.
259. Restoration and trans. by Fitzmyer, *Wandering Aramean*, 92–93.
260. For a discussion of this text see ibid.

serves to provide a positive counterpart for 17:23 in terms of Son of Man eschatology: do not attend to earthly messianic figures; the Son of Man will come as a heavenly figure!

No clear parallels for the other two correlatives can be found. Q 17:26–27 and Q 17:28–30 are so similar to each other in structure that they can only have been conceived together or, alternatively, one created on the pattern of the other. Since they are not obviously patterned on 17:24, and since they do not continue the theme of 17:24 ("where will the parousia be?"), it is possible that the two existed independently as prophetic sayings which castigated the audience for its obliviousness and unpreparedness in the face of the impending disaster.

3. Q 17:37b. The correlative in 17:24 is concluded by the cryptic saying ὅπου τὸ πτῶμα, ἐκεῖ συναχθήσονται οἱ ἀετοί.[261] Bultmann treats it as a profane proverb which was taken into the Synoptic tradition and interpreted eschatologically.[262] Jülicher, comparing it with Wis 6:12 ([σοφία] εὐχερῶς θεωρεῖται ὑπὸ τῶν ἀγαπώντων αὐτήν) argued that it was an undoubtedly authentic saying of Jesus which expressed the "certainty of entering into the kingdom of heaven—without struggle and violence . . ."[263] For Jeremias the saying was a threat, analogous to Luke 12:54–56: the signs of the times are visible, the vultures circle, the catastrophe is imminent.[264]

A striking parallel for Q 17:37b—perhaps even its source—is found in Job 39:27–30 LXX:

> Is it at your command that the eagle (ἀετός) mounts up
> and sitting upon its nest the vulture (γύψ) spends its time
> upon prominent crags and in hidden places?
> From there he seeks for food,
> from a distance his eyes survey,
> his nestlings are stained with blood,
> and wherever there are dead, they are found straightaway
> (οὗ δ' ἂν ὦσι τεθνεῶτες, παραχρῆμα εὑρίσκονται).

Whether Q 17:37 is an authentic saying, threatening or otherwise, is impossible to say; Jesus may well have adapted or repeated wisdom

261. Reconstructions: Schulz, *Spruchquelle*, 280–81; Steinhauser, *Doppelbildworte*, 299–300; Zmijewski, *Eschatologiereden*, 510; Polag, *Fragmenta*, 76. All agree on this form as that of Q.

262. Bultmann, *Tradition*, 99 [103]; similarly Schulz, *Spruchquelle*, 282; Manson, *Sayings*, 147.

263. Jülicher, *Gleichnisreden* 2:137 [trans. by auth.].

264. Jeremias, *Parables*, 162; similarly Steinhauser, *Doppelbildworte*, 304–5; Marshall, *Luke*, 669.

sayings such as Job 39:30. Its "original" function is impossible to recover because we have no way of establishing its original interpretive context (if indeed proverbs can be said to have a single context!). All that can reasonably be discussed is the proverb as it occurs in its present literary context. In Q, as in Job, the saying evokes the keen sight and swiftness with which the eagle locates its prey (living or dead) and applies this metaphor to the parousia.[265] Its ominous tone is in keeping with the threatening and dark metaphors which surround it.

4. Q 17:34–35. The apocalypse closes with an apocalyptic threat in the form of a double metaphor (Q 17:34–35). Since the Matthaean τότε is undoubtedly redactional, Luke's λέγω ὑμῖν may reproduce the original introduction of the Q saying.[266] Whether 17:34–35 ever existed as an independent judgment saying is a matter of dispute. Schulz appears to deny this, but does not justify his position further.[267] But if 17:34–35 was specifically formulated as a continuation of the preceding correlative, it is curious that its meaning is not clearer. Dodd observes, "It is not even clear whether the one taken or the one left has the better lot."[268] This suggests that the double saying was not deliberately composed to explain Q 17:26–27, 28–30, but is instead an originally independent saying and that it now functions as commentary word. The same conclusion is suggested by the presence of the logion in *Gos. Thom.* 61 where it appears without any connection to apocalyptic sayings.[269] The original significance of the saying is disputed. Dodd thought that it referred to

---

265. Acting on the assumption that eagles do not take carrion, Jeremias (*Parables*, 162 n. 46) argues that a mistranslation is present here: *nešer/nišra* was translated as ἀετός rather than γύψ, "vulture," because of a confusion over the meaning of the Semitic word. This thesis is unconvincing for two reasons: (*a*) *Nešer* in the MT is always translated by ἀετός and never by γύψ. Moreover, ἀετός is expressly distinguished from γύψ in Lev 11:14 and Deut 14:12–14. (*b*) More importantly, eagles *do* take carrion, as Aristotle (*Historia animalium* 9.32 [618B-19A]) and Pliny (*Natural History* 10.3) noted in regard to the περκνόπτερος (= tawny eagle?) or "mountain stork." The same, incidentally, is suggested by Job 39:30 and confirmed by modern observation. Eagles are opportunists and systematically steal prey from ospreys and vultures. This applies to *Aquila chrysastos* (golden eagle) and especially to *Aquila heliaca* (imperial eagle), *A. rapax* (tawny eagle) and *Haliaetus albicilla* (sea eagle), all of which are native to Greece, Asia Minor, North Africa and the eastern Mediterranean.

266. Thus Schulz, *Spruchquelle*, 280–81; Schnackenburg, "Abschnitt," 225; Steinhauser, *Doppelbildworte*, 202.

267. Schulz, *Spruchquelle*, 281, 282. It is unclear whether Bultmann (*Tradition*, 117 [123]) regards 17:34–35 as distinct from 17:26–27, (28–30).

268. Dodd, *Parables*, 64–65.

269. Schrage (*Verhältnis*, 126–27) attempts unconvincingly to derive Thomas from Luke in spite of the fact that the Sahidic version of Luke is not particularly close to Thomas and that Thomas uses ⲡⲟⲩⲁ . . . ⲡⲟⲩⲁ, which almost certainly corresponds to the original εἷς . . . εἷς and to the Aramaic *wᵉḥad . . . wᵉḥad*.

"the selective effect of the call of Jesus."[270] Geiger also refers it to Jesus' call: it is "a summons to discipleship even in the face of family and social ties . . ." and is related to 12:49–53 and 14:26–27.[271] But to interpret 17:34–35 as a discipleship saying is, as Steinhauser rightly observes, strained.[272] The passive verbs παραλαμβάνεται and ἀφίεται should be understood as *passiva divina*.[273] Accordingly, they must be taken to refer to the eschatological separation of the elect.[274] For this reason Q 17:34–35 is best regarded as an independent prophetic judgment threat which stresses the universality of judgment, its unexpected arrival and the fact that it will not respect familial or communal bonds.

What is the compositional effect of the joining of these sayings? The Son of Man saying in 17:24, connected to 17:23 by an epexegetical γάρ, serves to interpret the latter. But this juxtaposition of messianic expectations with Son of Man imagery presents interpretive difficulties. According to Vielhauer, 17:23–24 presupposes the (post-Easter) identification of the messiah with the Son of Man and polemicizes against the notion that the Son of Man might come in an earthly fashion.[275] Zmijewski accepts that the primitive church had identified the Son of Man with the messiah but doubts that this is the issue here. Instead, 17:23–24 treats two distinct matters: it first rejects the view that there will be messianic pretenders prior to the parousia (v. 23), and then provides the basis for correct apocalyptic expectation (v. 24): ". . . it is not so much a matter of the problem of an identification of messiah and Son of Man; it is instead a matter of the opposition to the pseudo-messiahs who appear before the parousia . . . and of *the* coming Son of Man."[276] But this does not pay enough attention to the epexegetical γάρ which signals that v. 24 provides the basis for the counsel of v. 23. The contrast is not between the one messiah/Son of Man and the many false messiahs, but between earth and heaven, and between concealment in the desert or in a chamber and conspicuous, public manifestation. There will be no mistaking it when it comes. Consequently the claims of pseudo-messiahs are self-

---

270. Dodd, *Parables*, 65 n. 1.

271. Geiger, *Endzeitreden*, 138.

272. Steinhauser, *Doppelbildworte*, 212.

273. Luke's future passive forms are probably a secondary smoothing of the original wording of Q. The present tenses are, nevertheless, to be interpreted in reference to the future, as ἔσονται shows.

274. Thus Jeremias, *Parables*, 53; Zmijewski, *Eschatologiereden*, 54; Steinhauser, *Doppelbildworte*, 212–13.

275. Vielhauer, "Gottesreich," 76. Similarly Laufen, *Doppelüberlieferung*, 372–73; Schulz, *Spruchquelle*, 284.

276. Zmijewski, *Eschatologiereden*, 416 [emphasis original; trans. by auth.].

evidently specious. The addition of the proverbial saying 17:37b rein-forces this point: the gathering of eagles provides a highly visible aerial indication of the presence of prey or carrion. The parousia will likewise be unmistakably visible[277] and will occur with the swiftness character-istic of eagles.

Attached to this cluster (Q 17:23, 24, 37b) are two more correlatives (17:26–27, 28–30). Here the emphasis shifts from the general visibility of the event to its effect: for those who are oblivious, the parousia will come as an unanticipated, unheralded disaster, destroying all. Implicit is a striking contrast between two modes of existence and their conse-quences: those who are unprepared eat, drink, plant and build; the disaster will destroy them to a man (καὶ ἀπώλεσεν πάντας bis). But the Q community eschews these mundane activities in its pursuit of the king-dom, and will escape the eschatological disaster. Q 17:26–27, 28–30 amounts to a threat of judgment upon all the unprepared—which means in the wider context of Q, the impenitent and those who reject Q's preaching of the kingdom. The double metaphor in Q 17:34–35 must likewise be interpreted as a threat of judgment. It not only implies that there will be no warning prior to the judgment; it also raises the ominous spectre of the tearing asunder of the closest of human ties: family, co-workers and village society. As in other Q passages which deal with the parousia (12:39–40, 49, 51–53), it is treated as an ominous and gloomy happening, not a point of joyful liberation.

Schürmann is probably correct in regarding 17:23–24 as the crystal-lization point for this cluster of sayings.[278] The order in which the rest of the sayings were added cannot be determined with any certainty. The overall effect, nevertheless, is clear: the parousia will come in a highly visible and spectacular fashion; divine judgment will overwhelm those who, like the contemporaries of Noah and Lot, are impenitent and therefore oblivious and unprepared. And divine judgment will be uni-versal and will penetrate the closest of human relationships.

Lührmann notes that the two pericopae which follow the Q apoca-lypse, Q 19:12–27 and 22:28–30, likewise deal with the subject of judg-ment. Their connection with Q 17:23–35 is no doubt on the basis of the

---

277. Thus Lührmann, *Redaktion,* 73; Laufen, *Doppelüberlieferung,* 373. Schenk (*Synopse,* 120–21) argues (implausibly) that 17:23–24, 37 is directed at the exponents of a realized eschatology (such as Paul encounters at Corinth) which affirms that baptism effects perfected eschatological existence.

278. Schürmann, "Menschensohn-Titel," 139. Schürmann argues that 17:23–24 + 26–30 existed at one stage, and was subsequently expanded in a pre-Lucan stratum or by Luke himself with 17:31, (32), 33, 34–35, 37; 18:1–8.

common theme of judgment.[279] The parable of the pounds (19:12–27) continues the description of judgment in particularly ominous tones and Q 22:28, 30 provides the positive counterpart for the threats of 17:23–34; 19:12–27. Those who respond positively to the message of the kingdom, that is, the followers of Jesus, will escape judgment and will in fact participate in the judgment of unfaithful Israel.

Comparison with Mark

Comparison of the Q apocalypse with Mark and with the later developments in Matthew and Luke reveal how little Q is interested in direct parenesis. The Marcan apocalypse is obviously parenetic in intention: it is replete with admonitions to the community to watch ($\beta\lambda\acute{\epsilon}\pi\epsilon\tau\epsilon$, 13:5b, 9, 33), pray ($\pi\rho\sigma\epsilon\acute{\nu}\chi\epsilon\sigma\theta\epsilon$, v. 18) and stay awake ($\grave{\alpha}\gamma\rho\nu\pi\nu\epsilon\hat{\iota}\tau\epsilon$, v. 33; $\gamma\rho\eta\gamma\rho\epsilon\hat{\iota}\tau\epsilon$, vv. 35, 37). The apocalypse is constructed as encouragement and admonition to the community as it awaits the parousia. Like Q, Mark expects deceivers. But Mark describes the "false christs and false messiahs" as coming $\grave{\epsilon}\pi\grave{\iota}\ \tau\hat{\omega}\ \grave{\sigma}\nu\acute{\sigma}\mu\alpha\tau\acute{\iota}\ \mu\sigma\nu$, i.e., as Christian messianic pretenders who identify themselves with Jesus by means of the $\grave{\epsilon}\gamma\grave{\omega}\ \epsilon\grave{\iota}\mu\acute{\iota}$ formula.[280]

There are important points of contrast between Q and Mark. First, the false messiahs of Q 17:23 are not identifiably Christian but are, more likely, the messianic figures such as those Josephus mentions. Q's warning $\mu\grave{\eta}\ \grave{\epsilon}\xi\acute{\epsilon}\lambda\theta\eta\tau\epsilon,\ \mu\grave{\eta}\ \pi\iota\sigma\tau\epsilon\acute{\nu}\sigma\eta\tau\epsilon\ (\mu\grave{\eta}\ \delta\iota\acute{\omega}\xi\eta\tau\epsilon)$ is not even necessarily directed at a Christian audience although, to be sure, community members are the proximate audience. Second, the character of Q's apocalypse is less parenetic and more prophetic than Mark's: the tone is threatening and the parousia is described in ominous terms more suitable to prophetic preaching than to intra-community parenesis. Whereas Mark expressly notes the positive side of the events with the phrase $\kappa\alpha\grave{\iota}\ \tau\acute{\sigma}\tau\epsilon\ \grave{\alpha}\pi\sigma\sigma\tau\epsilon\lambda\epsilon\hat{\iota}\ \tau\sigma\grave{\nu}\varsigma\ \grave{\alpha}\gamma\gamma\acute{\epsilon}\lambda\sigma\nu\varsigma\ \kappa\alpha\grave{\iota}\ \grave{\epsilon}\pi\iota\sigma\nu\nu\acute{\alpha}\xi\epsilon\iota\ \tau\sigma\grave{\nu}\varsigma\ \grave{\epsilon}\kappa\lambda\epsilon\kappa\tau\sigma\acute{\nu}\varsigma\ \dots$, Q represents the parousia as a disaster which overwhelms the world. The ambiguous $\epsilon\grave{\iota}\varsigma\ \pi\alpha\rho\alpha\lambda\alpha\mu\beta\acute{\alpha}\nu\epsilon\tau\alpha\iota\ \kappa\alpha\grave{\iota}\ \epsilon\grave{\iota}\varsigma\ \grave{\alpha}\phi\acute{\iota}\epsilon\tau\alpha\iota$ is as close as Q comes to a positive note. Finally, while Mark concedes that the time of the parousia is unknown (13:32, 33), he provides a virtual apocalyptic timetable (vv. 6–7, 14, 19–20, 21–23, 29, 30). Q more insistently maintains the unexpectedness of the coming of the Son of Man, although it appears to regard it as imminent (Q 3:7–9; 12:54–56).

---

279. Lührmann, *Redaktion*, 75.
280. See W. Kelber, *The Kingdom in Mark* (Philadelphia: Fortress Press, 1974) 114–15, and those cited in 115 n. 18.

The logia apocalypse, in short, is much more directly the prophetic proclamation of coming judgment than it is community-directed parenesis. It is undeniable that such preaching has an indirect parenetic effect. In form, however, it corresponds much more to preaching to the unconverted, warning them to repent before the catastrophe overtakes them.

The respective redactions of Mark and Q by Matthew and Luke reveal that parenetic interests dominated. Matthew fuses the first part of the Q apocalypse (24:26–28) with the Marcan description of the parousia. The second part (24:37–41) was used to reinforce the assertion that the time of the end is unknown (24:36 = Mark 13:22) and to buttress the parenetic materials which follow. Although the influence of Mark is less evident in Luke 17, parenetic motivation is no less obvious. Luke systematically subverts the *Naherwartung* of Q by his insertions in 17:20a and 17:22 despite the fact that he maintains the motifs of the swiftness and unexpectedness of the end. These motifs he turns to parenetic purposes, as his reference to Lot's wife shows. As elsewhere, Luke uses originally eschatological sayings to emphasize the urgency of the demands of everyday Christian living.

Summary. Analysis of the compositional principles governing the juxtaposition of the originally independent sayings constituting Q 17:23–35 and comparison with the Marcan, Matthaean and Lucan apocalypses reveal that the dominant tendency in Q is in the direction of prophetic preaching of the end to the impenitent, with emphasis upon its unexpected nature and its catastrophic consequences. Community-directed parenesis is not its primary intention. Threat of judgment and destruction is Q's real interest in transmitting these sayings.

THE PREACHING OF JUDGMENT IN Q

The preceding five complexes of Q sayings—3:7–9, 16–17; 7:1–10, 18–35; 11:14–26, 29–33, 39–52; 12:39–59 and 17:23–35—account for about one-third of the bulk of Q.[281] Analysis of the principles of composition of the sayings and reconstruction of the redaction history of the units within each of these complexes (to the extent that such reconstruction is possible) reveal several common features which invite the conclusion that these four blocks belong to the same redactional stratum.

---

281. See R. Morgenthaler, *Statistische Synopse* (Stuttgart and Zurich: Gotthelf, 1971) 70–85. Based on Morgenthaler's statistics, these pericopae account for 1281 of the 4005 Matthaean Q words (31.9%) or 1293 of the 3790 Lucan Q words (34.1%).

Projected Audience

Although, of course, the *actual* audience of these Q speeches is the community itself, i.e., those already sympathetic to the preaching of the kingdom, the *projected audience* consists of the impenitent and the opponents of community preaching. These Q speeches project, so to speak, "over the heads" of the proximate audience to those who do not "produce the fruit of repentance" (3:7), and those who cynically approach John claiming national privilege (3:8). They are the "children" who perversely refuse the summons of the τέκνα σοφίας (7:31–35), the opponents who blindly reject the signs of the kingdom (11:20, 29–32), the murderers of the prophets (11:49–51), those who violently oppose the kingdom (Q 16:16) and those who live oblivious to the imminent catastrophe of the coming of the Son of Man (12:54–56; 17:23–37). Even though some of the individual components single out smaller groups such as the Pharisees and scribes for special criticism (11:39–48, 52), the target group of the final form of the Q woes and the five speeches as a whole is much broader: it includes all of Israel or "this generation" (7:1–10, 31–35; 11:29–32, 49–51).[282] Deuteronomistic theology which characterized Israel as habitually impenitent and therefore in danger of judgment and final condemnation is in evidence at several points.[283] One cannot help getting the impression that the redactor of this part of Q holds out little hope for Israel's conversion. Original missionary fervor has turned into sectarian polemics.

While the ostensible or implied audience is "this generation," it is, of course, hardly likely that Q was broadcast as a whole to outsiders as missionary propaganda, or circulated as a polemical tract. It is conceivable that individual components of various speeches—e.g., 3:7b–9, 11:31–32; 12:54–56 or 17:26–30—originally had an actual function in missionary preaching. But in Q their function is markedly different. In their redactional arrangement these sayings articulate the conflict between the Q group and their Jewish contemporaries over the preaching of the kingdom. Conflict with outsiders, as Lewis Coser has shown,[284] actually serves a positive and constructive purpose as a means to define more clearly group boundaries, to enhance internal cohesion

---

282. Lührmann, *Redaktion*, 93.

283. E.g., 3:7–9; 7:31–35; 11:47–48, 49–51. On this, see Jacobson, "Literary Unity," and idem, "Wisdom Christology," passim.

284. Coser, *Functions*, 33–38, 87–95; also J. H. Elliott, *A Home for the Homeless: A Sociological Exegesis of 1 Peter* (Philadelphia: Fortress Press, 1981) 112–18.

and to reinforce group identity. This stratum of Q articulates its conflict with "this generation" in terms which provide a transcendental legitimacy for the community: those who have believed in the preaching of the kingdom and who themselves engage in that preaching stand on the side of John the Baptist, Jesus, the prophets sent to Israel, and ultimately, on the side of Sophia and God. The rejection and persecution which the Q preachers encounter is rationalized within the framework of the deuteronomistic understanding of history as one of perpetual disobedience. Thus, while ostensibly directed at the "out-group," these polemical and threatening materials function in fact to strengthen the identity of the "in-group" and to interpret for them the experience of persecution, rejection and even the failure of their preaching of the kingdom.

Forms

The only two *miracle stories* which Q contains are to be found in this stratum. Notwithstanding the fact that Q is well aware of the miracle tradition (see 7:22; 10:20; 11:14–15; 17:5–6), it is obvious that the motive for relating these stories lies not in an interest in the miraculous as such, but in the pronouncement of Jesus which is occasioned by them. The miracle stories which are selected function as chriae, that is, as short, pithy sayings which are given a brief introduction or setting. They fall into the class of chriae which Theon of Alexandria terms χρεῖαι ἀποκρι-τικαί (responsorial chriae), or sayings which are elicited in response to some circumstance.[285]

It is the form of chria (or apophthegm) which is typical of this stratum of Q. Q 3:7–9; 7:1–10; 7:18–23; 7:24–26; 11:14–15, 17–18a and 11:16, 29 all qualify as such. In several instances, it appears that these chriae have served as the condensation point for other related sayings:

Chria		Appended Sayings
3:7–9	+	16–17
7:18–23	+	24–26
7:24–26	+	27, 28, (31–35)
11:14, 15, 17–18a	+	19, 20, 21–22, 23, 24–26
11:16, 29	+	30, 31–32, 33, 34–36

285. Theon of Alexandria (L. Spengel, ed., *Rhetores Graeci* [3 vols.; Leipzig: Teubner, 1853–56] 2:97–98): ἀποκριτικαὶ δέ εἰσιν αἱ μήτε κατ᾽ ἐρώτησιν, μήτε κατὰ πύσμα, λόγον δέ τινα ἔχουσαι, πρὸς ὅν ἐστιν ἡ ἀπόκρισις, οἷον Πλάτων ποτὲ Διογένους ἀριστῶντος ἐν ἀγορᾷ καὶ καλοῦντος αὐτὸν ἐπὶ τὸ ἄριστον, ὦ Διόγενες, εἶπεν, ὡς χαρίεν ἂν ἦν σου τὸ ἄπλαστον, εἰ μὴ πλαστὸν ἦν· οὔτε γὰρ Διογένης περί τινος ἠρώτα τὸν Πλάτωνα, οὔτε ὁ Πλάτων πυνθάνεται αὐτοῦ, ἀλλ᾽ ἁπλῶς πρὸς τὸ ἄριστον καλεῖ αὐτόν, ὅπερ ἐστὶ τῶν οὐδετέρων.

In contrast to Mark, the Q chriae are not concerned with legal matters but criticize instead the response of "this generation" to the preaching of the kingdom.

The chriic form is employed to encapsulate various sayings of Jesus and John. The sayings most typical of this stratum are *prophetic judgment sayings and apocalyptic words:* Q 3:7b–9, 16–17; 11:19b, 31–32, 47–51 (a woe oracle in almost classical form!); 12:39–40, 49, 51–53, 54–56, 58–59 and 17:34–35. All of the "prophetic correlatives" occur here: 11:30; 17:24, 26–27, 28–30. In addition, there are several sayings which, while not originally prophetic in form, have been employed in Q redaction to articulate a threat against those who fail to apprehend the preaching of the kingdom: 11:20 (a kingdom saying); 11:23 (a proverb?); 11:24–26 (a teaching on demonology); 11:33 (an exhortation to preach); 11:34–36 (a warning about clear moral vision); 12:39 (a hortatory parable); 12:54–55 (a weather proverb); 12:57–58 (a sapiential admonition) and 17:37b (a wisdom saying). It is worth noting that the judgment sayings and apocalyptic words in Q 3:7–9, 16–17; 11:14–26 and 11:16, 29–32, 33–36 occur as responses to particular situations; in other words, they too occur as chriae.

Motifs

Corresponding to the high frequency of prophetic forms is the preponderance of motifs related to the theme of judgment. The imminence of judgment is implied in 3:9, 17; 11:51b; 12:51–53, 54–56. The parousia will be universal and highly visible (17:24, 37b) and its occurrence, sudden and unheralded (12:39–40; 17:26–27, 28–30, 34–35). Neglect of repentance (3:7b–9; 11:31–32) and refusal to respond positively to John, Jesus and the Q preachers as the envoys of Sophia constitute the grounds for judgment and condemnation (7:31–35; 11:19–20, 24–26, 29–32, 33–36, 49–51; 12:57–59).

As Q 16:16 and 11:49–51 evidence, the rejection of Q's preaching had been taken to the point of violence. Throughout, Israel is regarded as blind and obdurate. It is a "brood of vipers," obstinate and perverse children (7:31–34), an "evil generation" (11:29) and, as the logic of the Beelzebul story dictates, partisans of Satan. That Israel has already had more than enough reason to repent and respond is a pervasive conviction; for this reason the positive response of Gentiles (7:1–10; 11:31–32) serves to highlight Israel's unfaithfulness and even more than this, it acts as an *Unheilszeichen* for her. Gentiles will enter the kingdom and stand better in the judgment than those to whom God's messengers were originally sent.

The presence of common forms (especially prophetic sayings and chriae), shared motifs and agreement in projected audience unite these five complexes and suggest that they derive from the same redactional stratum. But what of the rest of Q? What literary relation do the other clusters of Q sayings bear to this stratum characterized by the announcement of judgment? Does the preaching of judgment represent the most primitive layer in Q, or was this the controlling motif of the final redaction as Lührmann suggests?

5

Sapiential Speeches in Q

We have seen that a significant portion of Q, including both the opening sequence and the closing pericopae, is controlled by motifs relating to the coming of the Son of Man and the judgment of the impenitent. Conflict and polemic against outsiders stand clearly on the horizon of these groups of sayings. Shaped by the experience of the rejection of the preaching of the kingdom, this stratum of Q relies heavily upon the deuteronomistic understanding of history for the interpretation of this experience of failure. The predominantly negative view of Israel which this experience of rejection elicited stands in sharp contrast to the rather positive and optimistic view of Gentiles.

What of the rest of Q? Significant blocks of Q are either untouched or only marginally influenced by these motifs: 6:20b–49; 9:57–62 + 10:2–16, 21–24; 11:2–4, 9–13; 12:2–12; 12:22–34; 13:24–30. In this chapter it will be argued that these clusters or "speeches"[1] are controlled instead by sapiential themes and devices and, notwithstanding several important interpolations, are directed at the Q community in support of its radical mode of existence. The first and most prominent of these speeches is 6:20b–49.

THE INAUGURAL SERMON Q 6:20b–49

Disagreements between Matthew and Luke in the extent and order of materials in this speech are substantial. It is apparent, nevertheless, that Matthew is responsible for a very large measure of the rearrangement.[2] He reproduces not only material parallel to Luke 6:20b–49, but many Q

---

1. Throughout this chapter I will refer to these clusters of sayings as "speeches." This is intended only as a convenient designation rather than as a generic term. In the final chapter I will show that these "speeches" in fact conform to the genre of "instruction."
2. Although most ascribe this editorial work to Matthew, Betz (*Essays*) argues that the rearrangement is pre-Matthaean.

texts found elsewhere in Q, Marcan sayings transferred from other locations and special material. This arrangement is almost certainly secondary to Luke, who reproduces the Q material in a continuous block with a minimum of editorial transitions.[3] Moreover, there is little in 6:20b–49 which does not appear to be a Q text; the Lucan woes are the only real exception.[4] If we accept the Lucan order as generally reproducing that of Q, the Q speech divides easily into five sections:

6:20b–23	Programmatic statement: the beatitudes
6:27–35	Admonitions (1): love of enemies and non-retaliation
6:36, 37–38	Admonitions (2): mercy, judging and generosity[5]
6:39–45	Warnings to teachers
6:46, 47–49	Peroration

The Beatitudes[6]

It is generally agreed that the first three beatitudes (Q 6:20b, 21a, b) and the fourth (Q 6:22–23) did not form an original unity. This is evident from a comparison of various features of the beatitudes: the first three use the formula μακάριοι οἱ + substantive while the fourth uses μακάριοί ἐστε ὅταν; the first three are bipartite, consisting of a beatitude and a ὅτι clause but the fourth has a beatitude and an imperative with a motive

---

3. Luke 6:39a, εἶπεν δὲ καὶ παραβολὴν αὐτοῖς, is probably Lucan. See 5:36; 20:9, 19; 21:29 (all additions to Mark); and 4:23; 6:39; 12:16, 41; 13:6; 14:7; 15:3; 18:1, 9; 19:11 (in non-Marcan material). Δὲ καί is found in Luke 26x, Acts 7x, but in Matt 3x, Mark 2x, John 8x.

4. The close parallelism between the Lucan woes and beatitudes excludes the possibility that the woes circulated independently of 6:20b–23. Schürmann (Lukasevangelium 1:339) defends the view that despite some evidence of Lucan redaction, the woes are pre-Lucan. He argues (1) that James 4:9 and 5:1 betray knowledge of the woes, (2) that Luke nowhere else shows himself to be so creative, and (3) that several words are un-Lucan: οὐαί (from Q, 10:13 [bis]; 11:42, 44, 47, 52; 17:2; diff Matt, 11:43, 46; from Mark, 21:23; 22:22), πλούσιος (from Mark, 18:25; 21:1; red, 18:23; Sondergut, 18x) and πεινάω (1:53 [Sond]; from Mark, 6:3; from Q, 6:21). Though the origin of the Lucan woes continues to be a problem, Schürmann's arguments are not particularly convincing. The resemblance between Luke and James is not sufficient to turn a parallel into a source. Even though the words cited by Schürmann (in #3) are not unambiguously redactional elsewhere, their use here is virtually dictated by the context. If, ex hypothesi, Luke wished to create contrasts for sayings which use μακάριος and πτωχός, what else would he have used? See further, C. M. Tuckett, "The Beatitudes: A Source Critical Study," NovT 25 [1983] 196 n. 12, and the literature cited there.

5. Matthew treats 5:48 // Luke 6:36 as the conclusion of 5:43–47. Schürmann (Lukasevangelium 1:357) notes with regard to Luke and Q that 6:36 deals not with the love of enemies, but mercy, and therefore fits better with 6:37–38 than it does with 6:27–35.

6. Reconstructions: Schulz, Spruchquelle, 76–78 [6:20b–21]; 452–54 [6:22–23]; Worden, "A Philological Analysis of Luke 6:20b–49 and Parallels," 75–76, 88–161; Polag, Fragmenta, 32; Steck, Israel, 22–27 [6:22–23 only].

clause; and the first three depend upon a logic of eschatological reversal, while the last uses the motif of eschatological reward. Finally, 6:20b–21 presupposes the general human conditions of poverty and suffering, while 6:22–23 is oriented toward the specific situation of persecution of the Christian community.

It is uncertain whether Q's first three beatitudes were formulated in the third person (so Matthew) or in the second (so Luke).[7] In either case they are addressed to a rather wide group of socially and economically disadvantaged persons. The association of vv. 22–23—undoubtedly on the basis of the catchword μακάριος—narrows the application to a group which is not simply "poor" but also persecuted, i.e., to a group of early Christian preachers.

Several have argued that 6:23c is a secondary addition to the "persecution beatitude."[8] Steck observes that v. 23c fits poorly with the logic of vv. 22–23b. It does not seem to undergird v. 23b (ὁ μισθὸς ὑμῶν πολὺς ἐν τῷ οὐρανῷ), which already provides an adequate motive clause for v. 23a.[9] Moreover, three parallels to the persecution beatitude are found in early Christian literature, but none contains a phrase corresponding to v. 23c: 1 Pet 4:14; *Gos. Thom.* 68 and *Gos. Thom.* 69a. The absence of a phrase corresponding to 6:23c in any of the other persecution beatitudes suggests that this is a secondary addition.

The cluster of beatitudes in 6:20b–23 thus contains (at least) three components: 6:20b–21, a *Grundwort*,[10] which was expanded and reinterpreted by vv. 22–23b. Verse 23c is a further expansion of vv. 22–23b, introducing the deuteronomistic motif of Israel's persecution of the prophets. Determination of the stages at which these units were combined must await a discussion of the entire sermon.

Q 6:27–35

Q 6:27–35 represents a very carefully structured set of admonitions

---

7. For a tabulation of opinion, see Schürmann, *Lukasevangelium* 1:329 n. 25; Schulz, *Spruchquelle*, 77 n. 128. The use of the third person is the more usual in beatitudes (see Dupont, *Béatitudes I*, 272–82), but this in itself does not aid in determining whether Q is innovative or traditional in this respect.

8. Steck, *Israel*, 258–59; Schulz, *Spruchquelle*, 456 n. 404; Jacobson, "Wisdom Christology," 53.

9. Steck, *Israel*, 259. Trilling (*Israel*) suggests that v. 23c has the sense of "Your reward is great, for the prophets were also persecuted (unjustly) in previous times (and nevertheless were vindicated and inherited life)" [trans. by auth.]. However, Steck (*Israel*, 258 n. 4) properly points out that there is no attestation for the notion of "the reward of the prophet" in contemporary Judaism.

10. Thus Schürmann, "Basileia-Verkündigung," 137–39.

and motive clauses, constructed from several originally independent sayings.

The wording, order and extent of this Q section are controverted. Matthew's hand is visible in the creation of the introductory formulae in 5:38 (39a?) and 5:43 (44a?).[11] But did Matthew divide the Q complex into two units (vv. 39–40, 42, and 44–48) or did Luke insert the originally separate sayings on retaliation and generosity (6:29, 30, [31]) into the midst of the sayings on love of enemies (vv. 27–28, 32–35)? Bultmann, Schulz and Zeller take the latter view, and accordingly assume that Luke 6:34, 35a, b—which recalls this interpolation—is Lucan.[12] They point to the change from second-person plural to singular in 6:29–30 and the more logical Matthaean construction (i.e., 5:44, 45 // Luke 6:27–28 + 35c).[13] However, Matthew is responsible for the formulation of vv. 38, 43; he is to be credited with the radical rearrangements of Q materials in Matt 10 and in the woes against the Pharisees; and he has apparently edited and transferred the Golden Rule (6:31 // Matt 7:12) to provide a summary for the catechetical section introduced by 5:17–20. This suggests that his "more logical" arrangement is secondary and that Luke's more difficult one is the earlier.

Agreements between Matthew and Luke allow at least part of Q to be reconstructed without serious difficulty: ἀλλὰ ὑμῖν λέγω τοῖς ἀκούουσιν[14] [Matt: ἐγὼ δὲ λέγω ὑμῖν]· ἀγαπᾶτε τοὺς ἐχθροὺς ὑμᾶς . . . προσεύχεσθε περὶ [ὑπὲρ] τῶν ἐπηρεαζόντων [διωκόντων] ὑμᾶς. Luke offers two sets of parallel commands (vv. 27b, c; vv. 28a, b) while Matthew has only a single pair (vv. 44b, c). Though some regard the longer Lucan form as redactional,[15] Cadbury showed that Luke tends to avoid, not create, such parallelism and hence the longer form may better represent Q.[16]

The admonition to love one's enemies was evidently followed by imperatives on non-retaliation and generous giving (6:29–30 // Matt 5:39b, 40, 42), the Golden Rule (6:31 // Matt 7:12) and the motive clauses which ground the love

---

11. It is disputed whether the Matthaean antitheses are entirely redactional creations, entirely traditional, or a combination of the two. In view of the fact that the third (5:31–32), fifth (5:38–42) and sixth (5:43–48) antitheses have Lucan parallels which lack the formula ἠκούσατε ὅτι ἐρρέθη, and because the third antithesis involves the transposition of a Q text (from Luke 16:18), it seems most reasonable to assume that *at least* these are redactional formulations. Thus Bultmann, *Tradition*, 135–36 [143–44]; R. A. Guelich, "The Antitheses of Matthew v. 21–48: Traditional and/or Redactional?" *NTS* 22 (1976) 444–57. See further, M. J. Suggs, "The Antitheses as Redactional Products," *Essays on the Love Commandment* (Philadelphia: Fortress Press, 1978) 93–107.

12. Bultmann, *Tradition*, 96 [100]; Schulz, *Spruchquelle*, 120–21, 130–31; Zeller, *Mahnsprüche*, 101–3. Harnack (*Sayings of Jesus*, 59–60 [45]) and Schmid (*Matthäus und Lukas*, 227–28) also argue for the primacy of Matthaean order.

13. Zeller, *Mahnsprüche*, 101; Josef Schmid, *Matthäus und Lukas*, 228; Schulz, *Spruchquelle*, 121.

14. Zeller (*Mahnsprüche*, 102) argues that both introductions are redactional and that Luke v. 27a is formulated in relation to the redactional woes (6:24–26). Lührmann ("Liebet eure Feinde"), however, points out that there are similar and corresponding locutions at the end of the speech (6:47, 49) and throughout the rest of Q.

15. Schulz, *Spruchquelle*, 128 (apparently); Fitzmyer, *Luke I–IX*, 638.

16. Cadbury, *Style*, 85–88; also Schürmann, *Paschamahlbericht*, 2.

command (6:32–33 // Matt 5:46–47).[17] Whether the second conditional sentence (6:33) read ἀσπάσησθε τοὺς ἀδελφοὺς ὑμῶν (Matt) or ἀγαθοποιῆτε τοὺς ἀγαθοποιοῦντας ὑμᾶς (Luke) is uncertain.[18] If it is the former, then the conditional probably serves as the motive clause for v. 28a (εὐλογεῖτε);[19] if the latter, it provides the motive for v. 27c (καλῶς ποιεῖτε).

Verse 34 also presents difficulties since it lacks a parallel in Matthew. It is curious, nevertheless, that δανείζω occurs both in vv. 34, 35a and in Matt 5:42 (diff Luke 6:30). There are several way of accounting for this "reminiscence." One might suppose that Luke changed an original injunction to generous lending in Q into the more general admonition καὶ ἀπὸ τοῦ αἴροντος τὰ σὰ μὴ ἀπαίτει, but preserved a reference to lending in his redactional extension of the conditionals (vv. 34, 35a). If so, he created v. 34 on the pattern of vv. 32, 33,[20] but by doing so he introduced the idea not only of lending (not present in 6:30) but of lending without expectation of return—which goes beyond Matt 5:42. Alternatively, Matt 5:42 may be a reminiscence of Luke 6:34, 35a. In this case, Matthew omitted Q 6:34–35 in his division of 6:27–35 into two antitheses, but preserved a reference to it when he rewrote Luke 6:30 (= Q) which, like 6:29 // Matt 5:39–40, originally had to do with the seizure of goods, not generous lending.[21]

Neither option is without difficulties. The first must assume that Luke removed the reference to lending from 6:30 but then created a motive clause (v. 34) which has no clear antecedent. Moreover, it supposes that Luke, contrary to his usual practice, creates parallelism. The second option creates the same problems for Q as the first does for Luke: v. 34 would lack an obvious referent if Luke 6:30 is the original reading of Q. One means to avoid these difficulties is to suppose that Q 6:30 originally concerned lending and corresponded to Matt 5:42, and that Luke 6:34 belonged to Q. Because of its position between 6:29 and the generalizing statement in 6:31, Luke changed 6:30 into a summary of 6:29 and an anticipation of 6:31, but thereby obscured its link with 6:34.

This set of imperatives and motive clauses ended with ". . . you will be sons of

17. Reconstructions: Q 6:29–30: Schulz, *Spruchquelle*, 121–23; Zeller, *Mahnsprüche*, 55; Worden, "Philological Analysis," 178–214; Polag, *Fragmenta*, 34. Q 6:31: Schulz, *Spruchquelle*, 139; Zeller, *Mahnsprüche*, 117; Worden, "Philological Analysis," 214–30; Polag, *Fragmenta*, 36. Q 6:32–33: Schulz, *Spruchquelle*, 129–30; Worden, "Philological Analysis," 230–89; Polag, *Fragmenta*, 34.

18. Ἀγαθοποιέω (Matt-/Mark-/Acts-) occurs only in Luke 6:9 (Mark, ἀγαθὸν ποιῆσαι, Matt, καλῶς ποιεῖν) and in 6:33, 35. Καλῶς ποιέω: Matt 1/Mark 1/Luke-Acts 2. Schulz (*Spruchquelle*, 129), Schmid (*Matthäus und Lukas*, 229 n. 4) and Schürmann (*Lukasevangelium* 1:354 n. 81) hold that ἀσπάσησθε (Matt 2/Mark 2/Luke-Acts 6) is original, but the case is not very compelling.

19. Thus Schürmann, *Lukasevangelium* 1:354; Worden, "Philological Analysis," 281. In this case "greet" must be taken to imply an invocation of a blessing of peace.

20. Schürmann (*Lukasevangelium* 1:353–54) argues that v. 34 is secondary to vv. 32–33 since it is not strictly symmetrical with the latter. While vv. 32–33 speak of receiving equal treatment, ἀποβάλωσιν τὰ ἴσα means "to receive back what is lent" rather than "to receive reciprocal treatment." See BAGD 381.

21. Schürmann (*Lukasevangelium* 1:354; "Basileia-Verkündigung," 137–38) advocates a yet more complex solution: v. 34 is a secondary but pre-Lucan *Parallelbildung* which in turn presupposes an earlier addition of 6:30 // Matt 5:42 to the original cluster, 6:27–28, 32–33, 35.

the Most High; for he is kind to the ungrateful and the selfish" (Luke 6:35c //
Matt 5:45).[22] But whether vv. 35a, b belonged is again unclear. Verse 35b (καὶ ὁ
μισθὸς ὑμῶν πολύς), if it derived from Q, serves as the motive clause for and
presupposes the three imperatives in 35a ("love . . . do good . . . lend"). There is
little warrant to ascribe v. 35b to Lucan redaction; μισθός is not obviously
Lucan,[23] and v. 35c already provides an adequate motive clause for v. 35a.

We can be relatively certain of the presence in Q of vv. 27–28, 29, 30
(with δανείζω?), 31, 32–33, 35c and in some doubt regarding vv. 34, 35a,
b. If the doubtful verses belonged, this section of Q displays a rather
elaborate structure: three of the imperatives (love, do good [or bless],
lend) are further supported by the rhetorical questions in vv. 32–34, and
summarized in 35a, b.[24] The concluding clause (v. 35c) provides a motive
clause of another sort, appealing not to reason or the promise of reward,
but to the notion of *imitatio Dei*.

That 6:27–35 is composite is obvious. The first four imperatives are
formulated in the second-person plural and all agree in placing the
imperative in first position. Verses 29, 30, on the other hand, are in the
second-person singular and follow the form τῷ + participle + imperative (or prohibitive).[25] Most see in vv. 29–30 the combination of two
originally independent sayings: an admonition concerning the seizure of
goods and a much more general admonition to generous giving (or
lending).[26] It goes without saying that the Golden Rule (6:31), formulated in the second-person plural, had a widespread and independent
circulation apart from this particular context. Verses 32–33 obviously
refer back to and presuppose vv. 27–28 while v. 34, which seems to have
been formed on analogy to the preceding verses, grounds 6:30 (with
δανείζω).

22. Reconstruction: Schulz, *Spruchquelle*, 128–29; Worden, "Philological Analysis,"
291–306; Polag, *Fragmenta*, 34.
23. Μισθός: Luke 6:23 (= Matt), 35; 10:7 (Matt: τροφή). It is generally thought that
Luke changes Q's (= Matt) τίνα μισθὸν ἔχετε (Matt 5:46) to ποία ὑμῖν χάρις (6:32, 33, 34).
Thus Harnack, *Sayings of Jesus*, 62 [46]; Schulz, *Spruchquelle*, 129; Schmid, *Matthäus und
Lukas*, 229 n. 4; Dupont, *Béatitudes* 1:163 n. 1; Schürmann, *Lukasevangelium* 1:353 n. 77.
Wrege (*Bergpredigt*) thinks it is pre-Lucan. Χάρις occurs only in Luke (8x, 4x meaning
'reward') and in Acts (17x).
24. Lührmann ("Liebet eure Feinde," 420) considers v. 34 as Lucan and hence also vv.
35aγ and 35b. However, he ascribes 35aα (ἀγαπᾶτε τοὺς ἐχθροὺς ὑμῶν) to Q. Jacobson
("Wisdom Christology," 56) observes that the love command in 35aα forms an *inclusio*
with 6:27.
25. See above, n. 17 for reconstruction. Schulz, Zeller and Polag agree in reconstructing the form: τῷ ῥαπίζοντί σε . . . στρέψον . . . καὶ τῷ θέλοντι . . . ἄφες, τῷ αἰτοῦντί
σε δός, καὶ τὸν θέλοντα ἀπὸ σου δανείσασθαι μὴ ἀποστραφῇς.
26. Thus Bultmann, *Tradition*, 83, 135 [87, 143]; Schürmann, *Lukasevangelium* 1:349;
Lührmann, "Liebet eure Feinde," 427; Zeller, *Mahnsprüche*, 55.

The core of this Q speech appears to be the love command (vv. 27b, 28) which has been expanded and elaborated in various ways. Schürmann suggests that the earliest elaboration of vv. 27–28 was 32–33, 35a, c and that vv. 29–31 and 35b came later.[27] Since vv. 29, 30, 31 appear to be an insertion which interrupts the connection between the imperatives (vv. 27–28) and their elaboration (vv. 32–33), this solution is plausible. We should include v. 35a along with vv. 32–33 since the conditional clauses require some positive summarizing conclusion. But the fact that v. 35a is followed by *two* motive clauses, and the differences between them in logic and content, suggest further editing. Schürmann prefers v. 35c to v. 35b as the original conclusion.

This is an eminently satisfactory solution: vv. 27–28, 32–33, 35a, c form a coherently structured piece of rhetoric, which was later supplemented by vv. 29–31, 34 and 35b. It produces a composition expressing sentiments that resemble not only Sir 4:10,

γίνου ὀρφανοῖς πατὴρ καὶ ἀντὶ ἀνδρὸς τῇ μητρὶ αὐτῶν
καὶ ἔσῃ ὡς υἱὸς ὑψίστου καὶ ἀγαπήσει σε μᾶλλον ἢ μήτηρ σου,

Be like a father to orphans and instead of a husband to their mother;
you will then be like a son of the Most High, and he will love you more than does your mother,[28]

but also Seneca *De Beneficiis* 4.26.1,

Si deos . . . imitaris, da et ingratis beneficia;
nam et sceleratis sol oritur et piratis patent maria,

If you are imitating the gods, then bestow benefits upon the ungrateful;
for the sun rises also upon the wicked and the sea lies open also to pirates.[29]

It has already been noted that vv. 29, 30 and 31 appear to be additions, and that v. 34 (and 35aγ) can be no earlier than the addition of v. 30. Verse 35b, which finds an almost exact counterpart in 6:23, may have been an insertion prompted when 6:20–23 was brought into relation with 6:27–35.

27. Schürmann, "Basileia-Verkündigung," 137; *Lukasevangelium* 1:357.
28. The Hebrew text reads somewhat differently:

היה כאב ליתומים	Be like a father to orphans,
ותמור בעל לאלמנות	and as a husband to widows,
ואל יקראך בן ויחנך	and God will call you "son" and be gracious to you,
ויעילך משחת	and will rescue you from the grave.

29. Translation according to Loeb edition (3:257). Epictetus (*Diss.* 3.22.54) describes the Cynic as God's messenger, who manifests love of enemy: ". . . he must needs be flogged like an ass, and while he is being flogged he must love the men who flog him, as though he were the father or brother of them all" (Loeb 2:149).

The association of the beatitudes (vv. 20b–23) with the following material has two bases: there may have been an original catchword connection between 6:22 (ὅταν μισήσουσιν ὑμᾶς) and 6:27 (τοῖς μισοῦσιν ὑμᾶς).[30] Additionally, both clusters of sayings deal with the theme of mistreatment and hatred (6:22–23b, 27–28, 29). From this two conclusions can be drawn. First, 6:22–23b must have already been attached to 6:20b–21 before the beatitudes were connected with 6:27–35 since the persecution beatitude contains the basis of association.[31] And second, v. 29, which also concerns maltreatment, and probably the other two insertions, vv. 30 and 31, were already part of the unit when the beatitudes were connected. As suggested above, v. 35b may have been added at the time of the joining of vv. 20b–23 and 27–35.

Schulz refers to both 6:29–30 and 6:27–28, 32–36 as "prophetic," arguing that they represent charismatic intensifications of Torah. To support this he cites the λέγω ὑμῖν formula of 6:27a and posits a similar introduction for 6:29 (Matt 5:39).[32] In his view, Q 6:27–28, 32–33 represents a radicalized interpretation of Lev 19:18,[33] Q 6:29a reinterprets the *ius talonis* of Exod 21:24–25, of Lev 24:20 and Deut 19:21; and Q 6:29b (Matt 5:40) presupposes and reinterprets the rabbinic exegesis of Exod 22:26–27.[34] There are two problems with this. First, apart from the entirely conjectural nature of Schulz's conclusion that λέγω ὑμῖν introduced Q 6:29–30, it is not obviously a "prophetic" formula; "I say to you" and similar asseveratives are also found before ethical admonitions in the *Testaments of the Twelve Patriarchs* where no prophetic knowledge is assumed.[35] Second, that these sayings are intended as reinterpretations or radicalizations of the Torah is far from obvious in Q; only in Matthaean redaction, with its use of the formula ἠκούσατε ὅτι ἐρρέθη, does

30. Lührmann ("Liebet eure Feinde," 413) points out that Matthew also provides the basis for a catchword connection of 5:11 with 5:44 in his use of διώκω in both verses.

31. Thus Schürmann, "Basileia-Verkündigung," 137. Jacobson ("Wisdom Christology," 52) holds that 6:22 presupposes the connection of 6:20b-21 with 6:27-35, i.e., that 6:22 is a later insertion. But this only raises the question, On what basis was 6:20b-21 connected with 6:27-35?

32. Schulz, *Spruchquelle*, 123–24, 131–32, 138–39. Schulz acknowledges the redactional nature of the formula in Matt 5:39 but insists on its presence here "since in the Q tradition it is a prophetic saying . . ." (p. 122 [trans. by auth.]).

33. Ibid., 134; similarly, Lührmann, "Liebet eure Feinde," 426.

34. Schulz, *Spruchquelle*, 125, referring to Wrege, *Bergpredigt*, 76–77. *Mek. Exod* to 22:25-26: "During the night one may take as a pledge a garment worn by day, and during the day one may take as a pledge a garment worn by night. And one must return the garment worn by day for the day and the garment worn by night for the night . . . You must not deprive [your neighbor] of the garment which is becoming to him" (trans. Lauterbach, *Mekilta*, 3.150–51).

35. See below, p. 210.

the idea of Torah reinterpretation come to the fore. The command ἀγαπᾶτε τοὺς ἐχθροὺς ὑμῶν (second-person plural!) does not obviously recall Lev 19:18: ἀγαπήσεις τὸν πλήσιον σου.[36] It is much closer in form and content to a host of admonitions from sapiential sources and from Hellenistic popular philosophy.[37] Likewise, once disassociated from Matthaean redaction (Matt 5:38), the admonition concerning non-retaliation loses any explicit connection with legal texts; as Zeller shows, it belongs instead to the wider realm of wisdom instruction.[38] Q 6:30, as Schulz himself concedes, entails no radicalization of the Torah. On the contrary, it is at home in the ethical teachings of second-temple Judaism:[39]

> Sir 4:3–5: Do not add to the troubles of an angry mind, nor delay your gift to a beggar; do not reject an afflicted suppliant, nor turn your face away from the poor; do not avert your eye from the needy, nor give a man occasion to curse you.

> Tobit 4:7–8: Give alms from your possessions to all who live uprightly, and do not let your eye begrudge the gift when you make it. Do not turn your face away from any poor man, and the face of God will not be turned away from you. If you have many possessions, make your gift from them in proportion; if few, do not be afraid to give according to the little you have.

The strategy of the speech is not to command by legal pronouncement or prophetic announcement, but to persuade by argument and rhetorical question. The closest material and stylistic analogies for the speech are

---

36. Zeller (*Mahnsprüche*, 103) observes that even Matthew did not efface the difference between the legal quotation (5:43) which uses the singular, and the Q saying which uses the plural.

37. Zeller, *Mahnsprüche*, 104–6 cites various sapiential parallels: Counsels of Wisdom 36–38: "Unto your opponent do not evil; your evildoer recompense with good; unto your enemy let justice [be done]" (Pfeiffer, *ANET*³ 426). Ahikar (Syr. A) 2:20: "My son, if your enemy meets you with evil meet him with wisdom" (Harris, *APOT* 2.730). Ahikar (Syr. B) 2:20: "My son, if your enemy meets you with evil, meet him with good" (Harris, *APOT*, 2.730). T. Benj. 4:2–3: "For a good man does not have a blind [dark] eye, for he is merciful to all, even though they may be sinners. And even if persons plot against him for evil ends, by doing good this man conquers evil, being watched over by God." T. Jos. 18:2: "And if anyone wishes to do you harm, you should pray for him along with doing good, and you will be rescued by the Lord from every evil" (trans. Kee, *OTP*, 826, 823). Several Hellenistic texts may be cited: Diogenes Laertius 8:23: Pythagoras bade his followers "not to make friends into enemies but to turn enemies into friends" (Loeb 2. 341). Musonius Rufus 10: "For to scheme how to bite back the biter and to return evil for evil is the act not of a human being but of a wild beast . . . But to accept injury not in a spirit of savage resentment and to show ourselves not implacable towards those who wrong us, but rather to be a source of good hope to them is characteristic of a benevolent and civilized way of life" (trans. C. E. Lutz, *Musonius Rufus* [New Haven: Yale University, 1947] 79).

38. Zeller, *Mahnsprüche*, 57–58.

39. Schulz, *Spruchquelle*, 126; see further Zeller, *Mahnsprüche*, 59–60.

found not in prophetic collections but in sapiential and popular philosophical works. The same holds for the conclusion of the speech: the motifs of imitation of God and of the righteous as υἱὸς θεοῦ are thoroughly at home in the wisdom tradition and in Hellenistic popular philosophy.⁴⁰

Q 6:36, 37–38⁴¹

Matthew and Luke agree in the relative order of these sayings (6:36, 37, 38 // Matt 5:48; 7:1, 2). However, while Luke uses 6:36 as a transitional saying introducing 6:37–38, Matthew employs it as a conclusion for his sixth antithesis. Since Q already has an adequate conclusion for 6:27–35 in v. 35c, and since Matthew's οὖν in 5:48 is undoubtedly redactional,⁴² it seems advisable to regard Luke's formulation—which includes asyndeton in v. 36 and καί connectives in v. 37—as original.⁴³

Although Schulz treats Q 6:37a, (b), 38c as a prophetic utilization of a wisdom saying, perhaps originally introduced by λέγω ὑμῖν,⁴⁴ there is little to sustain this opinion. Indeed the saying corresponds to a typical sapiential admonition, consisting of a prohibitive followed by a motive clause, and wisdom literature provides several parallels to both the basic motif of the saying and its inherent logic.⁴⁵ The assumption of a prophetic *Sitz* is unnecessary, and the evidence for a λέγω ὑμῖν introduction is entirely lacking.

Q 6:37a, (b), 38c may have circulated as an independent sapiential admonition, conceivably in a cluster of sayings such as is found now in

---

40. Georg Fohrer, υἱός, *TDNT* 8 (1972) 354–55; Zeller, *Mahnsprüche*, 107–8.

41. Reconstruction: Schulz, *Spruchquelle*, 130, 146–47; Worden, "Philological Analysis," 309–41; Zeller, *Mahnsprüche*, 110; Schürmann, *Lukasevangelium* 1:360, 362–64; Polag, *Fragmenta*, 34–36. It is clear that 6:36, 6:37a and 6:38c stood in Q. The fact that both Matthew and Luke speak of judging (i.e., condemning) in Matt 7:2a // Luke 6:37b may indicate that 6:37b also belonged to Q. That 6:37c (ἀπολύετε καὶ ἀπολυθήσεσθε) or 6:38a, b (δίδοτε καὶ δοθήσεται ὑμῖν . . .) derived from Q is more difficult to establish. These admonitions, in contrast to 6:37a, b, are positive. Moreover, at the Lucan parallel to Mark 4:24b, Luke omits ἐν τῷ μέτρῳ μετρεῖτε μετρηθήσεται ὑμῖν, presumably because he wishes to avoid a doublet with 6:38c. On the other hand, Luke may have inserted v. 38c into 6:37–38 under the influence of the Marcan text!

42. Οὖν: Matt 57x: from Mark 2x; from Q 5x; 13x diff Luke; red or *Sond*: 37x.

43. Since Luke otherwise tends to avoid parataxis, the use of καί in 6:37a (twice) is probably traditional. See Cadbury, *Style*, 142–45.

44. Schulz, *Spruchquelle*, 147–48.

45. Sir 28:1: ὁ ἐκδικῶν παρὰ κυρίου εὑρήσει ἐκδίκησιν, T. Zeb. 5:3. P. Insinger 33.8: "Violent vengefulness against the god brings a violent death." 33.20: "He who does harm for harm, his offspring will be harmed" (trans. Lichtheim, *Literature III*, 211–12). For further examples, see Zeller, *Mahnsprüche*, 115–16. Sayings expressing the symmetry between act and consequence are found throughout wisdom literature: e.g., Prov 13:20; 17:13; 22:22–23; Sir 7:1, 3, etc.

1 Clem 13:2.[46] In Q, however, it further develops the preceding speech on love of enemies and, more specifically, explicates the programmatic injunction to imitate divine mercy (6:36). Again, Q moves in the realm of popular philosophy. The motif of imitation of divine virtue is a common *topos*,[47] and appears especially in Hellenistic Judaism. In Ps-Aristeas, when asked by the king how one can become φιλάνθρωπος, the sage recalls the sufferings of humankind and says,

ἐπινοῶν οὖν ἕκαστα πρὸς τὸν ἔλεον τραπίσῃ καὶ γὰρ ὁ θεὸς ἐλεήμων ἐστιν, (208)

Therefore, if you consider these things you would be inclined to mercy, for God also is merciful.[48]

The effect of the juxtaposition of 6:37–38 and 6:36 is twofold: to interpret the ethic of non-condemnation as an act of mercy,[49] and to see this mercy as imitation of divine action. This motif binds 6:36, 37–38 closely with 6:27–35.

Q 6:39–45[50]

Synoptic comparison shows important disagreements between Matthew and Luke in the reproduction of these sayings. The balance of probability, however, is in favor of Lucan originality. The saying concerning "blind guides" (6:39 // Matt 15:14) has been inserted into the middle of a Marcan pericope (Mark 7:1–23 // Matt 15:1–20) where its position is obviously secondary. Matthew uses the saying on disciples

46. See also Polycarp *Phil.* 2:3. On the relation of these to the synoptic tradition, see Koester, *Synoptische Überlieferung*, 12–16, 115–18.

47. Musonius Rufus, fr. 17; Epictetus *Diss* 2.14.12; Seneca *Ad Lucilium epistulae* 95.50; idem, *De ira* 2.16.2. The idea is found already in Plato, *Theaetetus* 176B. See W. Michaelis, "μιμέομαι," *TDNT* 4 (1967) 661–62.

48. Text: André Pelletier, ed., *Lettre d'Aristée à Philocrate* (SC 89; Paris: Editions du Cerf, 1962) [trans. by auth.]. See also Ps-Aristeas §§ 182, 188, 205, 210, 254; Philo *Conf. Ling.* 41.

49. Although the evidence is not incontrovertible, the probability is that Luke's οἰκτρμόνες and οἰκτρίμων are original. Matthew uses τέλειος redactionally at 19:21 (Mark 10:21). As Manson (*Sayings*, 55) observes, "'Merciful' is regularly an epithet of God in the OT, while 'perfect' is never applied to God." See further, Trilling, *Israel*, 192–94; Schürmann, *Lukasevangelium* 1:360; Schulz, *Spruchquelle*, 130; Worden, "Philological Analysis," 311–13.

50. Reconstruction: Q 6:39: Schulz, *Spruchquelle*, 472–73; Schürmann, *Lukasevangelium* 1:367–68; Worden, "Philological Analysis," 342–48; Polag, *Fragmenta*, 36. The introduction, εἶπεν δὲ καὶ παραβολὴν αὐτοῖς, is Lucan (see above n. 3). Q 6:40: Schulz, *Spruchquelle*, 449–50; Worden, "Philological Analysis," 348–54; Steinhauser, *Doppelbildworte*, 187–88; Polag, *Fragmenta*, 36. Q 6:41–42: Schulz, *Spruchquelle*, 147; Worden, "Philological Analysis," 354–69; Polag, *Fragmenta*, 36. Q 6:43–45: Schulz, *Spruchquelle*, 316–18; Worden, "Philological Analysis," 369–439; Polag, *Fragmenta*, 36.

and their teachers (6:40 // Matt 10:24–25) in his mission speech, which is a secondary construction from various Q, M and Marcan texts. The remainder of the material has been broken up by Matthew through his insertion of M traditions (Matt 7:6, 15, 19–20) and relocated Q sayings (Luke 11:9–13 // Matt 7:7–11; Luke 6:31 // Matt 7:12; Luke 13:23–24 // Matt 7:14; Luke 13:25–27 // Matt 7:22–23). Q 6:43–45 is used twice by Matthew, once in the Sermon on the Mount, and once in conjunction with his saying on the blasphemy of the Spirit (12:31–37), which is itself a conflation of Mark and Q.

It is clear that this section of Q is composed of several originally independent sayings: 6:39, 40, 41–42, 43–44, and 45. Evidently the basis for the association between v. 39 and vv. 41–42 is the common motif of impaired vision and the importance of sighted instruction or correction. Since 6:40 does not share this motif, it is most likely that 6:40 was already attached to 6:39 prior to its association with vv. 41–42. Schürmann rightly observes, "Presumably no one would have encumbered the coherence of vv. 39, 41–42 so severely by a subsequent addition of v. 40."[51]

The following cluster of sayings (6:43–45) is also composite. Q 6:43 is a proverb which has been interpreted by means of 6:44a (ἕκαστον γὰρ δένδρον ἐκ τοῦ ἰδίου καρποῦ γινώσκεται). The metaphor of the grapes and figs (44b), which is a Stoic commonplace[52] and which also occurs in James 3:12 in the context of warnings to teachers, provides further grounding for vv. 43, 44a. Although similar in logic, the next saying (6:45) is probably an originally independent saying since it has to do specifically with speaking rather than with deeds. Following Bultmann, Wanke correctly observes that 6:45 functions as a "commentary word" for 6:43–44 and has the effect of narrowing the significance of the "fruits" of 6:43–44 from "deeds" to "teaching" or "instruction."[53] Since 6:41–42

---

51. Schürmann, Lukasevangelium 1:370 [trans. by auth.]; similarly Steinhauser, Doppelbildworte, 192; Wanke, "Kommentarworte," 213. Soiron (Logia Jesu, 84–85) appears to hold that Luke interpolated vv. 39 and 40 as independent logia.

52. In Stoic literature it is used to express the impossibility of one acting against nature. See Epictetus Diss. 2.20.18–19: "Such a powerful and invincible thing is the nature of man. For how can a vine be moved to act, not as a vine, but like an olive, or again an olive to act, not as an olive, but like a vine?" (Loeb 1:377). See also Marcus Aurelius 4.6.1; 8.15; 8.46; 10.8.6; 12.16.2. Plutarch De tranquillitate anima 472F: ". . . we do not expect the vine to bear figs nor the olive grapes, but, for ourselves, if we have not at one and the same time the advantages of both the wealthy and the learned, of both commanders and philosophers; of both flatterers and the outspoken, of both the thrifty and the lavish, we slander ourselves, we are displeased, we despise ourselves as living an incomplete and trivial life" (Loeb 6:213). Seneca Ad Lucilium Epistulae Morales 87.25: "Good does not spring from evil any more than figs grow from olive trees" (Loeb 2:337).

53. Bultmann, Tradition, 83 [87]; Wanke, "Kommentarworte," 214–15.

also concerns correction and direction—i.e., the function of teachers—it seems most likely that 6:45 had already been attached to 6:43–44 when this unit was connected with 6:41–42 and 6:39–40.

What is the significance of this composition? In trying to establish a thesis that the Q community was in conflict with Jewish revolutionary groups, Hoffmann argued that the "blind guides" of v. 39 are the Zealot leaders. On this understanding, Q criticizes the Zealots for presuming to judge others while overlooking their own faults and for failing to produce the true fruits of repentance (6:43–44), namely, love of enemies and rejection of violence.[54] But if 6:39–45 is anti-Zealot criticism, it is highly oblique: nothing in the speech touches on the principal political tenets of the Zealot movement, and Hoffmann's interpretation of μὴ κρίνετε as a rejection of revolutionary violence seems forced.

Jacobson contends that vv. 39 and 42 are redactional insertions which shift the address from the disciples to the opponents of Q.[55] These insertions he connects with the polemic against "this generation." Even before Jacobson, Schürmann had argued that 6:39–45 should be understood as an anti-Pharisaic collection.[56] In support of this he observed that the phrase ὁδηγοὶ τυφλῶν in Matt 15:14 (which he takes to be a closer approximation to Q than Luke 6:39)[57] recalls what may be a Pharisaic self-designation found in Rom 2:19: πέποιθάς τε σεαυτὸν ὁδηγὸν εἶναι τυφλῶν. According to Schürmann Q 6:40, which expresses the rabbinic idea of the master-student relationship,[58] is to be interpreted ironically or sarcastically: because their leaders are blind, Pharisees' disciples are of necessity blind too.[59] On this view, 6:41–42 has to do with the reasons why Pharisees are unable to teach others, and vv. 43–45 continue this polemic: "They teach badly (v. 45), produce bad fruit (vv. 43–44) and for that reason cannot be good."[60]

---

54. Hoffmann, "Die Anfänge," 149. See below, chapter six, for Hoffmann's anti-Zealot reading of the temptation story.

55. Jacobson, "Wisdom Christology," 62–65, 95–96. The reasons for ascribing v. 42a (?) to redaction appear to be connected with the absence of a parallel to this in *Gos. Thom.* 26 (ibid., 57–58).

56. Schürmann, *Lukasevangelium* 1:366–79.

57. Schürmann (*Lukasevangelium* 1:370 n. 177) argues that the Matthaean declaratory form of the saying is closer to the original than Luke's double question, although he also asserts that the questions are pre-Lucan rather than Lucan!

58. See *Sipra* 25.23: "[God says to Israel] 'You are my servants.' It is enough for the servant that he be as his master" [trans. by auth. from Str-B 1.578]. Also *Exod. Rab.* 42.5.

59. Schürmann, *Lukasevangelium* 1.370 [trans. by auth.]; similarly Wanke, "Kommentarworte," 214: "The rabbi's pupil is bound by his own self-understanding to the tradition represented in the form of his teacher. Guidance which forgets its basic commitment is 'blind'" [trans. by auth.].

60. Schürmann, *Lukasevangelium* 1:370 [trans. by auth.].

Since Schürmann and Jacobson concede that neither 6:40 nor 6:41–42 originated as a specifically anti-Pharisaic saying,[61] their interpretation rests, first, upon an anti-Pharisaic interpretation of 6:39 and the effect which this exerted on the entire passage and, second, upon an ironic interpretation of 6:40. However, the image of "blind guides" or "the blind leading the blind" was a commonplace in the ancient world; there is no reason to constrict its application to the Pharisaic opponents of the community.[62] If indeed 6:39 were directed at Pharisees, one would expect direct address or perhaps even a woe instead of the conditional formulation of Matthew or the rhetorical question of Luke. The point of the saying is not to establish at the Pharisees' expense that the disciple always emulates his master (and his faults!), but to fault those who strive to go beyond their master, i.e., those who *do not emulate their master*. In the context, the saying implies that the "blind guides" are those who try to outstrip their master by judging others. Thereby they fail to emulate divine mercy and show themselves to be blinded. Instead of using 6:40 as an ironic comment, Q actually subscribes to this model of discipleship (as other Q sayings such as 9:57–58 imply as well).[63] Q 6:36 recommends

---

61. Schürmann (*Lukasevangelium* 1:370) and Wanke ("Kommentarworte," 213) hold that 6:40 as an independent saying had a positive christological significance. Schürmann even concedes that prior to its connection with vv. 41–45, 6:39–40 "might have originally addressed teachers in the community: they should not be blind guides (v. 39), but pay attention to the word and manner of Jesus (v. 40)" (p. 370). Both Wanke ("Kommentarworte," 214) and Steinhauser (*Doppelbildworte*, 192) hold that vv. 6:39–40 were already anti-Pharisaic. With reference to 6:41–42, Schürmann (*Lukasevangelium* 1:372) notes that the second-person singular address does not suggest an originally polemical *Sitz* and ὑποκριτά is not reserved only for Pharisaic opponents (see Matt 24:51; Luke 12:56).

62. Xenophon *Mem.* 1.3.4; Sextus Empiricus *Outlines of Pyrrhonism* 3.259: "Now the expert artist does not teach the expert, for neither of them *qua* artist needs teaching. Nor does the non-expert teach the non-expert any more than the blind can lead the blind (ὥσπερ οὐδὲ τυφλὸν ὁδηγεῖν δύναται τυφλός) (Loeb 1:499). Idem, *Against the Professors* 1.31. Philo *De virtutibus*, 7: "But some making no account of the wealth of nature pursue the wealth of vain opinion. They choose to lean on the blind rather than one with sight and with this defective guide must of necessity fall" (Loeb 8:167). Horace *Epistles* 1.17.4: "ut si caecus iter monstrare velit." *T. Rub.* 2:9: αὕτη [ἀγνοία] τὸν νεώτερον ὁδηγεῖ ὡς τυφλὸν ἐπὶ βόθον καὶ ὡς κτῆνος ἐπὶ κρημνόν. Dio Chrysostom 62.7; Plato *Respublica* 8.554B.

63. Interestingly, Neusner ("The Pharisees in the Light of the Historical Sources of Judaism," *Formative Judaism: Religious, Historical and Literary Studies* [Brown Judaic Studies 37; Chico, Calif.: Scholars Press, 1982] 80) observes that the materials concerning the Pharisees prior to 70 CE tend to concern cultic matters, and (surprisingly) do not show "much interest in defining the master-student relationship, the duties of the master and the responsibilities and rights of the disciple, the way in which the disciple should learn his lessons, and similar matters of importance in later times." If this is so, the sayings upon which Schürmann et al. stake their case may be rabbinic (i.e., post-Yavnean) and not Pharisaic at all, and the Christian examples may be the earliest versions!

the imitation of divine mercy; 6:39, seen in the context of vv. 36, 37–38, 40–42, recommends imitation of the διδάσκαλος (Jesus) who exemplifies the ethic of non-judgment as well as non-retaliation, love of enemies and startling beneficence. Q 6:39–45, of course, takes particular aim at teachers (actual or imagined) who do not follow Jesus in his radical lifestyle and ethic. But there is no compelling reason to suppose that 6:39–42 is formulated with outsiders and opponents in mind; on the contrary, it has a parenetic intent similar to what is encountered in Rom 14:2–23 and James 4:11–12.

Q 6:46,47–49

Matthew has recast this Q pericope in the form of a judgment scene by revising the "Lord, Lord" saying, by introducing the phrase "in that day" and by interpolating a judgment saying from another context in Q (7:22–23 // Luke 13:26–27). By contrast, Luke's version of the "Lord, Lord" saying reveals fewer signs of editing, as most critics recognize.[64]

The parable of the two builders, which has several rabbinic parallels,[65] may well have circulated independently as an admonition to act upon what one has been taught. Whether 6:46 ever existed as an independent saying is virtually impossible to determine. Schulz treats it as a prophetic saying.[66] But the extreme brevity of the saying as well as the fact that both 6:46 and 6:47–49 speak of "doing my words" (ἃ λέγω, μου οἱ λόγοι) suggest that 6:46 may have been formulated specifically as an introduction for the parable.[67]

In the Q context, 6:46, 47–49 serves as the conclusion to the inaugural sermon (6:20b–49). Some have urged that κύριε, κύριε is an address to the

---

64. Schürmann (Lukasevangelium 1:381) notes the Matthaean character of τὸ θέλημα τοῦ πατρός μου (Matt 12:50; 21:31; 6:10; 26:42), ὁ ἐν τοῖς οὐρανοῖς (frequently in Matt), βασιλεία τῶν οὐρανῶν (Matt 34x). He argues that πᾶς ὁ + participle (Matt 7:21a) has been influenced by Luke 6:47, 49, that εἰσέρχεσθαι εἰς τὴν βασιλείαν recalls Matt 7:13–14 (diff Luke 13:24) and that ἀλλά following a negation is a Matthaean locution. In favor of Lucan priority: Bultmann, Tradition, 116 [122]; Fitzmyer, Luke I-IX, 644; Lührmann, Redaktion, 56; Polag, Fragmenta, 38; Schenk, Synopse, 34–35; Schmid, Matthäus und Lukas, 244–45; Gerhard Schneider, "Christusbekenntnis und Christliches Handeln," Die Kirche des Anfangs (Freiburg: Herder & Herder, 1978) 10–13. Hahn (Titles, 91) argues for Matthaean priority but ignores the obviously Matthaean vocabulary.
65. M. 'Abot 3:18; 'Abot R Nat. (A) 24.
66. Schulz, Spruchquelle, 428; Heinrich Greeven, Gebet und Eschatologie im Neuen Testament (Gütersloh: Mohn, 1931) 62; Schneider, "Christusbekenntnis," 13.
67. Thus Schürmann, Lukasevangelium 1:300 n. 3. That this is a creation ex nihilo must be doubted, since a very similar phrase occurs in P. Egerton 2.2 in Jesus' response to questioners: τί με καλεῖτ[ε τῷ στό]ματι ὑμ[ῶν δι]δάσκαλον· μ[ὴ ἀκού]οντες ὃ [λ]έγω. See on this, John Dominic Crossan, Four Other Gospels (Minneapolis: Seabury-Winston, 1985) 74, 79.

eschatological judge.[68] But while this interpretation is correct for Matthew, it is not particularly suited to Q. Here κύριε appears to be the respectful address of a disciple to his teacher.[69] Reproaches such as 6:46 and contrast parables are found in other sapiential and didactic contexts. Jacobson observes that the figure of a ruined house occurs at the end of several wisdom collections, including

Prov 9:13–18	concluding	Prov 1—9
Job 27:13–23	concluding	Job 3—27
Qoh 12:3	concluding	Qoh 1—12
Prov 15:25	concluding	Prov 10—15

and a more general allusion to ruin in Prov 24:21–22 concludes Prov 22:17—24:22.[70] It can be added that many sapiential instructions end (or sometimes begin) with descriptions of the rewards which await those who attend to the instructions, and the consequences for those who do not. For example:

Prov	1:29–33	Threat and promise concluding Wisdom's speech (1:20–33)
	2:20–22	Promise and threat concluding an instruction (2:1–11)
	4:18–19	Promise and threat concluding an instruction (4:10–19)
	5:22–23	Summarizing threat concluding an instruction (5:1–23)
	7:24–27	Call to attention and threat concluding an instruction (7:1–27)
	8:32–36	Call to attention and contrast saying concluding Wisdom's speech (8:1–36)
Sir	6:32–37	Call to attention and promise concluding an instruction (6:18–37)
	24:19–22	Invitation and promise concluding Wisdom's speech (24:1–22)

---

68. Thus Hahn, *Titles*, 91–92; Schenk, *Synopse*, 35; Schneider, "Christusbekenntnis," 13. Schulz (*Spruchquelle*, 429) ascribes 6:46 (and 6:47–49) to the younger "Hellenistic Jewish Christian" stratum of Q and connects the κύριε address with the κύριος statements of the parousia parables of Q (Q 12:42–46; 19:12–19). He comments, "Materially it is not really distinct from 'Maranatha' (1 Cor 16:22) and the other instances of κύριος in statements about the parousia (e.g., 1 Thess 4:15–18; 1 Cor 5:5, etc.) of the pre-Pauline Hellenistic Jewish Christian tradition . . ." [trans. by auth.].

69. Thus Bultmann, *Tradition*, 116 n. 2 [122 n. 1]; Manson, *Sayings*, 60; Betz, "An Episode in the Last Judgment (Matt 7:21–23)," *Essays*, 132–33; Jacobson, "Wisdom Christology," 62. For documentation of the use of κύριε, meaning "teacher," see G. Dalman, *The Words of Jesus* (trans. D. M. Kay; Edinburgh: T & T Clark, 1902) 327–31.

70. Jacobson, "Wisdom Christology," 110 n. 84. Jacobson refers to J. F. A. Sawyer, "The Ruined House in Ecclesiastes 12: A Reconstruction of the Original Parable," *JBL* 84 (1975) 519–31.

Warnings are typical in didactic contexts, as *Cebes' Tablet,* a well-known piece of popular philosophy, shows. The teaching takes the form of an exegesis of an inscription in the Temple of Cronos. The sage warns,

> If you pay attention and understand what is said, you will be wise and happy. If, on the other hand, you do not, you will become foolish, unhappy, sullen and stupid and you will fare badly in life. (3.1)

He continues, evoking the myth of the Sphinx,

> Foolishness is the Sphinx. Foolishness speaks in riddles of these things: what is good, what is bad, and what is neither good nor bad in life. Thus, if anyone does not understand these things he is destroyed by her, not all at once, as a person devoured by the Sphinx died. Rather, he is destroyed little by little, just like those who are handed over for retribution. But if one does understand, Foolishness is in turn destroyed, and he himself is saved and is blessed and happy in his whole life. As for you, then, pay attention; do not misunderstand.[71]

Viewed in the context of sapiential and didactic literature, Q 6:46, 47–49 provides a good example of the warnings which typically conclude these instructions.

The Composition of the Q Sermon

Compositional analysis has shown that a rather complex process contributed to the formation of 6:20b–49. We have already suggested that the association of the beatitudes with the admonition to love one's enemies presupposed that 6:22–23b was already part of the beatitudes, and that 6:35b may have been inserted into 6:35a, c at the time of this addition. Q 6:36 provides a transition between 6:27–35 and 6:37–38. Whereas the first half of the speech concerns violence, generosity and mercy, Q 6:39–45 is unified by the concern with speaking and teaching (or correcting). In typically sapiential style, the speech closes with a mild reproach and a contrast saying designed to express the urgency of attending to the teacher's words.

Analysis of the constituent forms and motifs of the speech reveals a predominantly sapiential idiom. The imperatives in 6:27–35, 36, 37–38 and 41–42 belong to the category of sapiential admonitions,[72] and most find parallels in motif within other sapiential literature and popular

---

71. Trans. J. T. Fitzgerald and L. M. White, *The Tabula of Cebes* (SBLTT 24; Graeco-Roman Religion 7; Chico Calif.: Scholars Press, 1983).
72. See Zeller, *Mahnsprüche,* passim.

moral philosophy. Bultmann classifies only the beatitudes and Q 6:46 as prophetic or apocalyptic sayings.[73] As we have noted, however, the "prophetic" designation is more appropriate to the Matthaean version of the "Lord, Lord" saying than it is to the Q version; as Bultmann himself states, κύριε, κύριε is the address of a student to the teacher.

The beatitudes pose a more complex problem. It is, of course, well known that the form is common in sapiential literature. But as Augustin George observed, the beatitudes of Jesus are not the simple moral or religious exhortations of wisdom; they are proclamations of eschatological salvation.[74] And unlike both sapiential beatitudes and the majority of those found in apocalyptic books, the Q beatitudes do not function as *conditions of salvation* or admonitions concerning how one ought to act;[75] instead they pronounce blessing upon a group defined by social and economic circumstances: poverty, hunger, sorrow and persecution. In Q they pronounce blessing upon the community. Even though the Q beatitudes should be considered as a development beyond both sapiential and apocalyptic beatitudes,[76] they share many of the structural and formal features of the sapiential beatitude, in particular, serialization and placement at the beginning of an instruction.[77] Recently Hans-Dieter Betz has made a suggestion which sheds light upon the relation of the beatitudes to traditional wisdom. The beatitudes are "anti-beatitudes": they stand in contrast to the views of the conventional wisdom

---

73. Bultmann, *Tradition*, 109–10 [114–15] (6:20b–21, 22–23); 116 [122–23] (6:46).

74. A. George, "La 'Forme' des Béatitudes jusqu'à Jésus," *Mélanges bibliques rédigés en l'honneur de André Robert* (Travaux de l'Institute Catholique 4; Paris: Bloud et Gay, 1957) 398–403; also J. M. Robinson, "The Formal Structure of Jesus' Message," *Current Issues in New Testament Interpretation: Essays in Honor of Otto A. Piper* (New York: Harper & Row, 1962) 91–110, 273–84, esp. 98, 278 n. 25.

75. A few apocalyptic beatitudes pronounce proleptic blessing on the elect or on those who will witness the eschatological events: Dan 12:12; 1 Enoch 58:2; Sib. Or. 3.371–72; Pss. Sol. 17:50; 18:7; 2 Enoch 66:7. Most others are exhortations to faithfulness, wisdom, perseverance and the like: 2 Enoch 42:7–14; 44:4; 52:1–5; Pss. Sol. 4:26; 1 Enoch 82:4; 99:10. See further, Eduard Schweizer, "Formgeschichtliches zu den Seligpreisungen Jesu," *NTS* 19 (1972–73) 121–26; Jacques Dupont, *Les Béatitudes*, Vol. 2, *La Bonne Nouvelle* (EBib; Paris: Gabalda, 1969) 324–38.

76. See the excellent study of R. A. Guelich, "The Matthaean Beatitudes: Entrance-Requirements or Apocalyptic Blessings," *JBL* 95 (1976) 415–34.

77. Beatitudes occur in *series* (usually in pairs) in: Tob 13:14; Pss 31 (32):1–2; 118 (119):1–2; 127 (128):1–2; 136 (137):8–9; Sir 14:1–2; 25:8–9; 2 Enoch 52:1–5 (blessings and woes); 42:6–14. Beatitudes are frequently found at the beginning of a speech or psalm: Pss 1:1; 31 (32):1–2; 40 (41):1; 111 (112):1; 118 (119):1–2; 127 (128):1–2; Sir 14:1–2; 26:1; 1 Enoch 10:6–7. Perhaps the closest parallel to the two-part structure of the Q beatitudes is found in Tob 13:14: "How blessed are those who love you; they will rejoice in your peace. Blessed are those who grieved over all your afflictions; for they will rejoice for you upon seeing your glory."

that those who dwell in affluence and safety are blessed.[78] Parallels to these may be found in Cynic teachings; but in Q the criticism of wealth is based not on philosophical reflection but upon an apprehension that the imminent kingdom will bring about a radical transformation of human life. Seen in this light, the Q beatitudes, while not typically sapiential in content, could well be characterized as the "radical wisdom of the kingdom." Other examples of such radical wisdom are to be found in the immediate context: in 6:27–35, 36–38, 39–45. In a programmatic fashion, the beatitudes signal the radical nature of the kingdom and the behavior which it calls forth. Both the beatitudes and the admonitions are sapiential forms infused with eschatological content; both evince the presence of the kingdom, its radical nature and its radical demands.

If the contents of Q 6:20b–49 are overwhelmingly sapiential, so too is the structure and organization. The collection opens with a programmatic statement in the form of four beatitudes; the body of instructions consists of sapiential admonitions (many expanded by motive clauses, rhetorical questions and assorted metaphors), and it closes with a typically sapiential warning. This structure is paralleled in many wisdom collections, for example, in Prov 1. The instruction is prefaced by a series of infinitives (1:2–6) ending with the programmatic statement "The fear of the Lord is the beginning of wisdom" (1:8). Then follows the instruction proper (1:8–19), which begins characteristically with "Hear, my son," and contains a series of admonitions (some with motive clauses). The speech closes with a reproach of Wisdom (1:20–33) describing the fate of the foolish and concluding with the contrast saying,

> For the simple are killed by their turning away,
> and the complacence of fools destroys them;
> but he who listens to me will dwell secure,
> and will be at ease, without dread of evil.

Another example is found in Prov 3:13–35.[79] The instruction begins with a beatitude (3:13: "Blessed is the man who finds wisdom") and a praise of

---

78. Betz, "The Beatitudes of the Sermon on the Mount (Matt. 5:3–12)," *Essays*, 17–36. Betz cites Gladigow ("Makarismus") who discusses the "beatitude of the wise" which arises from critical reflection upon conventional wisdom. In Cynic teaching, e.g., values are reversed: poverty is praised instead of riches, and poverty is regarded as the precondition of freedom, virtue, wisdom and happiness. Betz (p. 17) cites Sir 25:8 (μακάριος ὁ συνοικῶν γυναικὶ συνετῇ) as an "anti-beatitude" to the conventional wisdom that a wealthy and beautiful wife is desirable.

79. Murphy (*Wisdom Literature*, 57–58) divides this into two instructions: 3:13–24 and 3:25–35. A. Barucq (*Le Livre des Proverbs* [Sources bibliques; Paris: Gabalda, 1964] 62–65) divides it into three: 3:13–20 (éloge de la Sagesse); 3:21–26 (éloge de la prudence et du discernement) and 3:27–35 (conseils pour les rapports sociaux).

Wisdom (3:14–20). Then follow several admonitions (3:21–30) and the concluding contrast saying,

> The Lord's curse is on the house of the wicked;
> but he blesses the abode of the righteous.
> Towards the scorners he is scornful, but to the humble he shows favor.
> The wise will inherit honor, but fools get disgrace.
>
> (3:33–35)

Like Q 6:20b–49, both of these instructions conclude with a contrast saying concerning secure dwelling places. Several other examples of sapiential instructions will be examined in chapter seven, but these two examples suffice to show that the inaugural Q sermon is patterned on one form of sapiential speech.

The only element within 6:20b–49 which falls outside the scope of the sapiential idiom of the speech is 6:23c. As noted above, this phrase fits poorly with the rest of the beatitudes. Moreover, it reflects the deuteronomistic notion of Yahweh's sending of the prophets to Israel, and Israel's habitual rejection and murder of them. Since this theology is dominant in the redactional stratum discussed in the previous chapter, it is best to treat 6:23c as an interpolation made from the perspective of that redaction. It has the effect of focusing the beatitudes especially upon the experience of rejection and opposition, an experience which appears to have been especially important in the consciousness of the redactor of the speeches characterized by the motif of the announcement of judgment over "this generation."

Summary. Q 6:20–49 is composed of sapiential forms, organized into a sapiential instruction, and expressing an ethic which responds to the radical character of the kingdom. Only 6:23c belongs to a secondary level of redaction.

Q 9:57–62; 10:2–16, 21–24

This block of Q material breaks easily into three sub-sections: 9:57–62, on discipleship; 10:2–16, instructions for mission; and 10:21–24, a thanksgiving and concluding beatitude.

Q 9:57–62

Three chriae concerning discipleship begin the collection.[80] Despite the common theme, it is clear that the three do not form an original

---

80. It is unlikely that 9:61–62 was from L (thus Manson, *Sayings*, 72; Fitzmyer, *Luke I–IX*, 833) because of the close parallels in construction between 9:59–60 and 9:61–62.

unity. The second (9:59–60) suggests that discipleship is even more urgent than filial obligations toward one's deceased parents—obligations which in Mishnaic law took precedence over the recitation of the Shema' or the Shemone Esreh.[81] Similarly, the third pronouncement (9:61–62), which probably alludes to the story of the calling of Elisha in 1 Kgs 19:19–21, indicates that the service of the kingdom is even more urgent than Elijah's summons, which at least allowed Elisha to bid his parents farewell. The first saying, however, is quite different. Although the interlocutor's avowal "I will follow you wherever you go" leads to the expectation that the retort will concern discipleship, it is in fact a statement about the Son of Man. Of course it has a bearing on discipleship: the assertion is meant to provide a structural homologue for discipleship:[82] the mode of existence of the Son of Man is to be the pattern for the life of the disciple.

That 9:57–58 was not always attached to 9:59–60 is suggested not only by its differing logic and structure but also by the fact that 9:58 appears to have circulated as an independent saying. A slightly gnosticized version of the saying is found in *Gos. Thom.* 86:[83]

> Jesus said: [The foxes have their holes] and the birds have [their] nest, but the Son of Man has no place to lay his head and rest.[84]

Luke may have composed the saying, although, as Martin Hengel points out, it is as likely that Matthew omitted it because it added nothing to Matt 8:21–22 = Luke 9:59–60 and was therefore unnecessary for "his compactly arranged composition" (*The Charismatic Leader and His Followers* [trans. J. Greig; New York: Crossroad, 1981] 4 n. 5). Using Vassiliadis' criteria (see above, chapter two), a good case can be made for its inclusion in Q: it occurs in a Q context, it coheres theologically and stylistically with other parts of Q, it displays no obvious signs of Lucan redaction (except perhaps κύριε, δὲ καί and εἶπεν δὲ πρὸς αὐτόν—all in the introductions), there is a possible reason for Matthew to have omitted it, and it appears in the Lucan "great interpolation."

81. See *m. Ber.* 3:1 and Hengel, *Charismatic Leader*, 8–9 and n. 21. F. Gerald Downing ("Cynic and Christians," *NTS* 30 [1984] 588, 592) notes that 9:59–60 is comparable to examples of Cynic disregard for burial customs.

82. See Theissen, *First Followers*, 26–27.

83. Schrage (*Verhältnis*, 168–69) contends that *Gos. Thom.* 86 depends upon the Coptic translation of the NT on the basis of the following agreements: (*a*) the addition of possessive pronouns to "holes," "nest" and "head," (*b*) the addition of a second ογνταγ (= ἔχουσιν) and (*c*) the use of ма, "place," instead of τωн (= ποῦ). However, the first feature is simply a Coptism (see A. Guillaumont, "Les Sémitismes dans l'Evangile selon Thomas: Essai de classement," *Studies in Gnosticism and Hellenistic Religions* [EPRO 91; Leiden: E. J. Brill, 1981] 192) and the use of ма with ογνταγ/мнтq appears to be usual for translating ἔχω + ποῦ (cf. Luke 12:17) or other similar adverbs (see Crum 154B). On the other hand, the differences between Thomas and the Sahidic NT (the omission of "of heaven," "nest" in the singular and the use of εριкε ντεqапе rather than ñρεкт τεqапе [cf. Till §343]) indicate independent development.

84. Trans. by Lambdin, *NHLE*, 127.

This may have originally been a piece of pessimistic wisdom about humankind in general;[85] in Q, however, Son of Man has come to be used as a christological title and the saying as a whole has been given a setting relating to discipleship: the Son of Man provides the pattern for all Christian discipleship.

Several authors have suggested that there is an allusion to the heavenly Sophia who could find no dwelling place on earth (cf. 1 Enoch 42:1–2).[86] Jacobson opines that its position in Q recommends this interpretation: following 7:35, which describes the rejection of the Son of Man, one of the τέκνα σοφίας, 9:57–58 likewise employs sapiential motifs to describe the rejection of the Son of Man. Accordingly he assigns 9:57–58 to the stage of Q redaction which reflects the opposition between Jesus and "this generation," as well as the strong presence of wisdom motifs.[87] This interpretation seems far-fetched. Q 9:57–58 says nothing of rejection and it does not state that the Son of Man *could not* find a place of rest or that he subsequently found one among the angels (as in 1 Enoch 42). Instead the saying describes the vagrant existence of the Son of Man. As such, it provides the motivation for the radical detachment enjoined by the second and third chriae. If Q 9:58 was originally a proverb or independent Son of Man saying, it was apparently re-cast in the form of a chria, and then attached to 9:59–62 to provide a structural homologue between the Son of Man and his followers, and thus to motivate and legitimate their radical pattern of discipleship.[88]

Q 10:2–16

The next set of sayings deals with mission. Although Luke's setting of the speech (10:1) is undoubtedly secondary,[89] he has preserved the order of the Q sayings better than Matthew, who fused the Marcan mission charge with that of Q. Comparison of Q with Mark suggests that the core of the tradition consisted of (at least) the "equipment instruction"

---

85. See Bultmann, *Tradition*, 28 [27]; C. Colpe, υἱὸς τοῦ ἀνθρώπου, *TDNT* 8 (1972) 432–33.

86. T. Arvedson, *Das Mysterium Christi. Eine Studie zu Mt. 11.25–30* (Uppsala: Lundequistska; Leipzig: Lorentz, 1937) 210 n. 9; Hamerton-Kelly, *Pre-existence*, 29; Hoffmann, *Studien*, 181–82; Grundmann, "Weisheit," 181; Jacobson, "Wisdom Christology," 132.

87. Jacobson, "Wisdom Christology," 132–33, 145–46.

88. Similarly Schürmann, "Menschensohn-Titel," 132; Wanke, "Kommentarworte," 217.

89. For a discussion of the Lucan redactional terms present, see Jeremias, *Sprache*, 183; Hoffmann, *Studien*, 284–85; Schulz, *Spruchquelle*, 404 n. 4.

(10:4 // Mark 6:8–9), and instructions concerning acceptance (10:5–7 // Mark 6:10) and rejection (10:10–11 // Mark 6:11).[90]

As the Matthew-Luke comparison shows, the Q mission speech began with Luke 10:2 // Matt 9:37–38 including perhaps a reference to Jesus speaking (10:2a // Matt 9:37a). Schulz views the commissioning speech as a unitary composition from the beginning.[91] This is unlikely. The harvest motif introduced in 10:2 does not reappear in the rest of the sermon; in 10:2 "the Lord of the harvest" is the immediate "sender" of the workers, while both 10:3 and 10:16 imply a chain in which Jesus is the proximate sender; 10:2 exists independently in *Gos. Thom.* 73; and as Zeller observes, the command to pray for more missionaries is not directed to those sent out in v. 3, "but to Christians who might be imagined to be gathered for prayer prior to the commissioning, as in Acts 13:1–3."[92] There is, in short, a change of addressee between 10:3 and the following equipment instruction.

It is frequently observed that the use of "harvest" in 10:2b is distinctive since it applies to missionary activity a metaphor usually found in the context of apocalyptic judgment.[93] Moreover the Q missionaries appear in a role elsewhere reserved to the angels, namely, the gathering of the eschatological "harvest" (cf. Mark 13:27; Rev 14:15; Matt 13:39–41). Hoffmann remarks, "Therefore the 'mission' for Q is no different from the harvest time, but is itself an eschatological occurrence."[94] Both Bornkamm and Lührmann urge that since "harvest" is regularly used as an image for God's judgment of the Gentiles (Joel 4:1–21; Isa 24:13; Mic 4:11–13; Rev 14:15), the "harvest" in 10:2 should be seen to include the in-gathering of the Gentiles.[95] Caution is in order here, however, since this metaphor also occurs with reference to Israel alone (Hos 6:11; 4 Ezra 9:1–25, 29–37). In the level of redaction outlined in chapter four, Q supplies evidence of a Gentile mission; however, 10:2 is not incontrovertible evidence of that mission.

90. See Hahn, *Mission*, 43.
91. Schulz, *Spruchquelle*, 409.
92. Zeller, "Redaktionsprozesse," 404 [trans. by auth.]. Zeller (pp. 404–5, 409–10) accordingly detects a shift in *Sitz im Leben* between 10:3–12 (instructions for missionaries) and 10:2–16, 21–22 (parenesis in the churches established by those missionaries).
93. Joel 4:1, 13; Isa 18:3–7; 24:13; 27:12–13; Jer 51:33; Hos 6:11; Mic 4:11–13; 4 Ezra 4:28–32; 2 *Apoc. Bar.* 70:1–10.
94. Hoffmann, *Studien*, 290 [trans. by auth.]; similarly Hahn, *Mission*, 40; Schulz, *Spruchquelle*, 410.
95. G. Bornkamm, "End-Expectation and Church in Matthew," *Tradition and Interpretation in Matthew* (Philadelphia: Westminster Press, 1963) 18; Lührmann, *Redaktion*, 60.

Q 10:3 has somewhat stronger connections with the rest of the speech. Hahn suggests that some sort of commissioning belonged with the mission speech from the outset although he does not think that 10:3 itself was that commissioning.[96] The Marcan version of the mission charge also uses ἀποστέλλω (6:7) though in Mark it occurs in the narrative framework rather than as a saying of Jesus. However, there are enough similarities between Mark 3:13–15 and Mark 6:7 to raise the strong suspicion that 6:7 is a redactional construction influenced by 3:13–15.[97] Hence the agreement between Mark 6:7 and Q 10:3 at this point may be simple coincidence. As to 10:3 itself, it can easily stand on its own and may well have been an originally independent saying.[98] Nevertheless, 10:3 with its description of missionaries as "sheep" is particularly apt for 10:4–7, which enjoins them to travel without provisions or money (i.e., in an exposed and defenseless manner). Schulz rightly observes that the sheep-wolf contrast is not used as it is in other Jewish writings to denote "Israel-Gentile";[99] the saying clearly recognizes existing threats to the lives of missionaries, but these threats come not from Gentiles but from fellow Jews. While acknowledging the dangers, the saying conveys a fundamental optimism concerning the mission; the forewarnings do not obscure the conviction that the mission is authorized by God and a part of the eschatological manifestation of the kingdom.[100] Hence, although 10:3 may have been originally independent, it coheres well with the rest of the speech and may be, as Hahn claims, a relatively early accretion to the instructions.[101]

The core of the mission charge appears in Q 10:4–11, as the Mark-Q comparison shows.[102] Mark's version is somewhat less detailed and

---

96. Hahn, *Mission*, 43, 44–45.

97. Both introductions employ the words προσκαλεῖται, ἀποστέλλω, ἐξουσίαν ἐκβάλλειν τὰ δαιμόνια/ἐξουσίαν τῶν πνευμάτων τῶν ἀκαθάρτων, κηρύσσειν (3:14; 6:12).

98. Thus Paul Hoffmann, "Lk 10,5–11," 50; Laufen, *Doppelüberlieferung*, 250–51; Polag, *Christologie*, 99.

99. Schulz, *Spruchquelle*, 413.

100. G. Bornkamm, λύκος, *TDNT* 4 (1967) 310: "The disciples are herewith warned of the danger which threatens them . . . but they are also comforted, for this is no unforeseen disaster, but exposure to danger is involved in the very fact that they are sent out by Jesus." Similarly J. Jeremias, ἀμνός, *TDNT* 1 (1964) 340. Both cite *Tanch. Toledot* 32b (= Str-B 1.574): "Hadrian said to R. Jehoshua [ca. 90 CE]: 'There is something great about the sheep [Israel] that can persist among seventy wolves [Gentiles].' He replied: 'Great is the Shepherd who delivers it and watches over it and destroys them [the wolves] before them [Israel].'"

101. Hahn, *Mission*, 45; see also Dieter Georgi, *Die Gegner des Paulus im 2. Korintherbrief* (WMANT 11; Neukirchen-Vluyn: Neukirchener, 1964) 208.

102. Reconstructions: Schulz, *Spruchquelle*, 404–7; Laufen, *Doppelüberlieferung*, 201–46; Hoffmann, *Studien*, 263–87.

provides a slightly different instruction. While it forbids the carrying of a purse or bread, it permits both sandals and a staff. By contrast Q allows neither provisions nor sandals. The radical comportment of Q is usually taken as a sign of its antiquity,[103] and the Marcan account is viewed as a relaxation of the earlier, more stringent demands. The Q version contains several elements not found in Mark: the greeting of peace, the command to greet no one on the road,[104] the proverb ἄξιος γὰρ ὁ ἐργάτης τοῦ μισθοῦ (τῆς τροφῆς) αὐτοῦ, the command to "eat whatever is placed before you"[105] and the references to healing and proclaiming that ἤγγικεν (ἐφ' ὑμᾶς) ἡ βασιλεία τοῦ θεοῦ. While the proverb, which also occurs in 1 Tim 5:18 and *Did.* 13:1, may be a secondary accretion, it is usually agreed that the greeting of peace and the description of missionary activity are very ancient. Dautzenberg rightly observes that in comparison with Mark, Q provides a much less abstract conception of the preaching of the kingdom and one which appears to be closer to the actual situation of preaching:

> The essential difference between the preaching of the kingdom of God in Mark 1:14–15 and in Q lies in the fact that the preaching of the kingdom in Mark 1:14–15 seemingly has been divorced completely from its connection with the preaching and living situation which was typical of Jesus' preaching and partly also of the Q group, and became definable as pure teaching or pure "kerygma."[106]

Formally and materially the most intrusive passage is 10:13–15,[107] which is directed not at the community but at its opponents and which reflects the experience of the rejection of Q's preachers. These woes are clearly secondary interpolations, appended because of the mention of the rejection of missionaries in 10:10–11. Some think that 10:12 was part

---

103. Thus Hahn, *Mission*, 42; Rudolf Pesch, *Markusevangelium* 1:328–30; Vincent Taylor, *The Gospel According to Mark* (London: Macmillan & Co., 1966²) 304; Laufen, *Doppelüberlieferung*, 252–53; Hoffmann, *Studien*, 240; Schulz, *Spruchquelle*, 408 and n. 32; Gnilka, *Markus*, 237.

104. On the presence of this in Q, see Laufen, *Doppelüberlieferung*, 213–14; Schürmann, "Reminiszenzen," 121; Bosold, *Pazifismus*, 43–51. On the interpretation of this saying, see most recently, Bosold, *Pazifismus*; B. Lang, "Grussverbot oder Besuchverbot (Zu Lk 10,4b)," *BZ* NF 26 (1982) 75–79.

105. This also appears in *Gos. Thom.* 14b. Hoffmann (*Studien*, 276–83) argues that all of v. 8 is a Lucan creation, but Laufen (*Doppelüberlieferung*, 219–20) observes that v. 10a is formulated as an antithesis to v. 8a (which is not normal Lucan technique) and hence at least v. 8a belongs to Q. Moreover, since Matthew conceives chap. 10 as instructions for the Israel mission (cf. 10:5–6), he would have good reason to eliminate Luke 10:8b.

106. Dautzenberg, "Wandel," 22 [trans. by auth.].

107. Reconstruction: Schulz, *Spruchquelle*, 360–61; Laufen, *Doppelüberlieferung*, 228–30.

of the original mission speech,[108] while Bultmann regards it as an originally isolated prophetic saying which derives from the same situation as
10:13–15.[109] However, the phrase τῇ πόλει ἐκείνῃ obviously depends
upon 10:10–11, and for that reason 10:12 cannot have existed independently of 10:10–11. Moreover, as Lührmann points out, the similarities between 10:12 and 10:14 cannot be accidental; the most probable
solution is that 10:12 is a redactional construction used to connect the
woes to the mission charge.[110]

It is noteworthy that both 10:13–15 and 10:12 make an unfavorable
contrast of Israel's fate with that of the Gentiles. Moreover, 10:13–15
bases its condemnation of the Jewish towns on the predicted repentance
of Gentiles. As with 7:1–10 and 11:31–32, Gentile faith is interpreted as a
condemnatory sign for Israel. The force of this condemnation is all the
more prominent because of the fact that Tyre and Sidon themselves had
frequently been singled out as targets for condemnation in the OT (Isa
23; Jer 29 [47]; Ezek 28:11–12, 22–23; Zech 9:2–4; Amos 1:9–10; Joel 4:4–8)
and both had been represented as enemies of Israel (Ps 82 [83]:8; Amos
1:9–10; 3:11 LXX; Joel 4:4–8; 1 Macc 5:15).

The mission charge concludes with an antithetic saying concerning
acceptance and rejection of the missionaries.[111] That this saying was an
originally independent saying secondarily associated with the mission
speech is suggested not only by the fact that it is intelligible on its own,
but also because several variant forms exist: Mark 9:37 (Luke 9:48); John
5:23; 12:44–45; 13:20; 1 Thess 4:8; *Did.* 11:4 and Ignatius *Eph.* 6:1. Nevertheless, the connection of 10:16 with the mission charge was a natural
one. It displays several similarities to 10:3: both anticipate the rejection
of the preaching, and both represent the missionaries as the emissaries

108. See Schulz, *Spruchquelle*, 418 n. 102.
109. Bultmann, *Tradition*, 112 [118].
110. Lührmann, *Redaktion*, 62; thus Hoffmann, *Studien*, 288; Laufen, *Doppelüberlieferung*, 274–75, 286.
111. Matthew's formulation (10:40) with δέχομαι may be influenced by Mark 9:37 (=
Matt 18:5) and by the saying (10:41) with which he associates it, which uses δέχομαι
twice. This new context probably also accounts for the elimination of the negative
clause. Although a few (Harnack, *Sayings of Jesus*, 89; Hoffmann, *Studien*, 285–86)
regard the Lucan form as secondary—principally because of Luke's preference for
ἀκούω in contexts having to do with reception of preaching (red in Luke 5:1, 15; 6:17, 27;
8:21; 10:39; 11:28; 15:1; 16:29, 31; 19:48; 21:38; frequently in Acts)—this usage is also
attested in Q (6:46, 49; 11:31). Moreover, Luke's tendency is to avoid, not introduce
antithetic parallelism (Cadbury, *Style*, 88). The majority of critics consider Luke to be
original here: Bussmann, *Redenquelle*, 65; Streeter, *Four Gospels*, 278; Bultmann,
Tradition, 153; Schmid, *Matthäus und Lukas*, 278–79; Polag, *Christologie*, 70; Lührmann,
Redaktion, 110–11; Schulz, *Spruchquelle*, 457.

of Jesus.[112] As comparison with the variant forms shows (esp. *Did.* 11:4; Ignatius *Eph.* 6:1), sayings such as 10:16 were used elsewhere to legitimate the message and activity of missionaries.[113] In Q, 10:16 provides an apt legitimation and justification for the missionaries' response to the rejection mentioned in 10:10–11.

Q 10:21–22, 23–24[114]

Despite the apparently new beginning signaled by the prayer formula, 10:21–22 belongs with the preceding material. The thanksgiving was prefaced with "at that time/hour . . . he said" which clearly connects it with the foregoing material.[115] Ταῦτα/αὐτά in 10:21, moreover, seek their referents in 10:2–16.

Form-critical analysis shows that 10:21–24 is composed of two basic units: a thanksgiving[116] and a beatitude. The basis for the juxtaposition of the two resides in the similarities in subject matter and in structure. In the beatitude, the disciples are pronounced blessed because they witness the events which are portents of the kingdom.[117] The original referent of ταῦτα in 10:21 is probably the same: the events which signal the presence of the kingdom.[118] In addition, both sayings presuppose a "revela-

112. Thus Hoffmann, *Studien*, 293, 304; Laufen, *Doppelüberlieferung*, 281; Jacobson, "Literary Unity," 421.

113. The closest Jewish parallel is the principle of agency found throughout rabbinic literature: שלוחו של אדם כמותו "The agent of a man is like him." See *Mek. Exod* 12:6 (= Lauterbach, 1.40–41); *m. Ber.* 5:5; *b. B. Mes.* 96a; *b. Hag.* 10b; *b. Qidd.* 42b, 43a; *b. Menah.* 93b; *b. Nazir* 12b. See P. Borgen, "God's Agent in the Fourth Gospel," *Religions in Antiquity* (Festschrift E. R. Goodenough; Studies in the History of Religions 14; Leiden: E. J. Brill, 1968) 137–48. Schulz (*Spruchquelle*, 458) denies that ἀποστέλλω here recalls the Shaliah institution and derives it instead from the deuteronomistic conception of the prophets as those sent by Sophia. But this requires further nuancing since, as Steck (*Israel*, 286 n. 9) points out, 10:16 modifies this schema "insofar as Christian preachers are not simply in a continuous line of prophets and emissaries whom God or Wisdom sends (as the late Jewish preachers), but are sent by Jesus, who takes the place of God or Wisdom for them, and who for his part is sent by God." Thus it appears that the agent principle has been brought into relation with the Dtr view of the prophets (at least in Q redaction).

114. Reconstruction: Schulz, *Spruchquelle*, 213–14, 419–20; Hoffmann, *Studien*, 104–6; Kloppenborg, "Wisdom Christology," 132–35; Polag, *Fragmenta*, 46–48.

115. It is unclear which of the introductions is closer to Q. Ἐν ἐκείνῳ τῷ καιρῷ is redactional in Matt 12:1; 14:1, but Luke's ἐν αὐτῇ τῇ ὥρᾳ may also be redactional as it is in 7:21; 20:13 (and in *Sond*, 2:38; 13:31; 24:33; Acts 16:18, 33; 22:13).

116. For a detailed analysis of the form, see James M. Robinson, "Hodajot-Formel," 194–235.

117. Similar beatitudes—but with a future reference—are found in *Pss. Sol.* 17:44 and 18:6: Μακάριοι οἱ γενόμενοι ἐν ταῖς ἡμέραις ἐκείναις ἰδεῖν τὰ ἀγαθὰ κυρίου, ἃ ποιήσει γενεᾷ τῇ ἐρχομένῃ.

118. Thus Schulz, *Spruchquelle*, 217; Hoffmann, *Studien*, 110; W. D. Davies, "Knowledge in the Dead Sea Scrolls and Matthew 11:25–30," *HTR* 46 (1953) 137. Lührmann (*Redaktion*, 65) thinks that "it is intended in a generalizing way," while Bultmann

tion schema" similar to what Dahl identified from Pauline and deutero-
Pauline materials.[119] This schema speaks of the mystery which was
formerly hidden, but now revealed (1 Cor 2:6–10; Rom 16:25–26; Col
1:26; Eph 3:4–5, 9–10). Although the term "mystery" is not used, the
same temporal distinction of "formerly hidden/now manifest" is explicit
in 10:23–24 and presupposed in 10:21. The thanksgiving also draws a
social demarcation: revealed to the νήπιοι but hidden from the σοφοί.
The beatitude may in fact also contain a hint of this demarcation: the
somewhat puzzling use of βασιλεῖς[120] may be clarified on the supposition that Q here evokes the notion that the bearers of the eschatological
message (e.g., John in 7:24–26) as well as its recipients (10:21; 12:27) are
precisely not the wise and wealthy. Revelation instead comes to the
simple and poor!

As most surmise, 10:21–22 is itself composite. Verse 22 is no longer a
thanksgiving, nor does it presuppose a revelation schema; instead it is a
self-recommendation of the revealer and concerns the mediation of
revelation, indeed the exclusivity of that mediation. The repetition of the
key words πατήρ and ἀποκαλύπτω suggests that 10:22 serves as an interpretive addition to 10:21. It is disputed whether v. 22 is a secondary
expansion or a "commentary word."[121] The latter view is probably to be
preferred since, although v. 22 repeats two words of v. 21, the two
sayings differ markedly in form, structure and motif. The effect of the
association of vv. 21 and 22 is to introduce a new focus: the unique
authority of Jesus and the exclusivity of his mediation of revelation.[122]

(*Tradition*, 160 [172]) (rather unnecessarily) supposes that the reference is to a lost
Jewish writing.

119. Nils A. Dahl, "Form-critical Observations on Early Christian Preaching," *Jesus in
the Memory of the Early Church* (Minneapolis: Augsburg Publ. House, 1976) 31–36, esp.
32–33; also Dieter Lührmann, *Das Offenbarungsverständnis bei Paulus und in paulinischen
Gemeinden* (WMANT 16; Neukirchen-Vluyn: Neukirchener, 1965) 124–33.

120. Matthew's δίκαιοι is almost certainly redactional and Luke here is original. See
Schulz, *Spruchquelle*, 420, and literature cited there.

121. Q 10:22 as a secondary addition: Hoffmann, *Studien*, 109; Schulz, *Spruchquelle*,
215; Marshall, *Luke*, 431; J. Blank, "Die Sendung des Sohnes: Zur christologischen
Bedeutung des Gleichnisses von bösen Winzern, Mk 12,1–12," *Neues Testament und
Kirche. Für R. Schnackenburg* (Freiburg: Herder & Herder, 1974) 30–31. Q 10:22 as an
originally independent saying: Bultmann, *Tradition*, 159–60 [171–72]; Hahn, *Titles*, 309;
Percy, *Botschaft*, 260; Lührmann, *Redaktion*, 65; Wanke, "Kommentarworte," 218.

122. J. Jeremias (*The Prayers of Jesus* [SBT 2/6; London: SCM Press, 1967] 49)
interprets 10:22a as a reference to the handing on of teaching, while Eduard Norden
(*Agnostos Theos* [Leipzig: Teubner, 1913] 288–89) understands the πάντα as gnostic
secrets. However, the closest parallels to 10:22a show that πάντα is best understood as
"authority." Dan 7:13: καὶ ἐδόθη αὐτῷ [υἱῷ τοῦ ἀνθρώπου] ἐξουσία. 1 Enoch 69:27: "And
the sum of judgment was given to the Son of Man." Matt 28:18; John 3:35; 13:3; 17:2:
καθὼς ἔδωκας αὐτῷ ἐξουσίαν πάσης σαρκός. Corpus Hermeticum 1.32: ὁ σὸς ἄνθρωπος
συναγιάζειν σοι βούλεται, καθὼς παρέδωκας αὐτῷ τὴν πᾶσαν ἐξουσίαν.

While it refrains from explicitly identifying the Son with Sophia, 10:22 draws upon the mythologoumena associated with Sophia which represent her as God's intimate and as the sole mediatrix of knowledge of the divine.[123]

The Composition of Q 9:57–62 + 10:2–16, 21–24

From a compositional perspective, the core or crystallization point for this rather diverse collection of sayings is undoubtedly the instructions for mission in 10:4–11. As comparison with Mark suggests, this cluster existed in the pre-Q tradition and has been expanded in Q in several ways.

The most readily identifiable addition is 10:13–15. Despite the fact that the woes differ markedly from 10:4–11 in form, tone, implied audience and tradition-historical provenance,[124] they were attached to the mission instructions presumably because of the mention of rejection in 10:10–11. Verse 12 is the redactional clasp holding the two units together. The woes thus provide a concrete illustration of the prophetic words spoken against the towns which reject the message of the kingdom. But 10:13–15 and the redactional verse 10:12 cohere both materially and formally not with the sapiential portions of Q but with those sections characterized by the announcement of judgment (3:7–9, 16–17; 17:23–37), the call to repentance (3:7–9; 7:31–35; 11:29–32) and the motif of opposition between Israel and the envoys of the kingdom (7:31–35; 11:49–51; 13:34–35; Matt 11:12–13) and the consciousness of the ramifications of Gentile faith (7:1–10; 11:31–32; 13:28–29). In light of this, it seems most appropriate to regard 10:12, 13–15 as deriving from the same redactional stage as the judgment speeches.

The remainder of the speech is somewhat more difficult to situate with respect to compositional stages. To the original mission instructions were added two sayings, 10:2 and 10:3. As noted above, 10:3, though originally independent, serves as a particularly appropriate introduction to mission sayings which enjoin a defenseless and dependent posture for missionaries. Q 10:16 provides the counterpart to 10:3, resuming the motif of "sending." As Jacobson observes, 10:3 and 10:6 form an

---

123. For documentation, see Kloppenborg, "Wisdom Christology," 129–47.

124. Luke 10:13–15 belongs to the orbit of the deuteronomistic view of history according to which Israel stands in danger of condemnation if she fails to repent. See Steck, *Israel*, 286 and nn. 7, 9; 288 n. 5. In Q tradition, this is taken one step further: the fact or prospect of Gentile faith serves as an *Unheilszeichen*, auguring the imminent rejection of Israel by God.

inclusio,[125] bracketing the original mission words. An original catchword association may be detected between Q 10:10 // Matt 10:14 (δέχομαι [Luke = Matt], ἀκούω [Matt]) and the concluding saying which also uses δέχομαι (Matt) or ἀκούω (Luke). Manson rightly observed that 10:16 follows "more effectively" after 10:12 than after 10:13–15.[126] From this he concluded that the original Q order was 10:12, 16, 13–15. But the more likely solution is that the interpolation of 10:12, 13–15 has broken up a prior connection between 10:10–11 and 10:16.

The status of 10:2 is more difficult to access. Jacobson argues that v. 2 as well as v. 7b belong to "late redaction," i.e., *subsequent* to the addition of 10:12, 13–15. He points out that both sayings enjoyed an independent circulation, both conceive of Christian missionaries as ἐργάται and both serve to "conform the mission instructions to early Christian mission praxis."[127] But such reasons do not help us situate 10:3, 7b with regard to 10:13–15. Equally problematic is Lührmann's attempt to link 10:2 with 10:13–15 on the grounds that "harvest" implies consciousness of the Gentile mission and Gentile membership in the community.[128] As seen above, "harvest" is not always invested with the significance of the judgment or gathering of the Gentiles. Even if 10:2 does point to engagement in a Gentile mission, this in itself does not provide a basis for distinguishing 10:2 from 10:3–11, 16. If 10:8b belonged to Q, there was already consciousness of the problems attending a mission to the Gentiles. A much more decisive observation is that 10:2 signals a shift in setting from missionary instructions as such to the broader setting of advice to a community involved in the preparation and commissioning (10:2) of preachers. The same shift is signaled by Q 10:7b, which is no longer directed at the itinerant preachers but at those who are expected to *support* missionaries. Thus 10:2 and 10:7b appear to be later additions to 10:3–11, 16.

The three chriae (9:57–58, 59–60, 61–62) articulate the radical demands which characterize the following of Jesus. Q 9:57–58 programmatically conceives discipleship as imitation of the lifestyle of the Son of Man. The basis for the association of 9:57–62 with the mission sayings is presumably the similarity of this homeless and radically obedient mode of existence of the disciples to the itinerant and penniless existence of Q's envoys of the kingdom. The effect of the juxtaposition of the chriae with

---

125. Jacobson, "Lc 10,2–16 and Parallels," 421.
126. Manson, *Sayings*, 77. See also Zeller, "Redaktionsprozesse," 404.
127. Jacobson, "Lc 10,2–16 and Parallels," 421.
128. Lührmann, *Redaktion*, 60.

10:3-16 is noteworthy: it broadens the original mission instruction by setting them within the more comprehensive framework of a speech on discipleship. For Q preaching the kingdom and following Jesus are one. It cannot be determined whether the three chriae are antecedent or subsequent to the addition of 10:2 and 10:7b; they cohere equally well with the original missionary instructions, and with the expanded version.

The relation of Q 10:21-22, 23-24 to the rest of the discipleship/mission sermon is more difficult to determine. Although originally composed of several independent units, the cluster is unified by the theme of the reception and acceptance of the revelation of the kingdom by the "simple"—presumably, the followers of Jesus in the Q community. Meyer regards 10:21-22 as so foreign in its soteriological orientation that it must be deemed to be a very late accretion to Q.[129] Whereas the rest of Q places the onus for repentance upon humankind, not God, 10:21-22 takes the opposite view. Jacobson's point is similar: 10:21-22 should be relegated to a stage subsequent to the addition of 10:12, 13-15. Whereas 10:12, 13-15 and other pericopae belonging to this stage (e.g., 7:31-35; 11:49-51) relativize the position of Jesus by placing him alongside other envoys of Sophia, 10:21-22 describes him as the sole mediator of divine knowledge. Moreover, it lays the stress not upon the culpability of Israel, but upon God's own initiative in selectively disclosing revelation.[130]

It must be said at once that 10:22 implies a Christology which surpasses the christological understanding evinced by 7:31-35 and 11:49-51. But to argue that this stratum of redaction relativized Jesus' position by viewing him simply as another of Sophia's envoys does an injustice to 11:29-32, 33-36 and the christological ramifications of that Q composition and especially to 12:8-9 which makes confession *of Jesus* the definitive measure of salvation. The redactional stratum from which 7:31-35; 11:14-36; 11:49-51 and 13:34-35 derive indeed places Jesus in the line of envoys of Sophia; but this does not mean that Q has a "Sophialogy" rather than a Christology. On the contrary, 7:1-10 and 11:14-23 imply that response to the ἐξουσία of Jesus is viewed in the same way as response to the preaching of the kingdom. Jesus is not just a herald of the kingdom, but the final and definitive herald, and the coming Son of Man.

The inconsistency which Meyer and Jacobson detect in the soterio-

---

129. Meyer, "Community," 84.
130. Jacobson, "Wisdom Christology," 141, 144.

logical assumption of 10:21–22 must be seen in the context of the group self-definition and polemics of cults under pressure. A curious ambiguity exists, for example, in documents such as the *Manual of Discipline* which, on the one hand, treats new members as volunteers (*hanniddabîm*), issuing a variety of prescriptions and rules which have free will as their presupposition (e.g., 1QS 1:11), and on the other, regards participation in the new covenant a matter of special divine election (3:13–4:26). A similar ambiguity is found in the *Hodayoth* (1QH 15:15–17; 4:21–22). Revelation of eschatological mysteries is a consequence and mark of divine election, and it is wholly a matter of divine initiative (1QH 11:7–8); but at the same time community polemics regarded those on the outside as no less culpable for their ignorance or rejection of divine instruction. In a similar way, 10:21–22, 23–24 articulates the community's self-understanding as the privileged recipients of the revelation of the kingdom. But this in no way affected their ability to hurl invective and condemn outsiders for non-acceptance of their preaching.

As a cluster of sayings which deals principally with the reception of God's eschatological revelation and manifestation of the kingdom, 10:21–24 is best seen as a counterpart and antithesis to 10:13–15, which castigates the Galilean towns for their rejection of the signs of the kingdom. The theme of response to the eschatological events is a dominant one in the redactional stratum outlined in chapter four. John's disciples are directed to events which indicate the identity of Jesus as the Coming One, and Israel is condemned for failing to respond to similar events: 11:20–26, 29–32, 33–36; 12:54–56. Q 10:21–22, 23–24 offers comfort and legitimation to a community engaged in a mission which has met with opposition, rejection and persecution.[131]

Summary. Beginning as a cluster of instructions specifically for missionaries, the composition was augmented by framing sayings (10:3, 16) and by the addition of 10:2 and 10:7b. Both of these sets of additions signal a shift in *Sitz im Leben* from missionary instruction to instruction for a church engaged in the sending and support of missionaries. The three chriae, 9:57–62, fit well with this broader outlook. Rather than treating the specifics of instructions for mission, they deal with discipleship in general, interpreting it as an emulation of the homeless and detached life style of Jesus, the Son of Man. Thus the speech shifts from a mission discourse to a discipleship instruction. Two groups of sayings

---

131. Schenk (*Synopse*, 58) describes 10:21–22, 23–24 as the high point of Q, serving to legitimate its sayings.

signal another shift. The addition of 10:12, 13–15 and its counterpart, 10:21–24 derives from a context in which the preachers have experienced the failure of their preaching among their Jewish co-religionists. The failure is rationalized in two ways: through polemics and threats against those who refused the message of the presence of the kingdom, and positively by appeal to the sapiential and apocalyptic motifs of special disclosures of saving knowledge to a specially privileged group of elect.

Q 11:2–4, 9–13

Q 11:2–4, 9–13 comprises a short instruction on prayer.[132] Redaction by the evangelists has obscured the original Q introduction, although both Matthew and Luke agree in the use of a form of προσεύχομαι and an imperative (Matt, προσεύχεσθε; Luke, ὅταν προσεύχησθε, λέγετε). As indicated in chapter two, Matthew's placement of the prayer is influenced by the presence of the theme of prayer in a block of his special material which he interpolates in 6:1–18. Not only is his placement secondary, the wording of the prayer in Matthew is usually taken to be a development of the original.[133]

As the Lucan context shows, the prayer has been connected with a cluster of sayings on prayer. The first of these sayings (11:9) is a trio of imperatives and promises which, as Piper notes, "are almost embarrassing in the scope of what is encouraged and promised."[134] This is continued by a trio of maxims (connected by γάρ) which serve as a motive clause for the imperatives.[135] The almost exact agreement between 11:9 and 11:10 in the choice of verbs and their order (αἰτέω, δίδωμι/λαμβάνω, ζητέω, εὑρίσκω, κρούω, ἀνοίγω) diminishes the likeli-

---

132. Reconstruction: Schulz, *Spruchquelle*, 84–86, 161–62; Zeller, *Mahnsprüche*, 127; Steinhauser, *Doppelbildworte*, 69–73; Polag, *Fragmenta*, 48–50. David Catchpole ("Q and 'The Friend at Midnight'") has recently argued that 11:5–8 belonged to Q and that 11:9 served as the conclusion for the parable. Convinced that 11:9 is incomplete without any objects for the three verbs ("ask," "seek," "knock"), Catchpole finds the necessary objects in 11:5–8 (which he rewrites with the conclusion λέγω ὑμῖν· ἐγερθεὶς δώσει αὐτῷ ὅσον χρῄζει). But the *Gos. Thom.* version of the saying (92) shows that there is no need to explicate the objects.

133. See Joachim Jeremias, "Das Vater-Unser im Lichte der neueren Forschung," *Abba: Studien zur neutestamentlichen Theologie und Zeitgeschichte* (Göttingen: Vandenhoeck & Ruprecht, 1966) 152–71, and the older literature cited there; J. Carmignac, *Recherches sur le 'Notre Père'* (Paris: Gabalda, 1969); Schulz, *Spruchquelle*, 86 and n. 201.

134. Piper, "Evidence of Design," 412–13.

135. Minear (*Commands of Christ*, 115) regards 11:10 as "an innocuous and unnecessary restatement" of 11:9. This conclusion overlooks the function of this verse, which is to ground the imperatives with a general rule about human experience.

hood that 11:10 ever circulated independently of 11:9.[136] More likely,
11:9-10 was composed as a unit from the beginning. The imperatives
"ask," "seek," and "knock" now serve as metaphors for prayer, but there
is no reason to suppose that 11:9-10 was always used in that context.[137] It
is noteworthy that *Gos. Thom.* 92 uses a variant of the saying in the
context of searching for revelation.[138] Structurally 11:9-10 provides an
excellent example of a sapiential exhortation, consisting of imperatives
with a carefully balanced motive clause. Indeed the content and logic of
the saying also point to a sapiential origin. Piper comments,

> That gnomic apperception, rather than religious insight or prophetic
> announcement, is the ostensible basis of appeal in this verse is demon-
> strated by the strikingly unqualified πᾶς, the predominance of habitual
> present rather than future tenses (λαμβάνει, εὑρίσκει) and the continuing
> absence of clear references to divine agency.[139]

The wisdom admonition (11:9-10) has been strengthened further by a
double rhetorical question (11:11-12) which evokes ordinary human
experience and invites a *qal wehomer* conclusion about God's willingness
to answer prayer. The conclusion is made explicit in 11:13. It is indeed
only with the addition of these rhetorical questions and the *qal wehomer*
conclusion that it becomes clear that the "asking" and "seeking" of v. 9
have to do with petitionary prayer. Moreover, there is a slight shift
in perspective between 11:9-10 and 11-13: in the former "receiving,"
"finding" and "opening" are represented as the inevitable and expected
effects of persistent actions, whereas in 11:11-13 the superabundant
generosity of God is the cause of all good gifts. These observations
probably signal that vv. 9-10 and vv. 11-13 represent two originally
independent traditions.[140]

136. Cf. Jeremias (*Parables*, 159), who asserts that 10:10 is an independent gnomic
sentence springing from the experience of the beggar: "[H]e has only to persist, to take
no refusal, be unscared by abuse, and he will receive a gift."
137. "Seeking" can occur in a variety of contexts: seeking God, Wisdom (Prov 8:17),
the Law (Sir 32:15; *b. Meg.* 6b), revelation (*Gos. Thom.* 92) or the kingdom (Luke 12:31).
"Knocking" occurs in later rabbinic literature as a metaphor for prayer (*b. Meg.* 12b; *y.
Ber.* 1.2d.62 [Str-B 1.458], but also for the study of the Law (*Pesiq. R.* 176a). See further
Piper, "Evidence of Design," 413 n. 10.
138. *Gos. Thom.* 92: Jesus said, "Seek and you will find. Yet, what you asked Me
about in former times and which I did not tell you then, now I do desire to tell, but you
do not inquire after it" (trans. Lambdin, *NHLE*, 128).
139. Piper, "Evidence of Design," 413. Piper acknowledges that the passives in v. 9
might be construed as divine passives (thus Jeremias, *New Testament Theology*, 11 n. 3)
but points out that this interpretation is certainly not demanded.
140. Thus Bultmann, *Tradition*, 87 [90]; Josef Schmid, *Matthäus und Lukas*, 242; Piper,
"Evidence of Design," 414-15; Minear, *Commands of Christ*, 117. However, both Schulz
(*Spruchquelle*, 163) and Zeller (*Mahnsprüche*, 128) think that 11:9-13 is a traditional

Schulz agrees that 11:9–13 is an example of a wisdom saying but insists that it is represented by Q as a prophetic pronouncement.[141] In support of this he points to various "prophetic" features: the "prophetic" λέγω ὑμῖν formula, and the prophetic question τίς ἐξ ὑμῶν. This view may be challenged on two counts. First, from the point of view of authority claim, this cluster of sayings does not attempt to promote itelf on the basis of a special disclosure of divine will or a revelation of future divine purpose; instead it seeks to *convince* by argument and analogy from ordinary human experience. Second, Schulz's form-critical observations are open to challenge. The assumption that λέγω ὑμῖν necessarily bespeaks a prophetic consciousness is questionable.[142] Here, as in many hortatory and sapiential contexts, it serves to introduce imperatives, not revelatory disclosures about the future or about divine secrets.[143] Likewise τίς ἐξ ὑμῶν is not primarily prophetic; semantically the questions introduced by this formula are equivalent to οὐδείς statements, which belong to the realm of general wisdom and popular philosophy.[144]

The Composition of Q 11:2–4, 9–13

Although a reconstruction of the stages of growth of Q 11:9–13 must remain subjective, it is clear that the association of 11:2–4 with the following cluster of sayings presupposes that 11:9–10 (which contains no obvious reference to prayer) was already attached to 11:11–13. The connection of the prayer (11:2–4) with 11:9–13 is perhaps not simply a matter of common theme, but dependent also upon the catchwords (ἐπι)δίδωμι and ἄρτος[145] and upon the common motif of God's provision of material needs.

---

unity. Zeller states, "The thoroughgoing catchword connections, which use αἰτεῖν and διδόναι, make it likely that the rhetorical questions served from the beginning as illustrations at least of v. 7" [trans. by auth.]. There is, however, no corresponding catchword connection with the other verbs in 11:9, and the phenomenon to which Zeller points may be no more than the association of two originally independent sayings by catchword.

141. Schulz, *Spruchquelle*, 163.

142. Curiously, even though he concludes that Luke's κἀγὼ λέγω ὑμῖν is secondary, Schulz states, "The exclusion of the introductory formula as secondary does not mean that this prophetic saying was not introduced by λέγω ὑμῖν in its original oral form" [trans. by auth.].

143. See below, pp. 209–10.

144. See below, page 219 and nn. 195, 196.

145. Matthew uses the contrasting pairs "bread/stone" and "fish/serpent" whereas Luke has "fish/serpent" and "egg/scorpion." Matthew's contrast is between useful and useless items, while Luke has in mind good and harmful gifts. Manson (*Sayings*, 81) suggested that all three contrasts stood in Q and that Matthew and Luke each

This instruction coheres with other parts of Q. Formally, it employs the typical sapiential admonition with a motive clause (cf. 6:27–28, 32–33; 6:37–38; 6:42, 43–44). Like 6:27–35, it portrays God as a generous patron, and as in 12:4–7, 22–31 it counsels the members of the community to rely completely upon God for provision of their daily needs. In both the prayer and 6:27–35 there is an assumed correspondence between the actions of God and those of Jesus' followers: generosity and forgiveness are marks both of God and of the children of God. The invocation of God as πάτερ in the prayer finds a counterpart in 6:27–35 which represents discipleship as *imitatio Dei* leading to divine sonship. It may be added as well that an ecclesial rather than a missionary *Sitz* of 11:2–4, 9–13 is the more probable. Thus it belongs to the same sphere of interests and applications as the inaugural sermon (6:20b–49) and to the expanded version of the discipleship "speech" (9:57–62 + 10:2–11, 16).

Schürmann holds that the Lord's Prayer served as the starting point (*Grundwort*) for this collection and that 11:9–10, 11–13 functions as a commentary word or *Erganzungswort*.[146] This is possible, but cannot be proved; the reverse is also possible. For our purposes it is sufficient to observe that 11:2–4, 9–13 is a composition from smaller units with a preponderance of sapiential logic and idiom, and functioning as an instruction on prayer. In its form, motif and style it coheres with other sapiential portions of Q.

Q 12:2–12

The composite nature of Q 12:2–12 is immediately evident. Q 12:2 is an originally independent wisdom saying,[147] encountered in four other forms in Mark 4:22, *P. Oxy.* 654.4–5 and *Gos. Thom.* 5 and 6. The next saying, for which Matthew 10:27 may provide the more original wit-

---

eliminated one. Grundmann (*Lukas*, 235) contends that only one pair stood in Q and that Matthew and Luke each supplemented it. The better solution is to suppose that Q had two pairs, and that Matthew or Luke altered one. The Matthaean version is frequently preferred (see Marshall, *Luke*, 469, for a summary of the arguments), but the motives for Luke's alteration remain obscure. W. Foerster (ὄφις, *TDNT* 5 [1967] 579–80) points out that bread and fish were staple foods for inhabitants of Galilee, but this in itself proves nothing with respect to Q. Steinhauser (*Doppelbildworte*, 71–72) argues that since Luke already mentioned the borrowing of bread in 11:5–8 (*Sondergut*), he would have reason to avoid the repetition of "bread" in the following verses. But Catchpole ("Q and The 'Friend at Midnight'," 414) thinks that Luke is repeating the combination of "serpent" + "scorpion" used earlier in 10:19.

146. Schürmann, "Basileia-Verkündigung," 151.
147. Reconstruction: Schulz, *Spruchquelle*, 461–62.

ness,[148] can also stand on its own, as *P. Oxy.* 1.8 and *Gos. Thom.* 33a show. Synoptic comparison shows that this was followed by a cluster of sayings, 12:4–7, which also appears to be composite.[149] In 12:4–5 the emphasis falls upon the fear of God's power to destroy which outweighs any human destructive capability.[150] But 12:6, 7b does not concern God's destructive abilities but is a *qal wehomer* argument in support of God's providential care.[151] Q 12:7a, ἀλλὰ καὶ αἱ τρίχες τῆς κεφαλῆς ὑμῶν πᾶσαι ἠρίθμηνται, seems intrusive and may, as Zeller suggests, have been added to emphasize the special status of humanity in God's providential care.[152]

That 12:8–9 did not originally belong to the preceding is immediately clear both from the abrupt change in content, tone and form, and from the fact that a variant occurs independently in a different Marcan context (8:38).[153] The same may be said of 12:10, for which variants are attested in Mark 3:28–29, *Did.* 11:7 and *Gos. Thom.* 44, and which

148. Many critics hold that Luke 12:3 is original and that Matthew introduced the imperative to accord better with the preceding instructions to the disciples. Thus Hoffmann, *Studien*, 156; Lührmann, *Redaktion*, 50; Manson, *Sayings*, 106; Percy, *Botschaft*, 212–14; Polag, *Fragmenta*, 58; Schenk, *Synopse*, 83; Josef Schmid, *Matthäus und Lukas*, 274; Schulz, *Spruchquelle*, 462. However, the possibility of Lucan redaction is also strong. As Schmid observed (*Matthäus und Lukas*, 272), Luke 12:4 begins a new theme (for Luke), and 12:2–3 serves to conclude the previous discussion of hypocrisy. But since 12:1 cannot be traced to Q, this association is necessarily secondary. Laufen (*Doppelüberlieferung*, 162–63) rightly points out that Matt 10:27 fits better with the following verses than does Luke 12:3. In fact, 12:3 represents as *still future* what Matthew *and* Luke 12:4–7 require in the present, namely, the disclosure of "what was spoken in the dark." Luke can alter the sense of 12:3 because he, unlike Matthew, is not referring to the preaching of Jesus which is continued by his disciples, but to secret hypocrisy which, he holds, will be unveiled in the future. The Q exhortation to fearless preaching (12:4–7) clearly accords better with the Matthaean formulation than it does with the Lucan. Supporting Matthaean priority in this regard: Laufen, *Doppelüberlieferung*, 162–63; Wanke, "Kommentarworte," 222; Wernle, *Synoptische Frage*, 72; Strecker, *Weg*, 190; Harnack, *Sayings of Jesus*, 83 [60]; Meyer, "Community," 39–40; Neirynck, "Study of Q," 61; J. Horst, οὖς, TDNT 5 (1967) 553.

149. Reconstruction: Schulz, *Spruchquelle*, 157–59; Zeller, *Mahnsprüche*, 94; G. Dautzenberg, *Sein Leben*, 138–39. All prefer the Matthaean wording.

150. Grundmann (*Lukas*, 253) suggests that the devil is meant, but it is much more probable that the reference is to God. See Jas 4:12; Str-B 1.580–81.

151. A parallel to this is found in a story about R. Simeon b. Yohai (ca. 150 CE) in *Gen. Rab.* 79.6: "R. Simeon b. Yohai and his sons were hidden in a cave for thirteen years . . . At the end of the period he emerged and sat at the entrance of the cave and saw a hunter engaged in catching birds. Now whenever R. Simeon heard a heavenly voice exclaim from heaven 'Mercy' it escaped but if it exclaimed 'Death!' it was caught. 'Even a bird is not caught without the assent of Providence,' he remarked, 'how much more then the life of a human being'" (trans. H. Freedman and M. Simon, *Midrash Rabbah* [10 vols.; London: Soncino, 1939; reprinted 1961] 2:730). Also quoted in *y. Seb.* 9.38d.22 (Str-B 1.582–83); *Eccl. Rab.* 10.8 §1; *Esther Rab.* 3.7 (on 1:9).

152. Zeller, *Mahnsprüche*, 95.

153. Reconstruction: Schulz, *Spruchquelle*, 66–67; Pesch, "Über die Autorität," 26–30; Polag, *Fragmenta*, 58.

seemingly uses the term "Son of Man" to mean "the earthly Jesus" rather than "the coming Son of Man" as in 12:8–9.[154] Q 12:11–12 brings another shift in tone and form, and a variant of this saying occurs in a completely different Marcan context (13:11).[155]

The Composition of Q 12:2–12

Evidently, the core about which these sayings were gathered is 12:4–7, consisting of two imperatives ($\mu\dot{\eta}$ $\phi o\beta\epsilon\hat{\iota}\sigma\theta\epsilon$ . . . $\phi o\beta\epsilon\hat{\iota}\sigma\theta\epsilon$ $\delta\dot{\epsilon}$ $\mu\hat{\alpha}\lambda\lambda o\nu$) and a *qal wehomer* argument attached to the admonitions by a resumptive $\mu\dot{\eta}$ ($o\hat{v}\nu$) $\phi o\beta\epsilon\hat{\iota}\sigma\theta\epsilon$ (v. 7b). The tone and idiom are sapiential. In its rhetorical structure it coincides with several other Q texts, e.g., 6:27–31, 32–35; 11:9–13; 12:22–31, which also begin with admonitions (6:27–28; 11:9; 12:22b) buttressed either by rhetorical questions and examples drawn from everyday experience (6:32–34; 11:11–12; 12:24–26, 27–28) or by proverbial assertions (11:10; 12:23) or both.

Schulz dissents from this view and regards 12:4–7, especially the motif of the fear of God who can destroy in Gehenna, as characteristically prophetic.[156] But this is unnecessarily restrictive since the motif of the fear of God is a regular occurrence in wisdom literature.[157] Exhortations to courage in the face of martyrdom are found in a variety of contexts, not all of them especially "prophetic." The apocalyptic parenesis of *1 Enoch* (95:3; 96:1–3; 97:1; 102:4–5; 103:4) characteristically consists of an imperative followed by a grounding statement frequently introduced by "for" and predicting the punishment of the oppressors and the blessedness of the elect.[158] These might indeed be deemed "prophetic" insofar as they predict future events and appeal to special insight on the part of a seer. But alongside these exists an exhortation in a much more sapiential idiom, *1 Enoch* 101:

> Examine the heavens, you sons of heaven, and all the works of the Most High; and be afraid to do evil in his presence . . . Do you not see the sailors

---

154. Reconstruction: Schulz, *Spruchquelle*, 246–47; Polag, *Fragmenta*, 58.

155. Reconstruction: Schulz, *Spruchquelle*, 442–43; Polag, *Fragmenta*, 60.

156. Schulz, *Spruchquelle*, 160; similarly Bultmann, *Tradition*, 119 [126].

157. The exhortations "Fear the Lord" and "Fear no other except him" are found in Prov 3:7; 7:1; 24:21; Eccl 5:6; 12:13; Sir 4:8, 21; 7:31.

158. E.g., *1 Enoch* 95:3: "Fear not the sinners! For the Lord will again deliver them into your hands, that you may carry out against them anything that you desire" (trans. E. Isaac, *OPT* 76). G. W. Nickelsburg ("The Apocalyptic Message of 1 Enoch 92–105," *CBQ* 39 [1977] 308–28) notes the similarity of these exhortations to the OT holy war oracles (Num 21:34; Deut 3:2; Josh 8:1) which ground the exhortation in the description of the defeat of Israel's enemies as a *fait accompli*. He also notes similarities with the oracles of blessing of Deutero-Isaiah (43:1; 44:2–5; 51:7–8; 54:4–8; cf. 35:4).

of the ships, how their ships are tossed up and down by the billows and are shaken by the winds, and they become anxious? On this account (it is evident that) they are seized by fear, for they will discharge all their valuable property—the goods that are with them—into the sea; they think in their hearts that the sea will swallow them up and they will perish in it. Is not the entire sea and all her waters, and all her movements the very work of the Most High? Has he not ordered her courses of action and her waters —(indeed) her totality—with sand? . . . Do not the sailors of the ships fear the sea? Yet the sinners do not fear the Most High.[159]

Here as in Q, the appeal to fear God is not made on the basis of predictions of apocalyptic destruction, but by analogy with ordinary human experience of destruction. Another text remarkably similar to Q 12:4–7 is found in 4 Macc 13:14–15:

μὴ φοβηθῶμεν τὸν δοκοῦντα ἀποκτέννειν· μέγας γὰρ ψυχῆς ἀγὼν καὶ κίνδυνος ἐν αἰωνίῳ βασάνῳ κείμενος τοῖς παραβᾶσι τὴν ἐντολὴν τοῦ θεοῦ. (Cf. also 9:7; 10:4, 19)

Let us not fear him who thinks that he kills. Great is the trial of soul and the danger laid up in eternal tribulation for those who transgress the commandment of God.[160]

In 4 Maccabees the exhortation is based upon the philosophical proposition that the demands of reason and piety, which are rewarded with eternal life, far outweigh any mundane considerations such as human attachments and bodily safety.[161] Wis 3:1–9 takes another tack: the death of the righteous is not a cause for apprehension since their souls "are in the hand of God and no torment will ever touch them."

Although Q 12:4–7 has remarkable similarities with 4 Macc 13:14–15 (which is certainly not prophetic), it is closest in logic and structure to 1 Enoch 101: confidence to face the dangers of martyrdom is grounded in the fear of God whose providential care is all-pervasive, as nature and human experience themselves teach. There is nothing distinctively prophetic about 12:4–7.[162] Even if the two λέγω ὑμῖν formulae (12:4, 5b diff

159. Trans. E. Isaac, *OTP* 82.

160. Text and trans., Moses Hadas, *The Third and Fourth Books of Maccabees* (New York: KTAV, 1976) 213.

161. See esp. 4 Macc 15:1–9 and the thorough discussion of Dautzenberg, *Sein Leben,* 139–46.

162. Boring (*Sayings of the Risen Jesus,* 167–68) hesitates to designate 12:4–7 as oracular in origin but instead describes it as reformulated or re-presented by Christian prophets. He cites the use of λέγω ὑμῖν in 12:4, 5, and φίλοι, "which might have the prophetic overtones that this word had in the Johannine community," the similarity to Rev 2:10 (which probably is an oracle) and the theme of persecution (which Boring regards as typical of prophetic sayings). It should be noted that τοῖς φίλοις μου is probably Lucan (φίλος: Matt 1x [from Q]/Mark -/Luke 15x [1x from Q; at least 2x red;

Matt) and ὑποδείξω δὲ ὑμῖν (12:5a diff Matt) belonged to Q,[163] the discourse would not be significantly altered in a prophetic direction. Λέγω ὑμῖν (or its equivalent) followed by an imperative is a characteristically sapiential locution, occurring frequently in the parenetic sections of the T. 12 Patr.[164] In the absence of specifically prophetic forms, formulae and disclosures, 12:4–7 is better classified as a sapiential admonition to courage in the face of possible martyrdom.

To this "kernel" have been added two sayings, Q 12:2 and 12:3. The juxtaposition of the two is probably based on their common use of a contrast between hidden and revealed. The effect of this juxtaposition is important, since it transforms an originally independent wisdom saying (12:2), which had no necessary connection with missionary exhortation (as Gos. Thom. shows), into a legitimation of the mission. Wanke comments, "What occurs in the preaching of Jesus' disciples is comparable to the eschatological, revelatory action of God."[165] Moreover, Q 12:2 assumes a programmatic function with respect to what follows: it asserts in proverbial form the "divine necessity" of the disciples' preaching. The mission of the Q disciples is viewed not as a human undertaking but as an expression of God's deliberate and inevitable revelation of what is hidden. In contrast to the way in which Luke uses 12:2 (3)—to refer to the future disclosure of secret hypocrisy (cf. 12:1)—Q understands the disclosure of τὸ κεκαλυμμένον, presumably the kingdom, to be occurring in the present, in the preaching of the disciples. Hence the entire compo-

---

10x Sondergut or red]/Acts 3x). Rev 3:10 contains a rather specific prediction of impending arrest in connection with the exhortation to courage. Luke 12:4–7, however, contains no such predictive elements which would require a prophetic speaker, and exhortations to courage are too widely spread to be considered as a criterion for identifying Christian oracles.

163. Schenk (Synopse, 84) includes the two λέγω ὑμῖν formulae; Polag (Fragmenta, 58) also includes ὑποδείξω ὑμῖν. But the latter is redactional; apart from Luke 3:7 (= Q) it occurs only in Luke-Acts (6:47; 12:5; Acts 9:16; 20:35). See Jeremias, Sprache, 149. In 12:4, 5 λέγω ὑμῖν may be from Q, but Luke may have inserted it in 12:4 to mark a change in theme (thus Laufen, Doppelüberlieferung, 161). For a discussion of this, see Neirynck ("Study of Q," 61–62), who regards the formulae as Lucan.

164. The formula occurs in Prov 24:23, ταῦτα δὲ λέγω ὑμῖν τοῖς σοφοῖς; in parenetic sections of 1 Enoch (91:3; 94:1, 3, 10) and frequently in T. 12 Patr. with a following imperative: T. Rub. 6:5 (mss); T. Levi 16:4 (mss); T. Naphth. 4:1 (mss); T. Gad 5:2; T. Benj. 9:1 (mss). Several related formulae are attested: διδάσκω ὑμῖν + imperative, T. Rub. 3:9. διὰ τοῦτο ἐντέλλομαι ὑμᾶς + infinitive/ἵνα, T. Rub. 6:8; T. Sim. 7:3; T. Levi 13:1; T. Jud. 13:1; 17:1; T. Benj. 12:1. (παρ)αγγέλλω ὑμῖν + imperative/ infinitive, T. Jud. 21:1 (mss); T. Zeb. 5:1. παραινῶ ὑμῖν + imperative, T. Gad 6:1. παρακαλῶ ὑμᾶς + imperative, T. Rub. 4:5 (mss). ὀρκῶ ὑμᾶς τὸν θεόν + infinitive, T. Rub. 6:9. ἐπιμαρτύρομαι ὑμῖν + infinitive, T. Rub. 1:6. See also Zeller, Mahnsprüche, 155–57.

165. Wanke, "Kommentarworte," 223 [trans. by auth.]. Manson (Sayings, 106), perhaps unduly influenced by the Lucan setting, thinks that 12:2 is a "warning to the opponents of Jesus that a time is coming when their doings will be exposed."

sition, Q 12:2 + Q 12:3 (= Matt 10:27) + Q 12:4–5, 6–7, is both a legitimation of the mission and an exhortation to bold preaching of the kingdom. The mission is controlled in every respect by divine providence, in its very inception and throughout its prosecution.

Although composed of originally independent sayings, 12:2–7 has a unitary thrust. With Q 12:8–9, however, new motifs and interests appear. As Lührmann notes, 12:8–9 has to do with *confession* rather than *preaching*.[166] Moreover, the confession has an explicit christological focus lacking in the preceding material. Formally, too, 12:8–9 is distinctive. Widely regarded as a "sentence of Holy Law" with its origin in prophetic speech,[167] it moves beyond the essentially sapiential idiom of 12:2–7, introducing the motif of apocalyptic reward and punishment. The addition of 12:8–9 was undoubtedly occasioned by the forensic allusions in 12:4 and especially 12:11–12. As Lührmann points out, 12:8–9 is not simply a warning against apostasy, directed at the community members who find themselves under examination in the synagogues. It is a warning to the hearers of the community's preachers.[168] As with the addition of 10:12, 13–15 to the mission instruction, which shifted the focus from the community itself to the targets of its preaching, 12:8–9 effects a similar shift from community to outsiders.

The next Q saying, 12:10, is even more strongly directed at outsiders.[169] Irrespective of how the saying was created and what it originally intended, it is particularly enigmatic in its Q context. In itself it

---

166. Lührmann, *Redaktion*, 52. Hoffmann (*Studien*, 306) relates the secret preaching of 12:2a, 3a to the "confession before men" of 12:8–9, and the public manifestation of 12:2b, 3b to the appearance before the Son of Man but this strains credulity.

167. Ernst Käsemann, "Sentences," 77; Lührmann, *Redaktion*, 51; Schulz, *Spruchquelle*, 69; Schürmann, "Menschensohn-Titel," 141; Boring, *Sayings of the Risen Jesus*, 165–66. Klaus Berger, ("Zu den sogenannten Sätzen heiligen Rechts," *NTS* 17 [1970] 10–40; "Die sogenannte 'Sätze heiligen Rechts' im NT," *TZ* 28 [1972] 305–30) has strenuously argued against a prophetic origin of these sentences, but in view of the content of at least some of the NT sentences, 12:8–9 included, his sapiential derivation seems implausible.

168. Lührmann, *Redaktion*, 52; thus Hoffmann, *Studien*, 156; Schenk, *Synopse*, 86; Wrege, *Bergpredigt*, 158. Käsemann ("Sentences," 77) appears to allow 12:8–9 only the function of pronouncing "blessing and curse on those members of the community who confess and those who deny . . ."

169. We shall prescind from a host of questions regarding this enigmatic saying, such as its relation to Mark 3:28–29, its tradition-history and function as an independent saying. For a discussion of the problems see M. E. Boring, "The Unforgivable Sin Logion Mark III 28–29/Matt XII 31–32/Luke XII 10: Formal Analysis and History of Tradition," *NovT* 18 (1976) 259–79; C. Colpe, "Der Spruch von Lästerung des Geistes," *Der Ruf Jesu und die Antwort der Kirche* (Festschrift J. Jeremias; Göttingen: Vandenhoeck & Ruprecht, 1970) 63–79; E. Lövestam, *Spiritus Blasphemia: Eine Studie zu Mk 3:28* (Lund: Gleerup, 1968); Marshall, *Luke*, 516–19; Schulz, *Spruchquelle*, 246–50; Robin Scroggs, "The Exaltation of the Spirit by Some Early Christians," *JBL* 84 (1965) 359–73; Suggs, *Wisdom*, 51–55; Tödt, *Son of Man*, 118–20, 312–18; Wrege, *Bergpredigt*, 156–80.

appears to depreciate the status and importance of the Son of Man not simply by relegating him to a position inferior to God or to Wisdom (as in 7:31–35), but by declaring that "speaking a word against him" is forgivable. In the immediate context, this produces a flat contradiction since 12:8–9 announces that rejection of Jesus—who in Q is clearly identified with the Son of Man—will bring about decisive eschatological rejection! As seen in the wider Q context, 12:10 is equally anomalous. Elsewhere Q implies that rejection of Jesus, his words and works, carries with it the gravest of consequences (see 10:13–15; 11:20–23, 24–26; 11:31–32, 33–36; 11:49–51; 13:34–35).

There are several possible explanations for the enigma of 12:10. (1) Following Tödt, many critics see in the saying a distinction of two eras of preaching: that of the earthly Jesus, in which rejection was forgivable (provided that the opponents repent now), and that of the Spirit-endowed preachers in which rejection would be a deliberate affront to the manifest workings of God through his Spirit.[170] Understood in this way, 12:10 would be a qualification or correction of 12:8–9: while rejection of the earthly Jesus by Jewish opponents is not decisive, rejection of his envoys in the post-Easter situation is.[171] According to Schenk, 12:10 explains why in spite of Israel's rejection of Jesus, the Q community continues its preaching to Israel. This is Israel's last chance for response![172] (2) Following patristic exegesis, Barrett and Higgins hold that "speaking against the Son of Man" pertains to those outside the church but only Christian apostates are in a position to "speak against the Spirit."[173] (3) Interpreting both halves of the saying as referring to the earthly Jesus, M. J. Lagrange contends that the saying distinguishes between the lowly appearance of Jesus and the divine workings manifest through him.[174] (4) Finally, R. Scroggs interprets "Son of Man" as

---

170. Tödt, *Son of Man*, 119. Earlier exponents include A. Fridrichsen, "Le péché contre le Saint Esprit," *RHPR* 3 (1923) 366–72; G. Bornkamm, "End-Expectation and Church in Matthew," 34. See also Eduard Schweizer, Πνεῦμα, *TDNT* 6 (1968) 397; C. Colpe, Υἱὸς τοῦ ἀνθρώπου, *TDNT* 8 (1972) 452; Wrege, "Zur Rolle des Geistwortes," 373–77; Meyer, "Community of Q," 47; Schulz, *Spruchquelle*, 248; Schenk, *Synopse*, 88.

171. Thus Schürmann, "Menschensohn-Titel," 137; Wanke, "Kommentarworte," 224; Hoffmann, *Studien*, 152 (if 12:10 followed 12:8–9 in Q); Schenk, *Synopse*, 88.

172. Schenk, *Synopse*, 88.

173. C. K. Barrett, *The Holy Spirit and the Gospel Tradition* (London: SPCK, 1947, repr. 1966) 106–7; A. J. B. Higgins, *Jesus and the Son of Man* (Philadelphia: Fortress Press, 1964) 130 (Higgins here regards the Matthaean setting as that of Q and offers this interpretation for the independent saying); idem, *The Son of Man in the Teaching of Jesus* (SNTSMS 39; Cambridge: At the Univ. Press, 1980) 88–89 (neither Luke nor Matthew preserves the original Q setting).

174. M. J. Lagrange, *L'Evangile selon Saint Marc* (6th ed.; Paris: Gabalda, 1942) 76; similarly Lövestam, *Spiritus Blasphemia*, 48–49. Polag (*Christologie*, 163) holds a similar

referring to the *coming* Son of Man, and suggests that the Q saying derived from a community in which "the exaltation of the Spirit had so overshadowed the kerygmatic content of the gospel that one could even utter blasphemies against the Son of Man without incurring God's wrath."[175]

There are problems with each of these interpretations. That 12:10 espouses two distinct preaching eras finds no other support in Q. On the contrary, 10:16 treats the rejection of the disciples' preaching as identical with rejection of Jesus. And 12:10 notwithstanding, Q uniformly regards the rejection of Jesus as cause for eschatological condemnation (11:20–23; 11:31–32, etc.) This observation applies equally to Barrett's proposal that the saying distinguishes between outsiders and apostates. There is nothing in the context of 12:10b to suggest that "speaking against the Spirit" has to do with post-baptismal apostasy. While Lagrange's conjecture is possible for 12:10 as an isolated saying, it is impossible for Q since Q uses Son of Man as a title of dignity, not to refer to Jesus' humble guise. Even more importantly, 7:22–23; 10:13–15; 11:20 and 11:31–32 show that Q made no attempt to distinguish between Jesus and the power at work in him. Similarly, an enthusiastic interpretation might be plausible for the isolated saying—or perhaps in a setting such as *Did.* 11:7—but it accords badly with the rest of Q.

Q 12:10 is joined to its context by several catchwords, πᾶς ὅς (vv. 8, 10), ὁ υἱὸς τοῦ ἀνθρώπου (vv. 8, 10), ἅγιον πνεῦμα (vv. 10, 11), and by the motif of rejection or denial of Jesus (vv. 8, 10). The context makes it quite clear that the emphasis falls upon 12:10b, not upon 12:10a. The warning against blaspheming the Spirit is a threat directed at the synagogue *audience* of the spirit-inspired defense of the disciples in 12:11–12. As in 10:13–15, an editor has inserted into an essentially community-oriented speech a saying which takes aim at opponents, warning them that opposition invites disastrous consequences. This explanation admittedly does not venture an interpretation of 12:10a. However, the emphasis does not fall upon this half of the saying but falls upon the second. It should be noted that neither Matthew nor Luke was successful in integrating 12:10a fully into their respective Gospels.[176] One must

---

position: 12:10 is directed against false teachers "who by means of a false interpretation of the earthly Jesus blaspheme the Spirit at work in him" [trans. by auth.]. He does not clarify what false teachers he has in mind.

175. Robin Scroggs, "The Exaltation of the Spirit by Some Early Christians," 364; similarly Suggs, *Wisdom,* 53–54.

176. Of the two, Luke was perhaps the more successful. Schuyler Brown (*Apostasy and Perseverance in the Theology of Luke* [AnBib 36; Rome: Pontifical Biblical Institute,

reckon with the possibility that Q was likewise unable to integrate 10a into its theology. For Q the element of threat was paramount. Those who resist the manifestation of the Spirit at work in Christian preachers will not be forgiven.

With the following saying the tone changes again from threat to exhortation, and from a word directed at opponents to one directed at the community. Of course, 12:11–12 describes the forensic scene which the two preceding sayings presuppose, and as we have already suggested, it was this element (along with various catchwords) which occasioned the association of 12:8–9 and 10 with 12:11–12. Although strictly speaking, 12:11–12 goes beyond the sapiential logic of 12:4–7, it coheres with the exhortations in 12:4–7 and 12:22–31 in its hortatory stance and especially in its use of the phrase μὴ μεριμνήσατε. Both Schürmann and Zeller regard 12:11–12 as a relatively late addition to 12:2–9, serving as a transition to 12:22–31.[177] However, 12:2–7, 11–12 forms a coherent unit, unified by mode of address (second-person plural imperative), tone (hortatory and comforting), setting (a situation of persecution) and function (to encourage fearless preaching). Q 12:8–9, 10 depart from these features significantly: 12:8–9 shifts to the form of a "sentence of Holy Law" aimed at outsiders, and 12:10 is a prophetic threat directed at those who reject Christian preaching. Thus is seems that two polemical sayings have been interpolated into 12:2–7, 11–12 on the basis of catchwords and thematic associations. This is not unlike the case of the mission speech, which consists of a composite but coherent community-directed speech into which prophetic threats have been inserted.

1969] 107–8) points out that 12:10a may be seen in the context of sayings such as Acts 3:17 and 13:27 which indicate that Jewish complicity in the death of Jesus does not lead to the ultimate rejection of the Jews, because they had acted in ignorance. But rejection of the offer put forward in the apostolic preaching is unforgivable. It must be said, however, that 12:10a does not make this point particularly well. There is no hint that ignorance is the basis for the lesser gravity of "speaking a word against the Son of Man," and in any case there is no real attempt to mitigate the effect of 12:8–9.

Matthew's conflation of Mark 3:28–30 and Q produces almost unbearable tensions. The Q saying is placed in proximity to 12:28 (Luke 11:20), which declares that Jesus—who is the Son of Man—performs exorcisms ἐν πνεύματι θεοῦ. This can only imply that blasphemy of Jesus is equivalent to blasphemy of the Spirit. Matthew then interpolates another Q passage having to do with speaking (12:32–35 // Luke 6:43–45), and concludes it with the warning "I tell you, on the day of judgment, men will render account for every careless word they utter" (12:36). This severely attenuates any exculpatory implications of 12:32a.

177. Zeller, *Mahnsprüche*, 191 n. 234 (without explanation). Schürmann ("Menschensohn-Titel," 137) asserts that 12:8–9 formed the original conclusion for 12:(2–3), 4–7, and that the force of 12:8–9 was then mitigated by the addition of a commentary word, 12:11–12 + Matt 10:23.

Comparison of Q with Mark shows that Mark has used 4:22 (cf. Q 12:2) and 13:11 (cf. Q 12:11–12) in approximately the same manner as Q. The saying about the revelation of what is hidden (4:22) is placed by Mark in the context of his treatment of the mystery of the kingdom of God. Attached to the saying about the lamp,[178] 4:22 "speaks of the provisional reign of the secret which is, for a time, entrusted to a few but is destined to be manifest to all very soon."[179] Thus as with Q 12:2, the Marcan saying has to do with the post-Easter proclamation of the disciples.[180] The main difference between Q and Mark is one of idiom: Q 12:2 is a wisdom saying while Mark offers a paradox. In Q the manifestation of τὸ κρυπτόν in the disciples' preaching is regarded as the inevitable result of a "law of eschatological disclosure." On the other hand, Mark employs an apocalyptic idiom: the hiding is for the sake of later apocalyptic disclosure.

Mark, like Q, uses 13:11 as a *Trostwort* for those who face proceedings in a synagogue. Whereas the Q saying derives its specific connection to the situation of preaching from its association with 12:2–7, Mark 13:11 receives that connotation by juxtaposition with 13:9: ". . . and you will be beaten in synagogues; and you will stand before governors and kings for my sake, to bear testimony before them." Again the most noticeable difference between Mark and Q is that of idiom: while Q uses this word of comfort directly in the context of instruction to the community, Mark casts it in a section which describes the "signs of the end" (13:6–8, 9–10, 12, 13, 14–17, 18–27), where it functions explicitly as apocalyptic parenesis.

Q 12:8–9 finds a Marcan parallel in 8:38.[181] As the context of this saying shows (Mark 8:27—9:1), Mark uses 8:38 as an exhortation to preparedness for martyrdom. As such it is directed at members of the community and not, as in Q, at a wider audience (including opponents). Mark's parallel to Q 12:10, Mark 3:28–29, apart from its significantly

178. Some hold that only the connection of 4:21, 22 is pre-Marcan: Ambrozic, *Hidden Kingdom*, 103; Rudolf Pesch, *Markusevangelium* 1:247–48. Others think that 4:21–25 is pre-Marcan: Jeremias, *Parables*, 91; J. Gnilka, *Die Verstockung Israels* (SANT 3; Munich: Kösel, 1961) 40 n. 67; G. Lindeskog, "Logia-Studien," *ST* 4 (1951–52) 157–60 and others. Schneider ("Bildwort," 197–99) argues that Mark was responsible for joining vv. 21 and 22.

179. Ambrozic, *Hidden Kingdom*, 103.

180. Thus most critics: see Ambrozic, *Hidden Kingdom*, 103–4; Gnilka, *Markus* 1:180; Laufen, *Doppelüberlieferung*, 167, and the authors cited in n. 71.

181. On the complex question of which version is the earlier, see W. G. Kümmel, "Das Verhalten Jesus gegenüber und das Verhalten des Menschensohns," *Jesus und der Menschensohn. Für Anton Vögtle* (Freiburg: Herder & Herder, 1975) 210–24; R. Pesch, "Über die Autorität," 25–55.

different wording, is quite distinct in its setting. Situated in the Beelzebul accusation, it evidently interprets the Beelzebul accusation as an instance of blasphemy against the Spirit. Q indeed also regards the Beelzebul accusation as symptomatic of the blindness of Jesus' opponents and as a matter of utmost seriousness. But Q applies the blasphemy saying to the more specific situation of opposition to the preaching of the disciples and, more particularly, to the rejection of the Spirit-inspired *apologia* of the disciples before the tribunal.

On the whole, the Marcan usage of these four sayings is quite similar to that of Q. Comparison with Mark does, however, set the sapiential character of 12:2 into sharper relief, and it reveals the directly hortatory nature of 12:11–12. Q 12:10 is more clearly related to the situation of post-Easter preaching than it is in Mark and 12:8–9 perhaps represents part of that preaching.

Summary. This block of Q consists of a hortatory speech, Q 12:2 + Q 12:3 (= Matt 10:27) + Q 12:4–5, 6–7 + Q 12:11–12, into which have been inserted two prophetic and threatening sayings, 12:8–9 and 12:10.

Q 12:22–34

Almost immediately following in Lucan sequence is another cluster of Q sayings. Q 12:22b–31 comprises a small collection on the topic of concern over the necessities of life, and this is followed by a saying on the acquisition of wealth. There is even a possibility that the chria in Luke 12:13–14 and the parable of the rich fool (12:15–21) came from Q.[182]

Q 12:22b–31[183]

Q 12:22b–31 gives the impression of a carefully constructed set of

---

182. Schürmann ("Reminiszenzen," 119–20) holds that Luke 12:13–15 and 16–21 preceded 12:22–31 in Q, linked by the catchwords πίε/πιῆτε (12:19; Matt 6:25 [mss!] diff Luke), φάγε/φάγητε (vv. 19, 22), ἀποθήκη (vv. 18, 24) and θησαυρίζω (12:21; Matt 6:19 diff Luke). He observes that διὰ τοῦτο λέγω ὑμῖν (12:22 // Matt 6:25) follows more logically upon 12:13–21 than it does on 12:11–12, and conjectures that Matthew may have omitted 12:13–21 because it did not fit well into the Sermon on the Mount. It could be mentioned too that 12:13–14 resembles the chriic form and the challenging tone of Q pronouncements in 9:57–58, 59–60, 61–62. (Luke 12:15 is redactional). The parable of the rich fool, especially its application (12:21), coheres well with criticism of riches found in Q sayings such as 12:33–34 and 16:13. Although Vassiliadis does not treat 12:13–14 or 16b–21, his criteria (above, chapter two) for inclusion in Q would seem to be satisfied: both units occur in a predominantly Q section of Luke, and they cohere both stylistically and materially with other Q texts.

183. Reconstruction: Schulz, *Spruchquelle*, 149–52; Zeller, *Mahnsprüche*, 82; Polag, *Fragmenta*, 60–62; Steinhauser, *Doppelbildworte*, 215–23.

admonitions concerning anxiety over daily needs, beginning with διὰ τοῦτο λέγω ὑμῖν and concluding with the promise that those who seek the kingdom will receive provisions from God. There are some signs of editorializing. Q 12:25 is regularly regarded as intrusive in this context since its imagery differs from that of 12:22b–24 and it breaks the continuity between 12:24 and 12:26–28. It may have been an independent rhetorical question serving as an admonition which was attached to the speech on the basis of the catchword μεριμνάω.[184]

On the remainder of the speech, opinion is divided. Bultmann defends the view that 12:22b–23 is an originally independent wisdom admonition which was successively expanded by 12:24, 26–28 and 12:29–31.[185] More recently, Zeller has continued this line. The use of an illustration from experience (i.e., 12:24, 26–28) to buttress an admonition corresponds to one of the conventional structures of OT sapiential admonitions.[186] However, as Zeller points out, the admonition μὴ μεριμνᾶτε τῇ ψυχῇ (ὑμῶν) τί φάγητε μηδὲ τῷ σώματι ὑμῶν τί ἐνδύσησθε already has one grounding statement in 12:23.[187] Moreover, the respective logics of the two motive clauses differ. Verse 23 counsels against anxiety in regard to food, on the basis that food is not the ultimate human concern. Q 12:24, 26–28 attempts no ranking of human concerns and needs with respect to each other but instead compares humans with lesser creatures in respect of their expectation of divine provision.

Zeller's solution is to regard 12:22b–23 as an independent exhortation which was joined to another consisting of 12:24, 27–28, 29, 30b. This cluster was then expanded by vv. 25 and 26 (made necessary by the addition of v. 25), and then two sayings: a "Jewish-Christian" saying, ". . . for all the nations of the world seek these things" (12:30a), and a kingdom saying, "Instead, seek his kingdom, and these things will be yours as well" (12:31).[188] The segregation of 30a, 31 from 29, 30b is not convincing, however. In view of the referential pronouns ταῦτα, τούτων and

184. Thus Bultmann (Tradition, 81, 88 [84, 92]), who thinks that it was a profane proverb. Similarly Fuchs, "Jesus' Understanding," 105; Jeremias, Parables, 103, 214; Wrege, Bergpredigt, 119; Schulz, Spruchquelle, 152, 154; Steinhauser, Doppelbildworte, 230.

185. Bultmann, Tradition, 88 [92]; Fuchs, "Jesus' Understanding," 105.

186. E.g., Prov 3:11–12; 23:6–8; 24:19–20, etc. See Zimmerli, "Concerning the Structure," 178–84.

187. Zeller, Mahnsprüche, 86.

188. Ibid., 86–87; similarly idem, "Redaktionsprozesse," 400. Zeller excludes v. 31 from the original composition "because its eschatological outlook fits badly with the sapiential perspective of the preceding" (Mahnsprüche, 87 [trans. by auth.]). Verse 30a is excluded because v. 30b provides a sufficient grounding and because 30a functions "more as a parenthesis" (ibid.).

αὐτοῦ in vv. 30a and 31, neither 30a nor 31 can be viewed as an originally independent saying. Verse 31, moreover, seems to be formulated specifically as an antithesis to vv. 29, 30a, whether or not μὴ ζητεῖτε is original in v. 29.[189]

Schulz and Merklein, on the other hand, see no compelling reason to partition the unit into *Grundworte*, commentary words and secondary expansions.[190] Indeed it seems unlikely that 12:24, (26), 27–28 ever circulated independently of 12:22b–23. Verses 24, (26), 27–28 are tailored precisely to provide the motive clauses for the admonitions in 22b and only for those admonitions, treating them in order: first eating, then clothing. This suggests either that 12:22b–24, 26–28 was an original unity, or that 12:24, 26–28 was an early addition composed expressly for 12:22b–23.

With 12:29–31, however, the situation is different. These verses introduce drinking alongside eating and use περιβάλλω instead of ἐνδύω and ὁ πατήρ rather than ὁ θεός (vv. 24, 28). In addition to the vocabularic shift, there is a shift in logic. The admonition in 12:29 is grounded by means of a polemical contrast with the Gentiles and no longer by means of observations drawn from nature. In view of these features, it seems best to regard 12:29–31 as an originally independent admonition attached to 12:22b–24, 26–28 on the basis of catchword and thematic associations.

Whatever its actual literary history, 12:22b–31 may be characterized as an amalgam of sapiential admonitions and justifications. Even 12:25 which is undoubtedly an insertion does not depart from the sapiential character of the speech. Schulz takes a dissenting view, that the speech is prophetic in nature. As evidence for this contention he adduces the introductory formulae (διὰ τοῦτο) λέγω ὑμῖν and τίς ἐξ ὑμῶν.[191] However, as has been noted already, the λέγω ὑμῖν formula with a following

---

189. Schulz (*Spruchquelle*, 151) and Steinhauser (*Doppelbildworte*, 220) hold that Matthew's μεριμνήσητε is original because the rest of the speech uses this verb. But it is equally possible that Matthew introduced the verb precisely for the same reason and in order to form a bridge to his redactional verse 6:34. Incidentally, both 6:31 and the redactional verse 6:34 use the aorist whereas the rest of the Q speech employs the present tense. Hence Luke's μὴ ζητεῖτε . . . ζητεῖτε δέ may be original. Thus Jeremias, *Sprache*, 218; Schmid, *Matthäus und Lukas*, 236.

190. Schulz, *Spruchquelle*, 154; Merklein, *Gottesherrschaft*, 179. Merklein toys with the possibility that Matt 6:25a + 33 (Luke 12:22b–23 + 31) was an independent prophetic word which was expanded by a sapiential unit, but rejects this as too hypothetical.

191. Schulz, *Spruchquelle*, 153; similarly Steinhauser, *Doppelbildworte*, 230. Merklein (*Gottesherrschaft*, 177–78) regards only "I say to you" as prophetic. Boring (*Sayings of the Risen Jesus*, 168) rejects the view that 12:22–31 is prophetic in origin but proposes that it is a word of Jesus to which prophetic formulae have been added.

imperative is better regarded as sapiential in character,[192] and in view of the statement which follows the formula, its use in 12:27 can scarcely be deemed "prophetic." Nor can the formula "who among you . . ." be seen as prophetic. Although, as Greeven and Jeremias point out, the formula τίς ἐν ὑμῖν/τίς ἐξ ὑμῶν appears in the prophetic speech in the OT,[193] in those instances it introduces *real questions*. Berger rightly notes that in the Gospel materials the formula expects the answer "No one!"[194] The question is semantically equivalent to a statement introduced by οὐδείς. Locutions of this kind are to be found in a variety of types of literature, including sapiential works[195] and even Epictetus—who is hardly inclined to prophetic speech.[196] Consideration of the content of 12:25 also makes the designation "prophetic" unlikely: on the contrary, the verse is a sapiential reflection on ordinary human experience.

The most problematic verse is 12:31, which Schulz and Merklein characterize as "prophetic."[197] The mention of the kingdom indeed seems to introduce an eschatological aspect. But does this mean that the saying is prophetic? It is often observed that the use of ζητέω with τὴν βασιλείαν is nowhere attested in Jewish apocalyptic literature.[198] The metaphor of "seeking" is, however, frequently associated with the pursuit of Sophia.[199] Moreover, as Zeller points out, the structure of 12:31 is not too unlike sapiential sayings such as[200]

Honor the Lord with your substance
. . . then your barns will be filled with plenty . . .

(Prov 3:9–10)

Wisdom tradition is indeed familiar with the notion that those who seek Sophia first are rewarded with security and provisions. Perhaps the

---

192. See above, n. 164.
193. Greeven, "Wer unter euch . . . ?" 238–55; Jeremias, *Parables*, 103. But unlike Schulz, both Greeven and Jeremias treat the formula as an indicator of *dominical* sayings. For OT examples, see Isa 42:23; 50:10; Hag 2:3.
194. Berger, "Materialien," 31–33.
195. Prov 18:14; Sir 10:29; 12:13–14; *T. Job* 37:6.
196. Epictetus *Diss.* 1.22.1: "And who among us (τίς δ' ἡμῶν) does not assume that righteousness is beautiful and becoming?" (Loeb 1:143). Ibid., 1.27.19: "Who among you (τίς ὑμῶν) when he wishes to go to a bath goes to a mill instead?" (Loeb 1:177). See also 2.17.8.
197. Schulz, *Spruchquelle*, 154; Merklein, *Gottesherrschaft*, 178. Boring (*Sayings of the Risen Jesus*, 168) comments that it is not legitimate to label "all the wisdom materials in the synoptic tradition as prophetic without further evidence. In this case, the evidence seems to be insufficient."
198. Jeremias, *New Testament Theology*, 33; Zeller, *Mahnsprüche*, 91.
199. See Prov 2:4; 14:6; 15:14; 18:15; Qoh 7:25; Wis 6:12; Sir 4:11–12; 6:27; 51:13.
200. Zeller, *Mahnsprüche*, 86, 91.

most dramatic example is Wis 7:7–14, in which Solomon reports that his search for Sophia also resulted in his acquisition of "all good things" and "uncounted wealth." Promises of security and provisions are found elsewhere:

> He who obeys her will judge nations,
> and whoever gives heed to her will dwell secure.

(Sir 4:15)

> Search out and seek, and she will become known to you
> and when you get hold of her, do not let her go
> for at last you will find the rest she gives
> and she will be changed into joy for you.

(Sir 6:27–28; also 51:28)

While the introduction of the apocalyptic aspect is novel, the logic and basic motif of 12:31 is quite in keeping with the sapiential teaching on divine provision and providence.

All of the elements of the speech are in accord with sapiential idiom: the use of an imperative followed by a motive clause; the appeal to observation of nature;[201] the formulae "I say to you" and "who among you" and the promise of security to those who seek. Although not an original unity, Q 12:22b–31 has been formulated in a consistent idiom and with a clear intention: to counsel a community of poor against anxiety. Schürmann and Zeller have suggested that the *Sitz im Leben* of the speech is instruction to wandering charismatics.[202] This may be the case for 12:22b–28, which can be viewed as a counterpart for 10:4–7. However, the verb "seek" in 12:31 does not seem to be an appropriate term to describe the activity of preaching the kingdom.[203] One would

---

201. See, e.g., Prov 6:6–11. A close parallel to 12:24, 27 is found in *1 Enoch* 2:1—5:5, which consists of a series of imperatives (κατανοήσατε, ἴδετε, καταμάθετε, διανοήθητε, γνῶτε) which direct attention to the regularity of the cycles of nature (in contrast to human irregularities). The sapiential character of this section has been demonstrated by R. A. Coughenour, "Enoch and Wisdom: A Study of the Wisdom Elements in the Book of Enoch" (Ph.D. diss., Case Western Reserve Univ., 1972) 100–105. The main difference between *1 Enoch* 2:1—5:5 and Luke 12:22b–31 is that Enoch goes on to make apocalyptic predictions of punishment and salvation (5:5–9) which are lacking in the Q speech (although present in the extension of the speech, 12:39–59).

202. Schürmann, "Basileia-Verkündigung," 158; Zeller, *Mahnsprüche*, 93. In his comments on wandering Cynic preachers, Epictetus (*Diss.* 1.9.9) states that if they live "in harmony with nature" they will, like the animals, have everything appropriate to their way of life. However, the ideal of a "simple life" is not restricted to Cynics, but is found, among other places, in Epicurus: "Thanks be to blessed Nature because she has made what is necessary easy to supply and what is not easy unnecessary" (fr. 67; C. Bailey, *Epicurus: The Extant Remains* [Oxford: At the Clarendon Press, 1926] 136).

203. Schulz (*Spruchquelle*, 153) takes the view that "seeking the kingdom" is not primarily apocalyptic in scope but means "keeping the commandments and Law of God" and is similar to the rabbinic phrase "to take on the (yoke of the) kingdom of

expect κηρύξατε δὲ τὴν βασιλείαν αὐτοῦ καὶ ταῦτα προστεθήσεται ὑμῖν. Moreover, the negative reinforcement provided by the appeal to *Gentile* behavior makes more sense in an argument directed at a *community* which defines itself over against other existing groups than it does in an exhortation for individual preachers. As with the case of 9:57–62; 10:2–12, 16, it is likely that Q 12:22b–31 began as exhortations directed at missionaries, but was supplemented in such a way as to widen its intended audience to the community at large. Evidently, this community is, like its missionaries, in need of words of comfort that God will provide the physical necessities for those who comport themselves wholly toward the kingdom.

Q 12:33–34[204]

Despite the fact that 12:33–34 conforms to the familiar structure of an admonition plus motive clause (introduced by γάρ), it is usually held that v. 34 is a secondary accretion to v. 33.[205] The admonition itself finds partial parallels in contemporary Jewish exhortation to collect heavenly treasures by doing good deeds (especially almsgiving),[206] although the disdain for earthy acquisitions is somewhat peculiar.[207] The addition of 12:34 makes it clear that one cannot value both earthly and heavenly

---

heaven" (*m. Ber.* 2:2). M. '*Abot* 3:5 provides an interesting parallel: "He who takes upon himself the yoke of the Law, from him shall be taken away the yoke of the [earthly] kingdom and the yoke of worldly care; but he who throws off the yoke of the Law, upon him shall be laid the yoke of the kingdom and the yoke of worldly care" (trans. Danby). In spite of this parallel, there is no sign in Q that "seeking the kingdom" was interpreted with respect to keeping the Law. Although it is not clear in what this "seeking" concretely consisted, it is expressly contrasted with comportment toward material concerns, and perhaps related to the prayer for the coming of the kingdom in 11:2.

204. Reconstruction: Schulz, *Spruchquelle*, 142–43; Steinhauser, *Doppelbildworte*, 236–38; Polag, *Fragmenta*, 62. With minor variations, all take the Matthaean version to represent that of Q.

205. Matt 6:19–20 (diff Luke 12:33) speaks of θησαυρούς while 6:21 (Luke 12:34) uses the singular. Moreover, the assertion to the effect that one's values control one's desires (12:34) has no real logical connection with the contrast of imperishable and perishable treasures in 12:33. See further Zeller, *Mahnsprüche*, 77–78; Steinhauser, *Doppelbildworte*, 246–47; Bultmann, *Tradition*, 84 [87]. Bultmann points out that 12:34 might be a proverb.

206. Tobit 4:8–11 and Sir 29:11–12 treat almsgiving as "treasure" which is laid up and can rescue from affliction. *Pss. Sol.* 9:9: ὁ ποιῶν δικαιοσύνην θησαυρίζει ζωὴν ἑαυτῷ παρὰ κυρίῳ. Also 1 Enoch 38:2; 4 Ezra 8:33; 2 Apoc. Bar. 14:12; 24:1; 2 Enoch 50:5; *m. Pe'a* 1:1; *t. Pe'a* 4:18. See further Wilhelm Pesch, "Zur Exegese," 362–64; Percy, *Botschaft*, 90–91.

207. The sapiential and rabbinic texts cited in the previous note only recommend that wealth be used in the service of good. A more consistently negative view of possessions is found at Qumran (see 1QS 11:2; 1QpHab 8:10–12; 9:2–6; 12:3–10) though in these instances it is the wealth of the Jerusalem hierarchy which is criticized, not wealth in general. See on this H. Braun, *Spätjüdisch-häretischer und frühchristlicher Radikalismus* (BHT 24; 2 vols.; Tübingen: J. C. B. Mohr [Paul Siebeck], 1969²) 1:35–37, 58–59, 77–80.

"treasures"; the pursuit of earthly concerns will result in loss and in the failure to obtain imperishable treasures.[208] The either/or formulation reminds us of another Q saying, 16:13: "It is impossible to serve (both) God and mammon." The association of 12:33–34 with the preceding cluster of sayings is undoubtedly due to the common theme of exhortation to refrain from engagement in the pursuit of physical needs or wealth. By itself 12:33–34 might have emphasized the second half of the admonition, θησαυρίζετε δὲ ὑμῖν θησαυροὺς ἐν οὐρανῷ, but in its present context the stress falls upon the prohibition, μὴ θησαυρίζετε. The force of this saying is prohibitive, not positive.[209]

Schulz again insists upon the prophetic character of 12:33–34 and conjectures that the "prophetic" λέγω ὑμῖν formula originally belonged to the saying. This conclusion is predicated upon the "prophetic" character of the preceding speech, and upon the formal similarity between this saying and other alleged prophetic sayings (e.g., 11:9; 12:4).[210] However, as we have seen, λέγω ὑμῖν—even if it did belong to 12:33a—is not a clear index of prophetic speech. There is in fact nothing at all prophetic about the saying. Bultmann and Percy observe that there is no eschatological motivation to the saying.[211] Its structure and argumentation as well as its immediate context identify it as sapiential.

If it could be assumed that 12:13–14 and 12:16–21 also derived from Q, the entire complex would take on a carefully balanced structure. Like the discipleship-mission speech (Q 9:57–62; 10:2–11, 16), this block begins with a chria in which Jesus himself rejects any involvement in earthly and material pursuits. The parable of the rich fool reinforces the point of the ultimate absurdity of material gain. Although it serves as a conclusion for the parable, 12:21 (οὕτως ὁ θησαυρίζων αὑτῷ καὶ μὴ εἰς θεὸν πλουτῶν) goes beyond the actual point of the story, preparing for Q 12:33–34, which likewise asserts an antinomy between earthly and heavenly treasures. For Q, commitment to the pursuit of both is impos-

---

208. See Percy, Botschaft, 91; Zeller, Mahnsprüche, 80–81. Zeller notes that the juxtaposition of Matt 6:21 with 6:20 evokes the notion of a heart anchored in heaven such as is encountered in T. Job 36:3: "[Job's heart] is not fixed on earthly concerns, since the earth and those who dwell in it are unstable. But my heart is fixed on heavenly concerns, for there is no upset in heaven" (trans. R. P. Spittler, OTP, 857).

209. Thus Schulz, Spruchquelle, 144. There is no indication that "treasuring up treasures in heaven" meant "acquiring a treasury of meritorious deeds." Curiously, Schenk (Synopse, 93) proposes that the saying concerns heavenly rewards obtained from acts of confession and love of enemies. But the context gives no indication of this meaning.

210. Schulz, Spruchquelle, 143.

211. Bultmann, Tradition, 104 [109]; Percy, Botschaft, 91.

sible. Framed by the opening chria and parable and the concluding warning and aphorism (12:33–34), the main portion of the speech (Q 12:22b–31) consists in a carefully constructed set of admonitions which counsel by means of sapiential appeals absolute dependence upon divine care.

Q 13:24–30, 34–35; 14:16–24, 26–27; 17:33; 14:34–35

The last major block of Q material is found in Luke 13:24—14:35, broken up only by a few items of Lucan *Sondergut* (13:31–33; 14:1–6, 7–14, 28–33). As argued above, Q 17:33 is one of the few Q texts dislocated by Luke;[212] Matthew's location of the saying (after 10:37, 38 // Luke 14:26–27) is to be preferred.

The content of this section of Q is quite diverse: it begins with a "two ways" motif (13:24),[213] moves to threats of exclusion from the kingdom (13:25–27, 28–30), a lament (13:34–35), the parable of the great supper (14:16–24) and concludes with discipleship sayings (14:26–27; 17:33; 14:34–35). The common denominator is a concern for entry into the kingdom—either a description of the radical demands imposed on those who are in the service of the kingdom or threats issued to those who do not respond to the preaching of the kingdom.[214]

Q 13:24

The first saying employs the metaphor of the "two paths" (Matt) or the "narrow door" (Luke). Matthew's image is of two roads, each leading to a city gate ($\pi\acute{\nu}\lambda\eta$), the narrow one to life and the wide one to destruction, while Luke envisages a single narrow door ($\theta\acute{\nu}\rho\alpha$) which is difficult to enter. Opinion is sharply divided in regard to the form of the Q

---

212. See above, chapter four, pp. 158–59.

213. Although some suggest that Luke 13:23 derives from Q (Jeremias, *Parables*, 195 n. 9; Schmid, *Matthäus und Lukas*, 244; Mussner, "Das 'Gleichnis,'" 113), the presence of several Lucanisms—the introduction of a discourse by a question; $\epsilon\hat{\imath}\pi\epsilon\nu$ $\delta\acute{\epsilon}$; an interrogative $\epsilon\hat{\imath}$ following "Lord" (only in Luke); $\tau\acute{\imath}s$, $\epsilon\hat{\imath}\pi\epsilon\nu$ $\pi\rho\acute{o}s$, $\kappa\acute{\nu}\rho\iota\epsilon$ (used of the earthly Jesus); $\sigma\acute{\omega}\zeta\omega$ without an object as a term for salvation—makes it more probable that 13:23 is a Lucan construction. See Jeremias, *Sprache*, 231; Schulz, *Spruchquelle*, 310, and authors cited in n. 358; A. Denaux, "Der Spruch," 326–27; Steinhauser, *Doppelbildworte*, 148–49.

214. It is for this reason that we do not treat the two growth parables (13:18–19, 20–21) in this context in spite of their proximity to 13:24–30. They concern the vigorous and ineluctable growth of the kingdom from something small and hidden to something of amazingly large proportions, rather than entry into the kingdom as such. Materially, they seem to relate to sayings such as 12:2, which likewise implies that the kingdom will be manifest by some hidden yet powerful internal dynamism.

saying,[215] and it is not impossible that both Matthew and Luke have altered Q.[216] The minimal Matt-Luke agreements suggest that the Q saying began with an imperative (εἰσέλθατε/ἀγωνίζεσθε εἰσελθεῖν διὰ τῆς στενῆς θύρας [πύλης?]) followed by a motive clause introduced by ὅτι which contrasted the unsuccessful attempt of the many to enter the door with the success of the few.

Q 13:25-27

Reconstruction of the next saying is also fraught with difficulties. Common to both Matt 7:22b–23 and Luke 13:26–27 are several features: the protest of those who are rejected, the pronouncement "I do not know you" and the allusion to Ps 6:9. But the saying cannot very well have begun with the protest "Lord, did we not eat with you . . ." Some introduction is required, but Matthew and Luke differ widely in their versions of it. Matt 7:13a is perhaps to be preferred, though it is not impossible that Luke's catchword θύρα figured into the introduction as well.[217]

215. For the priority of Matthew: Harnack, *Sayings of Jesus*, 67–68 [50]; Bultmann, *Tradition*, 93 [97]; Schmid, *Matthäus und Lukas*, 244; Steinhauser, *Doppelbildworte*, 149–50; Schulz, *Spruchquelle*, 309–11; Schenk, *Synopse*, 102. For the priority of Luke: Bussmann, *Redenquelle*, 77; Wellhausen, *Evangelium Matthaei*, 31; H. Conzelmann, *The Theology of Saint Luke* (London: Faber & Faber, 1960) 109; J. Jeremias, πύλη, *TDNT* 6 (1968) 923; Loisy, *Evangiles synoptiques* 1:635; Manson, *Sayings*, 175; Streeter, *Four Gospels*, 283–84.

216. Whereas Matt 7:13a speaks of a gate, 7:13b-14 mentions a gate and a road. "Those who enter through it" (7:13c) makes more sense if taken to refer to "gate" rather than its immediate antecedent, "road." Accordingly, Zeller (*Mahnsprüche*, 139), Hoffmann (*Studien*, 195) and Denaux ("Der Spruch," 322–23) suggest that Matthew introduced the idea of the "two ways" motif. This could also account for the change of "door" to "gate." On the other hand, some argue that Luke added ἀγωνίζεσθε (Schulz, *Spruchquelle*, 310; Jeremias, *Sprache*, 232; Zeller, *Mahnsprüche*, 139 and others), although the word is not obviously Lucan. Schmid (*Matthäus und Lukas*, 244) and Bultmann (*Tradition*, 93 [97]) hold that Luke avoids antithetic parallelism. This may indeed be correct, and ὀλίγοι in 13:23 may be a reminiscence of the Q saying (cf. Matt 7:14b). Ἰσχύω may also be Lucan (Matt 4x/Mark 4x/Luke, 2x red, 2x diff Matt, 4x Sond; Acts 6x). Schulz (*Spruchquelle*, 311) holds that the meal scene (13:25–29) has led to the elimination of the "two ways" motif and the alteration of "gate" to "door." But this does not account for the tension within the Matthaean saying nor the tension between 13:24 and vv. 25–27 (see below). However, the use of the future tenses in 13:24b may be occasioned by the description of the eschatological meal (13:25–27) in which some try to enter and cannot. Luke's own interpretation of the scene is made clear from ἀφ᾽ οὗ: enter before it is too late (cf. 13:1–9)!

217. The agreements between Luke 13:25 and Matt 25:10-12 appear to justify the suspicion that Matthew and Luke are drawing on the same tradition, but whether it originally served as the introduction to 13:26–27 is another matter. Awkward shifts in *Bildlogik* created by Luke 13:25 suggest editorial intrusion: the metaphor of a narrow door (13:24) becomes a closed door (13:25), and the exclusion of latecomers gives way to the rejection of evildoers (13:26–27). The thoroughgoing use of the second-person plural is probably Lucan (see Cadbury, *Style*, 124–25) and the entire Lucan section (13:22–30)

It is a little easier to determine the original intent of Q 13:26–27. Just as Matthew was responsible for relocating the exclusion saying to the end of his Sermon on the Mount it is likely that he too reformulated it as a condemnation of Christian pneumatics and false prophets rather than Jesus' Jewish contemporaries.[218] His juxtaposition of the saying with materials directed against false prophets (Matt 7:15–23) permitted the introduction of references to prophesying, exorcisms and thaumaturgy. Q is better preserved by Luke 13:26–27,[219] which with an introduction such as Matt 7:22a may have circulated as an independent prophetic threat.[220]

Q 13:28–29, 30

The following Q saying (13:28–29 // Matt 8:11–12) is a prophetic oracle which is easily separable from its present context, as indeed is demonstrated by the fact that Matthew relocated it to his version of the healing of the centurion's son.[221] In spite of Lucan editorial activity

employs the metaphor of a festal meal, a motif which is already seminally present in 13:29 (= Matt 8:11) but due to Lucan redaction in 13:37, 14:15 and 22:30. Schulz (*Spruchquelle*, 425) and Mussner ("Das 'Gleichnis,'" 117, 121) see the original introduction in Matt 7:22a. There is little or nothing in 7:22a which is identifiably Matthaean: πολλοί is usually traditional in Matthaean sayings of Jesus (from Mark, 19:30; 24:5 [*bis*]; 26:28; from Q, 7:13; 10:31; 13:17; Sond or red: 22:14; 24:10, 11 [*bis*], 12; at 8:11 [diff Luke 13:29] Luke lacks a parallel), as is ἐκείνη ἡ ἡμέρα used eschatologically (24:36 = Mark; 24:19 = Mark; 24:22 [Mark: αἱ ἡμέραι]; 24:29 = Mark).

218. Similarly Bultmann, *Tradition*, 117 [123]; Mussner, "Das 'Gleichnis,'" 117; Hoffmann, "Πάντες," 200–201; Hahn, *Titles*, 90–91; Schulz, *Spruchquelle*, 424–26.

219. Lucan redaction is possible in the use of ἐνώπιον (Matt–/Mark–/Luke 22x/Acts 13x; see Cadbury, *Style*, 204); ἀφίστημι is perhaps Lucan (Matt–/Mark–/Luke 4x/Acts 6x) although it is found in the LXX of Ps 6:9; words with the ἀδικ-root are very common in Luke-Acts and infrequent elsewhere: ἀδικία: Matt–/Mark–/Luke 3x/Acts 2x. ἀδικέω: Matt 1x/Mark–/Luke 1x/Acts 5x. ἀδίκημα: Acts 2x. ἄδικος: Matt–/Mark–/Luke 4x/Acts 1x. Hahn (*Titles*, 123 n. 159) contends that κύριε κύριε belonged to Q, but it is more likely that it has been inserted from Matt 7:21. Matthew elsewhere inserts κύριε at 8:2, 6 (?), 21 (?), 25; 9:28; 14:28, 30; 15:22, 25; 16:22; 17:4, 15; 18:21; 20:30, 31, 33; 25:37 (?), 44 (?); 26:22.

220. See Bultmann, *Tradition*, 117 [123]; Schulz, *Spruchquelle*, 426; Hoffmann, "Πάντες," 201–2. Karl P. Donfried (*The Setting of Second Clement in Early Christianity* [NovTSup 38; Leiden: E. J. Brill, 1974] 62–68) has argued that 2 *Clem* 4:5 (ἐὰν ἦτε μετ᾽ ἐμοῦ συνηγμένοι ἐν τῷ κόλπῳ μου καὶ μὴ ποιῆτε τὰς ἐντολάς μου ἀποβαλῶ ὑμᾶς καὶ ἐρῶ ὑμῖν· οὐκ οἶδα ὑμᾶς πόθεν ἐστέ, ἐργάται ἀνομίας) is based upon an early sayings collection such as Q. Since a saying closely parallel to Matt 7:21 is quoted in 2 *Clem* 4:2, Donfried is obliged to make the tenuous argument that 7:21 // Luke 6:46—in the Matthaean form—was already found with Luke 13:26–27 in Q. However, Koester (*Synoptische Überlieferung*, 79–84) has shown that 2 *Clem* conflated Matthew and Luke. See, however, Betz (*Essays*, 145) who argues that 2 *Clem* 3—4 betrays knowledge of a pre-Matthaean Sermon (which is already developed beyond Q).

221. Thus Schmid, *Matthäus und Lukas*, 254; Käsemann, "Beginnings of Christian Theology," 100; Schulz, *Spruchquelle*, 324.

visible in the joining of the saying to 13:25–27, there is no good reason to doubt that Luke reproduces the relative order of the sayings in Q.[222] But to accept the Lucan placement of the saying does not obviate all of our problems. There is also disagreement between Matthew and Luke concerning the order of the two halves of the saying. Taking the Lucan order to be primary (vv. 28, 29), some have argued that the oracle is composite, consisting of a threat against unbelieving Jews in the second-person plural (v. 28) and a promise of Gentile salvation in the third (v. 29).[223] The considerations against this, however, are decisive: ἐκεῖ ἔσται ὁ κλαυθμὸς καὶ ὁ βρυγμὸς τῶν ὀδόντων cannot serve as an introduction to an originally independent saying, but it is quite acceptable as its conclusion. More likely, Luke brought this phrase forward in order to form a bridge with the preceding saying, in particular, the command "Depart from me."[224] This means that the following subordinate clause, ὅταν ὄψησθε ᾽Αβρααμ . . . ὑμᾶς δὲ ἐκβαλλομένους ἔξω, must also have been reformulated by Luke. The use of the second-person address is consistent with Lucan redaction elsewhere,[225] as is the insertion of πάντας τοὺς προφήτας (for which a parallel is missing in Matthew).[226] The Matthaean

222. Bruce D. Chilton (*God in Strength*, 185) argues that neither Matthew nor Luke reproduced the original position of Q, on the basis that Justin quotes 13:26–30 but omits 13:28–29 (*Apol.* 16.11–12). However, Justin reproduces not a continuous block of material, but scattered Matthaean and Lucan texts in no particular order. His quotation proves nothing about the original order of Q sayings.

223. Trilling (*Israel*, 88) and Strecker (*Weg*, 100) argue that the two sayings were joined by the catchword "kingdom of God." Similarly Schürmann, "Basileia-Verkündigung," 165; Schlosser, *Règne de Dieu*, 614.

224. Thus Hoffmann, "Πάντες," 207; Schulz, *Spruchquelle*, 323, and authors cited in n. 1; Dieter Zeller, "Das Logion," 223; Meyer, "Community," 16; idem, "Gentile Mission," 411–12; Dupont, "Beaucoup," 156. Against this Josef Schmid (*Matthäus und Lukas*, 255) holds that Matthew "the systematician" regrouped the saying when he transferred it to 8:5–13. Strecker (*Weg*, 100) opines that Matthew created antithetic parallelism and unified the saying by the consistent use of the third-person plural. Schlosser (*Règne de Dieu*, 609–11) suggests that the reformulation of the saying by Matthew—who emphasizes more strongly than Luke the contrast between Gentile and Jews—was occasioned by the connection of Matt 8:10 (Jesus' response to the centurion's statement). But none of these positions deals satisfactorily with the problem raised by ἐκεῖ introducing 13:28. Schürmann ("Basileia-Verkündigung," 164–67) holds that 13:28 did not circulate as an independent saying but was a *Zusatzwort* for 13:26–27, and 13:29 was a secondary expansion of 13:28.

225. See Cadbury, *Style*, 124–25; Hoffmann, "Πάντες," 207. Schmid (*Matthäus und Lukas*, 256) argues for the originality of ὄψησθε on the grounds that Luke tends to omit or replace forms of ὁράω (e.g., in Mark 14:62 // Luke 22:69). However, as Cadbury points out (*Style*, 176) this is frequently to change a Marcan statement of *perception* into one of *fact* (e.g., in Luke 3:21; 8:45; 9:30, 37; 22:69). In the present instance, as well as in 17:22 and 22:27, "seeing" is crucial to the Lucan point.

226. See Jeremias, *Sprache*, 209. Πάντες τῶν προφητῶν occurs, apart from Matt 11:13 (with "Law"), only in Luke-Acts: Luke 11:50 (diff Matt); 13:28; 24:27 (*Sond*); Acts 3:18, 24; 10:43.

form of the saying has a better claim to represent Q in spite of a few possibly redactional touches.[227]

Once the Matthaean order of the saying (8:11–12 // Luke 13:29, 28) is taken to be original, there is no need to suspect it as composite. On the contrary, it is intelligible as a unitary, antithetically formulated prophetic pronouncement. As the structure of the saying indicates, the prediction of the coming of Gentiles[228] functions in the same way as related sayings in 10:13–15 and 11:31–32: the participation of Gentiles in the kingdom serves as an *Unheilszeichen* for the "sons of the kingdom" and heightens the contrast between responsive Gentiles and impenitent Israel.

The motif of eschatological reversal is underlined by a *Wanderlogion* which occurs in several different settings: Matt 19:30 // Mark 10:31 (concluding a discipleship saying), Matt 20:16 (concluding the parable of the laborers in the vineyard) and *P. Oxy.* 654.3 (cf. *Gos. Thom.* 4).

Q 13:34–35[229]

Q 13:34–35 coheres with some of the characteristic emphases of 13:24–30. It is, of course, a matter of debate whether 13:34–35 was preserved in its Q order by Luke or by Matthew or whether both Matthew and Luke have transferred the saying to new locations.[230] The principal reason for

227. It is uncertain whether λέγω ὑμῖν (Matt 8:11) stood in Q (thus Schulz, *Spruchquelle*, 323) or whether Matthew added it from 8:10. Some regard Matthew's "many" as redactional (Schulz, *Spruchquelle*, 323–24; Schmid, *Matthäus und Lukas*, 256), but as n. 217 indicated, πολλοί is usually traditional in sayings. Moreover, there would be good reason for Luke to omit it since it contradicts his earlier statement in 13:24. Zeller ("Das Logion," 223) remarks that Matthew himself is not overly optimistic about the number of the elect (7:13–14; 19:30; 22:14; 24:10–12). This too suggests the originality of "many" here. Citing Matt 13:28, Schulz (*Spruchquelle*, 324), Trilling (*Israel*, 88), Chilton (*God in Strength*, 191–92) and Strecker (*Weg*, 100) urge that "sons of the kingdom" is from Matthew. However, οἱ υἱοὶ τῆς βασιλείας in 13:38 refers to Christians (cf. v. 43); in 8:12 it refers to Jews. This, coupled with the likelihood that the second-person plural address in Luke 13:28 is Lucan, makes it probable that Matthew reproduces Q. The clearest instance of Matthaean redaction is τὸ σκότος τὸ ἐξώτερον (cf. 22:13 [red]; 25:30 [red?]) which is probably secondary to Luke's ἔξω.

228. For a thorough analysis of the tradition-history of this saying, see Zeller, "Das Logion."

229. Reconstructions: Schulz, *Spruchquelle*, 346–47; Hoffmann, *Studien*, 171–72; Steck, *Israel*, 48–50; Polag, *Fragmenta*, 66.

230. The originality of the Matthaean context (23:34–36, 37–39) is defended either on the grounds that 23:37–39 appears to be the continuation of the sapiential quotation begun in vv. 34–36 (thus Bultmann, *Tradition*, 114–15 [120–21]; Robinson, "LOGOI SOPHON," 104; Meyer, "Community," 25–26) or on the grounds that the association of these two sayings is more natural than the Lucan context (thus U. Wilckens, Σοφία, *TDNT* 7 [1971] 515; Schenk, *Synopse*, 81; Lührmann, *Redaktion*, 45). Against the originality of Matthew's setting, three points have been raised: (1) The temporal positions of the respective speakers differ (in the former, it is prospective; in the latter, retrospective) (Haenchen, "Matthäus 23," 56–57; Steck, *Israel*, 47). (2) The two do not form one continuous saying but two discrete judgment words. (3) It seems unlikely that

suspecting the Lucan setting is the fact that it appears next to Luke 13:31–33, connected by the catchword "Jerusalem."[231] But it is equally likely that it was 13:31–33 that was attracted to 13:34–35, not *vice versa*. Whatever the case, we shall consider 13:34–35 here because of its thematic affinities to 13:24–30.

Q 13:34–35 provides perhaps the clearest example of the deuteronomistic conception of history according to which God or Sophia continually sends prophets to Israel (or Jerusalem) in order to call her to repentance. In fact, 13:34–35a was originally a Sophia-oracle. The phrase ποσάκις ἠθέλησα ἐπισυναγαγεῖν refers to the entire course of Israelite history and thus requires a speaker appropriate to that vantage point. This, however, creates problems for the interpretation of v. 35b, "And I tell you, you will not see me until you say, 'Blessed is he who comes in the name of the Lord.'" Steck assumes that the entire saying (including v. 35b) is pre-Christian, expressing the idea that Sophia will absent herself from the world (see Sir 15:7; *1 Enoch* 42) but will return in the "wisdom of the Son of Man" (see *1 Enoch* 48:1–2, 7; 49:3–4; 51:3).[232] But the evidence for a "return of Sophia" is not strong; besides, the λέγω ὑμῖν formula in 13:35b seems to be used as it is in 11:51b to mark a change of speaker (i.e., from Sophia to Jesus). It seems to me preferable to regard 13:34–35a as a pre-Christian Sophia saying to which has been added a Christian saying referring to the coming of the Son of Man (13:35b).[233]

Q 7:35, which characterizes John and Jesus as τέκνα σοφίας and describes their rejection by "this generation," and 11:49–51, in which Sophia speaks as the one who sends prophets to Israel and who will bring judgment upon those who reject those prophets, provide the closest Q parallels for 13:34–35. But similar themes are also available in the immediate Q context in the judgment sayings 13:26–27 and 13:29, 28, which threaten Israel with exclusion because of their non-response to

---

Luke would have removed 13:34–35 from its context in chap. 11 had he found it there. For these reasons, many reject the Matthaean setting of the saying. Thus Soiron, *Logia Jesu*, 45–46; Bussmann, *Redenquelle*, 73; J. Schmid, *Matthäus und Lukas*, 332; Manson, *Sayings*, 102; Strecker, *Weg*, 113; Schulz, *Spruchquelle*, 349; Jacobson, "Wisdom Christology," 210–11.

231. Thus Conzelmann, *Theology of Saint Luke*, 133; J. Schmid, *Matthäus und Lukas*, 332; Lührmann, *Redaktion*, 45; Steck, *Israel*, 45; Schulz, *Spruchquelle*, 347.

232. Steck, *Israel*, 56–57, 234–39. Schulz (*Spruchquelle*, 358–60) agrees that Sophia is the speaker throughout, but holds the oracle to be a Christian composition *in toto*.

233. Thus Harnack, *Sayings of Jesus*, 169; Wilckens, Σοφία, 515; Felix Christ, *Jesus Sophia* (ATANT 57; Zürich: Zwingli, 1970) 141–42; Hoffmann, *Studien*, 177; Neirynck, "Study of Q," 66.

God's envoys. As a prophetic oracle of judgment,[234] 13:34–35 coheres well both formally and materially with the preceding Q sayings (assuming the Lucan order to be that of Q), and the entire cluster 13:26–30, 34–35 has its closest affinities with the stratum of Q redaction described above in chapter four.

Q 14:16–24[235]

Matthew's setting of the parable of the great supper (22:1–14) is obviously secondary; it has been attracted to the Marcan parable of the wicked husbandmen (21:33–46 // Mark 12:1–12). In Luke, the parable occurs in a group of table sayings in which Jesus successively addresses lawyers and Pharisees on the legality of a Sabbath cure (14:1–6), then his fellow guests on the subject of accepting invitations (14:7–11), and then his host concerning whom to invite in order to secure a reward in "the resurrection of the just" (14:12–14). Finally, Jesus responds to a guest's exclamation (14:15) with the parable. The Lucan setting is uninfluenced by the Marcan framework; instead the parable is found alongside special material, attached no doubt because of the common themes of invitation and dining, and the catchwords κεκλημένος (vv. 7, 8, 12, 17, 24) and δεῖπνον (vv. 12, 16, 24). Although the meal setting for 14:1–24 is undoubtedly a product of Lucan redaction, there is no reason to doubt that Luke is reproducing this text in its relative Q position.

It is widely acknowledged that Matthew redacted the parable extensively, adding vv. 11–14, and that Luke has created the two successful invitations (14:21b, 23) as an allegory for the successive evangelizations of Jews and Gentiles.[236] But seen within the context of Q 13:24–30, 34–35, it is difficult to avoid the conclusion that in Q the invitation to the dinner was also understood allegorically as invitations to the kingdom and to its "dinner" already mentioned in 13:29, 28.[237] Schulz opines that the

---

234. The present ἀφίεται should be construed as a future (thus Hoffmann, *Studien,* 174). Ἰδού introduces judgment words in 1 Sam 2:31; 2 Sam 12:11; 1 Kgs 11:31; 14:10; Ezek 5:8; Jer 20:4; 28:16, etc. See H. Wolff, "Die Begründungen der prophetischen Heils- und Unheilssprüche," *Gesammelte Studien zum Alten Testament* (TBü 22; Munich: Chr. Kaiser, 1964) 10.

235. Reconstructions: Hahn, "Das Gleichnis," 51–60; Vögtle, "Einladung," 172–90; Schulz, *Spruchquelle,* 391–98; Polag, *Fragmenta,* 70.

236. See Jeremias, *Parables,* 67–69; Hahn, "Das Gleichnis," 51–56.

237. An allegorization of the story is suggested by 14:24 (Matt omit) which is introduced by λέγω γὰρ ὑμῖν and thus addresses not the servants but the audience of the story, and which interprets the feast as "my [presumably Jesus'] feast." Schulz (*Spruchquelle,* 397–99), Schenk (*Synopse,* 108), Polag (*Fragmenta,* 70) and Jeremias (*Sprache,* 241) concur in ascribing 14:24 to Q (in spite of the Lucanism ἀνήρ). But the case for the inclusion of 14:24 is far from decisive: see Neirynck, "Study of Q," 63–64.

contrast is between the righteous and the pious represented by the Pharisees, on the one hand, and the "tax collectors and sinners" or *'am ha-'ares*, on the other.[238] In view of the polemic against the Pharisees found elsewhere in Q this is not impossible. However, the logic of the parable would seem to suggest otherwise. As Percy points out, *all* of Israel—pious and sinners—are invited.[239] The same conclusion is suggested by the immediate Q context which alludes to Jesus' mission to his countrymen and to Sophia's sending prophets to Jerusalem (not just the Pharisees, or pious), and to the rejection of the "sons of the kingdom," i.e., Israel. The second invitation, which presupposes the failure of the first, more naturally suggests a mission to the Gentiles than it does a call to the *'am ha-'ares*.[240] The parable treats the complete failure of the first invitation as contrary to expectation and the second invitation as something of a surprise. But this turns out to be quite in keeping with other Q texts, which react with anger and incredulity to Israel's rejection of the preaching of the kingdom (7:31–35; 10:13–15; 11:49–51; 13:34–35) and with a measure of surprise to the positive response of Gentiles (7:1–10; 11:31–32). And from a compositional point of view, 14:16–24 is quite in keeping with the themes developed in 13:26–27, 29, 28, 30, 34–35 which concern the invitation to repent and respond to preaching, the threat of the exclusion of Israel and the eschatological reversal of the respective fates of Israel and the Gentiles.

Q 14:26–27; 17:33[241]

Of a quite different character are the three sayings which follow: 14:26; 14:27 and 17:33. The evidence suggests that the three were originally independent sayings which were only secondarily joined. The first saying (14:26) occurs twice in *Gos. Thom.*, once in conjunction with the "cross saying" (55) and once by itself (101). Mark has parallels to the second and third (Mark 8:34–35) while John 12:25 records a version of the third saying alone. The three sayings concern discipleship, not sectarian polemics, and it is undoubtedly this common thrust which accounts for their association.

Like other Q discipleship sayings (such as 9:59–60), Q 14:26 demands a transvaluation of commonly accepted social and religious norms, here

---

238. Schulz, *Spruchquelle*, 400, 401, 402. See also Jeremias, *Parables*, 177; Jülicher, *Gleichnisreden* 2:432.

239. Percy, *Botschaft*, 39.

240. Similarly Lührmann, *Redaktion*, 87.

241. Reconstructions: Schulz, *Spruchquelle*, 446–47, 430–31, 444–45; Polag, *Fragmenta*, 70, 78; Laufen, *Doppelüberlieferung*, 304, 321–22; Lambrecht, "Q-Influence," 279.

expressed as the renunciation of family ties.[242] Analogies to this demand are found in Cynic and Stoic teachings which counsel separation from family as a means to the absolute freedom from attachments and other hindrances to the pursuit of philosophy.[243] For Q, of course, the motivation for abandonment of family is not the pursuit of philosophy, but radical demands imposed by the dawning kingdom.

The next Q saying, 14:27, continues the theme of the radical nature of discipleship. Its original significance is a matter of debate.

Several conflicting interpretations have been offered: Although it is tempting to argue that the saying is a church construction which has Jesus' cross in view, Bultmann rightly points out that σταυρὸν αὐτοῦ/ἑαυτοῦ excludes the view that "the cross" had become a special Christian cipher for martyrdom.[244] The saying may reflect Jesus' anticipation of the possibility of his own death and that of his followers.[245] Or the saying could refer more generally to the necessity for preparedness for suffering and martyrdom.[246] Schlatter and, more recently, Hengel hold that the image of carrying one's cross may come from Zealot usage (although they are unable to cite specific Zealot sayings to this effect).[247] Referring to Ezek 9:4–6 (the marking of the faithful in a situation of apostasy), Dinkler sees an allusion to the cultic marking of the faithful with the sign tau or X, which in the post-Easter situation was interpreted in the light of the cross of Jesus.[248] Rudolf Pesch, who holds the Marcan version of the saying to be more original than Q, modifies this thesis slightly and argues that the parallel of

242. Duty to one's parents was a serious obligation throughout the ancient world. In Judaism, see Deut 5:16 and the rabbinic interpretation of the Fourth Commandment: Str-B 1.705–9; also Prov 1:8; Sir 7:27–31; Ps-Phocylides 8; Sib. Or. 3.593–94; Josephus Contra Apionem 2.206; Ps-Menander 2. Greek and Roman parenesis: Xenophon Memorabilia 4.14.19–20; Ps-Isocrates Ad Demonicum 16; Menander Monosticha 332; Polybius 6.4.14; Ps-Pythagoras Carmen Aur. 1–4; see J. W. Hewitt, "Gratitude to Parents in Greek and Roman Literature," American Journal of Philology 5 (1931) 30–48.

243. The idea of separation from family in the interests of philosophy may be as old as Socrates, who was accused of subverting family relations (Xenophon Mem. 1.2.51–55). (Ps-) Diogenes (Ep. 7, to Zeno) recommends against marriage, as a means for avoiding undue burdens. Musonius Rufus was much more favorably inclined to marriage (frags. 14–15) but warned that when a father hinders one from the pursuit of philosophy, he should be disobeyed and the will of Zeus, who commands that men be good, be followed (frag. 16). Epictetus (Diss. 3.22.45–49, 67–72, 81–82) describes the true Cynic as free from all ties of possessions, family and home. See further, Hommel, "Herrenworte"; A. D. Nock, Conversion (London: Oxford Univ. Press, 1933; repr. 1961) 164–86.

244. Bultmann, Tradition, 161 [174]; similarly Rudolf Pesch, Markusevangelium 2:60; Schulz, Spruchquelle, 431.

245. Schürmann, Lukasevangelium 1:453; Laufen, Doppelüberlieferung, 312–13.

246. Thus apparently Bultmann, Tradition, 161 [174] (but see 163 [176]!); J. Schneider, σταυρός, TDNT 7 (1971) 579; Schulz, Spruchquelle, 432–35; Rudolf Pesch, Markusevangelium 2:60.

247. Schlatter, Evangelist Matthäus, 350–51; Martin Hengel, Die Zeloten (AGSU 1; Leiden: E. J. Brill, 1961) 265–66.

248. Erich Dinkler, "Jesu Wort vom Kreuztragen," Neutestamentliche Studien für R. Bultmann (BZNW 21; Berlin: Töpelmann, 1954) 110–29.

"denying oneself" and "taking up the cross" suggests that the saying concerns confession. "Receiving his *tau*," his confessional sign, was a confession requirement (only later re-interpreted with reference to martyrdom).[249] Finally, Percy argues that the saying does not refer to martyrdom as such but to the enduring state of discipleship characterized by derision, contempt and hatred by others.[250]

Despite the uncertainty surrounding the original significance of the word, both the immediate and the wider Q contexts indicate that "to bear his (own) cross and come after me" serves as an admonition to preparedness for martyrdom and more generally as an enjoinder to self-renunciation.[251] Both 6:22–23b and 12:4–7 indicate that martyrdom is a possibility to be reckoned with and accepted, while 9:57–58, 59–60, 61–62; 12:22–31, 33–34; 14:26 and 16:13 advocate a self-renunciatory posture which takes the form of denial of material, social and familial obligations. The phrase ἔρχεται ὀπίσω μου (14:27b) implies, like 9:57–58, that the radical lifestyle of Jesus provides the pattern for community members.

That 14:27 (for Q) concerns the possibility of martyrdom is made perfectly clear by the next saying, 17:33 // Matt 10:39, which functions as a commentary word for 14:27. This wisdom saying finds parallels both in Greek and in rabbinic literature, and as a free-floating saying it could have assumed a variety of meanings.[252] The fact that a variant form of this wisdom saying is also found in Mark joined to the "cross saying" (Mark 8:34–35) probably indicates that quite early on the saying came to serve as support for early Christian teaching on the prospect of martydom. This is the clear significance in Q.

Q 14:34–35[253]

The concluding saying of this group is the "salt saying" (14:34–35). The reconstruction and interpretation of this saying are also plagued by many uncertainties.

249. Rudolf Pesch, *Markusevangelium* 2:60.

250. Percy, *Botschaft*, 170–73. Percy refers to A. Fridrichsen, "Ordet om a baere sit Kors," *Gamle spor og nye veier* (Festschrift L. Brun; Kristiana, 1922) 17–34 [unavailable to me].

251. Similarly Schulz, *Spruchquelle*, 432–33; J. Schneider, σταυρός, 579; Laufen, *Doppelüberlieferung*, 312–13.

252. In *b. Tamid*. 66a a very similar saying is used to counsel asceticism. Epictetus (*Diss.* 4.1.165–70) comments that Socrates was saved by death, not by flight (ἀλλ᾽ ἀποθνῄσκων σῴζεται, οὐ φεύγων, 165) and continues, "for [the sake of] true freedom, which cannot be plotted against and is secure, will you not yield to God, at his demand, what he has given [viz., your life]? . . . If not, you will be a slave among slaves" (172–73; Loeb 4:303).

253. Reconstructions: Schulz, *Spruchquelle*, 470–71; Polag, *Fragmenta*, 72; Steinhauser, *Doppelbildworte*, 332 (reconstructs only 14:34).

There are several initial questions: (1) Can salt in fact lose its flavor? The best answer seems to be that salt produced from the Dead Sea contained an admixture of various contaminants which could taint the flavor and which remained as useless material if for some reason the salt dissolved.[254] (2) The use of μωραίνω, "to be foolish, make foolish," is peculiar. Some have suggested that the confusion is due to a mistranslation of תפל, "tasteless," as תפלה, "folly."[255] This is possible, but it hardly explains what the saying could have meant in Greek! The cognate μωρός occurs at least three times with the meaning "insipid,"[256] and hence it is possible that μωραίνω could have this meaning too. (3) The metaphorical significance of salt is far from clear. On the strength of some rabbinic texts, W. Nauck argues that salt is a metaphor for wisdom.[257] In the Q context there is really nothing to suggest this interpretation although it might be suitable for Matt 5:13. Cullmann observes that in all three Gospels the word is directed at disciples and that salt, according to Lev 2:13, *Jub.* 21:11; *T. Levi* 9:14 and Mark 9:49 [D it], is connected with acts of sacrifice. He suggests accordingly that "salt" connotes the spirit of self-sacrifice.[258] This interpretation is perhaps possible for Mark 9:49–50 although even there the context suggests that salt is meant specifically as a purifying agent rather than as a metaphor for sacrifice.[259] Although the Q context contains words having to do with preparedness for martyrdom (14:27 + 17:33), the logic of 14:34–35 does not strongly suggest a sacrificial interpretation for the saying.

Jeremias argues that the saying is a threat directed against the impenitent in Israel.[260] Indeed, the phrase βάλλειν ἔξω occurs in the opposition saying in 13:29, 28, and similar phrases such as βάλλειν εἰς πῦρ (3:9) and βάλλειν εἰς φυλακήν (12:58) are used in prophetic threats against Israel. However, the immediate context of 14:34–35 has more to do with discipleship than judgment. Steinhauser draws attention to the similarity between 14:34–35 and another discipleship saying, 9:61–62 (which also uses εὔθετος).[261] He interprets the saying as referring to those disciples who might reject the radical demands of discipleship and thus become "stupid."[262] It should be noted that both the inaugural sermon

254. See Jeremias, *Parables*, 169; F. Hauck, ἅλας, *TDNT* 1 (1964) 229.
255. Jeremias, *Parables*, 168; Marshall, *Luke*, 595; Rudolf Pesch, *Markusevangelium* 2:117.
256. Diocles *Fragmenta* 138; *Comica Adespota* [in *Comicorum Graecorum fragmenta*] 596; Dioscurides *De Materia medica* 4.19.
257. W. Nauck, "Salt as a Metaphor in Instructions for Discipleship," *ST* 6 (1952) 165–78.
258. O. Cullmann, "Das Gleichnis vom Salz: Zur frühesten Kommentierung eines Herrenworts durch die Evangelisten," *Vorträge und Aufsätze* (Tübingen: J. C. B. Mohr [Paul Siebeck], 1966) 192–201, esp. 198–99.
259. See, on Mark 9:49–50, Rudolf Pesch, *Markusevangelium* 2:116–18.
260. Jeremias, *Parable*, 168–69. Similarly Schulz, *Spruchquelle*, 472; Rudolf Pesch, *Markusevangelium* 2:118 (apparently).
261. Steinhauser, *Doppelbildworte*, 347.
262. Ibid. Steinhauser (pp. 346–47) also attempts to relate μωραίνω in 14:34 to the

(6:20b–49) and the instruction of anxiety (12:22b–31, 33–34) conclude with sayings which warn the hearers of the consequences of disregarding the teachings: ruin (6:47–49) and loss due to theft (12:33). In the present instance, the saying warns that those who do not take seriously the demands of discipleship outlined in 14:26, 27 and 17:33 will be cast forth like insipid salt.[263]

The Composition of Q 13:24—14:35

What is the redactional intention and composition-history of this block of Q sayings? In this section of Q we are confronted by two basic types of materials: sapiential admonitions and discipleship sayings on the one hand, and prophetic pronouncements and threats against impenitent Israel on the other.

The first saying is a sapiential admonition consisting of an imperative with a motive clause introduced by ὅτι. The metaphor of two ways[264] or the narrow door[265] is a well-known parenetic *topos*. In spite of this, Schulz asserts that in Q the saying is prophetic in character: the imperative is "prophetic" and the parallelism of the saying is a mark of "prophetic improvisation." Schulz even conjectures that an original prophetic λέγω ὑμῖν formula has fallen away when the saying was com-

---

redactional stratum of Q to which the wisdom texts Q 7:35; 11:49–51; 13:34–35; 10:21–22; 11:31–32 also belong. This attempt, in my view, is not very successful or, indeed, enlightening. Luke 14:34–35 might be termed sapiential inasmuch as it uses an everyday occurrence—perhaps even in proverbial form—as a metaphor for discipleship. But it does not employ the deuteronomistic schema or the motif of Lady Wisdom which characterized these other sayings. The mere use of μωραίνω is not sufficient to establish the connection.

263. Schenk (*Synopse*, 112), Manson (*Sayings*, 132) and G. Bertram (μωρός, TDNT 4 [1967] 838) also interpret the saying as a discipleship word.

264. The most famous example of the "two ways" is that of Prodicus of Ceos, quoted by Xenophon (*Mem.* 2.1.21–34) but it was popularized in Cynic parenesis: two roads lead to happiness, one short, rising against the hill and difficult to endure (i.e., the Cynic way) and the other long, smooth and easy (Epistle of Diogenes 31; A. J. Malherbe, ed., *The Cynic Epistles* [SBLSBS 12; Missoula, Mont.: Scholars Press, 1977] 130–31). Lucian's satire *Rhetorum praeceptor* describes one path to Lady Rhetoric as "little traveled, narrow (στενή), briery and rough" and the other as "level (πλατεῖα), flowery and well watered" (7–8). The metaphor was used in Judaism to describe the paths of salvation and damnation: Jer 21:8; Prov 12:28; Sir 15:17, etc., and in *T. Asher* 1:3; 2 Enoch 30:15; 1 Enoch 94:1–5; *Mek. Exod.* 14.28; Philo *Spec. Leg.* 4.108; *Plant.* 37. See M. J. Suggs, "The Christian Two Ways Tradition: Its Antiquity, Form and Function," *Studies in New Testament and Early Christian Literature* (NovTSup 33; Leiden: E. J. Brill, 1972) 60–74.

265. *Tabula Cebetis* (15) states that true education is found only at the end of a small door (θύρα) and an infrequently traveled, rocky, rough and very narrow (στενὴ πάνυ) path.

mitted to writing.[266] But one does not need to presume prophetic authority to assert that the path to salvation is a difficult one; that was a virtual truism in antiquity. Zeller rightly regards 13:24 as a sapiential admonition, comparing it to the admonitions of Prov 1—4 which exhort listeners to adhere to the path of wisdom, for it leads to life.[267] More specifically, 13:24 is a summons to discipleship: the "narrow door/gate" corresponds to radical requirements of love of enemies, non-retaliation and mercy (6:27–36), to the admonitions to renounce home and social obligations (9:57–62; 14:26), to the exhortations to disdain wealth (6:20b; 12:33–34; 16:13) and to the admonishment to depend totally upon divine care in the situation of poverty and even persecution (12:4–7, 11–12, 22–31).[268]

In 13:25–30 the *Bildlogik* shifts abruptly from difficult paths and narrow doors to *locked* doors, and from the "few" who endure the arduous demands of discipleship, to "many" Gentiles who will stream into the kingdom. If Q 13:24 is not a prophetic form, there can be little doubt about the following sayings, 13:(25), 26–27 and 13:29, 28, 30. These two prophetic pronouncements concern not discipleship but judgment and exclusion from the kingdom. The connection of 13:26–27 with 13:24 seems to depend primarily on the catchword πολλοί (and θύρα if this came from Q) and on the common motif of successful and unsuccessful attempts to enter (the kingdom). The prophetic threat in 13:26–27 was originally directed not at Christian charismatics, as Matthew has it, but at unresponsive recipients of Christian preaching. It is sometimes thought that οὐδέποτε ἔγνων ὑμᾶς (Luke: οὐκ οἶδα ὑμᾶς πόθεν ἐστέ) is an adaptation of the formal synagogue ban.[269] Q itself provides a closer parallel in the apocalyptic threat that the Son of Man will deny those who deny Jesus (12:9). Percy draws attention to the similarity of Q 13:26–27 to the threat against Capharnaum in 10:15: the mere fact of having witnessed Jesus' miracles, especially as the residents of Caphar-

---

266. Schulz, *Spruchquelle*, 311–12. Schulz follows Bultmann, who terms the saying both a wisdom saying (*Tradition*, 77 [81]) and "characteristically prophetic" (119 [126]). See also H. Windisch, "Die Sprüche vom Eingehen in das Reich Gottes," ZNW 27 (1928) 163–92, esp. 165–66; Denaux, "Der Spruch," 328.

267. Zeller, *Mahnsprüche*, 140.

268. Wilhelm Michaelis, ὁδός, TDNT 5 (1967) 74: "In the foreground is the conditional severity of the requirements which Jesus puts to His disciples."

269. Adolf Schlatter (*Evangelist Matthäus*, 261) cites *b. Mo'ed Qat.* 16a, concerning R. Simeon b. Rabbi (ca. 220) and Bar Qappara (ca. 220), which uses the formula איני מכירך מעולם, "I never knew you." Similarly Str-B 1.469; 4.293; Otto Michel, "ὁμολογέω," TDNT 5 (1967) 208. This formula, however, occurs quite late and has to do with a *minor* ban, the *nezipah* (see Jastrow, *Dictionary*, 891), lasting not less that seven days (*y. Mo'ed Qat.* 3.81.50).

naum did, and the mere fact of having eaten with Jesus and having listened to his teaching, are no guarantee of final salvation.[270] Q 13:26–27 not only looks back on the failure of Jesus' contemporaries to respond, but probably also reflects the experience of the Q preachers described in 10:4–10 who understood themselves as representatives of Jesus (10:16) and who like him preached and took up temporary residence in various Galilean or Syrian towns. Q 13:26–27 reflects the general lack of success of those preachers, and like 3:7–9; 10:13–15; 11:31–32; 12:8–9, pronounces judgment on those who fail to respond appropriately.

In a similar vein, Q 13:29, 28 also represents a prophetic pronouncement which announces the impending exclusion of Israel from the kingdom and the inclusion of the Gentiles. The association of this saying with the preceding is probably due to the catchword πολλοί and to the common motif of exclusion of Jews from the kingdom. Again, the reason for exclusion can only be Israel's inadequate response to the preaching of the kingdom. Taken in isolation, Q 13:29 implies only an eschatological pilgrimage of Gentiles, not an active Gentile mission.[271] But when viewed alongside 7:1–10 and 11:31–32, which speak of *actual Gentile belief*, and alongside 10:13–15, which predicts Gentile faith in a hypothetical situation, it becomes more likely that 13:29, 28 has in view an actual Gentile mission.[272] Moreover, for Q the kingdom is currently in the process of self-manifestation (10:23–24; 11:20; 12:2; 13:18–21), and the mission of the Q preachers is part of the eschatological harvest (10:2). Thus it is pointless to insist that the coming of the Gentiles is still a future act of God,[273] since Q evidently understands itself to be participating in and spurring on that very act of God's manifestation of his kingdom.

---

270. Percy, *Botschaft*, 111–13.

271. Zeller, "Das Logion," 92–93; Hahn, *Mission*, 57; Käsemann, "Beginnings of Christian Theology," 88; Steck, *Israel*, 287 n. 2; Schulz, *Spruchquelle*, 326; Hoffmann, *Studien*, 293.

272. Thus Lührmann, *Redaktion*, 86; Schenk, *Synopse*, 105. Meyer ("Community," 17–18, 28) holds that the Q group "accepted the Gentile mission as a *fait accompli*" and although they did not engage in it themselves, they understood it as a warning sign to impenitent Israel (p. 28). Rudolf Pesch ("Die Voraussetzungen und Anfänge der urchristlichen Mission," *Mission im Neuen Testament* [Quaestiones disputatae 93; Freiburg: Herder & Herder, 1982] 67) takes a similar position to this. Schulz (*Spruchquelle*, 326) greatly overreaches the evidence when he says that the Q community rejected a Gentile mission in favor of the apocalyptic expectation of a future eschatological pilgrimage of Gentiles.

273. E.g., Käsemann, "Beginnings of Christian Theology," 88: "If the Gentile mission (to use the not wholly correct expression) is the proper and eschatological work of God himself, then any human attempt to anticipate it is seen as an arrogant invasion of a right God has reserved for himself."

The combination of the two prophetic words, concluded aphoristically by 13:30, reflects motifs seen elsewhere in Q. Q 13:26–27 announces the exclusion of the countrymen of Jesus from the kingdom and 13:29, 28 highlights the culpability of Israel by predicting Gentile inclusion in the kingdom. Israel's lack of faith will indeed provoke a drastic eschatological reversal: the formerly privileged will lose their special status to newcomers.

The polemical thrust of 13:25–27, 28–30 is continued in 13:34–35, a judgment oracle, and 14:16–24, which like 13:28–30 implies Gentile participation in the kingdom as a result of Israel's refusal. This theme of judgment runs through these sayings as a unifying thread.

With 14:26, 27; 17:33 and 14:34–35, however, we are back to discipleship. Thus our section of Q opens with an admonition to enter through the "narrow door/gate" and closes in the same vein with a series of four sayings which evince the radical nature of discipleship in the Q community. Here, indeed, is the description of the "narrow door"! Following Jesus entails radical self-denial and preparedness to die. It is for this reason that "few" chose to enter the narrow door, and others are cast off like worthless salt.[274]

As was the case with the discipleship-mission speech, and the speech on martrydom and persecution, it appears that an originally community-directed hortatory cluster of sayings (13:24 + 14:26, 27 + 17:33 + 14:34–35) was expanded by polemical sayings directed not against adherents of Q's preaching, but against those who rejected it. The original hortatory unit forms a rounded discourse on the nature of discipleship, with a programmatic statement about the nature of discipleship, specific instructions on following Jesus and a concluding warning. Into this "speech" has been interpolated a cluster of prophetic words. As in the case of other such interpolations into Q speeches, the method of attachment is catchword composition and thematic association. Since it is 13:24 which provides the point of attachment for the prophetic words, it is most likely that the discipleship speech was prior (from a *literary* point of view) and that the prophetic threats are secondary interpolations.

---

274. Wanke ("Kommentarworte," 226) and Laufen (*Doppelüberlieferung,* 331) hold that 14:27 and 17:33 were carried by and directed at wandering missionaries. This may be so, but as part of a larger unit (13:24 + 14:26, 27; 17:33; 14:34–35) they are directed (like 9:57–62) at a much wider audience, namely at all those who seek to enter the kingdom.

WISDOM SPEECHES AND THE FORMATION OF Q

The analysis of the preceding "speeches" reveals a rather complex composition-history for many of the clusters of sayings. Not only is there evidence of the amplification of individual sayings by the addition of secondary expansions and commentary words, and the condensation of groups of such smaller units into thematically organized "speeches," but there is evidence that once formed, these speeches were further elaborated by means of various interpolations and extensions. Six blocks of Q material have been treated in this chapter: the "inaugural sermon" (Q 6:20b–49), an instruction on discipleship and mission (9:57–62 + 10:2–16, 21–24), an instruction on prayer (11:2–4, 9–13), two groups of sayings concerning anxiety about mission (12:2–12) and daily existence (12:22b–31, 33–34) and a final speech on the demands of discipleship (13:24—14:34; contains several interpolations).

Many features common to these speeches suggest that they belong together in the same compositional phase and had a very similar intention and audience.

Implied Audience

In the case of the judgment speeches treated in the previous chapter, the ostensible audience was "this generation," i.e., impenitent Israel. Elements of this are to be found here but to a much lesser extent. Impenitent Israel is addressed in Q 10:(12), 13–15, 12:8–9, 10; 13:26–27, 28–30, 34–35 and 14:16–24. The speeches in the main are addressed not to outsiders and opponents, but to members of the community. The tone is hortatory and instructional, not polemical or threatening. These speeches are dominated by simple commands, sometimes buttressed by rhetorical questions or appeals to general experience or to observation of nature, by calls to a radical form of discipleship understood as "following Jesus" and by rather astonishing promises of God's favor and providential care for those who commit themselves to him. Mild warnings are found (Q 6:47–49; 9:61–62; 12:33–34; 14:34–35) and the speaker chastises his audience for not observing his words (6:46) and for their little faith (Q 12:28, ὀλιγόπιστοι)—but not for their lack of faith or rejection of the kingdom! This is quite different from the sharp rebukes and threats which characterize those sections organized around the theme of the announcement of judgment. It is difficult to avoid the conclusion that the six "speeches" treated in this chapter were originally intended as exhortations to the community.

Several of the individual sayings and small clusters of sayings which are included in the speeches may have had their *Sitz im Leben* in the instructions given to and carried by wandering charismatic preachers (e.g, 6:29? 10:4–11; 12:4–7, 22b–28; 14:27 + 17:33). But as finished compositions, they are directed not only at wandering preachers, but at the community as a whole. Since this community is apparently still engaged in the sending out of missionaries (see 10:2), it preserves these instructions and applies them to discipleship in general. These sapiential speeches address a wide variety of situations which arise in the community: interaction with outsiders, fraternal correction and teaching, the acquisition of and attachment to possessions, prayer, martyrdom and discipleship in general.

Characteristic Forms

The compositions analyzed in chapter four were dominated by sayings forms such as chriae and prophetic words. Sayings forms predominate here too. But it is the sapiential, not the prophetic, element which comes to the fore. A large number of the sayings can be classed as sapiential admonitions of the form second-person plural (or, less commonly, singular) imperative with or without a motive clause.[275] Some of these imperatives are introduced by the formula λέγω ὑμῖν, also a sapiential locution.[276] As part of the motive clauses, one finds a wide variety of wisdom forms: rhetorical questions which appeal to ordinary reason (Q 6:32–35; 11:11–13; 12:6–7, 23, 25), apodoses which express the symmetry between act and consequence (Q 6:37–38; 11:4, 9) and appeals to the observation of nature (Q 6:35c; 12:6–7, 24, 26–28, 25, 30, 33). In addition, there are several beatitudes (Q 6:20b, 21, 22–23b), proverbs and wisdom sayings (6:39, 40, 43, 44, 45c; 10:7b; 11:10; 12:2, 34; 13:24b; 14:34), sayings introduced by τίς ἐξ ὑμῶν (11:11–13; 12:25) and parables (6:47–49 and 13:18–19, 20–21, which coheres with this stratum). Of course, wisdom is not the exclusive preserve of these "speeches." It could be noted that proverbs and wisdom sayings are also found in the judgment speeches (e.g., 7:35; 11:17b–18, 21–22; 11:33, 34a; 12:54–55; 17:37). But there is an important difference in their usage: these function not to reinforce ethical imperatives, but to undergird the pronouncements of judgment.

Among these speeches in Q are also found some rather specialized

---

275. Plural: Q 6:27–28, 31, 35a, b, 36, 37–38; 11:9–10; 12:3–4, 6–7, 22b–23, 24, 26–28, 25, 29–31, 33–34; 13:24. Singular: Q 6:29, 30, 41–42.
276. Q 6:27; 11:9 (diff Matt); 12:4 (diff Matt), 5 (diff Matt), 22. See above, n. 164.

instructions which go beyond what is usually understood as sapiential admonitions: the sayings regarding mission (10:2, 3, 4–11, 16), the promise of the assistance of the Holy Spirit (12:11–12) and the pronouncements on discipleship (14:26, 27; 17:33). There is no reason, however, to divorce these elements from the rest of the sapiential speeches since these cohere with the radical ethic and lifestyle articulated in the admonitions and beatitudes, and build on the already-existing promises of God's providential care for his envoys. The same may be said of the three (or four) chriae which occur in 9:57–58, 59–60, 61–62 and 12:13–14. While these do not fall into the form-critical classification of wisdom sayings, maxims or admonitions, they contain such forms (9:58, 60b, 62), and they counsel the same mode of radical existence as that expressed by the beatitudes and admonitions.

The most obviously non-sapiential forms are clearly not formative from a compositional point of view. Q 10:13–15; 12:8–9, 10; 13:26–27, 28–30 and 34–35 represent prophetic woes, threats and pronouncements of doom upon the impenitent, in each case, interpolated into an earlier speech. Coherent with these threats is the parable of the great supper, which like 10:13–15 and 13:28–30 contains the theme of Gentile salvation and which implies a threat against Israel, and the apocalyptic thanksgiving and beatitude (Q 10:21–22, 23–24) which serve as a counterpart to the prophetic oracles of judgment. Q 10:21–24 pronounces blessed those who see (and believe!) the manifestation of those eschatological events which Israel has ignored, and declares that such a restrictive manifestation of the knowledge of the kingdom and of the identity of Jesus is indeed a matter of divine plan! This both provides legitimacy for the community and explains satisfactorily their lack of success in the mission field.

Characteristic Motifs

From a thematic standpoint there is a homogeneity to the community-directed speeches. Running throughout them are indications that the community placed a high religious and symbolic value on *poverty*. In view of 12:13–14, 33–34 and 16:13 this poverty was probably not involuntary, and it is possible that the term "the poor" was used as a self-designation for the community.[277] In any event, the "poor" are pronounced blessed (6:20b) and the envoys of the community emulate this poverty in the most radical form (10:4)—outdoing even Cynic preachers,

277. Similar designations appear in 1QpHab 12:2–10; 1QH 2:32–34; 5:13, 18, 20–22; 18:14.

who at least were permitted to carry a purse and staff![278] The provision of the necessities of life should be left to divine care (11:3, 9–13; 12:22b–31). *Renunciation of violence* and self-defense and a corresponding attitude of forgiveness and mercy—understood as *imitatio Dei*—is found not only in the inaugural sermon (6:27–28, 29, 32–34, 35, 36, 37–38) but also in the discipleship and mission instruction (10:3, 4, 5–6) and in the instruction on prayer (11:4). Corresponding to the renunciation of self-defense is a confidence in God's providential protection (12:4–7, 11–12, 22b–31). Throughout these portions of Q *discipleship* is conceived in the most radical social and personal terms. It is rigorous in the extreme (13:24), involving separation from family and rejection of the norms of macro-society (9:59–60, 61–62; 14:26) and preparedness for poverty, homelessness and martyrdom (9:57–58; 12:4–7, 13–14, 22b–31, 33–34; 14:27; 17:33; 16:13). More positively, it is understood as imitation of the merciful and generous God (6:27–30, 32–35, 36, 37–39) and as "following" or "listening to" or "coming to" Jesus (6:40, 46, 47–49; 9:57–62; 14:26, 27).

In contrast to the redactional stratum characterized by the announcement of judgment, in which Gentile faith is called as evidence against Israel, the wisdom speeches use "Gentile" pejoratively (Q 6:33 diff Luke; Q 12:30). It is unwise to infer too much from this locution alone, since it might be formulaic and could have survived (and in fact did) in an environment sympathetic to Gentiles. However, there are few other indications of sympathy to Gentiles in this stratum of Q—apart from a possible relaxation of the food laws (Q 10:8?). This perhaps justifies the conclusion that the wisdom portions of Q derived from a Greek speaking Jewish Christian community which had not yet engaged fully in a Gentile mission. The references to Gentiles in the later judgment speeches indicate that the community eventually developed sympathies for Gentiles.

The driving force behind the radical ethic and comportment of the community comes undoubtedly from the conviction that the kingdom is dawning. The kingdom provides the motivation for the voluntary poverty of the community (6:20b); it is both the content (10:9) and the *raison d'être* of missionary preaching (12:2 and probably 13:18–21) and it

---

278. See Epictetus *Diss.* 3.22.50; *Vita Secundi* (B. E. Perry, ed., *Secundus the Silent Philosopher* [New York: American Philosophical Assn., 1964] 68–69); (Ps-) Crates *Epp.* 16; 23; 33 (A. J. Malherbe, ed., *The Cynic Epistles*, 67, 73, 83). Teles (E. O'Neil, ed., *Teles [The Cynic Teacher]* [SBLTT 11; Missoula, Mont.: Scholars Press, 1977] 44H [pp. 45–47]) states that one does not even need a wallet, and Musonius Rufus (19) suggests that it is better to need no garments but a cloak, and to go about barefoot.

is the focal point of all activity and expectation (9:62; 11:2; 12:29–31). With some justification this stratum of Q could be termed "the radical wisdom of the kingdom of God." The dawning kingdom motivates the radical ethic of Q, and in turn the community members, by their mode of symbolic action (voluntary poverty, non-violence, love of enemies, etc.), point to the presence of the reign of God among them.

The prophetic forms identified above also display a distinct thematic profile. Q 13:34–35 and 14:16–24 (in the Q context) provide excellent examples of the deuteronomistic understanding of history which controlled the organization of Q's announcement of judgment. The addition to the "persecution beatitude," 6:23c, draws upon the same theology of history and should be grouped with these. Q 10:(12), 13–15 and 13:29, 28 contain the polemic contrast of Jewish and Gentile response which occurs also in 7:1–10 and 11:31–32. The similarities between the interpolated sayings (6:23c; 10:12–15, 21–24; 12:8–10; 13:26–30, 34–35; 14:16–24) and the judgment speeches described in chapter four are striking with respect to implied audience, form and theme—so striking, in fact, that it must be concluded that those sayings derived from the same redactional perspective as that manifest in the judgment speeches.

The Structure of the Sapiential Speeches

There are a few structural features which likewise invite the conclusion that the sapiential speech components of Q were redacted together. Four of the speeches begin with a programmatic pronouncement in the form of a wisdom saying or a declaratory sentence: Q 6:20b–21 (three beatitudes); 9:57–58 (a Son of Man saying which has marked similarities with wisdom sayings); 12:2 (a wisdom saying) and 13:24 (the commonplace of the "two ways" or the "narrow door"). If 12:13–14 derives from Q it would serve as a programmatic saying which sets the tone for the rest of the speech. The core of the speeches consists of imperatives and instructions. But they are presented not as a set of unstructured commands or assertions, but in the form of balanced and developed arguments, using symmetrical assertions, rhetorical questions, *qal wehomer* arguments and appeals to nature and human experience. This is especially clear in the inaugural sermon and in the exhortations to fearless preaching (12:2–7, 11–12) and reliance on God's provision (12:22–31, 33–34) but also true of the instruction on prayer.[279] Finally, it has already been pointed out that several speeches conclude

---

279. See Piper, "Evidence of Design," 411–18.

with a warning or description of what might occur if the teacher's counsel is not followed (6:46, 47–49; 12:33–34; 14:34–35).

Wisdom Speeches as the
Formative Component of Q

The presence of important similarities in implied audience, constituent forms, motifs and themes and even structure and argumentation suggest that the six "wisdom speeches" belong to the same compositional level in Q. It remains to discuss the relationship of this stratum to that in which the motif of judgment dominates. If it were the case that these two sets of materials existed in Q as discrete and separate blocks, it would be virtually impossible to establish the relative priority of either from a literary or compositional point of view. Indeed it might be possible that both were constitutive from the beginning. But such is not the case. As the analysis has shown, sayings which contain the deuteronomistic and judgment motifs appear to have been interpolated into and around the wisdom speeches. Q 6:23c is just such an example of an insertion into an originally sapiential collection. We have noted, moreover, that although there is reason to suppose that 6:22–23b was joined to 6:20b–21 *before* the association of the beatitudes with the following admonitions, there is no corresponding reason to suppose that 6:23c was added at that early stage. Q 10:13–15 is another instance of an insertion into a previously existing speech. In this case, it seems that 10:12 is a redactional clasp penned by the redactor who added 10:13–15. Moreover, the lengthy cluster of sayings dealing with the parousia in 12:39–59 seems to have been appended to 12:22–31, 33–34 on the basis of catchwords, and the same is true of 13:25–30, attached to 13:34 by catchword and thematic association. This kind of technique for accomplishing the interpolation is indeed characteristic:

Interpolation	*Mode of Association*	*Connected with*
1. Q 6:20b–49		
6:23c	thematic: persecution	6:22–23b
2. Q 9:57–62; 10:2–16, 21–24		
10:12, 13–15	thematic: rejection	10:10–11, 16
	thematic: acceptance/rejection	10:16
10:21–24	catchword: ἀκούω	10:16
	catchword: πάτερ	11:2–4
	thematic: prayer/thanksgiving	11:2–4
3. Q 12:2–12		
12:8–9, 10	thematic: forensic scene	12:4–7, 11–12
12:10	catchword: ἅγιον πνεῦμα	12:11–12

4. Q 13:24—14:34

13:25-30   { catchwords: πολλοί, θύρα(?)   13:24
                { thematic: failure to enter

Thematic and catchword connections may provide a partial explanation for the insertion of the larger judgment speeches between the wisdom speeches. It has already been noted that the connection between the inaugural sermon and the following judgment speech (beginning with 7:1–10) may be due to the catchwords κύριε (6:46; 7:6) and λόγος (6:47, 49; 7:7), and that 12:39–59 is attached to the preceding speech by the catchwords κλέπτης and διορύσσω. Similarly, the Baptist complex ends with a Son of Man saying (7:34) and the discipleship mission speech begins with one (9:57–58). The Beelzebul/request-for-a-sign complex may be attached to the preceding speech (11:2–4, 9–13) by the catchword "kingdom" (11:2, 17, 18, 20).

Conclusion

The analyses of the blocks of material controlled by the motif of the preaching of judgment, and of the "wisdom speeches" in Q and the examination of the literary relation between these two strata, has led to the conclusion that a collection of sapiential speeches and admonitions was the formative element in Q.[280] This collection was subsequently augmented by the addition and interpolation of apophthegms and prophetic words which pronounced doom over impenitent Israel. Given the techniques of interpolation and insertion, it is reasonable to assume that the "wisdom speeches" were *already in a written form* when they were glossed. Otherwise one would expect a greater degree of homogeneity and fewer abrupt transitions. To say that the wisdom components were formative for Q and that the prophetic judgment oracles and apophthegms describing Jesus' conflict with "this generation" are secondary is *not* to imply anything about the ultimate tradition-historical provenance of any of the sayings. It is indeed possible, indeed probable, that some of the materials from the secondary compositional phase are dominical or at least very old, and that some of the formative elements are, from the

---

280. Zeller (*Mahnsprüche*, 191–92) posits six sayings complexes standing behind Q, each formed around the kernel of a warning: 1. Luke 6:20–23; Matt 5:39b, 40, 42; Luke 6:31; Matt 5:44b–47; Luke 6:36; Matt 7:1, 2b, 3–5; Luke 6:43–46; Matt 7:24–27. 2. Luke 10:2–8a, 9–11a, 12, 16 (?). 3. Luke 11:2–4; Matt 7:7–11. 4. Luke 12:2–3; Matt 10:28–31; Luke 12:8–9, 10. 5. Matt 6:25–33, 19–21. 6. Luke 12:35–37 (?), 39–40; Matt 24:45–51a. He considers also the possibility that Matt 24:26–28; Luke 17:26–27, 30; Matt 24:40–41 constituted a seventh pre-Q complex. He observes that "they are obviously aimed not at outsiders, but at those who confess Jesus" (191 [trans. by auth.]).

standpoint of authenticity or tradition-history, relatively young. Tradition-history is not convertible with *literary history*, and it is the latter which we are treating here.

The results of our analysis of the literary or compositional history of Q will now provide the basis for an investigation of the "place" —or more correctly, the changing places—of Q within the spectrum of a late antique sayings collections. But before we can address the problem of the *Gattungsgeschichte* of Q, it is necessary to examine one final pericope, the temptation story.

6

The Temptation Story in Q

Q is composed predominantly of sayings forms. As the preceding analysis shows, some are compiled into coherent speeches and clusters of thematically related pronouncements, while others are strung together rather loosely. One pericope, however, stands out as anomalous in this compilation of speeches and sayings: the temptation story (Q 4:1–13).[1] While most of the Q materials are simple sayings, chriae or short "speeches," Q 4:1–13 is a three-part dialogue with a relatively detailed narrative framework. More importantly, it is a true *narrative*, albeit one in which speech plays a central function. The account poses difficulties for the interpreter because certain features suggest that it did not belong to either of the two redactional stages outlined above. It was nonetheless part of Q and was added, presumably, because it served some function in respect to other Q sayings and within the framework of the collection as a whole.

The temptation story in Q has often proved something of an embarrassment. Some indeed went so far as to deny that it belonged to Q at all! A. W. Argyle, for example, reasoned that since the account unmistakably quotes the LXX and for that reason must have been formulated in a Greek-speaking milieu, it could not possibly have belonged to Q.[2] Argyle's conclusion was predicated on the surprisingly tenacious hypothesis that Q was composed in Aramaic. As we have seen above, the evidence will not sustain this conclusion. But even if a written Aramaic form of Q once existed, the temptation account could have been added after the collection had been translated into Greek, a solution already suggested by Bultmann.[3]

---

1. Reconstructions: Schulz, *Spruchquelle*, 177–81; Hoffmann, "Versuchungsgeschichte," 208–9; Zeller, "Versuchungen Jesu," 61–62; Polag, *Fragmenta*, 30–32.
2. Argyle, "Accounts of the Temptation," 382.
3. Bultmann, *Tradition*, 328 [354]. Similarly Zeller, "Versuchungen Jesu," 62. An attempt to rescue an Aramaic version of the account was made by Bruce Metzger ("Scriptural Quotations in Q Material," *ExpT* 65 [1952–53] 125). He suggests that a

Lührmann excluded the temptations, but for a slightly different reason. "The temptation story . . . falls so far outside the scope of the remaining Q material, that I would suggest that Luke and Matthew independently of each other took it over from another tradition."[4] The anomalous character of the story must, however, be balanced against the strong Matthew-Luke agreements, especially in the speech portions, which in fact make the account among the strongest of candidates for membership in Q. Lührmann's treatment of the account is, however, symptomatic of the discomfort that critics have felt with Q 4:1–13.

A LATE ADDITION TO Q?

Many features of the temptation story show it to be a *Fremdkörper*.[5] It is, first of all, one of the few true narratives in Q, along with the two miracle stories in Q, 7:1–10 and 11:14. But in the latter two instances, the narrative component is of marginal interest and they are rightly regarded as apophthegms. The temptation story also contains a large speech component. But it can scarcely be treated as a chria or apophthegm, which, typically, are brief accounts leading to a witty or memorable saying. The temptations belong rather to a narrative genre which uses speech as the servant of narrative. Narrative movement is effected through dialogue. To this point we shall return later.

It is not simply the narrative nature of 4:1–13 which distinguishes it from the rest of Q. The *form* of the story, with its three-part debate as well as its mythic motif, is quite unparalleled in Q. Explicit biblical quotations (here from the LXX)[6] are rare; only in this account and in 7:27 are biblical quotations introduced by γέγραπται. In addition, the title ὁ υἱὸς τοῦ θεοῦ is not found elsewhere in Q although the absolute υἱός occurs in 10:22 (which is a secondary expansion of 10:21). The notion of miracle articulated here differs too. The implication of the devil's invi-

---

translator familiar with the LXX would naturally have accommodated the original Aramaic to LXX wording. But to this A. W. Argyle ("Scriptural Quotations in Q Material," *ExpT* 65 [1952–53] 285–86) retorted that if this were so, then other OT allusions in Q which are not entirely septuagintal should also have been similarly assimilated.

4. Lührmann, *Redaktion*, 56 [trans. by auth.]. Similarly Allen, "Book of Sayings," 274.

5. Thus Hermann Mahnke, *Versuchungsgeschichte*, 186–87; Jacobson, "Wisdom Christology," 40; Polag, *Christologie*, 146–51; Zeller, "Versuchungen Jesu," 61–62.

6. The septuagintal character of the quotation from Deut 6:16 (Q 4:12) is clear from the agreement with the LXX in κύριον τὸν θεόν σου (MT: yhwh 'ᵉlohekem). The quotation of Deut 6:13 (Q 4:8) agrees with LXX (mss A; 82) in the use of προσκυνήσεις instead of φοβηθήσῃ, although assimilation of these LXX manuscripts to Luke 4:8 is also possible.

tations is that the Son of God is or should be a miracle worker. But in the rest of Q, miracles are treated not so much as deeds *of Jesus* as they are events *of the kingdom* whose presence or impending coming they portend (7:22; 10:9; 11:20). Their expected function is to produce repentance in those who witness them (10:13–15). Nothing in the temptation story—either in the devil's invitations or in Jesus' responses—suggests this understanding of the miraculous. Finally, the direct confrontation between Jesus and the devil (who is here called ὁ διάβολος, not βεελ-ζεβούλ or σατανᾶς as elsewhere in Q) is unique; elsewhere Jesus' opposition comes from "this generation."

In these important respects the temptation story does not share the form, style or theological orientation of either of the two major redactional strata outlined in the preceding chapters. Nor is there an indication that it existed in the early stages of Q. It has every appearance of a later interpolation.

THE REDACTIONAL SIGNIFICANCE OF THE TEMPTATIONS

If Q 4:1–13 was an addition to Q, two questions arise immediately. Why was the story added? And what significance does it have within the structure of Q? These questions are best distinguished. The first is redaction-critical and concerns the proximate intentions of the redactor who added the account. The second has to do with the function of the story within the collection as a whole and impinges upon the question of the genre of Q, which will occupy us in the final chapter.

If the story were to be interpreted independently of its present literary context, the possibilities are legion.[7] However, we are interested only in the account as it functions in Q. This means that any presumptive

---

7. The literature is vast. For surveys, see Mahnke, *Versuchungsgeschichte*; Pokorný, "Temptation Stories"; Dupont, *Versuchungen*; Erich Fascher, *Jesus und Satan: Eine Studie zur Auslegung der Versuchungsgeschichte* (Hallische Monographien 11; Halle [Saale]: Niemeyer, 1949); Schnackenburg, "Versuchung Jesu." More specialized studies: James M. Robinson, *The Problem of History in Mark* (SBT 1/21; London: SCM Press, 1957) 26–32. H.-G. Leder, "Sündenfallerzählung und Versuchungsgeschichte," *ZNW* 54 (1963) 188–216 (and the rejoinder by J. Jeremias, "Nachwort zum Artikel von H.-G. Leder," *ZNW* 54 [1963] 278–79); W. R. Stegner, "Wilderness and Testing in the Scrolls and in Matthew 4:1–11," *BR* 12 (1967) 18–27; A. B. Taylor, "Decision in the Desert," *Int* 14 (1960) 300–309; G. H. P. Thompson, "Called-Proved-Obedient," *JTS* NS 11 (1960) 1–12; G. Friedrich, "Beobachtungen zur Hohepriestererwartung in den Synoptikern," *ZTK* 53 (1956) 300–2; E. Lohmeyer, "Die Versuchung Jesu," *Urchristliche Mystik* (Darmstadt: Wissenschaftliche Buchgesellschaft, 1958²) 83–122; Hoffmann, "Versuchungsgeschichte"; A. Feuillet, "La récit lucanien de la tentation," *Bib* 40 (1959) 613–31; Schottroff and Stegemann, *Jesus von Nazareth*, 72–77; Zeller, "Versuchungen Jesu," 69–72; Pokorný, "Temptation Stories," 125–26.

meaning must relate to other elements in Q. Put differently, we must assume that it was added because it was seen to resonate with one or another feature in the rest of the collection.

It is unlikely, for example, that the Q temptations serve as an apology for Jesus' power to exorcise. While this is a plausible interpretation of the Marcan story, it is unsatisfactory for Q precisely because of the paucity of exorcisms in Q. Similarly, to interpret the account as a demonic attempt to thwart the salvific plan of God, or as the beginning of the recapitulation of Israel's history, is more appropriate to Luke or Matthew, both of whom offer literary products in which salvation history figures importantly.

There are four major interpretations which the Q context may permit:

Polemic Against Israel

The story may have appealed to an editor of Q because of the implied contrast between the obedience and fidelity of Jesus and the infidelity of Israel. Although, as some critics observe,[8] the wilderness experience of Jesus does not parallel exactly that of Israel, Q 4:1–13 contains many allusions to that incident. All of the Deuteronomy quotations are taken from Deut 6–8, which recalls Israel's disobedience, and the account uses the terms (ἀν)άγω, ἐν τῇ ἐρήμῳ (εἰς τὸν ἔρημον), ἐκπειράζω and τεσσαράκοντα, all found in Deut 8:1–20.[9]

By confirming Jesus' absolute dependence upon God,[10] the story could be seen to establish him as an anti-type to Israel, which lacked precisely this virtue in the wilderness. On this view, the temptation account would have been incorporated into Q because it implied a criticism of Israel's unfaithfulness. The body of Q, of course, is replete with sayings accusing "this generation" of impenitence, non-response to prophetic preaching and even vaticide. Utilizing the deuteronomistic understanding of history, Q regards disobedience and impenitence as endemic in

---

8. Rudolf Kittel (ἔρημος, TDNT 2 [1964] 658) argues that "forty days" is not to be associated with the "forty days" of Deut 8 but rather with the forty-day fasts of Moses (Exod 34:28; Deut 9:9, 18) and Elijah (1 Kgs 19:5, 8).

9. See further, Mahnke, Versuchungsgeschichte, 62–72, 109–13, 133–36, and the literature cited there; Harald Riesenfeld, "Le Caractère messianique de la tentation au désert," La Venue du Messie: Messianisme et Eschatologie (RechBib 6; Brussels: Desclée de Brouwer, 1962) 51–63.

10. Schnackenburg ("Versuchung Jesu," 113–20) insists that the account depicts "messianic temptations" (against Bultmann; see below), not in the sense of emphasizing the performance or non-performance of specific "messianic acts" (as for Hoffmann; see below) but by relating the attempt to hinder the kingdom of God through the provocation of his agent to disobedience (esp. p. 120).

Israel's history. The temptation story, with its allusions to one of the earliest expressions of that disobedience, may have struck the editor of Q as particularly apt for his polemical purposes.

While this interpretation is possible, it is not entirely congruent with Q's polemic. Q's complaint with "this generation" is not that it does not rely upon God for sustenance and guidance, but that it has failed to respond to the preaching of the kingdom, i.e., by repenting. The redactor of the Q temptation story has made no attempt to draw out this contrast or other polemical implications of the account. The apparent focus is upon the obedient Jesus, not the disobedient Israel.

Paradigmatic Interpretations

Bultmann rejected the claim that the temptations were designed to be specifically "messianic" temptations of Jesus and argued that the Q temptation story functioned as a paradigm of obedience suitable for post-baptismal catechesis.[11] This has been developed more recently along slightly different lines by Luise Schottroff and Wolfgang Stegemann. Assuming the psychological-existential principle that anxiety about the necessities of life enslaves and victimizes humans to the extent that they are able to think, feel and do only what that anxiety dictates, Schottroff and Stegemann interpret the teaching of Q as a utopian answer to such anxiety and its dehumanizing effects.[12]

On this view, the temptations do not represent unique (or messianic) temptations *of Jesus*; instead they are paradigmatic and symbolic for the Q community's self-understanding. What is objectionable in each of the devil's proposals is not its source (i.e., the devil) but its substance. The invitation to produce (or hope for) miraculous provisions of food is rejected as demonic because by entertaining such illusions, the subject is ruled by anxiety rather than by God. The second (Matthaean) temptation rejects the illusory hope that God will orchestrate a spectacular rescue from death. This illusion tacitly acknowledges the supremacy of death; Jesus' response implies that the human is finally ruled not by death, but by God. The final temptation rejects the imperium Romanum *and* Zealot aspirations, again because both usurp divine rule and because both make the subject a victim of her/his powerlessness.[13]

There is some support for this interpretation elsewhere in Q. Q 12:4–

---

11. Bultmann, *Tradition*, 256 [274]. This interpretation is adopted by Feuillet ("Le récit," 613–21) and Thompson ("Called-Proved-Obedient," 1–12).
12. Schottroff and Stegemann, *Jesus von Nazareth*, 70.
13. Ibid., 74–75.

12 and 12:22–31 counsel against anxiety in regard to both daily needs and the situation of persecution. Q also stresses the absolute dichotomy between God and money (16:13), between earthly and heavenly treasures (12:33–34). The view of God operative in Q is for Schottroff extremely authoritarian but it is not the authoritarian God of the upper classes who functions to preserve their interests and privileges. The God of the marginalized strengthens them to take responsibility for their own lives even when no spectacular deliverance from their disadvantagement is forthcoming.

From a redaction-critical point of view, this interpretation seems over-subtle. Schottroff's contention that the account is designed to overcome the victimizing effects of anxiety, fear of death and political ideology reflects a modernizing, existential or psychoanalytic concern which can scarcely be ascribed to a first-century author. Moreover, this interpretation is predicated upon the assumption that members of the Q community were *involuntarily poor* and were from the lowest levels of society.[14] The message of Q served therefore to compensate for their abject economic circumstances and to provide a means by which the poor could avoid the dehumanizing effects of poverty. But it is questionable whether the Q group was constituted in this way. The mission-and-discipleship speech (9:57–62 + 10:2–16) and Q sayings such as 12:29–31, 33–34; 16:13 imply that possessions were *real* options, albeit ones to be rejected. Moreover, as Gerd Theissen has observed, our sources indicate that the earliest followers of Jesus were taken from the "middle classes" of fishermen, artisans and tax collectors.[15] Discipleship and abandonment of home, possessions and wealth are uniformly regarded as *voluntary* for Q. If the social situation of the group is seen in this light, then the function and message of the temptation account would have to be re-evaluated. The poverty of the community was not a social circumstance which required compensation, but a form of symbolic action which reinforced their prophetic proclamation of the kingdom.

Another paradigmatic interpretation is possible. With his rejection of the invitation to produce food for himself and by answering with Deut 8:3, Jesus provides a model of the voluntary powerlessness and absolute dependence upon God which Q elsewhere enjoins. It is well known that the Q missionaries are told to travel without money or provisions (10:4),

---

14. Ibid., 65–69, 77, 105–6, 108.

15. Gerd Theissen, "Zur forschungsgeschichtlichen Einordnung der soziologischen Fragestellung," *Studien zur Soziologie des Urchristentums* (WUNT 19; Tübingen: J. C. B. Mohr [Paul Siebeck], 1979) 27–28.

and that the community at large is instructed to rely completely upon God for all of its material needs (12:4-7, 22-31). Jesus' refusal in the temptation account provides both a legitimation and a structural homologue for this mode of behavior. In a similar vein, Theissen has argued that the saying "Foxes have their holes, and the birds of heaven their nests, but the Son of Man has no place to lay his head" (9:58) had the important symbolic function of legitimating and undergirding the radical (homeless) lifestyle of the Q missionaries.[16] Q 9:57-58 functions with respect to the following mission speech in the same way the temptation story functions with regard to all of the ethical injunctions throughout the whole of Q.

The third temptation rejects the service of power and wealth as demonic. Likewise, 16:13 opposes the service of money to the service of God; 6:20b and 10:21 award to the poor and simple a religious status which is denied to the wise and wealthy. The second temptation is somewhat more difficult to interpret. Dieter Zeller suggests that it offers a word of caution to those who, having believed sayings such as 12:4-7, are too eager to test God's providential care in the face of death.[17] In my view it is better seen as a refusal to exercise power for self-preservation or defense. This accords well with the admonitions which enjoin non-retaliation (6:27-30, 32-36), refusal to participate in judgment (6:37) and self-denial even in the face of death (14:27; 17:33). In short, the temptation account provides a paradigm and aetiology for the kind of behavior which Q elsewhere recommends for the followers of Jesus.

The usual objection to this kind of interpretation is that the temptations are vastly disproportionate to what an ordinary believer would ever experience.[18] This, however, overlooks the fact that equally fantastic (and contrived) stories are told of various Jewish and Christian heroes.[19] Such stories have anecdotal and biographical worth for those

16. Theissen, *First Followers*, 26: "From a sociological perspective, the ethical requirements of the idea of discipleship—a correspondence between Jesus and his followers—become a structural homologue between the attitudes of the wandering charismatics and the local communities on the one hand, and the Son of man on the other . . . [L]ike the Son of man, his disciples transcended the norms of their environment . . . The Son of man is not alone in being homeless and vulnerable (Matt. 8.20). The wandering charismatics, too, have forsaken everything . . . The Son of man is not alone in being persecuted (Mark 9.31); the same is true of his followers (Matt. 10.19)."

17. Zeller, "Versuchungen Jesu," 71.

18. Thus Dupont, *Versuchungen*, 97; Mahnke, *Versuchungsgeschichte*, 199-200.

19. The *Apophthegmata Patrum* provides several good examples. E.g.: "The devil transformed himself into an angelic form of light and appeared to one of the brothers and said to him, 'I am Gabriel who was sent to you.' But he replied to him, 'Behold,

who write stories about the saints; but their primary function was parenetic, as the *superscriptio* of the *Apophthegmata Patrum* shows.[20] The logic of the temptation story is this: the common believer should emulate those ideals of voluntary poverty, dependence upon God and powerlessness which Jesus displayed when confronted with temptations which are much more serious than what one would normally experience.

Christological Apologetics

A third possibility for explaining the redactional association of the temptations with Q relies upon an anti-enthusiastic and anti-thaumaturgic interpretation of the account.[21] Schulz contends that Q polemicizes against the "divine man" Christology upon which Mark drew.[22] Jacobson, for his part, thinks that the story is directed at "enthusiastic" tendencies which were present in the Q community itself and which are in evidence in the penultimate stage of redaction (11:2-4, 9-13; 17:5-6; 7:18-23).[23]

It is not easy to sustain this position at least in the context of Q. That the account rejects the notion that Jesus was a miracle worker is not at all clear. Throughout, the assumption is that Jesus *can* perform miracles should he wish to do so. His response is not to the effect that the miraculous as such is to be avoided; in fact the third temptation has nothing at all to do with a display of Jesus' thaumaturgic powers. Instead, the answers are directed at the *substance* of the miracles or acts proposed. In regard to Jacobson's proposals it should be noticed that 11:2-4, 9-13, although an expression of an enthusiasm or optimism

---

you have been sent to another of the brothers, for I am not worthy.' And immediately [the Devil] became invisible" (G. Zoega, *Catalogus codicum copticorum* [Rome: Congregatio de propaganda fide, 1810; repr. Leipzig, 1903] 305C [trans. by auth.]).

20. Codex Regius 2466 (= PG 65.71): Ἐν τῆδε τῇ βιβλίῳ ἀναγέγραπται ἐνάρετος ἄσκησις καὶ θαυμαστὴ βίου διαγωγή, καὶ ῥήσεις ἁγίων καὶ μακαρίων πατέρων, πρὸς ζῆλον καὶ παιδείαν καὶ μίμησιν τῶν τὴν οὐράνιον πολιτείαν ἐθελόντων κατορθῶσαι.

21. S. Eitrem (*Die Versuchung Christi* [Bihefte til Norsk teologisk tidsskrift 3/5.25; Christiana, 1924] 2-23) and Anton Fridrichson (*The Problem of Miracle in Primitive Christianity* [Minneapolis: Augsburg Publ. House, 1972] 124-26) suggest that the devil lures Jesus to perform magical acts—"absurd and fanciful miracles," as Fridrichson calls them (p. 126). This encounters several objections: Q nowhere else is concerned with the problem of magic. Moreover, the third temptation is in no way magical and the second is presumably not Jesus' act, but God's (even if it is instigated by Jesus). Finally, to interpret the changing of stones into bread as "absurd and fanciful" fails to take into account the situation of Jesus' hunger.

22. Schulz (*Spruchquelle*, 182) thinks that Mark was obliged to shorten his temptation account because of the Q polemic against "divine man" Christology.

23. Jacobson, "Wisdom Christology," 40, 93.

about God's extravagance as a giver of good things, does not suggest that members of the community thought of themselves as being able to produce these "good things" by means of thaumaturgy. The miraculous happenings described in 7:18–23 are primarily healings, yet 4:1–13 contains no references to healings or the like, and for this reason it is difficult to argue that 4:1–13 is directed against the view of Jesus (and his followers) as miracle-workers. Only Q 17:5–6 could possibly be construed as an instance of thaumaturgic enthusiasm, although it is better to regard this as simple hyperbole. Such evidence is a meagre foundation indeed upon which to build an interpretation.

Rejection of Zealot Messianism

Paul Hoffmann has recently made the suggestion that the Q temptation story functioned to explain and justify why the Q group did not participate in the Zealot movement.[24] The third temptation he takes as an invitation to accept the ideal of "political-messianic world rule."[25] The invitation to produce bread from stones evokes the current expectations of a messianic re-enactment of the manna wonder, while the second temptation concerns the hopes for a savior whose activities would naturally focus on the Temple.[26] That Jesus rejected all these invitations laden with Zealot implications indicated that divine sonship was not convertible with political messianism. Hence the Q group should follow the example of its leader in similarly rejecting the temptation to political involvement in revolutionary movements.

Hoffmann attempts to make this interpretation even more compelling by detecting anti-Zealot strains in the rest of Q. On his showing, the polemic against the "blind guides" (6:39) and the teachings on mercy (6:36), non-retaliation (6:27–28, 32–33) and judgment (6:37–38) are intelligible if seen as a rejection of Zealot ideology and practice. Similarly, two sayings in the mission speech may be regarded as anti-Zealot: "Behold, I send you as sheep among wolves" (10:3) and "Into whichever house you enter, first say 'peace be to this house' and if there is a son of peace there let your peace be upon him" (10:5–6).[27]

But is there sufficient warrant, either in the narrative logic of the

24. Hoffmann, "Versuchungsgeschichte"; idem, *Studien*, 74–78, 308–11, 326; similarly Bosold, *Pazifismus*, 63.
25. Hoffmann, "Versuchungsgeschichte," 214; thus Hahn, *Titles*, 159; Schulz, *Spruchquelle*, 187.
26. Hoffmann, "Versuchungsgeschichte," 215–16, 218. Hoffmann cites 4 Ezra 13:34–37; 2 Apoc. Bar. 35:1–5; 40:1; Josephus *Wars* 6.285–86.
27. Hoffmann, "Versuchungsgeschichte," 220–21.

temptation story itself, or from the rest of Q, to sustain this interpretation? The first temptation might be construed as an invitation to repeat the manna wonder, although it is by no means established that a manna miracle *was* expected from the Messiah.[28] Nor is there much evidence that the Zealots or the Sicarii claimed to be able to perform such miracles.[29] Hoffmann's interpretation encounters two further objections: "bread from stones" does not obviously parallel "bread from heaven" which is the usual designation for manna,[30] and the lack of an audience to witness the proposed miracle tells against its being an invitation to messianic self-manifestation. Similarly, there is no mention of witnesses

28. The evidence that the Messiah was expected to perform a manna-wonder is mostly circumstantial:
1. *2 Apoc. Bar.* 29:1—30:1 describes a period of abundance, including the "descent of the treasury of manna," associated with the manifestation of the Messiah. The Sibyllines (frag. apud Theophilus *Ad Autolycum* 2.36.29) mention the provision of manna in a renewed paradise (not specifically connected to the Messiah), and Rev 2:17 promises that the Risen Lord will provide "the hidden manna." The meaning of the latter reference is quite unclear, although B. Malina has made a good case for supposing that it refers to "extraordinary foods destined for the happiness of the world above" (*The Palestinian Manna Tradition* [AGSU 7; Leiden: E. J. Brill, 1968] 100–101). In this case, it would have nothing to do with messianic reenactment of the manna wonder.
2. Several of the prophets mentioned by Josephus seem to have consciously employed Exodus and Mosaic typologies. Theudas (*Ant.* 20.97–99) claimed to be able to part the Jordan; the unnamed prophets of *Wars* 2.259 (= *Ant.* 20.167–68) invited the masses to the desert where God would show them "signs of deliverance" (σημεῖα ἐλευθερίας); the Egyptian led his followers from the desert to the Mount of Olives, where he claimed to be able to repeat Joshua's destruction of a city (*Ant.* 20.169–70; *Wars* 2.261–62 gives a somewhat different account!); an unnamed prophet active during the procuratorship of Porcius Festus promised "salvation" to those who followed him into the desert; another unnamed prophet in the year 70 CE promised to produce τὰ σημεῖα τῆς σωτηρίας in the temple (*Wars* 6.285–86); and in 73 CE Jonathan, apparently one of the Sicarii, led a group into the desert promising to display σημεῖα καὶ φάσματα (*Wars* 7.438) Even though a manna miracle is not explicitly mentioned, it is undeniable that these prophets intended to perform miracles like Moses and Joshua.
3. The rabbinic evidence for the expectation of a messianic manna miracle is quite late. *Midr. Qoh.* 1.9 §1 (on 1:9) which contains this notion is attributed to R. Berekiah, a fifth generation Amora (ca. 350) speaking in the name of R. Isaac (probably Isaac II, third generation Amora, ca. 300).
29. The association of the prophets mentioned by Josephus with the Zealots or Sicarii is a matter of dispute, although *Wars* 2.264 states that the false prophets and brigands banded together (οἱ δὲ γόητες καὶ λῃστρικοὶ συναχθέντες), and *Wars* 7.437–38 implies that the sign prophet Jonathan (see n. 28) was one of the Sicarii. M. Hengel (*Die Zeloten* [AGSU 1; Leiden: E. J. Brill, 1961] 239) concedes that neither Theudas nor the Egyptian were Zealots "in the strong sense": "However, the prophetic-enthusiastic element must have also been at work among the Zealots: as the first example one could mention the founder of the sect, Judas, who is mentioned in the same breath with the enthusiast Theudas in Gamaliel's speech [in Acts]" [trans. by auth.].
30. Thus Zeller, "Versuchungen Jesu," 68; Jacobson, "Wisdom Christology," 38. In spite of the fact that Deut 8:3 does not state that the manna was "from heaven," the remainder of references to manna are virtually unanimous on this point. See Neh 9:15 (= 2 Esd. 19:15); Wis 16:20; Exod 16:4; Pss 77:24; 104:40; *Sib. Or.* frag. 3.49.

for the alleged "messianic self-manifestation" at the temple.[31] The third temptation, with its apparent rejection of political power, indeed amounts to a *de facto* rejection of Zealot ideology. But as Zeller observes, the quotation κύριον τὸν θεόν σου προσκυνήσεις καὶ αὐτῷ μόνῳ λατρεύσεις is hardly a convincing alternative to the revolutionary slogan of Judas the Galilean, μόνος ἡγεμὼν καὶ δεσπότης ὁ θεός.[32] Here if anything Jesus would be endorsing, not rejecting, Zealot ideology in this use of Deuteronomy!

An anti-Zealot interpretation of the other Q passages adduced by Hoffmann also seems forced. Indeed, it cannot be denied that as a matter of fact the Q group did not align itself with revolutionaries. But a *specifically* anti-Zealot interpretation of the sayings in the Sermon on the Mount/Plain and the Mission speech does not suggest itself.

Finally, the septuagintal character of the biblical quotations and the presence of non-Semitizing Greek[33] make it unlikely that the account belonged to a Palestinian sphere. On the contrary, it was formulated in a Greek-speaking milieu where Palestinian politics are not likely to have occupied centre stage. For these reasons, Hoffmann's anti-Zealot proposals must be set aside in favor of more plausible solutions.

Why was the temptation account added to Q? Given the nature and content of the collection, the most likely answer is that the redactor regarded the story as having paradigmatic and aetiological significance for the rest of Q. It served to illustrate and legitimate the mode of behavior and the ethos of the Q group. As hero and leader of the Q community, Jesus provided an example of the absolutely dependent, non-defensive and apolitical stance of his followers. It is possible, but much less obvious, that the polemical implications of the story played some role. Far less likely are the suggestions that the story was regarded *by the editor* as a christological apologetic or as a refutation of Zealot messianism.

THE STRUCTURAL SIGNIFICANCE
OF THE TEMPTATIONS

The questions of the redactional nature of Q 4:1–13 and the interests which its addition served are both diachronic in nature. To be distin-

31. Note the presence of crowds in all of the events mentioned by Josephus (see above, n. 28).
32. Zeller, "Versuchungen Jesu," 69. See Josephus *Ant.* 18.23.
33. The phrase εἰ υἱὸς εἶ τοῦ θεοῦ is hardly possible in a semitic language!

guished from these considerations is a synchronic question: that of the structural significance of the account. It has already been observed that the temptation story is somewhat anomalous within the context of a sayings collection. Does this anomalous element function in a special way? Did the addition of the account exert any significant influence on the genre conception of Q?

It is obvious that redaction can in some cases radically alter the understanding of the hermeneutical situation of a particular utterance. To take two related examples: many think that Jesus' word to Peter in Matt 16:17–19 and the Johannine farewell speeches originated as words of the Risen Lord. These might have appeared in post-resurrectional dialogues such as the *Epistula Apostolorum* or the *Apocryphon of John*. Their placement by the first and fourth evangelists prior to the resurrection significantly changed the way in which their origin is perceived and, correspondingly, the way in which they could be appropriated. Has the temptation story effected a similar change?

To bring the problematic into better focus, one should recall the characterization of Q by Boring and Kelber as the contemporizing and prophetic voice of the Exalted Lord in his church. Both concede that Q contained historicizing forms, but contend that *hermeneutically* it is the contemporizing component of Q which achieves dominance in the hierarchy of forms.[34] By contrast, Robinson has recently observed that by placing the temptation account between John's preaching and the Sermon on the Mount/Plain, Q "seems to be moving toward a biographical cast such as Mark 1 offers."[35] If our redaction-critical observations in regard to the relative lateness of the addition of Q 4:1–13 are sound, this would imply that Q was not tending toward a prophetic/contemporizing presentation of the words of Jesus, but away from it. Although Koester's argumentation is differently based, his conclusions are parallel. For Koester, the latest recensions of Q no longer epitomized the contemporizing and gnosticizing hermeneutic of the genre *logoi sophon* but had already moved in the direction of more "orthodox" theology.

One of the most troubling initial questions is that of the form of the pericope. Does its form represent a departure from the rest of the contents of Q and if so, of what importance is this? Some regard it as a sayings form and hence as little different from the rest of Q. Albertz

---

34. See above, pp. 34–37.
35. Robinson, "From Easter to Valentinus," 22.

called it a controversy story,[36] while others compared it with rabbinic exegetical debates or with haggadic midrashim.[37]

To focus on the sayings component is somewhat misleading. Q 4:1–13 differs from typical Synoptic controversy stories in its overall (non-chriic) construction, in its mythic setting and in the fact that it lacks the usual motif of a challenge to the validity of the Law. Here the validity of the Law is explicitly presupposed. And unlike most Synoptic controversy stories, Q 4:1–13 is not reducible to a saying of Jesus enclosed in a brief setting. It is, as many recognize, a scribal creation,[38] not a piece of tradition belonging to the oral phase of transmission (at least in the present form). In view of the *dramatis personae*, the mythic setting and the fact that the purpose is not exegesis, the analogy of a "rabbinic dispute" is not apposite. Mahnke aptly remarks that "it is not that Jesus is described as learned in the Scripture, or even as more learned than the devil, but as controlled by and obedient to the Scripture . . ."[39]

Rather than focusing on the speech component, H. A. Kelly has examined the underlying motif of temptation. He produced several parallel stories from second-Temple Judaism in an effort to illuminate the form of the Q temptation.[40]

Expanding on Gen 15, the *Apocalypse of Abraham* relates that immediately following his conversion, Abraham is instructed to prepare for a divine revelation (chap. 9).[41] This preparation consists of a fast and a forty-day journey (chaps. 10—12) on which he is accompanied by an angel, Yahoel. The preparation ends with an act of sacrifice (chaps. 12—15). During the sacrifice Azazel attempts to trick Abraham into offering an unclean bird (chap. 13). When this fails, he informs Abraham that his angelic companions intend to kill him. At

36. M. Albertz, *Die synoptischen Streitgespräche* (Berlin: Trowitzsch, 1921) 41–48. Bultmann (*Tradition*, 256 [275]) treats the temptation story in his section on "Historical Narratives and Legends" but comments that Christian scribal activity gave it in Q the form of a controversy story patterned on Jewish models (see n. 37). See also Schulz, *Spruchquelle*, 184.

37. Bultmann (*Tradition*, 254 [272]) compares Luke 4:1–13 with *Sipre Deut.* §307; *b. Sanh.* 43b; *b. Yoma* 56b; and *Tanh. B.* Bereshith §20 (8a), which contain debates in which questions and answers are given in the form of biblical quotations. In *p. Shek.* 5.49b R. Hanina b. Pappai (ca. 300 CE) disputes in this way with the lord of the demons (see Str-B 1.391). Gerhardsson (*Testing*, 11–12) and Polag (*Christologie*, 146) call the story a haggadic midrash.

38. Thus Bultmann, *Tradition*, 272; Schulz, *Spruchquelle*, 184–85; Gerhardsson, *Testing*, 11–12; Jacobson, "Wisdom Christology," 36–46; Mahnke, *Versuchungsgeschichte*, 198–99.

39. Mahnke, *Versuchungsgeschichte*, 198 [trans. by auth.].

40. Kelly, "The Devil in the Desert."

41. Now available in a new translation by R. Rubinkiewicz and H. J. Lunt in *OTP*, 689–705. The text dates from ca. 80–100 CE. On this, see James H. Charlesworth, *The Pseudepigrapha and Modern Research* (SBLSBS 7S; Chico, Calif.: Scholars Press, 1981) 68–69.

this, Yahoel declares that the tempter is "ungodliness" and identifies him as
Azazel and drives him off. His faithfulness thus tested, Abraham is allowed to
ascend to heaven where he receives various apocalyptic visions (chaps. 15—29).

Similar accounts develop God's testing of Abraham in Gen 22: *Jubilees* (17:16)
presents a scenario recalling Job 1—2 in which Abraham's faithfulness had
already been tested in ten trials (17:17–18) when Mastema obtained permission
to test Abraham one time further (17:16). Abraham's willingness to sacrifice
Isaac again demonstrated his faithfulness, Mastema was put to shame and the
sequence ends with God's promise to Abraham. *Gen. Rab.* 56.4 gives a dialogical
version of Samael's tempting of Abraham. Samael quotes Job 4:2, "If a thing be
put to you as a trial, will you be wearied?" Abraham retorts that even if he is
accused of murder, he will obey God. *B. Sanh.* 89b develops this into a three-part
debate between Abraham and Satan. Satan attempts to dissuade and dishearten
Abraham by quoting Job 4:2–5, suggesting that Abraham will not be able to
comply with God's command; Abraham responds with Ps 26:1, "I will walk in
my integrity." Satan continues with Job 4:6, suggesting that Abraham's fear of
God should guarantee that he will not lose his son; Abraham retorts with Job 4:7,
implying that no one who is innocent has ever perished. Finally, Satan tries Job
4:12 and Gen 22:8, hinting as to the final outcome of the test, and suggesting that
Abraham need not continue, but Abraham answers with a proverb, "It is the
penalty of a liar that should he even tell the truth, he is not listened to."

Even though the rabbinic examples derive from a somewhat later date
than the Gospels and Q, this does not mean that the motif of the testing
of Abraham was a later innovation. It is clear not only from *Jubilees* and
the *Apocalypse of Abraham* but also from Sirach (44:20–21) and 1 Macc
2:51–68 that the testing of Abraham was already a dominant *topos* in the
recounting of his life and that he had come to be regarded as a model of
fidelity in temptation.

Testing, of course, occupies a prominent position in the Job literature.
In the *Testament of Job*, not mentioned by Kelly, the notion of testing is
developed considerably:[42]

Job is converted from idolatry (chaps. 2—3) and receives a revelation that a
nearby temple is dedicated to the devil. Job asks for and receives the authority to
destroy the temple (3:5) but is warned that this action will provoke retaliation
(4:1–5). He is told that if he endures his sufferings faithfully, he will prosper and
be resurrected and rewarded (4:6–9).

Satan attempts an initial deception which Job thwarts by his superior knowledge (6:1—7:12). Satan then attacks Job's possessions (chap. 16), his children
(chaps. 17—19), all to no effect. Job's wife is successfully deceived (chaps. 22—
23) but Job is not. Nor are the three kings able to cause him to swerve in his faithfulness. Finally, a theophany resolves the conflict, and Job reconciles his friends
to God.

---

42. Available in a new translation by R. P. Spittler in *OTP*, 829–68. The work derives
from the first century BCE or CE.

Whereas the Abraham stories had to do with Abraham's reliance on God and his promises, this temptation story focuses on the opposition of God's revelation and Satanic deception. Job has knowledge of heavenly realities which proves superior to the trickery of Satan, and to the reasonings of his wife and his friends.[43] It is this knowledge which Satan attempts to undermine, and which in the end permits Job's athletic endurance of testing. The testing in fact confirms the genuineness of his knowledge of the true God, and it forms the basis for his final reward.

The motif of the temptation or ordeal of the wise and faithful man is common enough,[44] and in the next chapter, we shall show that this motif commonly occurs at the beginning of wisdom collections. The testing stories mentioned here are similar enough in structure and function to invite comparisons with the Q temptation account. In both the Abraham stories and the Q temptation the testing occurs away from society; Job's testing does not occur in a desert, but it happens after the elements which tie him to society (possessions, children, health) have been removed. The testers (human or otherwise) attempt to cause the hero to speak or act in such a way as to nullify his original commitment. The conclusions of the stories are not uniform: the Job story ends with a theophany and Job's restoration to his former position in society, the *Apocalypse of Abraham* concludes with a series of revelations and the Q account closes simply with the statement that the devil departed. In both the Abraham and Job stories, the testing of the hero serves to confirm the presence of a fundamental virtue which is requisite for living a righteous life before God: faithfulness and obedience in the case of Abraham and knowledge of heavenly realities in that of Job.

Like these other testing stories, the Q temptation is a true narrative in spite of its large sayings component. It is susceptible to both actantial and syntagmatic analyses, as Jean Calloud's work shows.[45] Yet this narrative, like the other temptation accounts, is of a special type, for its

43. See J. J. Collins, "Structure and Meaning in the Testament of Job," *SBLASP* (1974) 1.35–52, esp. 40–41.

44. See J. H. Korn, ΠΕΙΡΑΣΜΟΣ: *Die Versuchung des Gläubigen in der griechischen Bibel* (BWANT 72; Stuttgart: Kohlhammer, 1937).

45. Calloud, *Structural Analysis*, 47–108. Calloud notes the peculiarity of the story which, in syntagmatic terms, fails to proceed past the (anti-) mandating sequence (i.e., the devil's invitation that Jesus perform a task) in each of the three tests. In actantial terms, the devil offers himself in the role of "anti-sender" (thus replacing the Spirit, which occupies this position in the original sequence). But in each case, Jesus refuses to invest himself in the position of (anti-)subject by his refusal to accept the mandate of the devil. Thus each sequence aborts before the performance syntagm. Calloud aptly calls the story "an immobile narrative since it runs in a circle and returns to its starting point at the end" (p. 72).

essence is that *nothing happens*. The hero does not respond to the devil's (or "sender's") invitation to cease his act of sacrifice (*Apoc. Abraham*), or to curse God and re-invest Satan in the position of God (*Test. Job*), or to accept an inferior set of values and an anti-god as God. To use Calloud's phrase, these are "immobile narratives."

The "immobility" of the narrative serves an important function: it demonstrates the virtue of the hero and thereby advances a larger narrative movement. Temptation stories are pregnant with meaning for the material which surrounds them. The testing story so to speak projects a "heroic career" for which it will serve as an explanation or anticipatory confirmation. It is not related simply for the parenetic and paradigmatic value which it might possess (however important that may be), but because it serves to explain or make intelligible other parts of the hero's "story" or to legitimate and guarantee the reliability of his teachings or the revelations which have been entrusted to him.

Testing stories have a function comparable to that of qualifying and ordeal stories which are found in Graeco-Roman biography, though the latter are usually cast in a realist rather than in a fantastic or mythic mode. The function of the ordeal or test is to confirm the presence of virtue or valor or wisdom. Alexander's taming of the anthropophagic Bucephalus served as confirmation of the Delphic oracle's claim that the boy would rule the world, and of Philip's expectation of a "new Heracles."[46] Plutarch's lives of Theseus and Lycurgus offer other examples of qualifying tests:[47] Theseus—who later became king of Athens—undertook a dangerous overland journey, during which he encountered numerous challenges (7.1–12.3) which confirmed in him the "valor of Heracles" (6.6), thus qualifying him to assume the throne. Lycurgus, the famous legislator of Sparta, displayed his sense of justice when offered the opportunity to participate in a plot against the youthful legitimate Spartan heir and to install himself and a co-conspirator on the throne. By trickery he preserved the life of the true heir, ensured that he assumed the throne, and he was thereby recognized by his fellows as virtuous and just.

It is worth pointing out that in several instances the ordeal or quali-

46. *Vita Alexandri Magni* [Pseudo Callisthenes] 15.1–2; 17.1–4. See Helmut van Thiel, ed., *Leben und Taten Alexanders von Makedonien: Der griechische Alexanderroman nach der Handschrift L* (Texte zur Forschung 13; Darmstadt: Wissenschaftliche Buchgesellschaft, 1974) 24–25.
47. Trans. B. Perrin, *Plutarch: The Parallel Lives*, Vol. 1, *Theseus and Romulus—Lycurgus and Numa—Solon and Publicola* (LCL; Cambridge: Harvard Univ. Press; London: Heinemann, 1914).

fying test is preceded by birth oracles or divine disclosures concerning the hero: *Apoc. Abr.* 9 relates God's promise of divine relation to Abraham, *Test. Job* 4:6–9 has a promise of resurrection and reward, *Ps-Callisthenes* 15 contains a saying of the Pythia about Alexander and *Theseus* 3.4–5; 6.2–3 relates an oracle of the Pythia about Theseus. Q also has an oracle (3:7–9, 16–17) preceding the testing sequence.

The special character and especially the placement of the testing story after the predictions of John and just before the beginning of Jesus' main activity (preaching) conforms the opening sequences of Q to the narrative pattern shared by the legends about Abraham and Job, and the Graeco-Roman hero biographies. This conformity with a typical biographical pattern confirms, in my view, Robinson's suggestion that Q was moving *toward* a narrative or biographical cast. The fusion of Q with the Marcan narrative in Matthew and Luke only continued what had already begun in the last stages of Q redaction.

Of course, Q is not a "Gospel." It is still primarily a speech or sayings collection. Yet there is also movement in the direction of biography. As we shall see in the next chapter, this is not so surprising nor is it unique: forces active in other sentence collections of late antiquity—in particular the need for legitimation—sometimes led to the addition of introductory narratives or other legitimating sequences.

7

Q and Ancient Sayings Collections

Can Q be located within the context of ancient sayings collections, or is it, as Neirynck alleges,[1] *sui generis?* As the foregoing analysis indicates, the compositional history of Q is rather complex, and while the formative aspect of Q is sapiential and instructional, other materials have been interpolated. In this light the question just asked should be rephrased, Is it possible to understand each of the compositional stages in Q within the context of antique sayings collections, and are the developments perceptible within Q's own literary evolution intelligible in terms of the compositional options available in sayings genres and the dynamics of those genres?

Robinson's seminal essay attempted to situate Q on a trajectory of Jewish, Christian and Gnostic sayings collections.[2] This trajectory began with OT wisdom books such as Proverbs and terminated in Christian circles in the second century. Inasmuch as primitive Christianity in general and Q in particular owed much to the sapiential traditions of the OT, Robinson's procedure is quite sound. Nevertheless, there is considerable evidence that the purveyors of wisdom recognized the international nature of their medium.[3] Jewish collections are no exception. Proverbs on one hand, and *m. 'Abot* on the other, are indebted to non-Jewish sapiential traditions for their presentation of wise sayings. Two factors in particular suggest that any attempt to discuss the genre of Q should consider non-Jewish parallels. Q contains several chriae, a form which is not indigenous to Jewish (or Near Eastern) collections, but very common in Greek circles. Second, the very fact that Q was composed in Greek, not Hebrew or Aramaic, makes it *a priori* likely that resonances with Greek wisdom or sentence collections will be found.

1. Neirynck, "Q," 716.
2. Robinson, "LOGOI SOPHON."
3. This point has been made convincingly in respect of late Egyptian collections by Miriam Lichtheim, *Late Egyptian Wisdom.*

To examine all antique wisdom collections is an impossibly large task. It will not be attempted here. We shall, however, sketch three of the modalities available for presenting collections of wise sayings: the Near Eastern "instruction," the Hellenistic gnomologium and the chriae collection. We shall attend not only to morphological and structural features of these collections ("outer form"), but to such features as attitudes, setting, tone, purpose, implied speaker, projected audience and hermeneutical setting ("inner form").[4] The rationale for this is simple: collections with similar or even identical morphologies may nevertheless function in quite different ways and imply very different things about their putative speaker and the means by which their intended audience are intended to respond to their contents.[5]

THE INSTRUCTION GENRE

Wise sayings may be serialized in a variety of ways: in collections of proverbs loosely organized; in disputes or dialogues; or in speeches addressing a student or son. A few Near Eastern proverb collections are extant,[6] but these do not offer real analogies to Q, which, although it contains proverbs, is in no way comparable to collections such as Prov 10:1—22:16. Egypt and Israel have bequeathed to us several examples of wisdom literature in the form of a dispute or dialogue (The Dispute of a Man with his Ba; The Eloquent Peasant; Job). But Q is not concerned with the "reflective" side of wisdom—the place of humankind in the universe, the purpose of life, the benefits of piety. The major form of prescriptive wisdom in both Egypt and other parts of the Near East is the *instruction*. There are two reasons for this choice of the instruction genre as the starting point: First, Near Eastern instructions represent the oldest extant wisdom materials, dating from the third millennium BCE. And second, this genre is relatively easily defined and appears to have been very stable for well over two thousand years.

4. Wellek and Warren, *Theory of Literature*, 231: "Genre should be conceived, we think, as a grouping of literary works based, theoretically, upon both outer form (specific metre or structure) and also upon inner form (attitude, tone, purpose—more crudely, subject and audience). The ostensible basis may be one or the other;... but the critical problem will then be to find the *other* dimension, to complete the diagram" [emphasis original].

5. Doty ("Concept of Genre," 435, 439–40) likewise advocates a flexible approach to genre definition which takes into account not only morphology but setting, content, mood, function, intention and other typicalities.

6. In addition to Prov 10—22:16 and 25—29, see W. G. Lambert, *Babylonian Wisdom Literature* (Oxford: At the Clarendon Press, 1960); E. I. Gorden, *Sumerian Proverbs* (Philadelphia: University Museum, 1959).

The (Egyptian) Instruction

In Egypt, prescriptive wisdom is almost exclusively the domain of the "instruction" (sb3yt), a genre for which there are many examples.[7] The proverb collection is not a common literary form. The characteristics of the instruction genre are relatively well defined. The following features are to be noted:[8]

Morphology

The instruction almost always begins with a *title* employing some variation of the formula

h3t-' m sb3yt irt.n NN n s3.f
dd.f

Beginning of the instruction made by NN for his son.
And he says:[9]

Attribution to a named sage is a regular feature of this formula. Only a minority of instructions for which incipits survive are anonymous.[10] In most cases, the instruction is ascribed to a figure of some distinction and authority: a king (Amenemhat; Merikare [ascribed to King Khety?]), vizier (Ptahhotep; Kagemni [ascribed to Kaires?]), priest (Amenemhat [high priest]; Ankhsheshonq), scribe (Amunnakhte; Khety; Nebmare-Nakht; Aniy) or other figure of authority (Amenemope; Amenotes [= Amenhotep]; Djedefhor; Sehetepibre). The strong preference for named collections and the tendency to ascribe them to figures of importance point to the requirement of the genre for an authoritative guarantor of the instruction.[11] This no doubt also explains the extensive use

7. By itself, the word sb3yt is not a reliable indicator of the genre since it also appears in laments, onomastica and calendars. On this see Brunner, "Die 'Weisen,'" esp. 33; R. J. Williams, "Sages of Ancient Egypt," 7.

8. On what follows, see Brunner, "Lehren"; H. H. Schmid, *Wesen und Geschichte*, 8–84; Kitchen, "Basic Literary Forms."

9. Similar introductions appear in Amenemhat, Amenemhat (high priest), Amenemope, Amunnakhte, Aniy, Djedefhor, Instruction According to the Ancient Writings, Hori, Instruction of a Man, Khety, Merikare (restored), Nebmare-nakht (restored), Ostracon from Deir el-Bahri, *P. Louvre* 2414, Pentaweret, Ptahhotep, Qagebu, Sehetepibre.

10. The Instructions of a Man, Instructions According to the Ancient Writings and the Ostracon from Deir el-Bahri are anonymous. *P. Louvre D.* 2414 begins, "the instruction of *P3-wr-dl*," which is probably a personal name rather than a title. See Hughes, "Blunders," 54.

11. Brunner ("Lehren," 117) notes, "Neither in other literary products (apart from the prophecies and laments which are closely related to the instruction) nor in creations such as pictorial art or architecture is the name of the creator transmitted; indeed, apart

of official titles and epithets in some collections. Amenemope, for example, lists the 19 titles and epithets of the teacher and ten for his student. Even in the anonymous Instructions According to the Ancient Writings and the ostracon from Deir el-Bahri, an element of authorization is present in the association of the teaching with venerable writings or the ascription to a "scribe of the House of Life."[12]

A common though not constant feature of the instruction is a *prologue* or *exordium*. The prologue may contain a variety of motifs, of which the simplest is the exhortation to hearken to the instructions. Such prologues are found in Amunnakhte, the Instructions of a Man, and Sehetepibre. With only two or three exceptions the earliest prologues consist principally of such exhortations.[13] In later instructions longer exordia are attested and other motifs occur, sometimes alongside the exhortation to hearken. Amenemope begins with a long statement of its intended function:

> To know how to refute the accusation of one who made it,
> and to send back a reply to one who wrote it;
> To set one straight on the paths of life,
> and to make him prosper on earth;
> To let his heart settle down in its chapel
> as one who steers him clear of evil;
> To save him from the talk of others
> as one who is respected in the speech of men. (1.5–12)
> Give your ears and hear what is said,
> give your mind over to their interpretation. (3.9–10)[14]

Other prologues give details regarding the occasion of the teaching, and in doing so move in the direction of narrative prologues. Khety situates his instruction on the scribal profession during a southward journey to place his son in the writing school of the royal residence. The instruction of Ptahhotep is prefaced by a short account in which the aged sage requests permission of the Pharaoh to train a successor (4.2–

---

from our 'authors,' Egyptians transmitted only royal names. The reason may lie not only in the special appreciation which this genre enjoyed, but clearly also in the life experience which the writer brought into the instruction, and which was felt to be constitutive [for the work]' [trans. by auth.].

12. The "House of Life" consisted of several departments, including a scriptorium, library for important magical and religious texts and a medical department where the sick could be treated. It was apparently a centre of theological expertise and for the composition of hymns and spells. Relevant texts are conveniently collected by A. H. Gardiner, "The House of Life," *JEA* 24 (1938) 157–59.

13. Kitchen, "Basic Literary Forms," 247.

14. Unless otherwise specified, the English translation of the text will be that listed in appendix I.1.

5.7). More explicitly biographical are the prologues of Amenemhat the priest and Ankhsheshonq.[15] The former consists of an autobiographical account of the accomplishments, offices and virtues of the priest. Dating from early Ptolemaic times, Ankhsheshonq builds a prologue around the motif of the "ordeal or testing of the sage," relating a tale of accidental involvement in a conspiracy against the king, the discovery of the plot, the execution of the major conspirators and the imprisonment of Ankhsheshonq. As in Ptahhotep, the sage requests permission to instruct his son (1.9—5.14). His instruction, written on sherds, was eagerly read by the Pharaoh and "his great men" (5.15–17) although we are not told whether their enthusiasm led to Ankhsheshonq's release. In both Amenemhat and Ankhsheshonq, the narrative prologue enhances the reputation of the sage by associating him—by a variety of means—with the highest and most influential echelons of Egyptian society. The function of this association is presumably designed to provide legitimacy and authority for the instruction.

The fundamental form-critical unit of the instruction is, as McKane has rightly emphasized,[16] the imperative or admonition; the wisdom sentence or proverb occurs in large numbers only in the later works such as Ankhsheshonq, and even in such works the imperatival form is dominant. Although the imperative may stand alone as a monostichic command such as "Do not make an evil man your companion" (*P. Louvre D.* 2414 2:2), binary units are the rule in the earliest instructions: "Beautify your house in the necropolis/perfect your abode in the West" (Djedefhor 2). Or the imperative may be supplemented by motive clauses, final clauses, conditionals or maxims serving to strengthen the imperative. In Ptahhotep the instruction is presented in complex units consisting typically of imperative(s), final clause(s) (or motive clauses), conditionals and grounding maxims. For example, Ptahhotep 1:

> Do not be arrogant because of your knowledge, [imperative]
> but confer with the ignorant man as with the learned, [imperative]
> for the limit of skill has not been attained [motive]
> and there is no craftsman who has (fully) attained his mastery. [motive]
> Good speech is more hidden than malachite, [maxim]
> yet it is found in the possession of women slaves at the millstones. [maxim]

15. Several badly damaged fragments preserve the beginning of *P. Insinger* which seems to have contained a self-presentation of the sage who announces his allegiance to "the way of God" (fr. 1, lines 3–4) and a call to attention (fr. 1, line 5). See Guiseppe Botti and Aksel Volten, "Florentiner-Fragmente zum Texte des Pap. Insinger," *Acta Orientalia* 25 (1960) 30.

16. McKane, *Proverbs*, 3; similarly Lang, *Weisheitliche Lehrrede*, 31–36.

As to the internal organization of the admonitions, a variety of techniques are evidenced. (1) Several collections make no attempt at all at organization of their contents. Imperatives or imperatives with supplementary clauses are strung together in no discernible order; topics are raised, dropped and re-opened. There are numerous examples of this type of (non-)organization.[17] (2) Catchword association is also attested, although this is not a technique which is ordinarily sustained for a long list of maxims. Ankhsheshonq (8:2–6) provides several examples:

> *Learning* and foolishness belong to the people of your town; respect the people of your town;
> Do not say, "I am *learned*," [but] set yourself to become wise.
> Do not do a thing that you have not first *examined*.
> *Examining* makes your good fortune.
> If you *examine* three wise men about a matter, it is perfected;
> the outcome lies with the great god. [emphasis added] '

(3) Arrangement of instructions or maxims in thematic clusters characterizes the instructions of Aniy, which consists of approximately three hundred admonitions organized into clusters relating to religious duties, family matters, neighbors, women, drunkenness, etc. The Ptolemaic Counsels of Piety of Sansnos is a one-topic instruction containing imperatives bearing on religious duties. Ankhsheshonq groups some of its instructions by a combination of thematic clustering, formal analogy and catchword:

> S[erve your] god, that he may guard you.
> Serve your brothers, that you may have good repute.
> Serve a wise man, that he may serve you.
> [+ 3 more aphorisms introduced by "serve"]
> (6.1–6)

> Do not spare your son work when you can make him do it.
> Do not instruct a fool, lest he hate you.
> [+12 additional prohibitions introduced by the prohibition *m-'r*]
> (7.3–17)

Whereas the basic unit in Sansnos, Ankhsheshonq and Aniy tend to be monostichic or binary, Ptahhotep uses multi-segmented admonitions which are grouped to form short clusters of sayings dealing with such matters as disputants and leadership. Like catchword composition, however, the "cluster" technique is not consistently sustained through-

---

17. Djedefhor, Kagemni, Hori, Amenemhat, Instructions of a Man, Amunnakhte, *P. Louvre* 2377, Ostracon from Deir el-Bahri.

out Ptahhotep; many of the instructional units occur in no discernible order, and topics treated in the small clusters are broached again later on in the collection.

(4) The most sophisticated type of organization appears in Amenemope (ca. 1400 BCE?) and *P. Insinger* (late Ptolemaic period). In both the sayings are organized into "chapters"—30 in Amenemope and 25 in *P. Insinger*. Amenemope employs multi-segmented units consisting of not only imperatives, but motive clauses, programmatic statements, final clauses and concluding maxims.[18] For example, chap. 24 (on accusations):

> Do not listen to the accusation of an official indoors,
> and then repeat it to another outside.
> Do not allow your discussions to be brought outside
> so that your heart will not be grieved.
> The heart of a man is the beak of God,
> so take care not to slight it;
> A man who stands (at) the side of an official
> should not have his name known (in the street).

In *P. Insinger* monostichic maxims and admonitions are grouped topically into numbered chapters of instructions. Moreover, each chapter is punctuated with a cluster of seven sentences, consisting of two paradoxical couplets, two conclusions and the refrain "The fate and the fortune that come, it is the god who sends them."[19]

In the youngest Egyptian wisdom materials, those composed in the slightly pre-Ptolemaic or the Ptolemaic periods in either Demotic or Greek, some notable variations of the instruction form occur, partially under the influence of Greek conventions. The most obvious deviation from the older form is the fact that in both *P. Insinger* and Ankhsheshonq, the *wisdom sentence* is as frequent as the *imperative/admonition.*[20] McKane comments,

> Thus almost half of *Onchsheshonqy* is not Instruction at all. It is not therefore homogeneous with respect to form as the other examples of the Instruction are.[21]

The fact remains, however, that both Ankhsheshonq and *P. Insinger* call themselves "instructions" (Ankhsheshonq 4.17; *P. Insinger* 2.1, 21; 5.12,

---

18. See the detailed analysis of Amenemope by McKane (*Proverbs*, 110–17).
19. On this see Lichtheim, "Papyrus Insinger," 297.
20. See Gemser, "Instructions."
21. McKane, *Proverbs*, 120.

etc.) Moreover, Ankhsheshonq is explicitly framed as an instruction of a
father to a son, and *P. Insinger* seems also to have been conceived on this
pattern.[22] In other words, while wisdom sentences are present, in the
overall hierarchy of structures, the imperatival, instructional and prescriptive aspect dominates.[23] The conclusion to be taken from this is that
the instruction genre was rather flexible not only in regard to its modes
of internal organization but, in the later period, also with respect to its
constituent units.

A second notable aspect of later wisdom works is preponderance of
monostichoi instead of binary units. The lack of the use of extended
motivations following an imperative is particularly striking.
Ankhsheshonq, for example, contains only one multi-segmented unit
comparable to those of the older instructions (17.18–20),[24] and a relatively small number of imperatives with motive clauses.[25] Lichtheim
mentions two factors which contributed to the dominance of monostichic precepts and maxims: the underlying disinclination of Demotic
writers to adapt the vernacular—which was primarily a language of
legal and business documents—"to the formal, elevated style required of
poetry," and the influence of the monostichic precept and maxim characteristic of the *Sententiae Menandri* and other Greek gnomologia.[26]

The dominance of monostichoi and the large number of wisdom
sentences in Demotic instructions did not obviate the possibility of
structuring the sayings. The careful organization of the precepts and
maxims of *P. Insinger* into topical chapters with concluding formulae has
already been noted. Lichtheim also observes that Insinger overcame the
limitation of the monostich by creating thematic clusters, by attaching a
generalizing explanation to an admonition:[27]

---

22. The Florentine fragments of *P. Insinger* (fr. 1, line 5) contain the admonition to
attention typical of other instructions.

23. Lichtheim (*Late Egyptian Wisdom*, 5–6) also rejects Gemser's and McKane's
evaluations of Ankhsheshonq, pointing out that wisdom sentences are also common in
older instructions.

24. 17.18–20: "If you have grown up with a man and are faring well with him, do not
abandon him when he fares badly. Let him attain his house of eternity. He who comes
after him will support you." Compare the form of the instructions in Ptahhotep:
conditional + imperative(s) + motive clause.

25. For a convenient list, see McKane, *Proverbs*, 121.

26. Lichtheim, "Papyrus Insinger," 288, 304–5; idem, *Late Egyptian Wisdom*, passim.
That Menander's sentences were known in Egypt is certain: papyri fragments from the
third century BCE are extant (*P. Michaelidae* 5) and a substantial Greek-Coptic version of
Menander has recently been published by D. Hagedorn and M. Weber, "Die griechisch-
koptische Rezension der Menandersentenzen," *ZPE* 3 (1968) 15–50.

27. Lichtheim, "Papyrus Insinger," 289.

Do not trust a fool at any time in an undertaking.
The property of a wise man is lost through being left in the hand of a fool.
(12.12–13)

Sometimes two monostichoi are connected syntactically and logically:

It is not the wise man who saves who finds a surplus.
Nor is it the one who spends who becomes poor.
(7.15–16)

Ankhsheshonq does not demonstrate the same level of organization as Insinger. Nevertheless, various kinds of groupings exist. We have already noted the grouping of admonitions by catchword, formal analogy and thematic association. The same technique may be observed in the treatment of wisdom sayings: 8.17–9.4 contains ten sayings each having the form, The blessing (or wealth: *rnnt*) of *x* is *y*; the twelve sayings of 21.1–12 all employ the formula, There is no *x* which does/is *y*.[28] The striking formal similarity suggests that the author/editor of Ankhsheshonq not only collected wisdom sayings and admonitions, but created his own on the analogy of those he found in tradition in order to formulate strings of sayings with common formulae.

That the Ptolemaic collections were formulated under the influence of Greek conventions is seen not only in the preference for monostichoi. The Greek rhetorical device of the sorites or climax has been used to organize five sayings in Ankhsheshonq (22.21–25). Greek influence is also to be observed in the third-century BCE (Greek) Counsels of Amenotes. Although ostensibly the work of Amenhotep, son of Hapu, a distinguished sage and later divinized man from the 14th century BCE,[29] its initial admonitions, φρόνησιν ἄσκει μετὰ δικαιοσύνην· ὁμοίως θεοὺς σέβου [καὶ] γονέας, reflect the priorities of Greek parenesis.[30]

While the tendency to attribute instructions to named sages is a regular feature of the genre, pointing to the requirement of legitimation of the sayings, the Egyptian collections do not follow a common direction in other matters. The use and non-use of exordia belong to all periods, although the fully biographical prologue is observed only in

28. For further examples, consult Gemser, "Instructions," 145–46.
29. See Wilcken, "Zur ägyptisch-hellenistischen Litteratur." On Amenotes/Amenhotep see now Wildung, *Imhotep und Amenhotep*.
30. Honoring the gods and one's parents appear as the first precepts in many collections: Xenophon *Mem.* 4.4.19–20; Ps-Isocrates *Ad Demonicum* 16; Ps-Pythagoras *Chryse epe* 1; Ps-Menander 2; Plutarch *De liberis educandis* 7E; *Dicta Catonis* (monostichoi) 1–2; Sayings of the Seven Sages (Boissonade, ed., *Anecdota Graeca* 1:135). In others, although these precepts are not listed first, they are designated as the most important: Ps-Phocylides 8; Menander *Sententiae* 322.

Ankhsheshonq. It would also be premature to posit a linear development in the internal organization of collections: highly organized instructions are found both early and late; the same is true of those collections displaying no particular internal order.

Setting and Tone

McKane has provided a detailed analysis of the intended setting and tone of the Egyptian instructions. Rather than rehearsing his analysis, it will suffice to summarize his results.[31] Many of the Egyptian instructions seem to have been intended for use in schools. An examination of the titles, prologues and contents of Ptahhotep and Kagemni indicate that they functioned as educational manuals for apprentice statesmen. The tone of the instructions is prudential, emphasizing careful speech and behavior, intellectual discipline, discretion and good judgment in matters of state and fairness and impartiality towards suppliants. Merikare, Djedefhor and Amenemhat are somewhat more specialized since they are framed as instructions of a Pharaoh to the crown prince, and give advice which is primarily applicable to the heir apparent. Nonetheless, these too probably served as instructions for apprentice statesmen; Amenemhat, for example, is known through 194 ostraca written by schoolboys during the New Kingdom.[32]

Many of the remaining instructions come from somewhat lower levels of the scribal establishment. Khety, Nebmare-nakht and Pentaweret concern a rather elementary stage in scribal education and spend considerable space defending the profession as superior to other occupations. Aniy, Amenemope and Amunnakhte also appear to have their settings in the "middle classes" of Egyptian society, not the highest reaches of the administration. Both Aniy and Amenemope reflect popular piety and imagine for their addressees only modest attainment in the scribal hierarchy.[33]

Finally, a few works appear to be aimed at a rather general audience. These include the Instruction of a Man, which amounts to a piece of political propaganda in support of the monarchy, couched in language

---

31. McKane, *Proverbs*, 51–150; see also Brunner, "Lehren," 121–39; H. H. Schmid, *Wesen und Geschichte*, 9–16.

32. R. J. Williams ("Sages of Ancient Egypt") reports that Amenemhat is also preserved on six papyri, one leather roll and three writing boards.

33. See R. J. Williams, "Piety and Ethics in the Ramessid Age," *Journal of the Society for the Study of Egyptian Antiquities* 8 (1978) 131–37; F. L. Griffith, "The Teaching of Amenophis," *JEA* 12 (1926) 230; McKane, *Proverbs*, 98–99, 106–7; Brunner, "Lehren," 130–34.

designed to appeal to the *petites gens*.[34] While *P. Insinger* reflects careful structuring and degree of reflection on abstract matters, it is concerned with ordinary virtues and vices rather than matters pertaining to public administration.[35] *P. Louvre D.* 2414 focuses almost exclusively on domestic and familial topics, and Ankhsheshonq, despite the setting of its introduction in the royal court, is replete with rural, agricultural and working-class imagery.[36]

In spite of their wide variety of *Sitze im Leben*, Egyptian instructions from the earliest to the latest reflect the fundamental theological conviction that order or Maat (*m3't*) pervades both the cosmic and the human spheres and forms the basis for all sagacious action.[37] For this reason it would be mistaken to construe the instructions directed at administrative officials as counsels of unprincipled opportunism. Quite the contrary. Such instructions counsel action which is in harmony with the cosmic order established by the gods at creation and re-established and preserved by each king, who is regarded as the source of Maat. Hence Kagemni admonishes, "Do maat for the king [for] maat is that which God loves! Speak maat to the king [for] that which the king loves is maat!"[38] Merikare advises the monarch, "Speak maat in your house so that the magnates who are on earth may respect you . . . Do maat, that you may live long on the earth" (45, 46–47).

Egyptian instructions presuppose a fundamental order governing all human affairs, and attempt to promote action according to that order. Although specific admonitions are issued, Maat is not compassed by any command or combinations of commands. Rather Maat is a "basic value"[39] which undergirds every instruction. For this reason the educational process is not simply one of memorizing commandments, but

---

34. For a discussion of this text, see Kitchen, "Egyptian Wisdom Literature," 197–98.

35. Although it was widely copied by schoolboys, *P. Insinger* is probably not the product of a school. See Lichtheim, *Late Egyptian Wisdom*, 107, 185.

36. See the analysis of Lichtheim (*Late Egyptian Wisdom*, 13–92), who emphasizes Ankhsheshonq's dialogue with non-Egyptian wisdom.

37. For discussions of Maat see Aksel Volten, "Der Begriff der Maat in den ägyptischen Weisheitstexten," *Les Sagesses du Proche-Orient ancien* (Paris: Presses universitaires du France, 1963) 73–101; Siegfried Morenz, *Egyptian Religion* (trans. A. Keep; London: Methuen & Co., 1973) 112–36; Brunner, "Lehren," 117–19; Kayatz, *Studien*, 86–119. H. H. Schmid (*Wesen und Geschichte*, 17–24) takes the view that Maat is not an eternal order which governs action but an order which is constituted through wise action (p. 22). This represents a one-sided interpretation, as has been shown by Fox, "Two Decades," 122.

38. Inscription of Kagemni. Published, E. Edel, "Inschriften des Alten Reiches II: Die Biographie des *K3j-gmjnj* (Kagemni)," *Mitteilungen des Instituts für Orientforschung* 1 (Berlin, 1953) 225–26 (trans. Morenz, *Egyptian Religion*, 115).

39. Morenz, *Egyptian Religion*, 117.

rather the inculcation of an understanding of the order which underlies all action. Its aim is to produce "the truly silent man" (*grw m3'*), that is, one who is wise, discreet and cautious, but also modest, and just in all his behavior.[40]

The Hermeneutic of Egyptian Instructions

In the Egyptian instruction, the hermeneutic is in accord with the fundamental tone and presuppositions. By "hermeneutic" I mean two things: the way in which the instruction represents its mode of production or creation (the "authorial fiction," or "projected speaker") and the mode of appropriation which it recommends for itself. Two elements constituting the "authorial fiction" are remarkably constant. Virtually all instructions are ascribed to named sages, usually of some reputation, and the instruction is almost invariably portrayed as parental teaching. Both aspects have significance. Commenting on biblical wisdom, J. Williams has pointed out that the "father" stands as a symbol for the preservation of traditional, even archaic values.

> The point where the individual meets the tradition is in relationship with the "father," a figure which includes the parent but which is also a metaphor of several kinds of guide. The individual internalizes the voice of the fathers and obeys it by guarding himself against disorder (folly).[41]

For Egyptian wisdom, with its conservative comportment, and its tendency to undergird and affirm societal values, the motif of parental instruction was ideal for governing the "authorial fiction." As a primordial creation of the gods and as the eternal norm for all action, Maat, the primary focus of all instruction, must be transmitted and established in every historical period and at every level of society. The most apt metaphor for evoking this historical and societal continuum is the typical, repeatable situation of the "father-son" instruction. Thus in its conception, the instruction contains two moments, one historical and archaizing, and the other contemporizing. It derives its legitimacy by association with a venerable sage from the past, but it also addresses its audience in the present by means of the fiction of parental instruction.

Williams attempts to distinguish the "aphoristic wisdom of order," which rests on the collective voice of the "fathers," from the "wisdom of counter-order" characterized by individual insight and criticism of tradition:

40. Ibid., 118.
41. J. G. Williams, *Those Who Ponder Proverbs*, 42.

> The authority of the "voice" uttering the aphoristic wisdom of the fathers is that of a human subject, but it is not the authority of the individual. Even though all proverbs must originate with or be composed by some person, ... their intention is not to set the individual speaker in the forefront.[42]

This view, however, fails to explain the consistent ascription of instructions to named sages and the corresponding paucity of collections credited to anonymous collectivities. As I have argued above, these facts point to the requirement of the genre for an authoritative guarantor of the sayings. For that reason, sages of distinction are chosen. Even Ankhsheshonq and Amenotes, whose counsels are rather pedestrian, are ascribed to venerable and distinguished sages. The rationale for this strategy is simple: those who by their sagacity have earned and kept high office, or who are attended to by kings, officials and scribes, are living demonstrations of their own teachings.

It is important to note, however, that the teaching is never considered to be the *creation* of the sage. On the contrary, it is something which he transmits and which his own experience confirms.[43] It is perhaps for this reason that many instructions are represented as coming from persons close to the king or from the king himself, who is, for Egyptian theology, the very source of Maat. In fact the instructions of Amenotes come from one who was recognized as a god in his own right, at least in the neighborhood of Thebes and Deir el-Bahri.[44] The tendency of the instructional genre is, then, not only to associate wise words with a named sage, and indeed one whose reputation can serve as an authoritative guarantor, but also to associate the sage with the source of Maat, and ultimately, with Maat herself.

In regard to the mode of response which the instruction envisages, it is important to note, in the first place, that the instruction is authoritative: "[I]t demands unreserved acceptance and is not offered for critical

42. Ibid., 27. Von Rad (*Wisdom in Israel*, 192) argues that if wisdom sentences were dealing with individual subjective judgment, "they would lack any ultimate binding force; for in order to contribute to a valid knowledge of experience, the span of an individual life is much too short; it requires the reflection and sifting of generations. The legitimacy and worth of these teachings really resides primarily in the fact that they are validated by a long teaching tradition."

43. Thus Brunner, "Lehren," 118.

44. The provenance of the teachings of Amenotes is Deir el-Bahri. Wildung (*Imhotep und Amenhotep*) has assembled all of the texts relevant to Amenhotep (Amenotes). Amenotes, originally a scribe of Amenophis III, was by Ptolemaic times renowned as an assistant to Amun, a healing god and a divine sage. Wildung (pp. 298–302) points out that Amenhotep and Imhotep, who in their lifeworks established Maat by conquering chaos, were naturally viewed as pre-eminent sages and as mediators between the gods and humanity.

consideration."[45] In this crucial respect, instructions differ from proverb collections, which often contain contradictory statements requiring a mediating reflection in order to determine which counsel is appropriate for a given occasion. At the same time, however, the instructions are not intended to be treated as commandments to be memorized by the pupil. Nor, in spite of the fact that the instuctional genre is ultimately associated with Maat, do the teachings have the force of divine laws.[46] It is the task of the student not only to attend to the actual words of the teaching, but to perceive behind each word the fundamental ethos which informs it, and to assimilate that ethos. Only in this way can the sage "speak Maat, do Maat." The individual precepts serve to point the pupil to a comprehensive framework of meaning and order which is to control his every action.

Other Near Eastern Instructions

Wisdom collections which display an instructional intention are extant in Sumerian, Akkadian, Babylonian, Aramaic and, of course, biblical Hebrew, although they are neither so numerous nor so well defined in form as the Egyptian instruction. We will examine those collections of prescriptive wisdom in which jussive or imperatival forms are dominant in the hierarchy of structure, or in which an instructional intention is clear: Shuruppak (Sumerian/Akkadian), the Counsels of Wisdom, Shube-awilum, the Advice to a Prince, and the Counsels of a Pessimist (Babylonian), Ahikar (Aramaic/Syriac) and the wisdom instructions preserved in Proverbs[47] and Sirach. In spite of the diversity of languages of composition, there are important shared elements, and indeed elements in common with the Egyptian instructional genre.

Morphology

These collections do not employ a consistent introductory formula analogous to that of the Egyptian instruction, and in several cases the

---

45. McKane, *Proverbs*, 51.
46. See Morenz, *Egyptian Religion*, 118.
47. Although the final redaction of Proverbs in effect makes the entire book instructional, the sub-collections which are usually regarded as instructions properly so-called are Prov 1—9; 22:17—24:22; 24:23–34 (perhaps a miscellany) and 31:1–9. Prov 10—22:16 (sometimes further divided into 10—15 and 16—22:16) and 25—29 (subdivided into 25—27 and 28—29) are sentence collections displaying very little internal order, and relatively few imperatival or jussive forms. The "sayings of Agur" (30:1–14) is a sapiential meditation, 30:15–33 is a miscellany and 31:10–31 is a Wisdom poem in the form of an alphabetic acrostic. See on this, U. Skladny, *Die älteste Spruchsammlung in Israel* (Göttingen: Vandenhoeck & Ruprecht, 1962); McKane, *Proverbs*, 1–22; Murphy, *Wisdom Literature*, 49–53.

title and prologue are effectively fused. Nevertheless, most instructions have a title. Only the Advice to a Prince appears to be both untitled and anonymous.[48] A simple introductory formula characterizes most of the instructions in Proverbs:[49]

משלי שלמה בן־דוד מלך ישראל	1:1	παροιμίαι Σαλωμῶντος υἱοῦ Δαυιδ, ὃς ἐβασίλευσεν ἐν Ἰσραηλ.
גם־אלה לחכמים	24:22	ταῦτα δὲ λέγω ὑμῖν τοῖς σοφοῖς.
דברי למואל מלך	31:1	οἱ ἐμοὶ λόγοι εἴρηνται ὑπὸ θεοῦ.

Ahikar begins in a manner reminiscent of Egyptian instructions: "[These are the w]ords of one named Ahikar, a wise and ready scribe, who taught his son. For he said: Surely he shall be a son to me." In both Shuruppak (classical Sumerian) and Shube-awilum the incipit contains the ascription of the collection to a named sage, a brief description of the sage and the occasion of the instruction, and an exhortation to listen (Shuruppak 1–13; Shube-awilum I 1–16). Shuruppak, in fact, periodically repeats a modified version of the title and exhortation throughout the instruction (78–87; 147–57) and concludes with a similar formula (278–82).

Influence of the Egyptian instruction genre on Prov 1—9 and 22:17—24:22 is widely acknowledged.[50] While an explicit title and ascription are lacking for 22:17—24:22—perhaps removed when this instruction was incorporated into the larger composition[51] —22:17 contains the characteristic exhortation to listen and the general description of the instruction as "sayings of the sages." The prologue (22:17–21) continues in the vein of Egyptian instructions, stating the intended function of the teaching. The prologue of Prov 1—9 is similarly structured: after the title and ascription (1:1) comes a series of infinitives (strongly reminiscent of the beginning of Amenemope) stating the purpose of the collection (1:2–

---

48. Lambert (*Babylonian Wisdom Literature*, 96) suggests that the Counsels of Wisdom may have been anonymous, but the fragmentary state of the incipit hardly permits a firm conclusion.

49. The sentence collections of Proverbs begin in a similar way: see 10:1; 25:1; 30:1.

50. The case for influence has been put most forcefully by McKane (*Proverbs*) and Kayatz (*Studien*). See also Lang, *Weisheitliche Lehrrede*; Murphy, *Wisdom Literature*, 49–52, 54, 74. That 22:17—24:23 borrows from Amenemope or a related text is quite likely. The view that Amenemope depends upon Proverbs was convincingly refuted by R. J. William, "The Alleged Semitic Original of Amenemope," *JEA* 47 (1961) 100–106. Recently I. Grumach (*Untersuchungen zur Lebenslehren des Amenope*; Münchner Ägyptologische Studien 23; Munich and Berlin: Deutscher Kunstverlag, 1972) has tried to reconstruct an Egyptian instruction which served as the source of both Prov 22:17—24:23 and Amenemope, but the reconstruction is quite conjectural.

51. *BHK* restores the title as *dibrê hakamîm*.

6), a programmatic statement (1:7) and a set of admonitions on the topic of attending to parental instruction (1:8–19).

We have argued above that the tendency of the instruction genre to ascribe the sayings points to the need of the genre for legitimation. Nowhere is this clearer than in Prov 1—9. The prologue concludes with a "wisdom speech" (1:20–33) which in effect identifies the voice of the parent-teacher with that of the divine Sophia crying aloud in the street, admonishing the "simple" to receive instruction. The entire instruction is thus given not only the legitimacy which accrues to it from its ascription to the legendary sage-king of Israel's past, but more importantly, a transcendental authorization from the very source of wisdom itself. The strategy of the prologue of Sirach is remarkably similar: it begins with the programmatic statement "All wisdom comes from the Lord" and continues with a meditation on the heavenly Sophia and the posture appropriate to her reception. The intention is clear: to link the body of the instructions with Lady Wisdom, who as God's gift to humankind (1:9, 10, 19, 26) is the source of all human sagacity. The same tendency, incidentally, can be observed in the prologue of Shube-awilum:

> Hear the counsel of Shube-awilum, whose understanding is like Enlil-banda, the experienced counsel of Shube-awilum, whose understanding Enlilbanda gave him. From his mouth comes everlasting order for the people. (I 1–6)

As in Egyptian instructions, the prologue may also be narrative and biographical in form. Ahikar is the best example of such an introduction:

The prologue relates a tale, beginning in the vein of Ptahhotep, of the aged Ahikar requesting permission of Esarhaddon to train his adoptive son Nadan as successor. Nadan, however, proves treacherous and plots to have his father disgraced and executed. Ahikar is protected by a friendly officer and thus escapes death. After a lacuna in the manuscript (which may have contained an account of Ahikar's rehabilitation)[52] follows the instruction.

Two points are of interest in Ahikar's prologue. First, like the narrative

---

52. There is disagreement between the versions of Ahikar in regard to order: Aramaic version: (1) title; (2) story of Nadan's adoption and treachery; (3) [lacuna]; (4) instructions. Syriac version (S1): (1) Ahikar's adoption of Nadan; (2) instruction [21 admonitions introduced by "my son"]; [rest of mss is missing]. Syriac version (S2): (1) title; (2) adoption of Nadan; (3) instruction [75 admonitions introduced by "my son"]; (4) betrayal of Ahikar; (5) rehabilitation of sage and imprisonment of Nadan; (6) second instruction ["the parables of Ahikar"]; (7) death of Nadan. Ethiopic version: (1) title; (2) 15 instructions. The Greek Aesop does not detail an initial instruction of the boy, reserving the admonitions until after Aesop's (= Ahikar's) betrayal and rehabilitation, and after Linus' (or Ennus' = Nadan's) imprisonment.

prologue of Ankhsheshonq, it is formed around the motif of the "testing" or "ordeal" of the sage. As will be seen below, the same motif is formative for the narrative prologue of the *Sentences of Secundus*. The motif of testing or temptation appears also in the prologue of Prov 1—9 (1:10–11) and even more prominently at the beginning of Sirach's instruction:

> My son, if you come forward to serve the Lord,
> prepare yourself for temptation . . .
> Accept whatever is brought upon you,
> and in changes that humble you be patient.
> For gold is tested in fire,
> and acceptable men in the furnace of humiliation.
>
> (2:1, 4–5)

This motif of the ordeal of the wise man also permeates the first chapters of the Wisdom of Solomon (1:16—2:20). Its appearance at the beginning of these collections does not seem to be pure coincidence. One of the central virtues which these collections try to inculcate is that of self-control and clear-headedness in every conceivable situation. In Ahikar, as in Ankhsheshonq and Secundus, the testing/trial story seems designed to demonstrate in narrative form precisely what Sirach states aphoristically: "For gold is tested in fire and acceptable men in the furnace of humiliation" (2:5).

Second, the use of a narrative prologue with the wisdom instruction lends a narrative and biographical dimension to the whole collection.[53] This point is perhaps best illustrated by noting the varieties of titles which have been applied to Ahikar. The (earliest) Aramaic version is presented as instructional and sapiential: "[These are the w]ords of Ahikar, a wise and ready scribe." The Ethiopic version, which contains only sayings, is similarly titled. But the Syriac version begins, "The proverbs, to wit, the story of Ahikar" and the Armenian (B) version bears the title "The History and Conversation of Khikar." In Arabic it is designated as "The Story of Haiqar the Wise."[54] Because of the presence of a biographical prologue (as well as other narratives), some of the editors of the Ahikar material regarded it as primarily biographical in

---

53. Lindenberger (*Proverbs of Ahiqar* [Baltimore and London: Johns Hopkins Univ. Press, 1983] 19–20) has amassed evidence to suggest that the Ahikar narrative is of a different origin from the proverbs. Whether the narrative was an independently circulating story, or composed expressly for the proverbs is a matter of debate.

54. The versions are conveniently collected in F. C. Conybeare, J. R. Harris, and L. A. Smith, *The Story of Ahikar* (Cambridge: At the Univ. Press, 1913²). See also L. Pirot, "Ahikar," *DBSup* 1 (1928) 199–200.

intent rather than instructional. The Syriac version illustrates well the ambivalence of a collection such as Ahikar. The line between instruction and biography is not easily defined but easily crossed.

As in the Egyptian instruction, the title and prologue often function either implicitly or explicitly to legitimate the words of instruction. This is accomplished by various strategies: by simple ascription to an eminent sage; by the use of a narrative prologue which demonstrates the sage's qualifications; or, as in the case of Prov 1—9, Sirach and Shube-awilum, by associating the sage with the source of divine wisdom itself.

In regard to the body of the instruction, the most idiosyncratic form occurs in the Advice to a Prince, which is given as omens rather than admonitions, although the intent is clearly instructional: "If a king does not heed justice his people will be thrown into chaos" (1). The imperative or prohibitive, frequently supported by motive or final clauses, is the more usual form. These may be monostichic or binary units displaying parallelism, as the instructions of Shuruppak tend to be, or more complex units akin to what was characteristic of Ptahhotep and Amenemope. For example:

> When confronted with a dispute, go your way; pay no attention to it;
> Should it be a dispute of yours, extinguish the flame,
> (for) disputes are a covered pit
> (and) a strong wall that scares away its foes.
> They remember what a man forgets and make the accusation.
>   (Counsels of Wisdom 36–40)

> And you should set forth with a [companion].
> He who goes with a companion is [entr]u[sted] (to him).
> He who goes with an experienced man goes in peace.
>   (Shube-awilum I 14–16)[55]

The form of multi-segmented admonition is characteristic of Prov 1—9, 22:17—24:22 and 31:1–9.[56] It also occurs throughout Sirach.

The spectrum of organizational modes employed in Egyptian instructions may be seen here too. Collections such as the Counsels of a Pessimist and portions of Shuruppak display very little obvious overall structure, apart from some catchword associations and grouping of sayings which are formally analogous. The Counsels of Wisdom and Ahikar attempt to organize their admonitions thematically. Aramaic

---

55. Smith ("Wisdom Genres") has provided a superb rhetorical analysis of Shube-awilum demonstrating its strong affinities with biblical instructions.

56. For an analysis, see Murphy, *Wisdom Literature*, 54–68, 74–76, 81–82; Lang, *Weisheitliche Lehrrede*, passim.

Ahikar col. vii groups six or seven sets of instructional units (imperatives + motive or result clauses + aphorisms), all on the subject of discreet and careful speech. This technique, however, is not sustained throughout the instructions. The Counsels of Wisdom more successfully applies the principle of thematic clustering, but it is also much shorter, containing monostichic and multi-segmented admonitions divided into eight or ten topically coherent groups.

There is no consensus in regard to the structure of Prov 1—9. Skehan tried to show that it was organized around seven poems of 22 lines each,[57] but this view has attracted no significant following. It may be said only that the form of multi-segmented topical instruction dominates Prov 1—9, although there is considerable variation in the length and construction of each instruction. Moreover, several non-instructional units are present.[58] The editor of 22:17—24:22 states that his instruction consists of "thirty sayings" (22:20)—which recalls the 30 chapters of Amenemope—but despite the efforts of various commentators to divide it into 30 sayings,[59] the actual structure remains obscure. As in Prov 1—9 the dominant form is the multi-segmented admonition, although a few isolated wisdom sentences also occur (24:5-6, 7, 8-9). And as in Prov 1—9, there is no clear pattern governing the overall order of instructions.

G. Sauer rightly observes that Sirach also lacks an overarching order despite the fact that speeches of Wisdom occur at the beginning (chap. 1), middle (chap. 24) and end (chap. 51) of the book.[60] But deliberate structuring may be observed at the level of Sirach's sub-collections. Roth has demonstrated that the first half of Sirach (1:1—23:27) consists of

---

57. Patrick Skehan, "The Seven Columns of Wisdom's House in Proverbs 1—9," *Studies in Israelite Poetry and Wisdom* (CBQMS 1; Washington, D.C.: CBA, 1971) 9–14; "Wisdom's House," ibid., 27–45. The alphabetizing (22-line) schema is clear only in Prov 2:1–22, and Skehan had to resort to rearrangement of materials in order to construct his seven "columns." See Murphy, *Wisdom Literature*, 56.

58. McKane (*Proverbs*, 7) distinguishes (a) units which are formally instructions (1:8-19; 3:1–12, 21–35; 4; 5; 6:1–5, 20–35; 7:1–5, 24–27), (b) developments or relaxations of the instruction form (2; 3:13–20; 6:6–11; 7:6–23) and (c) various other elements (1:20-33; 6:12-15; 8; 9). Murphy (*Wisdom Literature*, 54–63) finds 12 instructions (somewhat more broadly defined than McKane's instructions) in Prov 1—9 and identifies only 1:20-33 (a Wisdom speech) and 6:1-19 (a miscellany) as non-instructional. Prov 8:1–36 is treated as both a Wisdom speech and an instruction.

59. See the varying divisions of McKane, *Proverbs*; B. Gemser, *Sprüche Salomos* (HAT 16; Tübingen: J. C. B. Mohr [Paul Siebeck], 1963²); R. B. Y. Scott, *Proverbs, Ecclesiastes* (AB 18; Garden City, N.Y.: Doubleday & Co., 1965). W. Richter (*Recht und Ethos* [SANT 15; Munich: Kösel, 1966] 25–40) finds only ten sayings. See further, Murphy, *Wisdom Literature*, 74.

60. See G. Sauer, *Jesus Sirach* (JSHRZ 3/5; Gütersloh: Mohn, 1981) 494.

four units, each beginning with a programmatic statement concerning Sophia and her pursuit:[61]

1:1—4:10	Prologue: 1:1—2:18	Body: 3:1—4:10 (topical instructions introduced by "my son")
4:11—6:17	Prologue: 4:11–19	Body: 4:20—6:17 (miscellaneous instructions; some topical organization)
6:18—14:19	Prologue: 6:18–37	Body: 7:1—14:19 (miscellaneous instructions; some organization by topic, catchword and formal analogy)
14:20—23:27	Prologue: 14:20—15:10	Body: 15:10—23:27 (miscellaneous instructions)

Roth proposes a three-part division of the second half of Sirach along somewhat the same lines,[62] but this is not so obvious as the structure of the first part. This is not to say that there are no signs of structure in chaps. 24—51. On the contrary, there are several topically organized instructions (e.g., 31:12—32:13, on dining manners; 35:1–12, on showing mercy; 38:1–23, on sickness and death).[63]

The organizational techniques typical of the Egyptian instruction recur: catchword composition, association by formal analogy, thematic clustering. Again, it is not possible to posit linear developments within the instructional genre, at least with regard to internal organization. While topical organization is common enough, it is not present in every collection surveyed, and even where topical organization is employed, it is not sustained throughout the long instructions such as Prov 1—9, Ahikar and Sirach.

Setting and Tone

That these Near Eastern collections had their *Sitz* in palace or scribal schools is not as clear as it was for the Egyptian instruction. Advice to a Prince has to do with matters of governance and statesmanship, and undoubtedly was employed in palace circles. The instruction to Lemuel (Prov 31:1–9) affords the clearest biblical example of this sort of instruction. The Counsels of Wisdom might have served as an educational manual for high officials, although only one section (81–94) is

---

61. Roth, "Gnomic-Discursive Wisdom," 60–61.
62. Ibid.
63. See further, Sanders (*Ben Sira and Demotic Wisdom*), who notes the use which Ben Sirach makes of Proverbs, but the higher degree of organization which he imposes upon his material.

directly applicable to statecraft; the rest is rather general wisdom admonitions. Ahikar is similar. Some of the instructions concern the behavior of a vizier before the king (vii 100–108) and thus accord well with the authorial situation described in the narrative prologue. But much of Ahikar is general wisdom instruction, and a few sayings (ix 129–31) seem to address persons of rather low economic status.[64] It should be noted that the Syriac and Greek (Aesop) versions of Ahikar do not correspond in content with the Aramaic version and lack the instructions aimed particularly at high officials. It appears that the teachings associated with the sage were changed to suit the intended audience; it may well be that Aramaic Ahikar itself already evidences the transformation of an official manual into a somewhat more popularizing wisdom book.

The original *Sitz* of the instructional collections of Proverbs is still a matter of dispute. Gerstenberger tried to trace sapiential admonitions to clan wisdom (*Sippenweisheit*) passed on in the course of parental instruction.[65] But McKane and Whybray, pointing to the pronounced similarities with Egyptian instructions, hold that the Israelite instructional genre originated not as a vehicle of popular, proverbial wisdom, but had its setting in court schools.[66] This view has much to recommend it. On the one hand, it is *a priori* likely that the Israelite court mirrored the Egyptian practice of providing schools for the training of high officials. There is ample evidence of the engagement of the Solomonic court in the pursuit and transmission of wisdom (1 Kgs 4:29–34; 10:1–10; Prov 25:1). Prov 31:1–9 and portions of 22:17—24:22 are quite suitable for instruction of high public officials. On the other hand, Prov 1—9 is not specifically suited to this task. Recognizing this, McKane conjectures that the instructional form has been "democratized" and transformed into a "broadly-based instruction for the community and especially for the young men of the community."[67] This is perhaps the best solution. The use of Proverbs in the post-exilic period indeed presupposes that it had moved from the narrow court circles to the lay, scribal class. The Egyptian instruction itself experienced a similar "democratization," as the examples of Aniy and Amenemope and, later, of *P. Insinger* and Ankhsheshonq show.

64. McKane, *Proverbs*, 156.
65. E. Gerstenberger, *Wesen und Herkunft des apodiktischen Rechts* (WMANT 20; Neukirchen-Vluyn: Neukirchener Verlag, 1965).
66. McKane, *Proverbs*, 19, 22–23; R. N. Whybray, *Wisdom in Proverbs* (SBT 45; London: SCM Press, 1965).
67. McKane, *Proverbs*, 9. See also Murphy, *Wisdom Literature*, 52–53.

The content and tone of Sirach indicate that its setting was in a lay scribal school. In a manner reminiscent of Khety, Pentaweret and Nebmare-nakht, Sir 38:24—39:11 extols the scribal profession, contrasting it with other less desirable occupations.[68] Sirach's statement that "the wisdom of the scribe depends upon the opportunity of leisure" (38:24: ἐν εὐκαιρίᾳ σχολῆς) and Sophia's invitation to lodge in her school (51:23: ἐν οἴκῳ παιδείας, Heb. *bêt midraš*) also point to the use of the instruction in scribal schools.

Hermeneutic

The Near Eastern instructions surveyed display the same authorial fiction as that of Egyptian instruction: parental instruction. It is especially prominent in Ahikar, Shuruppak, Shube-awilum, the Counsels of Wisdom, Prov 1—9; 22:17—24:22; 31:1-9 (instructions of Lemuel's mother!) and Sirach.[69] Only in the Advice to a Prince and the Counsels of a Pessimist is the motif entirely wanting. The fiction of father- (or mother-) son instruction fits well with the generally conservative comportment of all of these instructions. To use Williams' term, such collections express the "wisdom of order," emphasizing stability and continuity in society.

As with the Egyptian instruction, the sage is regarded as a tradent and interpreter of ancient wisdom rather than its creator (see Prov 1:5–6). This is expressed most succinctly by Sirach:

> [The sage] will seek out the wisdom of all the ancients,
> and will be concerned with prophecies;
> he will preserve the discourses of notable men
> and penetrate the subtleties of parables;
> he will seek out the hidden meanings of proverbs
> and be at home with the obscurities of parables.
> (39:1b-3)

In several instances (Shube-awilum; Prov 1—9; Sirach) the task of handing on and interpreting wisdom is placed under the auspices of divine Wisdom and thereby provided with a transcendental warrant. The sage in effect becomes a mouthpiece for the divine source of wisdom.

---

68. On this see R. J. Williams, "Sages of Ancient Egypt," 10; Sanders, *Ben Sira and Demotic Wisdom*, 61–63.

69. In the sentence collections (Prov 10—22:16 and 25—29), by contrast, the address "my son" is quite infrequent (19:27; 27:11), although both place a high premium upon filial obedience to parental instruction (10:1; 13:1; 29:17).

The appropriation of the wisdom instruction calls for a hermeneutic quite distinct from that required by the instruction's sister genre, the proverb collection.

A rather special hermeneutic is appropriate to collections such as Prov 10—22:16 (comprising mostly proverbs) and 25—29 (containing proverbs and admonitions). As is the case of many proverb collections, conflicting advices are given. Prov 26:4-5 provide an excellent example of diametrically opposed counsels for dealing with a fool. Other sayings may be true, but only under certain circumstances: "Poverty and disgrace come to him who ignores instruction" (Prov 13:18a). Still others seem empirically false: "The Lord does not let the righteous go hungry, but he thwarts the cravings of the wicked" (Prov 10:3). A clue to the hermeneutical key to sayings of this sort is given by Prov 26:7, "Like a lame man's legs, which hang useless, is a proverb in the mouth of fools," and 25:11, "A word fitly spoken is like apples of gold in a setting of silver."

A proverb, which is only "true" in a very restricted sense, depends upon skillful application. Proverb collections demand a hermeneutic of "fittingness."[70] Indeed the deliberate juxtaposition of contradictory counsels such as occurs in Prov 26:4-5 forces the student to confront the hermeneutical requirements of the genre. The presence of conflicting counsels, half-truths and even apparent falsities should not, however, lead to the conclusion that proverbial thinking is fundamentally subjective or determined by utilitarian principles. As many have emphasized, a concept of world order akin to Maat is an essential ingredient of Israelite wisdom.[71] The hermeneutic of collections of wisdom sentences is determined by what Gemser has aptly termed "the obstinate presupposition of a hidden order."[72] The criterion of "fittingness" is governed by a larger notion that in spite of the ambiguity of aphoristic wisdom and the limitations of human knowing, there is a created order which should form the basis of all action. Ultimately the wisdom sentences aim at inculcating an understanding of *sdqh*, the principle which allows the sage to apply proverbs "fittingly."

The response which the instruction envisages is much more direct than that of the proverb collection. Contradictory counsels are avoided, or at least not deliberately juxtaposed. The admonitions are not offered for deliberation or debate over their applicability; they are given as authori-

---

70. I am indebted to Dr. Raymond C. Van Leeuwen, of Calvin College, for helping me clarify my thinking on this issue. The term is his.

71. See H. Gese, *Lehre und Wirklichkeit in der alten Weisheit* (Tübingen: J. C. B. Mohr [Paul Siebeck], 1958); Gemser, "Spiritual Structure," H. H. Schmid, *Wesen und Geschichte*, 1–7, 198–99; J. Crenshaw, "'esa and dabar: The Problem of Authority/ Certitude in Wisdom and Prophetic Literature," *Prophetic Conflict* (BZAW 124; Berlin: Walter de Gruyter, 1971) 116–23; E. Würthwein, "Egyptian Wisdom and the Old Testament," *SAIW* 113–33; R. E. Murphy, "The Interpretation of Old Testament Wisdom Literature," *Int* 23 (1969) 291–93. Zimmerli ("Concerning the Structure") had argued for a contingent and subjective understanding of wisdom but later modified his view in "Place and Limit."

72. Gemser, "Spiritual Structure," 211.

tative commands requiring obedience. This latter point deserves to be emphasized, especially in light of the assertions that wisdom admonitions, in view of their experiential and subjective foundation, are non-authoritative and derive their legitimacy only from the cogency of the experiential rule which is articulated in the motive clause. Zimmerli states,

> A command appears categorical; counsel is debatable. It should be considered and pondered. It should be clear before it is transformed into deed. Thus, obedience is not the virtue of the wise, in terms of a general inculcation of hearing, but *d't* and *tbwnh* . . .[73]

It goes without saying, of course, that deliberation and reflection are virtues of the sage which the instruction genre enjoins. But this does not obviate the authoritative aspect of the genre. As with the Egyptian instructions, attribution to a named and renowned sage is a dominant feature. It is hardly ornamental. It points to the requirement for external authorization. Nor is it accidental that several instructions implicitly identify the voice of the sage with the divine source of wisdom and order. Kayatz has rightly underscored the influence of the notion of world order (Maat) upon the instructions of Prov 1—9.[74] Thus external legitimation of the instructions is present in two ways: from the sage/ tradent whose experience confirms the sagacity of his counsel; and from the divine source of wisdom, who is not only the teacher of order, but the originator of the primordial order of creation. The expression of the authority of the wisdom admonition differs in mode from other authoritative commands. The admonition does not, for example, rely on the prophetic "Thus says the Lord"; instead, it is framed in terms of an appeal to experience—the experience of the sage/tradent, and that of the addressee. But underlying this is a profound claim of authority: the authority of divinely created order.

Although the instructional genre neither envisages nor recommends the debate and deliberation which sentence collections require, the ultimate intention is the same: to inculcate an appreciation for the divinely ordained order and to promote action in accordance with that order. It is in the final analysis the effort to instil a comprehensive view of reality as orderly (though not necessarily predictable and entirely

---

73. Zimmerli, "Concerning the Structure," 180. For a summary of the criticisms of this view, see Crenshaw, "Problem of Authority/Certitude," 116–23.

74. Kayatz, *Studien*, 76–134.

intelligible). Submission to the instruction of the teacher/parent is the beginning of the initiation into this world view.

Sirach is perhaps the most reflective on the issue of appropriation. In 39:1-3 (cited above), he lays out his hermeneutic of appropriation. The student learns and transmits the sayings which he has received; he penetrates the obscurities of the sayings, with the result that

> he will be filled with the spirit of understanding;
> he will pour forth words of wisdom
> and give thanks to the Lord in prayer.
> He will direct his counsel and knowledge aright,
> and meditate on his secrets.
>
> (39:6-7)

The goal is not memorization. It is the assimilation of a world view which is itself generative of more wisdom. Roth aptly summarizes Sirach's hermeneutic as "from understanding to explanation, from assimilation to exposition, from learning to teaching, from apprenticeship to mastery."[75]

Later Instructions

Although the pervasive force of Hellenism accounts for a gradual shift from indigenous Near Eastern literary forms to the more typically Greek forms of the gnomologium and the chriae collection as a vehicle for the presentation of wise sayings, there are some examples of the perdurance of the instruction.[76] Recently W.-P. Funk has drawn attention to a sapiential text, transmitted in three different versions: in Coptic parchment containing an instruction of Apa Antonius (Brit. Mus. 979);[77] a section from the *Teaching of Silvanus* (NHC VII 97:3—98:22); and an eighth- or ninth-century Arabic version (in Latin translation) of the pseudo-Antonian "Spiritualia Documenta Regulis Adjuncta" (PG 40.1077AB).[78] These three texts conform well to the instruction form as described above, containing programmatic aphorisms followed by imperatives with motive and result clauses, the address "O my son" and

---

75. Roth, "Gnomic-Discursive Wisdom," 63.

76. Lichtheim (*Late Egyptian Wisdom*, 191) notes the shift in Christian Egypt from aphoristic wisdom and loosely organized gnomologia such as the *Sententiae Menandri* and the *Sentences of Sextus* to the more complex form of the tractate or sermon.

77. Walter E. Crum, ed., *Catalogue of the Coptic Manuscripts in the British Museum* (London: British Museum, 1905) 407. The text is from the 10th or 11th century.

78. W.-P. Funk, "Ein doppelt überliefertes Stück." He concludes that the two Antonian instructions depend not on *Teach. Silv.* but upon an earlier instruction (pp. 18–19).

conditionals with imperatives. Moreover, the subject matter—the importance of discretion and careful choice of friends—is a familiar one in Egyptian instructions.[79]

The *Teach. Silv.* as a whole reflects many of the techniques of the instruction: ascription to a named sage (Silvanus), the repeated address "my son," topically organized multi-segmented admonitions and a "Wisdom Speech" (89:5—90:28) reminiscent of Prov 1:20–33.[80] Though it displays an eclecticism in its philosophical interests, reflecting Philonic, middle Platonic and Stoic streams of thought, Zandee has also drawn attention to contacts with Ptahhotep, Amenemhat and Aniy, and with OT wisdom.[81] Not only the content of Egyptian wisdom, but the form too, continued to exert influence on the Christian didactic tradition.

The hermeneutic of the Antonian instruction and the *Teach. Silv.* is similar to that previously encountered: the authorial fiction combines both a historical and legitimating moment (ascription to a famed sage/teacher) and a contemporizing moment (in the father-son address). The teaching of Apa Antonius (and *Teach. Silv.* 97.3—98.22) is quite conventional in both form and character. Schoedel, however, has observed a significant shift in other portions of *Teach. Silv.*[82] The motive

79. Ibid., 20. That Egyptian instructions have influenced the formation of Coptic monastic rules has long been recognized. See T. Lefort, "S. Pachôme et Amen-em-ope," *Muséon* 49 (1927) 65–74; Helmut Brunner, "Ptahhotep bei den koptischen Mönchen," *ZÄS* 86 (1961) 146–47; Siegfried Morenz, "Die koptische Literatur," *Religion und Geschichte des Alten Ägyptens* (Weimar: Böhlaus, 1975) 585. Lichtheim (*Late Egyptian Wisdom*, 194–96) most recently has drawn attention to the affinities of these late instructions with Demotic wisdom.

80. M. L. Peel and J. Zandee ("The Teachings of Silvanus from the Library of Nag Hammadi," *NovT* 14 [1972] 294–311, esp. 297–98) drew attention to similarities between *Teach. Silv.* and *Spruchweisheit* such as the *Sent. Sextus*, Proverbs, Sirach and Wisdom but noted the differences between the aphoristic character of *Sent. Sextus* and the "short discourses" of *Teach. Silv.* (p. 297). W. R. Schoedel ("Jewish Wisdom and the Formation of the Christian Ascetic," *Aspects of Wisdom in Judaism and Early Christianity* [Notre Dame, Ind.: Univ. of Notre Dame Press, 1975] 169–99, esp. 174–83) prefers to treat it as a development of Jewish wisdom forms which have come under the influence of the Hellenistic diatribe and Hellenistic hymns. In his 1974 Harvard dissertation, W. R. Poehlmann ("Addressed Wisdom Teaching in *The Teachings of Silvanus*: A Form-Critical Study"; abstract in *HTR* 68 [1975] 394) rightly distinguished between the instruction (or "addressed wisdom teaching") and the sentence collections, and convincingly showed that *Teach. Silv.* was most closely related to the former. He also drew attention to the continuation of the instructional form in Sirach, Wisdom, Tobit, James and the *Instructions of Pachomius*.

81. J. Zandee, "Die Lehren des Silvanus: Stoischer Rationalismus und Christentum im Zeitalter der frühkatholischen Kirche," *Essays on the Nag Hammadi Texts in Honour of Alexander Böhlig* (NHS 3; Leiden: E. J. Brill, 1972) 144–55, esp. 145. On philosophical influences, see J. Zandee, "Les enseignements de Silvain et le platonisme," *Les Textes de Nag Hammadi* (NHS 7; Leiden: E. J. Brill, 1975) 158–79; C. Colpe, "Schriften aus Nag Hammadi II," *RAC* 16 (1973) 121–23.

82. Schoedel, "Jewish Wisdom," 180–83. Schoedel also considers the extended motive

clauses move beyond the normal experiential appeal characteristic of the older sapiential admonitions and are determined instead by logic and metaphysics.

This undoubtedly signals a shift in the hermeneutic of appropriation: from one in which the sage offers counsels which are confirmed by his own career, and which the experience of the pupil will confirm as trustworthy, to one in which the sage, on the basis of his insights into the nature of the divine, instructs the pupil so that he may "live according to the mind" (93:2–3). The authority claim of the sage is in effect stronger than in the older instruction, since the student cannot confirm through his own experience the truth of the counsel but must accept the reliability of his teacher's insights. It is worth noting in this context that the presence of a Wisdom speech (89:5—90:28) and the concluding exhortation to "accept the wisdom of Christ" (118:2–3) reinforce this authority claim by identifying the voice of the sage with that of Christ and Sophia.

Despite the differences with the older instruction, *Teach. Silv.* aims at the inculcation of a world view which will form the basis for all action. In this respect, it is not unlike the older instruction. And in spite of the shift in the content of the motive clauses, the general form of wisdom instruction remains intact. The genre was flexible enough to accommodate changing applications. In this case, the genre was adapted to use in Christian circles to inculcate and undergird an ascetic disposition (cf. 117:13–29).

HELLENISTIC GNOMOLOGIA

Preliminary Remarks on Gnomologia and Chriae Collections

Whereas the instruction had a relatively clearly defined morphology, setting, tone and hermeneutic, and a remarkably stable form over more than two millennia, Greek wisdom collections (and those influenced by Greek collections) reveal much greater variation, especially in their morphology. Several preliminary comments are in order:

1. Byzantine and medieval times produced several large anthologies of wise sayings, some composed of the sayings and anecdotes of Hellen-

---

clauses of *Teach. Silv.* to be developments of distichic imperatives of "classical Jewish wisdom." He seems to use the sentence literature of Prov 10—22:16 and 25—29 as his model, and takes too little account of the extended motive clauses of the wisdom instruction as represented by Prov 1—9 and Sirach.

istic philosophers and moralists, some comprising biblical and patristic citations, and others mixed in nature. Most conspicuous among these are Johannes Stobaeus' *Anthologium* (V CE), the *Gnomologium Democrito-Epicteteum*, and the anthologies transmitted under the names of Johannes Damascenus (VIII CE?) and Maximus the Confessor (probably from IX CE).[83] From this period too comes the multi-author anthology of epigrams, usually known under the name the *Greek Anthology*.[84] Neither type of anthology was the creation of medieval or Byzantine authors, however. The origin of the *Greek Anthology* goes back to the *Stephanoi* (as their authors called them) of Meleagros of Gadara (fl. ca. 100 BCE), Philippus of Thessalonica (fl. ca. 40 CE) and Diogenianus of Heraclea (fl. 140–50 CE). Papyrus fragments of both single and multi-author anthologies of epigrams are extant from the third century BCE.[85] The same is true of anthologies of wise sayings: collections of chriae begin with Metrocles of Maroneia (IV-III BCE), and papyri fragments of gnomic anthologies are extant from the third century BCE. J. Barns has made a strong case for the supposition that anthologies of poetic sayings were in use in Plato's day (see *Leges* 7.811A) and the invention of this system of education is probably the legacy of the fifth century BCE.[86]

The crucial difference between *stephanoi* and gnomic anthologies or gnomologia is one of function: while gnomologia were intended for educational purposes, *stephanoi* were composed for entertainment.[87] For this reason, we shall leave the *stephanoi* out of consideration. Q's style of saying is not that of the polished and arty epigram, nor is its function in any way comparable with epigram collections.

2. Greek rhetoricians distinguished two basic forms of wisdom sayings,

---

83. Johannes Stobaeus: O. Hense, ed., *Johannis Stobaei Anthologium* (5 vols; Berlin: Weidmann, 1884–1912; repr. 1968). *Gnomologium Democrito-Epicteteum*: C. Wachsmuth, ed., *Studien zu den griechischen Florilegien* (Berlin: Weidmann, 1882) 162–207; Johannes Damascenus, "Sacra Parallela," PG 95.1046–1588; 96.1–442; Maximus the Confessor, "Loci Communes," PG 91.721–1018; see also Antonius Monachus, "Melissa," PG 136.765–1244. Leo Sternbach (*Gnomologium Vaticanum e codice Vaticano Graeco 743* [Texte und Kommentare 2; Berlin: Walter de Gruyter, 1963] 2–4) lists over 20 Byzantine gnomologia preserved in medieval manuscripts. Wachsmuth ("Gnomologium Byzantinum," *Studien*, 162–65) lists 19 collections.

84. Critical edition: H. Beckby, *Anthologia Graeca* (TuscB; 4 vols.; Munich: Heimeran, 1957–58).

85. For a list of early papyri fragments of epigram anthologies, see Barns, "Gnomologium," 134–35.

86. Ibid., 5–8.

87. On this see ibid., 135; Guéraud and Jouguet, *Un Livre d'écolier*, 1:xxxv–xxxvii (the text published by Guéraud and Jouguet, however, is not a gnomologium, but a school exercise book).

both having instructional potential: the gnome and the chria.[88] For Theon, the essential distinction rested on attribution: chriae are always ascribed to a person; gnomai are not.[89] Chriae might also relate actions as well as words, although as Lausberg rightly observes, even in the so-called practical (πρακτικαί) chriae the action has a semantic function.[90] It would be unwise to press Theon's distinction too far, however, since popular usage of the terms "gnome" and "chria" was notoriously imprecise.[91] The fact that most gnomai are transmitted with ascriptions to known sages would, by Theon's definition, tend to make them chriae. The *Gos. Thom.*, which calls itself λόγοι, is by virtue of the repeated formula "Jesus said" a collection of "declaratory" (ἀποφαντικαί) chriae. Or again, while both the *Sentences of Sextus* and the *Sentences of the Pythagoreans* are transmitted as gnomai, an almost identically structured collection credited to Cleitarchus is entitled πραγματικαὶ χρεῖαι.[92]

In spite of the vagaries of popular usage, one difference may be observed between collections of gnomai such as the sayings of Democritus, Epicharmus, Pythagoras and Isocrates, and the chriae collections of Diogenes of Sinope, Socrates, Bion, Simonides and Demonax. Whereas the former are in the main concerned to instruct, the latter have *also* a

---

88. For modern discussions of the two terms, see Lausberg, *Handbuch* 1:536–40; Spencer, "Biographical Apophthegms"; Horna and von Fritz, "Gnome." See also D. E. Aune, "Septem Sapientium Convivium (Moralia 146B–164D)," *Plutarch's Ethical Writings and the New Testament* (SCHNT 4; Leiden: E. J. Brill, 1978) 64–65. Aune prefers the terms "wisdom saying" and "wisdom story" to the ancient terms, but curiously, he regards "wisdom sayings" as equivalent to χρεῖαι in spite of the fact that most chriae correspond more closely to his "wisdom stories."

89. Theon of Alexandria's definition: χρεία ἐστὶ σύντομος ἀπόφασις ἢ πρᾶξις μετ' εὐστοχίας ἀναφερομένη εἴς τι ὡρισμένον πρόσωπον ἢ ἀναλογοῦν προσώπῳ (L. Spengel, ed., *Rhetores Graeci* [Leipzig: Teubner, 1854] 96). Theon implies that the transition from gnome to chria is a simple one: "Every gnome attributed to a person is a chria" (p. 96 [trans. by auth.]). Aphthonius of Antioch (Spengel, *Rhetores Graeci* 2:26), Nicholas the Sophist (ibid. 3:458–59) and Isidorus of Seville defined a gnome as a *dictum impersonale* and a chria as an ascribed saying. Isidorus (*Etymologicarum libri XX* 2.11.2 [PL 82, p. 131]) states, "Nam inter chriam et sententiam hoc interest, quod sententia sine persona profertur, chria sine persona numquam dicitur. Unde si sententiae persona adjiciatur, fit chria; si detrahatur, fit sententia."

90. Lausberg, *Handbuch* 1:538.

91. T. Klauser ("Apophthegm," *RAC* 1 [1950] 546) notes that in Roman times, chriae coalesced with gnomai and both were known as *sententiae*. Similarly von Fritz, "Gnome," 89; H. Gärtner, "Chria," *Der kleine Pauly* 1 (1965) 1161. According to Horna ("Gnome," 87–88) "chria" should not be listed alongside "gnome," "apophthegm" and "apomnemoneuma" since it can appear as all three. Crossan (*In Fragments*, 232) notes that Quintilian is unable to distinguish clearly between chriae and sententiae (see 1.9.3 and 8.5.3).

92. All three texts are published in H. Chadwick, ed., *The Sentences of Sextus* (Cambridge: At the Univ. Press, 1959).

biographical aspect, providing anecdotes from the sage's life.[93] This distinction, of course, cannot be absolute; we must be prepared to admit of more and less biographical interest in the relating of chriae. For our purpose, however, it will be convenient to treat gnomologia and chriic collections separately.

It is impossible to consider in detail all of the gnomologia and chriae collections extant. We shall restrict ourselves to a representative number of pre-Byzantine gnomologia (roughly, those discussed by Max Küchler),[94] and some early examples (many of them fragmentary) of chriae collections.

3. There does not appear to have been a consistent convention for the naming of collections. Several early gnomologia are preserved in damaged copies where both the incipit and the colophon are missing. In other cases the incorporation of collections into other literary works has obscured the original title (if there was one).[95] In still other instances the function of the title is absorbed by the σφράγις which occurs in the opening or closing lines and contains not only a statement of the purpose of the collection but the name of the putative author. Such is the case with both Ps-Phocylides and the prologue of the sayings of Epicharmus (*P. Hibeh* 1.1). Others bear titles, using the form γνῶμαι or χρεῖαι NN,[96] but a variety of other titular forms are also attested.

4. Despite the lack of a consistent titular convention, ascription of collections to named sages is the rule;[97] anonymous gnomologia are relatively rare.[98] The pressure to attribute sayings to a historical figure

93. Plutach (*Alexander* 1.2) notes that in composing a *bios* "some trivial act (πρᾶγμα βραχύ), a word (ῥῆμα), a jest (παιδιά) often shows up character far more than engagements, with thousands of dead, or pitched battles or blockades." For this reason, chriae were ideal for biographical purposes, as indeed the prologue of Lucian's *Demonax* implies.

94. See appendix I.2: "Gnomologia." Küchler (*Weisheitstraditionen*, 240–61) surveyed the contents of approximately 20 gnomologia (including the Christian *Sent. Sextus*) in preparation for his analysis of *Ps-Phocylides* and *Ps-Menander*.

95. E.g., the collection of chriae of Bion (Diogenes Laertius 4.47–51) is given without the original title. Contrast 6.32, 33, 91, 95, where Diogenes cites the title of his source.

96. E.g., the collections attributed to Menander (*P. Giessen* 348), Democritus (Diels and Kranz, *Vorsokratiker* 68 B 35), the Pythagoreans, and several of the large medieval gnomologia. Cleitarchus' sayings, as well as the collections by Metrocles of Maroneia (Diogenes Laertius 6.33), Hecaton (6.4, 32, 95; 7.26, 172) and Zeno (6.91) were entitled χρεῖαι.

97. This is true at the level of individual saying as well: although some sayings are transmitted anonymously as general folk wisdom, there was a strong pressure to attach sayings to concrete historical figures. This did not mean, of course, that there were not conflicting attributions of the same saying. Diogenes Laertius himself provides evidence of this, ascribing the saying "Friends share in common" once to Bion (4.53) and once to Pythagoras (8.10), and "Nothing too much" to both Thales and Solon (1.41, 63).

98. The principal exceptions are two fragmentary inscriptions, one from the

appears to derive from the need for an authoritative guarantor of the reliability of the saying. R. O. P. Taylor once commented,[99]

> We view a maxim as if it had an existence and authority of its own, apart from its author . . . But to them [Hellenistic authors], the maxim, however impressive, had to come from an accredited person to carry the greatest weight.

Rather than ascribing the wisdom to a king, vizier or priest, the Greek and Latin collections are more often credited to philosophers (Epictetus, Epicurus, Pythagoras, Secundus, Simonides of Ceos), poets (Chares, Epicharmus, Menander, Phocylides, Publilius Syrus, Theognis) or various sages (Aesop, Democritus [Democrates], Isocrates, Seven Sages). Several Hermetic collections, which employ variations of the typical instructional setting of a father teaching his son, place the sayings in the mouth of divine revealer figures (Nous, Hermes).[100]

A form not encountered in Near Eastern collections is the multi-author gnomologium or chriae collection. These include not only the late *Gnomologium Vaticanum*, *Gnomologium Vindobonense* (both chriae collections) and the Florilegium published by Schenkl (combining chriae and gnomai) but also works from a much earlier date.[101] From the second century BCE comes an anthology on the subject of fate which employs sayings of Euripides, Menander, "Theophrastus or Anaximines" and Demosthenes;[102] from the same period come two gnomologia on women and marriage, *P. Berol.* 9772 and 9773, each containing the sayings of several authors,[103] and a fragmentary gnomologium

---

gymnasium at Thera (IV BCE) containing five maxims, and the second from Miletopolitanus (Cyzicus; III BCE) containing 56 admonitions. (For bibliographical details, see appendix I.2.) In both cases, however, the sayings display such striking overlap with the Sayings of the Seven Sages, known from several collections, that it is highly probable that their source would be recognized even without explicit attribution. Both inscriptions appear to be patterned after the "pithy and memorable" sayings of the Seven Sages inscribed on the Temple of Apollo at Delphi (see Plato *Protagoras* 343B).

99. R. O. P. Taylor, *Groundwork of the Gospels*, 81; similarly Crossan, *In Fragments*, 229.

100. CH 11 (Nous to Hermes) contains a series of Hermetic "definitions" introduced by the exhortation to listen. Excerptum XI Stobaei contains 48 sententiae (κεφάλαιοι) with an opening and closing exhortation. Recently J. Mahé has published an Armenian collection of Hermetic "definitions" bearing the title "Definitions of Hermes Trismegistus to Asclepius" ("Les Définitions d'Hermes Trismégiste à Asclépius," *RevScRel* 50 (1976) 193–214).

101. For bibliographical details, see appendix I.2b, "Byzantine and Medieval Gnomologia and Chriae."

102. Barns, "Gnomologium," 126–37 (cf. Pack², 1574).

103. *P. Berol.* 9772 (Pack², 1568): W. Schubart and U. von Wilamowitz-Moellendorff, *Griechische Dichterfragmente* (Berliner Klassikertexte 5/2; Berlin, 1907) 123–28, *P. Berol.* 9773 (Pack², 1573): ibid., 129–30.

containing sayings of Euripides, Ps-Epicharmus and Menander, topically organized, is preserved on a papyrus dating from ca. 250–210
BCE.[104]

M. 'Abot would seem to belie our assertion that multi-author collections were not
indigenous to the Near East. Yet there are compelling reasons for regarding m.
'Abot not as a continuation of biblical wisdom genres—either the instruction, or
the proverb collection—but as a representative of Hellenized wisdom. Neusner
observes that the most striking difference between the sayings materials from
Qumran and those in Pharisaic-rabbinic circles is "the persistent attribution to
living, immediate authorities of the bulk of Pharisaic-rabbinic tradition."[105]
Fischel points out three further differences: first, unlike biblical and apocryphal
wisdom books, m. 'Abot ascribes authorship to many authorities; second,
"sequels in time do not play a role in biblical wisdom collections" and, third, the
traditional elements of parallelism and alphabetic acrostics disappear in m.
'Abot.[106] These observations deserve to be underlined. M. 'Abot lacks the main
characteristics of the instruction and is much closer in form to doxographic compositions or to the collections of the Sayings of the Seven Sages.[107] Fischel
provides an eminently satisfactory explanation of this: Tannaitic literature came
under the influence of cynicizing chriae, adopting not only various motifs (self-
control, self-sufficiency, contentment with a simple life), but the practices of
telling stories about sages and attributing wise sayings to them.[108] M. 'Abot is
thus "hardly the 'New Testament of Judaism,' as it has been incongruously
called, but rather its Diogenes Laertius."[109]

The reason for the strong preference for named sayings collections
resides, as Taylor rightly notes, and as has already been seen in the
instructions, in the need for an authoritative guarantor of the teaching.
Even when the gnomologium conveys quite conventional and non-
controversial wisdom, ascription to a named sage is usual. One could
surmise that the competition of religious, philosophical and ethical
systems which characterized the Hellenistic and imperial periods reinforced the already strong pressure to attach sayings to an authoritative
figure. The chriic form, for which attribution is an intrinsic part, was
ideally suited to the combination of caustic wit, pointed polemic and
radical ethical command which Cynics popularized. In this case, anonymous pronouncements were scarcely an option; the radical comportment of the teaching dictated the necessity of attachment to a historical
figure.

104. P. Hibeh 1.7; see Pack², 1569.
105. Neusner, "Types and Forms," 367.
106. Fischel, "Transformation of Wisdom," 74–75.
107. On this see Saldarini, Scholastic Rabbinism, 20–21.
108. See Fischel, "Story and History"; idem, "Cynicism and the Ancient Near East."
109. Fischel, "Transformation of Wisdom," 75.

The Hellenistic Gnomologium

The use of individual gnomai in literary works is already attested in Homer and especially in Hesiod's *Works and Days,* although neither of these is a gnomologium.[110] The first instances of compositions made up solely of gnomic verses come from the sixth century BCE: Theognis and Phocylides. The pseudo-Hesiodic "Counsels of Chiron," of which only a few fragments survive, may also come from this period. Probably by the fifth century, and certainly by the fourth, gnomai from the poets were collected and used in education.[111] Numerous examples of verse anthologies on papyrus—some of them school exercises—attest the continued collection and use of gnomai in education throughout the Hellenistic and imperial periods.[112] While poetic gnomai were employed at elementary stages of education as writing exercises and to inculcate basic ethical ideas,[113] gnomologia also became the vehicles of the more specialized teaching of the philosophical schools, especially in Epicurean and Pythagorean circles.

Morphology

Apart from consistent attribution to named sages, the gnomologia under examination display no uniformity in the use or form of exordia or prologues. More than half have no prologues at all. Those which do reveal a range of introductions. Ps-Phocylides begins by emphasizing the sagacity of the putative teacher and the importance of his counsels. Like Prov 1—9 and Sirach, the prologue of this Hellenistic Jewish gnomologium connects the counsels of the sage with a divine source:[114]

ταῦτα δίκησ᾽ ὁσίῃσι θεοῦ βουλεύματα φαίνει
Φωκυλίδης ἀνδρῶν ὁ σοφώτατος ὄλβια δῶρα,

110. The term "gnomologium" has no special claim to antiquity as a *terminus technicus.* The earliest usage of the terms γνωμολογία, γνωμολογικός, γνωμολογικῶς refers only to sententious style. Horna ("Gnome," 75) points out that none of the texts cited in the lexica (e.g., LSJ 354) establishes the word as a technical term; only in Byzantine times was "gnomologium" so used. However, antiquity did not bequeath to us any better term; sayings collections are not discussed in the *Progymnasmata* of Theon of Alexandria, Hermogenes of Tarsus or Aphthonius of Antioch or in the rhetorical treatises of Aristotle or Quintilian.
111. Aeschines 3.15: διὰ τοῦτο γὰρ οἶμαι παῖδας ὄντας τὰς τῶν ποιητῶν γνώμας ἐκμανθάνειν, ἵν᾽ ἄνδρες ὄντες αὐταῖς χρώμεθα. See Barns, "Gnomologium," 5–8.
112. See Guéraud and Jouguet, *Un Livre d'écolier* 1:xxxv-xxxvii.
113. Marrou, *History of Education,* 150–59.
114. For a discussion of the provenance of Ps-Phocylides, see Pieter van der Horst, *The Sentences of Pseudo-Phocylides* (SVTP 4; Leiden: E. J. Brill, 1978) 3–83; John J. Collins, *Between Athens and Jerusalem* (New York: Crossroad, 1983) 143–48; Küchler, *Weisheitstraditionen,* 261–302.

These counsels of God by his holy judgments
Phocylides the wisest of men sets forth, gifts of blessing.
(1–2)

The simple hortatory prologue is seen less frequently than in the instruction genre. The sayings of Aesop (which bear some relation to the instruction genre) are introduced by the exhortation ἄκουσον τῶν ἐμῶν λόγων, τέκνον, καὶ φύλαξον ἐν τῇ καρδίᾳ σου (Life "W" §109). A modification occurs in two Hermetic sayings collections:

(Title) Nous to Hermes
(Exordium) Retain well my discourse, O Hermes Trismegistus, and remember what I said (to you) . . . Listen, O child, what is the nature of God and the All. (CH 11)

(Title not extant)
(Exordium) Now my child, I shall recount in brief sentences (κεφαλαίοις) the order of being. You will understand the things I say if you remember what you have heard. (*Fragmenta Stobaei* 11)

The (Golden) Sayings of Democritus [Democrates] begin not with an exhortation but with a promise to the reader:

γνωμέων μεν τῶνδε εἴ τις ἐπαΐοι ξὺν νόωι
πολλὰ μὲν ἔρξει πράγματ᾽ ἀνδρὸς ἀγαθοῦ ἄξια,
πολλὰ δὲ φλαῦρα οὐχ ἔρξει,

If one gives ear to my maxims with understanding
one will do many deeds worthy of a good man,
and will not do much mischief.[115]

The incipit of the *Gospel of Thomas* employs a two-part form (title + exordium) reminiscent of the prologues of instructions such as Ptah-hotep and Amenemhat I. However, Thomas requires of his readers not just attention, but hermeneutical skill to penetrate the opacity of the sayings:

(Title) These are the secret sayings which the living Jesus spoke and which Didymos Judas Thomas wrote down.

(Exordium) And he said, "Whoever finds the interpretation of these sayings will not experience death." (NHC II 32, 10–14 [trans. Lambdin, *NHLE*, 118])

Statements of purpose of varying length, sometimes accompanied by exhortations to listen, are found in several collections. The prose portion

115. Text: Diels and Kranz, *Vorsokratiker* 68 B 35 [trans. by auth.]. Democritus is presumably Democritus of Abdera (from V BCE). See Stewart, "Democritus and the Cynics," *HSCP* 63 (1958) 179, 187–88.

of *Dicta Catonis*, consisting of 57 monostichoi,[116] is introduced by a prologue in which Cato, the putative speaker, addresses his son (*fili karissime*), describes the purpose of his instruction (viz., that the son may attain glory and honor), and concludes with the admonition

> igitur praecepta mea ita legito, ut intellegas
> legere enim et non intellegere neglegere est,
> Therefore, so read my precepts as to understand;
> for to read and not to understand is to give them the go-by.
> (Loeb 593)

Books 2—4 of the *Disticha Catonis* begin with prefaces which exhort and promise benefits to the reader. For example:

> sin autem cura tibi haec est ut sapiens vivas,
> audi quae discere possis, per quae semotum vitiis deducitur aevum:
> ergo ades et quae sit sapientia disce legendo,
> (2.7–10)
> But if your serious aim is a life of wisdom,
> hear what you may learn of things
> that ensure a course of life divorced from vice.
> Come then and, as you read, learn what wisdom is.
> (Loeb 605)

Dating from ca. 280–250 BCE, *P. Hibeh* 1 contains what may be the prologue to Axiopistus' collection of the sayings of Epicharmus.[117] Although somewhat longer than the prologue of the *Dicta Catonis*, it contains similar features—a description of the application and intended function of the gnomai, and an exhortation,

> Within this book are many and manifold advices for you to use towards a friend or foe, while speaking in the courts, or the assembly, towards the rogue or the gentleman . . . Within it too are maxims wise: obey them, and you will be a cleverer and a better man for all events . . . He who learns these maxims well shall appear a wise man in the world and never talk but good sense if he remembers every word. (1–3, 5–7, 15–16)[118]

In a rather extensive preface, Ps-Isocrates (*Ad Demonicum* 1–12) relates the purpose of his writing, namely to provide counsel on how "to

---

116. That the monostichoi of *Dicta Catonis* are not abridgments of the disticha (books 1–4), but go back to a collection similar to the Sayings of the Seven Sages, has been argued by Skutsch, "Dicta Catonis," esp. 365–66. See also J. W. Duff and A. M. Duff, *Minor Latin Poets* (LCL; Cambridge: Harvard Univ. Press, 1935, repr. 1961) 587.

117. Thus D. L. Page, *Select Papyri*, Vol. 3, *Literary Papyri: Poetry* (Cambridge: Harvard Univ. Press; London: Heinemann, 1970) 439. Diels (*Vorsokratiker* 1:194) suggests a late-fourth-century BCE date for Axiopistus.

118. Restoration and translation by Page, *Select Papyri* 3:440–44.

win repute as men of sound character" (4). He then undergirds his instructions both philosophically, with an excursus on the enduring quality of virtue and the transient nature of wealth, and by means of the examples of other virtuous men, including Heracles, Theseus and Demonicus' father (8–12).

The sole example of a gnomic collection with a narrative and biographical prologue is offered in the Greek *Life of Aesop* (§§101–23). The close relation of the admonitions preserved in §§109–10 to Menander's monostichoi has often been noticed, and it appears that Aesop's ethical instructions were derived from that source.[119] However, the story of Aesop's service to Lycurgus of Babylon, his adoption and instruction of a son, and his betrayal and later rehabilitation is obviously borrowed from the Ahikar story. The extant *Lives of Aesop* contain much more than this "oriental episode," and in view of their extensive narrative components cannot be classified simply as gnomologia.[120] It appears, however, that the first century CE compiler of the *Life of Aesop* borrowed a Greek version of the sayings of Aesop with a prologue formed around the motif of the ordeal of the sage and rewrote the ethical instructions under the influence of Menander.[121]

Considerable variety is observed in the actual form of the sayings contained in gnomologia. A large number of collections are dominated by jussive or imperatival sayings, either monostichoi, as is the case with the *Delphic Precepts* from Thera and Miletopolitanus and the *Dicta Catonis* (monosticha), or more complex formulations displaying parallelism, strings of related imperatives or imperatives with motive clauses.[122] Several gnomologia mix imperatives with wisdom sayings,[123] while a smaller number are composed solely or predominantly of aphorisms (Democritus; Publilius Syrus). Iamblichus reports that the Pythagorean

---

119. See S. Jaekel, *Menandri sententiae* (Leipzig: Teubner, 1964) 132–36.

120. Critical edition of Lives "G" and "W": B. E. Perry, *Aesopica* (Urbana: Univ. of Ill. Press, 1952).

121. Perry, *Aesopica* 5: "Qui primum hanc Vitam in Aegypto composuit, is ipse, potius quam quivis alius, inter alia ab Aesopo aliena et Achicari quoque historiam sibi in promptu iacentem in rem suam vertisse putandus est." That Ahikar was already well known to Greek writers is suggested by Clement of Alexandria (*Strom.* 1.69.4; see also Eusebius *Praep.* 10.4) who reports that Democritus derived his teachings from Βαβυλόνιοι λόγοι ἠθικοί written on ἡ 'Ακικάρου στήλη. According to Diogenes Laertius (5.50), Theophrastus wrote a book entitled 'Ακίχαρος.

122. E.g., *Sentences of Aesop; Gnomologium Epictetum;* Ps-Isocrates *Ad Demonicum;* Ps-Menander; Ps-Phocylides; Ps-Pythagoras *Chryse epe;* Sayings of the Seven Sages.

123. E.g., *Sentences of Cleitarchus; Dicta Catonis* (disticha); Epicharmus; Epicurus *Kyriai doxai; Gnomologium Vaticanum Epicureum; Menandri Monostichoi; Sayings of the Pythagoreans; Sentences of Sextus; Gos. Thom.*

'Ακούσματα were framed as answers to three questions—τί ἔστιν; τί μάλιστα; and τί πρακτέον—and dealt with both ethical matters and dogma.[124]

Many gnomologia are arranged without regard to verbal or formal features or subject matter. Alphabetic organization is typical of the monostichoi of Menander[125] and Publilius Syrus, but attested also in the *Sayings of the Pythagoreans*.[126] Catchword composition and association by formal analogy are in evidence in other collections such as the *Gos. Thom.*,[127] *Sentences of Cleitarchus* and *Sent. Sextus*. Occasionally examples are found of extended groupings which build to a rhetorical climax, of which the five-member sorites at the beginning of the *Sent. Sextus* (1–5) offers an instance. Barns has noted a few instances of anti-logical arrangement of sayings, the purpose of which, presumably, is to introduce a student to both sides of a philosophical or ethical question.[128] More common than this is grouping by subject matter, a technique which is observed throughout Ps-Phocylides and Ps-Isocrates as well as the Byzantine *Gnomologium Democrito-Epictetum*, and within smaller clusters of sayings in Chares, *Chryse epe*, Ps-Menander, Ps-Pythagoras, *Sentences of Cleitarchus* and *Sent. Sextus*.

Setting and Tone

Ample evidence exists to show that some gnomologia, mainly composed of sayings from older poets and from writers such as Menander, were used in schools as writing and spelling exercises, and to inculcate basic ethical values. But other collections appear to have been employed at a somewhat higher level of moral instruction, either within schools or in the home. In these gnomologia certain emphases are characteristic: piety toward the gods, honor of parents, keeping oaths, social and sexual propriety and moderation in all forms of behavior.[129] There are of course features distinctive of individual collections: Ps-Isocrates is characterized by a pragmatism tinged occasionally by lofty moral idealism; the

---

124. Iamblichus *De vita pythagorica* 18.82.

125. Alphabetic organization is seen not only in the 877 sentences of the *Menandri Monostichoi*, but also in several of the smaller papyrus collections. See Jaekel, *Menandri Sententiae*, 3–25.

126. H. Schenkl, "Pythagoreersprüche in einer Wiener Handschrift," *Wiener Studien* 8 (1886) 262–81.

127. See Crossan, *In Fragments*, 154–55, for a tabulation of the catchwords used.

128. E.g., *P. Berol.* 9772, 9773. See Barns, "Gnomologium," 1–4.

129. E.g., Ps-Isocrates *Ad Demonicum*; Ps-Phocylides; the *Sentences of Aesop*; Chares; Cleitarchus; the *Sayings of the Pythagoreans*; *Dicta Catonis*; Publilius Syrus; Democritus; Ps-Menander.

Sentences of Cleitarchus stress self-sufficiency, self-control and deliberation as the marks of a sage; and Ps-Phocylides offers practical ethics with a few distinctively Jewish features.[130]

It is equally clear that some sayings collections functioned in philosophical communities either as catechisms or as convenient summaries of the principal doctrines.[131] The ἀκούσματα or σύμβολα of the Pythagoreans represent the oldest form of transmission of Pythagorean teachings.[132] Some, at least, were formulated in such a way that only the initiated could understand. For example, "Do not step over the beam of a balance" was understood as advice to give heed to matters of justice.[133] The sayings are rightly termed αἰνίγματα, "riddles," by Plutarch who tried his hand at interpreting some of them (*Quaest. conviv.* 8.7). Reference to specifically Pythagorean doctrines and writings in the *Chryse epe* suggests too that this was employed for the instruction of disciples.[134]

For Epicurean communities the *Kyriai doxai* or "Principal Doctrines" (= Diogenes Laertius 10.139–54) encapsulated basic ethical teaching. Epicurus himself describes the intended functions: For those who were unable to study the longer treatises, epitomes such as the *Kyriai doxai* provided the main outlines of the system to be committed to memory. And for the more advanced they afforded a convenient summary.[135] The so-called *Gnomologium Vaticanum Epicureum*, which bears the title Ἐπικούρου προσφώνησις, and a fragmentary Epicurean gnomologium from the second century CE, both of which contain sentences found in the *Kyriai doxai*, may have functioned similarly.[136]

130. E.g., 103–4, mention of the resurrection of the body; 147–48, prohibition of eating meat which has been torn by wild animals. For a discussion, see Van der Horst, *Pseudo-Phocylides*, 185–88, 211–12.

131. Stewart ('Democritus and the Cynics') has argued that the preservation of the Golden Words of Democritus was due to its use by Cynics. The Cynic Demetrius (in Seneca *De Beneficiis* 7.1–2) quoted sayings of Democritus extensively, and it is quite plausible that they also found acceptance among the so-called hedonistic Cynics (Bion, Menippus, Lucian).

132. See Burkert, *Lore and Science*, 166–68. As early as ca. 400 BCE Anaximander of Miletus produced a commentary on the *symbola* (Diels and Kranz, *Vorsokratiker* 58 C 6), and Aristotle (*On the Pythagoreans* frag. 192) quotes many of the sayings.

133. Aristotle *On the Pythagoreans* frag. 192; Diogenes Laertius 8.17–18; Plutarch *De liberis educandis* 12E.

134. Diogenes Laertius, who appears to quote a version of the Golden Words in 8.22–24, understood these maxims as instructions for disciples.

135. See Epicurus "Epistle to Herodotus" (apud Diogenes Laertius 10.35). Betz ('The Sermon on the Mount: Its Literary Genre and Function,' *Essays*, 1–16) shows that the *Kyriai doxai* functions as an epitome and was designated as such by later authors.

136. See P. von der Muehll, *Epicuri Epistulae tres et Ratas Sententiae* (Stuttgart: Teubner, 1966²) 60–69 [Gnomologium Vaticanum]; A. Vogliano, "Frammento di un nuovo 'Gnomologium Epicureum,'" *Studi Italiano di Filologia Classica* NS 13 (1936) 267–81.

In Christian circles, the *Gos. Thom.* provides a good example of a sayings collection which functioned presumably as an instrument of instruction. It is not possible to determine whether an organized community was involved. Like the Pythagorean *symbola*, the Thomas sayings are formulated so that they require interpretation in order to become efficacious. This interpretation may have been supplied in a communal or "school" context, or it may have depended upon individual "research" and insight.

Hermeneutic

In only a small number of gnomologia is the speaker represented as a father engaged in parental instruction. Both the *Sentences of Aesop* (influenced by the setting of the *Sayings of Ahikar*) and the *Dicta Catonis* are framed in this way, and in Ps-Isocrates the author speaks *in loco parentis*. It is not surprising that in keeping with the metaphor of domestic transmission of values the comportment of these collections is on the whole conservative, conventional and supportive of general societal values.

More commonly the authorial fiction employs not the metaphor of parental instruction but that of a sage or poet, usually of some distinction, handing on his wisdom. The interest in the legitimation of the sayings is clear in the preference for attribution of sayings to known sages. We have already noted in Ps-Phocylides the association of the sage and his sayings with a divine source. This is not peculiar to Ps-Phocylides. Chiron the centaur, to whom the Precepts of Chiron are attributed, was the son of Cronos and was known for his wisdom and piety. It was from him that Heracles is said to have learned virtue, and other heros learned hunting, medicine and other arts.[137] The divine origin of the teaching is clear in the case of the Hermetic collections, but also for Pythagorean teaching: Pythagoras was commonly held to be divine offspring, and his moral teachings were reputed to have derived from the Delphic oracle.[138] The close association of the Seven Sages with the Delphic oracle accounts, no doubt, for the fact that maxims such as "Know thyself," usually attributed to Chilon, are described by Seneca as

137. See Apollodorus *Bibliotheca* 1.9; Plutarch *Pericles*, 4. H. von Giesau, "Chiron," *Der kleine Pauly* 1 (Munich: Deutscher Taschenbuch Verlag, 1979) 1149.

138. On Pythagoras' divine origin, see Iamblichus *De vita pythagorica* 1–8; Diogenes Laertius 8.4–5. According to Aristoxenus (Diogenes Laertius 8.7, 21), Pythagoras received most of his ethical doctrines from Themistoclea the Delphic priestess, and Aristippus of Cyrene states that he was named Pythagoras because "he uttered the truth as infallibly as did the Pythian oracle" (8.21; Loeb 2:339).

oracular.[139] Finally, the incipit of the *Gos. Thom.* locates the ultimate source of the sayings in the "living Jesus"—a term over whose significance there is some uncertainty,[140] but which, when interpreted in the light of sayings such as 28, 38, 52, 59 and 111a, must connote a divine figure akin to Sophia.

It would go beyond the evidence to conclude that the attribution of sayings to a *divine* source was a characteristic of gnomologia; many do not display leanings in this direction. It would be more accurate to say that the evident pressure to seek legitimation for the sayings led in some cases to associations with various divine figures. But legitimation might be accomplished in other ways.

It is not possible to determine in every case the response which a gnomologium intended for itself. There are, however, important clues preserved in several of the collections. Three basic hermeneutical modes may be seen: the hermeneutic of "fittingness," that of obedience and assimilation of a wisdom ethos and that of "penetration and research."

1. In the prologue of the collection of Epicharmea (*P. Hibeh* 1), Axiopistus exhorts his readers to obey his maxims that they may become "cleverer and better." At the same time he is aware that skill is required if the maxims are to be applied well:

ποττὸ πρᾶγμα περιφέροντα τῶνδ᾽ ἀεὶ τὸ συμφέρον,

Bring round to your subject whichever of [the maxims] is apt. (1.9)[141]

This hermeneutical skill is precisely what was earlier termed "fittingness"—the art of knowing how to use maxims which are true and useful only if wisely applied, and which cannot be incorporated into any generally coherent theoretical framework. Although no statement of hermeneutic is given, the same mode of appropriation seems to be required for the *Menandri Monostichoi*, which occasionally offers conflicting maxims:

---

139. Seneca *Ad Lucilium epistulae* 94.27–28.

140. Although later gnostic works tend to situate revelation in a post-resurrectional setting, Koester ("One Jesus," 167), Robinson ("From Easter to Valentinus," 23) and J. A. Fitzmyer ("The Oxyrhynchus Logoi of Jesus and the Coptic Gospel According to Thomas," *Essays on the Semitic Background of the New Testament* [SBLSBS 5; Missoula, Mont.: Scholars Press, 1974] 368–69) point out that there is nothing in either Greek or Coptic to support a post-resurrectional interpretation. Robinson aptly observes the question of the setting of the sayings is largely irrelevant to Thomas. See further, Stevan L. Davies, *Gospel of Thomas*, 82–85.

141. Trans. Page, *Select Papyri* 3:443.

γυναικὶ μὴ πίστευε τὸν σαυτὸν βίον.
(142)
γυνὴ δικαία τοῦ βίου σωτηρία.
(149)

Do not entrust your life to a woman.
A just woman is life's salvation.

Publilius Syrus offers similar instances, requiring skillful application:

Bonum ad virum cito moritur iracundia.
(87)
Tarde sed graviter sapiens <mens> irascitur.
(695)

With the good man anger is quick to die.
A wise man grows angry slowly but seriously.

Or again:

Deliberando discitur sapientia.
(162)
Deliberando saepe perit occasio.
(163)

Deliberation teaches wisdom.
Deliberation often means a lost opportunity.

2. Another group of gnomologia prescribes a hermeneutic which is much closer to that of the instruction. They require not debate and reflection over the usefulness or applicability of maxims but obedience to them. It is this response which Ps-Phocylides expects of his listeners:

ταῦτα δικαιοσύνης μυστήρια, τοῖα βιεῦντες
ζωὴν ἐκτελέοιτ᾽ ἀγαθὴν μέχρι γήραος οὐδοῦ,

These are the mysteries of righteousness;
living thus may you live out a good life, right up to the threshhold of old age.
(229–30)

We are fortunate to have Epicurus' own words on the response which he intended for his instructions:

Exercise yourself in these and kindred precepts day and night, both by yourself and with a companion; then never, either in waking or in a dream, will you be disturbed, but will live like a god among men.[142]

---

142. Epicurus "Epistle to Menoeceus" (apud Diogenes Laertius 10.135; Loeb 2:659).

Epicurus required the memorizing of his maxims,[143] and later Epicurean communities took an oath of obedience to Epicurus and his teachings, an oath which made the Epicureans among the most conservative and stable of all philosophical sects.[144] Nevertheless, the intent was not to produce mimics but disciples who through observance of Epicurus' στοιχεῖα τοῦ καλῶς ζῆν[145] might attain to a perfect and untroubled state. Individual maxims are indicative of the comprehensive world view which is the real goal of Epicurean instruction. In this sense, the sayings require not only adherence, but study, reflection and interpretation.

Ps-Isocrates reflected on the relation between learning maxims and acquiring good character:

> But it is not possible for the mind to be so disposed [to noble behavior] unless one is fraught with many noble maxims; for, as it is the nature of the body to be developed by appropriate exercises, it is the nature of the soul to be developed by moral precepts. (*Ad Demonicum* 12; Loeb 1:11)

The function of precepts was further explored by Seneca some centuries later. In response to the Stoic Aristo who deprecated the use of precepts in philosophical training, Seneca insisted that precepts as well as ethical dogmatism could lead to a perfect condition of mind. Precepts arouse and catalyze virtue which is latent in the soul; they give specific advice where dogma gives general counsel; and they strengthen one's judgment concerning good and evil.[146] Posidonius of Apameia, a major influence on Seneca's thought, seems to have allowed an independent non-dogmatic section of his moral philosophy, sufficient for ordinary persons to inculcate order in the soul.[147] The *pars praeceptiva* employed precepts and *ethologiae*—characterizations or illustrations of various virtues, akin to chriae[148] —in order to educate regarding the good.

3. The Pythagorean *symbola* require a third type of hermeneutic. As noted above, many of the sayings were formulated in a deliberately

---

143. Epicurus "Epistle to Herodotus" (apud Diogenes Laertius 10.35). Cicero confirms this practice in *De finibus* 2.7.20: "...every good Epicurean has got by heart the master's *Kyriai Doxai*... since these brief aphorisms or maxims are held to be of sovereign efficacy for happiness" (Loeb 103).

144. Philodemus *Peri parresias* (A. Olivieri, ed., *Philodemi* ΠΕΡΙ ΠΑΡΡΗΣΙΑΣ *Libellus* [Leipzig: Teubner, 1914] frag. 45, 8–11). See De Witt, "Organization and Procedure," 205; Malherbe, "Self Definition," 47–48.

145. Epicurus "Epistle to Menoeceus" (apud Diogenes Laertius 10.123).

146. Seneca *Ad Lucilium Epistulae* 94.28–29, 32, 34.

147. Ibid., 95.65–67. See on this, A. Dihle, "Posidonius' System of Moral Philosophy," *JHS* 93 (1973) 50–57.

148. Quintilian (*Institutio oratoria* 1.9.3–4) lists sententiae, chriae and ethologiae as basic parts of Roman elementary education.

obscure fashion in order to prevent outsiders from understanding.[149] Some, it is true, were formulated quite unambiguously, even containing motive clauses: "One ought to beget children so as to leave behind for the gods people to worship them."[150] Nevertheless, the dominant understanding of the Pythagorean sayings was that they required not simple compliance but interpretation. Thus the prohibition against eating black-tail, while taken literally by some,[151] was understood by Plutarch and others as an injunction against spending too much time with persons of evil character.[152] Interpretation thus was integral to the process of assimilation of the ethos of Pythagorean teaching.

The incipit of the *Gos. Thom.* recommends a similar hermeneutic. In fact, *Gos. Thom.* 1 proposes a hermeneutic of appropriation which is perfectly symmetrical with its hermeneutic of production: the "living Jesus" speaks "hidden sayings" (λόγοι ἀπόκρυφοι) to Thomas, who writes them down; correspondingly, the reader is to penetrate the opacity of the written word by means of a hermeneutical key which would unlock the secret of life (i.e., not experiencing death). Here interpretation and salvation coincide.[153] The second saying further elucidates the soteriological and hermeneutical program of Thomas:

> Jesus said: Let him who seeks continue seeking until he finds. When he finds, he will become troubled. When he becomes troubled, he will be astonished, and he will rule over the All. (trans. Lambdin, *NHLE*, 118)

Given the context, which calls for the interpretation of Jesus' words, what seems to be described here is a process of "sapiential research" wherein the student passes through the perplexity of gnomic formulation to a state of "rest" and "rule." In this connection Davies has drawn attention to the parallel with Wis 6:17–20,[154] a sorites which traces a sapiential-soteriological progression beginning with "the most sincere desire for instruction" and ending with immortality, nearness to God

---

149. Iamblichus *De vita pythagorica* 161: "He was accustomed to reveal manifold and complex truths to his pupils in a symbolic manner, by means of very short sayings" [trans. by auth.].

150. Ibid., 86 [trans. by auth.]. Incidentally, Iamblichus mentions that some of the precepts have motive clauses, others do not and still others were supplied with motive clauses by outsiders.

151. Aristotle frag. 194; Porphyrius *Vita Pythagorae* 45; Diogenes Laertius 8.19. Diogenes (8.19) also reports a prohibition against eating erythrinus, the heart or womb of animals, beans and red mullet.

152. Plutarch *De liberis educandis* 12E. On this see Burkert, *Lore and Science,* 174–76.

153. The Pythagorean *Chryse epe* also have as their goal immortality for the student: ἢν δ᾽ ἀπολείψας σῶμα ἐς αἰθέρ᾽ ἐλεύθερον ἔλθῃς, ἔσσαι ἀθάνατος θεὸς ἄμβροτος, οὐκέτι θνητός (71–72).

154. Stevan L. Davies, *Gospel of Thomas,* 37–40.

and "a kingdom." Thomas' refrain "Whoever has ears to hear, let him hear" (8, 21, 24, 63, 65) continually alerts the reader to the need for penetration and interpretation if the sayings are to become efficacious.

There is no absolute dichotomy between the hermeneutics of "penetration and research" and "obedience" since in the latter, as Sirach shows, it is a matter not simply of the reception and memorization of traditional sayings, but also of reflection on their hidden meanings and implications (Sir 39:1–3). The goal of this mode of wisdom is to produce those who, through their assimilation of the sapiential ethos, become exponents of that ethos and sources of new wisdom. The difference between this and the hermeneutic prescribed by the Pythagorean *symbola* and the *Gos. Thom.* is one of degree: the deliberate use of obscure sayings only highlights the need for penetration and enlightened exegesis. And the result of the hermeneutical process is represented not simply as assimilation of a sapiential ethos, but as the acquisition of immortality.

CHRIAE COLLECTIONS

A third modality for presenting wise sayings is found in the chriae collection. The credit for the invention of this genre appears to go to Metrocles of Maroneia, a fourth-century Cynic who compiled the chriae of Diogenes of Sinope (Diogenes Laertius 6.33). The genre enjoyed continued popularity in Cynic circles, serving as a vehicle for propaganda, and was adopted by others for, among other things, elementary education.

Morphology

It is not possible to establish a consistent titular convention in chriae collections because many of the extant collections preserved on papyrus are missing both the incipit and colophon and some of those incorporated into Diogenes' *Lives* have lost their titles and prologues in the editorial process. As to the matter of attribution, however, there can be no doubt since the naming of the sage is intrinsic to the very form of chria. Some collections, moreover, were transmitted not only under the name of their sage/speaker, but also with the name of the collector: Metrocles of Maroneia, Hecaton, Zeno of Citium[155] and Lucian of Samosata. That all of these collectors were philosophers themselves is

---

155. See Diogenes Laertius 6:33 (Metrocles); 6.4, 32, 95; 7.26, 172 (Hecaton), 6.91 (Zeno).

an indication that chriae collections served important functions within philosophical circles, most likely for the preservation and propagation of the teaching of various "schools."

In only a few cases are exordia or prologues identifiable. Lucian begins his *Life of Demonax*, which consists of a long series of chriae, by giving his reasons for writing, citing both biographical and instructions motives:

> It is fitting to tell of Demonax for two reasons—that he be retained in memory by men of culture as far as I can bring it about, and that young men of good instincts who aspire to philosophy may not have to shape themselves by ancient precedents (παραδείγματα) alone, but may be able to set themselves a pattern (κανών) from our modern world and to copy that man, the best of all the philosophers whom I know about.[156]

Continuing with a brief biographical preface, he recounts Demonax' birth, his precociousness as a youth, his distinguished teachers, similarities to Socrates and Diogenes and his high repute among the Athenians. Demonax' acceptance was not entirely universal, however. Lucian relates an incident designed to strengthen the parallels between Socrates and Demonax:

> He too had his Anytus and his Meletus who combined against him and brought the same charges that their predecessors brought against Socrates, asserting that he had never been known to sacrifice and was the only man in the community uninitiated into the Eleusian mysteries.[157]

Unlike Socrates, however, Demonax endeared himself to the mob with some clever though caustic remarks, and thereby escaped stoning.

A narrative prologue also occurs in the second-century *Sentences of Secundus*,[158] in this instance emphasizing the motif of the ordeal or testing of the sage. After giving the reasons for Secundus' "Pythagorean" vow of silence, there is an account of his encounter with Hadrian, who threatens to execute the sage if he refuses to speak (while privately instructing the executioner to execute him if he does speak). Unable to coerce Secundus, Hadrian recognizes the superiority of the "law" to which the philosopher adheres, and begins to ask questions of Secundus. After delivering (in writing) a rather pointed speech on providence in which he displays the typically Cynic virtue of παρρησία, Secundus

156. Trans. A. M. Harmon, *Lucian* (LCL; 8 vols.; Cambridge: Harvard Univ. Press, 1979) 1:142–43 (all references will be to the pages of the Harmon edition).

157. Loeb 1:149. For Anytus and Meletus, see Plato *Apol.* 23E-28A.

158. On the dating, see B. E. Perry, *Secundus the Silent Philosopher* (Ithaca, N.Y.: Cornell Univ. Press, 1964) 1, 22 (all references will be to the pages of the Perry edition).

responds, again in writing, to twenty questions put him by the emperor.[159]

Both the prologue of *Demonax* and that of *Secundus* contain apologetic features which serve to legitimate these two otherwise unknown philosophers.[160] Lucian achieves this by his laudatory preface, and especially by the comparisons with Socrates and Diogenes. The entire preface of *Secundus* focuses on the "Pythagorean" vow of silence taken by the sage,[161] and the testing of this by Hadrian. It serves, presumably, to underline the legitimacy of Secundus' claim to observe the Pythagorean way of life and implies that he is a capable exponent of its teaching.[162]

The appearance of the motifs of the reproach of the sage or his rejection or his ordeal is not surprising. Cynic teaching, following Antisthenes, had emphasized that suffering and pain were beneficial,[163] and Dio Chrysostom represents Diogenes as the ideal Cynic "king," solitary, poor, homeless, unrecognized and suffering.[164] Heracles, Odysseus and Socrates were for this reason favorite examples in Cynic teaching.[165] Dio uses the example of Heracles to show that it is the duty

159. *Secundus*, 68–75. Perry (*Secundus*, 4–6) agrees that this collection is best classified as a chriae collection, but observes that the question-and-answer format finds parallels in Plutarch's *Banquet of the Seven Sages* (esp. 153C-D). He notes, moreover, that the opening sequence bears some relation to martyrologies: "Secundus is idealized and dramatized as a man who accepts death fearlessly in defense of his principles and in defiance of the state" (p. 6). See further, L. W. Daly, "The Altercatio Hadriani et Epicteti philosophi and the Question-and-Answer Dialogues," *Illinois Studies in Language and Literature* 24 (1939) 1:50–51.

160. Apart from a few scattered anecdotes, Lucian is the only source for our knowledge of Demonax. Philostratus (*Vita Sophistarum* 1.26) and the Suidas Lexicon (ad loc.) mentions an Athenian Secundus who was a rhetorician. But apart from the fact that both lived in Athens, nothing said of the rhetorician coincides with what is contained in *Secundus*.

161. The author of *Secundus* evidently operates under the misconception that the Pythagorean vow of silence was lifelong. It was in fact a five-year probationary vow. See Diogenes Laertius 8.10; Philostratus *Vita Apollonii* 1.14–15. It is unlikely that any Pythagorean would risk martyrdom for the sake of a probationary vow of silence. The sensational nature of the story along with its misconceptions indicates perhaps the popular character of *Secundus*.

162. Apart from the mention of the vow of silence (see n. 161 above), nothing in the prologue identifies Secundus as Pythagorean. His dress is Cynic (*Secundus*, 68–69). E. Zeller (*Die Philosophie der Griechen* [3 vols.; Leipzig: Reisland, 1922–23⁵] 3/2:125 n. 2) states that no influence of Pythagorean doctrine is evident in the "definitions" (*Secundus*, 78–91). Perry (*Secundus*, 9) emphasizes the eclecticism of Secundus, which includes Cynic contempt of women. Only in regard to *form* does it imitate Pythagorean teaching. Hadrian's questions are all framed in the τί ἐστι form typical of the Pythagorean ἀκούσματα.

163. Diogenes Laertius 6.2: "He [Antisthenes] demonstrated that pain is a good thing by instancing the great Heracles and Cyrus, drawing the one example from the Greek world and the other from the barbarians" (Loeb 2:5). The fundamental treatment of this subject is Höistad, *Cynic Hero*.

164. Dio Chrysostom *Or.* 9.9–10. See Höistad, *Cynic Hero*, 195–96.

165. For a thorough documentation, see Höistad, *Cynic Hero*, 195–220.

of the philosopher to submit to ill treatment and suffering; it is this in fact which reveals him to be the true king (*Or.* 47). The Cynic's response to threat and ignominy is patience, taking the form of witty or ironical or caustic words which ridicule or reprimand those who insult or abuse him.[166] By their endurance of rejection and threats, Demonax and Secundus show themselves to be true sages (at least by Cynic standards).

Legitimation is achieved by a more complicated device in *m. 'Abot.* *'Abot* 1:1–15 employs a "transmissional sorites"[167] which traces the transmission of the Torah from God's giving of the Law to Moses, through Joshua, the elders and the prophets, to the men of the Great Synagogue and a series of pairs of authorities ending with Hillel and Shammai.[168] Into each link of the sorites from the men of the Great Synagogue to Hillel and Shammai is inserted a trio of sayings, usually admonitions introduced by אומר.[169] The composition not only traces the "historical" transmission of the Torah (from a rabbinic perspective) and sets up a chain of authoritative interpreters, but also endows the maxims and precepts of each master with a special force which accrues to them by virtue of their association with the Torah and its legitimate tradents.

As both the extant collections which are labeled χρεῖαι and the ancient discussions of the chria show, the form admitted of a range of structures. While attribution to a named authority was a constant, a chria could consist in an aphorism introduced by ἔλεγε or ἔφη ("declaratory chria"), or it might be framed as the response to a question (ἐρωτηθεὶς δέ ποτε . . . ἔφη) or as an exclamation evoked by some circumstance. It might consist of a single grammatical period, or several. It could involve an action or a saying or both. And it might even contain two sets of pronouncements, one answering the other ("the double chria").[170]

---

166. E.g., Dio *Or.* 9.9: Like Odysseus, Diogenes endured insults at the Isthmian games. "For he really resembled a king and lord who in the guise of a beggar moved among his slaves and menials while they caroused in ignorance of his identity, and yet was patient with them, drunken as they were and crazed by reason of ignorance and stupidity" (Loeb 1:407–9).

167. See Fischel, "Use of Sorites," esp. 124–29. Fischel points out the similarity between *'Abot* 1:1 and Diogenes Laertius 9.116 which relates the succession of philosophers from Timon to Sextus Empiricus and Saturninus. See also the seminal essay of Bi(c)kerman, "La Chaîne."

168. After some intervening sayings the chain is resumed with Johanan b. Zakkai (2:9) who passed the Torah on to five disciples (2:10). It is usually held that the original chain terminated with Hillel and Shammai and that Johanan is a later addition. See Finkelstein, "Pirke Aboth," esp. 126; Saldarini, "End of the Rabbinic Chain."

169. The three-saying structure breaks down toward the end of the chain.

170. See Quintilian 1.9.4 and the *Progymnasmata* of Theon, Hermogenes and Aphthonius (Spengel, *Rhetores Graeci* 2:96–106 [Theon], 5–7 [Hermogenes], 23–25 [Aphthonius]).

Most of the extant chriae collections display this variety in their sayings; in only a few is there a noticeable homogeneity. From a formal perspective the most consistent collection is *Secundus*. All of the sayings or "definitions" are framed as responses to the question τί ἐστι . . . ; recalling the form characteristic of the Pythagorean *acousmata*.[171] Of the sub-collections which constitute *m. 'Abot*, some are relatively homogeneous in form.[172] As noted above, 1:1–15 contains admonitions and maxims arranged in groups of three and attributed to the sages in the transmissional sorites. Another collection of first-century masters (3:1–14) is similarly homogeneous, consisting mainly of maxims. However, the small cluster of Hillel sayings in 2:5–7 is more varied, with five admonitions (2:5), five aphoristic descriptions of types of humans (2:6), a circumstantial chria in Aramaic (2:7a) and a series of sayings taking the form "the more . . . the more . . ." (2:7b). In their formal heterogeneity, the Hillel sayings resemble the majority of papyrus chriae collections and those preserved by Diogenes and Lucian. Simple sayings, introduced with "he said," are set alongside a variety of more complex chriic forms (responsorial; circumstantial), some of them consisting of several grammatical periods.[173]

In an important analysis of the Diogenes chriae in Diogenes Laertius, Gunnar Rudberg noted some attempt at the ordering of small clusters of chriae.[174] There are instances of grouping by formal analogy,[175] association of sayings by catchwords or a series of catchwords[176] and, most commonly of all, grouping of chriae by common theme or subject

---

171. See above n. 162.

172. Finkelstein ("Pirke Aboth," 121–32) identified four major constituents, but in a later work (*Mabo le-Massektot Abot we-Abot d'Rabbi Natan* [New York: Jewish Theological Society, 1950]) added a fifth: (1) The chain of authorities and their maxims (1:1–15); (2) sayings of Johanan and his disciples (2:8–14); (3) sayings of various sages (3:1–14); (4) four who "entered the orchard" (3:17–20; 4:1–2, 20); (5) numerical sayings (5:1–18). Saldarini (*Scholastic Rabbinism*, 33) prefers to treat (3) and (4) as one section. Finkelstein ("Pirke Aboth," 15 n. 6) notes several other collections, including a cluster of Hillel sayings (2:5–7).

173. In the small chriae collection *P. Bouriant* 1 (5 chriae all introduced by ἰδών) some formal homogeneity is to be observed. However, the larger papyrus collections (*P. Vindob.* 29946; *P. Mich.* 41; *P. Hibeh* 17; *P. Hibeh* 182), and the chriae of Antisthenes, Bion, Crates and Diogenes in Diogenes Laertius, and Lucian's *Demonax* reveal little effort to use chriae of a single type or formal character.

174. Rudberg, "Diogenes-Tradition," esp. 39–42.

175. E.g., 6.65: four chriae in which Diogenes' question is introduced by "are you not ashamed..."

176. E.g., the chriae in 6.60–62 seem to be connected by the words "fig tree," "dog" and "courtesan."

matter.[177] Ordering is neither consistent nor complete, however. There are instances of doublets (6.46, 69) and considerable portions of the collection lack a recognizable order altogether. It is similar with other chriae collections of Diogenes. The Antisthenes (6.3–9), Bion (4.47–51) and Crates (6.91–93) chriae are varied in form and do not appear to be organized either by catchword, formal principle or subject matter. On the other hand, the Simonides chriae (*P. Hibeh* 17) all concern expenses, and the very fragmentary collection of sayings of Socrates (*P. Hibeh* 182) seems to be organized about the themes of Socrates and his wife and the vicious nature of desires. Lucian begins his collection with three sayings relating Demonax' opposition to sophists, but thereafter it is difficult to ascertain any ordering principle.

This schematic survey scarcely does justice to any one of the collections mentioned. Our intention is merely to show that the structuring techniques used in chriae collections are essentially those found in instructions and gnomologia: catchword, formal analogy and subject matter.[178] However, three differences are to be observed: first, because of the latitude in chriic forms, collections often contain strings of maxims or admonitions introduced only by "he said" interspersed with more complex responsorial or circumstantial chriae (or vice versa). In other words, small gnomic clusters could exist within chriae collections. Second, because of the nature of the chria, it is uncommon to find a series of sayings which are rhetorically structured to lead to a conclusion.[179] Chriae are self-contained units and although two or three may be linked by a common theme, they are seldom structured to build to a single conclusion. And third, whereas both instructions and gnomologia on occasion display careful (usually thematic) organization throughout the entire compositions, or at least in significant portions of them, chriae collections on the whole display somewhat less organization.

Setting and Tone

Although chriae were eventually employed in elementary education and as models for rhetorical training,[180] this was not their only, or indeed

177. E.g., 6.34, two sayings on Demosthenes; 6.36, two "discipleship" chriae, 6.37–38, criticism of piety; 6.40–41, several chriae mentioning animals, etc.
178. The medieval *Gnomologium Vaticanum*, a collection of chriae or apophthegms, is organized alphabetically by the name of the sage.
179. Occasionally one finds a syllogism *within* a chria. E.g., Diogenes Laertius 6.37: "[Diogenes] used to reason thus: 'All things belong to the gods. The wise are friends of the gods and friends hold things in common. Therefore all things belong to the wise'" (Loeb 2:39). On the "syllogistic chria," see Theon (Spengel, *Rhetores Graeci* 2:99).
180. See Quintilian 1.9; Seneca *Ad Lucilium Epistulae* 33; Diogenes Laertius 6.31;

their original, use. From the fact that it was philosophers such as Metrocles and Hecaton who first gathered the Diogenes chriae, Colson inferred that chriae served in philosophical propaganda.[181] This conclusion finds support in the statement of Lucian (quoted above) which makes clear the paradigmatic function of chriae for those "young men who aspire to philosophy."[182] Seneca, somewhat reluctantly, complied with a request of Lucilius for a collection of sayings of Zeno, Cleanthes, Chrysippus and other Stoics, but expressed the view that despite the utility of maxims, this was not the best way to learn philosophy.[183]

In the case of the Cynic chriae, their precise function is not entirely clear. Since Cynics were not organized into communities along the lines of the Epicureans or Pythagoreans, it seems unlikely that the chriae collections could have had the same function as the *Kyriai doxai* or the Pythagorean *acousmata*. But in spite of their reputation as loners, Cynics did take disciples. It may have been for the sake of such disciples that chriae were gathered. Seneca's Cynic friend Demetrius subscribed to the view that for philosophical education a few practical sayings were preferable to vast learning of a speculative nature.[184] Chriae would have served his purposes admirably.

That '*Abot* was employed in a setting akin to Greek philosophical schools is clear from its contents. The chain in 1:1–15, later extended to include Johanan b. Zakkai and his students (2:8–14), clearly served to legitimate the teaching tradition of early Pharisaic and rabbinic schools, probably even prior to the framing of Mishnah.[185] Although there is no proof of it, some of the smaller collections in '*Abot* such as the Hillel words (2:5–7)[186] or those of Johanan and his disciples (2:8–14) may also have been in use in the rabbinic academies prior to their incorporation into Mishnah.

There is no "typical" tone to be found among the chriae collections

---

Marrou, *History of Education*, 156, 172–75; Spencer, "Biographical Apophthegms," 99–107.

181. Colson, "Quintilian," 150.

182. Lucian *Demonax* (Loeb 1:142–43).

183. *Ad Lucilium Epistulae* 33.4–9. Contrast the view of Seneca's friend Demetrius (cited below).

184. Seneca *De Beneficiis* 7.1.3—2.1.

185. It is usually agreed that the original chain in 1:1–15 put Shammai before Hillel (see Finkelstein, "Pirke Aboth," 125–26; Saldarini, "End of the Rabbinic Chain," 99–100). This being so, it must derive from a time of Shammaite dominance, i.e., prior to ca. 90 CE. See in this regard, Bi(c)kerman, "La Chaîne," 261. Saldarini ("End of the Rabbinic Chain," 99 n. 10) argues that Johanan was added ca. 90.

186. See Georgi, "Records of Jesus," 538–39.

here treated. The Diogenes chriae exemplify the Cynic cardinal virtues, παρρησία, αὐτάρχεια and ἀναίδεια,[187] and frequently relate Diogenes' attacks on custom and convention, his ridicule of contemporaries and his anti-social asceticism. By contrast, the sayings of Crates are much milder,[188] and those of Bion betray a combination of Cynicism and hedonism. Demonax appears to represent the milder form of Cynicism, in contrast to the austere, almost misanthropic attitude of his contemporary Peregrinus.[189] Παρρησία and αὐτάρχεια are still the mark of his chriae, but not ἀναίδεια. Custom is held up to ridicule, but Demonax did not cultivate the vagrant and anti-social characteristics of the austere Cynics. Lucian describes him as a model of Cynic *philanthropia*:

> He never was known to make an uproar or excite himself or get angry, even if he had to rebuke someone; though he assailed sins, he forgave sinners, thinking that one should pattern after doctors, who heal sicknesses but feel no anger at the sick. (Loeb 1:146–47)

The Socrates chriae of *P. Hibeh* 182 reflect Cynic influence in their description of desires as "vicious" and in their condemnation of wealth;[190] but anti-social or misanthropic tendencies are not to be observed.

Though Cynicism exerted profound influence on rabbinic thought,[191] the chriae of *'Abot* do not place the Pharisaic and early rabbinic masters in confrontation with their peers. Nor is παρρησία a virtue for these teachers. The rabbis are not "Jewish Cynics." The central foci of the chriae of *'Abot* are Torah and the study of Torah and the virtues which flow from these: piety, discipline, humility, fraternal relations among scholars and good works.[192] All this is set within a framework which emphasizes the historical continuity and coherence of the teaching tradition of early rabbinism.

Hermeneutic

Whereas in the instruction and to a lesser extent in gnomologia, the metaphor of parental instruction was prominent in the construction of an authorial fiction, for chriae collections this metaphor is almost

---

187. See Dudley, *History of Cynicism*, 28–39.
188. Ibid., 42–53.
189. On this, see Malherbe, "Self-Definition," 50–59.
190. See E. G. Turner, "Life and Apophthegms of Socrates," *The Hibeh Papyri, Part II* (London: Egypt Exploration Society, 1955) 26–28.
191. See Fischel, "Cynicism and the Ancient Near East," 372–411; idem, "Story and History," 59–88; idem, "Transformation of Wisdom," 67–101.
192. See Saldarini, *Scholastic Rabbinism*, 9–23.

entirely wanting. The earliest title for *'Abot, mêlê 'abot*[193] conveys this idea, but this is virtually the only hint of the metaphor in the entire collection. The dominant hermeneutical model is that of a sage or a series of sages passing on wisdom to their fellows in the context of a continuous school tradition.

In the Cynic chriae the parental metaphor likewise is absent, and indeed, inapposite considering the general tone of collections. In his manifestation of παρρησία the sage stands over against society, not in continuity with it. This is obviously true of Diogenes who ridiculed the values and institutions of his contemporaries, but also true of the much milder Demonax. Yet while the Cynic was a solitary "voice in the wilderness," there is evidence from the first and second centuries CE that some regarded the Cynic as an envoy of God, sent, as Epictetus puts it,

> partly as a messenger, in order to show [mortals] that in questions of good and evil they have gone astray, and are seeking the true nature of the good and the evil where it is not, but where it is they never think; and partly, in the words of Diogenes, when he was taken off to Philip, after the battle of Chareoneia, as a scout. For the Cynic is truly a scout, to find out what things are friendly to men and what hostile; and he must first do his scouting accurately, and on returning must tell the truth, not driven by fear to designate as enemies those who are not such, nor in any other fashion be distraught or confused by his external impression. (*Diss.* 3.22.23–25; Loeb 2:139)

No convincing generalization can be made from a comment which may reflect Epictetus' Stoicism more than Cynic self-understanding. Some Cynics were ready to claim divine authorization for their mission,[194] but others, including Demonax, were hostile to religion. Thus it would be dangerous to conclude with respect to the *genre* of chriic collection that there was any immanent tendency to associate the sage with the divine, though this clearly was one of the hermeneutical options.

What mode of response does the chriae collection envisage? In most cases, we are able only to make guesses on the basis of the contents and general tone of the collections. *Secundus*, which consists of "definitions" on a range of subjects from ethics to cosmology, apparently functions as a kind of catechism for an eclectic popular philosophy which is framed in the guise of Pythagorean teaching.

---

193. *b. B. Qam.* 30a.

194. *Ep. of Socrates* 1.7 (A. J. Malherbe, ed., *The Cynic Epistles* [SBLSBS 12; Missoula, Mont.: Scholars Press, 1977] 222–23); Dio Chrysostom, *Or.* 13.9–11. On this, see Malherbe, "Self-Definition," 57–59.

With only one or two exceptions, the chriae of '*Abot* are what Theon termed declaratory (ἀποφαντική); the emphasis falls upon the saying of the sage, usually an admonition. The hermeneutic which '*Abot* appears to require is similar to that of Sirach: reception of the words of the sages, meditation upon them and assimilation of the ethos of the school tradition. Jose b. Joezer counsels,

> Let thy house be a meeting-house for the Sages and sit amid the dust of their feet and drink in their words with thirst. (1:4; Danby 446)

The advice of Johanan's student, Eliezer b. Hyrcanus, acknowledges the powerful, even dangerous, quality of wise words—words which require special attention and care in their appropriation:

> Warm thyself before the fire of the Sages, but be heedful of their glowing coals lest thou be burned, for their bite is the bite of a jackal and their sting is the sting of a scorpion and their hiss the hiss of a serpent, and all their words are like coals of fire. (2:10; Danby 449)

Since relatively few of the sayings are imperatives, the hermeneutic appropriate to the Cynic chriae is not a matter of obedience to the admonitions of the sage. Both Lucian's introduction to *Demonax* and the use to which Diogenes Laertius puts the chriae which he inherited indicate that chriae could be interpreted in a biographical way. This mode of hermeneutic is even operative in the occasional chria in '*Abot* (e.g., 1:7a, 8). However, biography is not the sole purpose of chriae. As the popular etymology indicates, chriae were preserved because they were "useful for life" (χρειώδης τῷ βίῳ).[195] The response appropriate to chriae is imitation or assimilation of the virtues displayed by the sage. Lucian, it will be remembered, states that his account of Demonax' chriae was for the purpose of providing παραδείγματα for those who aspire to philosophy. Although the chriae of famed Cynics were no doubt memorized by students, their purpose was presumably to provide ready examples of the παρρησία and αὐτάρχεια which were to be the mark of every Cynic. In this sense they were not simply to be rehearsed, but rather their guiding spirit was to be assimilated and expressed in all of the actions and words of the student.

Chriae collections, then, embody two moments, one biographical and "historicizing," and the other contemporizing and "useful." In collections

---

195. Theon *Progymnasmata* 5 (Spengel, *Rhetores Graeci* 2:97). *PSI* 85 contains a series of definitions pertaining to the chria, including the statement that it is called "chria," διὰ τὸ χρ(ε)ιῶδ<η>ς [ε]ῖν[αι] (Teresa Lodi, ed., *Papiri Greci e Latini* [Florence: Ariani, 1912] 1:157–58).

such as '*Abot* it is the "useful" dimension which is the more prominent; in *Demonax* biographical interest emerges, all the more so with Lucian's use of a biographical prologue. Evidently, the distinction between the chriae collection and the *bios* is a fine one.[196]

196. See Arnaldo Momigliano, *The Development of Greek Biography* (Cambridge: Harvard Univ. Press, 1971) 72–73.

8

Conclusion

From the foregoing sketch of three of the modalities for presenting wise sayings, important affinities with each stage of Q's compositional history are immediately evident. I have argued above that the formative component in Q consisted of a group of six "wisdom speeches" which were hortatory in nature and sapiential in their mode of argumentation. This stratum was subsequently expanded by the addition of groups of sayings, many framed as chriae, which adopted a critical and polemical stance with respect to Israel. The most recent addition to Q seems to have been the temptation story, added in order to provide an aetiology and legitimation for Q's radical ethic, but introducing at the same time a biographical dimension into the collection.

THE FORMATIVE COMPONENT
OF Q AS "INSTRUCTION"

The formative stratum has the strongest generic contacts with the genre of "instruction." Several observations support the cogency of this classification. First, while no title survives, lost perhaps like that of Prov 22:17—24:22 in the editorial process, it is clear from internal indications (6:46; 9:57–62; 10:3, 16; 14:26, 27) that these were transmitted as words of Jesus.[1] Second, the preponderance of the imperative signals proximity to the instructional genre. Clusters of imperatives, or imperatives with motive or final clauses, or supporting or summarizing aphorisms form

---

1. Koester ("Apocryphal and Canonical Gospels") suggests that Q may have circulated anonymously at first. I do not think this very likely in view of Q sayings such as 6:46; 9:57–58; 10:3, etc., which virtually demand attachment to a named sage, and more particularly, in view of the almost universal tendency of sayings genres to attach themselves to named sages. This obviously is no guarantee of the ultimate authenticity of any of Q's sayings. As in other cases, sayings from other sources may have been borrowed by Q and placed on Jesus' lips.

the bases and the central components of each of the six major speeches.[2] Moreover, in the structure of these imperatives, Q is not simply an agglomeration of sayings, but resembles the organizing techniques of some of the more sophisticated instructions.[3] Admonitions are organized thematically in a manner resembling Amenemope, the Counsels of Wisdom and parts of Sirach. In four of Q's speeches (6:20b–49; 9:57—10:16; 12:2–7, 11–12; 13:24—14:34), a relatively sophisticated structure is observed. Each cluster begins with a programmatic saying or group of sayings, setting the tone for the cluster (6:20b–23; 9:57–62; 12:2; 13:24), and then follows the imperatival or hortatory section. The instruction on prayer (11:2–4, 9–13) commences with Jesus' own prayer, which undoubtedly serves as a paradigm of prayer. The use of programmatic introductory sayings was also seen in Merikare and Sirach. And like several of the instructions in Prov 1—9, Q 6:20b–49 and 13:24—14:35 conclude with a warning to the prospective disciple.

Third, this stratum of Q falls within the parameters of the possible settings of instructions. We have noted a rather broad range of settings, from instructions of a crown prince (Merikare, Amenemhat [I]) or high royal official (Ptahhotep) to general wisdom instruction (Ankhsheshonq; Prov 1—9), to instructions within a religious community (Apa Antonius; *Teach. Silv.*). The Q speeches were presumably formulated for a setting of the latter type, although we have noted indications that some of the components may have functioned earlier in the more specific *Sitz* of instructions for wandering missionaries.[4]

There are two notable departures from the typical form of instruction. In contrast to the almost universal mark of the Egyptian instruction, and a usual feature in the other Near Eastern instructions, Q does not invoke the metaphor of parental instruction. And in contrast to the generally conservative comportment of the instruction, Q presents an ethic of radical discipleship which reverses many of the conventions which allow a society to operate, such as principles of retaliation, the orderly borrowing and lending of capital, appropriate treatment of the dead, responsible self-provision, self-defense and honor of parents. These two departures from the instructional form are clearly related. For a collection which advocates an ethic such as Q does, speaking, for example, of hating one's parents (14:26), the metaphor *par excellence* of historical

---

2. Q 6:27–35, 36–38, 41–42 (forming the basis for 6:20b–49); 10:4–11 (for 9:57—10:16); 11:2–4, 9–13; 12:3, 4–7, 11–12 (for 12:2–12); 12:22b–31, 33–34; 13:24 (for 13:24—14:35).
3. See appendix II for a formal analysis of the Q speeches.
4. See above, pp. 202, 220–21.

and social continuity would obviously be inappropriate. Q's rejection of the "wisdom of order" in favor of the "wisdom of the kingdom" forced it to adopt an authorial metaphor less fraught with conservative tone, namely that of a teacher (κύριος, 6:46).

In these two respects, Q has moved towards the form of gnomologium which does not habitually invoke the metaphor of parental instruction, and which on occasion contains instructions which are more appropriate to a small religious or philosophical community than to society in general. Moreover, gnomologia such as Ps-Isocrates (*Ad Demonicum*) and Ps-Phocylides display, like Q, consistent thematic structuring of their sayings.

Since the incipit, one of the usual points at which there are indications of the position and status of the projected speaker, is missing, the "authorial fiction" can be determined only through internal features. Q 6:40 and 6:46 imply that the speaker is represented as a teacher or master, and the following warning (6:47–49) implies that his words are to be taken with the utmost seriousness (though this warning in itself does not distinguish Q from other sapiential instructions which predict shipwreck for those who do not hearken). In 9:57–58 the teacher presents himself as a model to be imitated in his radical lifestyle, and the same is implied by 14:26, 27 and 17:33. While the metaphor of teacher or master is an important one, Q 10:3, 16 implies somewhat more. In these texts Jesus appears as the one who initiates the eschatological harvest and as the one whose message, as carried by his envoys, is equivalent to the voice of God. Steck rightly notes that 10:16 in effect places Jesus in the position of God or Sophia, as sender of the eschatological envoys.[5] This association of Jesus as the speaker of the wise sayings, with a heavenly source such as God or Sophia, is quite intelligible in the context of the instructional genre. Similar associations were observed in Prov 1—9, Sirach, Shube-awilum and many of the Egyptian instructions.

The strong potential—though not an ineluctable pressure—of the genre to associate the speaker of the wise words with the Divine makes intelligible the developments such as are visible in *Gos. Thom.* 1, which represents Jesus as a divine or semi-divine mediator of secret revelation. But developments within Q itself may also be explained on this basis: in the first major redaction and supplementation of the Q sapiential speeches, further indications of the functional unity of Jesus with

5. See above, p. 197 n. 113.

Sophia are introduced. Q 7:35 represents Jesus and John as Sophia's children; 11:49–51a places an oracle of Sophia in Jesus' mouth and then (11:51b) has Jesus resume the oracle in his own words; 13:34–35 appears to be another Sophia saying; and most dramatically, 10:22 draws upon the mythologoumena of Sophia for its description of the relation of the Father to the Son. In other words, the development seen at the second (polemical) stage of Q's literary development is an extension of the potentialities which were at work already at the first (sapiential) stage.

Throughout, the radical ethic of Q is associated with the proclamation of the kingdom and with the conviction that the kingdom is dawning. Kingdom sayings appear at the beginning of several of the speeches: 6:20b; 9:60, 62; 11:2–4 and 12:2,[6] and thereby bring ethics and eschatology into a close relationship. The imperatives are far from parenetic supplements to the kerygma. On the contrary, in their very structure they point to the presence of the kingdom. In an important article on the uses of proverbs in the Synoptic tradition, William Beardslee noted the confrontational, paradoxical and hyperbolic character of many of the Q aphorisms (and imperatives).[7] The intensified wisdom of Q plays a negative function of "deconstructing" the former world view of the hearer. Commenting on Q 17:33, Beardslee states,

> Here the reversal situation is so sharp that the imagination is jolted out of its vision of a continuous connection between one situation and the other [viz., losing and preserving one's life].[8]

Or again:

> . . . the proverb does have a distinctive usage in the Synoptics in which paradox and hyperbole challenge the typical proverbial stance of making a continuous project out of one's life, but a usage which paradoxically views this challenge as itself a way of life.[9]

The intensified wisdom of Q serves a positive role too. It not only disorients the hearer with respect to ordinary existence (e.g., with sayings such as 9:57–58, 59–60; 12:33–34; 14:26, 27; 16:13; 17:33), but it also reorients towards the new reality of the kingdom (6:20b) and God (6:35, 36; 11:9–13; 12:4–7, 22–31, 33–34). In this way, the sapiential speeches in Q, by means of their radical comportment, serve a properly kerygmatic function and point to the radical nature of the kingdom

6. On 12:2 as an implied Kingdom saying, see p. 210.
7. Beardslee, "Uses of the Proverb."
8. Ibid., 67.
9. Ibid., 69.

which is in the process of manifesting itself. Correspondingly, the imperatives specify the type of radical ethic which is to be characteristic of those who have responded appropriately to this new reality.

Thus the hermeneutic of appropriation can be described as the response to, and assimilation of, the radical mode of existence which the kingdom brings. This is in effect a transformation of the hermeneutic fundamental to the instruction. For the instruction, adequate response was measured not simply in terms of memorization and rehearsal of the various imperatives, but assimilation of the ethos of Wisdom or Maat. Both are conceived of as order immanent in the cosmos—an order to which all human action should conform. In Q, however, matters are more complicated. It is not the assimilation of "this-worldly order" but that of a new principle of human order. This new order is not in continuity with the old and requires a completely new response. Nevertheless, the ideological structure of Q must be seen in its relation to the structure of the wisdom instruction. Although Q infuses the form with new content, and although it shifts from a presupposition of this-worldly order to eschatological order, the basic hermeneutic of the instruction is preserved.

Can it be said that an instruction of this sort is "contemporizing" to the exclusion of all historicizing features? Several clarifications are in order here. In the first place, throughout the analysis of the "wisdom speeches" I have insisted that the dominant mode of address is sapiential, not prophetic. There is no indication that the λέγω ὑμῖν is that of the Exalted Lord speaking though the mouth of his prophets; it is rather the λέγω ὑμῖν of a teacher of wisdom speaking to followers. Q lacks the repetitive forms characteristic of prophet genres: "The word of the Lord came to . . . ," "Thus says the Lord," and "As I live." The mode of persuasion is not prophetic—by appeal to the authority of God—but sapiential, by rhetorical question and appeal to observation of nature and of ordinary human relations. Second, as a mode of linguistic organization, the instruction embodies two moments, one historicizing, signaled by the attachment of the wise sayings to a named sage (whether ancient or contemporary), and the other contemporizing. Moreover, it embodies both a "horizontal" (historical) dimension, and a "vertical" one in its potential to associate the speaker with the Divine. It is true that the historical and horizontal moment may be emphasized, as in Ahikar or Ankhsheshonq, through the use of a historical or biographical introduction, and likewise true that in instructions which lack such an exordium the historical aspect recedes. But it is nonetheless present, just as the contemporizing aspect is present even in an instruction such as Merikare which is ostensibly addressed only to ancient royalty.

While the *Gos. Thom.* seems to have developed the contemporizing side of the generic dialectic, Q moved in another direction. This movement may be seen in two phases, that of the redaction of the original speeches under the influence of the motif of the coming judgment, and that of the addition of the temptation story.

Q AS A CHRIAE COLLECTION

I have argued above that the wisdom speeches or, more properly, the "sapiential instructions" which represent the formative literary component were expanded by the addition of a variety of sayings of Jesus and John the Baptist. The *motifs* characteristic of this redactional stratum concern the announcement of judgment and the castigation of "this generation" for its lack of response to the preaching of the kingdom. Polemic replaces parenesis as the dominant tone. And the sapiential admonitions with all of their many auxiliary forms and figures are modified by the addition of prophetic announcements of judgment and apocalyptic words. This redactional stratum is also characterized by chriic forms.[10] In fact many of the judgment sayings are specifically formulated as the response of Jesus and John to specific circumstances or questions, i.e., as chriae. While these prophetic sayings may have originally circulated as sayings of the Exalted Lord speaking through early Christian prophets, in their literary setting in Q they are framed in a historicizing manner. Despite sayings such as Q 7:35 and 11:49–51 which interpret John and Jesus as prophetic envoys of Sophia, sayings are presented as sayings *of John and Jesus* rather than as oracles of Sophia. And there are no indications that Q represented itself to its intended audience as oracles of the Exalted Lord.

The expansion of the original set of sapiential instructions is quite intelligible when seen in the light of the compositional techniques typical of instructions, gnomologia and chriae collections. In all three, association of sayings by catchword and by thematic affinity is frequently observed. It has already been noted that the materials characteristic of the second recension of Q—those pericopae reflecting the motif of the announcement of judgment—have been attached to the sapien-

---

10. I.e., Q 3:7–9, 16–17; 7:1–10, 18–23, 24–28, (31–35); 10:21–22; 11:14–15, 16, 17–18a, 29–30.

tial instructions largely on the basis of catchword and thematic connections.[11] Viewing this expansion of Q from the standpoint of the morphology of the instruction, we are forced to the conclusion that redaction propelled Q outside the range of typicalities of the instruction. However, from the perspective of the morphology of chriae collections, the clusters of wisdom sayings absorbed into the second recension do not present any anomaly. As has been noted, chriae collections are not known for their homogeneity; they regularly juxtapose responsorial and circumstantial chriae with simple "declaratory" chriae or strings of sayings. Put briefly, the generic latitude of chriae collections permitted the original instructions to be absorbed into a related but distinct genre, that of chriae collection. In this sense, Colson and de Labriolle are well justified in regarding Q as the first Christian example of a chriae collection.[12]

When seen in the context of chriae collections, Q ranks with the most highly organized and structured of them. Not only are the instructional portions thematically grouped but there is thematic and topical organization among the sayings in the second recension. Q 3:7-9, 16-17 concern John's preaching of judgment; 7:1-10, 18-23, 24-28, 31-35 reveal Jesus' relation to John and their mutual opposition to "this generation"; and 17:23-37 deal with the coming judgment. Q 11:14-36, 39-52 affords the clearest example of conscious and considered organization of a large number of individual pronouncements. In the analysis of this section, we noted that the editor has arranged 11:14-26 and 11:16, 29-36 to form parallel sequences in which Jesus is first attacked, then defends himself and finally moves to the offensive using aphorisms and a concluding threat of judgment.[13] The woes in Q 11:39-52 provide an apt conclusion to this double sequence, by recapitulating the announcement of judgment (11:49-51) and by further developing the criticism of faulty moral vision enunciated in 11:34-36. Especially in the editing of 11:14-52, but elsewhere too, the redactor of this recension of Q displays organizational techniques found only in the most highly structured sayings collections. Q is very far from being a "random collection of sayings" and is erroneously regarded as a pure sedimentation of oral tradition. It is, on the contrary, a carefully constructed composition which employs literary techniques characteristic of other ancient say-

---

11. See above, pp. 243-44.
12. Colson, "Quintilian," 150; P. de Labriolle, "Apophthegma. B. Christlich," *RAC* 1 (1950) 547-49.
13. Chapter four, pp. 138, 147-48.

ings collections. In fact, in terms of its internal structure, it ranks some-what higher than works such as *Demonax* and the Diogenes chriae, and closer in level of organization (though not in type of organization) to '*Abot*.

In its tone and probable setting, this recension of Q falls within the parameters of other chriic collections, especially those current in Cynic circles. Not only is the radical ethical teaching carried over from the formative stage, but now confrontational and polemical anecdotes and sayings come to the fore. References to the homeless and wandering existence of the Q missionaries, and especially the prohibition of carry-ing a wallet or sandals, strengthen the affinities of Q with Cynic chriae. This is not to suggest that the Q group imitated Cynics or borrowed and adapted their ideology. The Jesus of Q is not a paradigm of Cynic παρρησία or, still less, of ἀναίδεια, as an expression of the freedom and self-sufficiency of the sage. The idiom of Q is controlled not by a philosophic notion of freedom, but by a historical and soteriological schema of God's constant invitation of Israel to repent, and by the expectation of the imminent manifestation of the kingdom—an event which calls forth a radical response in its adherents, and which produces conflict and polarization in the world. In actual fact, the preaching of the Q community is considerably less "philanthropic" than that of the mild Cynics such as Demonax, who regarded himself as a doctor to humankind. Q, by contrast, does not appear to hold out much hope for the repentance and salvation of "this generation." All that awaits it is judgment.

We have already noted the dialectic of historicizing and contempor-izing moments at work within the instruction. This dialectic is carried forth into the present stratum of Q: sayings are ascribed to a named sage, either John or Jesus; but at the same time, the sayings are obviously preserved because they serve some present need (χρεία!). Moreover, both Jesus and John are associated with the heavenly Sophia (Q 7:35; 10:22; 11:49–51). This strategy of legitimation—the association of the sage with a divine agent—finds some analogies in Cynic circles (though not by any means among all Cynics), and in '*Abot*. Thus the sayings obtain their weight, on the one hand, from ascription to a sage of distinguished reputation, and on the other, from the divine voice which is enclosed in the words of that sage.

It is safe to conclude that the instructional component in the second recension of Q maintained its original function, namely, to signal the presence of the kingdom and to evince its radical ethic. The confrontational and polemical sections serve another important instructional or educative function. Polemic serves the positive and constructive function of strengthening group boundary and self-definition. This is especially important in a group such as the Q community which both preached an ethic which departed markedly from macro-societal values, and experienced the failure of its preaching among its contemporaries. The telling of anecdotes relating Jesus' (and John's) lack of success and conflict with "this generation" served to establish the parameters of community self-understanding. The Q chriae which place Jesus in conflict with Israel function in a manner analogous to those Cynic chriae which relate the response of Diogenes, Antisthenes and Bion to reproach.[14] The sage's pithy reaction not only confounds the opponent but more importantly demonstrates that the matters over which the sage is reproached are virtues rather than causes for shame or reproach. In like manner, Jesus' responses turn the tables on his opponents and demonstrate to his followers the superiority of discipleship and pursuit of the kingdom. And like the Cynic chriae, Q's anecdotes introduce and reinforce the ethos of the community as a group of envoys of the kingdom who should be prepared for the typical reaction to envoys of the kingdom: rejection and even persecution.

THE FINAL RECENSION OF Q

The temptation story, which has been seen as something of an anomaly, is probably the latest addition to Q. The most likely reason for its addition was that an editor wished to exploit the account for its paradigmatic potential for showing that when faced with demonic temptation to do otherwise, Jesus himself conformed to the ethic of self-denial, voluntary poverty, refusal of means of self-defense or self-preservation and refusal to participate in power and wealth. The use of such a preface does not set Q in a category by itself. The *Sayings of Ahikar*, the *Life of Aesop* and *Demonax* all contain introductory narratives which show the sage to be exercising precisely the kind of behavior which he later enjoins upon his hearers.

The appearance of narrative-biographical introductions in sayings collections relates to the inner dynamisms of sayings genres. In all three

---

14. The Cynic reproach chriae follow a standard syntactical form: ὀνειδιζόμενός ποτε . . . ἔφη . . . E.g., Diogenes Laertius 6.4, 6 (Antisthenes); 4.47 (Bion); 6.49, 58, 66 (Diogenes). On this see R. Höistad, "Eine hellenistische Parallel zu 2. Kor 6, 3ff.," *Coniectanea Neotestamentica* 9 (Lund: Gleerup, 1944) 24.

genres treated—the instruction, the gnomologium and the chriae collection—the requirement of an authoritative guarantor of the saying is
strong. Legitimation is achieved with a variety of strategies, used individually or in concert: ascription of sayings to a distinguished sage or
hero, laudatory descriptions of the virtues and sagacity of the sage (e.g.,
Ps-Phocylides, Shuruppak), association of the speaker with a divine
source of wisdom, or juxtaposition of the sayings with another source of
authority such as the Torah (in 'Abot).

Another mode of legitimation is represented by a prefatory account
which demonstrates in narrative fashion that the sage is indeed worthy
of the hearer's attention. This strategy was adopted by collections of
widely divergent provenances: Amenemhat I, Ankhsheshonq, Ahikar,
Aesop, Lucian's Demonax and Secundus. It is obvious that the addition of
a narrative prologue introduces the possibility of a generic shift from
sayings collection to bios. The literary development of the Ahikar story is
a case in point. While the earliest Aramaic version is represented as
"sayings of Ahikar," later recensions of Ahikar sometimes preserve this
generic designation, but other times entitle it "the life of Ahikar." The
addition of the temptation narrative to Q is probably not enough to
allow us to claim a biographical genre for Q; however, its addition is one
step in that direction.

It is not entirely fortuitous that the initial narrative deals with the
temptation of the sage. We have already noted that the *motif* of the
testing or temptation of the wise man occurs in Near Eastern instructions such as Proverbs and Sirach.[15] Among the Cynics, the sage's
sufferings were understood on the model of the trials of Heracles and
the sufferings of Odysseus, and accordingly were reinterpreted as
badges of qualification rather than evils. For the Cynic, rejection, suffering, exile, reproach and trial were prerequisites and distinguishing
features of the true sage. In several of the instructions and chriae
collections discussed this motif of temptation or ordeal is formative for
the introductory narrative: the prologue of Ankhsheshonq relates the
sage's imprisonment, both Ahikar and Aesop are falsely accused and
imprisoned (and later rehabilitated), Demonax is reviled and almost
stoned by the Athenians and Secundus is put through an ordeal and
threatened with execution as a test of his "Pythagorean" vow. In all of
these cases, the testing or trial sequence illustrates in narrative form
what Sirach (2:1, 4–5) puts aphoristically:

15. See above, p. 279.

My son, if you come forward to serve the Lord, prepare yourself for temptation . . .
Accept whatever is brought upon you and in changes that humble you be patient.
For gold is tested in the fire and acceptable men in the furnace of humiliation.

Thus the temptation sequence in a sayings collection serves to demonstrate the trustworthiness of the sage, and hence, to undergird and buttress his teachings. This means that Q 4:1–13 not only functions paradigmatically to illustrate the particular ethic which Jesus enjoins in the body of the collection, it also functions to legitimate Jesus' authority as a sage who has endured temptation or ordeal. Although at first glimpse, the presence of a narrative introduction for Q might seem somewhat anomalous and even embarrassing, an understanding of the inner dynamisms of the genres of instruction and chriae collection shows that Q is by no means extraordinary in its use of a temptation story.

CONCLUSION

Though Q, like any of the other instructions, gnomologia and chriae collections surveyed, has its peculiarities, idiosyncrasies and unparalleled aspects, it is at the same time intelligible against the background of antique sayings genres. The shifts which have occurred in the course of Q's literary evolution from instruction to proto-biography do not present serious anomalies when viewed in terms of the generic typicalities and inner dynamisms of instructions, gnomologia and chriae collections. Both the instruction and the gnomologium had the potential for an esoteric hermeneutic as the Pythagorean *acousmata* and the *Teach. Silv.* show. The *Gos Thom.* has exercised the generic option to move in this direction, first, by developing the "authorial fiction" in such as way as to stress the association of the speaker of the wise sayings with the Divine, and second, by employing a hermeneutic of "penetration" when describing the intended response to the wise sayings. But Q followed another course. While the association of the speaker of the wise words with a divine agent (Sophia or God) is present both in the initial formative stage and in the second recension, the editing of Q strengthened the historicizing side of the dialectic, first by introducing chriae, and then by use of a biographical-narrative preface. These movements, it should be emphasized, do not represent a violation of the genre, or an attenuation

of the "natural" development of Q as a wisdom collection. The movement of Q from instruction to proto-biography simply exercised options
available within sayings genres in general. It is not the case that redaction of Q aborted a natural movement towards Gnosticism. And the
redaction of Q by the first and third Synoptists did not alter Q in quite so
dramatic a way as is sometimes assumed. Even before the incorporation
of Q into the narrative format of Mark in Matthew and Luke, Q had
already taken significant steps in the direction of a *bios* simply by
developing one side of the generic potentials and dynamisms of ancient
sayings collections.

Ancient Sayings Collections

1. EGYPTIAN AND NEAR EASTERN
SAYINGS COLLECTIONS

Egyptian

AMENEMHAT I [early II millennium BCE]

Text: W. Helck, *Der Text der "Lehre Amenemhats I für seinen Sohn"* (Kleine ägyptische Texte; Wiesbaden: Otto Harrassowitz, 1977).

Trans.: W. K. Simpson, *The Literature of Ancient Egypt* (New Haven: Yale Univ. Press, 1977³) 193–97.

(Title) Here begins the teaching which . . . Amenemhet made when he spoke . . . to his son . . . He said:

(Exordium) . . . hear what I shall say to you that you may be king of the land and rule the Banks and achieve abundance of good fortune.

(Body) Imperatives; imperative with extended motive clauses; autobiographical account of A.'s assassination; list of accomplishments; concluding imperatives.

AMENEMHAT (High Priest) [late II millennium BCE]

A. Gardiner, "The Tomb of Amenemhet, High Priest of Amon," *ZÄS* 47 (1910) 87–99.

(Title) Beginning of the teaching made by (12 titles and epithets) Amemenhat. He spoke thus to his children:

(Exordium) Autobiographical prologue; list of accomplishments and virtues.

(Body not extant)

AMENEMOPE, INSTRUCTIONS OF [mid II millennium BCE]

Text: I. Grumach, *Untersuchungen zur Lebenslehre des Amenope* (Münchner Ägyptologische Studien 23; Berlin and Munich: Deutscher Kunstsverlag, 1972).

Trans.: Simpson, *Literature,* 241–65.

(Title) The beginning of the instruction about life, the guide for well being, all the principles of court procedure, the duties of courtiers.

(Exordium) To know how to refute the accusation of the one who made it, and to send back a reply to the one who wrote it . . . (+ 6 more purpose clauses). (19 titles and epithets) Amenemope (2 epithets) for his son (10 titles and epithets).

(Body) 30 topical instructions beginning with an exhortation to hearken. Forms: imperative; imperative + motive clauses; imperatives + final clause; imperatives + extended motivation, etc.

AMENOTES, SON OF HAPU [Ptolemaic period]

Text: Ulrich Wilcken, "Zur ägyptisch-hellenistischen Literatur," *Aegyptiaca: Festschrift für Georg Ebers* (Leipzig: Wilhelm Englemann, 1897) 142–52.

(Title) Counsels of Amenotes.

(Body) Series of imperatives.

AMUNNAKHTE [II millennium BCE]

Text: G. Posener, "L'exorde de l'instruction éducative d'Amennakhte," *RdÉ* 10 (1955) 71–72.

Trans.: Simpson, *Literature*, 341–42.

(Title) The beginning of the instruction . . . which the scribe Amunnakhte made (for) his assistant, Hor-Min. He says:

(Exordium) Exhortation to hearken.

(Body) Imperatives; imperative + final clause; jussives.

ANIY [late II millennium BCE]

Text: E. Suys, *La sagesse d'Ani* (Analecta Orientalia 11; Rome: Pontifical Biblical Institute, 1935).

Trans.: M. Lichtheim, *Ancient Egyptian Literature*. Vol. 2, *The New Kingdom* (Berkeley and Los Angeles: Univ. of Calif. Press, 1976) 135–46.

(Title) Beginning of the educative instruction, the precepts of the way of life, made by (title) Aniy (titles) [for his son . . .] [He says:..].

(Body) Topical instructions. Typical forms: imperative + final clause + jussive + beatitude; imperatives + motive clause; imperative + circumstantial; imperative + motive clause + explication of motive clause; imperative + conditional + explication of imperative.

ANKHSHESHONQ [Ptolemaic period; written in Demotic]

Text: S. R. K. Glanville, *Catalogue of Demotic Papyri in the British Museum*. Vol. 2, *The Instructions of 'Onchsheshonqy* (London: British Museum, 1955).

Trans.: M. Lichtheim, *Ancient Egyptian Literature*. Vol. 3, *The Late Period* (Berkeley and Los Angeles: Univ. of Calif. Press, 1980) 159–84.

(Title missing)

(Exordium) Biographical narrative relating A.'s accidental involvement in a conspiracy, and his imprisonment. From prison he instructs his son.

(Sub-title) This is the instruction which the divine father Ankhsheshonq, whose mother was [. . .], wrote for his son on sherds . . .

And he said:

(Body) Monostichic maxims and imperatives; some connected by catchword, formal similarity, or thematic association; a few motive clauses; sorites at 22.21–25.

DJEDEFHOR (HARDJEDEF) [III millennium BCE]

Texts: (*a*) E. Brunner-Traut, "Die Weisheitslehre des Djedef-Hor," *ZÄS* 76 (1940) 3–9.

(*b*) G. Posener, "Le début de l'enseignement de Hardjédef," *RdÉ* 9 (1952) 109–20.

Trans.: Simpson, *Literature*, 340.

(Title) The beginning of the instruction which (titles) Djedefhor made for his son . . . He says:

(Body) Imperatives; imperative + motive clause.

DUAKHETY. See KHETY, SON OF DUAUF

HORI [late II millennium BCE]

Text: J. Cerný and A. H. Gardiner, *Hieratic Ostraca* I (Oxford: Griffiths Institute, 1957) plate VI.1.

(Title) Beginning of the educative Instruction made by (title) Hori. He says:

(Body) Undifferentiated instructions.

INSTRUCTION ACCORDING TO THE ANCIENT WRITINGS [late II millennium BCE]

Text: (Petrie Ostracon 11 = O. Brit. Museum 5631): Cerný and Gardiner, *Hieratic Ostraca* I, plates I–IA.

Trans.: A. H. Gardiner, "A New Moralizing Text," *WZKM* 54 (1957) 43–45.

(Title) Beginning of the educative instruction according to the Ancient Writings.

(Body) Undifferentiated imperatives.

INSTRUCTION OF A MAN FOR HIS SON [early II millennium BCE]

Texts and trans.: (*a*) K. A. Kitchen, "Studies in Egyptian Wisdom Literature I: The Instructions of a Man for his Son," *Oriens Antiquus* 8 (1969) 180–208.

(*b*) Idem, "Studies in Egyptian Wisdom Literature II: Counsels of Discretion," *Oriens Antiquus* 9 (1970) 203–10.

(*c*) G. Posener, "Section finale d'une sagesse inconnue," *RdÉ* 7 (1950) 71–84.

(*d*) E. Blumenthal, "Eine neue Handschrift der Lehre eines Mannes für seinen Sohn (P. Berlin 14374)," *Festschrift zum 150-jährigen Bestehen der Berliner ägyptischen Museums* (Berlin: Akademie Verlag, 1974) 55–66.

(Title) Beginning of the instruction made by a man for his son. He says:

(Exordium) Hearken to my voice, do not neglect (my) words, do not ignore what I shall say to you.

(Body) Undifferentiated imperatives. Form: imperatives; imperatives + result clause; imperative + extended motive clauses (on loyalty to the Pharaoh).

KAGEMNI [KAIRES TO HIS SON] [III millennium BCE]

Text: A. H. Gardiner, "The Instruction Addressed to Kagemni and His Brethren," *JEA* 32 (1946) 71–74.

Trans.: Simpson, *Literature*, 177–79.

(Title missing) [presumably: The beginning of the instruction made by Kaires for his son Kagemni].

(Body) Undifferentiated imperatives. Forms: conditional + imperatives + maxims serving as motive clauses + imperatives; imperative + circumstantial + imperatives + motive clause. Epilogue related (positive) reaction of K.'s children, and their success.

KHETY, SON OF DUAUF ("CHETI," "DUAKHETY") [early II millennium BCE]

Text: W. Helck, *Die Lehre des Dw3-Htjj* (Kleine ägyptische Texte; Wiesbaden: Otto Harrassowitz, 1970).

Trans.: Simpson, *Literature*, 329–36.

(Title) The beginning of the teaching which the man of Tjel named Dua-Khety made for his son Pepy,

while he sailed southwards to the Residence to place him in the school of writings among the children of the magistrates, the most eminent men of the Residence.

(Body) Satire on trades in form of aphorisms; praise of scribal profession; imperatives (no particular organization) concerning scribal schools. Forms: imperatives; imperatives + conditional + final clause; conditional + imperatives; imperatives + motive clause + imperatives; conditional + imperative + maxim as motive clause.

MERIKARE [ca. 2180 BCE]

Text: W. Helck, *Die Lehre für König Merikare* (Kleine ägyptische Texte; Wiesbaden: Otto Harrassowitz, 1977).

Trans.: Simpson, *Literature*, 180–92.

(Title) [Here begins the teaching made by King Khet]y for his son Merikare.

(Body) Organized topically. Typical forms: programmatic statement + conditional + imperative + motive clause; programmatic statement + 2 imperatives + final clause + imperative + motive clause; strings of imperatives.

NEBMARE-NAKHT [P. Lansing: P. Brit. Museum 9994; late II millennium BCE]

Text: A. H. Gardiner, *Late Egyptian Miscellanies* (Bibliotheca Aegyptiaca 7; Brussels: Editions de la fondation égyptologique reine Elisabeth, 1937) 99–116.

Trans.: Lichtheim, *Literature* 2:167–75.

(Title) [Beginning of the instruction in letter writing made by (titles) Nebmare-nakht] for his apprentice . . .

(Body) Praise of scribal profession; reproach of apprentice; satire on other professions; imperative + motive clauses; imperatives + final clauses; reproach. Satire of soldier's life.

OSTRACON FROM DEIR EL-BAHRI [Ptolemaic/Roman; Demotic]

Text and trans.: Ronald J. Williams, "Some Fragmentary Demotic Wisdom Texts," *Studies in Honor of George R. Hughes* (Studies in Ancient Oriental Civilization 39; Chicago: Oriental Institute, 1977) 270–71.

(Title) Here is a copy of a teaching that a [scribe of the House of Life] gave them (for) a little child who is very, very young.

(Body) Undifferentiated instructions. Forms: imperative + motive clause.

PAPYRUS INSINGER [Ptolemaic; Demotic]

Texts: (*a*) A. Volten, *Kopenhagener Texte zum Demotischen Weisheitsbuch* (Analecta Aegyptiaca 1; Copenhagen: E. Munksgaard, 1940); or,

(*b*) Idem, *Das Demotische Weisheitsbuch* (Analecta Aegyptiaca 2; Copenhagen: E. Munksgaard, 1941).

(*c*) Karl-Theodor Zauzich, "Berliner Fragmente zum Texte des Pap. Insinger," *Enchoria* 5 (1975) 119–22.

(*d*) G. Botti and A. Volten, "Florentiner Fragmente zum Texte des Papyrus Insinger," *AcOr* 25 (1960) 29–42.

Trans.: Lichtheim, *Literature* 3:184–217.

(Title/Exordium) Self-presentation of the author; exhortation to listen; introduction of first instruction: "The Teaching of the Work of God."

(Body) Monostichic maxims and admonitions; 25 topically organized instructions, each ending with 7 sayings including two paradoxical couplets, 2 summaries and the refrain, the fate and the fortune which come, it is the god who sends them. Organization by formal similarity, thematic association.

PAPYRUS LOUVRE D. 2414 [Ptolemaic; Demotic]

Text: A. Volten, "Die moralischen Lehren des demotischen Pap. Louvre 2414," *Studi in memoria di Ippolito Rosellini* (Pisa, 1955) 2.271–80 and plates XXXIV and XXXV.

Trans.: M. Lichtheim, *Late Egyptian Wisdom* (Orbis biblicus et orientalis 52; Freiburg: Universitätsverlag; Göttingen: Vandenhoeck & Ruprecht, 1983) 94–95.

(Title) The teaching of P3-wr-dl (which) he gave (to) his beloved son.

(Body) Imperatives with some maxims. Some grouping by formal analogy and catchword.

PAPYRUS LOUVRE 2377 V [II BCE; Demotic]

Text and trans.: Williams, "Some Fragmentary Demotic Wisdom Texts," 263–67.

(Title missing)

(Body) Undifferentiated imperatives. Forms: maxims; imperatives + motive clauses.

PAPYRUS LOUVRE 2380 V [II BCE; Demotic]

Text and trans.: Williams, "Some Fragmentary Demotic Wisdom Texts," 268–70.

(Title missing)

(Body) Badly damaged. Forms: maxims; imperatives.

PENTAWERET [P. Sallier I; late II millennium]

Text: Gardiner, *Late Egyptian Miscellanies*, 79.

Trans.: R. A. Caminos, *Late Egyptian Miscellanies* (Brown Egyptological Studies 1; London: Oxford Univ. Press, 1954) 303.

PTAHHOTEP [III millennium BCE]

Text: Z. Zába, *Les maximes de Ptahhotep* (Prague: Editons de l'academie tchéco-slovaque de sciences, 1956).

Trans.: Simpson, *Literature*, 159–76.

(Title) Teaching of (titles) Ptahhotep . . .

(Exordium) Account of circumstance of instruction.

(Sub-title) Here begins the maxims of good speech spoken by (titles) Ptahhotep, when instructing the ignorant to know according to the standard of good speech, being weal to him who will hear and woe to him who will disobey it. Thus he said to his son:

(Body) Topically organized instructions. Forms: conditional + imperative + maxim + final clause; conditional + imperatives + maxims; imperative + maxims; imperative + conditional + rhetorical question + conditional + imperative.

QAGABU [P. Anastasi IV; late II millennium BCE]

Text: Gardiner, *Late Egyptian Miscellanies*, 34.

Trans.: Caminos, *Late Egyptian Miscellanies*, 125.

(Title) [Beginning of the instruction made by (title) Qagebu, for his appre]ntice, (title) Inena . . .

(Body missing)

SAITE INSTRUCTION [I millennium BCE]

Description in G. Posener and J. Sainte Fare Garnot, "Sur une sagesse égyptienne de basse époque (Papyrus Brooklyn no 47.218.135)," *Les sagesses du Proche-Orient ancien* (Paris: Presses universitaires de France, 1963) 153–57.

SANSNOS, COUNSELS OF PIETY OF [Ptolemaic; written in Greek]

Text: E. Bernand, *Inscriptions métriques de l'Egypte gréco-romaine* (Paris: Les Belles Lettres, 1969) 165.

(Title) Sansnos, son of Pseno [. . .] writes:

(Body) Imperatives on subject of worshiping the gods.

SEHETEPRIBRE ("Loyalist Instruction" papyri, stele) [early II millennium BCE]

Text: G. Posener, *L'enseignement loyaliste: Sagesse égyptienne de Moyen empire* (Hautes études orientales 5; Geneva: Minard, 1976).

Trans.: Simpson, *Literature*, 198–200 (stele only).

(Title) The beginning of the teaching which [Sehetepribre] made for his children:

(Exordium) . . . I shall have you hear it and I shall let you know it: the design for eternity, a way of life as it should be . . .

(Body) 2 imperatives + several motive clauses; 2 imperatives + motive clause; imperative + final clause.

Other Near Eastern Instructions

ADVICE TO A PRINCE [I millennium BCE]

Text and trans.: W. G. Lambert, *Babylonian Wisdom Literature* (Oxford: At the Clarendon Press, 1960) 110–15.

(Title) None

(Body) Instructions imitating the style of omens: If a king does x, y will happen.

AHIKAR [originated in V–VII BCE]

Aramaic text: A. Cowley, *Aramaic Papyri of the Fifth Century BC* (Oxford: At the Clarendon Press, 1923) 204–48.

Text and trans.: F. C. Conybeare, J. R. Harris, and A. S. Lewis, *The Story of Ahikar from Aramaic, Syriac, Arabic, Ethiopic, Old Turkish, Greek and Slavonic Versions* (2d. ed; Cambridge: At the Univ. Press, 1913).

(Title: Aramaic) [These are the w]ords of one named Ahikar, a wise and ready scribe, who taught his son.

(Exordium) Story of Ahikar's adoption of Nadam, his betrayal by his son, the order to execute him, and the protection afforded him by a friendly officer [A.'s rehabilitation?].

(Body) Undifferentiated sayings; some catchword composition. Forms: Maxims; imperatives + motive clauses; imperatives; conditional + imperative.

COUNSELS OF A PESSIMIST [I millennium BCE]

Text and trans.: Lambert, *Babylonian Wisdom Literature*, 107–9.

(Title missing)

(Body) Maxims and imperatives; some catchword composition.

COUNSELS OF WISDOM [Akkadian; late II millennium BCE]

Text and trans.: Lambert, *Babylonian Wisdom Literature*, 96–107 [K 13770 contains possible incipit].

(Title?) A learned man [. . .] In wisdom. [. . .].

(Exordium?) Come, my son [. . .] to the command which [. . .] take my advice [. . .] One who is no savant [. . .] excelling in .[. . .].

(Body) Topical organization; thematic clusters; monostichic imperatives; imperative + motive clauses; maxims.

PROVERBS 1—9

(Title) The Proverbs of Solomon, son of David, king of Israel.

(Exordium) That men may know wisdom and instruction, understand words of insight . . . (1:16). Programmatic statement (1:7); exhortation to listen (1:8–19); Wisdom speech (1:20–33).

(Body) Multi-segmented admonitions with motive clauses; wisdom speeches; miscellaneous wisdom materials.

PROVERBS 22:17—24:22

(Title) [Words of the wise?]

(Exordium) Incline your ear, and hear the words of the wise, and apply your mind to my knowledge, for it will be pleasant if you keep them within you . . .

(Body) Multi-segmented admonitions; topical arrangement; wisdom sentences.

PROVERBS 24:23–34

(Title) These also are sayings of the wise.

(Body) Wisdom sentences; admonitions; example story about the sluggard.

PROVERBS 31:1–9

(Title) The words of Lemuel, king of Massa, which his mother taught him:

(Body) Admonitions on women, drinking and giving justice.

SHUBE-AWILUM [late II millennium BCE; Akkadian]

Text: J. Nougrayrol and E. Laroche, *Ugaritica V* (Mission de Ras Shamra 16; Paris: Geunthner, 1968) 273–90.

Trans.: D. E. Smith, "Wisdom Genres in RS 22.439," *Ras Shamra Parallels II* (AnOr 50; Rome: Pontifical Biblical Institute, 1975) 215–47.

(Title/Exordium) Hear the counsel of Shube-awilum whose understanding is like Enlilbanda, the experienced counsel of Shube-awilum whose understanding Enlilbanda gave him. From his mouth comes everlasting order for the people. [Zu]rranku, my child, carries his counsel to proclaim it.

(Body) Instructions, topically arranged.

SHURUPPAK, INSTRUCTIONS OF [III–II millennium BCE; Akkadian/ Sumerian]

Sumerian 1: Abu Salibikh [ca. 2500 BCE]: B. Alster, *The Instructions of Shuruppak* (Copenhagen: Akademisk Forlag, 1974) 10–20.

Sumerian 2: Adab version [ca. 2400 BCE]: ibid., 21–25.

Sumerian 3: classical version [ca. 1800 BCE]: ibid., 26–51.

Akkadian [ca. 1100 BCE]: W. G. Lambert, *Babylonian Wisdom Literature*, 92–95 (fragmentary).

(Title: Class. Sumerian) In those days, in those far remote days, in those nights, in those far-away nights, in those years, in those far remote years, in those days, the intelligent one, who made elaborate words, who knew the (proper) words, and was living in Sumer, Shuruppak—the intelligent one, who made elaborate words, who knew the (proper) words, and was living in Sumer,

Shuruppak gave instructions to his son . . .

(Exordium) My son, let me give you instructions, may you pay attention to my instructions! . . . Do not neglect my instructions. Do not transgress the word I speak.

(Body) Some thematic clusters; catchword composition; many undifferentiated groups of sayings; repetition of title + exhortation several times throughout the collection. Form: monostichic imperatives and maxims.

SIRACH

(Title absent; perhaps removed when the prose prologue was added)

(Exordium) Programmatic statement (1:1); meditation on Sophia (1:2–10) and the fear of the Lord (1:11–30); exhortation to prepare for temptation (2:1–6) and to wait on the Lord (2:7–11); 3 woes + 3 promises + exhortation (2:12–18); call to attention (3:1).

(Body) Multi-segmented admonitions; wisdom sentences; Wisdom speeches and hymns; topical arrangement of many of the admonitions.

Later Instructions

APA ANTONIUS (BM 979a) [IX–X CE; related to Teachings of Silvanus]

[Related texts: *Teach. Silv.* 97.3—98.22; Antonius Magnus "Spiritualia Documenta Regulis Adjuncta" PG 40 (1858) 1073–80]

Text and trans.: W. P. Funk, "Ein doppelt überliefertes Stück spätägyptischer Weisheit," *ZÄS* 103 (1976) 8–21.

(Title) Apa Antonius.

(Body) Programmatic statement on the wise man; admonitions of discretion; friendship; frequent interjection "O my son."

TEACHINGS OF SILVANUS (NHC VII 4)

Trans.: M. L . Peel and J. Zandee, "The Teachings of Silvanus," *The Nag Hammadi Library in English* (San Francisco: Harper & Row, 1977) 346–61.

(Title) The teachings of Silvanus.

(Body) Multi-segmented admonitions, some with extended motive clauses; frequent interjections ("my son"); Wisdom speech; miscellaneous wisdom sentences; beatitudes.

2. GNOMOLOGIA

Pre-Byzantine Gnomic Collections

**Dates represent presumptive date of composition, or earliest papyrus witness.

AESOP, SENTENCES OF (Related to Ahikar) [30 BCE–100 CE?]

Text: B. E. Perry, *Aesopica* (Urbana: Univ. of Illinois Press, 1952) 69–70, 101–2.

Anonymous PRAECEPTA DELPHICA [inscription from Thera; IV BCE]

Inscriptiones Graecae 12/3 (Berlin: Riemar, 1920³) no. 188, p. 1020 [related to the Sayings of the SEVEN SAGES, q.v.].

Anonymous PRAECEPTA DELPHICA [inscription from Miletopolitanus; III BCE]

Text: W. Dittenberger, *Sylloge Inscriptionum Graecarum* (4 vols.; Leipzig: Hirzel, 1920³) no. 1268 [Related to the Sayings of the SEVEN SAGES, q.v.].

AXIOPISTUS: See EPICHARMUS

CHARES [Pack², 240; IV–III BCE]

Text: Douglas Young, ed., *Theognis* (Bibliotheca Scriptorum Graecorum et Romanorum Teubneriana; Leipzig: Teubner, 1971²) 113–18.

CHIRON, HYPOTHEKAI [V BCE?]

Text: R. Merkelbach and M. L. West, eds. *Fragmenta Hesiodea* (Oxford: At the Clarendon Press, 1967) 143–44 (testimonia) 144–45.

Trans.: H. G. Evelyn-White, *Hesiod* (LCL; Cambridge: Harvard Univ. Press, 1914; repr. 1977) 72–75.

CLEITARCHUS, SENTENCES OF [II CE or earlier]

Text: H. Chadwick, ed., *The Sentences of Sextus* (Cambridge: At the Univ. Press, 1959) 73–83.

DEMOCRITUS: GOLDEN WORDS [V–IV BCE]

Text: Diels and Kranz, eds., *Vorsokratiker* 68 B 35–115.

DICTA CATONIS (DISTICHA CATONIS) [ca. 200 CE]

Text and trans.: J. W. Duff and A. M. Duff, *Minor Latin Poets* (LCL; rev. ed.; Cambridge: Harvard Univ. Press, 1935; repr. 1961) 585–639.

EPICHARMUS [collected by AXIOPISTUS; IV BCE]

Texts: (*a*) [P. Hibeh 1; 2]: B. P. Grenfell and A. S. Hunt, eds., *The Hibeh Papyri Part I* (Egypt Exploration Fund, Graeco-Roman Memoirs 7; London: Egypt Exploration Society, 1906) 13–16 [prologue and sayings].

(*b*) [Axiopistus]: Diels and Kranz, eds., *Vorsokratiker* 23 B 8–46 (47–54).

Trans. [P. Hibeh 1 only]: D. L. Page, *Select Papyri III: Literary Papyri and Poetry* (LCL; Cambridge: Harvard Univ. Press, 1970) 441–45.

EPICTETUS: GNOMOLOGIUM EPICTETUM

Text: Heinrich Schenkl, ed., *Epicteti Dissertationes ab Arriani Digestae* (Stuttgart: Teubner, 1916²; repr. 1965) 476–92.

EPICURUS: KYRIAI DOXAI [before III CE]

Text: P. von der Muehll, ed., *Epicuri Epistulae tres et Ratae Sententiae a Laertio Diogene servata, accedit Gnomologium Vaticanum* (Stuttgart: Teubner, 1922, 1966²).

EPICURUS: GNOMOLOGIUM VATICANUM EPICUREUM [cod. Vat. Graec. 1950; date uncertain]

Text: von der Muehll, ed., *Epicuri Epistulae*, 60–69.

EPICURUS: GNOMOLOGIUM EPICUREUM [P. Berol. 16369; Pack[2], 2574; II CE]

Text: A. Vogiliano, ed., "Frammento di un nuovo 'Gnomologium Epicureum,'" *Studi italiani di filologia classica* NS 13 (1936) 267–81.

HERMETICA: NOUS TO HERMES [CH 11]

Text and trans.: A. D. Nock and A.-J. Festugière, *Corpus Hermeticum* (4 vols; Paris: Les Belles Lettres, 1960) 1:147–66.

HERMETICA: Exerptum Stobaei 11

Text and trans.: Nock and Festugière, *Corpus Hermeticum* 4:54–60.

HERMETICA: DEFINITIONS

Trans.: J. Mahé, "Les Definitions d'Hermes Trismégiste à Asclepius," *Revue de sciences religieuses* 50 (1976) 193–214.

Ps-ISOCRATES: AD DEMONICUM [late IV BCE]

Text and trans.: G. Norlin, *Isocrates* (LCL; Cambridge: Harvard Univ. Press, 1928; repr. 1980) 4–35.

MENANDRI MONOSTICHOI [papyri frags. from III BCE]

Text: Siegfried Jaeckel, ed., *Menandri Sententiae* (Leipzig: Teubner, 1964) [contains 20 Papyri fragments + Menandri Gnomai Monostichoi].

Ps-MENANDER [III–IV CE?]

Trans.: Jean Paul Audet, "La Sagesse de Mènandre l'Egyptien," *RB* 59 (1952) 55–81.

MOSCHIONIS GNOMAI [II CE?]

Text: Schenkl, ed., *Epicteti Dissertationes*, 493–94 [related to Epictetus: Gnomologium].

MOSCHIONIS HYPOTHEKAI [II CE?]

Text: Schenkl, ed., *Epicteti Dissertationes*, 495–96 [related to Epictetus: Gnomologium].

PHOCYLIDES [VI BCE]

Text: B. Gentile and C. Prato, eds., *Poetarum Elegiacorum Testimonia et Fragmenta* (Bibliotheca Scriptorum Graecorum et Romanorum Teubneriana; Stuttgart: Teubner, 1979) 130–34 [testimonia], 135–40 [fragmenta].

Ps-PHOCYLIDES [I BCE–I CE]

Text: Young, ed., *Theognis*, 95–112.

Trans.: Pieter Willem van der Horst, *The Sentences of Pseudo-Phocylides* (SVTP 4; Leiden: E. J. Brill, 1978).

PUBLILIUS SYRUS [I CE]

Text and trans: Duff and Duff, *Minor Latin Poets*, 3–111.

Ps-PYTHAGORAS: GOLDEN WORDS (CHRYSE EPE) [before IV-III CE]

Text: Young, ed., *Theognis*, 86–94.

Ps-PYTHAGORAS: [SAYING OF THE PYTHAGORAEANS; II CE or earlier]

Texts: (a) Chadwick, ed., *Sentences of Sextus*, 84–94 [= collation of ms published by Heinrich Schenkl ("Pythagoreersprüche in einer Wiener Handschrift," *Wiener Studien* 8 [1886] 262–81) + 2 other mss].

(*b*) [apud Stobaeus Florilegium 3.1.30–44]: O. Hense, ed., *Johannis Stobaei Anthologium* (5 vols.; Berlin: Weidmann, 1884–1912; repr. 1968) 3:14–18.

(*c*) [Demophili similitudines seu vitae curatio ex Pythagoreis]: A. Mullach, ed., *Fragmenta philosophorum graecorum* (3 vols.; Paris: Didot, 1860) 1:485–87.

(*d*) [Demophili similitudines]: Mullach, ed., *Fragmenta* 1:488–96.

(*e*) [Demophili Gnomai Pythagoricai]: Mullach, ed., *Fragmenta* 1:497–99.

(*f*) [Pythagoreion Homoiomata]: Mullach, ed., *Fragmenta* 1:496–97.

Ps-PYTHAGORAS: AKOUSMATA (SYMBOLA) [before IV BCE]
Cited in: Aristotle *On the Pythagoreans* frag. 192; Diogenes Laertius 8.17; Iamblichus *De vita pythagorica* 18.82–87; Porphyrius *Vita Pythagorica* 42; Plutach *De liberis educandis* 12D-F.

SEVEN SAGES
Texts: (*a*) [apud Demetrius of Phaleron]: Hense, ed., *Johannis Stobaei Anthologium* 3:111–25 [= Stobaeus *Eclogae* 3.1].

(*b*) [apud Sosiades]: Hense, ed., *Johannis Stobaei Anthologium* 3:125–28 [Stobaeus *Eclogae* 3.1]

(*c*) [Gnomai of the Seven Sages]: J. F. Boissonade, ed., *Anecdota Graeca e codicibus Regiis* (5 vols; Paris, 1829; repr. Hildesheim: G. Olms, 1962) 1:135–44 [Codex Bibl. regiae 1630, p. 187].

(*d*) [Cod. Paris Gr. 2720 fol. 3ff.]: E. Wölfflin, "Sprüche der sieben Wiesen," *Sitzungsberichte der philosophisch-philologischen und historischen Classe der k. b. Akademie der Wissenschaften zu München* (1886) 287–98.

SEXTUS, SENTENCES OF [II CE?]
Text: Chadwick, ed., *Sentences of Sextus*.
Trans.: R. A. Edwards and R. A. Wild, *The Sentences of Sextus* (SBLTT 22; Early Christian Literature 5; Chico, Calif.: Scholars Press, 1981).

THEOGNIS [VI BCE]
Text: Young, ed., *Theognis*.

THOMAS, GOSPEL OF [I/II CE]
Text: A. Guillaumont, H.-C. Puech, G. Quispel, W. Till and Y. 'Abd al Masih, *The Gospel According to Thomas* (New York: Harper & Row; Leiden: E. J. Brill, 1959).
Trans.: T. Lambdin, "The Gospel of Thomas," *Nag Hammadi Library in English* (ed. J. M. Robinson; San Francisco: Harper & Row, 1977) 118–30.

Byzantine and Medieval Gnomologia and Chriae

Anonymous PHILOSOPHON LOGOI [Cod reg. 1166]
Text: Boissonade, ed., *Anecdota Graeca* 1:120–26.

Anonymous, GNOMAI SOPHON [cod. reg. 1630]
Text: Boissonade, ed., *Anecdota Graeca* 1:127–34 [= untitled copy of the SENTENCES OF CLEITARCHUS, q.v.]

Anonymous FLORILEGIUM
Text: H. Schenkl, "Das Florilegium ἄριστον καὶ πρῶτον μάθημα," *Wiener Studien*

11 (1889) 142.

GNOMOLOGIUM DEMOCRITO-EPICTETUM

Text: Curt Wachsmuth, *Studien zu den griechischen Florilegium* (Berlin: Weidmann, 1882) 162–207.

GNOMOLOGIUM VATICANUM

Text: Leo Sternback, ed., *Gnomologium Vaticanum e Codice Vaticano Graeco 743* (intro. by O. Luschnat; Texte und Kommentare 2; Berlin: Walter de Gruyter, 1963 = repr. of *Wiener Studien* 9 (1887) 175–206; 10 (1888) 1–49; 211–60; 11 (1889) 43–46, 192–242).

WIENER APOPHTHEGMATA or GNOMOLOGIUM VINDOBONENSE [Cod. Vind. theol. 149]

Text: Kurt Wachsmuth, ed., "Die Wiener Apophthegmensammlung," *Festschrift zur Begrüssung der in Karlsruhe vom 27. bis 30. September 1882 tagenden XXXVI Philologen-Versammlung* (Karlsruhe, 1882) 3–36.

3. CHRIAE COLLECTIONS

M. 'ABOT [II–III CE]

Text: P. Blackman, *Mishnayoth* (7 vols.; New York: Judaica, 1965³) 4:489–533.

Trans: H. Danby, *The Mishnah* (Oxford: At the Clarendon Press, 1933; repr. 1974) 446–61.

ANTISTHENES [apud Hecaton and Diocles]

Diogenes Laertius 6.3–9 (Hecaton), 12 (Diocles).

BION ῾Υπομνήματα καὶ ἀποφθέγματα χρειώδη

Diogenes Laertius 4.47–51.

CRATES [apud Zeno of Citium]

Diogenes Laertius 6.91–93.

DIOGENES OF SINOPE: CHRIAE [apud Metrocles of Maroneia and Hecaton]

Diogenes Laertius 6.33–73.

DIOGENES OF SINOPE: CHRIAE [P. Vindob. G. 29946; Pack², 1987; I BCE]

Text: C. Wessely, "Neues über Diogenes den Kyniker," *Festschrift Theodor Gomperz* (Vienna: Hölder-Pichler-Tempsky, 1902; repr. Aalen: Scientia, 1979) 67–74. Also W. Crönert, *Kolotes und Menedemos* (Studien zur Palaeographie und Papyruskunde 6; Munich: Müller, 1906; repr. Amsterdam: Hakkert, 1965) 49–53.

DIOGENES OF SINOPE: CHRIAE [P. Mich. inv. 41; Pack², 2086]

Text: Italo Gallo, *Frammenti Biografici da Papiri* (Rome: Edizioni dell' Ateneo & Bizzarri, 1980) 2.325–40.

DIOGENES OF SINOPE: CHRIAE [P. Bouriant 1 = P. Sorbonne 826; Pack², 2643; III–IV CE]

P. Jouguet and P. Perdizet, "Le Papyrus Bouriant n. 1. Un cahier d'écolier grec d'Egypte," *Kolotes und Menedemos* (Studien zur Palaeographie und Papyruskunde 6; Leipzig 1906; repr. Amsterdam: Hakkert, 1965) 148–61.

DIOGENES OF SINOPE: CHRIAE [Ostracon 5730 Preisigke; Pack², 1988; III–IV CE]

Text: H. Thompson, "A Greek Ostracon," *Proceedings of the Society of Biblical*

Archaeology 34 (1912) 197–98; repr. F. Preisigke, F. Bilabel, E. Kiessling, *Sammelbuch griechischer Urkunden aus Ägypten* (Wiesbaden: Harrassowitz, 1913–) no. 5730.

LUCIAN: DEMONAX [II CE]

Text and trans: A. M. Harmon, *Lucian I* (LCL; Cambridge: Harvard Univ. Press, 1913; repr. 1979) 142–73.

SECUNDUS [II CE]

Text and trans: B. E. Perry, *Secundus the Silent Philosopher* (APA Philological Supplements 22; Ithaca, N.Y.: Cornell Univ. Press, 1964).

SIMONIDES [P. Hibeh 17; Pack², 1459; III BCE]

Text: Grenfell and Hunt, eds., *Hibeh Papyri Part I*, 64–66.

SOCRATES: CHRIAE [P. Hibeh 1.182; Pack², 2084; III BCE]

Text: Eric G. Turner, ed., "Life and Apophthegms of Socrates," *The Hibeh Papyri Part II* (Egypt Exploration Fund, Graeco-Roman Memoirs 32; London: Egypt Exploration Society, 1955) 26–40.

Later Chriae and Apophthegm Collections

GNOMOLOGIUM VATICANUM

Text: Sternback, ed., *Gnomologium Vaticanum*.

SAYINGS OF THE NINE SAGES TO ALEXANDER

Text: Boissonade, ed., *Anecdota Graeca* 1:145–46 [Cod. Bibl. regiae 1630, p. 188].

WIENER APOPHTHEGMATA or GNOMOLOGIUM VINDOBONENSE [Cod. Vind. theol. 149]

Text: Wachsmuth, ed., "Die Wiener Apophthegmensammlung," 3–36.

Formal Analysis of the
Q "Wisdom Instructions"

1. Q 6:20b–49: THE INAUGURAL SERMON

a. 6:20a–23		Programmatic statement
	6:20a–21	3 beatitudes (poverty, hunger and weeping)
	6:22–23b	1 beatitude (persecution)
	6:22	beatitude
	6:23a, b	imperative + motive clause
b. 6:27–35		Admonitions: Love of enemies/non-retaliation
	6:27a	Introductory formula: "I say to you"
	6:27b, c, 28a, b	imperatives (love your enemies, do good, bless, pray)
	6:29a	imperative (turn the other cheek)
	6:29b	imperative (give your cloak)
	6:30	imperative (generous lending)
	6:31	imperative (golden rule)
	6:32–33	conditional + rhetorical question as motive for 6:27b, c, 28a
	6:34	conditional + rhetorical question as motive for 6:30
	6:35a, b	summary imperatives + motive clause
	6:35c	summary imperative + motive clause (*imitatio Dei*)
c. 6:36–38		Admonitions: mercy, judging and generosity
	6:36	imperative + motive clause (*imitatio Dei*)
	6:37a, b, 38c	imperatives on judging
	6:37a	imperative + motive clause (judging)
	6:37b (?)	imperative + motive clause (condemning)
	6:38c	motive clause
d. 6:39–45		Warnings to teachers
	6:39	rhetorical questions [Luke] or conditional [Matt]
	6:40	wisdom saying + elucidation (disciples and teachers)
	6:41–42	warning to teachers
	6:41	sarcastic question (why do you see the speck . . .)
	6:42a	sarcastic question (how are you able to say . . .)
	6:42b	reprimand + imperative + result clause

6:43–45	instruction on the nature of good teaching
6:43	wisdom saying (good and bad trees)
6:44a	wisdom saying supplementing 6:43 (tree known from fruit)
6:44b	wisdom saying supplementing 6:43 and 44a (figs from thorns)
6:45a	wisdom saying (treasures of the heart)
6:45b	wisdom saying elucidating 45a (from abundance of heart)
e. 6:46–49	Peroration
6:46	sarcastic question (why do you call me Lord?)
6:47–49	similitude of the two builders (strengthens 6:46)

2. Q 9:57–62; 10:2–11, 16:
DISCIPLESHIP AND MISSION SPEECH

a. 9:57–62	Three programmatic chriae on following Jesus
b. 10:2–11, 16	Mission sayings
10:2	aphorism + imperative + motive clause (the harvest is great . . .)
10:3	commission (I send you as sheep among wolves)
10:4–11	equipment and conduct
10:4	imperatives (take no provisions; greet no one)
10:5–6	imperative + conditional + jussive + conditional +jussive
10:7a	imperative
10:7b	wisdom saying justifying 10:7a
10:8–9	imperatives (on reception by towns)
10:10–11	imperative (on rejections by towns)
10:16	summarizing aphorism (*inclusio* with 10:3)

3. Q 11:2–4, 9–13: ON PRAYER

a. 11:2–4	Paradigm of prayer: The Lord's Prayer
11:2a	Introductory formula: "When you pray, say"
11:2b-4	Prayer
b. 11:9–13	Instruction on Prayer
11:9a	Introductory formula: "I say to you" (?)
11:9b	trio of imperatives + result clauses
11:10	trio of motive clauses in aphoristic form
11:11–12	2 rhetorical questions
11:13	*qal wehomer* conclusion

4. Q 12:2–7, 11–12:
EXHORTATIONS TO FEARLESS PREACHING

a. 12:2–3	Programmatic introduction
12:2	aphorism
12:3	imperative (based on statement of 12:2)
b. 12:4–7	Admonitions to fearless preaching
12:4–5	contrasting imperatives
12:6, 7b	*qal wehomer* conclusion supporting 12:4–5
12:7a	aphorism
c. 12:11–12	Final admonition and promise
12:11	conditional + imperative
12:12	motive clause

5. Q 12:22–31, 33–34: ON ANXIETY

[a. 12:13–14, 16–21]	[Programmatic chria and parable]
b. 12:22–28	Admonitions on anxiety
12:22a	Introductory formula: "Therefore I say to you"
12:22b	parallel imperatives (on food and clothing)
12:23	parallel motive clauses (food and clothing)
12:24	extended motive clause (on provision of food)
12:24a	appeal to observation of nature
12:24b	*qal wehomer* conclusion
12:25	rhetorical question (increasing one's stature)
12:26–28	extended motive clause (on provision of clothing)
12:26	rhetorical questions resuming 12:22b
12:27	appeal to observation of nature
12:28	*qal wehomer* conclusion
c. 12:29–31	Admonition to seek the kingdom
12:29	prohibitive (do not seek . . .)
12:30a	motive clause (negative example of the Gentiles)
12:30b	motive clause (God knows what you need)
12:31a	imperative (seek . . .)
12:31b	motive clause (promise)
d. 12:33–34	On keeping treasures
12:33a	imperative—negative (do not treasure up . . .)
12:33b	implied motive clauses (where moth . . .and thief . . .)
12:33c	imperative—positive (treasure up . . .)
12:33d	implied motive clauses (where moth . . .and thief . . .)
12:34	aphoristic summary.

6. Q 13:24; 14:26, 27; 17:33: THE NARROW DOOR

a. 13:34   Programmatic statement
   13:24a   imperative
   13:24b   motive clause
b. 14:26, 27; 17:33   Discipleship sayings
   14:26   condition: must hate father and mother
   14:27   condition: must take up his cross
   17:33   aphoristic conclusion: the one who loses his life . . .
c. 14:34–35   Peroration: Final warning

Bibliography

PRIMARY SOURCES

For bibliographical data on the antique sayings collections cited, see appendix I.

Other Sources Cited:

Aeschines
> G. de Budé and V. Martin, ed. and trans. *Eschine: Discours*. 2 vols. Paris: Budé, 1927; repr. 1962.

Aesopica
> Ben E. Perry, ed. *Aesopica*. Urbana: Univ. of Ill. Press, 1952.

Alexander Romance
> *See* Pseudo-Callisthenes.

Anthologia Graeca
> H. Beckby, ed. *Anthologia Graeca*. TuscB. 4 vols. Munich: Heimeran, 1957–58; repr. Darmstadt: Wissenschaftliche Buchgesellschaft, 1965[2].

Apollodorus *Bibliotheca*
> Sir J. G. Frazer, trans. *Apollodorus. The Library*. LCL. 2 vols. Cambridge: Harvard Univ. Press; London: Heinemann, 1921.

Apostolic Fathers
> Kirsopp Lake. *The Apostolic Fathers*. LCL. 2 vols. Cambridge: Harvard Univ. Press; London: Heinemann, 1912–13.

Aristeas (Pseudo-)
> A. Pelletier. *Lettre d'Aristée à Philocrate*. SC 89. Paris: Cerf, 1962.

Aristotle
> W. D. Ross, ed. and trans. *The Works of Aristotle*. 12 vols. London: Oxford Univ. Press, 1928–52.

Cebetis Tabula
> J. T. Fitzgerald and L. M. White, ed. and trans. *The Tabula of Cebes*. SBLTT 24. Chico, Calif.: Scholars Press, 1983.

Cicero
> H. Rackham, trans. *Cicero. De Finibus*. LCL Cicero, vol. 17. Rev. ed. Cambridge: Harvard Univ. Press; London: Heinemann, 1931.

Cynic Epistles
> Abraham J. Malherbe, ed. and trans. *The Cynic Epistles*. SBLSBS 12. Missoula, Mont.: Scholars Press, 1977.

Dead Sea Scrolls
  D. Barthélemy and J. T. Milik. *Qumran Cave I*. DJD 1. Oxford: At the Clarendon Press, 1955.
  Eduard Lohse. *Die Texte aus Qumran: Hebräisch und Deutsch*. Darmstadt: Wissenschaftliche Buchgesellschaft, 1971.
Dio Chrysostom
  J. W. Cohoon and H. L. Crosby, trans. *Dio Chrysostom*. LCL. 5 vols. Cambridge: Harvard Univ. Press; London: Heinemann, 1932–51.
Diogenes Laertius
  R. D. Hicks, trans. *Diogenes Laertius: Lives of Eminent Philosophers*. LCL. 2 vols. Cambridge: Harvard Univ. Press; London: Heinemann, 1925.
Epictetus
  W. A. Oldfather, trans. *Epictetus*. LCL. 2 vols. Cambridge: Harvard Univ. Press; London: Heinemann, 1925–28.
Epicurus
  G. Arrighetti, ed. *Epicuro Opere*. Turin: Einaudi, 1973².
  C. Bailey, ed. and trans. *Epicurus: The Extant Remains*. Oxford: At the Clarendon Press, 1926.
  P. von der Muehll, ed. *Epicuri Epistulae tres et Ratae Sententiae a Laertio Diogene servata, accedit Gnomologium Vaticanum*. Stuttgart: Teubner, 1966².
Hesiod
  H. G. Evelyn-Waugh, trans. *Hesiod, the Homeric Hymns, Fragments of the Epic Cycle, Homerica*. LCL. Cambridge: Harvard Univ. Press; London: Heinemann, 1914; rev. 1936.
Iamblichus *Vita Pythagorica*
  M. Von Albrecht, ed. and trans. *Iamblichi Chalcidensis ex Coele-Syria De Vita Pythagorica Liber*. Zurich: Artemis, 1963.
Lucian of Samosata
  A. M. Harmon, K. Kilburn and M. D. Macleod, trans. *Lucian*. LCL. 8 vols. Cambridge: Harvard Univ. Press; London: Heinemann, 1913–67.
Mekilta de-Rabbi Ishmael
  J. Z. Lauterbach. *Mekilta de-Rabbi Ishmael*. 3 vols. Philadelphia: Jewish Publication Society of America, 1961.
Midrash Rabbah
  H. Friedmann and M. Simon, trans. *Midrash Rabbah*. 10 vols. London: Soncino, 1939.
Mishnah
  Herbert Danby, trans. *The Mishnah*. Oxford: At the Clarendon Press, 1933.
Musonius Rufus
  Cora E. Lutz, ed. and trans. *Musonius Rufus: The Roman Socrates*. Yale Classical Studies 10. New Haven: Yale Univ. Press, 1947.
Nag Hammadi Library
  James M. Robinson, ed. *The Nag Hammadi Library in English*. San Francisco: Harper & Row, 1977.
Papyri Collections
  P. Hibeh: B. P. Grenfell and A. S. Hunt, eds. *The Hibeh Papyri*. Egypt Exploration Society, Graeco-Roman Memoirs 7, 32. 2 vols. London: Egypt Exploration Fund, 1906, 1955.

P. Oxy.: B. P. Grenfell and A. S. Hunt, eds. *The Oxyrhynchus Papyri*. Egypt Exploration Society, Graeco-Roman Memoirs. London: Egypt Exploration Fund, 1898–.

PSI: G. Vitelli and M. Norsa, eds. *Papiri greci e latini. Pubblicazioni della Società Italiana per la ricerca dei papiri greci e latini in Egitto*. 14 vols. Florence: Enrico Ariani, 1912–57.

Italo Gallo, ed. *Frammenti Biografici da papiri*. Vol. 2, *La biografia dei filosofi*. Rome: Editioni dell'Ateneo & Bizzarri, 1980.

Philo of Alexandria

F. H. Colson, G. H. Whitaker and Ralph Marcus, trans. *Philo*. 12 vols. LCL. Cambridge: Harvard Univ. Press; London: Heinemann, 1929–1962.

Philodemus *Peri parresias*

A. Olivieri, ed. *Philodemi* ΠΕΡΙ ΠΑΡΡΗΣΙΑΣ *Libellus*. Leipzig: Teubner, 1914.

Philostratus *Vita Apollonii*

F. C. Conybeare, trans. *Philostratus, Life of Apollonius of Tyana*. LCL. 2 vols. Cambridge: Harvard Univ. Press; London: Heinemann, 1912.

Philostratus *Vita Sophistarum*

Wilmer C. Wright, trans. *Philostratus: Lives of the Sophists*. LCL. Cambridge: Harvard Univ. Press; London: Heinemann, 1921.

Plato

H. N. Fowler, et al., trans. *Plato*. LCL. 12 vols. Cambridge: Harvard Univ. Press; London: Heinemann, 1914–29.

Plutarch *Lives*

B. Perrin, et al., trans. *Plutarch: The Parallel Lives*. LCL. 11 vols. Cambridge: Harvard Univ. Press; London: Heinemann, 1914–26.

Plutarch *Moralia*

F. C. Babbitt, et al., trans. *Plutarch: Moralia*. LCL. 16 vols. Cambridge: Harvard Univ. Press; London: Heinemann, 1927–69.

Porphyrius *Vita Pythagorae*

A. Nauck, ed. *Porphyrii Philosophi Platonici Opuscula Selecta*. Leipzig: Teubner, 1886; repr. Hildesheim: G. Olms, 1963.

Pre-Socratics

Hermann Diels and Walter Kranz, eds. *Die Fragmente der Vorsokratiker*. 3 vols. 6. Aufl. Berlin: Weidmann, 1951–52.

Pseudepigrapha of the Old Testament

R. H. Charles. *Apocrypha and Pseudepigrapha of the Old Testament*. 2 vols. Oxford: At the Clarendon Press, 1912–13.

James H. Charlesworth, ed. *The Old Testament Pseudepigrapha*. Vol. 1, *Apocalyptic Literature and Apocalypses*. New York: Doubleday & Co., 1983.

A.-M. Denis, ed. *Fragmenta Pseudepigraphorum quae supersunt graeca*. PsVTG 3. Leiden: E. J. Brill, 1970.

Pseudo-Callisthenes

Helmut Van Thiel, ed. and trans. *Leben und Taten Alexanders von Makedonien: Der griechische Alexanderroman nach der Handschrift L*. Texte zur Forschung 13. Darmstadt: Wissenschaftliche Buchgesellschaft, 1974.

Pseudo-Phocylides

Pieter W. Van der Horst, ed. and trans. *The Sentences of Pseudo-Phocylides*. SVTP 4. Leiden: E. J. Brill, 1978.

Quintilian
  H. Butler, trans. *Quintilian*. LCL. 4 vols. Cambridge: Harvard Univ. Press;
  London: Heinemann, 1920–22.
Rhetores Graeci
  L. Spengel, ed. *Rhetores Graeci*. 3 vols. Leipzig: Teubner, 1853–56.
Secundus
  Ben E. Perry, ed. and trans. *Secundus the Silent Philosopher*. APA Philological
  Supplements 22. Ithaca, N.Y.: Cornell Univ. Press, 1964.
Seneca *Ad Lucilium Epistulae*
  R. M. Gummere, trans. *Seneca: Epistulae Morales*. LCL. 3 vols. Cambridge:
  Harvard Univ. Press; London: Heinemann, 1917–25.
Seneca *Dialogi* (Moral Essays)
  John W. Basore, trans. *Seneca: Moral Essays*. LCL. 3 vols. Cambridge: Harvard
  Univ. Press; London: Heinemann, 1928–35.
Sentences of Sextus
  Henry Chadwick. *The Sentences of Sextus*. Cambridge: At the Univ. Press,
  1959.
Sextus Empiricus
  R. G. Bury, trans. *Sextus Empiricus*. LCL. 4 vols. Cambridge: Harvard Univ.
  Press; London: Heinemann, 1933–49.
Stobaeus
  O. Hense, ed. *Johannis Stobaei Anthologium*. 5 vols. Berlin: Weidmann, 1884–
  1912; repr. 1968.
Teles
  Edward O'Neil, ed. and trans. *Teles [The Cynic Teacher]*. SBLTT 11; Graeco-
  Roman Religion 3. Missoula, Mont.: Scholars Press, 1977.
Testaments of the Twelve Patriarchs
  Marius De Jonge. *Testamenta XII Patriarcharum*. PsVTG 1. Leiden: E. J. Brill,
  1970.
Theophrastus *De Sensu*
  G. M. Stratton, ed. and trans. *Theophrastus and the Greek Physiological Psy-
  chology*. London: Allen & Unwin, 1917; repr. Amsterdam: A. M. Hakkert, 1964.
Vita Prophetarum (Lives of the Prophets)
  C. C. Torrey, ed. and trans. *The Lives of the Prophets*. JBLMS 1. Philadelphia:
  SBL, 1946.
Xenophon *Memorabilia*
  E. C. Marchant and O. J. Todd., trans. *Xenophon IV: Memorabilia, Oecono-
  micus, Symposium, Apology*. LCL. Cambridge: Harvard Univ. Press; London:
  Heinemann, 1923.

SECONDARY WORKS

Allen, W. C. "The Book of Sayings Used by the Editor of the First Gospel," *Oxford
  Studies in the Synoptic Gospels*. Oxford: At the Clarendon Press, 1911. 235–86.
Ambrozic, Aloysius M. *The Hidden Kingdom*. CBQMS 2. Washington, D.C.: CBA,
  1972.

Arens, Eduardo. *The* ΗΛΘΟΝ *Sayings in the Synoptic Tradition*. OBO 10. Freiburg: Universitätsverlag; Göttingen: Vandenhoeck & Ruprecht, 1976.

Argyle, A. W. "The Accounts of the Temptation of Jesus in Relation to the Q-Hypothesis," *ExpT* 64 (1952–53) 382.

Bacon, B. W. "The Nature and Design of Q, the Second Synoptic Source," *HibJ* 22 (1923–24) 674–88.

Bammel, Ernst. "Das Ende von Q," *Verborum Veritas: Festschrift für Gustav Stählin zum 70. Geburtstag*. Wuppertal: Rolf Brockhaus, 1970. 39–50.

Barns, J. "A New Gnomologium," *ClassQ* 44 (1950) 126–37; 45 (1951) 1–19.

Barrett, C. K. "Q: A Re-examination," *ExpT* 54 (1943) 320–23.

Beardslee, William A. "Plutarch's Use of Proverbial Speech," *Semeia* 17 (1980) 101–12.

———. "Uses of the Proverb in the Synoptic Gospels," *Int* 24 (1970) 61–73.

Berger, Klaus. *Die Amen-Worte Jesu*. BZNW 39. Berlin: Walter de Gruyter, 1970.

———. "Materialien zu Form und Überlieferungsgeschichte neutestamentlicher Gleichnisse," *NovT* 15 (1973) 1–37.

Betz, Hans-Dieter. *Essays on the Sermon on the Mount*. Philadelphia: Fortress Press, 1985.

Bi(c)kerman, E. "La Chaîne de la tradition pharisienne," *RB* 59 (1952) 44–54; repr. *Studies in Jewish and Christian History Part II*. AGJU 9. Leiden: E. J. Brill, 1980. 256–69.

Black, Matthew. *An Aramaic Approach to the Gospels and Acts*. Oxford: At the Clarendon Press, 1967³.

Blank, S. H. "The Death of Zechariah in Rabbinic Literature," *HUCA* 12–13 (1937–38) 327–46.

Boring, M. E. *Sayings of the Risen Jesus*. SNTSMS 46. Cambridge: At the Univ. Press, 1982.

Bornkamm, Günther. "Evangelien, synoptisch. 2a. Spruchquelle," *RGG*³ 2 (1958) Sp. 758–60.

Bosold, Iris. *Pazifismus und prophetische Provokation*. SBS 90. Stuttgart: KBW, 1978.

Brown, J. P. "Synoptic Parallels in the Epistles and Form History," *NTS* 10 (1963–64) 27–48.

Brunner, Helmut. "Die Lehren," *Handbuch der Orientalistik*. 1/1, *Ägyptologie*, 2. Abschnitt, *Literatur*. Leiden and Cologne: E. J. Brill, 1970². 113–39.

———. "Die 'Weisen,' ihre 'Lehren' und 'Prophezeiungen in altägyptischer Sicht," *ZÄS* 93 (1966) 29–35.

Bultmann, Rudolf. *Die Geschichte der synoptischen Tradition*. FRLANT 29. Göttingen: Vandenhoeck & Ruprecht, 1921; 1970⁸.

———. "The Gospels (Form)," *Twentieth Century Theology in the Making*. ed. J. Pelikan. New York: Collins, 1969. 1.86–92.

———. *The History of the Synoptic Tradition*, trans. John Marsh. Oxford: Basil Blackwell, 1963.

———. "The New Approach to the Synoptic Problem," *JR* 6 (1926) 337–62; repr. *Existence and Faith*. London: Hodder & Stoughton, 1961. 35–54.

———. "The Study of the Synoptic Gospels," *Form Criticism*. trans. F. C. Grant. New York: Harper & Row, 1962; repr. of 1934 ed.

————. *Theology of the New Testament*. trans. K. Grobel. 2 vols. New York: Charles Scribner's Sons, 1951–55.

Bundy, Walter E. *Jesus and the First Three Gospels*. Cambridge: Harvard Univ. Press, 1955.

Burkert, Walter. *Lore and Science in Ancient Pythagoreanism*. Cambridge: Harvard Univ. Press, 1972.

Burkitt, F. C. *The Earliest Sources of the Life of Jesus*. Boston: Houghton Mifflin, 1910; London: Constable, 1922².

————. *The Gospel History and Its Transmission*. Edinburgh: T. & T. Clark, 1906.

Bussby, F. "Is Q an Aramaic Document?" *ExpT* 65 (1954) 272–75.

Bussmann, Wilhelm. *Synoptische Studien*. 2. Heft, *Zur Redenquelle*. Halle [Saale]: Buchhandlung des Waisenhauses, 1929.

Cadbury, Henry J. *The Style and Literary Method of Luke*. Harvard Theological Studies 6. Cambridge: Harvard Univ. Press, 1920; repr. New York: Kraus, 1969.

Calloud, J. *Structural Analysis of Narrative*. Semeia Supplements 4. Missoula, Mont.: Scholars Press; Philadelphia: Fortress Press, 1976.

Cameron, Ron. *Sayings Traditions in the Apocryphon of James*. HTS 34. Philadelphia: Fortress Press, 1984.

Carlston, Charles E., and Dennis Norlin. "Once More—Statistics and Q," *HTR* 64 (1971) 59–78.

Catchpole, David. "Q and the 'Friend at Midnight' (Luke xi.5–8/9)," *JTS* NS 34 (1983) 407–24.

Chilton, Bruce D. *God in Strength: Jesus' Announcement of the Kingdom*. Studien zum Neuen Testament und seiner Umwelt 1. Freistadt: Plöchl, 1979.

Colson, F. H. "Quintilian I.9 and the 'Chria' in Ancient Education," *CR* 35 (1921) 150–54.

Coser, Lewis A. *The Functions of Social Conflict*. London: Routledge and Kegan Paul, 1956; repr. 1968.

Crenshaw, J. L. "Prolegomenon," *Studies in Ancient Israelite Wisdom*. 1–60.

————. ed. *Studies in Ancient Israelite Wisdom*. New York: KTAV, 1976.

Crossan, John Dominic. *In Fragments: The Aphorisms of Jesus*. San Francisco: Harper and Row, 1983.

Dautzenberg, Gerhard. *Sein Leben bewahren: Ψυχή in den Herrenworten der Evangelien*. SANT 14. Munich: Kösel, 1966.

————. "Der Wandel der Reich-Gottes-Verkündigung in der urchristlichen Mission," *Zur Geschichte des Urchristentums*. Quaestiones Disputatae 87. Freiburg: Herder & Herder, 1979. 11–32.

Davies, Stevan L. *The Gospel of Thomas and Christian Wisdom*. New York: Seabury Press, 1983.

Davies, W. D. *The Setting of the Sermon on the Mount*. Cambridge: At the Univ. Press, 1966.

Dehandschutter, B. "L'Evangile de Thomas comme collection de paroles de Jésus," *Logia*. 507–15.

Delobel, Joël, ed. *Logia. Les Paroles de Jésus—The Sayings of Jesus: Mémorial Joseph Coppens*. BETL 59. Leuven: Uitgeverij Peeters and Leuven Univ. Press, 1982.

Denaux, A. "Der Spruch von den zwei Wegen im Rahmen des Epilogs der Bergpredigt (Mt 7,13–14 par. Lk 13,23–24). Tradition und Redaktion," *Logia*, 305–35.

Derrett, J. D. M. "You Build the Tombs of the Prophets," *SE* 4 (TU 102; Berlin: Akademie Verlag, 1968) 187–93.

De Solages, Bruno. *La composition des évangiles synoptiques.* Leiden: E. J. Brill, 1973.

Devisch, Michel. "Le document Q, source de Matthieu, problématique actuelle," *L'Evangile selon Matthieu: Sources, rédaction, théologie*, BETL 29. Gembloux: Duculot, 1972. 71–97.

De Witt, N. "Organization and Procedure in Epicurean Groups," *CP* 31 (1936) 205–11.

Dibelius, Martin. *From Tradition to Gospel*, trans. B. L. Woolf. New York: Charles Scribner's Sons, 1935.

Dodd, C. H. *The Parables of the Kingdom.* rev. ed. London: James Nisbet & Co., 1961; repr. 1965.

Doty, William G. "The Concept of Genre in Literary Analysis," *SBLASP* 3 (1972) 2:413–48.

Dudley, R. *A History of Cynicism.* Hildesheim: Olms, 1967; repr. of 1937 ed.

Dupont, Jacques. *Les Béatitudes I: Le problème littéraire—Les deux versions du Sermon sur la montagne et des Béatitudes.* EBib. Nouvelle édition. Brussels: Abbaye de Saint André; Louvain: Nauwelaerts, 1958.

————. "Beaucoup viendront du levant et du couchant . . . ," *SciEccl* 19 (1967) 153–67.

————. *Die Versuchungen Jesu in der Wüste.* SBS 37. Stuttgart: KBW, 1969.

Edwards, Richard A. "The Eschatological Correlative as *Gattung* in the New Testament," *ZNW* 60 (1969) 9–20.

————. *The Sign of Jonah in the Theology of the Evangelists and Q.* SBT 2/18. London: SCM Press, 1971.

————. *A Theology of Q.* Philadelphia: Fortress Press, 1976.

Finkelstein, Louis. "Introductory Study to Pirke Aboth," *JBL* 57 (1938) 13–50; repr. *Pharisaism in the Making.* New York: KTAV, 1972. 121–58.

Fischel, H. A. "Story and History: Observations on Greco-Roman Rhetoric and Pharisaism," *Americal Oriental Society, Middle West Branch: Semi-Centennial Volume.* Bloomington: Univ. of Indiana Press, 1969. 59–88.

————. "Studies in Cynicism and the Ancient Near East: The Transformation of a Chreia," *Religions in Antiquity.* Studies in the History of Religions 14. Leiden: E. J. Brill, 1968. 372–411.

————. "The Transformation of Wisdom in the World of Midrash," *Aspects of Wisdom in Judaism and Early Christianity*, ed. R. L. Wilken. Notre Dame, Ind.: Univ. of Notre Dame Press, 1975. 67–101.

————. "The Use of Sorites (Climax, Gradatio) in the Tannaitic Period," *HUCA* 44 (1973) 119–51.

Fitzmyer, Joseph A. *The Gospel According to Luke I—IX.* AB 28. New York: Doubleday & Co., 1981.

————. "The Priority of Mark and the 'Q' Source in Luke," *Jesus and Man's Hope.* 2 vols. Pittsburgh: Pittsburgh Theological Seminary, 1970. 1.131–70.

————. *A Wandering Aramean*. SBLMS 25. Missoula, Mont.: Scholars Press, 1979.

Fox, Michael V. "Two Decades of Research in Egyptian Wisdom Literature," *ZÄS* 107 (1980) 120–35.

Fuchs, Ernst. "Jesus' Understanding of Time," *Studies of the Historical Jesus*. SBT 1/42. London: SCM Press, 1964. 104–66.

Fuller, Reginald H. *The Mission and Achievement of Jesus*. SBT 1/12. London: SCM Press, 1954.

Funk, W.-P. "Ein doppelt überliefertes Stück spätägyptischer Weisheit," *ZÄS* 103 (1976) 8–21.

Garland, David E. *The Intention of Matthew 23*. NovTSup 52. Leiden: E. J. Brill, 1979.

Geiger, Ruthild. *Die lukanischen Endzeitreden: Studien zur Eschatologie des Lukas-Evangeliums*. Europäische Hochschulschriften 23/6. Bern and Frankfurt: Lang, 1976.

Gemser, B. "The Instructions of 'Onchsheshonqy' and Biblical Wisdom Literature," *VTSup* 7 (1960) 102–28; repr. *SAIW*, 134–60.

————. "The Spiritual Structure of Biblical Aphoristic Wisdom," *SAIW*, 208–19.

Georgi, Dieter. "The Records of Jesus in the Light of Ancient Accounts of Revered Men," *SBLASP* (1972) 2:527–42.

Gerhardsson, Birger. *The Testing of God's Son*. ConB NT series 2/1. Lund: Gleerup, 1966.

Gilbert, George H. "The Jesus of 'Q'—The Oldest Source in the Gospels," *HibJ* 10 (1911–12) 533–42.

Gladigow, B. "Der Makarismus der Weisen," *Hermes* 95 (1967) 404–33.

Gnilka, Joachim. *Das Evangelium nach Markus*. EKKNT 2/1–2. Neukirchen: Neukirchener Verlag, 1979.

Greeven, Heinrich. "Wer unter euch . . .?" *WuD* NF 3 (1952) 86–101; repr. *Gleichnisse Jesu. Positionen der Auslegung von Adolf Jülicher bis zur Formgeschichte*. Darmstadt: Wissenschaftliche Buchgesellschaft, 1982. 238–55.

Grundmann, Walter. *Das Evangelium nach Lukas*. THKNT 3. Berlin: Evangelische Verlagsanstalt, 1961³.

————. *Das Evangelium nach Matthäus*. THKNT 1. Berlin: Evangelische Verlagsanstalt, 1971².

————. "Weisheit im Horizont des Reiches Gottes: Eine Studie zur Verkündigung Jesu nach der Spruchüberlieferung Q," *Die Kirche des Anfangs: Für Heinz Schürmann*. Freiburg: Herder & Herder, 1977. 175–99.

Guéraud, O. and P. Jouguet. *Un Livre d'écolier du IIIᵉ siècle avant J.-C.* Publications de la Société royale égyptienne de Papyrologie, textes et documents. 2 vols. Cairo: Institut française d'archéologie orientale, 1938.

Güttgemanns, Ehrhardt. *Candid Questions Concerning Gospel Form Criticism*. trans. W. D. Doty. Pittsburgh Theological Monographs 26. Pittsburgh: Pickwick Press, 1979.

Haenchen, Ernst. "Das Gleichnis vom grossen Mahl," *Die Bibel und wir. Gesammelte Aufsätze*. Tübingen: J. C. B. Mohr [Paul Siebeck], 1968². 135–55.

————. "Matthäus 23," *ZTK* 48 (1951) 38–63.

————. *Der Weg Jesu*. Berlin: Walter de Gruyter, 1968².

Hahn, Ferdinand. "Das Gleichnis von der Einlagung zum Festmahl," *Verborum Veritas: Festschrift für Gustav Stählin*. Wuppertal: Rolf Brockhaus, 1970. 51–82.

———. *Mission in the New Testament*. SBT 1/47. London: SCM Press, 1965.

———. *The Titles of Jesus in Christology*. trans. H. Knight and G. Ogg. London: Lutterworth Press, 1969.

———. "Die Worte vom Lichte Lk 11,33–36," *Orientierung an Jesus: Für Josef Schmid*. Freiburg: Herder & Herder, 1973. 107–38.

Hamerton-Kelly, R. G. *Pre-existence, Wisdom and the Son of Man*. SNTSMS 21. Cambridge: At the Univ. Press, 1973.

Harnack, Adolf von. *Sprüche und Reden Jesu*. Beiträge zur Einleitung in das Neue Testament 2. Leipzig: Hinrichs, 1907. ET: *The Sayings of Jesus*, trans. J. R. Wilkinson. New York: G. P. Putnam's Sons; London: Williams & Norgate, 1908.

Hawkins, J. C. *Horae Synopticae*. Oxford: At the Clarendon Press, 1899, 1909²; repr. 1968.

———. "Probabilities as to the So-called Double Tradition of St. Matthew and St. Luke," *Oxford Studies in the Synoptic Problem*. Oxford: At the Clarendon Press, 1911. 95–140.

Hirsch, E. D. *Validity in Interpretation*. New Haven: Yale Univ. Press, 1967.

Hirsch, Emanuel. "Fragestellung und Verfahren meiner Frühgeschichte des Evangeliums," *ZNW* 41 (1942) 106–24.

———. *Die Frühgeschichte des Evangeliums II: Die Vorlagen des Lukas und das Sondergut des Matthäus*. Tübingen: J. C. B. Mohr [Paul Siebeck], 1941.

Hoffmann, Paul. "Die Anfänge der Theologie in der Logienquelle," *Gestalt und Anspruch des Neuen Testament*. Würzburg: Echter, 1969. 134–52.

———. "Jesusverkündigung in der Logienquelle," *Jesus in den Evangelien*. SBS 45. Stuttgart: KBW, 1970. 50–70.

———. "Lk 10,5–11 in der Instruktionsreden der Logienquelle," *EKK Vorarbeiten* 3. Neukirchen: Neukirchener Verlag; Zurich: Benzinger, 1971. 37–53.

———. "Πάντες ἐργάται ἀδικίας: Redaktion und Tradition in Lk 13,22–30," *ZNW* 58 (1967) 188–214.

———. *Studien zur Theologie der Logienquelle*. NTAbh NF 8. Münster: Aschendorff, 1975².

———. "Die Versuchungsgeschichte in der Logienquelle," *BZ* NF 13 (1969) 207–23.

Höistad, P. *Cynic Hero and Cynic King*. Uppsala: Bloms, 1948.

Holtzmann, H. J. *Lehrbuch der historisch-kritischen Einleitung in das Neue Testament*. Freiburg, Leipzig and Tübingen: J. C. B. Mohr [Paul Siebeck], 1892³.

———. *Die synoptischen Evangelien*. Leipzig: Engelmann, 1863.

Hommel, H. "Herrenworte im Lichte sokratischer Überlieferung," *ZNW* 57 (1966) 1–23.

Honoré, A. M. "A Statistical Study of the Synoptic Problem," *NovT* 10 (1968) 95–147.

Horna, K., and K. von Fritz, "Gnome," *PW* Supplement 6 (1935) 74–90.

Hughes, George R. "The Blunders of an Inept Scribe (Demotic papyrus Louvre 2414)," *Studies in Philology in Honour of Ronald James Williams*, ed. G. Kadish and G. Freedman. Toronto: Society for the Study of Egyptian Antiquities, 1982. 51–67.

Jacobson, Arland D. "The Literary Unity of Q," *JBL* 101 (1982) 365–89.

———. "The Literary Unity of Q: Lc 10,2–16 and Parallels as a Test Case," *Logia*. 419–23.

———. "Wisdom Christology in Q." Ph.D. diss., Claremont Graduate School, 1978.

Jastrow, M. *A Dictionary of the Targumim, the Talmud Babli and Yerushalmi, and the Midrashic Literature*. New York: Pardes, 1950.

Jeremias, Joachim. ʼΙωνᾶς, *TDNT* 3 (1965) 406–13.

———. *New Testament Theology*. Vol. 1, *The Proclamation of Jesus*. trans. John Bowden. London: SCM Press, 1971.

———. *The Parables of Jesus*. Rev. ed. London: SCM Press, 1972.

———. *Die Sprache des Lukasevangeliums*. MeyerK Sonderband. Göttingen: Vandenhoeck & Ruprecht, 1980.

———. "Zur Hypothese einer schriftlichen Logienquelle Q," *ZNW* 29 (1930) 147–49.

Jülicher, Adolf. *Einleitung in das Neue Testament*. Tübingen: J. C. B. Mohr [Paul Siebeck], 1894[1]; 1900[2]; 1906[5.6]; 1931[7] (with Erich Fascher).

———. *An Introduction to the New Testament*, trans. J. P. Ward. London: Smith, Elder, 1904; from 1900[2].

———. *Die Gleichnisreden Jesu*. 2 vols. Darmstadt: Wissenschaftliche Buchgesellschaft, 1976; repr. of 1910[2] ed.

Jüngel, Eberhard. *Paulus und Jesus*. HUT 2. Tübingen: J. C. B. Mohr [Paul Siebeck], 1979[5].

Käsemann, Ernst. "The Beginnings of Christian Theology," *New Testament Questions of Today*. London: SCM Press, 1969. 82–107.

———. "On the Subject of Primitive Christian Apocalyptic," *New Testament Questions*, 108–37.

———. "Sentences of Holy Law in the New Testament," *New Testament Questions*, 66–81.

Kayatz, Christa. *Studien zu Proverbien 1—9*. WMANT 22. Neukirchen-Vluyn: Neukirchener Verlag, 1966.

Kelber, Werner. "Mark and Oral Tradition," *Semeia* 16 (1979) 7–55.

———. *The Oral and the Written Gospel*. Philadelphia: Fortress Press, 1983.

Kelly, H. A. "The Devil in the Desert," *CBQ* 26 (1964) 190–220.

Kilpatrick, G. D. "The Disappearance of Q," *JTS* 42 (1941) 182–84.

Kitchen, K. A. "Basic Literary Forms and Formulations of Ancient Instructional Writing in Egypt and Western Asia," *Studien zu altägyptischen Lebenslehren*. OBO 28. Freiburg: Universitätsverlag; Göttingen: Vandenhoeck & Ruprecht, 1979. 235–82.

———. "Studies in Egyptian Wisdom Literature I," *Oriens Antiquus* 8 (1969) 189–208; 9 (1970) 203–10.

Klein, Günther. "Die Prüfung der Zeit (Lukas 12,54–56)," *ZTK* 61 (1964) 373–90.

Kloppenborg, John S. "Tradition and Redaction in the Synoptic Sayings Source," *CBQ* 46 (1984) 34–62.

———. "Wisdom Christology in Q," *LTP* 34 (1978) 129–47.

Klostermann, Erich. *Das Matthäusevangelium.* HNT 4. Tübingen: J. C. B. Mohr [Paul Siebeck], 1971 [4].

Knox, W. L. *The Sources of the Synoptic Gospels.* Vol. 2, *St. Luke and St. Matthew.* Cambridge: At the Univ. Press, 1957.

Koester, Helmut. "Apocryphal and Canonical Gospels," *HTR* 73 (1980) 105–30.

————. "Dialog und Spruchüberlieferung in den gnostischen Texten von Nag Hammadi," *EvT* 39 (1979) 532–56.

————. "GNOMAI DIAPHOROI: The Origin and Nature of Diversification in the History of Early Christianity," *Trajectories Through Early Christianity.* Philadelphia: Fortress Press, 1971. 114–57.

————. "Gnostic Writings as Witnesses for the Development of the Sayings Tradition," *The Rediscovery of Gnosticism.* Vol. 1, *The School of Valentinus.* Studies in the History of Religions 41. Leiden: E. J. Brill, 1980. 238–61.

————. *Introduction to the New Testament.* 2 vols. Philadelphia: Fortress Press, 1982.

————. "One Jesus and Four Primitive Gospels," *Trajectories.* 158–204.

————. "The Structure and Criteria of Early Christian Beliefs," *Trajectories.* 205–31.

————. *Synoptische Überlieferung bei den apostolischen Vätern.* TU 65. Berlin: Akademie, 1957.

Küchler, Max. *Frühjüdische Weisheitstraditionen.* OBO 26. Freiburg: Universitätsverlag; Göttingen: Vandenhoeck & Ruprecht, 1979.

Kümmel, W. G. *Introduction to the New Testament,* trans. H. C. Kee. Rev. ed. New York and Nashville: Abingdon Press, 1975.

————. *Promise and Fulfilment.* SBT 1/23. London: SCM Press, 1957; repr. 1974.

Lambrecht, Jan. "Die Logia-Quellen von Markus 13," *Bib* 47 (1966) 321–60.

————. "Q-Influence on Mark 8,34—9,1," *Logia,* 277–304.

————. *Die Redaktion der Markus-Apokalypse.* AnBib 28. Rome: Pontifical Biblical Institute, 1967.

Lang, B. *Die weisheitliche Lehrrede.* SBS 54. Stuttgart: KBW, 1972.

Laufen, Rudolf. *Die Doppelüberlieferung der Logienquelle und des Markusevangeliums.* BBB 54. Bonn: Hanstein, 1980.

Lausberg, H. *Handbuch der literarischen Rhetorik.* 2 vols. Munich: Hueber, 1960.

Légasse, S. "L'oracle contre 'cette génération' (Mt 23,34–36 par. Lk 11,49–51) et la polémique judéo-chrétienne dans la Source des Logia," *Logia.* 237–56.

Lichtheim, Miriam. *Ancient Egyptian Literature.* 3 vols. Berkeley and Los Angeles: Univ. of Calif. Press, 1975–80.

————. *Late Egyptian Wisdom Literature.* OBO 52. Freiburg: Universitätsverlag; Göttingen: Vandenhoeck & Ruprecht, 1983.

————. "Observations on Papyrus Insinger," *Studien zu altägyptischen Lebenslehren.* Freiburg: Universitätsverlag; Göttingen: Vandenhoeck & Ruprecht, 1979. 284–305.

Lindenberger, James M. *The Aramaic Proverbs of Ahiqar.* Baltimore and London: Johns Hopkins Univ. Press, 1983.

Linnemann, Eta. "Jesus und der Täufer," *Festschrift für Ernst Fuchs.* Tübingen: J. C. B. Mohr [Paul Siebeck], 1973. 219–36.

Logia. See Delobel.

Loisy, Alfred. *Evangiles synoptiques*. 2 vols. Ceffonds Près Monteier-en-Der: By the author, 1907–8.

Lord, Albert B. *The Singer of Tales*. Harvard Studies in Comparative Literature 24. Cambridge: Harvard Univ. Press, 1964.

Lührmann, Dieter. "Liebet eure Feinde (Lk 6,27–36/Mt 5,39–48)," *ZTK* 69 (1972) 412–38.

———. "Noah und Lot (Lk 17.26–29)," *ZNW* 63 (1972) 130–32.

———. *Die Redaktion der Logienquelle*. WMANT 33. Neukirchen-Vluyn: Neukirchener Verlag, 1969.

Luz, Ulrich. "Die wiederentdeckte Logienquelle," *EvT* 33 (1973) 527–33.

McKane, William. *Proverbs*. Philadelphia: Westminster Press, 1970.

McKnight, Edgar V. *Meaning in Texts*. Philadelphia: Fortress Press, 1978.

Mahnke, Hermann. *Die Versuchungsgeschichte im Rahmen der synoptischen Evangelien*. BBET 9. Frankfurt am Main: Lang, 1978.

Malherbe, Abraham J. "Self-Definition Among Epicureans and Cynics," *Jewish and Christian Self-Definition*. 3 vols. Philadelphia: Fortress Press, 1980–82. 3.46–59.

Maloney, Elliott C. *Semitic Interference in Marcan Syntax*. SBLDS 51. Chico, Calif.: Scholars Press, 1981.

Manson, T. W. "The Problem of Aramaic Sources in the Gospels," *ExpT* 47 (1935) 7–11.

———. *The Sayings of Jesus*. London: SCM Press, 1949; repr. 1971. Originally published 1937.

Marrou, Henri I. *A History of Education in Antiquity*. New York: Sheed and Ward, 1956.

Marshall, I. Howard. *Commentary on Luke*. Grand Rapids: Wm. B. Eerdmans, 1978.

Martin, R. A. *Syntactical Evidence of Semitic Sources in Greek Documents*. SBLSCS 3. Missoula, Mont.: Scholars Press, 1974.

Merklein, Helmut. *Die Gottesherrschaft als Handlungsprinzip: Untersuchung zur Ethik Jesu*. FzB 34. Würzburg: Echter, 1981².

———. "Die Umkehrpredigt bei Johannes dem Täufer und Jesus," *BZ* NF 25 (1981) 29–46.

Meyer, Paul D. "The Community of Q." Ph.D. diss., Univ. of Iowa, 1967.

———. "The Gentile Mission in Q," *JBL* 89 (1970) 405–17.

Minear, Paul S. *The Commands of Christ*. Nashville and New York: Abingdon Press, 1972.

———. "False Prophecy and Hypocrisy in the Gospel of Matthew," *Neues Testament und Kirche*. Freiburg: Herder & Herder, 1974. 76–93.

Moffatt, James. *An Introduction to the Literature of the New Testament*. Rev. ed. Edinburgh: T. & T. Clark, 1918.

Murphy, Roland. *The Forms of the Old Testament Literature*. Vol. 13, *Wisdom Literature*. Grand Rapids: Wm. B. Eerdmans, 1981. 49–53.

———. "Hebrew Wisdom," *JAOS* 101 (1981) 21–34.

Mussner, Franz. "Das 'Gleichnis' vom gestrengen Mahlherrn (Lk 13,22–30)," *Praesentia Salutis*. Düsseldorf: Patmos, 1967. 113–124.

Neirynck, Frans. "Q," *IDBSup* (1976) 715–16.

———. "Recent Developments in the Study of Q," *Logia*, 29–75.

Neusner, Jacob. *Early Rabbinic Judaism*. SJLA 13. Leiden: E. J. Brill, 1975.

———. *Rabbinic Traditions About the Pharisees Before 70*. 3 vols. Leiden: E. J. Brill, 1971.

———. "The Rabbinic Traditions About the Pharisees Before 70," *Early Rabbinic Judaism*. 73–89.

———. "Types and Forms of Ancient Jewish Literature: Some Comparisons," *HR* 11 (1971–72) 354–90.

Overbeck, Franz. "Über die Anfänge der patristischen Literatur," *Historische Zeitschrift* NF 12 (= 48) (1882) 417–72; repr. as a monograph, Basel: Benno Schwabe, 1954; Darmstadt: Wissenschaftliche Buchgesellschaft, 1966².

Parry, Milman. "Studies in the Epic Technique of Oral Verse-Making. I: Homer and Homeric Style," *HSCP* 41 (1930) 73–147; repr. *The Making of Homeric Verse*. (Oxford: At the Clarendon Press, 1971) 266–324.

Percy, Ernst. *Die Botschaft Jesu*. Lunds Universitets Arsskrift NF 1/49 no. 5. Lund: Gleerup, 1953.

Perrin, Norman. *Rediscovering the Teaching of Jesus*. New York: Harper & Row, 1967.

Pesch, Rudolf. *Jesu ureigene Taten*. QD 52. Freiburg: Herder & Herder, 1970.

———. *Das Markusevangelium*. HTKNT 2/1-2. 2 vols. Freiburg: Herder & Herder, 1974–76.

———. "Über die Autorität Jesu," *Die Kirche des Anfangs: Für Heinz Schürmann*. Freiburg: Herder & Herder, 1978. 25–55.

Pesch, W. "Theologische Aussagen der Redaktion von Matthäus 23," *Orientierung an Jesus—Zur Theologie der Synoptiker: Für Josef Schmid*. Freiburg: Herder & Herder, 1973. 286–99.

———. "Zur Exegese von Mt 6,19–21 und Lk 12,33–34," *Bib* 41 (1960) 356–78.

Peterson, Norman. "On the Notion of Genre in Via's 'Parable and Example Story: A Literary-Structuralist Approach,'" *Semeia* 1 (1976) 134–81.

Piper, Ronald A. "Matthew 7,7–11 par. Lk 11,9–13: Evidence of Design and Argument in the Collection of Jesus' Sayings," *Logia*. 411–18.

Pokorný, Petr. "The Temptation Stories and Their Intention," *NTS* 20 (1973–74) 115–27.

Polag, Athanasius. *Die Christologie der Logienquelle*. WMANT 45. Neukirchen-Vluyn: Neukirchener Verlag, 1977.

———. *Fragmenta Q: Textheft zur Logienquelle*. Neukirchen-Vluyn: Neukirchener Verlag, 1979.

Rad, Gerhard von. *Wisdom in Israel*. London: SCM Press, 1972.

Rigaux, Beda. "La petite apocalypse de Luc (xvii, 22–37)," *Ecclesia a Spiritu Sancto edocta*. BETL 27. Gembloux: Duculot, 1970. 407–38.

Robbins, Vernon K. *Jesus the Teacher: A Socio-Rhetorical Interpretation of Mark*. Philadelphia: Fortress Press, 1984.

Robinson, James M. "Early Collections of Jesus' Sayings," *Logia*. 379–87.

———. "Die Hodajot-Formel in Gebet und Hymnus des Frühchristentums," *Apophoreta: Festschrift Ernst Haenchen*. BZNW 30. Berlin: Alfred Töpelmann, 1964. 194–235.

―――. "Jesus as Sophos and Sophia," *Aspects of Wisdom in Judaism and Early Christianity*. Notre Dame, Ind.: Univ. of Notre Dame Press, 1975. 1–16.

―――. "Jesus – From Easter to Valentinus (or to the Apostles' Creed)," *JBL* 101 (1982) 5–37.

―――. "ΛΟΓΟΙ ΣΟΦΩΝ: Zur Gattung der Spruchquelle Q," *Zeit und Geschichte. Dankesgabe an Rudolf Bultmann*. Tübingen: J. C. B. Mohr [Paul Siebeck], 1964. 77–96.

―――. "LOGOI SOPHON: On the Gattung of Q," *Trajectories Through Early Christianity*. Philadelphia: Fortress Press, 1971. 71–113.

Rosché, T. R. "The Words of Jesus and the Future of the 'Q' Hypothesis," *JBL* (1960) 210–20.

Roth, Wolfgang. "On the Gnomic-Discursive Wisdom of Jesus Ben-Sirach," *Semeia* 17 (1980) 59–79.

Rudberg, Gunnar. "Zur Diogenes-Tradition," *Symbolae Osloensis* 14 (1935) 22–43.

Saldarini, Anthony J. "The End of the Rabbinic Chain of Tradition," *JBL* 93 (1974) 97–106.

―――. *Scholastic Rabbinism*. Brown Judaic Studies 14. Chico, Calif.: Scholars Press, 1982.

Sanders, J. T. *Ben Sira and Demotic Wisdom*. SBLMS 28. Chico, Calif.: Scholars Press, 1983.

Schenk, Wolfgang. *Synopse zur Redenquelle der Evangelien: Q Synopse und Rekonstruktion in deutscher Übersetzung mit kurzen Erläuterungen*. Düsseldorf: Patmos, 1981.

Schenke, Hans-Martin. "Die Tendenz der Weisheit zur Gnosis," *Gnosis* (Festschrift Hans Jonas). Göttingen: Vandenhoeck & Ruprecht, 1978. 351–72.

Schenkl, H. "Das Florilegium ἄριστον καὶ πρῶτον μάθημα," *Wiener Studien* 11 (1889) 1–42.

Schlatter, Adolf. *Der Evangelist Matthäus*. Stuttgart: Calwer, 1963[6].

―――. *Das Evangelium Lukas*. Stuttgart: Calwer, 1960[2].

Schleiermacher, Friedrich. "Über die Zeugnisse des Papias von unsern beiden ersten Evangelien," *TSK* 5 (1832) 735–68; repr. *Sämmtliche Werke*. Berlin: Reimer, 1836. 1. Abt., 2:361–92.

Schlosser, Jacques. *Le Règne de Dieu dans les dits de Jésus*. EBib. 2 vols. Paris: Gabalda, 1980.

Schmid, H. H. *Wesen und Geschichte der Weisheit*. BZAW 101. Berlin: Töpelmann, 1966.

Schmid, Josef. *Matthäus und Lukas: Eine Untersuchung des Verhältnisses ihrer Evangelien*. BibS(F) 23/2–4. Freiburg: Herder & Herder, 1930.

Schmidt, Daryl. "The LXX *Gattung* 'Prophetic Correlative,'" *JBL* 96 (1977) 517–22.

Schmidt, Karl Ludwig. "Die Stellung der Evangelien in der allgemeinen Literaturgeschichte," ΕΥΧΑΡΙΣΤΗΡΙΟΝ: *Festschrift Hermann Gunkel*. FRLANT 36. Göttingen: Vandenhoeck & Ruprecht, 1923. 2:50–134.

Schnackenburg, Rudolf. "Der eschatologische Abschnitt Lk 17,20–37," *Mélanges bibliques en hommage au R. P. Beda Rigaux*. Gembloux: Duculot, 1970. 213–34.

―――. *God's Rule and Kingdom*. New York: Herder & Herder, 1963.

―――. "Ihr seid das Salz der Erde, das Licht der Welt," *Schriften zum Neuen Testament*. Munich: Kösel, 1970. 177–200.

————. "Der Sinn der Versuchung Jesu bei den Synoptikern," *Schriften zum Neuen Testament*. Munich: Kösel, 1971. 101–28.

Schneider, Gerhard. "Das Bildwort von der Lampe," *ZNW* 61 (1970) 183–209.

————. *Parusiegleichnisse im Lukasevangelium*. SBS 74. Stuttgart: KBW, 1975.

Schottroff, Luise, and Wolfgang Stegemann. *Jesus von Nazareth: Hoffnung der Armen*. Stuttgart: Kohlhammer, 1978.

Schrage, Wolfgang. *Das Verhältnis des Thomasevengeliums zur synoptischen Evangelien*. BZNW 29. Berlin: Töpelmann, 1964.

Schulz, Siegfried. "Die Bedeutung des Markus für die Theologiegeschichte des Urchristentums," *SE* 2 (TU 87; 1964) 135–45.

————. "Die Gottesherrschaft ist nahe herbeigekommen (Mt 10,7/Lk 10,9). Der kerygmatische Entwurf der Q-Gemeinde Syrien," *Das Wort und die Wörter* (Festschrift Gerhard Friedrich). Stuttgart: Kohlhammer, 1973. 57–67.

————. *Q: Die Spruchquelle der Evangelisten*. Zurich: Theologischer Verlag, 1972.

Schürmann, Heinz. "Beobachtungen zum Menschensohn-Titel in der Redequelle," *Jesus und der Menschensohn: Für Anton Vögtle*. Freiburg: Herder & Herder, 1975. 124–47.

————. "Die Dubletten im Lukasevangelium," *Traditionsgeschichtliche Untersuchungen*. Düsseldorf: Patmos, 1968. 272–78.

————. *Das Lukasevangelium*. HTKNT 3/1. Freiburg: Herder & Herder, 1969.

————. *Der Paschamahlbericht*. NTAbh 19/5. Münster: Aschendorff, 1968[2].

————. "Protolukanische Spracheigentümlichkeiten?" *Traditionsgeschichtliche Untersuchungen*. Düsseldorf: Patmos, 1968. 209–27.

————. "Sprachliche Reminiszenzen an abgeänderte oder ausgelassene Bestandteile der Redequelle im Lukas- und Matthäusevangelium," *Traditionsgeschichtliche Untersuchungen*. 111–25.

————. "Die vorösterlichen Anfänge der Logienquelle," *Traditionsgeschichtliche Untersuchungen*, 39–65.

————. "Wer daher eines dieser geringsten Gebote auflöst . . ." *Traditionsgeschichtliche Untersuchungen*, 126–36.

————. "Das Zeugnis der Redenquelle für die Basileia-Verkündigung Jesu," *Logia*. 121–200.

Scroggs, Robin. "The Exaltation of the Spirit by Some Early Christians," *JBL* 84 (1965) 359–73.

Selwyn, E. G. *The First Epistle of Peter*. Grand Rapids: Baker Book House, 1981; repr. of 1947[2].

Simpson, W. K. *The Literature of Ancient Egypt*. New Haven: Yale Univ. Press, 1977[3].

Skutsch, F. "Dicta Catonis," *PW* 5 (1905) 358–70.

Smith, D. E. "Wisdom Genres in RS 22.439," *Ras Shamra Parallels II*. AnOr 50. Rome: Pontifical Biblical Institute, 1975. 215–47.

Soiron, Thaddaeus. *Die Logia Jesu: Eine literarkritische und Literargeschichtliche Untersuchung zum synoptischen Problem*. NTAbh 6/4. Münster: Aschendorff, 1916.

Spencer, Richard A. "A Study of the Form and Function of the Biographical Apophthegms in the Synoptic Tradition." Ph.D. diss., Emory Univ., 1976.

Steck, Odil Hannes. *Israel und das gewaltsame Geschick der Propheten*. WMANT 23. Neukirchen-Vluyn: Neukirchener Verlag, 1967.

Steinhauser, Michael G. *Doppelbildworte in den synoptischen Evangelien*. FzB 44. Würzburg: Echter, 1981.

Stendahl, Krister. *The School of St. Matthew*. ASNU 20. Lund: Gleerup, 1954; repr. Philadelphia: Fortress Press, 1968.

Sternbach, L. *Gnomologium Vaticanum e codice Vaticano Graeco 743*. Texte und Kommentare 2. Berlin: Walter de Gruyter, 1963; repr. of *Wiener Studien* 9 [1887] 175–206; 10 [1888] 1–49, 211–60; 11 [1889] 43–64, 192–242.

Stewart, Zeph. "Democritus and the Cynics," *HSCP* 63 (1958) 179–91.

Strecker, Georg. *Der Weg der Gerechtigkeit*. FRLANT 82. Göttingen: Vandenhoeck & Ruprecht, 1971³.

Streeter, B. H. *The Four Gospels*. London: Macmillan & Co., 1924; repr. 1951.

————. "The Literary Evolution of the Gospels," *Oxford Studies in the Synoptic Problem*. Oxford: At the Clarendon Press, 1911. 209–27.

————. "The Original Extent of Q," *Oxford Studies in the Synoptic Problem*, 185–208.

————. "On the Original Order of Q," *Oxford Studies in the Synoptic Problem*, 141–64.

Suggs, M. J. *Wisdom, Christology, and Law in Matthew's Gospel*. Cambridge: Harvard Univ. Press, 1970.

Taylor, R. O. P. *The Groundwork of the Gospels*. Oxford: Basil Blackwell, 1946.

Taylor, Vincent. *The Formation of the Gospel Tradition*. London: Macmillan & Co., 1935².

————. "The Order of Q," *JTS* NS 4 (1953) 27–31; repr. *New Testament Essays*. Grand Rapids: W. B. Eerdmans, 1972; London: Epworth Press, 1970. 90–94.

————. "The Original Order of Q," *New Testament Essays: Studies in Memory of T. W. Manson*. Manchester: Manchester Univ. Press, 1959. 246–69; repr. *New Testament Essays*, 95–118.

Theissen, Gerd. *The First Followers of Jesus*. London: SCM Press, 1978.

Till, Walter C. *Koptische Grammatik (Saïdischer Dialekt)*. Leipzig: Enzyklopädie Verlag, 1970⁴.

Tödt, Heinz E. *The Son of Man in the Synoptic Tradition*. London: SCM Press, 1965.

Torrey, C. C. *Our Translated Gospels*. New York: Harper & Row, 1936.

Trilling, Wolfgang. "Die Täufertradition bei Matthäus," *BZ* NF 3 (1959) 271–89.

————. *Das Wahre Israel*. SANT 10. Munich: Kösel, 1964³.

Turner, Nigel. *Grammatical Insights into the New Testament*. Edinburgh: T. & T. Clark, 1965.

————. "Q in Recent Thought," *ExpT* 80 (1968–69) 324–28.

Vassiliadis, Petros. "The Nature and Extent of the Q Document," *NovT* 20 (1978) 49–73.

Vielhauer, Philipp. *Geschichte der urchristlichen Literatur*. Berlin: Walter de Gruyter, 1975.

————. "Gottesreich und Menschensohn in der Verkündigung Jesu," *Aufsätze zum Neuen Testament*. TBü 31. Munich: Chr. Kaiser, 1965. 55–91.

————. "Jesus und der Menschensohn," *Aufsätze zum Neuen Testament*, 92–140.

Vögtle, Anton. "Die Einladung zum grossen Gastmahl und zum königlichen Hochzeitsmahl," *Das Evangelium und die Evangelien*. Düsseldorf: Patmos, 1971. 171–218.

_____. "Der Spruch vom Jonaszeichen," *Das Evangelium und die Evangelien*, 103–36.

_____. "Wunder und Wort in urchristlicher Glaubenswerbung," *Das Evangelium und die Evangelien*. 219–42.

Wachsmuth, Carl. *Studien zu den griechischen Florilegien*. Berlin: Weidmann, 1882.

_____. "Die Wiener Apophthegmensammlung," *Festschrift zur Begrüssung der in Karlsruhe vom 27. bis 30. September 1882 tagenden XXXVI Philologen-Versammlung*. Karlsruhe, 1882. 3–36.

Wanke, Joachim. "Kommentarworte. Älteste Kommentierung von Herrenworten," *BZ* NF 24 (1980) 208–33.

Weiser, Alfons. *Die Knechtsgleichnisse der synoptischen Evangelien*. SANT 29. Munich: Kösel, 1971.

Weiss, Bernhard. *A Manual of Introduction to the New Testament*, trans. A. J. K. Davidson. 2 vols. New York: Funk & Wagnalls, 1887–89.

Weiss, Johannes. *Die Schriften des Neuen Testaments*. Göttingen: Vandenhoeck & Ruprecht, 1907².

Weizsäcker, Carl. *Untersuchungen über die evangelische Geschichte und den Gang ihrer Entwicklung*. Gotha: Besser, 1864.

Wellek, R. and A. Warren. *Theory of Literature*. New York: Harcourt Brace Jovanovich, 1956³.

Wellhausen, Julius. *Einleitung in die drei ersten Evangelien*. Berlin: Reimer, 1905¹; 1911².

_____. *Das Evangelium Matthaei*. Berlin: Reimer, 1904.

Wernle, Paul. *Die synoptische Frage*. Leipzig, Freiburg and Tübingen: J. C. B. Mohr [Paul Siebeck], 1899.

Wilcken, Ulrich. "Zur ägyptisch-hellenistischen Litteratur," *Aegyptiaca: Festschrift für Georg Ebers*. Leipzig: Engelmann, 1897. 142–52.

_____. "Tradition de Jésus et kérygma du Christ: la double histoire de la tradition au sein du christianisme primitif," *RHPR* 47 (1967) 1–20.

Wildung, Dietrich. *Imhotep und Amenhotep: Gottwerdung in alten Ägypten*. Münchner Ägyptologische Studien 36. Munich and Berlin: Deutsche Kunstverlag, 1977.

Williams, J. G. *Those Who Ponder Proverbs: Aphoristic Thinking and Biblical Literature*. Sheffield: Almond Press, 1981.

Williams, Ronald J. "A People Come Out of Egypt," *VTSup* 28 (1974) 231–52.

_____. "The Sages of Ancient Egypt in the Light of Recent Scholarship," *JAOS* 101 (1981) 1–19.

Wink, Walter. *John the Baptist in the Gospel Tradition*. SNTSMS 7. Cambridge: At the Univ. Press, 1968.

Worden, Ronald D. "A Philological Analysis of Luke 6:20b-49 and Parallels." Ph.D. diss., Princeton Theological Seminary, 1973.

_____. "Redaction Criticism of Q: A Survey," *JBL* 94 (1975) 532–46.

Wrege, Hans-Theo. *Die Überlieferungsgeschichte der Bergpredigt*. WUNT 9. Tübingen: J. C. B. Mohr [Paul Siebeck], 1968.

▬▬▬. "Zur Rolle des Geistwortes in frühchristlichen Traditionen (Lc 12,10 parr.)," *Logia*. 373–77.

Wright, A. "Oral Teaching," *ExpT* 11 (1899–1900) 473–74.

Zeller, Dieter. "Die Bildlogik des Gleichnisses Mt 11 16f/Lk 7 31f," *ZNW* 68 (1977) 252–57.

▬▬▬. "Das Logion Mt 8,11f/Lk 13,28f und das Motif der Völkerwallfahrt," *BZ* NF 15 (1971) 222–37; 16 (1972) 84–93.

▬▬▬. "Prophetisches Wissen um die Zukunft in synoptischen Jesusworten," *TP* 52 (1977) 258–71.

▬▬▬. "Redaktionsprozesse und weckselnder 'Sitz im Leben' beim Q-Material," *Logia*. 395–409.

▬▬▬. "Die Versuchungen Jesu in der Logienquelle," *TTZ* 89 (1980) 61–73.

▬▬▬. *Die weisheitliche Mahnsprüche bei den Synoptikern*. FzB 17. Würzburg: Echter, 1977.

▬▬▬. "Der Zusammenhang der Eschatologie in der Logienquelle," *Gegenwart und kommendes Reich*. Stuttgarter biblische Beitrage. Stuttgart: KBW, 1975. 67–77.

Zimmerli, Walther. "Concerning the Structure of Old Testament Wisdom," *SAIW*. 175–207.

▬▬▬. "The Place and Limit of the Wisdom in the Framework of the Old Testament Theology," *SAIW*. 314–26.

Zmijewski, J. *Die Eschatologiereden des Lukas-evangeliums. Eine traditions- und redaktionsgeschichtliche Untersuchungen zu Lk 21,5–36 und Lk 17,20–37*. BBB 40. Bonn: Hanstein, 1972.

Index